DREAM CHILD – CREATION AND NEW LIFE IN DREAMS OF PREGNANT WOMEN

REGINA ABT – IRMGARD BOSCH – VIVIENNE MACKRELL

Dream Child

Creation and New Life
in Dreams
of Pregnant Women

Inspired by Marie-Louise von Franz

by

Regina Abt – Irmgard Bosch – Vivienne MacKrell

DAIMON

The authors and the publisher thank the "Marie-Louise-von-Franz-Foundation" for supporting and helping to realize this project.

The chapters by Regina Abt and Irmgard Bosch were translated from the original German by Valérie Nizon Rivkin.

Cover illustration:
"Die Beseelung des Kindes" (The coming to life of the child), Hildegard von Bingen.

Table of Contents

Translator's Note

The lively exchange with the authors rendered the otherwise secluded business of the translator especially engaging and stimulating. I am thankful to Regina Abt and Irmgard Bosch for their continual support and readiness to discuss all of the questions and problems I had in the course of the translation of this book.

I am also greatly indepted to Vivienne MacKrell, whose chapters here appear in the original, for her generous and meticulous assistance throughout the task.

My daily dialogue with this book has been for the most part immensely interesting and rewarding. I wish that I had had the benefit of knowing it when I was pregnant with our daughter. I would have realized then that spiritual and intellectual development and pregnancy complement – rather than exclude – one another, and that the passive and meditative brooding period culminating in the birth of a child, can and should be a most precious and wondrously rich time in a woman's life.

Valérie Nizon Rivkin

1. Foreword

Marie-Louise von Franz

Today there is an abundance of books about pregnancy, and even about dreams in pregnancy. The present study is a pilot test endeavoring to explore the types of dreams as objectively as possible. For this purpose, around 700 dreams were collected from pregnant women and examined. This first analysis already proved that the so-called archetypal dream motifs predominated, as was also to be expected. It is generally known that according to C.G. Jung an archetypal motif represents a symbolic image or gesture of universal human nature whose function it would appear to be, is to cope with typical situations happening in life. Thus, archetypal motifs occur frequently in crucial periods of transition, such as starting school, puberty, marriage, mid-life crisis, preparing for death and last but not least in the time before pregnancy or birth. What our study reveals surprisingly is the prodigious wealth and the variety and depth of the occurring motifs. Pregnancy seems to create an entire universe. As in the form of a rough sketch the foetus repeats the biological evolution, so is the creation of the universe psychically repeated in the birth of each human being; for, the universe only exists for us to the extent that it exists in our consciousness. This is what Jung calls the cosmogonic meaning of human consciousness.

In the last years, research in biology and medicine has resulted in tremendous progress in our field. This in turn caused a certain loss of the spiritual significance of pregnancy for woman. It has become reduced to a technological platitude. We have lost track of the religious awe and the mystery involved in the creation of a new human being. The dreams that follow and that have been interpreted according to Jung's method may help to reawaken this sense of awe and admiration. At the same time they lead us to innumerable new questions that we have not been able to answer here and that we hope will encourage a new generation of scholars to penetrate into this yet unknown territory.

Jungian psychology could be called a heuristic psycho-centric way of seeing; it is not only a new theory but indeed a new way of seeing. Moreover, it gives rise to new ethical questions regarding abortion, contraception, etc.. This, too, is new territory for us. But if for now this book can assist some pregnant women in feeling in harmony with themselves, then it will have fulfilled its goal.

Küsnacht, March 18, 1996

2. Introduction

Irmgard Bosch

During pregnancy, some women enjoy a feeling of security, as if they themselves were wrapped in a protective cloak – "like in a cloud." In connection with the fatigue normal for this time, a subtle psychic turning inwardly, an introversion occurs, accompanying and facilitating the anticipation of the child. A good many insecurities disappear, giving way to a new more centered self-confidence.

Other women in this phase of life feel much more insecure. They are additionally shaken by dreams and are more prone than usual to sinister forebodings, mood swings and even depression. For this there are many reasons, inner as well as outer ones.

One of the reasons is certainly the fact that pregnancy is no longer simply a matter of course. Even when a pregnancy was planned, the change is not made easy for women, given the values placed on profession, higher education and on freedom. In addition, problems often crop up in the partnership.

Pregnancy signifies something like "the hour of reckoning": What counts now, is woman's very own inner reality, and more often than not she has to get to know it first. There is no training available in which to find solutions to her problems; they are fateful and the general opinion on this subject is thoroughly contradictory. Instruction by the family, in particular by the mother, has virtually ceased to exist.

We lack the effective social and religious forms that people developed in the past, in order to regulate and to assist with the hazardous passages of human life (birth, puberty, marriage, illness, death). These *rites de passage*[1] – rituals of survival and of passing tests once constituted a kind of support system, particularly in the formative years. A feeling of being left to ones own devices in difficult times is common today – the other side of freedom.

Woman is challenged by pregnancy in a manner entirely different from what complies with the Zeitgeist that has increasingly moved away from the

[1] Arnold van Gennep, *The Rites of Passage*, The University of Chicago Press, 1980

forms of life that have traditionally been passed down, and instead has set new objectives for her. How can orientation occur for pregnant woman when she is confronted with questions regarding her own identity that seem foreign to her in the modern world? Pregnancy courses of all kinds may be of great help to her, but an expectant woman wants to find out more about herself.

Her own unconscious nature and in particular her dreams, can tell her most unerringly what no one else can tell her. In particular, when she faces those tormenting questions in case of an unwanted pregnancy, carefully taking into consideration her dreams can make orientation possible, because dreams are at once objective and personal. Conscious thought may be far removed from the psychic is-state, the state that dreams disclose to us. – Jung says: "Only what woman or man really is has healing power."

The present book is not like other traditional dream reference books. It spreads a wealth of present-day pregnancy dreams from many countries and tries to present possibilities of interpretation from an angle of contemporary depth psychology. Pregnant women and medical doctors, psychologists, mid-wives and pastors can gain from this book a more individual and more precise understanding of the spiritual process coming about in each pregnancy.

It would indeed be important for us all – not only for pregnant women, but with the aid of their dreams – to learn again how to understand better and in a more differentiated manner the time of pregnancy and its objective-psychic (i.e., archetypal) background. It seems to me at present as if we were facing the imminent loss of something essential: namely the focus on an inner meaning of life which we so often doubt, in which we can no longer "believe" wholeheartedly and to which we sometimes tend to shut our eyes; it is, how-ever, immensely present and has undeniable consequences. To take dreams seriously and to allow our consciousness some insight into their cryptic images, requires immersion on our part in a world that has become estranged from us.

No major work on pregnancy dreams from a Jungian viewpoint has been published so far.[2] It is for this reason that Dr. Marie-Louise von Franz made the suggestion that the foundation carrying her name, organize a comprehen-sive and new collection of dreams of pregnant women. Every one of us collab-orating on this project is deeply grateful to Dr. Marie-Louise von Franz for her inspirational tips, her encouragement and help over the course of many years.

---

[2] A recent American representative study analyzed dreams from the first three months of pregnancy and observed a significant predominance of archetypal dreams: Tho-mas Schroer, Archetypal Dreams during the first Pregnancy, in "Psychological Per-spectives," Vol. 14, No. 1, Los Angeles, 1984. Carol Baumann interpreted several pregnancy dreams from a Jungian perspective: "Psychic Experiences in Connection with Birth"; Edward Edinger studied several important motifs: *Anatomy of the Psyche*, Open Court, La Salle, IL, 1985 – we will quote No. 588 from it.

At the beginning of the project a large number of Jungian analysts in several countries were asked if they were able and willing to contribute to a collection of archetypal dreams from the period of pregnancy with the objective to study their purposeful origin. The following questions were to be investigated on the basis of the material available to us:

Do dreams of pregnant women differ from those of other women or from other dreams in woman's life? Does this involuntary expression of her psyche reveal anything about those questions mankind has been concerned with from the beginning of time? For example, about the beginning or the origin of life, the mysteries involved in the birth a new human being, or about the destiny of a child? Sometimes pregnant women are struck with the kind of terror that can only be compared to ancient consecrations. In their dreams, are there any healing archetypal solutions and aids visible that can be valid for women nowadays?

Jung writes: "All those moments of individual life, when the universal laws of human fate break in upon the purposes, expectations, and opinions of personal consciousness, are stations along the road of the individuation process."[3] It seems evident that a (wanted, and in particular an unwanted) pregnancy represents just that: a modification of personal planning and thinking through the universally valid human destiny. Does it therefore follow that stages of the individuation process in pregnancy dreams are perceptible?

They should also be perceptible in a planned pregnancy that follows its course determined not by the will of the ego but by nature, as it has been the experience of countless generations of women. Because nowadays the upbringing and education of women and girls are strongly oriented towards individual development, one of woman's most precious modern achievements is apparently sacrificed during pregnancy: her hard-fought-for independence. On the basis of the dreams, we wanted to research whether and to what extent these fundamental changes with all their voluntary and involuntary sacrifices could at the same time indicate steps on the way to individuation. The question could be raised whether and to what extent entering the nest-making phase – as is often claimed today – causes stagnation of the spiritual/intellectual development of woman: in other words, it would be interesting to see how dreams comment on such questions. One would also have to see from the dreams whether pregnancy represented merely a kind of way out or pretext and whether a genuine attitude towards it would first have to be developed.

We received an extremely large number of dreams (ca. 700) and these were selected chiefly in respect of their archetypal content. Although we mostly did not know the expectant women, we were occasionally able to speculate about the compensatory reference to the personal. However, our interests lay above all with the dream's archetypal content and its relation to pregnancy. The

[3] C.G. Jung, *Collected Works* (CW) 8, § 557, Bollingen Foundation, New York, 1960

classification and sorting of the dreams according to the main chapters may at times be conceived differently, for instance, when the dream comprises several motifs. We hope that the index at the end of the book will facilitate the looking up. Access to additional data of the material as well as to the original dream texts may be requested from the foundation.

At this point, on behalf of the initiator and the authors of the research project, I would like to extend our warmest gratitude to all those who, upon our enquiry, sent dreams to us and to the dreamers themselves. The Marie-Louise-von-Franz-Foundation in Zurich received a very large and mostly very impressive number of dreams from many different countries. Permission for publication and interpretation of the dreams was obtained in each case. We thank Regina Abt for her editorial work, Eva Wertenschlag and Ursula Kiraly for their meticulous proofreading and Dr. Rigmor Robert, Nacka/Sweden, for the classification and numbering of the dreams. In particular, we would like to express our gratitude to the Marie-Louise-von-Franz-Foundation for making possible the publication of the research conducted.

The works of depth psychology by Carl Gustav Jung and Marie-Louise von Franz constitute the theoretical foundation of the research we conducted. What follows now are a few very brief explanations concerning the methodology, so that later there will be no need to interrupt our flow of thought. Readers unfamiliar with Jungian psychology may ask themselves, why we had to draw upon so many parallels from mythology, intellectual history, fairy tales and folklore. Are such fantasies and images that after all, must be traced back to a world-view that has practically vanished, still appropriate? Can they still be valuable for dream interpretation today?

On the activity of the unconscious in the dream, Jung writes: "It (the unconscious) develops motifs that appear across time and across cultures in myths and fairy tales in similar form. These same primordial images pervade our dreams, fantasies and ideas even today."[4]

Therefore, besides bringing to mind the situation of the dreamer (which in our case is directly linked to the fact of pregnancy), according to Jung, the preparing of the ground in order to grasp the meaning of the dream consists of the so-called amplification of the dream motifs. By amplification, i.e., extension of the dream motifs by their parallels and analogies from evidence across time, we mean the comparative recording of motifs: we familiarize ourselves with the function, history and characteristics of the figure or action, in order to find out its psychological meaning.[5] When we follow this track we not only gain more precise knowledge of the surrounding field, but we also establish something like a personal relationship, an opinion and a feeling for the image and its peculiarity as a means of expression of a particular psychic process. An interpretation is only convincing once it works psychologically. It

---

[4] Seminars, Olten, 1987, Note 148

is a matter of practicing intuitive imagery, of letting ourselves be guided by certain recurring threads in the richness of the imagery and, of not losing ourselves in boundless association. This is what is important in the search for the meaning.

Jung differentiates between an objective and a subjective dream content. "Interpretation on the objective level" means that the persons and actions appearing are primarily connected with the outer reality. "Interpretation on the subject level," on the other hand perceives the protagonists, events and relationships as aspects of the dreamer him/herself. And it is the latter, subjective content of the dreams that is particularly important for the growing consciousness of the individual. Furthermore, Jung understands the entire dream content to be the inner reality of the dreaming subject; i.e., the dream consists of current images and possibilities of a person's overall psychic personality which, by an unknown degree, surpasses the conscious ego.[6] Interpretations on either the subjective or objective levels often do not exclude one another. One has to scrupulously weigh up which aspect discloses the meaning of the dream more convincingly.

Jung's discovery of the "final" meaning, namely the compensation of consciousness[7] is also one of the chief functions perceptible in a dream. Because in its own way a dream represents something of which consciousness is not (yet) aware, that it neglects, fails to appreciate or suppresses. The dream therefore corrects and compensates, often quite against conscious will but always related to a current issue. The question arises: who composes or creates these images? What creative psychic function is at work here?

In the course of many years of intensive research in thousands of dreams, Jung observed that in the depth of our being there is a powerful, natural impulse striving to arrange and to merge the multifarious and often contrary parts of our personality with their disparate tendencies. This appears to be a spiritual-psychic center which Jung opposed to the conscious ego and called it the Self or the totality of man. This "central organ of the soul" moreover

---

[5] This method strongly differs from Sigmund Freud's method of free association, who was the first to identify the unconscious as the source of dreams. As the key to interpretation Freud saw in the unconscious what corresponded to the culture of his time, that is to say, mainly repressed sexual desire. He assumed further that even in dreams the desire could not manifest openly but hiddenly, otherwise sleep would be interrupted. In order to uncover such repressed and sick making, entangled impulses ("complexes"), Freud successfully applied the method of free associating. However, he interpreted the images almost exclusively along the lines of his basic oedipal assumption.

[6] The terms 'subjective' and 'objective' are neutral in meaning. If the subject is everything as well as the actual object of the dream it is in fact difficult to speak in terms of 'objective' and 'subjective.' Nevertheless, these designations seem to have established themselves as useful aids for dream interpretation.

[7] C.G. Jung, CW 8, § 509 ff

encompasses the unconscious, the physical as well as the spiritual aspects. Impulses can emanate from there compensating for the one-sidedness of consciousness and presenting new perspectives in life.

The picturesque dream processes surging from and arranged by the Self, can throw light on how the dreamer is coping with the challenge of pregnancy; for instance, on what inhibits her, and what powers are available to her of which she had previously been unaware. From the viewpoint of our "larger personality," there are sometimes surprisingly new perspectives and deeply moving insights that we spontaneously perceive as true and that we cannot but sometimes designate as divine or numinous.

We hope that on the one hand our investigations will help to look at cryptic and shadowy images with less fear and on the other hand, not to deem immaterial those seemingly unimportant ones. In other words, to place more trust in the process of growth and in nature. According to Jung, even an approximate understanding of what our dreams are telling us is healing. With some patience we can learn to better understand the language of the unconscious and to get to know the particular way in which our unconscious larger personality looks at our life from within.

In the German language there is an old fashioned sounding expression for being expecting: "to be full of hope." We could apply it to our dream book: this baby is not only nine months old but has been growing in concealment over several years and has itself got very big and there were crises and veritable labor-pains. However, if it can be brought to the world at last, I am full of hope that it will realize its promise!

Figure 1. Isis as fish goddess with Horus as a child
(Egypt 1580-1100 B.C.)

3. Elements

3.1. Water and Water Animals

Regina Abt

We begin our work on dreams of pregnant women with a motif, which intrinsically belongs to the beginning. Not only does the life of a new child in the womb begin in water, but life without water is simply unthinkable. Where there is a lack of it on earth, there is desert, arid land, and where it flows there is vegetation, nourishment and life for animal and man.

Thus in antiquity water was always associated with *the origin of life* and with the creation of the world. It is therefore not surprising that prior to the birth of a child, to the beginning of a new human being, in dreams the unconscious brings to the surface images of primeval origin and new creation that are closely tied up with water. In order to better understand such dreams, we wish to allow ancient mythical fantasies and ideas speak; for they originate from the same depths as many dreams of pregnant women, they speak the same language, as it were, and can thus be used to add to and elucidate dream imagery. They also impart to us something of the deep emotional imprint with which dream images from great psychical depths leave the dreamer; for myths speak of great things, of the origin of the world, of gods and demons and of overpowering occurrences. Today we tend to judge dreams as immaterial because we are not able to recognize their larger background of meaning, that is, their psychic fertile ground.

From the very start, humankind imagined that the secret of the beginning of the universe lay in the depths of water. It therefore says in many cosmogonies, that is to say, in tales about the beginning of the universe, that at the beginning there was water. Our own biblical myth of creation begins with water above which glides the spirit of God. The Greek thinker Thales defined water as the prime element from which everything evolved. According to him, the earth rested on water and was surrounded by it. He also said that the

17

original surface of earth was water and that the first living beings were created in the water.[8] For Homer the universe is surrounded by Okeanos, the stream of origin which is also where the gods come from. Okeanos contains the germ cells from which the universe emerged.[9] In Babylon the earth rests on the primeval sea Apsu and is surrounded by it on all sides. From it – as from Okeanos – originate all springs and rivers. The Germanic cosmogony also speaks of the creation from the primeval sea: The "roaring" giant Ymir, out of whose limbs the world was supposedly created, is identified with the primeval sea.[10] In the ancient Egyptian creation myth we are told that in the beginning there was neither heavens nor earth. "Surrounded by dense darkness, the cosmos was filled with unlimited primeval waters – called Nun –, that concealed in its womb the male and female germs or the beginnings of the future world."[11] From these prehistorical waters earth emerges, entirely surrounded and supported by Nun. Nun is also the "old man," the "father of the gods," a cosmic god that existed already before the Chthonic primeval god known as Atum, the creator of the universe. From Nun, the primeval waters, Atum rose as his son. Just as in Egypt earth re-emerged annually from the muddy floods of the Nile, so is Atum too, the primeval mount, the first soil that emerged from the water.[12]

Already in ancient times, like isles out of the primeval waters of unconscious life, did such magnificent images of the creation of the world rise from man's psyche to the surface of his consciousness. We will discuss this in detail later on. But we can already say that in its mysterious unfathomableness, its flowing eternal mobility, water is one of the most important symbols for the unconscious from whose invisible depths all psychic life feeds and develops.

Many mythical tales speak about a *godlike child* living in the solitariness of the primeval element; a wonderful orphan symbolizing the beginning of creation. In Indian cosmogony, in the Rigveda, Vishnu is both the Creator of the cosmos and the cosmic ocean. In the shape of a boar he brings up young soil from the ocean. Sometimes, before his creation he rests as a godlike child on the coils of the gigantic water snake. According to other narratives, Narayama or Prajapati, the divine child in India was hatched out from an egg that was created from the primeval waters and now reposed in the cup of a water flower.[13] Harpokrates, the Egyptian sun child too, was represented like Prajapati on a floating lotus. Even geographically a little closer to us, we can find the mythical primeval child, particularly in ancient Italian and Cretan narra-

---

[8] R.B. Onians, *The Origin of European Thought*, 247 f
[9] W.H. Roscher, *Lexikon der griech. und röm. Mythologie*, 450 f
[10] *Ibid.*, p. 462
[11] *Ibid.*, p. 461
[12] H. Bonnet, *Reallexikon der ägyptischen Religionsgeschichte*, Verlag Walter de Gruyter, Berlin, 1971, pp. 535, 71
[13] K. Kerényi, *Humanistische Seelenforschung*, pp. 86, 91

tives and in ancient layers of continental Greek religion.[14] We shall deal further with this important imagery in the chapter on the child symbol. For the moment we wish merely to establish the close link between water and child; for in pregnancy we are also dealing with a child, in other words, with the creation of man or the original human consciousness born out of water, the original element, i.e., the unconscious.

The creation of humankind was sometimes directly related to water. According to Anaximandros, a Greek philosopher of the second century B.C., fish or fish-like beings that were at the same time phytogenic, were created from heated water. From these, it was thought, man had eventually come into being. At the beginning of the 19th century in Jena, the natural philosopher and natural scientist Oken claimed that the first uterus was the sea as it provided nourishment, mucus and oxygen for the foetus. The first embryos had been created in the sea, many had perished, others had gently drifted to the shore where their sheaths were ripped.[15] Although this doctrine was put forth by a natural scientist and philosopher of the last century, it reminds us of the ancient mythological idea of the child originating from water.

It is impossible for us to grasp even a small part of the infinite variety of images despite the fact that we have already penetrated a fair way into the symbolism of water. One could literally drown in it! For this reason, I shall only indicate a few important points, in order to go more deeply into them in the context of the dreams.

The almost universal meaning of water as the origin and support-system of all life is present in all traditions and rites that are to do with *fertility* of plant, man and animal, with procreative potency and regeneration. In ancient Greece bride and bride-groom were bathed in the river in the hope that they would thus be blessed with a large number of children. There was a widely known popular belief that said that if one bathed in the water of the spring of the Nile (believed to be the original spring), there would be more than three children to one birth. Rivers had procreative powers and were donors of semen. They stimulated growth in youths, who at the time of puberty had to sacrifice a lock of hair to it.[16] According to ancient middle-European popular belief, children as well as animals came directly out of fountains, ponds, lakes and streams. In our regions child-fountains and child-ponds can still be found today.

Fertility, among other things, always symbolizes regeneration in a wider sense, and hence healing. Regeneration and healing in turn are contingent on preceding purification. Wherever man sought *purification, healing* and *regeneration*, in springs, fountains and holy waters, water represented the elemen-

---

[14] *Ibid.*, p. 111
[15] *Ibid.*, pp. 94 f
[16] Onians, p. 229

tary substance of life. Many of our Christian churches were originally built on a pre-Christian sacred well. For instance, in the Rieder Valley in the canton of Uri in Switzerland, a fountain was built as an extension to the Chapel of the Black Madonna where to this day women come to pray to be blessed with a child. Wherever it was a matter of creating or regenerating life, there were female sanctuaries representing goddesses of the earth or mothers.

Just as the beginning of all life was thought to be in the water, so people believed that ultimate knowledge and the ultimate secret of life also rested in the depths of water. This was the common primeval perception. It is reflected in the belief in the many goddesses of Fate that obtained their knowledge from the bowels of the earth and from the water. Among them were the three Germanic goddesses of fate, called Parzen, sitting at the source of Urd at the foot of Yggdrasil, the world tree. The water of this source contained all the germs and possibilities, and all living beings developed from it. The source of Urd is also a fountain of youth, in which whatever drops into it is transformed back to its earlier purity, to its pre-natal origin.[17]

Everywhere in mythology we encounter the idea that the depths of water are linked with fate and with the future. We also find it in countless customs and *prophecies*. Young women see their future husband in the water. In the face of a threat of war, water turns a red color, etc.[18] In *The Concise Dictionary of German Folk Belief*, an enormous, highly useful collection of ancient customs and ideas, a large number of examples can be found. So-called "hydromantics" or fortune-telling from water, played an important role already in antiquity.

If we stand by deep, dark waters, by a brilliant and vividly swirling mountain brook or by a torrential cold river tearing down between towering walls of rock, we may also have fantasies that we do not produce ourselves. It is as if they came to us from the water, i.e., from our inner being, stimulated by the mysterious, flowing, reflecting, changing quality of water. If we have poetic abilities, then words are "formed" in us, ideas "rush by" and the "current" of creativity is set in motion. Ancient Irish texts describe, how for the Irish poets water was the place and means for *inspiration and revelation*. They sang its praises to obtain prophetic insights.[19] In the *I Ching*, the book of Chinese wisdom, in Chapter 7 ("The Army"), the ground water within the earth represents the powerful, creative source emanating from the divine nature of man.

Water also played an important role in romantic literature. On the one hand, it served to express ecstatic feeling and visionary seeing; on the other hand, it symbolized being overwhelmed by billows, maelstrom and surges of a melancholy mood that can end up in a desire for death. Infinitely many

[17] Brosse 13
[18] *Handwörterbuch d. dt. Aberglaubens*, Vol. 7, p. 1564
[19] *Dictionnaire des Symboles*, Vol. 2, p. 230

myths and legends of nymphs and naiads that were collected at that time, tell stories of the suggestive power of the sea waves, which can pull a person down till he/she drowns in the maternal waters. Psychologically, this signifies immersion in the world of sleep and dreams of the unconscious, in the night-world of the soul where a person can be torn away from everyday life. We shall see in our collection that there are dreams which clearly point to this danger.

We shall also encounter water as the *place of death* or of the Hereafter. For, according to archaic imagination, the dead return to where life began. Some Australian aborigines, for example, believed that the spirits dwell in water before they enter a woman's womb from where they are born as a child. Thus, apart from caves, trees and roots, water is the place through which the dead return to life. At the same time, the way to Hades also leads through water. All the dead have to drink from Lethe, the stream of forgetfulness before they enter Hades, the underworld; then the souls have to cross Acheron, the grue-some river of the underworld, to reach the land of the dead.[20]

From what has been said about water so far, it follows that given the constant movement of water, all its aspects are related to *change* and transfor-mation: creation and termination of life suggest change into a new state in the same way as do healing, regeneration, growth and the course of fate. The idea of change also exists in the Christian concept of baptism where it mainly implies spiritual change. The holy water of the church has a quality of creation as well as transformation. Through the *benedictio fontis*, the blessing of water before Easter, water is endowed with the divine quality to transform, in other words to give rebirth.[21] Inner man is renewed in the baptismal water. For the alchemists, the water used in their experiments carried a divine quality, for it served to "bring to the surface the concealed nature of man."[22] It was the "eternal water," moreover, that had the power to transform body into spirit. Behind this was in fact the same idea as was behind the rite of baptism. In St. John 7, 38, there is a passage about the rivers of living water that flow out of Jesus' belly and of Jesus saying: "If any man thirst, let him come unto me, and drink."

We can see how the visible appearance of water corresponds to a symbolic image innate in man, namely the image of a source of life in man's own soul. Jung says: "For indeed our consciousness does not create itself – it wells up from unknown depths. In childhood it awakens gradually, and all through life it wakes each morning out of the depths of sleep from an unconscious condi-tion. It is like a child that is born daily out of the primordial womb of the unconscious. In fact, closer investigation reveals that it is not only influenced by the unconscious but continually emerges out of it in the form of countless

---

[20] *Lexikon der griech. und röm. Mythologie*, Vol. 6, pp. 9 f
[21] C.G. Jung, CW 11, § 161
[22] *Ibid.*, § 161

spontaneous ideas and sudden flashes of thought.[23] Now the unconscious "night happening" including everything that does not reach consciousness but happens without our knowledge was thought to be like a river, gushing forth and flowing. This happening at the bottom of the unconscious, during sleep or dreaming, but equally in insanity or ecstatic exultation (*Entrückung*) in a sense is also fateful. Heraclitus says: "Dreaming, we labor on and contribute to the cosmic events ..."[24]

In the same way as water follows its own natural law of eternal movement, so it happens in a dream. At the most we can obstruct this unconscious source, however, it can never be eliminated. It is because it contains possibilities, life germs and substances of change and, because these internal sequences of imagery determine our fate, we are concerned in this book with the dreams of expectant mothers, the carriers of new life.

I believe it is evident to what extent water symbolizes maternity in mythology. In the Vedas, the waters are called *matritamah* = the most maternal. "Born of springs, rivers, lakes and seas, man at death comes to the waters of the Styx, and there embarks on the "night sea journey." Those black waters of death are the water of life, for death with its cold embrace is the maternal womb, just as the sea devours the sun but brings it forth again."[25] In this sense, water carries the projection of the mother, and the unconscious contains maternal meaning.[26]

The following pregnancy dreams are about the motif of the water and its maternal aspect. That which rises from the springs of the unconscious, maternal nature of woman, deals at the same time with what motherhood entails and with the entire physical and psychological condition of the mother. And if while studying these dreams it may seem to us that they differ little from the dreams other people have, we must nevertheless not lose sight of this background.

The following dream stems from a thirty-one-year-old woman in the second month of pregnancy. She had not really wished for this second pregnancy at this point in time when she was struggling with depression.[27]

---

[23] *Ibid.*, CW 11, *Psychology and Religion: East*, § 935

[24] Martin Ninck, *Die Bedeutung des Wassers im Kult und Leben der Alten*, Wiss. Buchgesellschaft, Darmstadt, 1967, p. 137

[25] C.G. Jung, CW 5, *Symbols of Transformation*, Bollingen Foundation Inc., New York, 1956, § 319

[26] *Ibid.*, § 320

[27] By the same woman: Dream No. 107, Chapter 6

Dream No. 1: [28]

> *I see a beach with trees and flowers. I am told that this is the original beach on which life or all living things or children are born. – I am travelling along the coast looking for the sites where someone had been born from the water. I only know of the rock where at her birth Venus rose from the water. I find it and explain to others that it is situated in Cyprus.*

The first part of the dream reminds us of one of those images of mythology that people have formulated across time. The dreamer is told something about the origin of life. Contrary to her personal perception of her own "making" of a child, i.e., carrying it to term and giving birth to it, this image emphasizes the origin emanating from the depths of the sea, that is to say, from the collective universally human unconscious. In the second part of the dream she is looking for Venus – in Greek, Aphrodite –, the goddess born from foam. We shall see shortly, how these two parts are related.

Aphrodite (Astarte in the Near East) was venerated by all Semitic peoples as a goddess of the moon (and also of Venus, the star) and also as the goddess of all female and terrestrial fertility. As a goddess of the moon she seemed to be in charge of female sexual life and responsible for the donation of dew that was vital for the fertility of plants. In particular she was a goddess for women and was as such venerated above all by women. In Babylon she was called the "the birth-making one." In addition, she was the goddess who would bless people with children. Originally, Astarte was associated with the moon. Her association with water, with life-giving moisture and with the sea ensued later, in Greek times. For, the moon directed the tides. Her animals were fish, dolphins, the pigeon, the hare, the sparrow, the rabbit, the ram – all highly fertile animals. Above all, Aphrodite who always appears adorned with flowers, is the goddess of gardens, flowers, of pleasure groves and of Spring. Let us recall the beginning of the dream: "I see a beach with trees and flowers ...." From the later Greek era, Aphrodite/Venus is known to us primarily as the goddess of matrimony and love.

Now let us recall the story of the creation of Aphrodite as it is told by Hesiod, for it reveals Aphrodite's strong association with water: when the progenitor Uranus did not allow the Titan children to emerge from the interior of the earth, Kronos, the youngest among them, with the aid of his mother Gaea, cut off his reproductive organ and threw it into the sea. Aphrodite was created from this act, emerging from the foaming billows. According to Homer, the west wind then dispatched her to Cyprus in soft foam on a sea wave.[29]

---

[28] Dreams that have not been translated or abbreviated are rendered in the same wording as the dreamers themselves wrote them down.

[29] W.H. Roscher, *Lexikon*, 394 ff

We can see from this dream that the young woman, quite unknowingly, is looking for both the secret of creation and of the maternal. Symbolically, the moment of Aphrodite's emerging from the sea is also the moment of becoming conscious of this powerful psychic component. This moment for a pregnant woman is, quite literally, pregnant with fateful significance. In the dream, she is looking for the rock at which Aphrodite / Venus rose from the water. It is not likely that the dreamer knew that in Paphos, Aphrodite was also venerated in meteorites that fell down from heaven. The rock may therefore represent a consolidated, larger feminine-maternal personality, the feminine Self for which the dreamer is ultimately looking.

The dreamer even knows where this place is – namely, in Cyprus. How much she knew about Aphrodite's connection with Cyprus, we cannot tell. She presumably did not know that Aphrodite's grave is exhibited in Cyprus to this day. Nowadays the story of her death is explained by the fact that on the days of the change of the moon and during lunar eclipses the moon temporarily disappeared. This caused the archaic peoples to fear that the great goddess had died. Legend also had it that the Near Eastern goddess periodically descended to the underworld, or the realm of the dead. For example, in the dry season (which would be winter here) fertility on earth would disappear with her until she would finally reappear in the rainy season, i.e., in Spring.

What significance could this amplification have for our dreamer? Whenever the great goddess of water, fertility and motherhood is constellated in a woman's life, so is her association with the land of the dead, which is suggested by her proximity to the depths of the water. This would also include the proximity to the "states of darkness of the soul" and to the eclipses during which man is deprived of light. We know that this dreamer was suffering from depression at the time of her pregnancy. However, Aphrodite / Venus is the goddess that resurrects time and again: she is the guardian goddess of women and of birth! Hence the dreamer may have faith in her deep feminine instinct that will help through difficult times.

The next dream comes from a twenty-four-year-old woman in the first month of her first pregnancy. She gave birth to a healthy baby-girl five weeks before due date. At this time both parents were taking their doctoral degrees at a university.[30]

Dream No. 2:

> *We were standing by the sea. There was lively rippling of not very high waves. The deep roaring of the rising of the wind could be heard in the distance. I expected the waves to rapidly become higher, but nothing*

---

[30] By the same dreamer: Chapter 5.6: No. 84, Chapter 5.5: No. 80, Chapter 7: 141, Chapter 5.2: No. 58

happened. Then I saw high wave formations of various shapes surge up in the distance. It looked magnificent and uncanny. They were at as far a distance as the horizon, and so this gigantic wave that washed everything away appeared quite unexpectedly. Everything became submerged by it.

This dream, too, begins with the state before the Creation. There is the peaceful murmuring of the sea. But then you hear the wind that sets those weird wave formations in motion and that finally drives this all-overpowering billow to the shore.

Let us, in this context, look at the following Indian myth of creation: Vishnu, who himself personifies the universe, entered the sea, in order once more to bring the universe into being. The ocean waves rippled softly as he moved them. Then a narrow aperture was formed between the waves; that was the chamber, the ether or the carrier of sound. The chamber resounded, and from the resonance rose the second element, air, in the form of a wind. The latter recklessly stretched itself into the distance, blowing ferociously and roaring mightily, thus agitating the waters. From the friction and the uproar fire was created. The fire consumed a large quantity of cosmic water, and from this void heaven was created, etc. ... [31]

The similarity to our dream is astounding. Even the sound produced by the wind is in it. In many creation myths the wind personifies the fertilizing element, so to speak. Chnum, the Egyptian ram-god, at once the god of air and wind, is also the donator of water and creator of all living beings, the guardian of the source of the Nile and the master of primeval water.[32] In *Symbols of Transformation*, Jung says: "To be born of water simply means to be born of the mother's womb; to be born of the Spirit means to be born of the fructifying breath of the wind." The Greek word *pneuma* denotes both wind and spirit. Jung goes on to quote Jesus' words to Nicodemus: "Verily, verily. I say unto thee, Except a man be born again, he cannot see the kingdom of God ... Marvel not that I say unto thee, Ye must be born again. The wind bloweth where it listeth, and thou hearest the sound thereof, but canst not tell whence it cometh, and whither it goeth: so is every one that is born of the Spirit." (St. John 3, 3 f).[33]

In our dream we are clearly dealing with birth from water and spirit. However the fertilization of the maternal water by the male *pneuma* causes a terrific tidal wave that submerges everything. We can imagine that far away, in the unconscious of the dreamer the conception of a new child has provoked strong emotions that now threaten to flood consciousness. The dream imparts a powerful image of the new pregnancy; it is clearly a spiritual event that will

[31] H. Zimmer, *Myths and Symbols in Indian Art and Civilization*, Bollingen Series VI, Princeton University Press, 1946
[32] H. Bonnet, 138
[33] C.G. Jung, CW 5, *Symbols of Transformation*, § 334, § 333

strongly affect the woman's body but also her spiritual side, her emotions, thoughts, fantasies and ideas. The dreamer does not appear to be particularly touched and at the end of the dream we are left with the impression that the dream never quite reached her. Perhaps this is to her advantage, for the wave washing everything away, might have taken her with it.

Ten days later she had a dream that will be discussed in the Chapter called "Horse" (No. 85). There, the young woman has to jump into the water where she then has to take hold of a horse and embark on an adventurous horse-ride. This seems like the continuation of the dream we have just discussed. Things are becoming more concrete: they are coming to the shore; they are coming closer! In another 14 days this will become even clearer:

Dream No. 3:

> *There was suddenly water spurting out from my ceiling like from a shower. I was quite frightened and tried to find some kind of a receptacle with which to catch it. The water squirted all over the room, as if driven by a wind. I was deeply disturbed by this happening.*

Here we have the same elements of water and wind but this time in the middle of the dreamer's room. She desperately tries to "grasp" what is happening, for now it concerns her very personal everyday life. The wind, blowing unruly, deregulates her orderly life. She has to find a way of coping with these unconscious feelings and thoughts (water and wind) that are breaking forth and to give them a receptacle and a direction. The new element is but a nuisance and frightening to her. She cannot yet grasp or comprehend the "impregnation" of the room of her own soul.

There are various dreams of high waves in our collection; for example, the following one of a twenty-nine-year-old woman in her fourth month, expecting her second child. The woman underwent treatment due to psychological difficulties triggered by the pregnancy or the earlier birth.

Dream No. 4:

> *As I was walking on the beach, waves were high, but I did not think they reached me. We two were walking on the beach. When I looked back, very high waves came surging toward us.*

Dream No. 5:

> *I'm on the beach with other people. There are huge breaking waves that partially inundate me. I apply all my strength and swimming skills to always come up again, in order to catch some air. But my daughter, who was further out on the beach, gets washed away. Nevertheless, somebody*

catches her and holds her high so that she can get air. I have to first rescue myself, in order to reach her and help her.

The gigantic waves come very close here and in a very threatening way, and the dreamer's child is being swept along as well. Many women suffer from depression during pregnancy, others are emotionally unstable, others again are anxious and feel they cannot cope. Children can feel this kind of distress – even if we try to hide it – and often become involved in it. This is why the mother must help herself first. The proximity of the archetype of the great goddess of water and motherhood seems to open doors, as it were, to the collective unconscious with its contents that are often foreign to us. The following dreams, in which extraordinary or treacherous animals emerge from the water, speak of those contents.

Dream No. 6 of a twenty-five-year-old woman, six months pregnant:[34]

> *It was night. I was with my son on a deserted beach. After we walked to the other end I realized I was so far away from nature and from myself that I could barely see the sea. At this place where we were the sea was enraged, full of big waves. We were on a higher place. We were looking at the sea and I was showing my son the waves coming and going. Suddenly the sea went up and almost made us wet. I thought of leaving but there appeared many geese trying to bite us. Despite my pregnant belly I took my son in my arms and ran away. The geese came after us, biting my son's legs.*

The deserted beach and the dreamer's feeling of being so far away from nature and from herself that she can hardly see the sea, suggest the young woman's feeling of having lost her way and of her melancholy mood. Now, what are the geese? The ancient Egyptians associated the goose with the origin of man. The "Great Cackler" was a cosmic primeval being, and the first human being was created from its egg.[35] In Rome, geese lived next to the temple of Juno, the mother-goddess, the patroness of matrimony and family. They watched over the capitol and according to the legend warned of attacking Teutons. In Greece, Aphrodite was represented riding on a goose.[36] Because geese exist in the water, on the earth and in the air, they play the role of a kind of mediator between the elements. As birds, they embody thoughts and intuition that attack the dreamer's conscious position by way of the agitated unconscious. As they belong to the maternal element and in this respect have the function of guards, we may assume that the dreamer, that is, her child or

---

[34] By the same dreamer: Chapter 3.1, No. 1
[35] Manfred Lurker, *The Gods and Symbols of Ancient Egypt: An Illustrated Dictionary*, Thames and Hudson, New York, 1980
[36] *Dictionnaire des Symboles*, Vol. 3, p. 306

Figure 2. Aphrodite riding on a goose (Rhodes, 470-460 B.C.)

the childlike side in her, somehow incurred the mother-goddess' disapproval. It is possible that a different attitude to motherhood or to her motherly role in the family is demanded by the unconscious.

In such a dream, the child can indeed mean her own child that gets exposed to danger by the onrush of the unconscious and the fear and insecurity in the mother's feelings.[37] Children's unconscious is often like a sponge, absorbing the mother's unconscious problems without being able to do anything against it. By the same token it may be her childishness that no longer befits her present motherly role and is therefore being criticized by the unconscious. In the first instance, we interpret the child on the so-called objective level, namely as the actual external child. In the second instance, the child is seen on the subjective level, in other words, as an inner figure on the inner stage of the psychic happening. The second interpretation, an essential component of Jung's understanding of dreams, is not easy to understand. However, in the course of this book we shall see, how helpful it is and how the meaning of a dream-happening can often only be found when we bring back the dream-happening from the projection onto the outside world, in order to contemplate it on the inner level. This way the energy can flow back to the dreamer, – the subject, and can occasion an inner change in her.

[37] Compare Chapter 7

Sometimes it is more useful to envisage our own childishness than to project everything onto our children although the latter is a much easier option!

A twenty-three-year-old woman had the following very powerful dream the night before the birth of her child:

Dream No. 7:

> *I was in a prehistoric landscape at sunrise, of the kind associated with the dinosaurs. I was on a slightly elevated spot looking down upon a large lake surrounded by volcano-like mountains and the sort of trees, now extinct, that grew at that time. Playing inside the lake were a great many dinosaurs of all sizes. I got the impression that there were a few adults and many young ones of various ages. The type of dinosaur in the dream is known to science as the* Brontosaurus, *whose long neck and massive body are distinctive traits. While watching them play, I realized that even the slightest "mistake" on their part, such as being hit by one of their tails as they dove under the surface of the water, would be utterly fatal for me. The sheer enormity of the animals was contrasted with the insignificance of myself, the human. At the same time, the sight of these ancient animals in all their living vitality was so awesome and beautiful, strange and wonderful, that I could not tear myself away from the spot where I was standing and continued to watch them for a long time. Then I awoke. As soon as I awoke, the first thought that went through my semiconscious mind was: "Now, very soon, your baby will arrive." That evening I did go into labor.*

The labor lasted 27 hours! Dinosaurs are in fact the ancestors of the mythological dragons that have presumably been derived from them. On this, Jung says the following: "These cold-blooded relics [snakes, crocodiles, etc. are included] are, in a way, uncanny powers, because they symbolize the fundamental factors of our instinctive life, dating from Paleozoic times." And: "So whenever life means business, when things are getting serious, you are likely to find a saurian on the way." When he is benevolent, he is "a tremendous force of organized instinct and pushes you over an obstacle which you would not believe possible to climb over by will-power or conscious decision. There the animal proves to be helpful."[38]

It is during birth that the deepest instincts from our infinitely remote past take the lead. Jung says that the saurian or primary worm is related to our primeval elementary centers from which derive the earliest psychic manifestations. The saurian, according to Jung, brings to light the contents of the unconscious.[39]

[38] C.G. Jung, *Dream Analysis*, The Seminars, Routledge & Kegan Paul, 1984, pp. 645-6

As we shall see in the Chapter *Creation Motifs*, according to the *I Ching*, the dragon is the cosmic energy in the first trigram that is behind all creative processes on earth. Its energy or power prevails over all creative things! Hence it represents tremendous primary energy similar to wind or water. What it brings forth from the unconscious is pure, still unconscious creation consisting of instinctive energy connected with psychic contents, in other words, spiritual energy. These are the images from the collective unconscious, from the deep waters – the archetypal images, as Jung called them. Not only on the level of the instinct but also in the psyche, the dragon personifies the "knowledge of nature," the knowledge of what lies ahead! (In Greek, *drako* = snake, also symbolizing the "knowledge of nature.")

Since the beginning of humankind, in the volcano-like primeval landscape, the sunrise has been an image for the birth of light or, psychologically, for the beginning of consciousness. As we shall be studying many dreams in this book, we shall repeatedly encounter the motif of the birth of consciousness in the context of the birth of a child.

In the dream, the dreamer is aware that one "mistake" the saurians make, be it only hitting her with the tail, could be fatal for her. The proximity of such stupendous instinctive forces is always dangerous for the minute human consciousness. Just as even today a birth can and will be associated with the death of mother and child, so can the onset of a pregnancy psychosis result in the submersion of consciousness in the unconscious. Here, woman is entirely dependent on Nature's not making any "mistake." Much could be said about the play of dinosaurs and about creative play in general. For the origin of creation is often in play, just as many people's creative deeds are first brought on in a playful way.[40] It is as if nature or creative imagination can flow out from the unconscious most freely and most undisturbed during play.

Perhaps the woman experienced something similar during the long delivery if, as she writes, she was in an inner conversation with the dream during the entire time (*like a continuing active imagination*). A very serious inner play!

The next two dreams stem from a twenty-seven-year-old woman in her first pregnancy during which she felt exceptionally healthy and good.

Dream No. 8:

> *I sat by the side of a river, fishing. The river was flowing strongly from left to right. I hooked something which proved to be very heavy. I raised it to the surface and was horrified to find I had brought up the skeleton of a prehistoric fish, "something very ancient." This frightened me extremely.*

---

[39] *Ibid.*, p. 334
[40] Cf. J. Huizinga, *Homo ludens: A Study of the Play Element in Culture*, J. & J. Harper Editions, New York, 1970; and U. Mann, *Der Ernst d. hl Spiels*

And a few months later:

Dream No. 9:

> *I sat by the side of a river, fishing. Again I hooked something which proved to be very heavy. As it neared the surface, I could see a round dark shape, darkly iridescent, a huge dark "sunfish," 3-4 feet across (when normally these are only 2-3 inches across). Again I experienced enormous fear, and picking up my fishing knife, severed the line.*[41]

Before we turn to the principle motifs of these two dreams, namely the fish, let us first carefully amplify the starting point, that is, the fishing by the river. The ancients imagined the darkness of the soul[42] like a stream, something flowing. There are countless tales where a person is carried off across waters into a fairy tale or awesome land of the hereafter. Sometimes he/she is thrown ashore again, sometimes the water turns into a death stream running between this life and the hereafter, like Acheron or Lethe in Greece, or the River Leiptr of the Teutonic Edda.[43]

The tales of a man/woman being carried off to an unknown destination describe the stream of destiny flowing incessantly like the unconscious soul's stream of images. We know how easily man/woman can drift away from reality through unworldly and naïve fantasies and thoughts, leading in extreme cases to the mental asylum. Conversely, ideas and symbols from the unconscious can motivate and set free tremendous new powers. Therefore, like the dragon and the wind, the river symbolizes energy from the unconscious.[44]

In fact, through the power of water, e.g., electricity, rivers supply us with energy. Before man had decided to utilize this energy with technology, the river simply symbolized life and fertility. Before building the dam of Assuan to extract energy from it, the Nile meant yearly flooding, growth in nature and life. For this reason rivers often represent feminine-maternal goddesses.[45] In popular belief, the flowing water from the river has both fertilizing and healing qualities. It cleanses and washes off disease and can, if you are not careful, take away your health.[46] Psychologically, contact with the stream of unconscious thoughts and feelings can be healing as well as fertile, provided it is undertaken with sufficient caution. In most parts of the world fishing is associated with countless taboos. The same goes for the relationship with the inner stream. If we succeed in coming closer to the dream stream in the right way and with due respect, we can rid ourselves of fallacious, misguided attitudes,

---

[41] By the same dreamer: No. 123, Chapter 7
[42] Martin Ninck, *Die Bedeutung des Wassers*, p. 136
[43] *Handwörterbuch d. dt. Aberglaubens*, Vol. 2, p. 1693
[44] C.G. Jung, *Seminare: Traumanalyse*, p. 473
[45] Heinrich Zimmer, *Mythen und Symbole*, pp. 117 and 123 ff
[46] *Handwörterbuch d. dt. Aberglaubens*, Vol. 2, p. 1681

and new impulses can emerge. Rivers have always been deities, powerful factors in the psyche and natural forces determining the destiny of human life.

If we consider the river as a stream of unconscious energies, of unformed psychic forces and cryptic motivations, then fishing must have to do with extracting something from this chaotic mass, this unconscious domain: some nourishment to feed on.

Let us now take a closer look at the symbol of the fish, one of the most important symbols. Jung has devoted five chapters to it in his work *Aion* alone. The symbolic images expressing the ideas related to the symbol of the fish in past centuries, help us to approach the general meaning of such a dream. As Jung explained on the basis of his research into symbolism, "Every psychic product, if it is the best possible expression at the moment for a fact as yet unknown or only relatively known, may be regarded as a symbol."[47] If a dream avails itself of an ancient symbol such as the fish, we can assume that the unknown element behind it is a psychic principle similar to what has been behind the living fish-symbol of earlier ages. The symbols of our dreams often seem to stem from a more ancient layer of our psyche, from antiquity or the middle-ages, or even from a prehistoric layer. Those images were represented and interpreted in the context of their time and age.

If by comparative analysis we succeed in translating them into the language of today, we have at least managed to gain a little more understanding of them. Although Jung says that we are replacing one symbol by another, we find that our own interpretation means more to us and gives us more satisfaction.

Let us now return from the symbol to the fish: It is remarkable to see, how respectfully and cautiously the fish was approached by popular customs. People suspected a certain magic power in it. Fishing, for instance, required specific behavior including eating prohibitions, regulations regarding the time and place of fishing, processions, sacrificial acts, keeping the waters clean (!), etc. On the isle of Farø, meeting a priest or a minister before fishing had to be avoided.[48] This could mean that the demonization and dismissal of numinous forces, through Christian ideas that were adopted in all those regions visited by Christian missionaries, had to be avoided!

Owing to their great fertility, fish were closely associated with women's fertility, that is to say, with the blessing of children. Fish dishes at wedding ceremonies, ritual baths and contact with fish were part of this. Many folk tales speak about how eating fish causes pregnancy. People also imagined the still unborn children as tiny little fish, before they were born from a fountain into the human world.

Fish also possessed higher knowledge. Many fairy tales tell of speaking and helping fish; Grimm's fairy tale, "The Fisherman and His Wife," is one example.

---

[47] C.G. Jung, CW 6, § 817
[48] *Handwörterbuch d. dt. Aberglaubens*, Vol. 2, pp. 1529 ff

Figure 3. Vishnu as a fish (India)

The Babylonian fish-god Oannes was also a god of wisdom. He imparted to men and women the knowledge of agriculture and culture. Just as there were sacred sources, ponds and rivers, so there were sacred fish whose behavior would be observed, for instance, during the time of feeding, in order to tell the future. People hoped to gain insights from them about the mysterious, fateful connections existing in the water (which, in fact, meant in the unconscious).[49]

At the beginning of the creation, where man first came into being, one often encounters the fish. In our language, it means the place where human consciousness came forth from the unconscious for the first time. In Argos, Greece, the first man was Phoroneus, the son of Inachos, the god of the river. In India, a tale is told of how, in the great flood, Vishnu, the great god of creation, appearing as a fish and also as a tiny golden fish, came to the rescue of Manu, the original man.[50]

The first Christians, from around 200 A.D. on, described Christ, or God-become-man, as a fish. In many religions, the fish is a symbol of the Savior. Christ, which in Greek is Ichthys, fish, also signifies the inexhaustible nourishment of the faithful during the feeding of the 5000; and the faithful are the fish that have been fished by the disciples, the man-fishers (the ones who have become conscious through Christ!). As Jung explains in *Aion*, Christ himself rose like a fish from the unconscious of the men and women of that time; an image, as it were, of the unconscious Self, the all-including wholeness. Christ as a fish means that man can perceive his wholeness or Self in his deep instinctive impulses and biological drives but also in his emotions and convictions. "When these emerge from the unconscious, they can either oppress or else 'nourish' and enrich consciousness."[51] Many other religions also felt this to be a numinous occurrence. It was Jung who, in the 20th century again made us aware of this; contrary to Freud, who held the view that the unconscious contained mainly repressed sexual desires, in other words, waste products of consciousness. One could compare this notion with the idea that the sea is but a container of shipwrecks and other rubbish produced by mankind.

Let us not forget to mention the particularly important link between the fish and the feminine. In the cults of the Near Eastern mother-goddess, Kybele, the fish was worshipped, and her priests were not allowed to eat it. The fish was also the sacred animal of Atargatis, the Syrian mother-goddess. Atargatis was venerated both as Derketo in the shape of a semi-fish and as Aphrodite in Asia Minor and in Greece[52]. Her temples were surrounded with

---

[49] Martin Ninck, *Das Wasser* 97

[50] Manfred Lurker, *Wörterbuch der Symbolik*, 209 f

[51] Emma Jung / M.-L. von Franz, *The Grail Legend*, Princeton University Press, 1970, p. 189

[52] Manfred Lurker, *Lexikon der Götter und Dämonen*, 50 7 ["Dictionary of Gods and Goddesses, Devils and Demons," London, New York: Routledge and K. Paul, 1987]

sacred fish ponds. Feminine contents of the unconscious of very great numinosity were at play here.

As our dreamer is a pregnant woman, we have to bear in mind the feminine-maternal aspects of the elements we have discussed.

The river, vigorously flowing from left to right, apparently corresponds to a psychic stream of energy flowing towards consciousness. The dreamer wants to fish there, perhaps to bring up unknown contents that have to do with the enchanting and inexplicable power, the deeper knowledge of the unconscious or even with a larger feminine personality, the Self.

"The fish, living in the darkness of deep water, is often illustrative of a content of the unconscious that lingers below the threshold of consciousness and in which instinctual and spiritual aspects are still merged in an undifferentiated state. Therefore, the fish is an inspirer, a bringer of wisdom and, at the same time, a helpful animal – at once insight and redemptive, instinctive impulse."[53]

Now, the surprising and strange thing about the first dream is the fact that the dreamer does not bring up a fish, but a prehistoric skeleton, "something very ancient," as she says and which gives her a fright. Perhaps she does not quite know what it means to bring up the contents of the unconscious. The dream shocks her: "Look, it is much deeper and much more ancient than you think!" The skeleton, representing the apparently imperishable basic structure of a body, comes from the most ancient layer of the beginning of life. The fish, as a new instinctive and emotional impulse relating to pregnancy and to a large extent to the development of woman and possibly also to the new child, has an inner "structure" (biol. *Stroma* or *reticulumin*) in a prehistoric layer. Such an archetypal structure, i.e., a hidden design, Jung discovered in the unconscious. It manifests itself as symbolic collective imagery and ideas shared by entire cultures and throughout the ages.[54] The dream seems to say that we are now dealing with things that link the dreamer's life and pregnancy with the most ancient layers of the soul and of life. No wonder therefore that the small ego of everyday life is startled by such insights!

Jung assumed that in those deepest levels of the collective unconscious, where independently of historic tradition or migration common mythological motifs and images are generated, that there, mind and matter were not differentiated; that in a sense there was an *unus mundus*, an all-embracing original entity.[55] Moreover, Jung observed that certain events seem to stem from this layer, conspicuous by their meaningful connection to both the concrete material reality and the psychic domain. He called them synchronistic events. The

---

[53] M.-L. von Franz / Emma Jung, *The Grail Legend,* p. 189

[54] M.-L. von Franz, *C.G. Jung, His Myth in Our Time,* C.G. Jung Foundation for Analytical Psychology, Inc., New York, 1975, p. 125

[55] Cf. C.G. Jung, CW 8, Chapter VII, *Synchronicity*

prehistoric fish skeleton seems to point to such a (usually invisible) original entity. Not only do the new feelings, emotions and instinctive reactions, elicited by the immense physical changes in a pregnant woman, derive from this original entity, but ultimately also the concrete child. When it comes to the deeper layers of the collective unconscious, we can no longer, according to Marie-Louise von Franz, differentiate between mind and matter, between inner and outer.[56] Here we come across some serious difficulties in our work on the dreams in pregnant women. For we shall see in the course of this entire book that the archetypal dreams in pregnant women frequently revolve around the domain of the *unus mundus*. In other words, we cannot be sure whether they refer primarily to psychic occurrences, i.e., to a psychic rebirth in the dreamer, or to the child about to be born, or to both. But about this more will be said later.

In the second dream, a few months later, the dreamer is again fishing by the river. This time, she pulls out a gigantic round, dark "sunfish," that is darkly iridescent and very heavy. In order to approach this highly powerful and paradoxical image, it is best to resort to alchemy.

Jung was the first to demonstrate how, at the time when chemistry and physics were still at the early stages of development, vital psychic contents were projected onto substances largely unknown at the time.[57] In their experiments, laboratory technicians or the alchemists would come across unconscious psychic experiences which they would formulate in a language that has become quite remote to us, full of seemingly abstruse symbolism. The unconscious in its essential contents was thus expressed in a medium that even the alchemists themselves only intuitively perceived as psychic reality. This lasted over millennia (the beginnings of alchemy are directly traceable to the ancient Egyptian times of the pharaohs).[58] In fact, alchemy led a clandestine existence in the shadow of the official religious and philosophical trends. It is thanks to Jung that this valuable reservoir of psychic experiences, often dealing with areas which have been neglected in the collective consciousness, such as the feminine and Nature, are now accessible to the consciousness of our day and age. Research in alchemy was continued by Marie-Louise von Franz and is far from being completed.[59] Some dreams seem to actually "make use of" alchemical symbolism, so that oftentimes, in the case of archetypal dreams, we are obliged to resort to alchemy.

In his extensive investigations into the fish symbolism of the Middle Ages, Jung shows that especially in alchemy, from the 11th century on, round, iridescent fish enjoyed a special status.[60] The alchemists named a round, shining

---

[56] M.-L. von Franz, *Projection and Re-Collection in Jungian Psychology*, p. 88
[57] Cf. C.G. Jung, CW 12, *Psychology and Alchemy*
[58] Cf. *Die Forschungen von M.-L. von Franz und Th. Abt*, unpublished
[59] Cf. *ibid*.

fish that was supposedly hot and burning, *stella marina*.[61] Picinellus says, this fish glowed but did not shine. It belongs to "fire without brilliance which though has the power to burn, is dispossessed of light."[62] We are reminded of our curious paradoxical dream vision of the "dark sunfish," that is dark and yet luminous. This must have to do with Paracelsus' *lumen naturae*, a light that becomes visible in nature's wisdom. This *lumen naturae* also shines in the water. It illuminates the darkness of the unconscious when, for example, we have discovered the meaning of a dream. The unexpected, helpful meaning of the dream lights up from the darkness of the unconscious, as it were, and opens our eyes!

Certain alchemists held the view that God himself began to glow in this submarine fire, in this glowing fish.[63] In other words, the human idea of wholeness was projected onto this fish. As we shall see in more detail in the chapter on creation motifs, roundness in itself has served as an ancient image of God. In a 15th century text, *isculus rotundus*, the round fish, carries within him a stone (among other things a symbol of the Self), the so-called "dragon stone."

It is dark and black and yet transparent and radiant.[64] This opposite nature inherent in *stella maris* with its creative and at the same time destructive fascination, has been described by other alchemists, too. There are other accounts of extreme contrast inherent in "Little Echeneis," a tiny fish from the depths of the ocean which, despite its minuscule size, has the strength to hold up huge liners. Jung interprets it (as well as the round fish in general) as the Self which, despite its tiny size in the ocean of the unconscious, disposes of tremendous strength.

When the Self is represented as a symbol of the fish, its state is that of an unconscious content.[65] On the one hand, the Self is only actually perceptible once it has entered our awareness; on the other hand, "experience has shown that it has existed for a long time, that it is older than the ego and that it primarily represents the *spiritus rector* of our destiny."[66]

Having amplified these aspects, we can now better understand why the dreamer experienced such enormous fear when she saw this dark sunfish. It is an image of God in its entire overwhelming and terrifying contradictory nature and magnitude that is shining at her from the depths of the unconscious. "Fear of God" is the right reaction here: it would mean a tremendous overrating of the ego, were it to try to integrate the Self in its totality into

---

[60] Cf. also C.G. Jung, CW 9/II, *Aion*, Chapters VI-XI
[61] *Ibid.*, § 197
[62] *Ibid.*, § 199
[63] *Ibid.*, § 200
[64] *Ibid.*, § 213
[65] *Ibid.*, § 219
[66] *Ibid.*, § 257

consciousness. For this reason, to cut the fishing line seems the right thing for the dreamer to do.

This second dream tells the dreamer once again, yet in a more powerful and more detailed manner, that in her pregnancy, all the physical, sexual and emotional impulses welling up from the unconscious, belong to her unconscious wholeness; or, in the language of the Middle Ages, to that which God has intended for her. To have a child also signifies inescapable fatefulness, for good or bad. Ultimately, "the fear of God" alone can endow woman with the readiness and willingness to bear what is to come, whatever it may be, and to sufficiently value her life as a mother, however it may turn out to be. The shining, dark fish symbolizes a shedding of light upon one's purpose in life originating from the personality's unknown psychic background. However, this should not be confused with "happiness" in the usual sense of the word as it encompasses a great deal more.

Dream No. 10:[67]

> *A kissing fish (a tropical fish) jumped up from a glass fishbowl. The kissing fish changed its appearance and became a colorful (like a rainbow) carp in front of me. It was so graceful.*

I shall only briefly discuss this dream that a mother had during her third pregnancy. Compared to a river or ocean, a glass bowl holds a small amount of water. You can calmly behold a fish in a bowl; it is now within your reach, as it were. In other words, it exists in the personal unconscious of the dreamer (more about the glass bowl in the plant chapter). The personal unconscious contains "acquisitions of personal life, everything forgotten, repressed, subliminally perceived, thought, felt."[68] These things are more familiar to us than the mythological motifs and images of the collective unconscious that can come into being anew everywhere and at any time, independent of any historical tradition or migration. The fish as an unknown substance is thus closer to consciousness. The "kissing fish," probably related to Eros, turns into a carp which, owing to the ripe old age it is known to reach, has been designated an animal of wisdom. In the past, it was thought that the carp wore a small stone over each one of its eyes "in the shape of a half-moon." This stone plays an important role in folk medicine.[69] Because of the "moonstone" the carp is seen as an animal of nocturnal wisdom, nocturnal light and of the feminine. Moreover, in the dream it contains all the colors of the rainbow, indicating thereby potential psychic wholeness.

---

[67] By the same dreamer: No. 94, Chapter 5.7
[68] C.G. Jung, CW 6, § 842
[69] *Handwörterbuch d. dt. Aberglaubens*, Vol. 4, pp. 1008 f

This dream seems to allude to a process of change taking place in the unconscious of the dreamer and developing into a larger inner "wisdom" containing all of life's richness of color. The image of the peacock with its multicolored tail is a popular motif in ancient alchemist prints and calligraphy. It is an essential characteristic of Juno, the mother-goddess who, like the peacock renewing its feathers every year, affords permanent renewal. It is therefore closely associated with all transformations in Nature.[70] In Alchemy, the *cauda pavonis*, a peacock's tail, appears shortly before completion of the work. In our dreamer, this transformation takes place on a deep instinctive level, but the beholding ego is delighted by it. The changing of colors seems to announce the coming "completion of the opus," the forthcoming birth. This dream does not contain any terrifying appearance of a paradoxical divine image, but instead seems to reassure the dreamer. In a later chapter, we will discuss another one of her dreams and find that this will still hold true.[71]

In an ancient Egyptian grave of the 19th Dynasty, there is an illustration in which, in place of a mummified human body, a carefully bandaged fish is shown. On a coffin of a later date one can see a fish above the mummy instead of the traditional Ba-bird, the bird of the soul. The fish is marked with the symbol for "body."[72] We could perhaps add here that the dreamer at this point would be best advised to concentrate on what is happening inside her body, to calmly "watch" the new being grow, and to anticipate the child with joy! And while she is focusing on the physical aspect, behind the fish there is the unconscious Self, her specific wholeness. Her present condition – that which she "lives in her body" – seems to correspond to the Self and to her growing into a whole personality.

Dream No. 11:[73]

> *I am in much pain. I am lying on the grass on the front yard. A cool breeze is blowing over me. I am as comfortable as possible with my pain. I am very weak and lifeless. My husband is worried. My brother-in-law suddenly appears and tells my husband to take me down to the lake, and have me swim out to the middle, where there is a large dead frog (the size of a car). He says this dead frog has a healing effect on people when they swim over it. My husband explains to me what my brother-in-law said. It all*

---

[70] C.G. Jung, CW 14/II § 58

[71] Dream No. 95, Chapter 5.7

[72] Erik Hornung, *Geist der Pharaonenzeit*, 168 [Idea Into Image: Essays on Ancient Egyptian Thought, Timken, New York, 1992]

[73] This dream stems from an essay by Th. Schroer, "Archtypal Dreams during the First Pregnancy," in *Psychological Perspectives*, Vol. 15, No. 1, 1984. With the kind permission of the author, several dreams from this essay will be used for our own interpretation.

sounds very logical to me. My husband helps me down to the lake. We both jump in and swim towards the middle, where the frog is. The water is a pleasing temperature, but very murky, dark and horrible smelling. I fully believe that this will heal my pain. When I reach the point where the huge dead frog is, I am appalled by the way it looks. It is rotten. Suddenly the weakness I felt when swimming disappears. I soar out of the water and into the sky. I feel no pain. I don't know where I am going, but I feel a great deal of sorrow at leaving my husband behind.

The dream begins with the dreamer suffering strong pain. We do not know why. Neither is it known to us why she is not in her bed but lying outside on the grass. It seems natural, though, to connect her pain and weakness to the fact that she is pregnant with the first child. Something is not going well in her pregnancy, either physically or psychologically, or both. Since we do not know the dreamer, we can only guess. As to the brother-in-law, without the dreamer's associations we cannot say why it is he who knows what needs to be done. On this personal level, much of what could be elucidated in a conversation with the dreamer, we have to leave open. So far we can only say that he presumably represents an animus aspect that actively does something in the face of this menacing situation and that he seems to know what must be done.

Together with her husband the dreamer is to swim out to the middle of this murky, stinking lake where there is a large dead, rotting frog. Firstly, the pond: unlike rivers, ponds and lakes are stagnant waters. Formerly people believed that they were so deep that there was a subterranean link to the sea.[74] In their still darkness, they were perceived as particularly unfathomable, even uncanny. In people's fantasies, they were inhabited by female and male water spirits, awesome water animals, e.g., snake-like fish, dragons (in places like Allgäu, Mecklenburg, Loch Ness!), child-abducting witches, viragoes, and sometimes dead souls. In order to pacify the awesome powers from the depths, cult worship, supplicatory processions and even sacrifices were needed.

On the other hand, it is known that ponds were considered as "children's reservoirs," from which, so it was said, children and even pets could be obtained. The earliest Christian churches very often had a sacred pond to which healing powers were ascribed. And even today we continue to hope for healing and alleviation of pain from mud baths!

It seems that for the dreamer healing can be found in this murky pond and stagnant, profound, earthy water. This image of the unconscious differs from the surge of the sea or the limpid flow of the river. The emphasis lies with death, decay and renewal of life which suggests healing. From the old and the decayed, new things can be born. The fact that the dreamer dives into the

---

[74] *Handwörterbuch d. dt. Aberglaubens*, Vol. 7, pp. 1558 f

water and swims out to the middle is important in this dream. Symbolically, it stands for active immersion in the unconscious as well as turning towards the center, the core of the personality and the Self. In the previous dreams, a more contemplative or cautious attitude to the unconscious was indicated, perhaps even withdrawal. Here, without hesitating, the dreamer jumps into the water, knowing instinctively that this is the right thing for her.

Everywhere in folklore, immersion and swimming have to do with transformation and renewal and with the introduction and initiation in a new outer and inner state. The same symbolism is behind baptism. We may thus assume that the healing process in our dreamer is related to a profound transformation.

Figure 4. Heket taking the queen to give birth

What is the meaning of the dead, rotting frog that is the size of a car and yet has healing power? Again, Egypt's marsh and river land is a rich source of information on the symbol of the frog. Frogs were among the 8 primary gods that existed already before the origin of the world. They are personifications of the primary forces of chaos. Here the frog is a chthonic animal pointing to the forces contained in the beginning of life.[75] Nun, the god of chaos or the primeval sea before the Creation, sometimes has a frog-head. Nun's female

Figure 5. Heket with 'Ankh,' the sign of life, bringing to life the child created by Chnum, the creation god, together with his 'twin brother,' his Ka-soul (his life force)

[75] Manfred Lurker, *Lexikon der Götter und Symbole der alten Ägypter*, 75 [The Gods and Symbols of Ancient Egypt: An Illustrated Dictionary, Thames and Hudson, New York, 1980]

equivalent is Naunet. In India, too, the frog belongs to the undifferentiated matter before the Creation. Moreover, it is the sacred animal of Heket, the Egyptian primeval goddess and midwife. She is a life-giver. "Together with the deities that create all human beings, she forms a child in the maternal womb and as a 'deliverer' supervises its birth."[76] We can find her image on sarcophagi, representing the patroness and life-creating power for life after death. She is worshipped together with Chnum, the god of creation.

Man has always been fascinated by the phenomenon of the frog's transformation from tadpole to an actual figure. It is because of this metamorphosis that the frog became a symbol of transformation. This also signified transformation into a new life after death.

This idea was taken up by early Christianity, and thus the frog became the actual symbol for resurrection.[77]

The first croaking of frogs signaled the revival of Nature. This was commonly associated with forthcoming rain, with water, with renewal of life, particularly in those regions where rain marked the long hoped-for end of drought.

In the dream, the frog is in the center of the lake. Symbolically it is the center of the unconscious or the place occupied by the Self. In the murky rotten stinking water, the chaos before the creation, lies the central substance that creates new life, heals and transforms. The motif of the initial chaos is reminiscent of the idea the alchemists had, according to which the very process of producing gold, that is, of the philosophical stone (Jung called it the individuation process), begins with the phase of Nigredo, which means of darkness. The phase of darkness is a time in which things are still vague, not yet discernible, a time of uncertainty and confusion and a time of disintegration and depression that has to be endured. It is also this dark, destructive aspect of the unconscious that we usually encounter in our first dealings with this. It includes instincts with their archetypal background which, according to Marie-Louise von Franz, generally appear first in chaotic form in the earth, in other words, as a projection. If we take a closer look at the seemingly bad dreams or the projections onto all the external negative influences we are subjected to, we can suddenly see that it makes sense and we can see the light.[78] The birth of the "divine child" also happens in this way: almost always out of chaos or a catastrophe, be it a flood or be it the Massacre of the Innocents. The new symbol of the Self is born in perfect darkness.

Our dreamer appears to be in a comparable state of unhappiness at the beginning of the dream. She is ill, weak and in pain. Many women experience this when they become pregnant. To begin with they feel badly, unsure, anx-

[76] H. Bonnet, *Reallexikon der ägyptischen Religionsgeschichte*, p. 285
[77] Manfred Lurker, *Lexikon der Götter und Symbole der alten Ägypter*, p. 65
[78] M.-L. von Franz, *Alchemy*, pp. 220, 221, 225

ious, troubled with physical discomfort, their vitality has diminished and they feel they are no longer in charge of their own life. The dream says that the dreamer has to immerse herself more deeply and that she has to completely surrender to the unconscious which feels so chaotic to her; for it is there that the child is created! The unconscious is the world of the instincts, of the most profound physical processes and the corresponding fantasies and images. It is there that she can obtain help and healing.

Why, however is the frog so repulsive, rotting, stinking – dead? And yet it has healing power? Even though we have great difficulty in accepting this paradox, this paradoxical quality is in the nature of the unconscious. It includes those contents of which we should be or once had been conscious, be it on the level of a culture or an individual. Oftentimes they behave like the contents of a rubbish bin: they rot and stink. The frog is an archetypal symbol, something that has never been fully conscious, which is why the comparison is a little lame. As we have seen, it has to do with the profound, instinctive and vital energy that helps to sustain birth, renewal and transformation. The decaying element is, in fact, a precondition for the revival of Nature. Thus, in Egyptian books of the dead, Osiris, the god of resurrection, was called "the lord of putrefaction and the lord of lush green."[79]

Now, it is possible that the condition of the frog has to do with this unconscious-chaotic-instinctive domain; a domain in which the feminine-maternal is rooted and which, in our Christian culture, has been occupied with various taboos and precautionary measures against its unpredictability. It is therefore likely that today's woman has not experienced access to this domain, which is so important for her physical and psychological well-being. What she really needs is Heket, a frog goddess! Therefore she must reestablish contact with this important archetype by going into the unconscious and sinking inwardly, as it were, without fear or reluctance and give herself over to the chaotic feelings and emotions. We can infer from the dream that she is well advised to do this and that there is no danger of an uncontrollable onset of depression or dissociation by the unconscious.

The final scene of the dream with her rising from the water into the air can be seen positively because she has presumably been cured from her suffering. This new condition could be likened to the alchemist phase of Albedo, which means whitening, and follows Nigredo. In this phase, writes Marie-Louise von Franz, we can observe things more calmly, more objectively and are less caught up in the emotional chaos. "Our standpoint is *au dessus de la melée*; we can stand on the top of the mountain and watch the storm beneath, which although it is happening we have no need to feel threatened by it."[80] The dreamer does not yet know where this elevated state will take her, and she feels

[79] E. Hornung, *Das Totenbuch der Ägypter*, Artemis, 1979, p. 215
[80] Cf. M.-L. von Franz, *Alchemy*, p. 222

great sorrow because she has to leave her husband behind. The motif of leaving the husband behind frequently comes up in pregnancy dreams.[81] The transition to the condition of a future mother or the initiation into a primeval female domain, such as birth, may be said to have ultimately always excluded men. Contrary to all efforts on the part of certain feminist tendencies, the unconscious seems to think that man cannot follow woman into this area, no matter how painful this may be for the relationship. On the other hand, he is clearly able to help her and to approach the unconscious and the unknown; whether he be an inner figure, an active, healthy, determined animus, or an open, tolerant husband, who does not shy away from all those chaotic feelings and emotions, which pregnancy can cause in woman. But he can only accompany her a little way: after that, she is alone and must find her own way.

With this dream, we are going to leave the symbol of water in pregnancy dreams. Because water is so often at the beginning of the creation, in some sense, this theme rejoins our last chapter on creation motifs. These motifs, which will meanwhile have been selected and treated, examine more closely still other aspects of the psychical experience. Finally, we shall try to see, whether or not there is a red thread running through all the chapters and whether we can recognize a meaning or logic behind the selection of the motifs we have made on the basis of the dreams.

[81] Cf. Th. Schroer, *Archetypal Dreams during the First Pregnancy*, p. 70

Figure 6. Mother Earth (Italian). Presumably an ancient mother-goddess named Tellus by the Romans, later named Terra Mater

3.2. Earth, Stones and Precious Stones

Irmgard Bosch

I. Earth

The abundance of meanings of the word "earth" is as immense as a multi-faceted landscape. The following examples may stimulate further reflection.

There is that ancient notion or image of the earth that in many cultures, including our own, has almost always been thought of as being somewhere below as well as being feminine. This is in clear contrast to the sky, which is perceived to be more spiritual. In the Chinese *I Ching*, like the image of the landscape under the sky, Kun, the earth is below and receiving. The ancient Egyptians, however, thought very differently: There, Nut, the goddess of the sky, arched over Geb, the god of the earth (Figure 7).

The fact that we view the earth as "this life" as opposed to "the life to come," is a result of the Christian influence. The Greeks of the classical age viewed the earthly deities or chthonic gods as gods of the hereafter and as the wise ones. They lived beneath the earth. In most cultures they indicate the beginning of the world. According to a pre-Greek myth widely propagated in the Mediterranean basin, Gaea, the goddess of the earth and the earth itself as deity, brought forth of herself her husband, Uranus, the starry sky. All gods and humans stem from them.[82]

Our earth is indeed the mother of all living creatures: it produces them, nourishes them, is their home and finally receives them in what seems like an eternal cycle. Since the Middle Ages, we have found these two ancient mother-of-the-earth-aspects in the most well-known Christian representations of the Madonna (Mary with the child and Mary as Pietà): holding on her lap not only the baby-son as the new life that has sprung from her, but also the dead man that has returned to her. However, as a remarkable contrast to this, in early Christianity, the great and liberating element of the young faith consisted in the very fact that Christ was the sole dead man who did not remain on earth:

---

[82] Karl Kerényi, *The Gods of the Greeks*, Pelican Books, London, 1958 and *Der Kleine Pauly, Gaia*, in *Lexikon der Antike in fünf Bänden*, Alfred Druckenmüllerverlag, Artemis, München, 1975

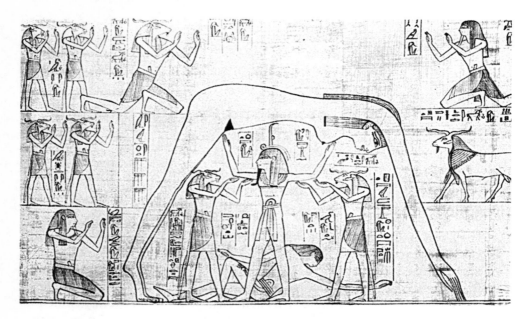

Figure 7. The God of the Air holding up Nut, the Goddess of the Sky, over Geb, the God of the Earth. (Drawing on the Grennfield papyrus, 21ˢᵗ Dynasty)

instead, he rose to heaven and to his father – rather than sinking back into his mother's lap. With the adoration of the Virgin Mary, something of the archaic faith in the "mother" was retrieved, however only a thousand years after its roots had been removed from the earth and had also settled in heaven.

Having looked back briefly into some intellectual history, let us return to the pregnancy dreams. In the first two dreams of this chapter, there is some suggestion that would point to the above-mentioned aspects of the earth as representing the primeval mother, the very source of all living beings. On the basis of the dreams, we shall consider in more detail the earth in terms of matter. Symbolically, the earth is comprised of mud, loam, clay, sand, dirt and other such things. We will go on to focus on stones, rocks, clefts, ravines, grottos and caves, for many dreams of pregnant women take us into the depths of the earth. Seeing a connection between the maternal uterus in which the child develops, the narrow passage through the birth canal and the archetypal cave-dreams pregnant women have, is certainly viable.

Since time immemorial, hills, mountains and valleys have continued to be associated with the beauty of the female body. In the domain of the "earth," there is a large range of the rich symbolism of the feminine and in particular of the mother.

Unlike the element of water, the earth appears less frequently in the dreams of pregnant women. Perhaps this has to do with the deep bond that unites us humans in our very essence with the earth. Indeed, according to 1. Moses 3, 19, "we have been taken from it" and shall return to it, which is why we can barely distinguish it as "other." The earth itself is, in the widest sense, our matter ("matter" comes from the Latin *mater*, "mother"). Figuratively speaking, it is that on which we stand, our "stand-point," and in every respect, the unconscious foundation of our existence.

Adolf Portmann, the great Swiss biologist and anthropologist, writes: "The child, itself the structure to be, has from the very start been adapted to this [our] geocentric environment, as an unknown whole, [so] that all of the maturing organisms' immediate experiences become geocentric."[83]

We are not conscious of this extensive reciprocity today. Earlier cultures were much more aware of this and made sacrifices to the earth as the mother-goddess in various forms.[84]

However, very ancient Greek myths tell of uprisings against her! The young hero rebels against the mother. Gaea had conceived all too indiscriminately and had given birth to odious monsters. There is, for instance, the story of Perseus' victory, which he gained by looking away from the dreadful, petrifying Gorgon Medusa, one of Gaea's granddaughters. The Jewish prophets, too, protested vociferously against the neighboring Near-Eastern mother-goddesses, whom, in the face of the One God of Israel, they considered "great" whores.

In the face of the radiant image of the Son of Man, all the multifarious heavenly and chthonic gods and goddesses eventually ceased to be venerable. The prevailing aspiration to the divine Union of Father, Son and Holy Ghost became the focus of interest. God appearing and being transformed on the soil of the earth might have resulted in man glorifying and praising the earth more than ever before. However, only in the Middle Ages, and only in the narrow context of the Holy Land, did the Christians honor the earth, and in particular, the Holy Grave (even though it was empty!). In the Jewish culture, the land of Israel has retained its numinous role. The idea that the entire earth would be sanctified by the incarnation of Christ never developed in the Christian world.

In modern times, we have become detached from the ecclesiastical-religious but also generally from the symbolic way of thinking; we have become "enlightened." We have now begun to explore the earth enthusiastically and with painstaking exactness, but have also inflicted more and more deep wounds on it. For, if – according to Jung – "mater" and "matter" are not only linguistically related but related in a far more consequential way, then we have wounded the "mother," i.e., the maternal principle. Now that, for the natural sciences, the earth has become nothing but matter, materialism takes on a variety of forms and shapes and often shows us a deadly grimace; just as if a

[83] Portmann, *Die Erde als Heimat des Lebens*, in: Eranos-Jahrbuch Vol. XXII, p. 473 ff
[84] Erich Neumann, *The Great Mother. An Analysis of the Archetype*, Bollingen Series 47, New York, 1955

kind of Gorgon, whose gaze already turned ancient men to stone, had re-emerged. If everything is but matter, though, then where do we stand? Another example: Don't images of horror and imminent danger stare us in the face once we think of the earth reacting to the ruthless exploitation of its resources? Do we not anticipate, almost paralyzed, the menacing climatic changes due to the deforestation of the rainforests? We live with the deep insecurity that the careless subjugation with which we have treated the earth in the past millennia might become our own undoing. As an antithesis to the widespread fear of the end of the planet earth as living space, for which mankind alone would be to blame, I wish to refer to C.G. Jung's statement that since the Renaissance, or the time when this a-symbolic, exact (Cartesian) and extremely successful "neutral" thinking began to be generally accepted, a new, ever increasing and henceforth much more conscious love began to flourish: the love for earthly beauty, for life on earth, for nature and for the body. In many places today a sense of and the will to assume responsibility for the earth as *Lebensraum* are gaining ground again.

Dream No. 12: A twenty-six-year-old woman (who was healthy and gave birth to a girl without complications) had this dream several times during what was her first pregnancy:

> *I am pulling up potato plants from a field*
> *An old, unknown woman comes up to me.*
> *Then I see that the potatoes are really nice little dolls in the earth.*
> *The old woman tells me that the dolls are my fetus.*
> *I am amazed and become filled with mixed emotions.*
> *Finally, I wake up very upset.*

Bending down to the earth and touching the ploughed soil cause unexpected consequences: an old, unknown woman appears as if the dreamer had summoned her with her gesture. Evidently, the old woman has something to do with what is now going on in the earth, and with the growing and maturing of the fetus in the pregnant woman's belly. – A mother-earth figure who is wiser than the young woman.

What the old woman now says sounds like an ancient myth. In fact the Etruscans told the story of peasants who ploughed a young boy from a furrow. They named him the "god of the day" ("Day"), and he made them wise. Thus, they gained wisdom from the earth.

To stoop down to the earth is an ancient gesture of worshiping the deities of the earth. People would invoke the chthonic gods (Greek *Chthonos* = "earth") by bending down low and with enshrouded heads. They venerated and feared their dark power so much that they stood in deep awe of these gods. Our dreamer cannot explain why she is suddenly confused and upset. We could paraphrase *"vocata et invocata,"* the saying that Jung had carved above his front door: at once invoked and not invoked the goddess was there, as if she belonged to the field.

Archetypal dreams often come with an awful fright. Sometimes the sleeping soul senses more acutely than our conscious ego the unfathomable and quite "other" that becomes manifest in a numinous experience. Sometimes the exact opposite may be true, too.

What is it that gives the dreamer such a fright that she wakes up confused and upset? Maybe she did not know that her pregnancy had to do with the earth and its deep dark layers. With this dream, she realizes that she and her body partake of Nature's fertility and of life and death. The latter is evoked by the restfulness of the earth. She begins to apprehend that she and her body are a part of Nature and thus not merely under the control of the ego but part of a higher, divine cycle of growth and decay. It is the primeval Mother Earth whom she meets in the "old, unknown woman" and who initiates her into this context. In view of the dimension her pregnancy assumes through the dream image, the fright and the "mixed feelings" are only too understandable and quite appropriate.

Mother Earth is ancient and has always been – from the beginning. As in the *I Ching*, she is also dark, in more than one way. According to Marie-Louise von Franz,[85] the image of the Great Mother is "… that of completeness in which everything is simply held together in one unified whole. Consequently, this feminine goddess all-Nature also possesses cunning, cruelty, wickedness, unfathomable depths of passion and the uncanny gloom of death, the smell of corpses and putrefaction in equal measure with the potentiality of new life and rebirth." Thus she not only gives birth or feeds, she also devours or slays – as in the examples of the mother goddesses Gaea, the Indian Kali, Ishtar and Hecate.

When the dreamer encounters her, she knows nothing of all this; she only feels something strange and frightening. Perhaps it makes her think of what people say at the graveside: "For dust thou art, and unto dust shalt thou return."[86] Or, the grain of wheat that falls into the ground where it perishes, in order to live[87] may come to her mind, which is even more relevant. Experiencing that her own fetus lies in the earth, something inside the dreamer "knows" that she herself is meant: that her belly is the earth, as it were, and that new life grows in it.

She has this dream repeatedly during her pregnancy, as if the unconscious were trying to tell her something important. Perhaps consciously she had imagined a heavenly little angel, something light and pure, coming down from "above," from heaven, so that – almost in the way of a compensation – the

---

[85] Marie-Louise von Franz, *Projection and Re-Collection in Jungian Psychology*, Open Court, La Salle, IL, 1980, p. 156
[86] Genesis, 3, 19, King James Version, Cambridge University Press
[87] St. John, 12, 24

dream now reveals the earthly side to her, her own fertility, figuratively as something earthy and chthonic. This knowledge, reaching her from unthinkable depths extends her field of consciousness and prepares her for the transition to a new form of life. This dream can therefore be interpreted as an obvious dream of initiation. Mother Earth herself initiates the woman into her secret. With a shudder, the knowledge of her partaking in a superhuman-divine happening is brought home to her.

About the following dream we were informed that before the present pregnancy there had been an abortion. Although the couple married after the abortion, there remained an uncertainty about whether or not they were going to stay together. The woman is a very creative artist, a practicing architect, and from childhood has been a very good dancer. It had been her decision to have the baby, despite the difficulties she experienced during pregnancy. The baby-girl was born healthy. Two years prior to this second pregnancy she had joined a psycho-analytical group. Her dreams at the time revealed that her unconscious was very concerned with the question of fertility. To give an example, her initial dream in the group was about an old woman who handed to her a little girl dressed in pink.

This dream was symbolically interpreted as pointing to a new creative activity as pregnancy was not an issue at the time.[88]

Dream No. 13:

> *I am playing with little figures of clay.*
> *There is a little girl of clay.*
> *Then she comes into life – like a human being.*

The clay figures again remind us of the biblical account of the Creation.[89] What is noticeable, however, is a stark contrast to the established tradition: this woman's dream suggests a somewhat unintentional play with clay figures. It is as if the possibility of creating a living being, a girl "somewhat unintentionally," existed in the material of clay itself, or in the process of play. In this activity, the woman is alone.

The image of the woman playing with clay figures relates to the first part of the dream which is about a primeval animal: a Brontosaurus. Hence it points to prehistoric times that, even in the mythical world of the Greeks, have become but a distant memory. According to a tradition we have already discussed above, Gaea created the earth and all living things after having brought forth her own husband Uranus, the starry sky.[90]

---

[88] Cf. Dream No. 156, Chapter 9
[89] Genesis, 3, 19
[90] Karl Kerényi, *The Gods of the Greeks* and Erich Neumann, *The Great Mother*, Princeton & London, 1955

It is not surprising then that there were myths of female primeval goddesses before, parallel to and outside the development of strongly patriarchal divine images. Even in ancient Judaism there were such trends, albeit outside of the official writings, in mystical literature, such as the Zohar and the Kabbala.[91] And even in the Bible we can find traces here and there of a female co-creator of the world. Her name is Sophia, the "wisdom" of God.[92] Sophia says:

> The LORD possessed me in the beginning of his way, before his works of old. When there were no depths, I was brought forth; ... When he prepared the heavens, I was there: ... Then I was by him, as one brought up with him: and I was daily his delight, rejoicing always before him; rejoicing in the habitable part of his earth; and my delights were with the sons of men.

This is a very arcane biblical passage! There is an allusion to the pleasurable, playful side of the creation and, interestingly, this is attributed to the feminine side of God. He is playfully surrounded by the wisdom of his "forewoman." How highly placed in this text is the role of the female co-creation – a role without which God could not have created anything intelligent – for, Sophia is his wisdom! Unfortunately, this passage stands rather alone and has become forgotten over the course of the Western intellectual history.

In India, on the other hand, the idea of Shiva and Shakti sharing the work of creation is still very much alive, and Tantrism, a religious-philosophical branch, remains popular to this day. There, Shiva is absolute being, invisible, and it is his strength or dynamism that in turn is visible, and that is the world. Because of the one-sidedness regarding the god of creation that characterizes our thinking, I wanted at least superficially to touch upon this remote example of different thinking.

The dream about playing with figures of clay can be compared to a so-called "big" dream. This kind of dream does not only address the individual, but contains a message for the entire tribe. If the dream is understood and taken seriously, then compensation by the collective unconscious for the collective conscious can take place. In a time where the collective consciousness sees pregnancy in an ambivalent, if not hostile, light, the dream could be saying in a clear and uninhibited fashion, that for the creation, as well as for the development of a human being, a playful and feminine element is at least as vital as the will-driven masculine element.

For our dreamer, the dream could suggest that even as a mother she will remain creative, in an unintentional, very natural way. Nowadays, putting one's profession last entails sacrifices for women; this is an important factor and a great relief, especially for this artistically inclined dreamer. As an answer

---

[91] Siegmund Hurwitz, *Lilith, The First Eve*, Daimon Verlag, 1992, *passim*
[92] Proverbs 8, 22-23; 26-31

to the problems of an unplanned pregnancy, this woman's unconscious has demonstrated to her how pregnancy could be valuable for her: although it may differ from professional creativity, it is none the less creative.

The following dream comes from a woman pregnant with her second child, a boy. The dreamer has contributed many dreams with detailed comments from her pregnancy. As to this dream, she notes that she was in a state of despair the day before and had had an argument with her husband. The following day she is cheerful again and full of energy, takes initiative and her husband is cooperative. About her cousin, Jackie, she writes: "She is friendly and kind. She can find solutions or the right things to say when everything seems hopeless." The dream has been slightly abbreviated:

Dream No. 14:

> *After a difficult descent down some steep narrow stairs during which the dreamer is being harassed by a fat fellow, whom she drives away by throwing stones at him, she hides behind large round slabs of rock by a river. These rocks, laid out in parallel rows, serve as a kind of a passage to the ocean. Groups of young people are playing there and having fun. The dreamer watches them from the distance. From then on she is with her English cousin J., whom she admires and loves. For J. is good, she can easily cope with unexpected, difficult situations. Together they now want to go over to the other shore and are looking for a passage through the rocks. J. goes in front. "But when I reach the cave I find the passage very narrow." In the end, it is very hard, she can barely get through, her head won't get through but she struggles and makes it. "I get stuck, but raising my head – I don't know how – I make it."*

It is possible that dreams about narrow passages, tunnels and caves in the earth, could be determined by an individual's own natal experience.[93] The motif of the narrow passage, in any case, illustrates an archetypal situation, similar to the one occurring before death[94] or in other times of crisis in life. We can compare the passage through the dark caves with introversion, or a psychic inward-turning. Whenever we have to make a grave decision or when duties collide causing unbearable pressure and every time we are in a state of worry or anxiety, we are psychologically in a narrow passage. Thus pregnancy can really feel like a crevice becoming forever more constricting! – At the unfathomable bottom of such imagery is the fear of the "devouring mother."[95]

As she goes down the narrow steps, she is harassed by this fat, young fellow

---

[93] An assumption of Artur Janov (*The Primal Scream*); however, there is no real evidence for it

[94] M.-L. von Franz, *On Dreams and Death*, Shambhala, Boston & London, 1986

[95] C.G. Jung, CW 5, Chapter VII

trying to flirt with her. This episode suggests that for the dreamer who is already close to the water, the masculine element and attitude now represent unwanted interference that she clearly rejects. It is not masculine but feminine assistance and support she now seeks. The happy young people playing in the rocks prompt the momentary yearning after the loss of a carefree youth. She is no longer destined to play in the rocks. Her destination is the ocean, and to reach it she has to make her way through the rows of rocks.

The large round stones are strongly reminiscent of the prehistoric stone arrangements of Brittany or other Atlantic coastal regions, with their alignments to which people have paid tribute for fertility rites since prehistoric times. More will be said about this in the section on stones and rocks.

To her pleasant surprise, her much admired cousin J. joins her. The feminine assistant comes to the rescue in a moment of crisis. Like Ariadne, who knows the way out of the rocky labyrinth, she securely guides the dreamer through the discomforts caused by the crevice.

We are dealing with the kind of assistance that has been rendered by women for women during the difficulties of pregnancy and delivery since the beginning of time. This assistance, moreover, often involves some secret knowledge passed down from one generation of women to the next, and to outsiders, therefore, could seem like magic or witchcraft. It is for this reason that midwives were often suspected of being involved with witchcraft.

J. assists and guides our dreamer through the passage by "struggling and making it." This struggle is important. The midwives' assistance during a birth also often involves struggling with life or death. Our dreamer admires her cousin's ability to always find appropriate solutions. J.'s superiority, springing spontaneously from the wholeness of a human being, is the result of her personality acting in agreement with her deeper Self. We do not know to what extent the real J. corresponds to the J. of the dream. In any case, it is her function to show the dreamer that she can get through and overcome the fear (narrowness) if she struggles for it.

This interpretation is confirmed at the end of the dream: "I get stuck, but raising my head – I don't know how – I got through it." The dreamer has been encouraged by J.'s example and empowered to the extent that she manages to get through the passage in an upright position. And almost accidentally, she adds the following crucial words: "I don't know how, I got through it." In other words, she managed to do it unconsciously, but correctly.

And indeed, whatever it is that comes to our rescue, we almost never "know" it beforehand. Marie-Louise von Franz once called it an instinctive "gliding over" to the right solution, upon which the conscious ego would hardly have chanced alone. The ego gets stuck only too easily in irreconcilable positions (here, the rocks), were it not for the regulating center, the deeper Self of the individual coming to its assistance with the instinctively correct attitude, whose source lies in the unconscious possibilities of the total personality.

II. Stones and Rocks, Monoliths

The element of the "earth" is often thought of as stone, as if it were something like its essence, its stone or "seed." Stones have also been considered the "bones" of the Mother Earth.[96]

Figure 8. Statuette of "Venus of Willendorf," approximately 30-40 thousand years old

There is something strangely fascinating about large natural stones. Is it their invulnerability, their age? Or, is it their glistening and glittering surfaces, the beautiful colors of granite and sandstone? Is it their "speaking silence," that unmistakable strength about them that has impressed man since the dawn of history? Mircea Eliade writes about the stone and how it affected prehistoric man: "... nothing was more immediate and autonomous in its full strength, nothing more magnificent and nothing inspired more awe than a majestic rock or a towering granite stone. Above all, the stone is 'being.' It always remains itself and exists through itself." This formulation has brought the image of the stone closer to the psychological image of the Self.

In all cultures of the world within living memory, the stone played a major role. In fact, we are coming back to the "Stone Age," where men and women found protection from the weather in the caves of the rocks and were confronted for the first time with the notion of something lasting, resistant to decay. We do not know which dates back further: the making of stone tools or the earliest symbols painted and carved on stone. Very early stone figures (aged approximately 20,000 years) that are clearly of human shape (anthropomorphic) sometimes represent full shapes suggesting female fertility (cf. *Venus of Willendorf*).

In all eras, stones were venerated in their natural formations; for instance, as Herms in their towering phallic shapes, or in their hollows, seen as symbols of the female womb (the Indian Lingam and Yoni).[97] The ancient Europeans would carve vulvae in certain places of rocks and caves.[98] Their consciousness of the *Terra Mater* was materialized in the stones.

[96] Mircea Eliade, *The Forge and the Crucible,* University of Chicago Press, 1978
[97] C.G. Jung, CW 13, § 123
[98] Marie König, *Unsere Vergangenheit ist älter, Höhlenkult Alteuropas*, illustration p. 143

Some very early cults revolved around the stone seat, the precursor of the regal throne. The king, as a son of the Great Mother, "mounted" it when he assumed power. In fact, the goddess Isis' symbol is the stone seat.[99]

Some of this ancient relationship with stone we can still feel today. We have a curious predilection for minerals and fossilization, for a particular pebble from the beach or we are mysteriously attracted to caves or large protruding stones. Stones can have "wakanda" to a large extent. C.G. Jung describes the quality "wakanda," similar to "mana," in the following way: "... wakanda (Oglala-Indian) can be better rendered by the word 'mystery' than by any other word; however, even this term is much too narrow: *wakanda* can mean secret, force, greatness, holy, old, alive, and immortal," qualities that, in popular belief, continue to be attributed to stones.[100]

The first monuments in the history of humankind have no doubt been natural stones. Some were venerated because they were thought to have come down from heaven. This is true even today for the Mohammedans' Kaàba in Mekka and in former times also the white stone at Delphi that was worshipped as omphalos, the navel of the earth. People liked to see a testimony to the gods in certain large stones but also a monument of conscious man in the infinite, pathless and awe-inspiring grand nature. Piles of rubble were attributed to Hermes, who was travel-wise and a patron of the travelers. In the pathless mountains and in remote areas, piles of rubble and little stone men are still associated with this meaning today. Their message is: someone has been here before, you can stay on this path, or: something has happened here that we must remember (cross of atonement, *Marterln* = stone niche with crucifix or saint's image). On the other hand, such marks may be saying: here has been a higher power, and man acknowledges this. This is where its presence has been felt and where it has struck fatefully – like the elements (blazes of lightning), and we shall not forget this: the stone monument bears witness to it.

A protected domain of a god and later temples were surrounded by stone-walls. There, the law of god and peace was supposed to reign. Large stones also marked boundaries and warned of transgression like guards. Boundary stones served as important juridical witnesses, and to this day the removal of boundary stones is a serious offence.

It is interesting to notice that monuments were erected spontaneously at a particular time of development in the most heterogeneous cultures and places on earth: the Ziggurats in Mesopotamia, the pyramids by the Nile and later in America, the stone circles, rows and dolmens of the Megalith culture in Ancient Europe and later the Christian domes. Like stones in Nature, these

---

[99] Erich Neumann, *Die Grosse Mutter*, p. 103. *The Great Mother*, Princeton & London, 1955

[100] Summarized in M.-L. von Franz, *Projection and Re-Collection*, pp. 67 ff

huge edifices belonged to the gods or god-kings. It is more than likely that, in their grandeur, they originally represented divinity itself.

Figure 9. Brittany, Presqu'île de Crozon

Later on, e.g., when the Celts settled in Europe and were already familiar with these stone arrangements from when they took over the land, the belief in the magic power of old stone monuments was maintained. Even though the original meaning had eroded, people related them to new, equally "real" rituals and new legends from their own intuition and dreams.[101] Mostly and probably rightly so people continued to associate them with fertility, that is, their orientation with respect to the constellation of the moon, sun and stars was used by the priests to determine sowing and harvesting. In many traditions and customs, fertility rites were conducted around stones, for example in Brittany, where it has survived to this day.[102] Scottish farmers know very well that they must never remove the standing stones – otherwise disaster will be brought upon them. Time and again, the Catholic church was obliged to prohibit pagan rites that were being conducted around the ancient stones – even by their own priests. In times as recent as the 19th century, women who could not become pregnant were said to have sought aid from the ancient stones (cf. Dream No. 15).

In his memories,[103] Jung writes about a certain large stone near the boundary of the garden where he played as a boy. He considered this stone to be "his stone" and would often sit down on it. Each time, he experienced a mysterious kind of identification with it so that he could not be sure whether he was the one sitting on the stone, or whether in fact he was the stone thinking that *he*

---

[101] Ingeborg Clarus, *Keltische Mythen*, Walter Verlag, Olten, 1991, p. 46 f

[102] *Handwörterbuch des deutschen Aberglaubens*, Bächtold-Stäubli, Berlin & Leipzig, 1927, "Stein"

[103] C.G. Jung, *Memories, Dreams, Reflections*, Vintage Books, New York, 1965, p. 20

was sitting on it. Whenever as a boy he was worried or uneasy, he could find peace and consolation in the stone. In the Middle Ages and in antiquity people thought that stones could grow, were animate and had a gender. Many legends talk about stones that have moved to their sites by themselves.

The imprints of polishing, scraping or beating catch the eye in many holy places and suggest that stones were considered to have some intrinsic secret numinosity within them. We can find imprints in prehistoric caves and rocks as well as at certain spots in pyramids or temples not to speak of the vast numbers of Christian churches.[104] Having received the benediction at the altar, all the men and women pilgrims in Santiago di Compostela in Northern Spain touch the marble pedestal of the stone statue of St. Jacob on the entrance hall of the cathedral. We are not only thinking of the Middle Ages but of our own age, and only having performed this deed will the pilgrimage be regarded as fully effective. The millions of fingers touching the marble stone have resulted in five deep-seated grooves! – Similarly, the same idea is behind the touching of the stones of the Western Wall of the temple in Jerusalem by devout Jews and Moslems.[105]

Today, just as several hundred years ago, in Karla, Middle-India, there are many large and smaller rocks along the steep winding path leading up to the cave temple. I saw how countless pilgrims, including women, laid flowers and offerings on the rocks and hollows and how, in passing, they lovingly rubbed red ocher – the ancient color of the realm of spirits – into the smaller holes. Not only is the temple hewed out of the rock but also the entire mountain with its rocks and stones are marked as sacred and consecrated. According to Mircea Eliade,[106] the red color symbolized the goddess' menstruation blood indispensable for the fecundity of the ploughed land. The stones were lovingly touched as well as the stone statue of the goddess, her stone breasts and her lap.

Many other sacred objects or gigantic stone figures symbolize in their grandiose image the mighty power of god. Examples of such places are: Abu Simbel in Upper Egypt, or the huge mandala-shaped Kailasa Temple near Ajanta in India, which have been directly carved out from the rock. If you continue to climb up the mountainside near this temple, you find it crisscrossed with innumerable, in parts incomplete, subterranean little temples, rosettes in the rock and other Mandala forms; the entire mountain has been turned into a temple.[107]

---

[104] M.E.P. König, *Unsere Vergangenheit ist älter*, p. 143

[105] In our hemispheres, the children's game "hide-and-touch" may be said to have preserved some of the magic of touching.

[106] M. Eliade, *The Forge and the Crucible*

Dream No. 15:

The dreamer is a woman with three children. She has had one miscarriage, and this is her fifth pregnancy. As with the previous pregnancy, it was neither planned nor wanted. And as before, she is considering abortion. She suffers from high blood pressure, insomnia, problems with her veins and some strange viral disease. Thanks to the psychotherapy the dreamer and her family are undergoing, family life becomes easier. A healthy boy was born. Here is the dream:

> *She goes towards a rock. She climbs it without difficulty, and it seems natural to her that it should be so. She wants to urinate, and she wants to enter the rock through a door, but she is not able to do so, though she had been able to do so at other times in the past. Her belly doesn't permit her to go through the door. She decides to go back home. There is a WC there and so she is able to urinate. The house looks like a shanty and is near the rock.*

In mythology, stones and rocks are sometimes given masculine characteristics and frequently also feminine ones. In European popular belief, there were practices where, through touching or sliding on a rock,[108] through disguising or dancing around erratic blocks, people hoped to obtain healing or help during pregnancy and for the forthcoming birth. *The Concise Dictionary of German Popular Belief* has the following entry on "stone": "Rites such as dancing around a stone ... are generally to be understood as fertility rites and have been maintained up until the most recent past." In Near-Eastern traditions we read about the stone birth of Mithras born of a rock ("petra genetrix").[109] There are many other birth legends that describe human births from a rock.[110]

It seems obvious in our dream that climbing the mountain has something to do with the pregnancy although the dreamer merely has the urge to pass water. Her situation with already three children is clearly problematic, and therefore both mentally and physically her pregnancy is, as it were, a stony road. Concretely and figuratively, "urinating" signifies a release of pressure and relief. Moreover, during the process of delivery, the so-called breaking of the waters brought about by the bursting of the amniotic sac is a great relief

---

[107] Ramana Maharishi, the South-Indian saint of this century, sat in "speaking silence." The Maharshi (Maha Rishi = great teacher) sat at the foot or in the cave of the Arunachale Mountain (= dawn/red sky/aurora) in which Shiva, or God himself, revealed himself to him; cf. C.G. Jung, CW 11, on the Indian saint, preface to Heinrich Zimmer, *Der Weg zum Selbst, Lehre und Leben des Ramana Maharshi*, München, 1989

[108] "glissade," cf. Mircea Eliade, *Die Religionen und das Heilige*, 252, quoted in *The Forge and the Crucible*

[109] *Der Kleine Pauly*, Mithras

[110] Mircea Eliade, *The Forge and the Crucible*

and not dissimilar to the everyday passing of water. Once the amniotic sac has burst, the longed-for end of the delivery is usually not too far off. The breaking of the waters is the first step towards a release of inner pressure.

The dreamer goes toward the rock as if it would cause her relief. She now wants to go inside the rock; however, she is in an odd situation: her big pregnant belly does not permit her to enter the rock through the door even though she remembers very well that she had gone through it before!

Let us imagine her situation: this fifth pregnancy is an almost unbearable burden and source of distress to her. She had not wanted the last pregnancy either and it ended with a natural miscarriage. Meanwhile, this time she is thinking of an abortion. It is possible that the WC she is looking for stands for abortion. However, her belly is already too big to find relief from the pressure and urge this way.

I suspect that the rock is a mother-symbol and as such will not allow an abortion. The hindrance is the large belly, that is, pregnancy itself. The dreamer wants to slip inside this symbol of the Great Mother as if to look for protection and help. Also, "climbing without difficulty" could mean that there is sufficient trust in the mother-principle even though, at the moment, things are beyond her control. And although she remembers that in the past she was able to, her condition now is such that she cannot slip in and simply flourish in the Great Mother. The dream draws her attention to herself and to the reality of her condition.

She then decides to go home. What does that mean? The realization of her situation happened near a rock and occasioned her to find her way back to the human domain, to home, where there is a human-sized WC, where she can finally pass water. The lysis of this dream is a true relief: "passing water" symbolizes it. It may mean talking to, loading off problems with a professional confidential person that results in relief, or a good cry with streaming tears. To cry is also to pass water, hence also a relief.

In the following part of the dream, it becomes clear that the dreamer does not have to remove herself completely from the rock, that is, from the protective domain of the Great Mother. She notices that her own little house, her own human space and her ego-consciousness that inhabits it, is very close to the rock representing the natural power of the maternal. On the whole this dream seems to say: our dreamer can find relief in real life and in her personal sphere, which is small in comparison with the all-mighty Nature, but it is also nearby and under its protection – a shanty next to a rock!

Dream No. 16:

Third week of a pregnancy of which the dreamer is not yet aware. – The dream stems from a large collection of highly "pregnant" dreams of a woman who takes herself away from her dramatic and complicated relationships to live by the deserted coast of Northern Scotland. She lives in a mobile home facing the ocean, with several children, endeavoring to find herself. She meticulously keeps a diary.

> *I am sitting, straddled on a tree trunk or wooden bench. I must be part of a group or live in a community, for there are many "friends and lovers" around me and they are indulgingly teasing me, as good friends do, because I "have visions."*
>
> *I, however, look up to the sky and see a vast hole in the sky, like a gigantic opening that is plugged with huge boulders and rocks of all sizes. In the very center there is a large knotted stick and I realize that there is a danger or possibility of this great opening being unplugged from above. This will cause both a terrible cataclysm from the falling boulders and rocks but also – and here the dream becomes very numinous – our first view into the Beyond! – I am full of awe. I point this out to my companions, but they again tease me.*

The dreamer is straddled on a tree trunk or on a wooden bench. Let us bear this in mind together with the friendly teasing by her friends as we follow her gaze up into the sky and try to take in her grandiose vision. Interestingly, it seems that judging by the description of the situation, she herself keeps her feet on the ground. And she is not even completely separated from her "friends" either. Although they cannot share her experience they merely indulge in teasing her. In other words, she is not fundamentally isolated and is still in touch with a more objective view of things and with common sense. This sheds a much more positive light on the otherwise uncanny dream.

Her vision shows her a vast hole in the sky "plugged" with boulders and slabs of rock. Although the hole is somewhat patched up, the dreamer is perfectly aware of the danger involved: in the center of the hole there is an enormous knotted stick; what would happen if the stick were pulled out from above, that is from the center of the sky? That would be disastrous and at the same time it would open up a view into the sky – "our first view into the Beyond"! – At last we would know what it is like: we could see God in his glory, surrounded by his cherubs as Ezekiel saw it. But perhaps we could see none of this, for the rocks and boulders tumbling down would have instantly buried beneath them the earth and all living creatures!

The dream-ego can see beautifully clearly both the chance and the danger involved. The formulation "our first view into the Beyond" betrays a fascination with this spiritual sight. We may infer that she had waited for a long time to catch that glimpse into the Beyond and, moreover, that this desire is shared by all humanity – "our" first view. There is a certain danger in this formulation: a tendency toward ego-inflation by an archetype. By the same token she clearly foresees the catastrophe in everything being smashed to pieces: A view into the Beyond would simultaneously entail the end of the world.

The dreamer is shaken by the impending danger but her companions are blind to this and are amused by it. Luckily, their attitude represents a healthy distance to such extraordinary visions, for which our dreamer is known. Interpreting this distance subjectively, we can assume that it is present in the dreamer herself and that it saves her from possibly becoming all wrapped up in a numinous fascination, that is, in the impending devastation of her ego.

At first, the hole in the heavens plugged with boulders and rock precariously kept together – "in the very center" – by a wooden stick, evokes a weird but highly ominous image, and the catastrophe the dreamer anticipates seems inevitable. A vault can only hold up provided the stones have been cut properly and obliquely (conically) and joined together skillfully, especially at the keystone, the central point at the top. The security of this point is crucial. But any one of these heavenly inhabitants – do we know who they are, these beings of the Beyond? – could pull away this rough stick at that very point. Could they be demons, one of whom might come up with the abominable idea of pulling out the stick and amusing himself at the rumbling and crashing rocks?

The idea that the heavens were attached with stones is in fact not that far-fetched. In many ancient cultures, it was believed that when God created the world, the first thing he did about the initial chaos was to separate above and below and then to firmly secure the vault of heaven, as if it were made of stone. According to the Jewish tradition, too, God separated the upper primeval waters from the "fountains of the depths" by placing the firmament in between them. He built the "firmness of heaven" that was believed to be immensely tough and strong, in order to prevent the upper waters from reuniting with the lower ones, thereby deflecting the return of chaos – which eventually was to happen with the Flood. (Luther created the word "firmness" for firmament, from Lat. *firmus* = "firm").

Therefore, we might say that "stony heavens" bring back an archaic image for the firmness of the vault of heaven as was held true over the course of many centuries and formulated in the "Ptolemaeic *Weltbild*" ca. 100 A.D. It bestowed upon the people the reassuring feeling that the heavens would not collapse and that the well-ordered creation would be sustained.

However, there is an important difference in this image: in antiquity, the heavens were imagined to consist of crystalline firmness and as a well put together vault of immense strength, supported by the tremendous powers of a giant or demi-god (e.g., in the Greek legend about Atlas, the giant or Heracles, the demigod).

Interestingly enough, according to an account written by an Hellenistic medical doctor by the name of Galen (b. 131 A.D.), the fear that the heavens could collapse existed already at that time: Galenos writes about a patient who suffered from the delusion that Atlas, exhausted by the weight of the vault, would shake off his burden and crush and kill everybody.[111]

What does "heavens could collapse" mean? The dream vision indicates that the greatest danger comes "from above," or from the realm of the intellectual and spiritual. If certain thoughts in their primary form fell down onto unprotected men and women, they would be overrun and crushed by them. This reminds us of the Apostle Paul's narrow escape in Damascus when he was virtually shattered – shocked and blinded for three days after having been struck by the lightning of insight.[112]

A similar kind of danger is present in this dream, too.

The gigantic figures of Atlas or Heracles go well with this strange "huge knotted stick" that is stuck in the center of the boulder. Could it be that some such tremendously violent, i.e., archaic powers are waiting to pull it out without warning? And what does the image tell us that the "huge boulders and rocks" as patching-up material are held together by no more than a knotted stick at the vault of heaven? Can such a vault hold up? It cannot, not even in the dream! Despite the fascination, the dreamer is seized by a terror.

In order to explore this dream further, I would like to take a look at a well-known dream, namely the dream about Jacob's ladder. Like our dreamer, Jacob is far away from home, living in uncertainty, wandering around in solitude. In Genesis, 28, 11-19 ff we can read:

> *… and he took of the stones of that place, and put them for his pillows, and lay down in that place to sleep. And he dreamed, and behold a ladder set up on the earth, and the top of it reached to heaven: and behold the angels of God ascending and descending on it. And, behold, the Lord stood above it, and said, I am the Lord God of Abraham thy father, and the God of Isaac: the land whereon thou liest, to thee will I give it, and to thy seed. … and in thee and in thy seed shall all the families of the earth be blessed. And, behold, I am with thee and will keep thee in all places whither thou goest …*
>
> *And Jacob awaked out of his sleep … And he was afraid, and said, "How dreadful is this place! This is none other but the house of God, and this is the gate of heaven". … and [he] took the stone that he had put for his pillows, and set it up for a pillar … And he called the name of that place Beth-el.*

Letting this account sink in a little, we detect the following similarities and dissimilarities, respectively. Both dreams have the motif of the "opening of the heavens" above man. Both dreamers are faced with very deep and solemn ideas. And astonishingly, both dreams contain the motif of the "stone." However, much more interesting are the dissimilarities: In Jacob's dream, a ladder firmly grounded in the earth touches the open heavens only with its top. The

---

[111] In: *Analytische Psychologie*, Vol. 9, No. 2, Basel, 1978, "On Depressive Delusions" by H.-W. Wilke
[112] Acts 9, 3

ladder embodies a link between heaven and earth, a bridge on which the angels and messengers of God go up and down. Though this vision inspires fear in Jacob, it also signifies the highest blessing, posterity and God's promise of everlasting protection. On this holy ground (Beth-El) he vows to erect with the stone an eternal monument and memorial to the grace of God. The angels are called in as messengers between the highest power and man to allay the unfathomable terror, in order to allow man to read "salvation" in the word of God.[113]

Our image of the inadequately patched hole in the heavens, furthermore, belongs to the frightening antinomical and incongruent motifs that are essentially cataclysmic. Marie-Louise von Franz describes them as amalgamations of different patterns and systems. It relates to the question of how "time" and "eternity" are interconnected. Interestingly, according to her interpretation, a "hole" is created in the center.[114] She writes: "The only place where the two systems combine is in that hole in the center, which means that time and eternity are united in a no-man's-land or indeed in a hole. Similarly, in our dream we can see the link between man and the Beyond represented through a "hole" in the center. Everything would thus depend, as it were, on this center, the "inner peep-hole" which, in our dream vision, is likewise "the window to eternity."[115]

This is the gist of the dream. And again, let us refer to Marie-Louise von Franz's writing:[116] "The hole as an experience of the Self breaks open the gates behind which our consciousness is imprisoned." However, for our dream we would have to add: it also breaks through the protection of the boundaries of our given inner personality! And because of that and rightly so, the boundary-experience inspires fear. Consciousness should listen to the obvious and serious dangers caused by the unconscious.

The dream about the knotted stick in the hole of the heavens plugged with stones is an unequivocal manifestation of the ambivalence inherent in numinous experience, at least as far as our dreamer is concerned: the longed-for gaze into the hereafter could seriously endanger, if not annihilate, the individual as well as all life on earth. The fact that our dreamer plays with the idea of someone pulling on the stick from above, which for the first time ever would afford man a look into the hereafter, reveals her passionate religious interest. However, there seems to be a direct connection to a dangerous inclination of wanting to approach the mysteries of the hereafter without taking the necessary precautionary measures. The dream warns the pregnant woman of this.

---

[113] Cf. Mircea Eliade, *Shamanism, Archaic Techniques of Ecstasy*, Bollingen Series, Princeton University Press, 1974

[114] M.-L. von Franz, *On Divination and Synchronicity*, Inner City Books, 1980, p. 110 f

[115] *Ibid.*, p. 122

[116] *Ibid.*, p. 123

Dream No. 17, The treasure, the music and the stone:

11th week, 4th pregnancy of which two have ended in miscarriages, intact family, easy deliveries. Mother has temporarily given up her professional activity.

This dream consists of the following separate images:

> *Dream vision of a treasure that must not be found by anyone because they would plunder it. Images of making music and of a stone that was cut into a beautiful shape and was just receiving the final polish.*

At first, we may doubt whether these images have anything to do with one another. However, all three images speak about something precious, two of them about something valuable and creative. Each one illuminates a different aspect.

As Marie-Louise von Franz writes,[117] we could hypothetically think of the invisible world of the collective unconscious as a "psychic energy field where the archetypes are the points of energy concentration. And just as in the case of a physical field, we can define close neighbor relationships, we can do so in the field of the collective unconscious." A rich variety of constellations and interactions exists among these points of energy concentration. These close connections, and sometimes even entanglements, of different archetypal images can entail specific traps for the interpretations, one of which is the danger of getting lost in associations. "Play" with fantasies is vital but can also lead us astray. We have to listen very carefully and try to see if there is an accord between the image and the interpretation. To sum up, it can be said: the three images all stem from some collective oscillating motion (likewise, "motif" derives from Latin *movere* = "to move"). However, how differentiated is the response of this woman's unconscious and how does it deal with present-day problems and perhaps with vital questions in general! Let us look at each image individually.

To begin with, a state of danger and a warning is being issued. There is a treasure. It must be hidden from thieves, from a collective keen on treasures. A treasure always implies value and possession concentrated in a certain place and needing to be vigilantly guarded.

What comes across here, I believe, is the necessity to keep such values to oneself. The great challenge involved in pregnancy is to carry to term something precious and valuable. This requires concentration on the woman's part, in order not to abandon what is growing and weak. Not only do we have here an individual growing who, unlike the collective, always requires a refuge, but we are dealing with woman's inner development and maturing process, which is too sensitive to be pulled into the "general" that only too often is also the common.

[117] *Ibid.*, p. 63

Pregnancy can be regarded as a profoundly collective feminine situation, for it is shared by absolutely every woman prepared to give birth. And yet, each one of the myriad women has her own very individual experience. It is a time in a woman's life – maybe the first time – when everything is entirely up to her: she alone, in the wholeness of her being, is in control.

Hence, the vision of the "treasure that must not be found because it would get stolen" could signify that this highly personal experience of an expectant woman is an opportunity and a step towards individuation that does not want to be displayed, gaped at, excessively discussed or subjected to mass opinion. The treasure would otherwise be "plundered," that is, violently extracted from the individual common fate that unites the two, i.e., mother and child. This dream, as well as Dream No. 23, hints at the danger of being robbed by collective opinions.

Many peoples' initiation rites have this remarkable characteristic of secrecy. Even in initiations into a life-stage that every individual goes through – in other words, when dealing with a quasi-collective step – the adepts often have to go into hiding, and each individual has to undergo the trials and pains on his/her own, often without speaking about it. Although the entrance into a new life-stage is a common fate, each and everyone has to walk through it alone and in his/her own manner – rather as at the time of death.

The "images of making music" throw light on another aspect of pregnancy: in dreams, "music" often refers to feelings, to joviality and to the heart in a positive sense that affects the environment harmoniously and pleasantly and that permits regular movement. Making music is a creative act, the unfolding of sound, where vibration and rhythm are created.

Beyond this, musical instruments often resemble a human figure. Large string or plucked instruments such as the cello, lute or contrabass in fact have a big "belly" and a "neck," and violas often have a little head on the top; producing sound, moreover, they generate something alive. For many a musician, their true lover and sole soul-mate is their instrument.

In some myths and fairy tales, making music and the singing storytelling of the bard are represented as genuine "creating." In his singing, Väinämöinen, the ancient Finnish bard, has real objects come alive before the audience. The most noteworthy visual representation of this is the image of Shiva Nataraja (Sanskrit: "Lord of Dance" and source of all movement), who, with the sound of his drum, creates the entire Universe. "Making music" thus represents bringing something into motion and awakening to life: a lovely image for being pregnant!

The last of the three images evokes the artistic aspect and the creation of "form" even more directly. It speaks for itself. However, on the basis of this example, I would like to point out that no matter how obvious the imagery seems, we should not as a rule jump from the dream motif to the concrete – in this case, the child: we would go very wrong, were we to translate one-to-one the "cutting of the stone" and its "final polish" into the embryo's quietly grow-ing in the maternal womb. In a dream, we must always bear in mind the translation into a symbolic language, and the task is to find a common ground.

Therefore, we must first investigate the meaning of the "stone." As has already been said above, it represents man's essentially indestructible inner core: the Self. This interpretation of the stone is known to us from Saint Niklaus von Flüe's own memory of a "dream in the maternal womb." He saw a stone and recognized in it "the continuity and steadfastness of his own being, realizing that he must never give up his inner vocation" ("*… die Feste und Stetigkeit seines Wesens, darin er beharren und von seinem Vornehmen nicht abfallen sollte*").[118]

If in our dream a stone "has been cut to a beautiful shape," it could mean that an important process of inner consolidation will shortly be completed.

The Swiss writer, Conrad Ferdinand Meyer, also uses the image of a stone in his poem, "In der Sistina." He has Michelangelo, the sculptor muse, medi-tate and speak as he is sitting in front of his just completed frescoes in the twilit chapel:

> *Den ersten Menschen formtest du aus Ton –*
> *Ich werde schon von härtrem Stoffe sein –*
> *Da, Herrgott, brauchst du deinen Hammer schon!*
> *Bildhauer Gott, schlag zu! Ich bin der Stein.*

The stone to be cut is an image for the essence of man himself. In it he is resilient, firm, earthly and malleable at the same time, and it is God who moulds him through his destiny. I therefore see in the almost completed stone both the process of growing into a new little human being as well as that of the pregnant woman. The dream suggests that pregnancy is intimately linked with the personal development of woman herself.

Let us now come back to the initiating image of the treasure that must be kept secret. It introduces the theme for the following two dreams where the treasure is being unfolded in the imagery.

Dream No. 18, The blue-red dice,[119] 7th week:

> *The dreamer comes to her psychoanalytical group. There is a feeling of solidarity though each participant is occupied with his or her own game or with an invention of some kind. Something is going to come of it, something new. They are pedagogic toys for children, and the players play with dice that have blue and red faces. Someone announces that Ana (the dreamer) is pregnant. The therapist says: "Ana is breathing another air"*

---

[118] Lectures by M.-L. von Franz, *The Dreams and Visions of St. Niklaus von Flüe*, Jung Institute, Küsnacht, 1957, pp. 11-16

[119] Cf. commentary on Dream No. 13 in which there are extracts from Dream No. 18

or "someone else is talking through Ana" or something to that effect.
Everyone in the circle is happy about this but they don't quite understand
it. R., a male participant, asks if this new thing "is inside my lungs, my
breasts and if it will come out through the lungs." The dreamer explains
it. Then they continue playing the game with the colored pieces.

The uncertainty of the future has often been likened to dice. Scientific investigations have shown that human gender is determined by an infinitesimal component, the presence or absence of a single gene. Today, we speak of "chance" referring to whether a boy or a girl is born, employing the terminology of dice. At the same time, we know that chance, that is, whatever falls to our lot, is part of a larger context. Scientists deal with it in probability theory while Jung tried to approach it in his ideas on synchronicity and *unus mundus*. Similarly, biology postulates a general organizational principle of Nature which, in the main, tends to create a balance between the genders.

Now, it is customary to choose pink for girls and blue for boys. Thus in our dream, the red and blue faces of the pieces may indeed point to the possible outcome in the game the group is playing, namely the "new" gender that will "come up." According to a more precise color symbolism, blue will be considered as the more suitable for the intellectual, red for the more instinctive basis of the new "invention." The pieces also have a "red basis."

The Jungian study-group might be likened to that generic background, as it were, Nature at work where each individual is working on something sensible, intelligent, new and spirited (a positive sign for this group!). The collective consciousness in this group is apparently constructive given its shared desire to create something.

We have known pieces in various forms and shapes from the earliest history of humankind. Through the millennia dice in particular were believed to have served as an oracle: what lot will befall me? It transpired that the negative expression "nothing but" fate or chance developed and became an antithesis to the notion of fate only much later. The literal meaning of fate and chance is the same.[120]

The dream about the dice may also be seen as an illustration of the way collective and personal processes in pregnancy interplay.

It is interesting that one of the "male" participants of the group cannot understand where the new being will come from. We consider him to be the dreamer's animus. Will it come out of the breasts, or from the lungs? He is simply too "high up" and is apparently afraid to deal with the flesh and blood. This reminds us of the great difficulties the dreamer had accepting the pregnancy (cf. introduction to 13). We empathize with her: as a dancer, she expe-

---

[120] M.-L. von Franz, *Projection and Re-Collection in Jungian Psychology,* Open Court, La Salle, IL, 1980, p. 63 and p. 94

riences her own body in terms of floating weightlessness. The weight of a huge belly gravitating towards the ground is an extreme contrast.

The fact that the entire group is "happy" about the news of the pregnancy suggests that the collective ground of her personality welcomes the child. This will facilitate the acceptance in the dreamer's consciousness.

Dream No. 19, The round stone (week 4):

Dreams of expectant women frequently comprise particularly fierce attacks directed to woman or child on the part of a man (often a stranger, sometimes the dreamer's own husband). He will often try to force her to make love or will actually rape her. We shall see in the chapter on man that, on the subjective level, we are dealing with an autonomous, negative, unconscious complex that is trying to take control of the ego. Contrary to the differentiated ego of woman, the "male aspect in woman" has often archaic, primitive features and has remained undifferentiated.

The dream:

> *I am with a stranger who wants to have sexual intercourse with me. As I try to fight, but he becomes so infuriated that, by means of magic powers and from a distance, he wants to operate my unborn child out of my belly. Only because I am holding a round stone in my hands – and because I am incessantly praying to God – am I able to stop him from doing this. The man comes closer, threatening me and gesticulating. We are surrounded by people smiling at me condescendingly.*
> *As long as I don't waver and continue praying, the man cannot do anything to me.*

This dream is about an assault by a real devil. As in Dreams No. 14 and 20, he is a "stranger." C.G. Jung[121] explains the fact that we often dream of strangers in function of their unconsciousness.

This fellow has magic powers. From a distance, he wants to surgically remove the child from the pregnant belly. Because the dreamer is only four weeks pregnant, it is possible that she is still unconsciously struggling pro or contra the child. "To surgically remove from a distance" suggests either black magic, or the more fatal, clinical abortion. What is required here, is psychic distance – a "neutral" attitude.

The dream-ego fiercely fights the stranger's impertinent advances. The dreamer manages to fend them off by holding a "round stone in her hands and continually praying to God." Although people standing around her are "smiling condescendingly," the man cannot touch her.

The group of people represents the public. Many women today may subcon-

---

[121] *Collected Works* 9/I, § 517 f, Routledge and Kegan Paul, 1969

sciously feel that they are laughed at for carrying a child to term, giving up a job and staying at home with the children ("where the walls are closing in on you"). The dream-ego's attitude must be admired all the more for it. This woman succeeds in concentrating her attention unwaveringly on the prayer and the stone; that is, she decidedly turns inwardly to the Self.[122] We have in the unremitting concentration on the round stone and prayer a remarkable example of contemplation: *contemplari* = "to observe unremittingly."

The devilish animus is not only after the woman but also the child. He seeks to control her, to make her pregnant himself. This way he could force on her his negative and destructive rigid opinions and destroy the nascent life in her – that, on the subjective level, signifies the most recent opportunity for her own development.

The negative animus is therefore not merely *lebensfremd* (unnatural) but actually also hostile to life, producing at this point ominous forebodings in our dreamer.

Holding a round object reminds us of the beads of a rosary, another aid for continuous attention during prayer. Moslems, too, employ a string of stone beads for prayer, and Hindus also tend to pray with strings of seeds. The purpose of the beads is to help those who are praying concentrate inwardly, on the Eternal, the Whole and the Indestructible made tangible by the roundness of the bead.

Through time, the stone in its firmness and durability has been perceived as an image of the Self. In this dream, appearing in the shape of a ball (round stone), the stone further embodies a perfect symmetry, causing any disturbing or interfering influence to be deflected. Whether it be a product of Nature – say a pebble, which through millennia of glacial erosion or the waves of the sea, or through strenuous and skilful cutting has become symmetric – a round stone is always an image of perfection which deeply touches us. In fairy tales, too, a sphere or a golden ball suggest the central value of the soul, the Self.[123]

I would like at this point to recall a dream by C.G. Jung. Only a few days before his death he saw in a dream "a large round stone somewhere high up, ... and on it was written: May this be your sign of unity and wholeness."[124] It is in this tenor that I understand the praying and the holding of the round stone as our dreamer's concentrating on the deepest essence of her being and her communion with God. This way she can fend off the horrible assault. This dream could be most valuable for her.

---

[122] Alfons Rosenberg, *Das Herzensgebet, Mystik und Yoga der Ostkirche*, p. 9

[123] Hedwig v. Beit, *Gegensatz und Erneuerung im Märchen*, p. 38 ff, and especially M.-L. von Franz, *The Interpretation of Fairy Tales*, Shambhala, Boston, 1996, p. 80 ff. These two volumes of the comprehensive reference book on the interpretation of fairy tales by H. v. Beit will henceforth be quoted as H. v. Beit / M.-L. von Franz, since all the fairy tale interpretations stem from M.-L. von Franz.

[124] M.-L. von Franz, *C.G. Jung*, Inner City Books, New York, 1975

III. Precious Stones

According to the Ptolemaic *Weltbild* (around 100 A.D.), the different cosmic spheres were seen as spiritual powers that had their corresponding "stone powers" here on earth. They could be imparted to men and women through precious stones. St. Hildegard v. Bingen (1098-1179) still worked with stone-medicine on that principle. This is an era when antique philosophy and natural science together with the Christian faith were about to establish a new bond between the rational and irrational.[125] Stones, and in particular precious stones, still belong to that category of things whose effects cannot be fully understood by means of chemical-physical analysis.

Of course, precious stones and metals in terms of symbols have played an exceptional role from time immemorial. They are the king's emblems and denote his original divine rank. Gold, the most immortal of all metals, plays the leading part in this. The jewels in a sovereign's crown represent much more in the subjects' minds than their material worth. Such stones often had names of persons and powers that were associated with them! That was the original reason why they were also put on weapons (for example, on Siegfried's sword, *Balmung*). Even today, people tell stories about diamonds that have either a propitious or ruinous effect on their owners. Places like Karlsburg in Bohemia, the German Imperial crown jewels in Nuremberg, and in particular, the English crown jewels in the Tower of London continue to be places of pilgrimage, despite the fact that the old idea of the Empire has long since lost its spiritual significance. It is evident that it is not so much the material value of the jewels that attracts all the attention. Ultimately, it is the symbolism that the wonderful image of "Heavenly Jerusalem" conveys with its gates and palaces ornamented with pearls and gems: it is something central but impenetrable that profoundly moves all men as the most "precious" in the soul as well as an image of the Self.

In many fairy tales, too, the precious stone is a symbol of the Self, and something precious that can only be attained by having overcome considerable obstacles. It is its hardness, its exceedingly slow maturation, its beauty and its crystalline-geometrical, regular form that in fact describe the qualities of the Self.[126] For this reason, we find that the beauty of precious stones is praised in all cultures. In the most fundamental and important concepts, the stone signifies "eternity." In the Bible it says: (Ex. 24, 10) "Sapphire is the ground beneath the Lord's feet" and in Hesekiel (1, 26): "His throne is designed like a sapphire," for "this represented the glory of the Lord." "Solomon's table" is made of a single emerald.[127]

---

[125] Hildegard von Bingen, *Heilkraft der Edelsteine*

[126] Hedwig v. Beit / M.-L. von Franz, *Symbolik des Märchens*, Francke Verlag, Bern, 1952, Vol. I, p. 568, and Vol. II, p. 224

[127] Emma Jung/M.-L. von Franz, *The Grail Legend*, Princeton University Press, 1970

Mircea Eliade tells of many Shaman traditions where healing crystals came down from heaven, or were brought back by a Shaman from his journey in the other world.[128]

In the highly differentiated Eastern wisdom of Tibetan Buddhism, there is a "path of diamonds" that corresponds to the "diamond-body" of Chinese alchemy.[129] C.G. Jung explains the Buddhist Amitabha meditation that describes a "floor made of transparent lapis lazuli" as its aim.[130] This means that at the end of the inner path an absolutely imperturbable, crystal clear state of consciousness can be attained. In his commentary on the Zosimos visions, Jung deals in greater detail with the connection between God, soul and stone.[131]

The lapis of the alchemists, the "stone of the wise" symbolizes the aim of the soul unified within the Self in man. The grail stone is a particularly clear manifestation of it, the central symbol of the Middle Ages and of the knightly quest. The "healing stone" already existed in the original Celtic preliminary stages of the Holy Grail legends and is not limited to Christian symbolism.[132]

In his "Cherubic Wanderer" the mystic Angelus Silesius (1624-1677) expresses this arcane connection beautifully:

> The soul is a crystal, the deity its shine
> The body you inhabit is their shrine

Dream No. 20, The first of three pregnancies, week 12:

> *I found many rings on the ground and put them on all my fingers. A strange man tried to rob me of all the rings. Then, an old woman appeared. She was the mother of the strange, wild man. She told him to give me only one ring that I could have: the ruby ring.*

Besides just being jewelry, rings have always and everywhere in the world been a symbol of connectedness, commitment and belonging.[133] Our dreamer chances upon these rings as if they were on her way, on her path of life. Given the high symbolic value of commitment and the fact that the dreamer puts rings on all of her fingers, we may assume that she has picked up things, e.g., opportunities, tasks that she will find fulfilling.

---

[128] Mircea Eliade, *Shamanism, Archaic Techniques of Ecstasy*, Bollingen Series LXXVI, Princeton University Press, 1974, p. 132 ff

[129] Jung / Wilhelm, *The Secret of the Golden Flower*, Kegan Paul, London, 1931

[130] C.G. Jung, CW 11, § 605 ff

[131] CW 13, § 110

[132] Emma Jung, M.-L. von Franz, *The Grail Legend*

[133] M.-L. von Franz, *Interpretation of Fairy Tales*, Shambhala, Boston & London, 1996, p. 81

"All my fingers" are her active possibilities to act, or valences in the human and professional domain, i.e., in matters of love, work, position, politics, society and family. In short, she is covered with obligations in all respects. And although a lot of rings may represent valuable adornment, in such excess it rather suggests overload and overburden. Thus, psychologically speaking, the dream-ego is made to enter a "brilliant" but crushing bond. Glory and glamour are no adequate substitute for the freedom and spontaneity that she would have to give up for the sheer number of inner and outer obligations wearing a ring on each finger would imply. There is, in addition, a threat of inner disorder. The ego-inflation is being attacked by strong self-doubt.

Acting as a kind of counterbalance to the overload of valuable commitments, the most dreadful compensatory onsets of self-doubt and self-aggression can arise in woman's unconscious. As we shall see, though, it is for her own good. Consciously she may simply suffer a dull, persistent feeling of inferiority or dissatisfaction and anger with herself. These feelings are embodied by the strange man who is trying to rob her of all those values or "valuables." He is the voice that, in her innermost nature, devalues and doubts everything that is important and precious to her. A common fact in such a situation is that the tormenting assaults of the animus get projected onto real men, who are seemingly suitable for this. Projections occur spontaneously and unconsciously. The inner world is experienced in the outer world, which is only too facile to do; however, there is also a danger of failing to see certain inner potentials.

At this critical point, our dream indicates – perhaps constellated through the pregnancy – positive development. In the face of the workings of the inner dynamics personified by the robber, the dream-ego is helpless. The woman is suffering terribly from attacks of feelings of inferiority, doubts and anger directed at herself. The dream, however, offers a ray of hope: an "old woman" appears unexpectedly.

Astonishingly, she is the mother of the strange wild fellow. It is interesting that it is she – just as in the fairy tale of "The Devil's Grandmother" – who has the power and is willing to help the human ego in her plight and to sort things out. There is in the dreamer a higher – we might also call it a "lower" – feminine principle. It consists in the absolute knowledge of the course of life and how to further it. Whenever it appears and in our dream, this figure has the power to set the soul right again. This often happens – quite contrary to the intentions of the ego.

The authority the old woman commands – her wild son obeys instantly – makes us think of a great goddess, or the wisdom of Nature or, in relation to an individual, of the self-image. She appears on the one hand, in order to pacify the conflict between the inflationary tendencies of the ego and the inner masculine aggressor. On the other hand she rectifies the situation by assigning to the dreamer only what is "due to her": the ruby ring. This could point to her future. In popular belief, a ruby has healing power, is associated with warm feelings and passionate love.

In our interpretation, this would mean: the only bond and commitment that is decisive for the woman and symbolized by the ruby ring is most likely the bond of love. Without additional information about her personal situation, we cannot infer whether this precious bond refers to the child to be, to her relationship with her husband or any other love relationship. What seems to be clear, though, is that any excess should be avoided.

The old woman embodies the regulating unknown center of the personality that always acts befitting the wholeness of the personality. She is an image of the Self. It is where impulses towards individuation come from and rarely without sacrifice or suffering. The fact that the "robber" is her son may be understood in terms of a matrix containing all psychic factors.

Let us now briefly touch on another aspect of the dream: the two opponents, the dream-ego and the wild fellow, behave in remarkably similar fashion. They both want "all" the rings, and both are obsessed, as it were, by a claim to totality. For this reason, it is likely that putting on all the rings, that is, the multiple adorning-of-oneself, is an expression of a persona-obsession by the ego. According to Jung, the "persona" is a force determined by the collective, a "segment of the collective-psyche"; it can completely occupy the individual ego and go as far as taking it over.

"Persona" is the outer form we show to the outside world and in which we wish to be seen. If the persona is very dominant, the individual melts into, for instance, rank, professional reputation, social status, or into the ideal image of the loving mother or father. Establishing one's persona is both unavoidable and necessary, and it also makes up a genuine part of our identity. After all, it represents our specific form, our "garment" in the world, and thus helps others orient themselves. The excess of more than "ten rings" in our dream, however, results in the individual's estrangement from herself, no matter how successful she may be. A woman so strongly tied up with her persona will often be attacked; life grows cold, the eros escapes her, she becomes hollow or mechanical and ends up merely as outer form. However, the dream seems to indicate that the woman found the rings actually lying on the ground, as though the adorning commitments befell her through fate.

On the whole, the dream seems to say that a much more personal, unique and individual relationship would be suitable for this woman. And, viewed subjectively, she seems capable of it as the old wise woman would appear to be an inner figure.

We may call her a Self-figure that puts order into and unites the diverging and life-disturbing, quarrelling tendencies of the personality. She is constellated as a positive mother more than ever during pregnancy.

The ruby may have to do with a particular passionateness of the dreamer. The dream seems to indicate that the dreamer's possibility to develop and the chance she is given lie in her individuality.

Dream No. 21:

Child was conceived during a six-months' trip through India. The dream occurred four months after the birth of a healthy, first baby-girl:[134]

> *Sarabel lay sleeping in her basket when an older, bearded man – who I knew was a kind of a bandit chief – came in. He went over to someone else, who looked a bit like him and was sitting at a table. Then he came near Sarabel, whereupon she awoke and laughed with him. The older man now told the younger one: "There is something quite extraordinary about that child: she actually 'radiates.'" Here, let me show you: And he picked her up and from her clothes pulled out a small ring.*
>
> *At that moment, I saw a young shepherd (Greek, Pan) holding in his hand a stick made of a branch. He was the one who had given Sarabel the small ring. It was made of scrap-gold and had a little heart made from wreathed twigs.*
>
> *"A Druids' heart," the old man said.*

Again, we are dealing with a robber; however, the situation here is very different. There are three bearded men: one is old, "a kind of a bandit chief," another one is like him but a little younger, and finally there appears a young shepherd, whom the dreamer immediately recognizes as Pan, the Greek god of shepherds and flocks. These three archaic and bearded men have a mysterious relationship with the child peacefully sleeping in her basket. The dreamer is only involved as a kind of onlooker, and although she knows that the old bearded man coming in is "a kind of bandit chief," she is not afraid that he would harm or kidnap the child. On the contrary, there even seems to be a degree of intimacy between him and the child from the onset: she awakens, and they laugh together.

Together with his saying "she radiates" (*abstrahlen*),[135] something wonderful happens: he brings out a small ring from the child's clothes, and at the same time, there appears in the room Pan, the god of herdsmen, who had given Sarabel the ring with a little heart wreathed from twigs – "a Druids' heart" the old man calls it.

---

[134] The following dreams also stem from the same dreamer: No. 36: Chapter 4.1, No. 65: Chapter 5.3, No. 92: Chapter 5.6, No. 99: Chapter 5.8, No. 112: Chapter 6, No. 24 at the end of this chapter

[135] Cf. Avo Harnik, *Seele und Kristall*, Diploma thesis at the C.G. Jung Institute in Zürich, 1982, pp. 28, 32: In Central Switzerland, all crystals and precious stones the people found in the mountains used to be called *Strahler* and the collectors of these stones were also called *Strahler*.

This dream takes up a familiar image: we all know and have loved from early childhood the picture of the shepherds gathered around the Christmas crib. This motif has been depicted an infinite number of times, and just as the oxen and donkey are somehow necessarily present at the birth of Christ, so are the shepherds! It is unthinkable that they would not be there, partly because of the Christian tradition, but mainly because of the archetypal correspondence. The interesting order in which the bearded shepherds appear I see as an analogy with the natural powers a child needs for its growth (cf. the role of the Chthonic and dark Cabiri as companions of the Great Mother). The origins of Pan are also likely to go back to a pre-Greek fertility god.[136] Finds dated from the 7th–3rd cent. B.C. depict Pan together with pregnant women. He was worshipped as a vegetation and fertility god.

There is something uncanny about this dream vision. The Greeks also felt this with respect to Pan: in their imagination, Pan would suddenly appear in the tranquility of noonday, giving a fright to men, women, flocks and nymphs in the forest. That is why, to this day, we use the term "panic" or "panic-stricken." In our dream, however, neither child nor mother feel any panic.

This dream scene is clearly a numinous image. It is an experience taking place in the depths of the unconscious. We notice that the dreamer gets along well with these archaic men and watches their actions free from any fear. This makes for very favorable conditions: a sleeping child in a bassinet surrounded by three bearded men suggests a very strong and completely natural, unconscious male (animus) side in this woman. There doesn't seem to be any conflict or fear related to these forces within her; she seems to live with them in complete harmony. The middle man even sits at a table, thereby partaking in real human life, whereas the bearded old man came in from outside, from Nature. The third one, whom she immediately recognizes as Pan, the Greek god of shepherds, appears unexpectedly and at a specific moment of the dream. He carries a shepherds' staff in his hand – the shepherd's or the god of flocks' emblem.

Let us not forget that the "good shepherd" is also one of the oldest names for Christ (e.g., St. John, 10, 14) and that at a time when the ancient gods of shepherds, such as Pan in the wake of Dionysos, and humane Hermes (who was at the same time a thief!) were still known.[137]

"This child actually 'radiates,'" says he and brings out from her clothes the little golden ring. What a lovely image for the "golden" or blissful aura of a small child! Precious stones and pearls often figure in fairy tales and will fall out of the hero/heroine's mouth or, in the form of tears, characterize their enriching and positive qualities.[138] It is often a gift of a good fairy; however, in

---

[136] *Der Kleine Pauly,* Lexikon der Antike, Kabiren, Pan

[137] For example, the well-known mosaic of the Good Shepherd in the Galla Placidia Chapel of Ravenna, 5th cent.

this particular volume (cf. footnote), they are three male Nature spirits called the tree *Haulemännerchen* in the woods that endow a poor girl with this gift!

Gold or precious stones "radiating" or falling down is an image of a child or adult's psychic richness that can profoundly move us.

The golden ring with the little heart made from wreathed twigs signifies not merely love, but rather a sense of being very close to someone.

We know Pan from the Greek, the Druids from Celtic antiquity. Both are a creation of the collective unconscious that can manifest itself anywhere (here in the dream of a Swiss woman).

The Celtic religion seems to have closely associated itself with Nature, and the Druids possessed great knowledge of it. The names of German landscapes, rivers, lakes and mountains frequently have Celtic origins. Some of the harmony and intimate relationship with Nature characteristic of the Celtic religion is apparent in this dream, too. Judging by their heroic legends, the Celts also must have been quite rough fellows.

Quite likely, the "heart of a Druid" would be a kind of quintessence of the Celtic religion and feeling and the highest manifestation of love. In our dream it would therefore signify a gift of a particularly true-to-Nature and Nature-loving inner attitude that would be binding for both mother and child (the ring).

If Pan is the one making a present of the small ring, he is certainly not an ordinary shepherd, let alone a robber. Perhaps he is one to rob people's ego-centered frills, their all too dominating "persona," in order to be more in touch with their deeper Self. Perhaps it may even be appropriate to quote Jesus' words here: "Behold, I come as a thief." (Rev. 16, 15)

The child is enveloped by such strong, perhaps rather archaic but absolutely benign, forces in her mother, and from them she receives the gift of an everlasting, binding love for Nature and access to its secrets. The preconditions for the child to thrive could not be better!

Dream No. 22:

The dreamer is 36 and has been married for seven years; the pregnancy was planned, and she is healthy. Her parents are both undergoing Jungian analysis. She was very keen to find out how her unconscious would react to the pregnancy.

> *Going to the doctor to get my last vitamin-injection to become stronger for pregnancy. An unknown man, helping me to get the coins into the parkmeter, "he slams the meter with his fist and suddenly it is as if I have hit the jackpot on a slot machine – piles of coins, then jewels begin to*

[138] For example, Grimm, *The Complete Grimm's Fairy Tales*, Pantheon Books, 1944, No. 13

pour out into my arms – diamonds, emeralds, etc.!" Putting all these into the car it has changed into a family-car, a station wagon. The doctor gives me the last injection and then "starts to roll me around this office, like a ride at an amusement park. I am laughing."

The doctor and the stranger are positive animus figures. Although the dreamer has a certain age and has had seven years of marriage without children, she becomes pregnant at a propitious moment. On the other hand, the difficulties she has in the dream, trying to get the coins into the parking meter, may suggest some sexual problems – certainly that would be the assumption of a more Freudian interpretation. Jung speaks of the slot in the alms box into which the value each individual owes has to be thrown. He interprets this in the following manner: If any problems arise when performing this deed, it would mean that the appropriate sacrifice cannot be made easily. In our dream, it suffices that an "unknown man" coming to her assistance, slams the meter with his fist, and it is as if she had struck lucky with a slot machine!

A masculine determined, unconscious impulse, a positive animus helps her make the offering she owes before she can take possession of the incredibly large treasure. Slamming the meter with the fist bespeaks substantial unconscious energy that cooperates most effectively – a rare windfall that has the dreamer give a loud laugh once she has put all the jewels in the car – and, to top it all, she has been given a "power-injection"! Finally the doctor rolls her around his office, which makes her think of an amusement park. This man too makes her spirits high, gets her going in a circular movement – always an image of wholeness.

After seven years of childless married life, pregnancy may well have felt like "hitting the jackpot." The car has already changed to a family car to make sure the treasure-child is safe. The entire dream is an expression of how the dreamer's unconscious welcomes the pregnancy and prepares her for it.

Dream No. 23: [139]

Week 8 of pregnancy. The dreamer associated the diamond with her pregnancy.

I am on the lower level of the subway system. A young black woman gives me a diamond. I put it deep into my pocket, not wanting people to know for fear they will steal it. When I reach the upper level, I feel safer.

While sleeping vis-à-vis waking is an *abaissement du niveau mental*, this dream reaches further down to a subterranean net of tunnels and corridors where people are no longer separated from one another in their homes. The underground railway system is an image for the collective unconscious, rather

---

[139] From: Edward Edinger, *Anatomy of the Psyche*, 1985

like ground-water.[140] Many folktales begin with a comparable murky, dark area, such as a thick forest, where the hero has lost his way searching for the "hard-to-attain-gems."

We do not know why the dream-ego finds itself in this dark area. It is possible that pregnancy made her go deeply into the unconscious, all the way into the bodily functions. This position allows her to have this extraordinary experience: the encounter with a black woman handing her a diamond. The dreamer calling her a black woman, we can assume that she herself is white. She instantly hides the jewel in her pocket for fear of "people" stealing it from her. Only once she is on the upper level does she feel safe. Psychologically speaking, she has returned to the more cognitive and perceptive levels of consciousness. It is also a more personal area as opposed to the collective, dark underground flooded with strangers. Encounters on the collective level can be fatal or vital for the individual – depending on how mature the ego, in this case the dream-ego, is. To apprehend the meaning and message of the encounter, it needs to be alert and to hold its ground.

Why could the treasure get stolen down there? Because a treasure from the unconscious is likely to disappear again. It may get swallowed back again. An interpretation of this could be that the personal value is being abused, disdained, betrayed and sold by the crowd, or that it would simply get lost and forgotten in the chaotic hustle and bustle. In this sense, it would also have been "robbed."

Who is that dark woman? Figures of the same sex, who are opposites in some way, could theoretically be shadow-figures. The woman stranger being black and appearing in the depths of darkness substantiates this idea. C.G. Jung explains "shadow" as follows: the shadow is generally those components of the personality that we – consciously and unconsciously – put into the shade: what we conceal from ourselves and others. It contains the experiences, personality traits and qualities that we would rather do without and that we have succeeded in repressing. This way we almost lose sight of them and are highly surprised when others perceive and reject them. They are mostly negative or embarrassing personality traits (e.g., suppressed ambition) from which we wish to free ourselves in this unfortunately inadequate manner. Both Freud and Jung understood the shadow to mean the repressed personality components inaccessible to day-consciousness, and in particular – in Freud's view – those components that could be conscious provided we were not afraid. Their encounter is the dark chapter of any analysis and at the same time the

---

[140] It unites the inhabitants of the world above, the conscious world, in a deeper-seated level by means of which all people communicate. More recent research in biology shows that analogously with the principles of communicating pipes, certain behavioral phenomena can manifest themselves at the same time in different places in the world.

most important precondition for a more whole personality. According to Jung, there are also "light" shadows: images of positive personality aspects that through lack of confidence we ignore and forget; thus they remain undeveloped.[141]

Now, a young white woman dreaming of a young black woman handing her a precious stone in the underground implies a rigorous separation between light and shade, yet at the same time, one that is doubly intertwined. If we consider the ego to be the (white) dreamer, then the black young woman is the shadow-image of the white woman or a kind of a double. But it is the fact of the white woman descending to the underground that has made the sisterly encounter possible.

No details are given as to why she had to go down. These are frequently painful and depressing processes. The descent can signify a certain stage of development. The Alchemists called it nigredo, "blackness" that no one can avoid. The soul is dipped into blackness (the Alchemists spoke of a prima materia, a transformation substance) and meets demons of multifarious shapes. In other words, the soul ultimately encounters its own blackness and gloominess, and the individual is faced with his or her own negative.

A descent into the deep layers of the unconscious can suggest depression. Quite a few biographies of saints tell of depressions and visits by demons and of their absorption taking them to powerful depths (e.g., Saint Niklaus von Flüe, or Saint Francis or the best known of them all, St. Anthony). It takes a strong and discerning ego-organization to find one's way up again.

However, I do not believe that our dream is about depression. Our common (collective) "underground" is that domain of our culture which is rather suppressed, dark, unconscious, and constitutes – along with many other forgotten or not yet perceived contents – our natural instinctive processes, our cultural and morally dubious physical and sexual sides. The religious side, too, is predominantly in the underground; that is, it has become unconscious and archaically undeveloped. It may well be the strong feelings and emotions kindled by the pregnancy that made the dreamer descend into the collective sphere to which she can now relate.

There is no negative tinge or threatening attribute associated with the "black woman." Moreover, the dream seems to clearly point out that black does not equal evil, even though the language of symbols often suggests this. In this dream, the darkness offers the highest value – the diamond.

And yet the "blackness" must not last too long: the dreamer thrusts the diamond deep down into her pocket and quickly makes for the light. Psychologically speaking, she finds herself not so much in a "feeling-low-mood" but rather on the level of the collective unconscious that is in sharp contrast to that

[141] Fundamentals on the personal and collective shadow in M.-L. von Franz's *Shadow and Evil in Fairy Tales*, Spring Publications, Inc., Dallas, Texas

of the individual, as the dream vision clearly shows. The "people" are an ominous, amorphous collective. Once the black woman has handed over the precious stone, it must under no circumstances be relinquished to the crowd; in other words, it must not be overly discussed, stared at, plucked apart or pulled off before the dreamer has appropriated it on the personal level and assimilated it in her consciousness (in the light).

As the dreamer herself assumes, the "pocket" in which she places the gem could symbolize her pregnancy. We could therefore infer that the pregnancy represents a gift to her and that the child is a "jewel." This is one way of interpreting this beautiful dream. However, we must also look at another aspect of the dream image. If, in the eyes of the dreamer, the pregnancy is so plainly precious, then why is there the mysterious black woman in the underground? Presumably she would not have had to go down there if, as it were, the dream only mirrored her attitude to pregnancy.

Let us look at this vision once more: the dreamer encounters a shadow-figure in an obscure, collective place, or in the collective unconscious and is personally handed by the black woman something uniquely precious: a diamond.

Who is this obscure, unknown counter-image of the dreamer rendering her rich provided she accepts the gift and rescues it out of the darkness? I think we can consider her as a self-image that must not be opposed to the "shadow." On the contrary, the Self encompasses and unites the opposites: it is the richer, deeper all-encompassing center of the dreamer that together with her – embodied by the diamond – completes her wholeness. Barbara Hannah writes: "In the beginning of an analysis, the shadow and the Self can appear as the same figure."[142] A pregnancy corresponds in several ways to an analysis.

According to the dreamer's commentary, she associates the precious stone with the pregnancy. This is no mistake but we may also look at it as on the whole a much more far-reaching step toward individuation. The self-knowledge the dreamer seems to have experienced is the fruit of an initiation taking place. The dark woman's gift quite rightly appears to be a precious secret needing to be safeguarded, for it concerns the very core of her being. It would seem that the reaction of the dream-ego does justice to it, that is, the dreamer is able to integrate the treasure of her dark side into the consciousness and transport it safely up to the level of her waking and personal life.

But what exactly is this precious diamond from somewhere deep down? It could be the deeply felt gift of her feminine wholeness that, thanks to the pregnancy, she is now able to accept and live consciously. Furthermore, it is the earthly, instinctive side of her femininity that has been brought to her consciousness.

[142] In: *The Problem of the Contact with the Animus*, Jungiana, Series A, Vol. 3, The Guild of Pastoral Psychology, Guild Lecture No. 70, London, 1962

We do not know anything about the personal circumstances of the dreamer. Therefore we can just say that this dream is as much about pregnancy as it is about the process of individuation, or rather about pregnancy as a step toward individuation. The dream testifies to a healthy psychic reaction.

Dream No. 24:

Traveling back from India, over a year prior to Dream No. 21, this dream is from the 7th week of pregnancy. Finally, a healthy baby-girl was born:

> *I dreamt that Felicitas brought us my mother-in-law's keys, and in the small box, there was also a pale-golden ring with a clear, transparent stone in the shape of a cross and a ball. If you look into the clear stone, you can see the color of a soft rose-pink in the center of the cross – like the highest concentration of everything.*

The dreamer has a deep love for her husband's mother. We can see from the delivery of the box that she also enjoys her mother-in-law's complete trust and a reciprocal love. Taking the keys over to mother-in-law's apartment signifies the possibility, moreover, of an invitation into the domain of the mother.

For the dreamer, the mother-in-law is the beloved, admired mother, thus an ideal personification of the Great Mother in her positive aspect.

Unusually fortunate apart from the strong love relation (also indicated in other dreams by this woman) is the mother – daughter (-in-law) relationship that is ordinarily all but free from obligation. Becoming a mother happens to the dreamer (who, at this point, is aware of her condition) rather like a confidential invitation, or a loving overture to new horizons; but, above all, it is without any constraints. The small box comes to her like a gift.

The key to "mother's" apartment made me think of the magic key that is given to Faust for his trip to the realm of the "mothers."[143] The key takes the searching man down into nocturnal depths. The word "the mothers" alone sounds "peculiar" to him. This is not the world of human beings: it is the "virginal, the non-enterable" – the very distant, ethereal world of the secrets of creation. Faust is supposedly permitted to cast an apprehensive look into the inaccessible archetypal background of life and death. Contemplating this key episode in Goethe's *Faust*, we have before us an immensely powerful vision of a writer and man. No matter how passionately he loved and studied the feminine being, it is foreign to him – as much as is the realm of the anima. The key takes him inevitably to the abysmal, and the unconscious. – Quite the contrary in our present dream! Here the key is precisely to open up the maternal world and to make it tangible. In this dream, the pregnant woman's own personal reality is being unlocked. No schemes or shadows impede her way: instead, she is being invited to enter a loving maternal world. The mother archetype is

---

[143] Faust II, Act 1

not the "quite other," the unenterable; instead, the "mother" makes available to her what is destined to be hers.

The meaning of the key is contained in the small box (that in itself represents a maternal symbol): next to the key there is a "pale-golden little ring with a clear stone." The pale-golden glint could suggest that it is an ancient ring, perhaps an heirloom handed down from mother to daughter. Perhaps the "pale" golden glint suggests that the full value of the gold, that is its spiritual significance, has not yet been fully recognized. As we have seen earlier, a ring has long been the symbol for a strong and binding attachment between two people and is understood as such all over the world. The shape of the ring signifies "eternity," the everlasting union, and the gold signifies the preciousness of it.[144]

The small ring in our dream "has a clear, transparent stone in the shape of a cross and a ball." The dreamer had attempted to illustrate this three-dimensional form by sketching it, but this is extremely difficult (even more so than the squaring of the circle!). Each individual must create her own image of it. The number of allegories of this most central of symbols, the Self, is formidable: often illustrated by the union of the cross and ball, or circle and square, we find it in a tremendous variety of mandala forms in all cultures.[145] Particularly renowned is the combination of circle and cross in the form of the Irish stone crosses. The early Christian halo of Christ consists of a circle and cross, to name but a few examples; also, let us not forget the many magnificent church window rosettes as well as Tibetan Tangcas.

The stone of the little ring is clear and transparent. Implicit in its transparency is its purity but also the clear understanding the dreamer has of the message of the dream: she can see "all the way into the center." And as she does this, she can see "a soft rose-pink in the center of the cross – like the highest concentration of everything."

What I find touching in this dream vision apart from its content is the simple language in which the dreamer describes it. That "highest concentration of everything" is certainly something that cannot in fact be expressed in words. "Of everything" is a humble way of speaking about the totality – that is, the unity of all life and all the opposites that converge in the center of the cross – a point where the "heart of Jesus" could be thought to be. The simple words, "highest concentration of everything," express this mystical point better than any other.

The center has a specific color in the dream: a soft rose-pink. It is to our dreamer the very quintessence of "everything": our life and thoughts, our entire being, our destiny and our religion in particular, for the rose-pink color happens to be in the center of the cross.

[144] For a more detailed analysis of the ring, cf. M.-L. von Franz, *Psychological Interpretation of Fairy Tales*, p. 79 ff and p. 93 f
[145] On this theme, cf. C.G. Jung, CW 9/II, p. 323 ff

Perhaps the image of the cross suggests that suffering is an essential part of perfection – illustrated by the ball. This would be the quintessence of our religion in keeping with the fundamental Christian idea, its "highest concentration," and as stated clearly in both the dream vision and text, "of everything." There is for me an undeniable ring of the opposites inherent in the nature of life, namely, affliction and joy, work and play, plenitude and emptiness. All this is manifest in the shade of the soft rose-pink. Color is always an attribute providing a closer description of the psychic contents of the dream vision. The image of the rose also comprises two strong opposites: the most splendid of all flowers has prickly thorns alongside with its beauty. Moreover, the pink color contains red – the color of passion and blood – united with the white of purity and innocence. The tension between these opposites is annulled, as it were, in what the dreamer calls the softness of the rose-pink. This softness also contrasts with the hardness of the crystal. It is, as it were, its human essence. The "rose-colored blood" is also used in the alchemical tradition as an image for Christian love.[146]

In the greater part of his work, Jung assumes that all psychic phenomena consist of opposites – of their polar tension and union. We have seen examples of such polarity in the soft rose-pink and the hard stone as well as in the symbol of the rose and in the combination of cross and sphere. Throughout the dream, there is polarity. Just as the soft rose-pink is seen by the dreamer as the highest concentration *of everything*, so we can recognize the stone, according to Alchemy, as *lapis* too. This stone symbolizes the new and whole human being that is highly relevant in pregnancy for every single future mother and child.

These particularly limpid dream images shed light on the processes taking place in the archetypal background of a pregnancy.

---

[146] Cf. Jungiana Reihe A Band 3: M.-L. von Franz, *C.G. Jung's Rehabilitation der Gefühlsfunktion in unserer Zivilisation*, p. 28 f

Figure 10. Ex. Voto. Nidwalden, Switzerland, 1741

3.3. Fire

Irmgard Bosch

Where there is fire, there is movement, transformation and change. Hence, during pregnancy, fire dreams are of particular interest. When interpreting fire dreams, we must tread very gently, for the element of "fire" constitutes strong ambivalence. Let us therefore begin by looking at some general aspects of fire symbolism.

In his epic poem, "The Lay of the Bell" (1800), Friedrich Schiller has managed to evoke the ambivalent character of fire in an unparalleled fashion. He outlined the quintessence of fire in the following lines:[147]

> *Wohltätig ist des Feuers Macht,*
> *Wenn sie der Mensch bezähmt, bewacht,*
> *Und was er bildet, was er schafft,*
> *Das dankt er dieser Himmelskraft;*
> *Doch furchtbar wird die Himmelskraft,*
> *Wenn sie der Fessel sich entrafft,*
> *Einhertritt auf der eignen Spur*
> *Die freie Tochter der Natur.*
> *Wehe, wenn sie losgelassen ...*

> What vapor, what vapor – God help us! – has risen? –
> Ha! The flame like a torrent leaps forth from its prison!
> What friend is like the might of fire
> When man can watch and wield the ire?
> Whate'er we shape or work, we owe
> Still to that heaven-descended glow,
> When from their chain its wild wings go,
> When, where it listeth, wide and wild
> Sweeps the free Nature's free-born Child!

[147] Friedrich von Schiller, *The Lay of the Bell*, in: The Poems and Ballads of Schiller, translated by Sir Edward Bulwer Lytton, Bart. Leipzig, B. Tauchnitz Jun., 1844

This is followed by a grandiose description of a blaze, at the gruesome end of which it says:

Hoffnungslos
weicht der Mensch der Götterstärke

And at length,
Wearied out and despairing, man bows to their strength!
With an idle gaze sees their wrath consume,
And submits to his doom!

The above emphasizes once more the sheer dimension with which we are confronted here.

In order to understand the content of a fire dream and because of the substantial ambivalence inherent in fire, we depend on the entire dream and its context. Fire is "the agent of transformation"[148]: its essence is perpetual movement and an uncontrollable transformation through heat; from the psyche's point of view, it is the power of libido that propels forward the process of life: "The attributes of light and fire characterize the intensity of the shade of feeling and thus express the psychic energy manifested through libido. When we worship God, the sun or fire, we automatically worship the intensity and power, in other words libido, the phenomenon of psychic energy."[149]

This is true above all for the life of the spirit: Buddha's teachings are venerated in the image of the sun wheel[150]; in the Bible, the magnificence of God is also described "like devouring fire"[151] or, in the words of Psalm 104, 4: "Who maketh his angels spirits; his ministers a flaming fire." Heraclitus,[152] the pre-Socratic Greek thinker saw fire as the primordial substance of the universe and all things in perpetual flux eventually returning to it. For him, the primordial source of being consisted in a constant fiery transformation of opposite forces.[153] In Plato's famous cave parable, the phenomenal world is rendered visible by fire. The doctrine of the Stoics[154] held that the all-creating primal fire was at the prime origin and that the fiery pneuma personified by logos penetrated everything.[155] C.G. Jung also points to this, speaking of: "... all the strong impulses of man ... seemed to the ancients like the compulsion of evil stars, *Heimarmene*, or ... the *compulsion of libido.*"[156]

---

[148] Mircea Eliade, *The Forge and the Crucible*
[149] C.G. Jung, CW 5, § 161 f
[150] *Ibid.*, ill. 20
[151] Exodus, 24, 17
[152] 6th century B.C., from Ephesos
[153] Heraclitus, *Der kleine Pauly*
[154] 3rd cent. B.C. to 3rd cent. A.D.
[155] Stoa, *Der kleine Pauly*

The Gnostics, too, e.g., Simon Magus,[157] assumed that there was a "primal fire." The New Testament establishes the same connection with the appearance of Christ on Earth: "But he that cometh after me is mightier than I ... he shall baptize you with the Holy Ghost and with fire" or, "I am come to send fire on the earth; and what will I, if it be already kindled?"[158]

Goethe's attitude to fire is known to be highly ambivalent. Awed by its fierceness, by the "ferocious volcanism," he celebrated fire where it signified love and was reconciled through love to the clarifying element of water:[159]

> *... ringsum ist alles vom Feuer umronnen;*
> *So herrsche denn Eros, der alles begonnen!*
> *Heil dem Meere! Heil den Wogen,*
> *Von dem heiligen Feuer umzogen!*

> And the lapping of fire touches all things around:
> Let Eros who wrought it be honored and crowned!
> Hail to the Ocean! Hail to the wave,
> The flood with holy fire to lave!
> Waters hail! All hail the fire!
> The strange event hail we in choir!

The nature of fire is certainly altered here. The rare union with water has transfigured it. Goethe alludes here to a first step of a "unification of the elements," such as the phenomenon of the rainbow. There is no doubt that Goethe was thinking in terms of the arcane tradition of the Alchemists.[160]

Now, to Moses God spoke unveiled and directly from the burning bush – which, miraculously, did not burn.[161] Even Moses, the strong (antlered!) holy man could not bear the radiance.[162] In the bleak desert by night Jehovah, appearing as a wandering pillar of fire, showed the way to the weary people of Israel.[163]

Many saints and mystics testified to experiencing God, accompanied by stupendous phenomena of fire and light, as we know from the accounts of the Apostle Paul on his way to Damascus[164] as well from St. Hildegard v. Bingen

---

[156] C.G. Jung, CW 5, § 102
[157] Acts, 8, 9
[158] Matthew 3, 11 and Luke 12, 49
[159] J.W. von Goethe, *Faust*, The Penguin Classics, Penguin Books Ltd., 1959, Part II, Act 2, p. 155
[160] M.-L. von Franz, *On Dreams and Death*, p. 115 f
[161] Exodus 3, 2
[162] Cf. *Faust II*, Act I
[163] Exodus 13, 21
[164] Acts 9, 3

(1098–1179), who left an authentic report on the experience of her own illumination:[165]

> *It happened in the year of 1141 … A fiery light suddenly flashed down from the open heavens. It penetrated my brain and set fire to my heart and whole chest, like a flame; it did not burn me, but it was hot … and suddenly I was given insight …*

Fire has always been perceived as a numen.[166] Gaining control over fire that was considered either divine or demonic is one of the highest achievements in the development of human culture. It is therefore not surprising that in myths it is often represented as theft, as a crafty "robbing the gods of something." The most famous of these myths is the one about Prometheus who, as a benefactor of humankind, stole fire from the gods and then was bitterly punished by them. Similar legends exist in India (theft of fire and nectar through Indra).

The ancient peoples and primitives imposed strict taboos on the kindling of fire. Only very few initiated individuals would have access to the secret and only through initiation rites and sacrifices. The knowledgeable, i.e., the smiths, alchemists, magicians or shamans, thus enjoyed great power and formed secret orders, and it was sometimes thought that they derived from the gods. Other peoples disdained them.[167] The creation of fire has always been associated with excitation, ecstasy, with strong emotions and bodily heat, and above all, with gaining control over it. For this reason, the ability to kindle fire signified an increase in power and consciousness.

Sometimes the rituals and techniques of kindling fire are clearly linked to the sexual domain and its initiation rites, such as for instance, fire rubbing, drilling and beating.[168] Fire kindling and human conception alike belong to ancient taboos still in force today.

It is noticeable that in folktales, demonic, luring women often have some connection with fire, the domain of strong affects: they always fan the flames, wailing, as if they needed to warm themselves: "Whew, whew, I am so cold!" (KHM 193) – an allegory for the artful, depleting and injurious nature of negative powers. We often feel that, in fact, they themselves are the victims and sufferers. However, what they claim with their greed only reinforces the evil (as happens in "Frau Trude," (KHM 53). In the end, witches frequently are consumed by their own fire, as in "Hansel and Gretel" (KHM 15), in "Fundevogel" (KHM 51) and in "Der Trommler" (KHM 193). From a psychological point of view, this could signify that the fire of negative affects is ultimately self-destructive. Sometimes it can suggest transformation – always accompa-

---

[165] E.g., at the beginning of her book, *Scivias*, p. 5
[166] C.G. Jung, CW 5, § 138 f
[167] Cf. Mircea Eliade, *The Forge and the Crucible*
[168] Cf. C.G. Jung, CW 5, e.g., § 211 ff

nied by immense suffering. We will briefly deal with the historical burning of witches below.

Fire is a never resting element. Indeed it is only thinkable and existent in the burning process and is therefore a primordial image of life. It is worth remembering that fire is frequently attributed to God, although God is perceived as the immutable in the stone image, as all-pervading in the water image, or as a hint of a spirit, ruach or pneuma in the element of air. And yet, it appears to me that the fiery element prevails in divine imagery. If it says in Exodus, 24, 17: "And the sight of the glory of the Lord *was* like devouring fire," it may at the same time suggest that men and women must not behold this glory unprotected.

Countless are the images of fiery deities, their fiery horses and carriage, arrows and spears and beams in all religions. To name but a few: Zeus with the lightning, Elijah, Jehovah and many others. The Christian halo is also founded upon the experience of light and fire. The Persian Parsi religion has been based on the central purport of fire-rites since Zarathustra.[169]

Fire both renews life and entails undoing of what has existed before. Fire is directly connected with destruction,[170] even when it is in the service of ritual or profane human activity: it always involves the killing of a sacrificial animal, offering earthly materials (including candle wax). To cause renewal, something has to be burnt. On the day of Pentecost, the Holy Ghost poured "tongues of fire" upon the heads of the Apostles; in witness of it, they "caught fire," and the ensuing ordeals were burning with it almost to physical destruction.[171]

Concretely, however, fire has warmed people since time immemorial. It has comforted them in the cold of the winter and kept them together; it cooked bread and grits long before the invention of the revolutionary metallurgy that made the savants very powerful and lead to an irrevocable turning-point in cultural history.[172] By means of its power of transformation, fire can transport the offerings upward to the gods.[173] Fire decomposes the old and confers upon the offering a new, higher form of being visible in immaterial scent and smoke. Likewise, the idea behind incinerating the dead (in contrast to the drawn-out process of putrefaction) is to transform the body into a spiritual body as speedily as possible. The same idea is behind "purgatory." The fire of penitence burns the sin and frees people from sin already here on earth, an example of this being the victim of purge in the Jewish tradition. Until not so many

---

[169] 6th cent. B.C.

[170] Shiva as Shankara (i.e., destroyer), *Tod der Semele*; see also Goethe's Ballad, *"Der Gott und die Bajadere"*

[171] Acts 2, 3

[172] Mircea Eliade, *The Forge and the Crucible*

[173] Cf. Ge 4, Cain and Abel

centuries ago, people tried to get rid of sorceresses and sorcerers by burning them. Hundreds of heretics were burnt, in order to purge the earth of evil. An example of this is the burning of two hundred Catharists in South France at the foot of Mount Segur in the 12th century. Today, it strikes us as a tragedy of Christianity that for too long we refused to recognize that the zealous hatred of the Inquisitors psychologically was no lesser purgatory (hellish fire), not to speak of the mass murder of the Jews, which is erroneously compared to the Jewish victims of purge ("Holocaust").

As keepers and preservers of the fire, women were placed in a saintly role within the community much earlier than the male smiths: even in patriarchal societies women possessed a unique power stemming from the fireplace with the maternal symbol of the kettle, or the kitchen stove seen as the central point of the family. In addition, their role as providers of carefully prepared food and certainly as child bearers reinforced this position of power. Furthermore, as the keepers of the public fire in Vesta's temple they held high offices of state. They had to guard the life and welfare of the entire city and state; they had to ensure it would never be extinguished. In Greece, Hestia was the goddess of the hearth. Women were responsible for the spirits of the ancestors that lived in the hearth and guaranteed the survival of the family. Perhaps this is a primordial image: men light the fire, women safeguard and keep it. One is as important as the other.

The ambivalence inherent in fire is not merely a question of degree. In ancient times, there may have been a similarly irrational absolute fear of the fire element, comparable perhaps to what is currently felt with respect to energy extraction from atom-splitting.

Already the Egyptians had a complex and contradictory relationship with fire. In the 11th hour of the *Amduat*, the *Egyptian Book of the Dead*, it tells of how the enemies of Re, the god of the sun, are thrown into a fire pit.[174] The Greeks also had a river of fire called Phlegethon into which they threw the criminals, and at the same time they lit sacred fires, e.g., the olympic fire guaranteeing peace during the games.

For a psychological study of fire symbolism, we can find a wealth of material in C.G. Jung's "Symbols of Transformation."[175] According to Jung, in dreams and fantasies fire is the most vivid expression of feelings and passions and above all represents the painful transformation of the soul. Being movement, it embodies the intensity of life. According to M.-L. von Franz, fire is particularly valuable for the process of individuation. She writes:[176] "No development can take place nor can a higher consciousness be attained without the fire of emotion [see above, Hildegard's words], which is why God says: 'So

---

[174] Cf. Erik Hornung, *Die Nachtmeerfahrt der Sonne*, p. 176
[175] C.G. Jung, CW 5
[176] Marie-Louise von Franz, *The Interpretation of Fairy Tales*, p. 191

then because thou art lukewarm, and neither cold nor hot, I will spew thee out of my mouth.' (Rev. 3, 16)" And from Origien[177]: Those close to me are close to fire. Those who are far away from me, are far away from the kingdom." – "Far away from the kingdom" means removed from life and God.

Like fire, the warmth and passion of human life can be suffocated when the ego of an individual is badly adjusted. Life grows cold. This often happens when a person is subject to an insurmountable craving for recognition and in the case of an underdeveloped shadow-integration by the ego, e.g., under the yoke of rigid moral principles and ideals. Behind this, there is sometimes a deep fear of the potential fires pertaining to a life lived intensely and fully. In his *Divine Comedy*, Dante has the most terrifying of all places, an ice hell, at the deepest end of the inferno, beneath the fire hell. It is only there that death is definitive, contrary to fire, which still harbors possibilities of transformation.

Finally, let us glance at a few well-known customs relating to fire. The ancient custom of the paschal fire symbolizing resurrection is still (or anew) observed by the Christian church. In Catholic churches, there is always an eternal light burning near the altar. It is the symbol of the perpetual veneration of God through his church and of His presence in it. Christian rites join the ancient pagan rites in Spring fires on hills with the crackling and "sparking" of objects being burnt down and fiery wheels. Resurrection after winter and death continues to be celebrated in this manner to this day. With the Midsummer Eve's bonfire, we celebrate the summer solstice; and we could not begin to think away the burning candles on the Christmas tree in the winter darkness. The candles on the bier of the departed or on graves (All Saints Day, Christmas, Easter) also signify perpetual life and immortality.

Sacred fires are mostly about rebirth in arenas of strong opposites, where a new aspect of life is about to be kindled.

Fire Dreams

In pregnancy dreams, too, fire makes ambivalent and highly complex appearances. The following dream expresses its power of transformation:

Dream No. 25 [nine weeks pregnant]:

> *I live in B in Ö. I am both as young as I was then, about ten, and at the same time my actual age.*
> *The fire is loose, and it has started in the houses in the west part of the area. The fire is now spreading in our direction.*

---

[177] Early Christian teacher, 185 – 253

There is only time to save a few things, and I will not have space for much in the car that will take us away from the fire.
I decide to save this dream journal, my dark altar painting (the same painting as in the dream of the 1.12.83) and a couple of my most precious books. That is, in fact, all I need from the home.
I am most upset and register with surprise that my father and the rest of the family seem rather indifferent.

In games and in the context of personality tests, the question – what would you take with you if you were sent into exile to a desert island? – is often asked. What do I need most in the long-term? This is the kind of question that individuals will ask themselves when it comes to a change at a certain point in life. Pregnancy signifies this kind of saying good-bye to the past.

Faced with the fire, there is little time for reflection. The dreamer decides on three things: her first priority is the analytical dream work, that is, to carefully watch the images from the unconscious; the second is an altar painting, presumably the one that is most sacred to her and that she has designed herself; the third is books, something to stimulate her spirit. That is all she wishes to take with her. We are offered a glimpse of something like a life-plan here, formulated spontaneously in the unconscious. This dream represents a confirmation issued by consciousness rather than a compensation.

There are not that many opportunities for a woman to grow up, but pregnancy is certainly one of them. It helps, even unconsciously, to take the right steps at the right time, even though they may not – generally or in our dreamer's case – be taken voluntarily.

These are by no means easy steps to take: leaving the childhood home involves an overwhelming and painful affect. The fire points to the dreamer's inner agitation, it clearly seems to say: soon this house will no longer exist, will no longer offer a refuge. The realization that childhood is over involves great personal pain. The collective side, that is, father and family, remain untouched; the loss is the dreamer's alone. Looking at it from the collective background (the family), the burning down of the childhood home is a normal and natural, fateful process and yet, for the individual person, it is as dreadful as fire and destruction.

However, the dreamer understands that, in fact, there isn't anything in that home she now needs, except for the three things. The triad suggests the compelling, dynamic character of the situation and its future development, just as in folktales. The three precious items are reminiscent of the three drops of blood on a white piece of cambric that a queen gives to her daughter as she sends her off to a foreign land.[178] They are a kind of magic maternal protection and are to stand the daughter in good stead in all situations.[179] Our dreamer

[178] Grimm, "The Goose Girl"

knows instantly what she wishes to take with her, and the decision is that of her waking ego. This is surprising as, in the dream, she is in addition "the child aged ten." We may assume that it is the child within her who feels the burning pain for the parental home.

She wants to rescue "three things" for her new life. Just as in "The Goose Girl," she chooses something like a magic protection, only her talisman does not come in the shape of a feminine symbol, such as the maternal drops of blood. (They rather suggest an earlier, more unconscious stage of womanhood which, through motherly powers, focusses upon and expresses the growing and unfolding of womanhood.) Instead, she wants to keep in touch with her deep core in a more modern and conscious fashion. At most, books could represent irritation for the individuation process. They of course embody a large amount of theoretical knowledge which is known to tend to lead us astray, and all the more so since there are "a couple" of them. We are not speaking of a heap or a suitcase full of books, and the dream is not criticizing the quantity of books in any way, even though they do constitute a third of "the most important." All things considered, they may express, how important it is to the dreamer to continue her studies in the present crisis.

If in the burning fire – that is, the pain of saying good-bye – we glimpse a fire of sacrifice and transformation, we can see in the car and its four wheels a motif of recovery and rescue: namely, an image of the Self. The meaning of "auto" is "self," and the automobile is that which moves by itself.[180]

Fire-dream No. 26 (resembles the one above):

> A neighbor came up to me to tell me that there had been a big fire near my house. I ran to the hill where my house was located. Many houses along the road were burnt out completely. There were two new and splendid houses beside mine. I felt pity on the owners.
> Fortunately my house was safe. The windows were bright for the lights of the lamps, which made me feel relieved.

Here, too, the dreamer's house is in danger but at closer examination, only the neighboring houses have been struck by the fire. What does this mean? It means that the dreamer's private sphere, her protective soul-chamber, was very nearly destroyed by a big fire. However, the fire – probably overwhelming, destructive emotions, spared it, and to the dreamer's relief, the windows are even lit up. Thus, much of what was dear to her has been destroyed by the fire, but the core of herself remains untouched. On the contrary, the windows are

---

[179] The "three gifts" are a recurring pattern in folktales, e.g., Grimm Fairy Tales "Cinderella" (21), "Allerleihrauh" (65) and many others. Cf. Max Lüthi, *Das Europäische Volksmärchen*, p. 38

[180] Robert Bosch, *Das Automobil als Selbst-Symbol*, unpublished lecture, 1990

"bright" – her inner being has been illuminated. Through pain, she has reached a higher level of consciousness.

New and handsome buildings in the immediate vicinity have been consumed by the flames. On the subjective level, this means that the dreamer has also had to make sacrifices and suffer losses but that her core has remained intact. She feels a great relief.

In Dream No. 27, a young woman who is pregnant for the first time (a planned pregnancy) dreamt of "jewels from a fire":

> *There was a big fire. I picked up a small box from the fire. Opening the box I found some shining jewels. The jewels were beautiful in my hands. It was an amazing experience.*

In this dream vision, fire clearly signifies a creative and productive process, for there is a small box in the fire which the dreamer bravely picks out. With this act, she shows her courage and determination in the face of the pain, i.e., the heat of emotions. She picks the fruit out of the fire, "pulls the chestnuts out of the fire." In other words, she can obtain something that in a psychic ardor has proven indestructible and steadfast.

The "small box" suggests the preciousness of it. It resembles a shrine which, in the form of the Ark of the Covenant (e.g., in ancient Judaism), contained the Holy of Holies of the entire people (more precisely, it became the seat of God). We also find the shrine of the Most Holy Sacrament, the tabernacle on Christian altars. The highest preciousness requires a protective and communicative form. Shining contents indicate a value that is generally held as highest. The small box represents the container of these values – the case that makes the precious content tangible for the woman.

We do not know what the process of the "great fire" refers to in this dream. The dreamer will know however – at least on a personal level! In any event, she can easily relate to the object that was born in the fire (the jewels shine in her hands), and she has fully grasped it.

This dream vision addresses a higher aim, which might exist behind personal passion, love or pain. Securing shining jewels from a fire evokes the image of a process resulting in something immortal and extra-temporal – rather like the Alchemists attempted to do with their complex opus aiming at the mysterious lapis, which embodied an immaterial, psychic or spiritual goal. It seems obvious that, in the depths of this fire, there lies a hidden, alchemical symbolism (which was discussed in the chapter on stones).

In "the three men in the burning furnace,"[181] we have an example of finding a treasure and mercy by withstanding the burning. They withstood the fire,

---

[181] Old Testament, Daniel 3

moved around in it unhurt, and to the horror of their tormentors, a "fourth" joined them, who looked godlike.

The high, heavenly origin of fire is represented by lightning and the low, chthonic origin of fire by volcanoes and fire spurting out of the earth. The two types of fire must be interpreted accordingly.

Dream No. 28 (dreamt around the time of conception):

> *My husband and I are in the South East of Africa and I am told by my father that there are great volcano eruptions at Buenos Aires and in Honolulu. I see the places like in an earth globe. Buenos Aires seems to be situated at Madagascar.*
>
> *We are in a town at the coast and across the water we see the island of Madagascar with an enormous volcano mountain. Burning and glowing material is thrown up from it's center, and smoke rises to the sky from it. We are not afraid of the volcano.*
>
> *I ask Thomas S. if it is true that Hitler offered this island to the Jewish people. Thomas answered that now Madagascar is the last safe place, where all wise people try to move.*
>
> *We are going to be shipped across the water by a ferry. There is a problem with our two dogs. They are not allowed to come with us. Stress and worry. The boat is to leave soon.*
>
> *We ask two Swedish tourists if they can look after our dogs for two weeks. They hesitate and say no. The man's father has pheasants in cages, therefore he cannot have our lively dogs running about. We try to find a dog pension. I also consider smuggling them along with me in the car.*

Together with her husband, the dreamer finds herself in the Southern Hemisphere, in fact, almost at the other end of the world. She feels as if, around the time of conception, she has been pulled away from her usual environment. She dreams of enormous volcanic eruptions in places that are far apart – Honolulu and Buenos Aires – but that she can still observe as if they were within sight. The dream-ego is confronted with "earthshaking," huge eruptions of enormous subterranean (that is, unconscious) heat boiling over everywhere. But all this is happening in the far distance. The dreamer and her husband watch the gigantic eruptions across the ocean on Madagascar: they see glowing lava, stones that are being hurled up and huge clouds of smoke. They feel no fear, but on the contrary, plan to take a ferry to the island with the volcano, in order to watch the spectacle from nearby. A friend explains to the dreamer the significance of Madagascar, which she had already heard about: Madagascar had almost become an "island for the damned," that is, the place where Hitler had wanted to deport the Jews, a dreaded place of exile, whereas today, the island is considered the last place of refuge for the clever and wise. The dreamer's own positive development is revealed in this answer:

"Madagascar," formerly a place of terror and punishment, is now a safe haven – a place of refuge for people who are clever and wise. This could mean that the dreamer has gained a more positive attitude to the spiritual world, that in earlier years had seemed to her rather like "isolation" (isola), or like a prison run by an appalling dictator. This is over now, and a volcano is exploding.

The island "Madagascar" stands out in this dream – we wonder why.

The name alone already sounds mysterious. It is distant and foreign to us Europeans; its location is almost antipodal, particularly with respect to Northern Europe. But it is not only the distance that has always made Madagascar seem fairy-tale-like and "otherworldly," as it were, but rather its isolated location far out in the Indian Ocean. "Madagascar," therefore, is the embodiment of exoticism. There are exotic plants and animals on this island, which do not exist in any other place. To reach it, one has to cross an ocean, which in a dream – just as in fairy tales – often signals a transition into another world, or further, into the unconscious.

Voyages abroad form the theme of many fairy tales, stories and myths: heroes or heroines searching for lonely islands, their multifarious journeys to a "glass mountain," to the moon or to the sun. Oftentimes, the goal of the journey is the "water of life" for an aging king or a treasure difficult to obtain, i.e., a means to renew life. Ultimately, it is about the search of an individual soul on *her* arduous path to individuation. Oceans – that is, unconscious domains – have to be crossed, and there is almost always a great danger lurking.

The dream-ego, accompanied by her inner masculine partner, has no doubts about venturing the crossing so as to see the fascinating eruptions at close range. At the last moment, though, there is a stumbling block – the travelers are forbidden to bring their dogs along. They are desperately looking for a place for the dogs, but because they don't succeed and no dog-home can be found, the dreamer is considering smuggling them over. These canine companions represent their owners' animalistic side: their instinct. They embody the unconscious security of an individual's emotional life as well as anticipation or intuition (scent), as we shall see later in the chapter on dogs.

Therefore, if it is not possible to travel with these vital and often life-saving powers, it is unlikely that the crossing could be successful. The adventure would merely be motivated by some intellectual impulse, a kind of daredevil curiosity which would be bound to end in failure. The dreamer could then be likened to the naïve little girl, who in the fairy tale, "Frau Trude,"[182] out of defiant curiosity and against all wise counsel approaches the terrible monster only to catch one good look and to immediately fall prey to her: without further ado, Frau Trude uses the little girl for firewood.

---

[182] Grimm's Fairy Tales No. 43, cf. also Sibylle Birkhäuser-Oeri, *The Mother: Archtypal Image in Fairy Tales*, Inner City Books, 1988

Examining our dream, we cannot help but feel that this global and yet cool interest in the volcanic eruptions without feelings of fear or alarm and the plan to get across to the fire island shaken by eruptions with ash and stones flying about, is similarly lacking in instinct. Without the dogs and their noses, our travelers would be in great danger. But the woman is not at all out of her wits, for despite obvious complications, she insists that the dogs come along "even if she has to smuggle them." Fortunately, the dreamer is in fact in touch with her instinctive powers despite her fascination for the exotic-eruptive natural events, and would under no circumstance leave the dogs behind. Thus, she is reduced to waiting and having to exercise patience vis-à-vis this mighty spectacle of Nature until things have calmed down.

But what is going on out there that the dreamer so wishes to study? Recalling that the dream was dreamt "around conception," we can perhaps guess the reasons for eruptions and tremor! A volcanic eruption might be compared to an enormous emotional discharge supplied from depths far removed from the personal; indeed, it could inundate the personal. Another very interesting fact in this dream is that the eruptions are happening at so far a distance, yet we can understand why the dreamer wishes to be closer. Perhaps the dreamer keeps the fiery world of emotions at some distance so that she cannot easily contact it but remains fascinated by it all the same.

However, this dream is clearly about an occurrence in Nature that reaches far beyond the personal. We can see that this woman has a strong unconscious drive for discovery and insight and that at the same time there is sound cohesion between her thirst for knowledge and her instinctive powers. This cohesion prevents her from exposing herself to the primary power of erupting emotions, to the hail of stones and fire.

It is likely that, on the subjective level, the wish to come closer to the "volcanic eruptions" corresponds to an attempt made by the ego to be more in touch with certain overpowering or uncontrolled emotions and to learn how to control them better (e.g., an onset of feelings of anger). The dream further shows a great discrepancy between an extremely deep psychic process and the dream-ego, which seems well-equipped, with the animus being exclusively in the company of men. Therefore, there cannot be an adequate crossing, it would be against instinct as the dream vision so clearly points out. The dream-ego's attitude not to undertake the crossing without the dogs is thus the appropriate one.

In the following example, we shall witness rumbling going on in dangerous proximity, beneath the earth. In her elaborate commentary, the dreamer tells us that she feels unwell that morning, has feelings of inferiority, is exhausted and depressed. She does not get out of bed and feeling oppressed by both her father and husband, refuses to cook.

Dream No. 29, slightly abridged (approximately in the 26th week):

> *I dream that in front of my terrace, they carry out or make disappear a mountain, that looks like leaning against the wall and door under our terrace. Then, it appears again, like a volcano, black, with prolonged stone slabs. But the lava doesn't appear.*
> *People come to look.*
> *I want to go to Andorra or Catalonia, that are nearby, around the hill that the volcano has made, but L. says that it will be dangerous and doesn't want me to. When we are there, I awake.*

What strikes one as being particularly oppressive in this dream is the following: the lava is not coming out even though the pressure from underneath is so enormous and has already forced up a volcanic hill that is moving right up to the dreamer's doorstep. In the commentary, she associates the elongated, black and cold looking stone slabs on the volcanic hill with a mechanical cold padlock. She writes that this padlock was painted onto a sticker on one of her three-year-old daughter's sweaters and that she did not like it because it was silver-black, uncanny, mechanical and cold. The sight of the volcano frightens her, leaving her hot while, on the terrace, it is cold.

All kinds of hostile counter-forces are at play here, and one of them is the ground ominously moving up and into the garden. The volcano is hot but its black color is "ominously cold." Everything is counteractive, strained and irreconcilable but there is no eruption. The boiling lava cannot exit.

This may well be the reason why the dreamer is feeling totally exhausted and frustrated, as she indicates herself: she probably has to suppress strong feelings of exasperation and anger, constantly and with an enormous effort, as they would otherwise break out at any moment and cause destruction. It seems that this woman is particularly irritated by the "mechanical," cold, hard and heartless nature of her situation. There is no human or friendly response to her suffering, for there is a padlock.

It is intriguing that this awful lock is attached to something belonging to her child. Could she have fallen into this leaden silence out of consideration for her child? Or is the child too great a burden for her? Perhaps what torments her – what the volcano that's unable to erupt and the distressing heat evoke – she cannot tell anyone. Her fear, rather like a steel lock, may prevent an outburst. Her own view of her situation is that husband and father are "obvious machos" and – as ever – she has to carry the entire burden alone.

As long as the volcano will not erupt, it is hard to see a way out. The dream only shows the manifest desire to get away from there, to escape into Nature – the mountains or Catalonia –, away especially from the oppressive human environment. Although escape may be the only option available now, the dreamer should be aware that these powers from below, which need to be brought to the light, are immense; they are already rumbling in her own garden, right beneath her terrace. These chthonic powers being "hot" seems to say that an instinctive-fiery process, going on inside her, badly needs to be unleashed. But instead of letting it run its course, she is made insecure and irritated by it; she also allows it to bother her friends, and as a result, it rocks the foundations of her well-established existence.

I would imagine that, so far, our dreamer has met the challenges of her life more or less passively and has seen herself as a victim. But now, something is fundamentally rebelling, something enormously strong: a subterranean fire that threatens to dismantle her old cornerstones (the garden, terrace – the world she has cultivated) and disallow her role of a victim. Perhaps her own sexual passion and/or her love of freedom that she has kept under control (padlock) are now demanding attention. Of course, the secret rumbling of the fire will persist until she realizes that it is her own fire and that it is very powerful. Only once having reached that point and using these very powers will she be able to defend herself and to become more herself. Pregnancy could be of valuable help to her, but it is understandable that, at the onset, she is quite terrified of these tremors.

Let us now look at the following, equally threatening fire-dream.

Dream No. 30 (7th week):

> *I'm in a haunted house, my house. I'm playing a board game with my mother, father and my brother. There are plastic mice on the board. The lights are all on in the house. But the mother wants to turn them off to see the mice glow in the dark. We each have a pack of matches. We light the entire pack at once and turn off the lights. It gives me an edgy feeling because I know I'll be left alone in the house later.*

If it were not for the haunted house, this would make a peaceful and happy picture of a family sitting around a board game. The family consists of four forms: a concentric group oriented towards the center; it forms a unity arranged in a circle, or rather a square, representing a simple and regular Mandala.[183] For this reason, we can infer that the family has a central meaning for the dreamer, on a subjective level; however, and according to Jung's understanding of the number four, it is more likely that this has to do with a problem regarding the dreamer's own wholeness.

The dream evidently revolves around the pieces on the board that have turned into self-glowing plastic mice. Although it is particularly bright in the house – all the lights are on – it is not quite "right" in there. Apparently, the brightness is supposed to drive away or shut out some element of darkness. A certain fear is palpable, and although there are no additional details in the text

---

[183] C.G. Jung, CW 9/I, § 627 ff

– the meaning of the curse is unknown to us – there is an unpleasant atmosphere from the very beginning.

Let us take a closer look at the constellation: a gathering of father, mother, son and daughter represents the primordial state, or the primordial "family" cell. Brother and sister still seem to be completely integrated in the bosom of the family despite the fact that the dreamer is twenty-eight years old, married and seven weeks pregnant. Relations' libido seems to be unbroken in the original family, that is, a collective group-libido whose dynamics are determined mainly (and as is mostly the case) by the mother. The mother expresses the needs of this living unit.

Psychologically, we must not restrict ourselves to the image of the family gathered around the board game as the exterior family situation of the dreamer; rather, the image points to something central in the dreamer herself. The core family and the haunted house are an allegory for the general present constellation of her psychic state. What is happening here touches her in her innermost center and in her own sense of order where, presumably, something essential has gone wrong: the lighting is not right. There is a false, exaggeratedly bright perspective of things.

Again, the arrangement of this regular Mandala-like form this game-playing family constitutes, is a representation of the early, virtually completely unconscious collective state of the "original family" before any kind of exterior interference could occur. Mother alone exerts influence here, and this feels much like a curse.

The board with the mice is in the center of the Mandala on which everyone's eyes are set. Something crucial must be happening there. However, since we are not familiar with the "mouse game," we must inquire into the meaning of being engaged in games in general. We know that playing is one of the most ancient communal human activities; in fact, it is an instinctive manifestation of life and as such far older than humankind (animal progeny!). What were supposedly pieces[184] and lines carved in stone from the Neolithic period could be interpreted as magic fields, as "game-boards," for there is a striking similarity between them and the fields that children draw with chalk on the pavement still today. Many elements of a magical world-view have been preserved in children's games.[185] The rules of the game are no different from the models of our own life-paths, which we must try to walk without making too many serious mistakes. And just like dice, to our lot falls either progress or stagna-

---

[184] Cf. Marie König, op. cit., p. 195

[185] In this ancient child's game (hopscotch) that in German is called "Heaven and Hell" or "Heaven and Earth," you have to skip along a certain path marked by boxes which have been colored-in and determined by casting a little stone (chance principle), without ever stepping on the lines. If you only slightly step on the line, you have to start from the beginning. This path becomes increasingly more difficult until you finally end up in either hell or heaven.

tion, good luck or bad luck, depending on how the dice were cast. Board games with mostly dice or figures are very likely to be related to the innumerable forms of oracle across times and cultures and we assume that this form of playing with fate is really ancient.[186] The transitions from triviality to serious-ness, fun to deeper meaning and from practice to magic are fluid and varied. The excitement to be derived from games lies in the very fact that boundaries can be crossed so easily, so confidently. Schiller says: "Man is a king when he plays." For, the pieces and figures are, just like puppets, no different from ourselves: little men and women representing and modeling us on the board. To play games requires sincerity as well as being prepared to lose. Ultimately, we play out our own lives, trying to master them in a kind of ritual, half seriously, half in jest. We have all experienced identifying with the figures and having to accept sacrificing them.[187] In this case, they are mice.

What is the significance of mice? They are not generally welcome in peo-ple's homes. They belong to the dark world, to dirt, scurrying secretly along the floors, nibbling away at our provisions, gnawing their way through ward-robes and doors (i.e., making connections where we do not want any!).

Tidiness-loving women are the first to shy away from these parasites and thus devil's animals (Mephisto, the dark Apollo), which can become quite a pest. What is particularly astonishing is that they lead an expansive life in the midst of us, in our homes – at least in the countryside. Moreover, we hardly ever manage to lay eyes on them when in fact they know every nook and cranny in the house far better than we do (and particularly those we wish not to know anything about). In this sense, they make for a useful image of certain hidden aspects of our own personality, our shadow-aspects, so to speak, which we tend to shy away from. C.G. Jung writes:[188] "The mouse is an animal of the soul, an image of a psychic reality that it is difficult to apprehend. It is a form of the soul that is closely linked to muscel, lat. *mus* = meet, to sexuality and fertility and the devil." And later he describes the mouse as "an animal that is related to the darkness of the soul." Now, the mother wants to have all the lights turned off as though the aforementioned perfect brightness would inter-fere with the game. And we learn why: one cannot see the mice; they do not glow enough to be noticed in the glaring brightness of electric lights.

The situation now becomes even more like an oracle. Since time immemo-rial, men and women have tried to fathom the impenetrable darkness of the future. All cultures developed oracles to try and divine their fate and to try to adapt their behavior correspondingly. There used to be, and there still are, birth oracles. We can see our dreamer's unconscious' inventing of a board

---

[186] Cf. M.-L. von Franz, *On Divination and Synchronicity,* Inner City Books
[187] M.-L. von Franz, *On Divination and Synchronicity*
[188] C.G. Jung, *Kindertraumseminar 1939/40*, Ed. by L. Jung and M. Meier-Grass, Walter Verlag, Olten, 1987, p. 351 ff

game with luminous mice in the context of this kind of oracle game, perhaps in order to find a way out of a life-inhibiting situation. Bright lighting would only permit rational analysis or illumination, which could impede oracle consulting, and which is also why the mother orders all lights to be turned off.

But now something quite unexpected happens in the dream: Mother's demand causes instant panic and frantic activity in the playing group, and as if struck by a terrible fear of the dark with which all four are "infected," each player lights an entire packet of matches at once just before the lights are turned off. There must have been a single darting flame or an explosion followed by instant darkness. A gentle twilight, which might have turned the mouse game into something constructive and valuable, could not be attained. I do not believe that the instantaneous burning-up of all the matches should be interpreted as "illumination" or a sudden insight. Rather I believe it to be a destructive panic reaction, even a catastrophe. Fear has consumed all personal reserves all at once. Once all the matches have burnt down, the flame is worth no more than a straw fire. The dreamer "has an edgy feeling" at the end of the dream as she knows that she is going to be left alone in the haunted house.

This ending sentence sounds like something a child who is afraid of the dark might say. The "game" did not work: there was a kind of short circuit. Perhaps the explanation of the ending lies in what is to come: this pregnant woman is still very apprehensive about "being left alone" in the future, that is, being independent, with a family of her own and responsible for her own actions.

Dream No. 31: [189]

> *It was in the Middle Ages. I lost the count's and countess' good graces when I defended some witches and allowed one to skip away, crying out loud: "The evil you see in others is within yourselves. Jesus said: Let weed and wheat grow together, so that you don't make the mistake of removing the wheat." I was also supposed to be burnt as a witch and fled, was betrayed, hidden by a priest, discovered and sentenced to be burnt at the stake together with him. I saw a niche from which light emanated, and a thin, blue veil. I crouched down and discovered a lovely little Madonna. I thought: "Even this lovely statue is now no use to you any more." I imagined all the stages of burning to death.*

It is as if this medieval dream scene pretended the problems addressed in it belonged to a distant past. Although the dream has found a suitable frame for the events described, it nevertheless paints a picture of the dreamer's current psychic condition. The woman has to suffer and feel in her imagination all the stages of burning at the stake.

---

[189] The first part of this dream will be discussed in Chapter 5.5, No. 83

Having lost "the count's and countess' good graces" signifies being in contradiction to the generally prevailing state of consciousness. The count and countess personify the rules of their time with which the dreamer does not feel comfortable. The dream-ego is in grave contradiction to these: it has been deprived of their "grace" by both the feminine role model (countess) and the masculine one (count), that is, there has been a rupture.

We are clearly dealing here with the dreamer's personal problem, but also with a collective problem of woman: something unresolved with which the Christian-Western cultures have long been struggling.

Dissenting life-styles and opinions are by no means easily tolerated in any society. The ideal of religious tolerance is only the crux of enlightenment. In Christian Europe of the Middle Ages, such people were easily accused of being in a pact with the devil, and those who defended "witches" were put on trial.

There is no doubt that the dreamer's unconscious considers such action deeply unchristian. Two thousand years ago, Jesus himself, so she declares in the dream, pleaded for a very different attitude regarding evil,[190] namely to let tare grow with the wheat. Jesus continues to say: "Let both grow together until the harvest: and in the time of harvest, I will say to the reapers, 'Gather ye together first the tares, and bind them in bundles to burn them: but gather the wheat into my barn.'" I understand this passage to mean that casting out the tares should only be done at the time of the "harvest" (a symbol for death and the Last Judgment), that is, only once we know what we have reaped. This parable gives "tare" the chance to transform itself here on earth.[191]

Now, we all tend to be rather quick to reject things that are not generally accepted. There were times when wearing trousers as a woman was enough for her to be called a witch. This just goes to show that the collective perceptions of the role models men and women represent are highly sensitive, intolerant and inconsistent.

A priest, who was courageous enough to hide the dreamer from her persecutors, must also be burnt. Historically speaking, there were many other such men. The priest in the dream represents a remarkably positive animus figure standing by the feminine dream-ego's ordeals like a brother.

The final image once again sheds light on the background of the conflict. Just before she is to go to the stake she sees a mysterious light shining out of a niche and a "thin, blue veil." She bends down and discovers a sweet little Madonna statue. The transparent blue of the veil might be interpreted as a sign of her heavenly, spiritual purity. However, the dreamer knows that even this lovely little statue cannot help her now – she has to suffer death at the stake. Reflecting further on the image of the veil, we are reminded of Maya's

---

[190] Mt. 13, 25-30
[191] Cf. the words of St. John: "He that is without sin among you, let him first cast a stone at her." Jn. 8, 7

veil to whom Mary is related in her quality of the worldly mother. This reveals to us the profound difference between the Christian ideal woman and the ancient Indian symbol. "Maya's veil" shimmers seductively in all the colors of this world, and, moreover, to such an extent that it conceals from man the true higher reality.[192] In contrast, the thin blue veil of the Mother of God is a sign of her otherworldly spiritual beauty.

In the course of the Christian history of symbols, time and again features of the ancient goddesses of the earth and the heavens were ascribed to the Christian Mother of God, particularly deriving from popular belief, that is, from down below: more earthiness in the Black Madonnas, more Nature symbols with the Madonna, a wreath of roses or corn ears, or the apple, more cosmic elements in her crown of stars and in the image of the crescent at her feet, not to mention many more. And yet, the "blue veil," presenting her as the most sublime, immaculate virgin and her femininity as more spiritual than physical, continues to prevail. Only baby-Jesus or departed Jesus are permitted to be seen on her lap.

Jung showed that the spiritually necessary elevation of Mary to a heavenly status of sublimity and immaculateness provoked a fearful schism in the Middle Ages. Humankind, and in this case women, were professed to be responsible for all the darkness in life, resulting in the disastrous propagation of an obsessive belief in witches.

Our dream leads to this situation. It was dreamt by a modern, intellectually inclined woman preoccupied with the question of her identity from the very depths of her soul. More often than not, such questions are related to collective role models, although her questions, extending to eras beyond her own, appear to be her own personal questions, or at least to reflect conflict-laden processes from her unconscious. It seems that the inner rebellion is so strong that she will have to be burnt, because she stood up for witches. In her defense, she quotes the words of Jesus, the gist of which has practically been forgotten. Though it may not be unknown, this is not a maxim prevalent or central to the official Christian doctrine. Jesus' parable is in no way a justification of witches or other villains. As Jesus himself had told it to the sinful Mary Magdalene, he merely meant that in this life the last word should not be spoken. Whether someone be a witch or a whore shall be known only at the time of "harvest." These kinds of conflicts are burning in the soul of our dreamer. They are of a strong, dangerously passionate nature.

In the dream, she comes up with better and more Christian solutions, and yet she has to be subjected to the flames of the fire. She has to endure the deep schism between the sweet Madonna and the witch until she will have found a more whole and truer feminine role model. This collective and chronic prob-

---

[192] The image here therefore suggests a one-sided spiritual attitude that, in Hinduism and Buddhism, possibly results in even stricter asceticism.

lem has such far-reaching ramifications that it requires unlimited devotion to confront and also causes great suffering, as is evoked by the death at the stake.

Speaking in the language of the dream, a new count and a new countess personifying the archetype reigning over our times and requiring a far wider horizon, would have to be found.

Figure 11. Grain harvesting (Sennedjem's tomb, Egypt, 18th Dynasty)

4. The Vegetable Kingdom

4.1. The Plant

Regina Abt

Pregnancy is like the vegetable kingdom, or so man close to Nature thought in the past. The fertilization of a seed caused the nine-month-long growth of a child in a secluded, dark and humid place comparable to the womb of the Earth. The fetus was like a plant whose growth and development continued after birth. Once fertilization had occurred, woman had to make sure the fetus grew into a healthy child. The child in her womb was like a flower in a vase filled with life-giving water, like a seedling implanted in fertile soil: it takes the sap from the maternal body, in order to grow.[193] Just as the farmers and gardeners made sowing and new planting dependent on the lunar cycle, so it was thought beneficial to plan conception around the new moon, so that plant or fetus could grow well. Woman's body was like a field or arable land that opened up to receive the seed of the child. "It was the garden of the human race into which secret forces sowed the seed. Woman would become mother by the direct implantation of a child into the womb that would give it human shape. Up to this point, the male had not yet come into the picture. Although people saw a connection between the sexual act and fertilization, they failed to recognize the biological causes of conception. The father may have been indispensable, however he was only of secondary importance. He helped to attach the embryo that he would subsequently 'manipulate,' ... and it was certain that in this way he gave the child the family imprint. Woman herself was merely a carrier, the fertile soil, the embryonic sheath of the fetus. ... For, ultimately the question was whether in fact children did not belong to the land, the soil of their ancestors rather than to their own parents. ... This ancient conception of the origins of life lasted until the middle of the 19th

---

[193] Cf. J. Gélis, *Die Geburt, Volksglaube, Rituale und Praktiken von 1500–1900*, p. 89 f

century, determining behavioral patterns in much of European rural population."[194]

In our age of advanced medical science and technological tools, such as ultra-sound, this aspect of child conception beyond the personal and the close association with the vegetal world has largely disappeared. This helpful allegory is no longer available to young women of our time. However, we still encounter it in dreams.

The following dream stems from a twenty-two-year-old woman who had previously had to opt for an abortion under very difficult circumstances. From the day she got married to another man, though, she wished to become pregnant again. She thus had a very positive attitude to her future motherhood.[195]

Dream No. 32:

> *The scene of the dream was in my new home to which I had moved only 3 weeks earlier following our wedding. The time in the dream was the morning shortly after breakfast. I was wearing my red dressing gown. The dream was thus placed into the morning following the night during which it was being dreamed. The doorbell rang and I went to answer it Standing outside was a young man carrying a big box of the type florists use for very large and expensive flowers. He asked me, "Are you Mrs. X?" I replied, yes, I was, and he handed me the box. I said, very surprised, "But I don't know of anybody who would send me flowers. Who sent these?" He smiled and motioned towards the card which was in an envelope attached to the box with tape. I opened the little envelope and found written on the card: "With love from the New Life." I was utterly thrilled, took the box inside and opened it on the dining room table which was in actual fact as well as in the dream, a totally square, dark 19th century mahogany table. Inside the box were 4 large white bulb-chrysanthemums. I took them out of their wrappings and placed them in a vase and deliberately put the vase exactly into the center of the square table. The young man who had delivered the box and I smiled and looked with utter pleasure at the wonderful white flowers. I said good-bye and left and I ran into the bedroom to call my husband and show him what had arrived for us.*
>
> *(I should add, that I had decorated the house for our wedding with such large bulb-chrysanthemums, as they are among my favorite flowers. I was told at the florist that in this country they are used only for funerals and were not appropriate for a wedding. I stuck to my guns and explained that I had lived in the East most of my life, studied Chinese and philoso-*

---

[194] *Ibid.*, p. 74 f
[195] By the same dreamer: No. 7, Chapter 3.1, No. 33 this chapter and No. 134, Ch. 7

phy for many years and associated something quite different with these flowers, which were the most auspicious symbols for marriage.)

This dream was dreamt at the very time of conception. Nine months later the "new life" had arrived! The dream does not require interpretation. However, we do want to investigate who the sender of the mysterious flowers may have been, and why the word of greeting from the "new life" appears in just this form – for this question addresses one of the fundamental problems of this book.

We receive flowers on all the important occasions of life. But most of all, flowers are used around death and funerals in our culture. Flowers were in fact considered heralds of death, and grave-yard flowers in particular were not supposed to be picked as they were thought to bring bad luck. Small children, sick people and nursing women were not to be given flowers. Flowers sent to a woman in childbed were considered nails in her coffin.

In perfect contrast to this aspect of death, flowers embody new life. In folklore, we frequently come across the motif of woman touching a flower, a tree or eating a fruit or vegetable, resulting in the conception of a child. Juno, the Roman Mother Goddess, conceived Mars without Jupiter's involvement, solely by touching a flower. In the different versions of the fairy tale "Rapunzel," the mother conceives a child having eaten lamb's lettuce, parsley or apples. In folk tradition, the explanation that children stem directly from flowers, vegetables or fruit is quite common.[196] Saint Roseline de Villeneuve's mother dreamt that she would give birth to a fragrant rose without thorns.[197]

Let us explore this double-significance of flowers a little further. In the Greek myth of Demeter and Persephone, the flower-picking Persephone is being abducted by her uncle, Hades, the god of the underworld. Consequently, Demeter, the goddess of corn and vegetation, has the earth turn sterile until Hades eventually agrees to a compromise the gods have reached: namely, to allow Persephone to spend two-thirds of the year with her mother on the earth. Thus, every year, Persephone appears in the blooming narcissus and returns to the earth fertility of vegetation, humans and animals. We perpetuate this myth to an extent when, in the autumn, we "bury" tulip and narcissus bulbs in the earth and long for their blooming in the forthcoming spring as a symbol of hope.

People have always compared the cycle of growth and decay of vegetation with that of human existence. It was believed that the souls were waiting, as it were, in the lap of the Mother Earth to be reincarnated in the body of a plant, animal or human. Many cultures that admitted the perpetuation of life, considered death like a dying plant growing back again and again from the roots.

[196] *Handwörterbuch d. dt. Aberglaubens* 1, pp. 1431-1433
[197] Jacques Gélis, *Die Geburt*, p. 93

The Komarius text,[198] an ancient Alchemist text interpreted by Marie-Louise von Franz, describes how in the underworld plants, i.e., bodies and spirits, lifeless and agonized are revived and restored to life by the inrush of fresh waters, life's healing element. In this text, the flowers represent a prima materia, the primary matter of the process of resurrection. For the ancient Egyptians, flowers, like corn, embodied an aspect of resurrection of the body.[199] When they had grains and flower bulbs sprout in the mummy-bandages of the dead, they took this as a sign of the dead person's completed resurrection.[200] Just as new life shot up from the ostensibly dead grain or bulb, so they believed in a new life growing out of the dead body. This is why it says in the Komarius text that at the moment of resurrection the plants are in bloom. Flowers generally are a common image of further existence after death.[201]

At the same time, flowers are related to birth, i.e., new life from the earth, inside which the bygone transforms itself into a new germ and death into resurrection, as in the myth of Demeter and Persephone. The image of the flower as a post-mortal form of existence is concomitantly the soul of the yet unborn. Hence a plant can be the seat of the soul of a deceased man or woman or, alternatively, that of a new child. It therefore makes sense that in our dream the new child appears as a white flower that we associate with funerals here but that in the Orient represents a good-luck sign of marriage and child blessing. Ghosts and figures from the Beyond are white or wear white. The dead go to the Beyond and from there come the newly born children. For all the peasant cultures, vegetation represented the psychic mystery of death and resurrection.[202]

The dreamer receives a parcel with four white chrysanthemums sent to her by a stranger. It contains knowledge that the dreamer does not yet have, namely, the knowledge of her having conceived that night. The sender-dream spirit apparently knows more that she does. It is the psyche's authority that can impart valuable knowledge to our dreamer. The dream spirit, designated as Mercurius by the Alchemists, is a spirit of love. The gift she is given contains the mystery of the new life, namely, the wisdom of Nature about death and birth. The number four carries a specific meaning.

Jung shows that, in retracing the history of symbols, the quaternity appears as oneness folded into four. Psychologically speaking, dividing the unintelligible multiplicity of chaos into four – e.g., the four cardinal points – amounts to letting previously unconscious contents enter consciousness. For, as soon as the unconscious content has reached consciousness, it disintegrates into four;

---

[198] Cf. M.-L. von Franz, *On Dreams and Death*, Shambhala, Boston & London, 1986
[199] Cf. also Dream 279
[200] Cf. Chapter 9
[201] M.-L. von Franz, *On Dreams and Death*, op. cit.
[202] *Ibid.*, p. 63

that is, it can only become an object of conscious experience thanks to the four fundamental functions of consciousness. It is perceived as something that exists (sensation), is recognized as this and distinguished from that (thinking); it proves acceptable, pleasant or unpleasant (feeling), and finally it is an object of presentiment as to where it comes from and where it is going (intuition).[203]

The quaternity is also an organizational schema of four fundamental aspects, such as the year and its four seasons. Hence, the number four represents wholeness that has entered consciousness. In dreams, it therefore often suggests the personality's achievement of consciousness and individuation or the birth of the totality of man.

The image the unconscious produces of the growing of a new child or the incarnation of a soul from the Beyond is the same as the image of attaining consciousness of a totality. Perhaps the mystery of new life consists in the fact that it already comprises completed wholeness during the vegetal phase. In addition, the departure point of growing is simultaneously the aim; thus, the cycle of life and death becomes complete. The symbol of the four white chrysanthemums must therefore already contain a degree of consciousness. How is this possible?

In her research into creation myths of various cultures, Marie-Louise von Franz discovered that "myths seem all to circle around, or to describe in a symbolic way, the mystery – which we shall never be able to solve – as to why there is consciousness and why consciousness has come from the unconscious, or always has been with what we now call the unconscious and always existed in it. We only can say that in every human being we meet with the same fact, namely, a preconscious totality in which everything is already contained, including consciousness ...."[204]

We may want to speculate about the possible deep-seated connections in the symbol of the white chrysanthemums. The dreamer evidently senses instinctively the momentousness of the mysterious gift and does the right thing: she places the four flowers in the middle of the square dining table. This table is not only the center of family life, where everyone meets to have a meal together, but is also a symbol of wholeness. Putting the flowers right in the center of the table, the dreamer positions the new life at the center of her own life. This is the right place for them, and the act corresponds to the importance of the gift.

The table at which we eat and where the food is provided is a feminine-maternal symbol. At the same time, its quaternity is an image of *reflected wholeness* or of the human struggle for consciousness.[205] We are thus dealing here with the dreamer as mother. Perhaps we could say that we must meet the

---

[203] Cf. C.G. Jung, *A Modern Myth*, CW 10, § 774

[204] M.-L. von Franz, *Creation Myths*, Shambhala, Boston & London, 1995, p. 108

[205] Emma Jung and M.-L. von Franz, *The Grail Legend*, Princeton University Press, 1970

113

wholeness of the child with our own wholeness, a task that is much more difficult to take on in real life than we would have thought at the time of conception or even later. All those things belonging to her own preconscious wholeness that a mother is not willing to let into consciousness and to realize (insofar as the unconscious required it) can impede the child's life and development.[206] This understanding, however, often only comes with years of experience.

Jung says that apart from the genetic laws, there is a kind of psychic causality between parents and child, a kind of influence from an unconscious background. Therefore, for the development of the child, a high degree of consciousness of the parents' own problems is of utmost importance. Moreover, says Jung, it is "that aspect of life that the parents (and ancestors, for we are here addressing the psychological, primordial phenomenon of the original sin) have never lived." In other words, a life that possibly could have been lived had the parents not evaded it. It is frequently a lack of care, fear or conventionality – plus the excuse of "not knowing" – that prevents parents from creating optimal conditions for their children's psychic growth. "Nature has no time for the excuse of ignorance. Ignorance equals blame."[207] This is the parents' share of personal responsibility and thus a moral problem.

There is, however, an area that lies beyond our responsibility. It is the original sphere of the child's soul, the collective soul of humankind from which child begins to emerge as it awakens to the initial instances of consciousness. Prior to this it is like a drop in the ocean. "Child's unconscious soul has infinite dimensions and is of incalculable age."[208] It is its unconscious wholeness that by far exceeds our powers of comprehension as well as a combination of collective factors going back to the line of ancestors. The symbol of the four white chrysanthemums is evocative of this, and it is from there that later on, in the form of projections, we become confronted with devils and demons. Puberty, moreover, is the time when they can be particularly belligerent. We can stand firm against them, provided we do not take them personally, for they are powers beyond our personal control. Neither must we let our own devils and demons join forces with them through our own unconsciousness. This would result in our identifying with the child's emotions and thus becoming stuck, so to speak, in the same mud – then, like the child, not knowing finally how to get out. There is not much we can do, but even that is hard. For the little bit we are ahead of the child consists merely of

---

[206] C.G. Jung, *Mysterium Coniunctionis*, CW 13, § 267. Jung says: "Wholeness can only be relative. In reality, we are dealing with the main aspects of the individual psyche as well as the collective unconscious."

[207] C.G. Jung, Introduction to Frances G. Wicke's *Analyse der Kindesseele*, in CW 1, § 90 f

[208] *Ibid.*, § 95

a small amount of consciousness that the child has not yet acquired – not very much in the face of divine powers, but nonetheless of utmost importance.

In view of certain fateful, higher intentions, having a child can for this mother involve a tremendous challenge to her personal development. In the light of this dream, it can no longer be an "incidental affair," and it is even less likely that this woman would want an abortion.

However, Jung never became weary of emphasizing that, in the psychology of the unconscious, there were always cases where the exception to the rule applied. About our next dreamer we know that at age nineteen she had an abortion under most problematic circumstances. This affected her very badly, knowing in addition that her religious parents considered abortion to be a crime, so they would harshly judge and ostracize her. Later, she would become happily married to another man and have children with him. However, during the abortion, at the end of the anesthesia, she dreamt:

Dream No. 33:[209]

> I dreamt that I saw four tulips. Two were yellow and two were red. They were completely closed and in their bud-state. They were arranged in a square with their stems meeting below in a bunch. A voice said: "Look!" I looked carefully at the buds, and while doing so, they slowly began to unfold, the green encasing petals pulled back and allowed the golden and red flowers to emerge fully. As the buds opened in this way, the light changed, too. An increasingly stronger, golden light from above appeared until the four tulips were fully open and stood in all their splendor in the full, golden light that flooded them. I was astonished and amazed at this beautiful sight and asked: "What does this mean?" The voice replied: "This means light and life." It was said in a tone of calm reassurance and caused a sense of peaceful certainty with which I awoke.

We have little to add to this wonderful and comforting dream. The death aspect of the flowers, referring to the abortion through which the dreamer suffered so, is being toppled by the unconscious' displaying an image of *reflected wholeness* (brought forth by the light), signifying life as well as the purpose of her life. In the light of this dream, it is evident that it would be wrong to judge the dreamer for moral reasons, nor should she judge herself for having had the abortion.

A twenty-six-year-old woman, during her first pregnancy, had the following dream several times:

---

[209] The same dream is interpreted in Chapter 7

Dream No. 34:

> *I am pulling up potato plants from a field. An old unknown woman comes up to me. Then I see that the potatoes are little nice dolls in the earth. The woman tells me the dolls are my fetus. I am amazed and filled with mixed emotions. I wake up very upset.*

We have already discussed this dream in detail elsewhere.[210] We find in it the motif of the new child as a vegetable, i.e., a potato, as we know it from popular tradition. Without going into the peculiarity of the potato again, let us try to understand better, why in fact, the unconscious or the dream, have chosen a plant as a symbol for a new child.

As Jung explained in a dream seminar, from the biological point of view, the nervous system of the plant is not sympathetic. "... there is no relation between that form of life and any nervous life at all. It is a prenervous condition, absolutely unimaginable to us; there is no possible connection in our consciousness" and yet the functioning of this vegetative state provokes fear. Jung goes on to say: "... we can compare preconscious life with the vegetative life of the lower animals, for all this fulfils itself in the individual in uterine life. What is merely vegetative at first later develops into the sympathetic nervous system, then the spinal cord, then the brain, so we almost repeat that growing up from plant life into human life."[211] The plant corresponds to that very early stage of human existence, then there is a stage of dim mental life, not capable of consciousness ...."[212]

So, the potato-dolls in the earth represent the earliest developmental stage of the new child, pointing at the same time, as formed dolls, to the future human being. We can therefore assume that this dream is the result of a kind of consciousness in the unconscious, a kind of form-giving or pre-conscious wholeness.

The dream causes mixed feelings as well as a strong emotional reaction in the dreamer. It evokes an image of pregnancy as part of Nature that she must let take its course, and it is as if for our dreamer this is something new, unfamiliar and upsetting. Perhaps she worries about the child that is growing inside her. Judging by the dream, she could simply relax, wait and see. She can

---

[210] Chapter "Child" and Chapter "Earth, Stones, Precious Stones"

[211] M.-L. von Franz, *On Dreams and Death*, Shambhala, Boston, 1986, p. 32: In the so-called "vigil hours" of the Osiris mysteries, the "vegetal resurrection" occurs in the fourth hour of the day (to be followed soon afterward by the "animal resurrection," which seems to have been a rebirth rite in which the dead man's *ka* renews itself). Then in the sixth hour it is said that the sky goddess Nut receives the deceased and brings him forth again as a child. (Cf. Figure representing vegetative resurrection, head of dead man emerging from blooming lotus flower)

[212] C.G. Jung, *Dream Analysis*, pp. 235-6

let Nature take its course, and Nature will yield her fruit when the time is ripe for it.

Dream No. 35 (abridged) The dreamer is twenty-six years old and expecting her first boy:[213]

> *My husband and I are together with another couple. They seem to be animal doctors or plant researchers. There are dogs around that she judges and treats. I am particularly impressed by a growing plant in full blossom. One of her pupils has cared for it with intense love and attention. The plant grows in a glass jar and it radiates health and comfort.*
> *We pass through large halls, like in the Museum of Nature History. I see large stuffed animals. Among them two giant whales, two giant otters in the size of lions, with huge teeth showing that they were beasts of prey. I am told that these animals once, in former ages, have inhabited the largest lake of Sweden, Vänern. I catch glimpses of many prehistoric animals, like the majestic Mammoths ...*

It seems as though we had before our eyes the evolution from plants to the primeval water animals through the prehistoric animals living on land to present-day pets. As a doctor, the dreamer has a scientific interest in all of this. What impresses her most, however, is the plant to which one of the pupils has given intense care. It is in full bloom and radiates health and comfort. It embodies the new life growing in the maternal womb. It does not grow in the garden or field but in a glass jar. We want to further explore this symbol.

According to an Alchemist text, *Liber Quartorum*,[214] a vessel has to do with the creation of man. The vessel "that is not dissolved by water and not melted by fire" is, Jung writes, like the work of God in the vessel of the divine seed, "for it has received the clay, moulded it and mixed it with water and fire." On the other hand, it seems to emerge from the text that it also has to do with the creation of souls that are brought forth from the seeds of the heavens. And then again, just as in Caesarius v. Heisterbach, the vessel itself is the soul: the soul is considered to be a spiritual substance of spherical nature, like the moon, or like a glass jug that has eyes in the front and at the back and sees the entire universe.[215] The jug, that is the soul, is the uterus, as it were, for the creation of humankind in the history of creation.[216]

---

[213] By the same dreamer: No. 28, Chapter 3.3, No. 91: Chapter 5.6, No. 80: Chapter 5.5, No. 75: Chapter 5.4, No. 44: Chapter 4.2

[214] C.G. Jung, CW 13, *The Visions of Zosimos*, § 113, Routledge & Kegan, 1968

[215] *Ibid.*, § 114

[216] The eyes that can see the entire universe symbolize the eyes of God or, in other words, the "consciousness in the unconscious" that is inconceivable to us and seems to be behind the wonderful plan of Nature which makes creation function.

The glass jug radiating health and comfort is also reminiscent of the Medieval bowl of the Holy Grail from the Grail legend. According to the perception of people of that time, the bowl dispenses material food and imparts spiritual solace, preserves youth and generally maintains life, heals knights wounded in battle, radiates light and fragrance and rejoices the heart.[217] According to the legend, the blood of Christ and his immortal psychic substance could survive in the vessel. It is ultimately an image of the human psyche where the religiousness, which has apparently died away, can be preserved.[218] It is in the individual psyche that God can be found and born, anew.

The glass jug of our dream with its growing plant may be said to be the "second uterus," and in a wider sense, an image of the soul as the foundation of creation and the birth of human consciousness. The soul is also the content of the jug, the blooming plant, the soul-flower, resurrection-body and the soul of the new child. Furthermore, it could be understood to mean readiness and willingness to accept the new, to care for it and allow it to grow: not only the physical child but also a psychic birth and process of attaining a higher level of consciousness.

This kind of psychic understanding of and incorporating of things, I believe, is also the theme of the next dream. The dreamer is pregnant with her third child. Prior to this, she had had the very difficult delivery of her daughter and preceding that, a still-birth when she was four months pregnant.

Dream No. 36:[219]

> *Last night I had a dream from which I awoke with a bunch of flowers in my hands. In the cellar of the children's home we had a kind of a greenhouse. I was apparently somewhat in charge there and had keys and wanted to get a plant for a teacher for the parents' meeting. A colleague who accompanied me thought it was unnecessary; moreover, I couldn't actually find anything in bloom, but I was so delighted by the tender and delicately green plants, that I took one for myself.*

A cellar is a symbol of femininity. It is (or used to be) humid, dark and below the ground – in the earth, as it were. In contrast to an attic, which is airy and dry and bright (because it usually has a window and is where, in the olden days, people used to hang washing or meats to dry), in the cellar there was kept the produce of the garden, an activity ascribed to woman. In the cellar, there were thus seeds, plants, bulbs, flower pots, potatoes, winter vegetables, fruits, preserves of all kinds and also butter, pickled cabbage, salted meats – as well as women's menstruation underclothes (which were only washed at monthly

---

[217] Emma Jung and M.-L. von Franz, *The Grail Legend*, p. 155
[218] M.-L. von Franz, *The Golden Ass of Apuleius*, Spring Publications, New York, 1970
[219] By the same dreamer: No. 24: Chapter 3.2, No. 64: Ch. 5.3, No. 99: Ch. 5.8

intervals). Women's "food-cellars" were certainly rather different from the men's cellars where wine and tools were kept.[220]

Our dreamer has the key to and is somehow in charge of this distinctly feminine place. She goes there to pick a tender fresh little plant, a particular one just for herself from the many the children's home has. The cellar may be seen as the uterus of a house, and nurturing plants and keeping and preserving food as a cultural means of ensuring survival over the wintertime. The new plants, which symbolically are the new children and ensure the survival of humankind, come from this very reservoir. An individual flowerpot is the personal "vessel" that the expectant dreamer represents in Nature's immense household so perfectly equipped for survival. I like the active role of our dreamer. She wanted the child – and look, here it is!

In another dream, a woman has a beet plantation on her windowsill. In their often human-like shape, beets are a pre-figuration of the future human being, rather like the potato dolls in Dream No. 34. At first sight, it may seem strange that there are so few examples of natural vegetation from the earth or the field in this dream collection on plant symbols and instead more cultivated plants in pots and vases. Taking a closer look, however, we can see that the symbol used by the unconscious – of a plant growing in a vessel – suggests far more emphasis on the individual than on plants in tilled fields.

Moreover, what seems to be important is the concept of the vessel and its capacity. Woman's body as vessel is not merely a kind of biological nutritive sheath for a growing embryo. Symbolically, it could be an allusion to how the dreamer accommodates it: that is, her inner attitude towards that new element which will occupy so much space in her life. Thanks to the modern examination methods, including ultrasound, intellectual knowledge and understanding are infinitely more precise than they were in the past. But are the medical insights adequate for the psychic adjustment, for an inner attention to the child and for coping with the fundamental change in the life of woman now? For, if the child, or symbolically the new precious content cannot be integrated, it can hardly flourish in our reality.

This feminine propensity to "have a capacity for" appears in the ancient Chinese description of Yin, as the feminine principle represented in the symbol of the house. The house was, of course, woman's sphere of activity. However, what I believe to be much more significant in the present-day context, is that the "feminine" seems to be a place where something alive can grow within the boundaries of the individual. Marie-Louise von Franz writes: "The Etruscans placed a little house on women's graves. ... An awareness and understanding of reality consisting of a certain structure with various segments in which things pertaining to reality can be hatched out – as in an egg – differentiated and realized, seems to be an aspect of feminine creativity." Therefore, if

---

[220] Jocelyne Bonnet, *La terre des femmes et ses magies*, p. 242

the essence of Yin, the feminine, is represented in the symbol of the house, it is because "the house cuts out a segment of space from the infinite universe and gives it a framework in which man can feel secure, akin to the maternal womb."[221]

From this standpoint, the vessel or feminine womb and body are, at the same time, an image of an underlying developmental principle: namely, that all development requires an appropriate framework – in other words, the right psychic attitude. By the same token, however, this represents restriction. Furthermore, this principle of creativity, which involves at once restriction and segmentation, is vital for all those realms of life whence truly new things are to be born. Thus, for a woman, introversion, often coupled with staying in the house, does not in any way exclude the advancement of her spiritual development. This time, our dreamer gave birth to a healthy baby boy.

[221] Cf. M.-L. von Franz: *C.G. Jung and the Problems of Our Time.* Analytical Psychology Club, Perth. The ideas on the receptacle discussed above developed from a conversation with Irmgard Bosch.

Figure 12. The birth of Adonis from a tree (Urbino 16th century)

4.2. The Tree

Regina Abt

The tree, as we encounter it in the following dreams, is one of the most profound symbols man has ever come to face from the depths of his own soul.

"Long ago, and long before man appeared on the earth, a mighty tree arose and grew way up into the sky. As the axis of the universe, it penetrated the three worlds. Its roots reached into the underworld; its branches extended to the dwelling of the gods. The water it soaked up from the earth became its sap; the rays of the sun made its leaves, blossoms and fruit grow ripe. Through it, the heavenly fire came down; its crown bore a resemblance to the clouds that caused the fertile rain to fall. It stood proud and upright connecting the Uranian universe and the Chthonic abysses. In it, the cosmos regenerated itself perpetually. Providing protection and nourishment to thousands of living creatures, it was the source of all life. Snakes crept amidst its roots, and birds sat on its branches. The gods chose it as their temporary abode."

With this paragraph, J. Brosse, the dendrologist and passionate tree-lover, begins his book on the mythology of trees. "This tree of the Universe," he writes, "can be found in nearly all traditions, from one end of the planet to the other, and we may assume that it has existed in all cultures – even in those places where its image has faded by now."[222]

According to J. Brosse, we owe the most powerful and magnificent representation of the Tree of the Universe to the written traditions of Germanic mythology, which were preserved by Scandinavian poets. The most famous description of Yggdrasil, the giant ash tree representing the axis and pillar of the universe, can be found in Snorri Sturluson's (from Iceland) notes in the *Edda*.[223] Its branches reach into the heavens. It extends into Midgard, the residence of humankind, and up to Asgard, the abode of the gods. One of its three roots extends into the underworld, enthroned by Aesir, the gods; the second root extends to the frost-giants, the predecessors of men; and the third root extends into Niflheim, the realm of the dead. Hvergelmir, the source of all

---

[222] J. Brosse, *Mythologie der Bäume*, p. 11 (translated by V. N.)
[223] *Edda*, p. 276 f

rivers that water the earth and make it fertile, lies by the side of the root in the realm of the dead. By the side of the second root is the spring of Mimir, providing wisdom and knowledge.[224] Beneath the third root lies the most divine of all sources, the Fountain Urd, which is carefully tended by the three Norns, the goddesses of Fate. They sprinkle the ash tree with water. This Fountain of Fate is also a Fountain of Youth. Here, the gods sit to hold counsel and court. Every living creature, every germ, every potentiality is born out of this Fountain. Odin (or Wotan in Germanic mythology), the highest and oldest of the gods – who is not only a god of war but also a master of wisdom and otherworldly arts – once consulted Mimir, the keeper of the Well of Wisdom. Mimir permitted Odin to drink from this Well if he would first sacrifice his own eye. In this way, Odin would attain visionary power despite his blindness. He would also acquire inner wisdom and the knowledge of the Runic characters. Finally, having purloined, too, the "mead of the poets" – which was of divine origin – he hung nine nights on Yggdrasil in order to attain even more magic powers.[225] Through his ritual death or sacrifice on the Tree of the Universe, Odin established a connection to the lower, invisible world of natural wisdom and to the source from which the cosmic tree feeds. This signified the highest insight, despite the fact – or perhaps even because of the fact – that he had to relinquish his vision in the outer world.

We can find a Yggdrasil type of Tree of the Universe in many other cultures, such as Middle- and North-Asian, Iranian, Indian, Babylonian and Egyptian.[226] In Nordic cultures, this Tree often exists as a pillar of the universe representing at once the axis and support of the vault of heaven. It stands in the navel of the earth, which is why there are so many so-called "navel holy places." "Some Germanic tribes erected pillars on hills, which were made of the trunks of enormous trees ... One of them, according to Saxon belief, is Irminsul, the pillar supporting the heavens. The Germans, too, built their houses around a carved tree trunk ... The roof represented the vault of heaven that was supported by the axis of heaven."[227]

The seven or nine-notched Shaman Tree of the peoples of Middle and North-Asia corresponds to the Pillar of the Universe on which the Shaman has to climb up through the heavenly spheres in order to reach the heavens.[228] The Shaman Tree is usually a fir tree, although with the Siberian Shamans, it is a birch. These trees were taken from the forest where the dead are buried, for they provide shelter to the souls of the ancestors.[229] This ritual, of which the

---

[224] A.V. Ström / H. Biézais, *Germanische und baltische Religion*, pp. 975, 254
[225] *Ibid.*, p. 117 f
[226] Holmberg, *Weltenbaum*, p. 52 f
[227] J. Brosse, *Mythologie der Bäume*, p. 17
[228] Holmberg, *Weltenbaum*, p. 133 f
[229] J. Brosse, *Mythologie der Bäume*, p. 17

tree is the center, consists of the Shaman climbing up the nine-crenate birch ladder of the heavens. The ladder represents the universe. It all takes place outside time and space, and the ancestral past becomes the present. The most crucial element of the event is the number nine: 9 steps on the ladder, 9 sacrificial bowls on the sacrificial alter, 9 sacrificers, 9 sacrificial animals, etc. At 9-year intervals the Swedish tribes would meet by the tree representing Yggdrasil for the renewal of the regal powers.[230] Nine is the number of months of pregnancy resulting in the human birth. However, not only renewal at the court but also the rites of the Shamans are closely linked to birth, in other words, to the renewal of consciousness through a connection with the world of the hereafter. For, the ruling collective consciousness embodied by the king is always in danger: in danger of becoming inflexible, of aging and becoming stale. Hence the need for periodic renewal, a theme dealt with in numerous fairy tales.

Both Yggdrasil and the Shaman Tree have their roots in the depths of the realm of the dead, the ancestral past, and extend into the heavens with their branches. It was believed in many cultures that the stars were attached to a cosmic tree (or the central mountain) by means of a thread or rope. The Tungusians of Northern Siberia believed that each man had a star in the firmament. In the view of the Turkish peoples, a star appears each time a man is born. These ideas are widely propagated and are by no means unfamiliar to us either. In medieval Europe they were generally considered to play a role in human life. We still say things like: "She was born under a lucky star" or "it is written in the stars" when we are referring to this person's destiny. The Slavs

Figure 13. Shaman Tree

believed that every birth caused a star to rise in the sky as well as the appearance of the goddess of birth on the earth.[231] Man always associated the stars

---

[230] *Ibid.*, p. 37

with the immutable laws of the order of the universe. Moreover, they served as a regular and never oscillating chronometer.[232] Thus they represented a framework that was subject to fate and within which the life of each human being unfolded.

As Holmberg explains, the idea of the tree of life is closely connected with the idea of a central world mountain or a navel stone in the heart of the universe, and in addition with the spring. All three are generally associated with great fertility and the Mother Goddess. In Eastern Europe, the navel stone, central mountain, tree of life and spring containing the blessed waters all belong to the abode of the mother of God. In ancient Egypt, the goddess of fate is often depicted at the foot of a large tree evoking the sky. The Sumerian goddess Nin-hursag is enthroned on a central world mountain, and likewise the Iranian goddess is enthroned on the mountain of paradise or navel. Thus she is a Regina coeli, a queen of the heavens. The great Oriental goddess of birth resides at the axis of the universe, at the center of the world spinning the thread of life that connects each man's star with the center. Verpeja (=spinner), an ancient Lithuanian deity of destiny sits in the center of the heavens and begins to spin the life-thread at the very moment of birth. She ties the end of the thread to the new star that has just risen and is now visible in the heavenly sphere. At the time of death, she severs the thread, the star falls and becomes extinguished. The cosmic mother-goddess is frequently depicted with a spindle. Urd (destiny), the eldest of the three Norns by the side of the fountain at the roots of Yggdrasil, also has a spindle.

Let us now take a look at the tree that stands at the beginning of the Christian myth: the tree of paradise. Its predecessor is the Kishkanu, the Sumerian tree of life that actually is the prototype of the Mesopotamian trees of life. In paradise, there are two trees: the tree with the serpent who leads the first parents into temptation and the tree of life. "And the Lord God said, 'Behold, the man is become as one of us, to know good and evil: and now, lest he put forth his hand, and take also of the tree of life, and eat, and live for ever.'"[233] And with this, or so we are told in the Old Testament, Adam and Eve were chased out of paradise. Later, in the New Testament, the tree of paradise becomes the tree of life in heavenly Jerusalem, which is identical with paradise.

Later, thanks to the Messiah, the Redeemer on the cross, the tree of life becomes the tree of the cross, or a tree of death as the symbol of a resurrected divine death. From the Early Fathers to the modern Mystics, the cross and tree of life have been considered a unity.[234] Golgotha, the summit of the cosmic

---

[231] Holmberg, *Weltenbaum*, p. 110
[232] *Ibid.*, p. 104
[233] Genesis, 3, 22
[234] J. Brosse, *Mythologie*, p. 267

mountain, becomes the pole of the world and the cross the cosmic tree. Even in pre-Christian Mexican depiction we can find the cross with leaves and branches, illustrating the connection between the cross and tree of life. It represents the entire cosmos.[235]

Although Christian and pre-Christian ideas were ultimately based on the same archetype, the Christian missionaries and bishops were relentless in their fight against the Germanic and Celtic holy trees and against pagan superstition, which believed these ancient giant trees to be divine. Eventually, after "the victory over the Barbaric cults there was only one tree left to be venerated: the hewn cross on which the Redeemer died."[236] And yet, as ever, we continue to find the image of the tree in the dreams of men and women today. The only difference is that we have largely lost sight of the religious context of it. Maybe we shall find it again, both on an inner and an outer level.

In her study of dreams of the dying, Marie-Louise von Franz has found that the tree often serves as a symbol of the mysterious relationship between death and life.[237] It is as if the tree somehow has to do with life continuing after death. According to folklore, the tree is the dwelling place of the dead souls which is why, for example, trees in cemeteries are populated with spirits and ghosts. Moreover, the tree brings forth the newborn children. In many regions in Switzerland, one can find the so-called *Kindlibaum* – little children's tree. Jung comments on the idea of man originally coming out of trees and eventually disappearing into them again: "The world of consciousness yields to the vegetative. The tree is the unconscious life which renews itself and continues to exist eternally, after human consciousness has ceased to exist."[238] As in the unconscious, in tree symbolism spatial and temporal limits, the boundaries between the here and now and eternity, the dead and the living, between past and future, seem to be removed.

This is probably why, as Jung explains, the Alchemists saw the union of opposites in the symbol of the tree: "... it is therefore not surprising that the unconscious of present-day man, who no longer feels at home in his world and can base his existence neither on the past that is no more nor on the future that is yet to be, should hark back to the symbol of the cosmic tree rooted in this world and growing up to heaven – the tree that is also man. In the history of symbols this tree is described as the way of life itself, a growing into that which eternally is and does not change; which springs from the union of opposites and, by its eternal presence, also makes that union possible. It seems as if it were only through an experience of symbolic reality that man, vainly

---

[235] *Ibid.*, p. 268
[236] *Ibid.*, p. 273
[237] M.-L. von Franz, *On Dreams and Death*, p. 25
[238] *Ibid.*, p. 25

seeking his own "existence" and making a philosophy out of it, can find his way back to a world in which he is no longer a stranger."[239]

Whenever in dreams of expectant mothers a tree appears, a link is established to the timeless mystery of death and renewal taking place at once within and without. Woman here is only a contributor, and her achievement consists in her submission to it. Furthermore, her responsibility for the child to be born is only relative, for the child is a star, as it were, attached to the thread of destiny of the Great Mother or a fruit on the cosmic tree of life. In some legends of saints, we read that before the birth of a saint, his mother sees a tree sprouting forth from her lap – a tree that bears delicious fruit or has an exquisite, sweet fragrance.[240]

Man always has been and still is fascinated by the tree that defying wind and weather, by day and night, day in, day out and over the years and long decades still remains firmly rooted in its place, in order to be that, which it is meant to be, and to become that, which it is meant to become. It is the image of our own perpetually changing life, from the past of our ancestors to the destiny of the future. The hereditary components and imprinting of our parents, grandparents and forefathers play a substantial part in our future life. Just as the tree, in its preconditioned nature, grows into its individual form, so too can we perceive our own individual growth and development. The tree is an image of the individuation process, the slow growth man traverses throughout the course of life. Thus, the giant tree rooted in the center of the universe is a symbol of man rooted in the Self.

The dreamer of the following dream was thirty-six at the time, married for seven years and now, at last, two months pregnant. The night before she had the dream, she begged the unconscious for a dream on the forthcoming birth. Then she dreamt:

Dream No. 37:[241]

> *I am in a line with a group of Indian women (from India, not America). All the women are pregnant. They are waiting until their turn comes to go up to a big tree and give birth. I am dressed like them, in a sari. One by one, the women go up to the tree, stoop down and give birth to their babies. My turn has not come yet.*

In many cultures, it was thought that certain trees could ease the pains of childbirth. In Africa and Sweden, for instance, there are holy trees that women would embrace in the hope of having an easier birth.[242] According to the Greek

---

[239] C.G. Jung, *Psychological Aspects of the Mother Archetype*, CW 9, I, § 198

[240] Cf. Jacques Gélis, *History of Childbirth: Fertility, Pregnancy and Birth in Early Modern Europe*, Northeastern University Press, Boston, 1991

[241] By the same dreamer: No. 22, Chapter 3.2

legend, Leto gave birth to Apollo and Artemis having touched a palm tree and an olive tree. The mother of Buddha is said to have given birth to him at the foot of a tree clasping both arms around one of the branches. There are plenty of references to the widespread custom of women giving birth in the neighborhood of, in front of or beneath trees. For, "the tree is the protector of the newborns. It facilitates the delivery and watches over the life of the little children. … The act of approaching or touching a tree can have a soothing, invigorating and fecundating effect."[243]

It is for this reason that old and in particular hollow trees are under protection and are objects of worship. They have maternal qualities. They bear fruit, provide shelter. They are the embodiment of rootedness and at the same time of death and the yearly renewal of vitality. This feminine, maternal aspect of the tree with its continual transformation throughout the year and to all appearances complete rejuvenation after the winter, conveys a feeling of incessant transformation or rebirth and thus of timelessness.

Before midwifery had been taken over by specialists in clinics, midwives played a vital part everywhere. They enjoyed great public esteem, and people thought they were endowed with special powers. The French call a midwife *sage femme*, or literally: a "wise woman." She may well be that same old woman of Grimm's fairy tales who like the *sage femme* is depicted with a spindle. In France, fairies too are called *sages femmes*, and it is likely that in archaic societies they were considered midwives. In addition, the fairy is knowledgeable and endowed with the art of magic and is thus closely associated with the dark powers in life. She plays an important part at the moment of birth just like the Germanic Norns at the foot of the cosmic ash or the Greek Moirae.[244] Gaelic priestesses living in the woods presumably took over this important part. The precursors of the fairies are the Gaelic Fates, who again are somewhat fused with the pre-Celtic Matres or Matrons. The latter are represented in a triad with an infant on the knees, presumably female foremothers of the Germanic "wise women" and midwives.[245] They go back to the Neolithic cults of Mother Earth, of the fertile-rendering waters and the moon. We can see that the dreamer's unconscious associates the forthcoming birth with the intrinsic maternal and fate-determining forces of the tree, which reach back into the Stone Age. It is as though a deep archaic layer in the dreamer has now been activated.

[242] J.G. Frazer, *The Golden Bough: A Study in Magic and Religion*, Macmillan, London, 1980 [or New York: St. Martin's Press, 1990]

[243] M. Eliade, *Die Religionen und das Heilige*, Wiss. Buchgesellschaft, Darmstadt, 1976, p. 352 / *Pattern in Comparative Religion*, Sheed and Ward, London and New York, 1958 (translated by V.N.)

[244] J. Brosse, *Mythologie*, p. 197

[245] *Ibid.*, p. 204

There is no other time in life when woman feels as acutely in touch with the perpetual and ever repeating life processes than during pregnancy. It gives her a feeling of protection, stability and confidence in the inevitability of a process all mothers have shared, throughout the ages. For, when her time has come, she must be near the tree and intimately close to this timeless natural process of transformation, which has always controlled pregnancy and birth. She is now an entirely collective being, and when the time is ripe, she has to submit to it as Indian women do. We assume that, for the dreamer, the latter represent shadow-figures who are particularly feminine (the sari being a very feminine garment) and close to Nature. The Indian world could thus be an image of the unconscious, that is, the "other," spiritual world, somewhere far away. In mythology, the tree being associated with the three goddesses of fate and the "wise women," or midwives, can be said to embody the great maternal aspect in herself into whose hands she now has to put herself. What a comforting and beautiful dream before a birth!

A twenty-nine-year-old woman, who had practically given up hope to become pregnant, dreamt (when five months pregnant):

Dream No. 38:

> *The image of the birth: a secular olive tree.*[246]

The secular tree is an age-old tree that has lived through the cycles of day, night and the seasons hundreds of times. From early on, man must have been fascinated by the idea of outliving long periods of time – of moons or annual cycles. We have no control over the incessant, recurring cycles: they are subject to a higher authority. Hence, the connection between tree and fate – which, as we have seen, is particularly pronounced in Germanic mythology.

Why, however, does she dream of an olive tree? Olive trees yield oil, the wonderful imperishable sap of life that is a staple food in all countries where olive trees grow. In Antiquity, there was no other word for oil, except olive oil – *Elaion* in Greek, *Oleum* in Latin. That is why this generic term was also used for oils made from other plants.[247] For the Hebrews, the olive tree was one of the most valuable gifts of Jehovah representing the actual symbol of the alliance into which he had entered with man. Olive oil was used for consecration. The Greek word, *Christos*, meant "the one anointed with dark oil." Anointing was one of the most frequent sacraments in the Christian church. After the examples of Christ, the Lord's Anointed and the prophets, the kings were anointed too. Only olive oil was used for that purpose. In Homeric Greece, but also in ancient Egypt, oil represented vitality, and statues of the gods were

---

[246] By the same dreamer: No. 153: Chapter 9, No. 164: Chapter 5.3, No. 172: Chapter 10, No. 168: Chapter 9
[247] J. Brosse, *Mythologie*, 231

anointed regularly with it. According to Marie-Louise von Franz, the idea behind this was that gods could only live as long as they were given life, i.e., affection from humankind.[248] Thus, oil has to do with creating a bond, and with eros. Oil also connects things that would otherwise grate against each other. So, oil has the characteristic of uniting opposites.

In Islam, the olive tree is the cosmic tree per se, the center and supporting column of the world. It is a tree of life, however, because of the oil that was also used for lamps (probably the only light available apart from fire), the blessed olive tree serves chiefly as a source of light. It is a wonderful and arcane divine tree that kindles the divine light.[249] The olive trees of the Greek plain of Eleusis were sacred to Demeter, the great goddess of grain and fertility. Anyone who damaged them was severely punished. But above all, the olive tree was the sacred tree of Athena. The trees consecrated to Athena were called Moria as opposed to elaia, the usual word for olive tree. Moira signifies "given as inheritance" (i.e., by the gods or fate). In the 2nd century, in the vicinity of Athena's sacred olive tree on the Acropolis, so the legend goes, there was a golden lamp that burned (with oil) for an entire year until it was refilled anew.[250] Athena's light is allied with the wisdom of the owl, her favorite animal. Owls sleep by day and see at night. Athena's light, therefore, has somehow to do with the night-light, with nocturnal wisdom, the knowledge of the obscure background of the soul.

To summarize this amplification, we could conclude that the olive tree has to do with food, light and the nocturnal wisdom of the feminine-maternal background of the soul. It comprises the sap of life that unites the opposites, the actual substance of the soul; it is imperishable and outlasts the life cycles. The uniting principle of the maternal unconscious is, in fact, the only thing able to solve an apparently irresolvable conflict or opposite in a marvelous and unexpected manner. The unconscious psychic background thus signifies destiny, for, whether or not we succeed in uniting the opposites ultimately depends upon our alliance with destiny or the gods.

With this fine and comforting image, the birth of a child and new life is placed in a wider context. Behind the process of birth and the destiny of the future life is a suprapersonal mother, as it were, dispensing eternal nourishment and knowledge. To the terrestrial mother, it brings home some of the religious attitude, common to all cultures where the Great Mother was venerated.

---

[248] M.-L. von Franz, *The Golden Ass of Apuleius,* Spring Publications, New York, 1970
[249] J. Brosse, *Mythologie,* 229 f
[250] *Idem.*

Dream No. 39:

> *Asleep, I can feel how I delight in having enough room in bed while my husband and child are away. In my dream, I experience how good it feels to stretch out and to relax completely. I spread out my arms – they grow into branches. My relaxed legs and pelvis become heavy; they grow into roots and branches. How wonderful! I am a tree! I awaken calm and happy.[251]*

The tree's being bound to the earth and rooted is experienced by the dreamer as something marvelous. We know that she subsequently had to keep still as there was an acute danger of a premature delivery. The exterior circumstances at that time seemed to demand of her a particularly high level of activity. However, the unconscious prepared her for complete immobility: not in the sense of prison or a deprivation of freedom, but rather of a natural fusion with the leisurely process of growth – a kind of sinking and settling into a vegetative state. In this natural process of growth and creation, the dreamer's feminine-maternal spreading and stretching-out provide a counterweight to the modern young woman so accustomed to being mobile and so detached from all natural bonds.

Figure 14. Nut as a tree-goddess, feeding the dead in the realm of the dead

The dreamer herself becomes the tree. Some Persian Nomads tattooed the body of a woman with a tree that had roots extending to her belly and branches to her throat.[252] The birth, growth and death of a tree are seen as analogous with the human life. Marie-Louise von Franz writes that, behind the visible exterior life, there is an inner growth that like a tree guided by its own laws, proceeds from birth to death. For this reason, mythologically speaking, the "greater man," the Anthropos, is fixed to a tree. Man seems to be hanging on

---

[251] Jacques Gélis, *History of Childbirth,* cf. title page: Myrrha's birth. Majolika cup, Urbino, 16th cent. Myrrha is represented as woman out of whose arms and head branches are growing, and whose feet are rooted in the ground. Same dreamer as in Dream No. 66, Chapter "Horse"

[252] *Dictionnaire des Symboles,* p. 106

the tree because "the conscious man constantly pulls away, trying to free himself and to act freely and consciously, and he is then painfully pulled back to the inner process."[253]

The tree – representing the inner process of achieving consciousness, or individuation – develops somewhere far back-stage of the psyche, as it were, ignoring consciousness. "Whenever the conscious and animal personality is in conflict with the inner process of growth, it suffers crucifixion; it is in the situation of the god suspended on the tree and is involuntarily nailed to an unconscious development from which it would like to break away but cannot."[254] Our dreamer's wonderful dream experience of turning into a tree possibly compensates for her fear of being "nailed down" and interfered with in her freedom. In reality, "being nailed down" signifies becoming and growing into that which we are meant to be. It has to do with our inner development, which Nature is in charge of, and with the mysterious creation of a new life woman is involved in. In the dream of an eagle and white horse (No. 89, Chapter "Horse"), she has to stand rooted in the ground until her hair has grown all the way to the ground. This dream image reminds her in a similarly salient way that, if she wishes to make allowance for her psychic needs, she has to accept that pregnancy, delivery and motherhood will involve a fair amount of patience as well as sacrificing her mobility.

Dream No. 40, A thirty-year-old dreamer (two months pregnant):

There was a beautiful peach tree, and I am about to eat the fruit.

We know of this dreamer that she is unmarried and holds a job, and that she has already had three abortions with two different partners. In her present pregnancy, she almost lost her baby in week twenty-six. Because she developed high blood pressure, she wound up needing to have an early Caesarean section. The dream occurred the night after she had learned that she was pregnant. She did not want the baby. Her partner only came back to her when the healthy child was born, albeit prematurely.

In this dream, we have a brief, but magnificently comforting response from the unconscious to the negative conscious attitude to the conception. It is as though the dreamer had been transferred to a garden-of-paradise-situation that does not at all correspond to the circumstances of her conscious life. Eating the fruit and becoming pregnant thereby is a widespread motif in fairy tales. In the Rumanian fairy tale, "The Cat," the queen only realizes that she is "with child" thanks to an apple from the Tree of Mary; and in the Grimm fairy tale about "The Juniper Tree," the mother conceives a boy when eating a juniper berry.[255] This time, it is a peach.

[253] M.-L. von Franz, *Shadow and Evil in Fairy Tales*, Shambhala, Boston, 1995, pp. 43-4
[254] *Ibid.*, p. 40

Contrary to the apple, the peach – in the Mediterranean regions – is considered an exotic fruit, and like all more or less apple-like looking exotic fruits, was called *malum*, i.e., in Greek, "apple" or "melon." *Melon citrion* was the lemon, *melon cydonion* the quince, *melon armeniacon* the apricot, *melon persicum* the peach, and so forth. We assume that the apples of the Tree of Life, for example, of the Hesperides Tree, were not classed as a particular variety of fruit, but as "the fruit of immortality" or mythical fruit.[256] This mythological context behind the peach tree is certainly relevant for any interpretation, although the personal associations the dreamer has would also have to be taken into account.

Both of the above-mentioned folktales begin with a childless marriage. For a king, who does not have a son or an heir, this means that the renewal of his kingdom is at risk. It is therefore highly significant when a queen becomes a mother through eating a fruit. The ancients venerated food-providing trees, and above all, fruit trees. The Latins had a goddess, named Pomona, who watched over the ripening of the fruit.[257] Fruit signified tree children or children of the maternal goddess. In "Ave Maria" [Hail Mary], they speak of "the fruit of thy womb." Fruits are gifts from Mother Nature, who was worshiped in the tree. The Germanic Norns were also depicted with a basket on their laps brimming over with fruit. Cinderella's mother, whose spirit resides in a hazel tree, gives her daughter three dresses – corresponding to the sun, moon and stars –, and she, too, symbolizes a cosmic mother-goddess. Thus, renewal at the royal household, which psychologically speaking, means renewal in the ruling collective consciousness, is associated with a powerful mother-figure. To begin with, it is perceptible only in the fruit-bearing tree, that is, on a quite unconscious, vegetative plane. In our dream, and in the tale "The Cat," it is a Tree of Paradise. This reminds us of the fruit in the Garden of Eden that led Adam and Eve into temptation. There, the fruit embodied Eros, on the one hand, and Knowledge, on the other. In the tale about the cat, the magical apple tree, or the realm of the vegetative and Eros, are assigned to the dark Great Mother living in a castle, far away in the middle of the sea. This means it is no longer part of our consciousness. However, it must be retrieved for the expected child, who in the folktale represents a future, higher personality, therefore suggesting wholeness.

As Jung shows in his work, "The Philosophical Tree," the fruit-bearing tree plays an important part in Alchemy. He quotes from *Turba Philosophorum*: "…

---

[255] Joh. Bolte / Georg Polivka, *Anmerkungen zu den Kinder- und Hausmärchen der Brüder Grimm*, II. 125, IV. 257, and A. Aarne & St. Thompson, *The types of the folktale* (Motif index), V 302, and: M.L. v. Franz, *The Cat, A Tale of Feminine Redemption*, Inner City Books, Toronto, 1999

[256] J. Brosse, *Mythologie*, p. 247

[257] *Ibid.*, p. 227

this most precious tree, of whose fruit he who eats shall never hunger."[258] And, "I say that that old man does not cease to eat of the fruits of that tree ... until that old man becomes a youth."[259] Accordingly, the fruit on this tree rejuvenates and provides wonderful, everlasting spiritual nourishment.

In Alchemy, the tree is seen as the image of the alchemical opus and the fruit as its result.[260] In the golden fruit of the philosophical tree, God Himself appears. A kind of divine birth takes place in the tree, an archetypal motif that we know from the sun-god Ra of the Egyptian culture, for instance, who was born out of a tree. We could therefore say that, in the dream, the "divine food" on the Tree of Life does not merely refer to the birth of the new child, but is also an allegory for a kind of spiritual food growing on the "tree of individuation." The Alchemists associated it with the motif of the birth of the Lord, which shows that it has to do with something divine, which, through this process of growth represented by the tree, has entered our life. This divine aspect complements the man of the here and now, making him a more complete being – for which the Alchemists used the image of *Anthropos*, the immortal man. Our dream image corresponds almost literally to the illumination of one of the Alchemists, quoted by Jung: "Here, I saw the fruits and herbs of Paradise, whereof my eternal man should thenceforward eat, and live."[261]

It seems as though behind our dream about conception lies the image of the eternal man. Hence, the idea of abortion would simply be unthinkable! It is as if our dreamer were now shown the sight behind the scenes of her conscious life, where love, conception, abortion and birth could easily be taken as being just an absurd way of complicating life.

Dream No. 40 (The dreamer is eight months pregnant):

> *I am with the women who are collecting their dreams for this research project. When I come home, my husband and son have brought home a Christmas tree. I am surprised because it is like a tall pole with only a few branches at the top with decorative red apples. My husband and son are very proud and happy.*

The dreamer has just come back from where certain dreams were being studied. The starting-point of the dream is also the place where people try to inquire about the depths of the psyche. The unconscious is clearly responding very positively, for it brings into her house the symbol of the Christmas tree: the tree of the birth of the divine child and of new light. It is her husband and

---

[258] C.G. Jung, *The Philosophical Tree*, in CW 13 § 403, *Alchemical Studies*, Routledge & Kegan Paul, London, 1967
[259] *Ibid.*, § 403
[260] *Ibid.*, § 404
[261] *Ibid.*, § 403, fn. 23

son (that is, presumably, her own animus and its further development in the son), who, through this spiritual task, have been able to recognize and "bring home" or "bring to consciousness" something from the depths of the unconscious. The dreamer is surprised by the strange appearance of the Christmas tree, which obviously does not look like an ordinary Christmas tree. There are apples hanging on the sparse branches of what appears more to be a "pole" than a fir tree.

In this form, the dream tree is actually reminiscent of the "Maypole," which can still be found in rural regions. It is a tree or a pole which, in the month of May, people bring out from the forest, decorate with branches, flowers, fruits and colored paper, then around which they celebrate and dance. The customs around the Maypole form part of the various Spring and fertility rites and are all festivals that celebrate Nature's power of perpetual renewal.[262] As we have already seen, fruits and branches, apples, pomegranates, poppy-heads, etc., belong to the female goddess – to representations of Ishtar, the Babylonian mother-goddess, for instance, or to the Cretan mother-goddess and finally to all pagan-peasant milieux where tree worshipping remains customary.[263]

We might thus conclude so far, that although the fir tree is a Christmas tree as we know it, it is apparently far more than we have known heretofore. The fir tree in the wilderness emphasizes even more the great Mother Nature than does the Christmas tree hung with lights. Death and renewal are parts of Nature, which is why the pre-Christian mother-goddess has always also been associated with death, the deceased and the underworld. The myth of Aphrodite, to whom the apple tree was consecrated, illustrates this – along with Adonis, her son-lover, the god of vegetation in Asia Minor, who dies and resurrects each year. According to this myth, Aphrodite, whose pride had been hurt, induced Smyrna (also Myrrha), a daughter of a king, to have an incestuous relationship with her father. When the latter realized what had happened, however, he persecuted his daughter, who then implored the gods' help and was changed into a tree. Nine months later, Adonis was born of this tree, whereupon Aphrodite immediately claimed him for herself.[264] Persephone, the goddess of the underworld, however, coveted him just as much, so that Zeus had to settle the dispute. Thus it came to be that Adonis spent one-third of the year with Persephone in the underworld and two-thirds with Aphrodite on the earth. Finally, Adonis would be fatally wounded by a wild boar on a hunt.[265]

---

[262] J.G. Frazer, *The Golden Bough*

[263] E. Neumann, *The Great Mother. An Analysis of the Archetype*, Bollingen Series 47, New York, 1955

[264] See J. Gélis, *History of Childbirth (The Birth of Myrrha)*

[265] J. Brosse, *Mythologie der Bäume*, p. 132

Aphrodite and Persephone represent those aspects of Mother Nature that are responsible for Nature's annual cycle of decay and rebirth. Mother Nature is the great Transformatrice, who has the gift of reawakening death to new life. This ability to transform is also inherent in the tree and thus in the feminine nature per se.

In our culture, magnificent trees bearing beautiful exotic fruit are often found in the "other world" – e.g., in *Frau Holle's* subterranean realm, in *Rübezahl's* garden, in the fairy tale, *Die Schöne der Welt,* or even at the bottom of the sea.[266]

In Christian mythology, the apple tree is clearly associated with the snake, temptation and thus with the Christian opposites of good and evil. Accepting the apple from the serpent, Eve, the human woman, commits an offence against God, the Father. By so doing, she brings to consciousness the opposites of male and female and of good and evil. Before this, she had lived with Adam in paradise in complete innocence. The Christian church stigmatized this act committed by Eve as the "original sin," which stigma has never ceased to weigh heavily upon the feminine-maternal self-image. For, if the feminine is responsible for the phenomenon of sin in the world, then the eternal feminine mystery of transformation and rebirth cannot be appreciated as a true value.

In his chapter on the philosophical tree,[267] Jung writes about the Alchemists' various fruit-bearing trees: the tree of paradise hung not with apples but with sun-and-moon fruit; or else, there was a sort of Christmas tree, adorned with the seven planets and surrounded by allegories of the seven phases of the alchemical process. The tree is sometimes alive and foliaged, and sometimes it is abstract.

Trees bearing blossoms and fruit in color and number symbolically suggest wholeness, that is, an all-embracing unity as the goal of the alchemical process. The fruit designated as the "golden apples of the Hesperides" represent the gold of the philosophers, the *aurum non vulgi*[268] – this means the indestructible, the most precious, the final goal of all the efforts of the alchemical opus, which does not refer to any ordinary gold but represents a spiritual value. The Christmas tree hung with lights – as well as the tree at whose summit the sun rises, which is another allegory of alchemy – ultimately signify growing towards a higher consciousness.

The fact that the fruits are apples and sometimes lights or gold means that this process of achieving consciousness is the same kind of process Eve initiated with her act. The ultimate goal is the birth of a new, precious value and of new insights. The apple, in particular, comprises the Christian problem of

---

[266] *Enzyklopädie des Märchens*, Vol. 1, pp. 622 f
[267] C.G. Jung, *The Philosophical Tree*, CW 13, § 398
[268] *Ibid.*, § 404

good and evil, which, as we have seen, involves for woman the split of her own feminine self-image.

To sum up, we could perhaps say that the Christmas tree of the dream actually joins together three planes or three trees. Firstly, the purely vegetative, unconsciously proceeding natural drama of death and renewal (an archaic tree of life embodied in the image of a wicked, emotional, murdering – as well as abundantly giving – mother-goddess); secondly, Eros and the feminine kind of knowledge (Eve and the Tree of Paradise), and finally, the joining together of both aspects with the spiritual dimension or that of meaningfulness (*arbor philosophorum*).

In an after-dinner speech on Christmas 1957, Jung said – referring to the Christmas tree: "It is an alchemical symbol, which signifies the genesis of the inward, the greater and nobler man: that is, the man who comes into being when a person has drawn all the *numina* out of the world and into himself. Then he notices that he contains a microcosm within himself, a 'treasure hid in a field.' Man and his soul become miraculous. To that, let us drink as a *momento vivorum et mortuorum* [memory of the living and the dead]."[269] We might add: and of those who are about to be born from one world into another!

Dream No. 42 (six months pregnant):[270]

> *I ascend the stairs of a solemn official building, a church or a palace. As I have passed some stairs, I see that some trees are growing inside the building. There are a couple of ordinary fir trees with reddish-brown, high, straight trunks. The remarkable tree is a huge oak, with a wet, black, shiny trunk. It is very, very old. It grows twisted and with large bumps. The trunk divides into immense branches that seem to support the ceiling of the huge hall. Every branch, diameter like a man's wrist, ends with a rounded club. It has no leaves or bars.*
>
> *I know it is a divine tree. I stand in front of it. I call for my husband, who is left on a lower store, to come and see it. He comes up and has our grand dog with him.*

At the beginning of the dream, the dreamer is ascending the stairs of a solemn building (a church or a palace). She notices that there are trees growing inside this building: ordinary fir trees and then an enormous, sacred oak. In dreams, going up the stairs, step by step, often indicates a way to a better view, or a process of obtaining knowledge, as it were, involving slow progress and spiritual work. As the stairs are in a public, important building, we can infer that something of universal validity is being addressed – something that

---

[269] C.G. Jung, *Word and Image*, edited by A. Jaffé, translated by Krishna Winston, Bollingen Series, Princeton University Press, 1979, p. 144

[270] By the same woman: No. 81 (Chapter Dog), No. 25 (Chapter Fire)

is of general interest to people. This might have to do either with the church, embodying a higher religious idea, or with a palace and a ruling secular attitude or idea. For centuries, church and palace – that is, religious and secular powers – dominated all cultural and spiritual life. This kind of building stands for an entire historical era, and at the same time, for a spiritual attitude that has been cultivated collectively. The dreamer is on her way to investigate it.

The extraordinary thing she recognizes is the fact that the entire building is supported by a tall, mighty, divine oak. There are other trees growing in this building, too. Realistically speaking, however, this would not have been possible in such a large building. According to the ideas of the Ancients, who often had a tree in the center of their huts or houses, constituting the axis of everything built around it, this would have been quite usual. In the North Asian cultures, the tree represented the center of the world as well as the heavenly pillar that supported the vault of heaven and allowed the Shamans an ascent through the heavenly spheres. In the Jewish-Christian tradition, the tree is associated with the pole that supports the temple and house like the spine in the human body.[271] Thus in our dream image, too, the temple and building both rest on the tree. However, before we investigate the deeper meaning of this image, let us try to find out why the dream has selected the oak as the magical, divine tree.

Before the fruit tree had been discovered the oak served as one of the most important food providers for the ancients. From the acorns they extracted a kind of flour from which they baked bread. Later oak groves and acorns in the sacred forests became more rare. In his ode to agriculture and basing it on ancient beliefs, Virgil prophesied that the slow disappearance of the acorn signaled the end of the Golden Age.[272]

In the past, the oak was a sacred tree not only in the entire Mediterranean region (which, in Antiquity, was still largely wooded), but also throughout Europe. The sacred oak was the most ancient Greek oracle in Dodona, consecrated to Zeus, where three female priestesses, the Pleiades practiced fortune-telling by listening to the sounds of the rustling oak leaves.[273] The Pleiades were the priestesses of the goddess Dione, who was married to Zeus in Dodona. She was an archaic goddess appearing at the very beginning of the creation of the universe. At the foot of the divine oak there was supposed to be a divine spring, as we have already seen with Yggdrasil. Dione corresponds to the Cretan great Mother Goddess (primarily known to us under local names, e.g., Dictynna). She was a great tree goddess, the patroness of the universe of plants and the provider of all nourishment. She is accompanied by doves (the Pleiades were also referred to as doves) and snakes. She is often depicted as a

271 *Dictionnaire des Symboles*
272 J. Brosse, *Mythologie der Bäume,* 231
273 *Ibid.*, p. 61 f

pillar statue because she was of cylindrical shape at the base – like a tree trunk out of which sprang the torso of the goddess.[274]

The oak of Dodona was not only the most important oracle in Greece, it was, like other divine oak trees, also a provider of rain. The sacred oak growing on the Roman capitol was also implored to send rain. The seven hills of Rome were originally covered with oak woods consecrated to Jupiter. The Temple of Vesta was surrounded by an oak copse, for the eternal fire kept by the Vestal virgins had to be fed by oak wood only.[275]

In pre-Christian times, the cult of the oak was common throughout Europe and was maintained long after conversion to Christianity had taken place. The sacred oak trees were huge, ancient trees that, presumably, were several thousand years old.[276] The ancient Germans considered these giant oaks to be divine ancestors – seeing that they were the oldest creatures still alive on earth and that could be traced back as far as the Creation of the world. The ancient Arcadians of Greece believed likewise that having appeared on the earth so much earlier, the oak had brought forth mankind and that they themselves had been oaks before they became humans. According to an ancient source, the ancient Hellenes, too, considered oak trees as "their first mothers."[277] Psychologically speaking, therefore, the oak stands at the rise of human consciousness.

In the Teutonic era, the oak belonged to Donar-Thor, the god of lightning. The Slavs, Lithuanians and Latvians, as well as the Finnish-Urgish Estonians, venerated the oak as being the highest god of thunder and lightning. The Finns likened the oak tree even more unequivocally to the cosmic tree whose golden twigs filled the heavens. The ancient Slavs, Celts and Germans held court in the shade of the old sacred oak, and this custom would survive for a long time to come, for, "the most Christian King Ludwig IX still adhered to it."[278]

In the culture of the Celts and old Teutons, each sacred oak was held to be a representative of the cosmic tree that is the supporting pillar on the earth upon which reposes the vault of heaven. One day, so they believed, this pillar would collapse and the heavens would fall onto the heads of men, and Ragnarök, the end of the world, would come. But after that, from Hel, the underworld, the gods Balder and his brother, Hödur, returned to the earth, and in the grass they found the golden plates of Odin with the sacred Runes that Odin

---

[274] *Ibid.*, p. 70
[275] *Ibid.*, p. 81
[276] *Ibid.*, p. 81: "In his *Historia plantarum*," published 1686-1704, the English botanist, John Ray, describes an oak that has a trunk of ten meters diameter, which would mean that it was over 2000 years of age."
[277] *Ibid.*, quoted from *Anthologia Palatina of Zonas* from Sardes
[278] J. Brosse, *Mythologie der Bäume,* p. 83

had once found at the foot of the cosmic tree.[279] Thus the knowledge of the cosmic tree lived on.

In order to gather a bit of the rich mythological material, let us try to summarize the most essential features of the sacred oak: It is a maternal provider of food and rain; it serves as an oracle (and again, we find here the archaic triad of the "mothers"); it is of "infinite age" and therefore both a creator and an ancestor of the human race. Furthermore, as the cosmic tree, it is the pillar of the universe and support of the heavens. The fascination of a 2000-year-old oak to which all this is ascribed, is quite beyond our grasp today, as is, too, the sacrilege of felling such a sacred tree in a missionary zeal or any other kind of ardor.

Thus, our dreamer has to discover that the church or palace is being supported by this kind of a divine oak, and that it had existed long before the building, which apparently had been built around it. It stands out amidst ordinary trees, and it is archaic and moist like a primeval animal. Moisture or water are part of the tree of the great mother, for the origin of all life is in the water.[280] However, the origin of all life is the unconscious, which is why in dreams water mostly suggests the unconscious.

The oak therefore symbolizes an immense central content of the unconscious that not only pertains to the origin of man but also to the center and support of our entire cultural and intellectual-historical development. The dream shows this with the "solemn building," a place or rather an allegory for the way man experiences and understands the world. The church and palace reflect man's grasp of the world, that is, what his consciousness has been able to assimilate from the world or from the totality of the unconscious. Man forgets about this achievement all too easily and tends to ignore the fact that there is a kind of central authority of the unconscious, namely the Self that is at the beginning and end of any process toward achieving consciousness. Hence the oak symbolizes the ancestor or primordial mother at the beginning of human consciousness as well as at the end of the world, at its downfall. The oak as the cosmic tree supports the entire cultural and spiritual "building" that has at once brought into being and represents human consciousness.

Jung says of the sacred giant oak that it is "the prototype of the *Self*, a symbol of the source and goal of the individuation process."[281] It is that "which keeps in place the innermost core of the world" that this numinous dream seems to be about. And what determines the fate of the dreamer and her future child, is the very same. All things outside, all man-made things including the human façade in fact only exist to the extent that they are sustained by something that is deeply and firmly rooted in the unconscious

---

[279] *Ibid.*, p. 91
[280] Cf. Chapter 3.1
[281] C.G. Jung, *The Philosophical Tree*, CW 13, § 241

and that last throughout the ages. The dreamer's unconscious has expressed this most pertinently with the picture of the sacred oak. Jung called it the Self, an indefinite word that can only be illuminated by the unconscious itself.

Dream No. 43 (five months pregnant):[282]

> *I come out of my "hut," and look towards the place where my friend's caravan used to stand. In precisely that space I now see three mighty beech trunks. I am enchanted and delighted, indeed quite overpowered (because the area so near the sea never allows for anything more than scrub and the odd gnarled pine or bent birch). I consider it as a miracle. But then I look up and notice that they are trunks only, lacking all upper branches and leafy crown. First I am puzzled and somewhat disappointed, when suddenly a voice speaks to me and explains: "These are the three supporting pillars. It is just a preparation – for they will soon hold the great glass roof – the protecting dome."*
>
> *The implication seemed to be, that the roof was going to be the really important part – the crowning glory. This was both saddening for it set the fourth apart from the other three, but at the same time the thought of this great protective dome filled me with security and comfort and warmth and growth.*

At the time of the dream the dreamer was expecting her fourth child. It would seem likely that the three trees are connected with the three children, for in folklore, the tree and life of a child often belong together. Even nowadays, people frequently plant a tree when a child is born. However, I believe this interpretation would be rather too superficial. The trees in this dream are of the kind we have already discussed – namely, leafless and without branches. They are most unusual trees, which the dreamer had never before noticed. They are mighty beeches, not barren and tousled by the sea wind nor anything like tiny crippled pines or birches. Because of the oily beechnuts, beeches have been considered vital food providers for ages. Legend has it that witches danced near beeches and also that there were small children's beeches. In addition, beech trees cannot be struck by lightning.[283] Beeches are often conspicuous in that they seem to attract each other in a peculiar manner. They are often very obviously grown or fused together, whether the trunks at the bottom or anywhere else for that matter where they very nearly touch each other. Then they look like people in an embrace. In old times, people believed that the souls of a couple in love outlived death in these trees.[284] This motif is

---

[282] The same dreamer: Nos. 59 and 60 (Ch. 5.3), No. 16 (Ch. 3.2), No. 114 (Ch. 6)

[283] *Handwörterbuch d. dt. Aberglaubens*, 2, p. 1692

[284] J. Brosse, *Mythologie der Bäume*, p. 187. This belief was widespread amongst the Celts.

familiar from the legend of Philemon and Baucis. Contrary to other trees, it may be for this reason that beech trees have been associated with Eros – or, in the case of our dream, are closely connected to maternal feelings on a very deep, vegetative level, as it were.

Now the voice does not speak to the dreamer of a fourth tree but of a glass roof that, supported by the trees as pillars, would form a dome. Thus the "fourth" is the glass roof and protecting dome. At first, the dreamer is disappointed, for she somehow expected a fourth pillar, or a fourth tree. It would appear, however, that the birth of the fourth child will not now take place in a purely vegetative sphere of the maternal Eros but somewhere else.

What do the three trees signify? Symbolically, the "three" in this case belongs to the earthy, or feminine. Ancient shrines consecrated to the Mother Goddess show a structural trinity (walls, stone ceiling) that are frequently complemented by a fourth, phallic single pillar.[285] The trinity also belongs to the dark aspect of fate of the Great Mother. Examples of this are Hecate, the goddess of the world of

Figure 15. Triple-faced Hecate

the Shades to whom statues were erected in the form of a woman with three dog-heads or three heads, further, the Norns, the three Germanic goddesses of fate, the Greek Moirae, the Roman goddesses of fate, and the Celtic and Egyptian moon-goddesses, etc.[286] It relates to the stages in which our destiny unfolds: the past, present and future. Thus, at a point in our life where destiny inevitably prevails, such as at the time of pregnancy or birth, the unconscious constellates the image of a rather archaic feminine trinity. It has to do with the dynamics of the natural course of a growing new life.

The protecting glass dome that stretches across the trees signifies a completion from triplicity to quaternity. Glass is transparent, and therefore, in Jung's words: "Transparent glass is something like solidified water or air, both of

---

[285] E. Neumann, *The Great Mother*
[286] *Ibid.*, pp. 217 f

which are synonyms for spirit."[287] In this passage, Jung also speaks of the *vas hermeticum* of alchemy, a vessel made of glass that was called uterus. He then mentions a vision Caesarius of Heisterbach (13th century) had in which the soul appeared as a spherical glass vessel. The glass roof with the supporting poles is reminiscent of the idea of the celestial dome resting on the cosmic tree. As the fourth completing element it must be dependent upon the trees or poles that support it. We could envisage the three trees as "Jacob's ladder," which has grown up and matured, as it were, from the past feminine-vegetative life, the domain of Mother Earth and of pregnancies, births and children. But just as the earth goddess' ancient caves and grottos were apparently flanked by a pole, a masculine upward pointing, procreative symbol, so it is possible that this dream vision is also trying to reveal the spiritual dimension or deeper meaning of maternity. For, just as the church, or *mater ecclesia*, represents a symbol of maternity, so, too, does the protecting dome.

Unlike the Christian church, it is, however, supported by three trees, which belong to the dark, earthy, physical and fateful aspect of the feminine. Moreover, because the trees had to grow before the glass roof could complete the dome, we may assume that it has to do with a renewal of spiritual or higher religious ideas, which have been generated from below, that is, from the depths of fate or the unconscious. The well-meaning efforts of the church today – to present a more popular image in the hope of reaching out to more people – have little to do with a renewal from below. Conversely, the maternal dome of our dream is a new church or rather a new religious attitude that has developed out of the feminine Self. It is for this that the dream is preparing the woman who is preoccupied with the forthcoming birth of a natural child. It seems to say: "There is much more to it."

The fourth element is something new and separate from the rest, which is painful to the dreamer. More often than not, spiritual development for a woman primarily involves a very painful process of detachment from the natural-biological life, a cutting-off from the nature-conditioned feminine that follows its course without any active contribution from her part. The fourth signifies the very different element, though one without which the first three cannot be complete. "... whenever we are dealing with totality, quaternity plays a role, no matter how primitive or high the ideas may be. The number four always expresses the coming into being of the essentially human aspect, in other words, of achieving consciousness."[288]

"This great protective dome filled me with security and comfort and warmth and growth." Just as the protective glass roof can only be built with the three trees and depends on their support, so the feeling of comfort and security can only be granted by this glass roof. Let us look at the three support-

---

[287] C.G. Jung, *The Spirit Mercurius*, CW 13, § 245
[288] C.G. Jung, *Kindertraumseminar 1939/40*, p. 96 (transl. V.N.)

ing trees as the dreamer's biological life forming the pillars of a "spiritual roof" (the glass roof). This clearly shows that the protecting dome and sacral building cannot exist without one or the other. The dome would thus be a mature, new religious attitude, genuine protection and a place of retreat – possibly the goal of woman's entire life. Such a dream could impel a strongly "biologically" oriented motherliness in the direction of the necessary spiritual dimension: "The important part – the crowning glory."

Dream No. 44 (nine months pregnant):[289]

> *The baby is born … I have to feed it, but I have hardly place to do it, because the car is full of people.*
> [This is followed by a longer scene in which the dreamer is on a trip with her husband, aunt, friends and other people and finally arriving at the sea-side.]
> *I see some apples on the floor, and look where they come from. There are two apple trees, one of normal size, and another, enormous, giant one. We climb up it, and upwards, excavating a tunnel through its inside. Now we are wearing black costumes like divers to protect ourselves from what could happen. Now follows a strange story. The excursion inside is led by a woman, who sees danger of water dripping over us and drowning the trunk inside with us in it. This water is a very clean, sweet and transparent sap flowing steadily in one direction. We notice it doesn't cause trouble for us. We go on upwards, and come out to one of the lower – considering the tree's size – side branches. It has a Romanesque structure. We have to explore it, and each one of us must have a nave. I place myself in front of the main nave, and look at all of them. There are symbols sculptured on the stone, a ram and other things. There isn't a roof, only stone arches that don't cover the naves. They look as if they have never been covered. I try to find the center, but can't. It seems asymmetric. I awake.*

At the time of this dream, the dreamer was expecting her second child, a boy, her first child being a girl. To begin with, she finds herself with her husband and relatives, friends and other people in a flurry of extraverted activity and mobility, so that she hardly manages to feed it. Initially, it looks as though this might be the problem or theme of the dream. She lacks the necessary peace for herself and the child. This could correspond to her conscious unwillingness to slow down and to attach more importance to the psyche, introversion and to what is growing inside her and needing to be fed. The dream, however, takes her precisely to that dimension, to the inside of a

---

[289] There are almost 100 dreams by this dreamer in our collection, thus one in almost every chapter.

tree trunk, the quintessence of darkness and introversion. But before this happens, she arrives at the sea, at the threshold of the great unknown and symbol of the collective unconscious. Indeed, she will have to kind of immerse herself in the water and will even need to wear a wet suit for it. There are apples lying on the beach. She is wondering where they might have come from – then, looking up, discovers the two apple trees.

As we have seen earlier, the apple is connected with the goddess of love and the feminine power of seduction, thus with Eros. It is also connected with the recognition of a gift of the feminine-maternal nature. This would be a possibility to recognize something emanating from the unconscious or even a preconscious state, similar to the situation taking place in the Garden of Eden. Our dreamer seems to find herself in this kind of position in the second part of the dream. The apple trees correspond to the tree of knowledge and the life-tree, the latter of which is surrounded by a stream with four arms, the life-tree (cf. Ge. 9, 10). At first, the dreamer sees only the apples or the nourishing and tempting aspects of the maternal unconscious. And yet, she herself is being seduced into seeing the cosmic tree and perceiving that life is determined by something similar to fate. Mother Nature always tempts us when we are fulfilling a biological purpose, be it love, founding a family or motherhood. Sooner or later, we realize that we have taken on far more than we had intended to – namely, a destiny. Young people are often afraid of entering a serious relationship, of getting married and having children. This is ultimately a fear of the three aspects of the goddesses of fate, viz., the fear of assuming one's destiny!

Now begins the trip into the unknown, led by an unknown woman. It is the motif of doubling that has already come up with the two trees and has to do with a previously unconscious content now approaching consciousness. Marie-Louise von Franz explains it in the following manner: "When we talk about the unconscious we use a concept which characterizes it as a kind of complete continuum, like a magnetic field. ... Then a content comes up and the moment it touches the threshold of consciousness it is cut into two parts, into a one and the other. The one is the aspect which I can state, while the other remains in the unconscious, and that is why, generally, when you have dream images of a complete double, you dream about a person doubled, or of two dogs, two cats, two trees or two similar houses, and so on."[290] Thus eating the apple from the tree of knowledge in paradise suddenly reveals to Adam the tree of life with the fruits of immortality, and this is of concern to God the Father. A process towards achieving consciousness has taken place.

This could also be true for the dreamer. Having found the apples, she then becomes interested in where they came from and discovers the two trees. It is as if she has now become conscious of the fact that behind the apples and the

---

[290] M.-L. von Franz, *Individuation in Fairy Tales*, Shambhala, Boston, 1997, p. 33

taste of Mother Nature – in other words, behind her marriage and motherhood – there was a cosmic tree, a cosmic principle, something far more powerful than herself. This is what she must investigate.

The unknown, second woman must be understood as an inner figure of the dreamer, an unknown side in her that she was previously unaware of. This side is evidently capable of undertaking this kind of excursion into uncertainty. It also knows the danger lurking about; it is closer to the unconscious than to the dream-ego. A part of the dreamer knows that entering the world of the unconscious is best done after having taken some precautions, for one might drown in the water.[291] Although the sources of the unconscious or the water inside the tree are evocative of the sap of life, of stimulating inner visions, fantasies, intuitions and creative ideas, we can also be inundated by them. It is therefore wise for the consciousness to adopt a cautious attitude and putting on wet suits reflects this sensible attitude. Let me explain what I mean: If, for instance, a drug user is pulled down into the depths of the unconscious, he or she lacks the wet suit that could protect the small human consciousness against the overwhelming power of the collective unconscious. It is indeed much better to approach the unconscious with due respect rather than to naively take a header into unknown waters. Later in the dream we shall return to this problem when discussing the motif of the nave.

Entering the trunk of the giant tree, the dreamer and her companions first end up in the dark. This corresponds to the starting point of many fairy tales, where the hero or heroine get lost in the woods. This is a way of indicating a state of introversion that our dreamer's consciousness accepts easily, which also involves being unable to see anything nor seeing a way out of a murky situation. Oftentimes, this is the point in psychoanalysis when people stop early, for they cannot wait to find out how they can be helped. However, the initial phase of work can easily be compared with digging one's way through the tunnel of a dark tree trunk! And then, it may take some time before it becomes clear that we can find the elixir of life that is indeed salubrious.

Entering or getting in touch with the collective unconscious is often described as "going down" – although this need not be the case. Our dreamer is ascending. She goes up towards the light, the sky and branches, presumably pursuing a spiritual goal (even though she does not yet know this). It is from there, and not from the earth below where water ordinarily seeps into the tree, that the clear, transparent sweet sap – the sap of life – drips down. It is a peculiar image, but bearing in mind the strange church alluding to a religious or spiritual problem later in the dream, it is deeply meaningful. The dreamer has to excavate herself up and out of the dark interior of the tree. This initial stage could be seen as an unconscious identification with the Great Mother. We can also look at it as a wholehearted dedication to the biological-feeding

---

[291] Cf. Chapter 5.1

and maternal side in the dreamer that she must overcome having already chosen the path towards a spiritual goal. However, she still has to enter the tree trunk, which could mean that she first has to experience her own blossoming in motherhood. Having so far led a very extraverted life, she does not know how to feed a child, for babies feed on this kind of unconscious vegetative or animal-like maternal quality. The path she is on now takes her through this maternal task upwards, towards the sweet sap of life. There will be no flood, for her effort to let some light permeate the darkness of her biological destiny will be rewarded with insight, only slowly, drop by drop, and will mean constant spiritual nourishment.

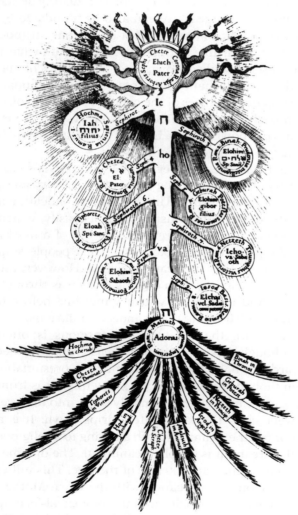

Figure 16. Tree upside-down: The Sepiroth-Tree (1626)

In Indian mythology, Asvatta, the tree of the gods, is said to have poured down from the tree top Soma, the drink of immortality. This conception may be linked with the water inside the tree of our dream, which runs down instead of up. Divine food comes from above. Asvatta is a tree which is upside-down, rooted in the heavens with branches reaching down to the earth. In the Middle Ages, the idea of the tree standing upside-down as an image of man was quite common. Jung quotes Plato, who said: "... seeing that we are not an earthly but a heavenly plant."[292] The idea behind this is that man as a spiritual being obtains nourishment or the elixir of life, as it were, from the heavenly, spiritual sphere.

However, our dream does not go as far in emphasizing the spiritual, for the giant tree is firmly rooted in the earth. It rather suggests a development taking an upward course, having begun from the lower, feminine-maternal, earthly domain. It is as if cutting upward through the tunnel has to begin there. It has sometimes struck me that the ideals of "women's liberation" cause women to become like an uprooted tree, free of all female obligations and restrictions, in order to achieve an independence that in fact should be of a spiritual nature. This way we run the risk of the elixir of life not seeping through either from above or below. For, the above and below of the living tree rooted in the earth form a natural unity that is the water as a cycle of movement of rising and dripping down. Thus, although woman can free herself from her restricting obligations, it is not always a genuine spiritual freedom that she gains. It would rather seem that the true liberation entails a slow, arduous process through her feminine destiny. It may be for this reason that the feminist discourse is often unpalatable and that men find it difficult to swallow. The continuation of our dream could provide an answer to the problem many women share today, namely, to reconcile their feminine destiny, in harmony with Nature, with the realization of their spiritual development.

The ascent through the tree trunk ends temporarily at the first lower side branches. There she finds something like ancient Romanesque arches and naves without roofs. These have to be investigated. Ordinary vessels (in German, the nave is called the ship or vessel of the church) were always perceived as feminine, for like a woman, they carry the sailor in their belly and guard him from the dangers of the deep. They usually have female names. The patroness of the seafarers is Isis – also, Maria or Stella Maris. This is the context in which we must see the nave. It has feminine connotations because it represents the lap of the Mother Church, which protects the devout from the dangers of the ocean and the unconscious. Jung thought that the church maintained a well-organized dogma and ritual that substituted actual religious experiences with a selection of suitable symbols.[293] Furthermore, rites and dogmas had been a safe way to cope with the unpredictable forces of the unconscious.[294] Like dreams, these are some kind of regulating signs created by the unconscious. Once they are no longer respected and valued and their function not appreciated anew, then the retaining walls, which used to guard against an inrush of the overwhelming contents of the unconscious, break down. They become replaced by an unquestioning faith in such things as science or the state, to name just two of the many possibilities, while in their shade the destructive beasts of the unconscious, such as power, violence, lying and all varieties of covetousness, are at work. The nave, representing the *Mater*

---

[292] C.G. Jung, *The Philosophical Tree*, CW 13, § 412, fn 11
[293] Cf. Jung, CW 12, § 36 f
[294] *Ibid.*, § 40

Ecclesia, is like a vessel symbolically allowing for a way of dealing with the contents of the collective unconscious.

On her way up through the tree, the dreamer comes to a church, where she is confronted with an essentially religious or spiritual problem. The man-made, albeit not complete, church whose naves have no roof is only vaulted by a Romanesque arch. At that point, for some reason, the construction was discontinued.

The Roman arches point to the Middle Ages. The round, stocky form of the Romanesque period still reminds us of caves and grottoes. They are forerunners of the structures of the Gothic period that reach up and dissolve into the spiritual sphere. The Middle Ages were characterized by an increased emphasis on feeling and the feminine, as well as personal relationships at the courts of love. This paved the way to a foundation for acceptance of the lower earth goddess encompassing love, Eros and maternity, which had so far been spurned by the ecclesiastical-Christian conception of the Virgin Mary.[295] These beginnings were, however, suppressed by the church, so that speaking in terms of the dream imagery, the new church did not receive a roof nor the new conception, a spiritual superstructure. It has remained unfinished to this day. The feminine in Nature does not exist in the ecclesiastical-religious Welt-bild, which is why the lower and the higher could never be joined together. The dreamer has now become conscious of this problem. She must take a good look at it, for it is likely to be important for her development.

Amongst the symbols on the walls the dreamer only recognizes a ram. The others, probably the signs of the zodiac, she does not recognize. In astrology, the ram is ascribed to the spring, the time of the awakening of Nature. According to Marie-Louise von Franz, it stands for aggressive impulsiveness, for a kind of unreflected, naïve initiative.[296] This can be woman's animus, manifesting itself in the form of the well-known kind of sudden intrusion that, looking back, leaves her angry and frustrated. The ram has unexpectedly and against her own will, given someone a push. Together with the lion, bull and some other animals, the ram belongs to the great animal goddess and represents her aggressive, masculine side. Therefore, it is as if these instinctive aspects, which Christian thought has found difficult to accept and to deal with, were somehow present in those Romanesque walls of the past. This would mean that these masculine aspects of the Great Mother had at least partially been admitted to the Christian Weltbild of that time.[297] These aspects appear to force

---

[295] Cf. M.-L. von Franz's essay: *Bei der Schwarzen Frau* in: *Märchenforschung und Tiefenpsychologie*, ed. by W. Saiblin, Wiss. Buchgesellschaft, Darmstadt, 1965

[296] M.-L. von Franz, *Die Erlösung des Weiblichen im Manne*, Insel Verlag, Frankfurt, 1980, p. 136

[297] Mary hides the sinners under her coat; cf. C.G. Jung, *Man and His Symbols*, Aldus/Jupiter Books Ltd., London, 1979, p. 118

themselves back into consciousness with the ideas of the present-day emancipation of women, along with all the difficulties they entail.

Now, why these unfinished walls in the branches of the huge tree? The giant tree or cosmic tree is a collective symbol representing the universe. It embraces all domains of life extending from the earth and snakes in the roots to the birds in the branches of the treetops and to the stars. It is an allegory for biological growth carrying the totality of life. Behind everything there would be, so to speak, a natural, large-scale plan of Nature similar to the growth of a tree. As the tree grows in a vertical fashion, i.e., from below upward, one could say that the development originates at the very roots of the Great Mother, deep down in the earthy-unconscious, and culminates in a differentiated form, with the branches reaching up to the sky, i.e., to consciousness. When man feels supported by such a natural plan of growth, as did the ancient cultures where the symbol of the cosmic tree was sacred, then he is part of a divine wholeness. The development of wholeness underlies his personal development much as the archetypes in the background of the collective psyche carry and influence the individual psyche.

The unfinished church touches on a problem that, in the course of the spiritual development of collective Christianity, has remained unresolved. For this reason, the dreamer feels impelled to explore it, for it affects her life, too.

We have seen that the cosmic tree or tree of life that sustains all life is a maternal-feminine symbol of wide-ranging implications. Reaching up and separating into various branches is analogous to the first differentiation, as it were, of the supra-feminine-maternal aspect aspiring to spirituality. This is where the dreamer finds the Romanesque church. It could indicate that at that time the religious approach of the church partially and consciously recognized the earthy-feminine-maternal element. The dreamer must understand why the construction was stopped at the time and what this discontinuance means to her.

She now tries to get a better view by trying to find the center. She realizes that this unfinished church does not have a proper center. In reality, very old Romanesque churches, such as St. Michael's Church in Fulda, Germany, have a very conspicuous center in the wonderfully simple form of a mandala with a central rotunda surrounded by eight pillars. In alchemy, the center plays an important part: it is called the *punctum invisibile*, which does not corrode and is therefore everlasting. It corresponds to the philosophical gold. This *punctum invisibile* – "invisible center" – that cannot be corrupted corresponds to the Self, the empirical notion coined by Jung. It appears in totality symbols, such as the cross, circle, square and mandala, but also in the figure of the "'supraordinate personality,' such as a king, hero, prophet, savior, etc. in dreams, myths and fairy tales."[298] The Self "proves to be an archetypal idea, ...

[298] C.G. Jung, CW 6, § 790

which differs from other ideas of the kind in that it occupies a central position befitting the significance of its content and its numinosity."[299] "... the Self designates the whole range of psychic phenomena in man. It expresses the unity of the personality as a whole."[300] If the unfinished church still does not have a center today, it is because it failed to pay sufficient attention to the central value, the invisible, eternal value – in other words, the Self. The dreamer awakens in the middle of her quest that is the center representing wholeness. We can assume that this is the purpose of the dream and that the dreamer should "wake up" to this problem and understand that her own psychic wholeness is being addressed here. It is thus an individuation dream that seems to say to the dreamer: This is the responsibility you must assume once your child has been born.

Dream No. 45, dreamer is 31 years old and six months pregnant:[301]

> *I was in a group of several women. The atmosphere was pleasant. A few women made music, and I was engrossed in dancing to it. Then we were supposed to paint ourselves as trees. What came out in my case was a kind of a cross, almost like a T, possibly with a snake entwined around it. It looked relaxed, and the leaves were still fresh and tender. I liked the tree. Then another woman was supposed to join us. My cousin, Pia, who has been wanting to get closer, came to me. Now we were asked to draw this woman as a tree and then to talk about it. I immediately knew what the tree should look like but just couldn't begin drawing it. I was blocked, knowing that she was my counter-image. All the branches originated in the ground. They were thick and the leaves tough and dark.*

The group the dreamer finds herself in seems to be a kind of "encounter group." The atmosphere is harmonious, people are making music. Before the dreamer starts drawing her tree, she is engrossed in dancing to the music. The tree she is supposed to paint apparently has to do with group therapy and with a deeper experience of the enigmatic growing process of her psyche. In most cultures, men and women dance on occasions that mark something that moves them, that is larger and higher than themselves. People dance before or after a hunt, military campaign, in connection with fertility, during sacrificial rites consecrated to the veneration of the gods and for many other reasons. Dancing activates the whole of man; in other words, his psychic forces, which lie beyond his consciousness and may affect his life at any pertinent moment. In this dream, it is a feminine rite enabling woman to be in touch with her deeper feminine layers. Dancing also signifies creativity, for Shiva created the

---

[299] *Ibid.*, § 791
[300] *Ibid.*, § 789
[301] By the same dreamer: No. 17 (Chapter 3.2)

world by dancing. Dancing was also a part of woman's mysteries.[302] To dance is body and soul moving in unison, as it were, and being in harmony with the unconscious.

Now the dreamer can paint her tree. Drawing trees is part of general or popular psychology. We do "tree tests" on children when we want to know more about them, and in encounter groups this is also done. What is peculiar though and rather surprising is the fact that her tree is cross-shaped and has a serpent entwined around it. What the unconscious brings up is certainly new for the dreamer. Nevertheless, it does not seem to affect her in any extraordinary way – "I liked the tree." Given the uncommon and striking symbolism of the image, however, her reaction seems somewhat lacking. She is taking the image too personally, as if it were merely an ego-reflection; she has not yet assimilated with her feeling the unfamiliar, numinous archetypal content of it.

Inquiring further into these motifs, in the Christian legend, for instance, we find the connection between tree and cross where the tree is both a tree of death and a tree of life.[303] This is why Christ crucified is so often represented as hanging on a blooming, fruit-bearing tree (e.g., St. Mary's Church in the convent of Fulda) – for the sufferings and the death of the Redeemer at the same time suggest the promise of redemption and eternal life. The tree as a cross also symbolizes the great mother of life as well as death containing in herself the most extreme opposites. In Christian mythology, these opposites (that are still united in the tree) eventually become an irreconcilable conflict in which Christ and all human nature is displayed on the cross. It is the conflict between above and below, heaven and earth, spirit and nature, good and evil, etc.

The tree and cross are also closely related in Manichaeism. According to the Manichaeans, trees contain a large part of the divine *Weltseele* or light substance, which they regarded as suffering because it is spread out in matter. They tended to equate it with the immortal Jesus crucified above matter. For them Jesus was the life and salvation of man, crucified in every piece of wood, "in which the wounds of passion our soul suffers reveal themselves, and the world receives meaning."[304] Jesus' passion takes place in each human being, and man's redemption is commensurate with God's Redemption in whose light man partakes through his living soul.[305] The aspect of the divine suffering taking place in the individual, in other words, the close relationship and even identification of the personal with the archetypal, thanks to which personal suffering can have meaning, is particularly strong here.

---

[302] Cf. Carol Baumann, *Psychological Experiences Connected with Childbirth*, in: *Studien zur analytischen Psychologie C.G. Jung's*, Rascher Verlag, Olten, 1955
[303] Cf. C.G. Jung, *Symbols of Transformation*, CW 5, Ill. 71, § 369
[304] Geo Widengren, *Manichäismus*, Darmstadt, 1977, p. 180
[305] *Ibid.*, p. 186

In the dream, the cross-shaped tree is rather suggestive of the form of an Egyptian *crux ansata*, a rope-cross signifying life, fertility and the renewal of life.[306] Moreover, it is a cheerful, green tree, relaxed and fresh, with tender leaves. As yet, there is no darkness about it that might suggest suffering.

Figure 17. Goddess with a snake (Legarit, ca. 2500 B.C.)

What does the snake have to do with it? In terms of amplification, the motif of the snake on the tree of paradise comes to mind. It demonstrated for the first time the conflict between good and evil that resulted in the original parents' expulsion from paradise. In this respect, the snake has something to do with the realization of something that can put an end to a state of bliss. In the dream, this happens with the image of the dark tree that is signaled by the snake image. In Gnosticism, Christ himself is the snake, and the Manichaeans represented Christ as the snake on the tree of paradise.[307] In the eyes of the Gnostic sects of the Ophites and Naassens (Ophis and Naas = snake), in the serpent were united not only the opposites of good and evil. The image of Uroborous, the serpent with its tail in its mouth, furthermore represented the dualistic theme of the eternal life cycle, that is: destruction and re-creation, the world and God, beginning and end, sin and deliverance (innocence), spirit and matter, etc.[308] The mercurial snake symbol expressing the psychic process of transformation can also be found with the Alchemists.[309]

Like alchemy, the Gnostic systems revolve around a circular process of development and transformation that in fact underlies all processes in Nature. We are used to the thought that development happens on a straight line beginning at point zero of a system of coordinates and ending somewhere else on this line. Such thinking tends to produce a view where pregnancy and birth and the future life of a child are seen as entirely dynamic, rather like a kind of an ascending stream rushing towards the happiness of mother and child. The snake, on the other hand, hints at Nature's own dynamics, which do not conform to the linear thinking our consciousness is geared to.

---

[306] C.G. Jung, *Symbols of Transformation*, CW 5, § 407 / § 411
[307] Cf. C.G. Jung, *Symbols of Transformation*, CW 5, § 593, ill. 37
[308] Cf. Hans Leisegang, *Gnosis*, Kröner Verlag, Leipzig, 1924, pp. 35, 99
[309] Cf. C.G. Jung, *Symbols of Transformation*, CW 5, § 150, Fig. 6

The veneration of the snake as a redeeming and saving force is widespread in certain Gnostic sects despite the fact that the Gnostics were quite aware of the paradoxical nature of the snake.[310] Jung says that "the serpent symbolizes the mysterious numen of the 'mother' ... who kills but who is at the same time man's only security against death, as she is the source of life."[311] Psychologically speaking, the serpent is a symbol of the unconscious. It signifies sudden and unexpected manifestations from the unconscious, painful and hazardous interventions in our conscious world and affairs with all its frightening ramifications. The snake stands for some autonomous impulses that are rooted in the deepest layers of the psyche. They extend all the way into the biological part of the psychic spectrum, even to the bodily functions. Because the snake is a cold-blooded animal, we can never have the kind of relationship with it which we have with, say, a dog; usually, the snake symbolizes a terrifying and incomprehensible aspect of Nature. Most people's attitude to snakes is one marked by fear, rejection of and repugnance to the entirely foreign and uncanny characteristics of the snake.

In the chapter on snake-dreams, we shall see that snakes belong to the goddesses of fate. When the cold-blooded nature gets its way, we are in its hands through fate – for better or worse. This applies to pregnancy, too. Many pregnant women do not exclusively enjoy a feeling of happiness, fertility, warmth and growth, but also feel nausea, fatigue and other physical discomforts to an equal extent. The process of growth goes on, to result in a birth or death, although each birth already carries death within it.

Not only are pregnancy and birth subject to Nature's obscure laws, but the future of the child is also in a dark veil, and we do not know what hazards the goddesses hold in store for it. A young mother may, or perhaps should, retain a degree of haziness and not reflect about all this too much in order to provide the necessary composure and calmness for the infant. In the case of our dream, however, the unconscious seems to give an important signal. At first the dreamer sees in the greening tree primarily the lovely, life-bestowing, stimulating aspect of pregnancy. This pleases her. The snake, which she only marginally perceives, adds a larger and more consequential element to it. The dreamer apparently does not quite realize this, but the second part of the dream clearly points in this direction.

What the dreamer has not been able to see or accept is a shadow-figure appearing in the dream as cousin Pia. All we know about her is that she had sought closer relations before. This means that a part of the dreamer on the inner dream-stage wants to be near her or, psychologically speaking, wants to become conscious. She corresponds to the other tree whose dark and tough branches ramify from the ground, and although the dreamer recognizes this

---

[310] Cf. Wilhelm Bousset, *Hauptprobleme der Gnosis*, Göttingen und Zürich, 1973, p. 124
[311] Cf. C.G. Jung, *Symbols of Transformation*, CW 5, § 452

at once, she draws it only reluctantly. This tree – according to the dream – is her counter-image, the image of her "other side." This side now lacks the light-green lightness. It is dark and tough and stuck to the ground. One might say that the image of this tree represents the unpleasant, burdensome part of the natural process of transformation in pregnancy. If the light aspect is too prevalent in consciousness, and motherhood is seen only in terms of happiness and love, then the dark side has to be repressed; otherwise it would interfere with the harmony of the picture. In reality, this upsets the harmony nevertheless, for children have a knack of provoking that unconscious shadow-side of the mother, which can be triggered by anger or irritation and lead to uncontrollable rages.

The proximity to the mythical image of the crucified serpent brings the dreamer's personal drama closer to a larger context: namely, the process of achieving consciousness of the opposites in nature that are united in the snake. The cross and crucifixion symbolize suffering through the process of becoming conscious of the opposites. We could put it this way: to the extent the dreamer can see and consciously accept her dark sides, consciousness reaches a kind of "natural equilibrium." By the same token she can apprehend her own darkness from which she is suffering as something embedded in the large context of Nature, encompassing the opposites of light and darkness, goodness and evil, or joy and sorrow. This cannot eliminate personal suffering, but unites it with a fundamental wholeness and, so the symbol says, contains the promise of deliverance. What this really means can only be surmised as the ultimate secret of our existence, provided we no longer imagine salvation in the strictly Christian sense – that is, the paradise where we would one day end up after death. It must have to do with a feeling of deliverance from the tormenting opposites in which every natural life is embedded. The tree or tree as a cross symbolizes the biological life of man. It carries both the suffering and the deliverance. Thus the serpent is hanging on what is at once the symbol of change and (in shamanistic religions) renewal, healing and rebirth. This also signifies a revalorization of individual life and of modern man's plight of being apparently hopelessly swamped in the masses.[312]

Our dream seems to suggest that as a result of an all too optimistic inclination a neurotic split has taken place. This happens whenever certain parts of the personality are repressed by consciousness. The dark, tough tree represents, as it were, the dark principle of life behind the shadow. To accept the shadow would mean at the same time to face the uncanny, threatening and fateful aspect of the dark feminine nature. Only in this way could the two trees or two sides of the mother archetype actually be joined together. This is the task the dream formulates (both trees should be painted). Thus the split can

---

[312] Cf. Gotthilf Isler, *Das rätoromanische Margaretenlied – eine seelische Tragödie*

be revoked and the "unnatural," one-sided conscious inclination complemented.

Figure 18. Celtic Mistress of the Beasts

5. Animals

Regina Abt

Until not so long ago, at least amongst the rural population of farmers, the animal was part of everyday life. It determined the daily rhythm of people's lives, which in their regularity, did not differ markedly from the animal's. The archaic hunter's relationships with the animal, however, were even closer, as he had to do his best to adapt to their lives since his own life directly depended on it. Being himself still very much guided by instinct, he had a particularly intimate bond with the animal upon which he depended. With an increasing development of consciousness which on the one hand enabled him to adapt to a certain order, i.e., to bridle his instincts,[313] man distanced himself from his instinct and thus from his empathy for and identification with the animal. He gained more and more power over the animal. Today many people are indifferent towards animals or see them merely as utility objects while others see them as a threat. On the other hand, the animal embodies a yearning after a "paradise lost," after a world in which Nature determines and regulates the life cycles and where the animal is integrated into a purposeful totality. Its unadulterated being, which submits to the natural laws without any "ifs" and "buts," touches people in their innermost cores, and they suffer in the face of the silent suffering of the animal. Thanks to his consciousness, man is apparently able to reduce his own suffering. Yet if despite this he despairs, his soul produces images that can convey meaning or a purpose to his own suffering. He remains connected to that higher law of Nature, which regulates life on the instinctive level in terms of acts, and on the psychic level in terms of images or conceptions. Jung says in one of the seminars: if man can trust the law of Nature, he will discover his own law, too.

Animals always seem to stand for "instinctive behavior," that is, in Jung's words, for the mode of behavior "of which neither the motive nor the aim is fully conscious and which is prompted only by obscure inner necessity."[314]

---

[313] C.G. Jung, CW 8, *Instinct and the Unconscious*, Routledge and Kegan Paul, 1960, § 412

Instinctive behavior can be life-saving for us. In her lecture on pets, Barbara Hannah writes that in all natural situations instincts are a better protection than all the intellectual wisdom in the world.[315]

Hence, to consciously reconnect with the animal instinct (not to regress to the level of the animal, which would involve returning to an unconscious state) results in a feeling of a return to Nature. Dreaming of a relationship or an encounter with an animal therefore often has a healing effect. In fairy tales, the helping animals, who must absolutely be trusted and obeyed because they alone know how to advise the heroine or the hero, are also the ones who bring them to their ultimate goal.

Pregnancy makes woman particularly close to an animal in as much as she has to submit to the biological course the same way an animal does. She feels best and most healthy when she surrenders to it just as an animal does. The less intellectual interference with her instinctive behavior there is, the better she will feel.

Animals do not only represent the physical instincts Jung designated as "typical modes of action,"[316] but together with his instinctive actions, man also experiences inner images or emotions. Jung designates these in the same passage as typical modes of perception: "These emotions, ideas and spiritual images are just as typical and collective as the patterns of instinctive actions. Sometimes the emphasis of our experience lies with the physical domain, with the instinctive action itself, and at other times, rather with the accompanying fantasies and emotions."[317] We are in-between these two poles – sometimes too far towards the instinctive pole, sometimes too far towards the archetypal or spiritual pole. But sometimes the two sides meet insofar as something begins on the instinctive, physical side that can only later be conceived as an idea. Then again, new ideas or an attitude that has changed might influence our instinctive behavior. Woman's attitude during pregnancy is very important. Pregnant women, for whom the maternal-feminine has negative connotations, often suffer from various physical discomforts.

We can see in dreams that sometimes a woman's attitude that is too one-sidedly instinctive can be compensated for or complemented through emphasis on a spiritual view.

On the other hand, an instinctive, more body-oriented behavior frequently appears to be given more weight.[318] I believe it safe to assume that women in our day and age whose behavior is generally much less guided by natural

---

[314] *Ibid.*, § 265

[315] B. Hannah, *The Cat, Dog and Horse Lectures,* ed. by Dean L. Franz, Chiron Publications, Wilmette, Illinois, 1992

[316] C.G. Jung, CW 8, *Instinct and the Unconscious*, § 273

[317] M.-L. von Franz explains this complicated phenomenon in an inimitably simple manner in: *The Psychological Meaning of Redemption Motifs in Fairy Tales*, Inner City Books, 1980, p. 51

instinct than, say, that of a farmer woman of past centuries, dreams of animals particularly frequently. Pregnancy is a time in life when the instincts primarily take charge. And yet, woman of today is perhaps more concerned with the meaning of her task than women were before. Here, she finds herself in deep water, for the meaning and purpose which were still taken for granted by the latter, or rather were never questioned, have largely been lost for today's woman with the disappearance of religious and social traditions. Her desire to have children is rarely due to the family's name having to be handed down or because the court has to have an heir, because this is what she is supposed to do or because the church prescribes it. However, without seeing the meaning of it, one is badly prepared for a transition to a new form of life. The "initiation" into maternity is becoming all too demanding.

As symbols, animals in pregnancy dreams can shed light not only on what the instinct means for the body but also the psyche. Symbols then help to understand what, on the psychic level, is "instinctively right" or "wrong." Likewise, we might say that woman can be put in touch again with her psychic and physical instincts through the animals that appear in her dreams.

When the dreams are about a dog, cat, horse, cow or pig, that is about domesticated animals, we assume that these contents are closer to consciousness and reveal themselves more easily to it than when the dream animals are wild ones or animals going back to a very primitive stage in evolution. According to mythology, the horse and dog, for instance, are mediators between the world of the beyond and the human world.[319] Sometimes dream animals are menacing, dangerous, unnaturally large or small or behave strangely. But they always have something to say about our instincts, how we handle them and consequently how faithful we are to our own, higher code or inner nature. In short, how we relate to our own *raison d'être.*

---

[318] In psychology, body-oriented methods of therapy occasionally have reproached Jungian psychology for being too spiritual and for neglecting the importance of body. Dream images, however, are the most unerring advisor, in order to find the balance between body and soul.

[319] For example, in Egypt, Anubis (jackal) paying his last respects to the dead or the oracle horses of the ancient Germans, who were regarded as the confidants of the gods.

Figure 19. Phanes-Eros in the egg, entwined by a snake

5.1. The Snake and the Tortoise

Vivienne MacKrell

In the history of our world about 190 million years ago, after amphibian life had crept out of the ocean, land-dwelling reptiles developed. This age of reptiles culminated in the dinosaurs – some small and others gigantic. As the climate changed and became colder, this era faded: the dinosaurs died out, and the age of mammals began. Today, there are comparatively few reptiles left, most commonly in the warmer regions of the world. They are all air-breathing, and being poikilotherms, are dependent on the temperature of their surroundings. Many hibernate in cold weather as they cannot tolerate extremes of temperature. They are all oviparous, and most abandon their eggs after laying them in sheltered surroundings. A few incubate their eggs internally, and the young are born alive. Maternal care, as such, is rare. Crocodiles, alligators, turtles and tortoises have persisted more or less unchanged since their very early days; some (including some snakes and lizards) have returned to life in the water but must still surface to breathe. They have horny or scaled skins which, in the turtle and tortoise, generally have the form of a thick, unyielding upper and lower shell within which the legs, tail and head can be withdrawn. They can live to a very old age; some of the giant tortoises can live to at least two hundred years of age. Lizards and snakes belong to the scaled reptile order, but are not such ancient types as the crocodiles and tortoises. Snakes evolved only at the end of the reptile age: there are no limbs, and they developed their familiar and unique swift, sinuous way of moving. Reptiles are most common in the tropics and subtropics; the frequency of their occurrence diminishes as one moves towards the poles. However, a common viper occurs at 67°N and appears in parts of southern Siberia. Hearing has degenerated, but vision, particularly of motion, is highly developed. Snakes have tactile sensation in the tongue, which is also olfactory, as well as in their scales. Especially pit vipers have a temperature sensitive organ to detect heat radiation from their prey.

Man has a deep aversion to most reptiles. Crocodiles and alligators are actively antagonistic if approached; turtles and tortoises usually disregard humanity. Most lizards and snakes prefer to avoid people, but a few may actively attack them. Apparently, human and monkey babies up to 2-3 years old have no fear of snakes and even readily play with them. When older, however – possibly from adult influence – they begin to fear them. Reptiles will approach or attack for food, but one cannot form a relationship with them, nor can they usually be trained. Snakes particularly seem to possess an inhuman, repellent, yet fascinating quality with their unwinking gaze and swift, slithering movements. One factor which seems to have captured man's imagination is the shedding of the snakes' whole skin when it becomes too small as the snake grows. In Antiquity the snake was viewed as the possessor of eternal life, conquering death and renewing itself by shedding its skin. Not all snakes are poisonous, but it was supposed that those which are, carried their own antidote for their own venom.

This lack of relationship to man, their unpredictability and potential danger, made them objects of veneration and fear. Death to man was only too apparent a fate, but the snake was eternal. Something unknown and numinous attracts projections, and the more unknown it is the more emotion is aroused and the greater the attraction or the fear. For primitive man, the psyche was present on the outside, and only in more recent history have projections into the outer world been withdrawn. Phylogenetically, reptiles are far removed from man's developmental history. Psychologically, they represent correspondingly remote layers of the psyche in the collective unconscious – unrelated, impersonal factors that underlie personal psychology. If a reptile appears in a dream, something of far-reaching and basic consequence is imminent sooner or later, which one can try to understand but which one cannot influence or control by willpower.

Anatomically, the vegetative life system and motor reflex responses, the approximately 80% of the nervous system over which one has little or no control, are associated with the snake brain, the feeling participation mystique of humanity upon which are placed the higher cognitive and voluntary motor centers. The parallel could be said to be the collective unconscious, upon which and from which one's personal psychology is perilously balanced and derived. In Antiquity, it was believed that the psyche, the life soul that lives on after death, was associated with the cerebrospinal marrow, and that after death, this turned into a snake which lingered in this form in association with the tomb and represented the genius, the procreative life element, that the psyche was felt to be.[320] The snake is both chthonic and spiritual, and psychologically, the unconscious as such, in both its mysteriously healing and equally dangerous aspects. The poisonous snake carries its own antidote; healing, in its meaning of making whole, comes from the unconscious. Dreams and other messages from the unconscious compensate the ego viewpoint. They try to make the ego aware of something beyond its boundaries. Psychic and psycho-

---

[320] R.B. Onians, *The Origins of European Thought*, Amo Press, 1973, pp. 206 and 249

somatic symptoms (which can be very debilitating) are a further stimulus for the enlargement of a too constricted ego consciousness. In Jung's view, a neurosis is the attempt of the unconscious to promote healing.

When a snake dream comes, it indicates that consciousness is especially far away from instinct. The conscious attitude is too much aligned with outer collective conventional precepts, which is particularly a problem for women in Western society. As there is no religious image for instinctually related pregnancy, one could expect the appearance of compensatory symbols in dreams such as the snake and other reptiles.

The snake is a paradoxical symbol and represents both instinct and spirit; it contains the opposites. In Christianity it was equated with Satan. In Norse mythology, as the Midgard serpent, it was the enemy of the upper god world. At Delphi, Apollo killed the python and took over the oracle from Gaia, but in Epidaurus, the snake was the healing companion of Asklepios. In the fairy tale "Three Snake Leaves," it brings healing, and in "The White Snake,"[321] the king, by eating the snake, gains access to the divine wisdom of Nature. In alchemy, the snake was the Uroborous but also Mercurius, who contains all the opposites and has the mercurial serpent aspect: it was related to the lapis, the transformative substance. In Jung's model of psychic activity, using the terms of the spectrum with the infrared (instinct) and the ultraviolet (spirit) poles, the snake carries both. The instinct manifests in matter, and the spirit – its meaning – manifests as an archetypal image. Sometimes the snake has wings, which would emphasize the spiritual aspect. The symbology of the snake is so vast that no attempt will be made to encompass it in this short chapter; it would need a book of its own. Some brief references are made in the text; the reader is referred to the notes below for some helpful amplifications.[322]

The following dream comes from the same lady who dreamt two dreams in the dog section. They were those of the puppy with the peacock (No. 78) and Anubis (No. 84). At the time of this dream she was 3 months pregnant.

Dream No. 46:

> *I dream about a metallic snake, it has something like sections, it is in my garden. I take my little daughter aside. It becomes real, poisonous, disgusting, black, it curls up. With large and black chimney scissors I catch its head and dominate or kill it (it is not dangerous anymore).*

---

[321] The complete Grimm's Fairy Tales, Pantheon Books Inc., Random House, 1972, pp. 94 and 98

[322] An excellent survey of snake symbolism by Marie-Louise von Franz can be found in C.G. Jung, *Kindertraumseminar*, Walter Verlag, Olten, 1984, p. 254. See also Hans Leisegang, *The Mystery of the Serpent in The Mysteries*, Bollingen Series XXX2, Pantheon Books, New York, 1955.

The dreamer also said that the snake was a mechanical toy – at first black, then yellowish. Chimney scissors are used when a fire is made, but in the dream they were larger than normal. I am presuming that these scissors were a tool which was used to grasp the wood or coal to put it on the fire, or to rearrange the fire so that it burned well. The garden was part of her grandmother's home, where she was looked after as a child. She grew up there (with her parents) in a strict, secluded family until she was eighteen.

The dreamer thus spent her formative childhood and adolescent years in subjection to the strict, controlling rules and advice of her family. Any outside influence was presumably viewed as threatening. She was not permitted to develop in the way her own instincts could have led her or to make her own decisions: "the family knew best." As she was an only child, she would be even more concentrated upon. This could have built up in her a rigid framework of unconscious precepts, which she automatically obeyed until such time as it became imperative for her to recognize and confront them in consciousness. In the religious sphere, especially in Catholicism, any spontaneous psychic manifestation, religious experience, past or present, has to find its place within the church dogma. Personal contact with the divine is regulated and mediated by the church to fit its rules, deviation is not permitted. Many meditative sects also prescribe a definite subject for meditation, where one has to follow the guru and his rules. Not so long ago in Europe, those who did not conform to the regulations were regarded as heretics and frequently burned at the stake. The individual approach to the feminine, with a personal relationship between man and woman, starting with the troubadours and the Courts of Love in the 10-11th centuries was promptly squashed. Women who were unusual – in that they were individuals rather than part of the collective image – were burned as witches; one of the last such cases occurred only two hundred years ago. We no longer do this, but anyone who does not fit is still regarded with distinct suspicion or even with active antagonism. This not only applies in the religious sphere but also in secular conventions. These conventions of collective consciousness may change but he or she who does not conform is regarded as a black sheep by the white flock. On a larger scale, this can result in tyrannical despotism with the subjugation or obliteration of the opposition. In a family, this could appear as: "This is the way we do things, do it our way." "Take our advice." "You are only a child, do what you are told." There is an underlying power: "Our way is *the way*, follow it" – veiled by an ostensibly sweet concern for the child's welfare but with disregard for its individuality.

Pregnant women are often almost smothered by advice. I remember one young woman in labor with her first baby who repeatedly said, "Just wait until I see my grandmother." Apparently she had been told dreadful stories about what could happen, and what to do if it did. Her labor was not particularly difficult, and as she put it, she was going to "tick the old witch off." Perhaps the only advice needed for a pregnant woman is to not take any advice, but to listen to what her own heart and guts tell her. Within this dreamer, a set of rigid, mechanical rules is coming alive – the rules in which the manifestations of the chthonic spirit, representative of the vital processes far from consciousness deep in the unconscious, have been compartmentalized. Jung says, "Snake dreams always indicate a discrepancy between the attitude of the conscious mind and instinct, the snake being a personification of the threatening aspect of that conflict."[323] At first, the snake was black – the unknown – then it became yellowish. Yellow is a color associated with light and intuition, indicating a possibility of conscious awareness. One has to become aware of one's unknown complexes before they can be confronted. So this lady is threatened by a conflict between her own personal instincts and the precepts instilled into her in her youth. She puts her young daughter aside: her childish femininity cannot deal with this, it needs adult ego action. She finds the snake disgusting and poisonous, and it has to be killed with force and determination. The rigid values within herself have to be destroyed with the same rigidity. Friends and relatives may say, "Don't do this or that," but she can successfully contend with this in the outer world only when she has consolidated her own inner values. Symbolically, she does this by dominating or killing the snake so that it is no longer dangerous. She uses scissors which are used to handle the fire. Fire is a transformative (or destructive) element which can be equated with the libido and emotions necessary for transformation – the alchemical retort has to be heated. So with the instrument she uses to keep her own transformation going, she depotentiates her own threat and kills the danger. One does not destroy collective values: they remain as they are. The snake's tail, symbolically the most dubious part of it, is not mentioned. This lady has to stop listening to the do's and don'ts from others, which constellate her own vulnerability, and has to try hard to become aware of her own feeling values and instincts and thus destroy her own rigid patterns. Childishness has to be set aside, ego determination is now needed to keep the fire going and to transform herself.

The following dream occurred in the first pregnancy of a twenty-six-year-old woman. The time of its occurrence is not known. It was a planned pregnancy.

Dream No. 47:

> *My husband and I were out walking in the landscape. We were climbing a mountain. Suddenly I almost stepped on a viper. I am very scared of snakes. I had a slight shock, but I talked to myself, saying: "Do not panic,*

[323] C.G. Jung, CW 5, § 615, translated by R.F.C. Hull, Bollingen Series XX, Princeton University Press, 1970.

just go peacefully in the other direction." The mountain behind me was rather steep, so I could not turn back. I turned to the right and there was another snake! I had a terrible shock, and it was as if I had a black-out in my memory. I do not know how I came down from the mountain. My husband must have helped me. I had just one thought in my head."This is too much, I cannot come through this passage."

Two days later, the dreamer had a miscarriage. She stated that she has always felt that the snake experience triggered the miscarriage, and that in the dream, she seemed to realize this when she saw the second snake. She has had two uneventful pregnancies since then, the first a year later.

Doubling of an image in a dream indicates that it is at the brink of conscious realization, and here there were two snakes. She described the first one as a viper, which could imply a malignant, poisonous snake. Suddenly it was there, and she almost stepped on it. One of the factors making the snake very uncanny and alien to man is its ability to appear and to disappear, suddenly and unexpectedly. The unpredictable can provoke fear especially if it is not understood. She felt she could avoid this snake by turning to another path to the right, the direction of consciousness, she attempts to repress it. However, the right path was blocked, too, and she could not go back, as it was too steep. She and her husband had climbed too steep a path and had become separated from the instinctual realm. The two snakes, possibly poisonous here, represent a definite threat and point to a physical danger; something material is going to happen in the outer world within her body. In the dream, this was a tremendous shock. The ego got into a state of panic and blacked out; she could not realize what was happening. She was not aware of how she got down from the mountain. The animus presumably helped as she was reduced to a purely reflexive activity. She felt that she could not come through this passage, possibly meaning that she would not be able to continue this pregnancy, which for her would be a transition from young woman to mother. To miscarry is to have one's maternal instinct denied material fulfillment. She did not have the support of her instincts as she was too high up, away from her body.

She felt that this dream triggered the miscarriage. This could be so, since a shock sometimes does, although I feel the dream could be seen more as a warning of an impending event.

The following dream occurred in the "last days of pregnancy" of a thirty-year-old woman who had had two uneventful previous pregnancies, four and six years earlier. At twenty-eight weeks, there was a threat of premature labor, which subsided after a week of bed-rest. There had been no reason to suppose that this delivery could be any problem. However, two weeks past her due date the baby had to be delivered by Cesarean section due to fetal distress, and the umbilical cord was found to be wound twice around the baby's neck. The baby fortunately was unharmed and healthy.

Dream No. 48:

> *I was at the hospital when a nurse came in and put the baby in my arms. There was a bathing tub where childbirth would happen. The water was clean. Suddenly we saw a snake moving in the bathing tub. First it was flat and transparent, but soon it was hard and coiled. I thought this was interesting because I compared it with the movements of the baby inside my womb. The other people were frightened and wanted to kill the snake. Tranquil and without fear I told them it was going away and would not harm anyone.*

It was not stated whether or not the dreamer was anxious because she was overdue. In my experience, when this happens there is a greater tendency for the mother to wonder if everything is going to be all right – will there be anything the matter with the baby? – and so on, and she had also earlier had the threat of going into premature labor. In view of the later physical events this dream could be seen as precognitive.

The focus of this dream is upon the delivery of the baby. The setting is in a hospital, a place of healing and where her baby will be delivered, and a nurse puts the baby safely in her arms. The bathing tub was full of clean water: no delivery had taken place there. In all religions, water is life substance; its necessity for mortal life makes it a very appropriate vehicle to carry the symbolic necessities for inner and immortal life, the life of wisdom and the spirit. Then, in the water where the delivery of a new life was anticipated, a fear-provoking element, the snake, appears. Something beyond her control threatens in the area of the baby's expected delivery. At first, it is almost not there, a mobile, vague threat; then it becomes three-dimensional and hard, coiled in a spiral, indicating the possibility of a negative fate for mother and child. New life and new death are close to each other as the dreamer compares the snake's movement with that of her baby in the womb. Her fearful companions, unknown shadow and possibly animus factors, want to kill the snake, but she remains calm, knowing that it will go away. If something unforeseen occurs in labor, anxieties promptly arise in both the mother and the attendants. Something must be done quickly, and the speed and fear of the outcome can be disorienting, most particularly for the mother, whose fear of the unknown ahead can surface and even cause her to panic. Thus the emphasis is that she should remain tranquil: a danger is going to arise, but it will go away, and as she has been told in the beginning of the dream, her baby will be safely in her arms, brought to her by a helpful feminine figure.

The dreamer of the next dream was thirty years old. Her first pregnancy, six years earlier, was ended by an induced abortion. In this, her second pregnancy, she was approximately thirty-five weeks pregnant. Four weeks earlier, there had been a threat of premature labor. She went into labor at term, developed a high fever and the baby, a healthy girl with no signs of infection, was delivered by Cesarean section. Although the cervix was well-dilated, vaginal delivery was not possible due to fetal malpresentation. The outer circumstances were uncertain. She desired this pregnancy, although it was unplanned, but her husband was doubtful about it, and future divorce was a possibility for her.

Dream No. 49:

> *I remember we wanted to unveil life's mystery. My husband, me and other people (it is not very clear to me who they are) are all sitting on a bed. There are brown seeds on the bed. They are about 3 cm in diameter. From inside, little gray snakes appear. There is an intense light inside the seeds, like a gleaming eye. We are a bit afraid of this. Three little snakes start to germinate and to dance in the air in front of us. This is a moment of great fear. We try to relate cautiously to the snakes, looking for some mystery's discovery.*

The start of this dream presents the need to try to understand the mystery of life rather than to concentrate on outer problems. In company with her husband, possibly an ambivalent or negative animus figure and unknown human psychic factors, she sits on a bed. A bed is a place of instinctual life: one is born there and dies there, one makes love there, it is where the opposites can unite or become evident, and most importantly, it is where in dreams and sleep one can become aware of the messages from the unconscious. The seeds are brown, the color of earth and the material reality of Mother Nature. Seeds are germs of new life, new potentials, these are like gleaming eyes with their own intense light. In his discussion of the unconscious as a multiple consciousness, Jung says: "Since consciousness has always been described in terms of the behavior of light, it is in my view not too much to assume that these multiple luminosities correspond to tiny conscious phenomena."[324] This is not ego consciousness but a consciousness inherent in the unconscious. The gleaming eye with its own light implies the presence of a subject within the unconscious. Insofar as an eye is a mandala, these eyes could be called the eyes of the Self. An impersonal irrational factor is alive and watching, something other than the ego has a consciousness. To the intellectual, rational, controlling mind this can be frightening. Three gray snakes develop from these seeds (which are 3 cm in diameter) and dance in the air. "Three signifies a unity, which dynamically engenders self-expanding, irreversible processes in matter and in our consciousness."[325] Gray is an in-between color, a mixture, con-

---

[324] C.G. Jung, CW 8, § § 388-396; quotation is from § 396. See also CW 14, *The Scintilla*, § § 42-50.

[325] Marie-Louise von Franz, *Number and Time*, Northwestern University Press, Evanston, Illinois, 1974, p. 106. Cf. also Chapter 6

scious or unconscious, of the black and white opposites. Essentially earth-bound animals, the chthonic snakes are dancing in the air – in their more spiritual realm. Earth and air come together, black and white come together, and the dynamic process is irreversible. Something which has its own light wants and needs to come into ego consciousness to supplement a perhaps too narrow conventional attitude.

One is reminded of the dreams of Kekulé of the dancing atoms and snakes, one of which caught hold of its own tail, which gave him the inspiration for the formula of the hitherto unknown benzene ring basis of organic chemistry.[326] It is parallel in that Kekulé's two dreams and the dream above point to a mystery. Dancing is a movement in harmony with something outside oneself; the dance of the atoms is not under conscious control, nor is the generation and development of a new life. One can choose to try to become pregnant or not; it just does or does not happen, but upon accepting it – not aborting it as she did before – it proceeds independently of conscious control. The pregnancy was unplanned – fate took a hand in it – an essential part of this lady's individuation. The idea that came to Kekulé in dreams had to be worked on by him to develop it. Similarly, this dreamer needs to work on the nature of her dream, and ask herself what this pregnancy, and this new dynamic process mean, both personally and more generally. She needs to reflect on the incarnation of the feminine spirit in matter, and to try to understand the way in which she serves and plays a part in the mystery. The lysis of the dream indicates a willingness to try to cooperate. The snake's appearance can also warn of the possibility of danger ahead in material reality, as indeed there proved to be.

In the week after the delivery, she had another two dreams both on the same night. The second dream has been interpreted in Chapter 3.2.

Dream No. 50:

> I am fighting with a prehistoric being, perhaps a dinosaur. All his entrails are out in the fight, but something remains latent as a seed for its subsequent development. However I have the feeling, at least for this time, the battle was won. I am playing with little figures of clay. There is a little girl of clay, and she comes into life like a human being.

The theme of this dream is a battle with a prehistoric antagonist: the dreamer is fighting a cold-blooded, destructive power. In outer life, there had been a conflict from which she and the baby both emerged alive and well. In pregnancy and at the time of birth, the feminine archetype of the mother is

---

[326] These dreams are detailed and discussed by Marie-Louise von Franz in: *Projection and Re-Collection in Jungian Psychology*, translated by William H. Kennedy, Open Court, La Salle and London, 1980, pp. 69 and 70

constellated, both in its womb aspect as a positive source of life and in its negative, destructive, death-like tomb aspect. The entrails, the part of the body which digest and absorb food, have been torn out, and the battle is won. The negative mother, the regressive pull of unconsciousness, can no longer eat everything up. For a woman with a negative mother complex, with doubts about her own feminine ground, the negative animus (the being was said to be masculine) can "eat up" all the "food" offered. For example, a woman in her first pregnancy wanted to breastfeed her baby when it was born. Her mother said, "I couldn't – so you won't be able to either," which reinforced her doubts about her own abilities to do so. However the negative mother and negative animus, which often go hand in hand to stifle the natural feminine development of a woman, lost, and the woman could successfully breastfeed. One could say that the positive nurturing aspect triumphed; her positive instincts won. In this dream, the battle had been won at least for this time, but something remained latent as a seed for future development. Archetypes are eternal: they cannot be destroyed. It remains to be seen in which image they will appear again.

The next dream occurred on the first pregnancy of a twenty-seven-year-old married woman. She had it in the night before she went to know the result of the examinations that would confirm her pregnancy. (She was about three months pregnant at the time.) She said that the dream atmosphere was uncanny and very impressive. A. is her best girlfriend from her adolescent time (about twelve years of age), and A. is now married with two children.

Dream No. 51:

> I was in the house of A., but it was an unknown house. It was night, and I wanted to close all the doors, because I felt fear that someone will come from the street and try to enter the house.
> Now I am in her room, and I looked outside through a door, and I noticed that two boys of about twelve years old came near. I tried to put them out of the house, but then I noticed that in the entrance of the house there was a huge snake lying there.
> I go to the main room and there were many other snakes, they were large, colorful and with strange drawings in their skins, like geometric patterns – spirals, labyrinths, etc. I am afraid and go up on the table, but the snakes didn't attack me and stayed on the floor, motionless.
> From the table, I looked down to the right side and I see two huge eggs, 25 to 30 cm each. They were different from each other and belonged to two snakes, and each egg had the color of the snake to whom they belonged.
> Now comes a small child and takes the egg of the snake that is more near the table where I am. I tell the child to let down the egg, on the floor. The

child let it fall but to my surprise, the egg didn't break, it was hard like of a coconut.'

The setting is at night in an unknown house, but it is that of A., whom the dreamer has known since adolescence – the time when the feminine in a woman begins to take shape. In the antique world, the chthonic underworld mystery cults, such as those of Isis and Eleusis, held their initiation rites at night. The light of solar consciousness, with its rational collective precepts, has gone, and the illumination comes from the unconscious itself in the form of mystery. In the Sabazius mysteries, the snake was the healing, transformative representative of the God. In the temple of Asklepios, the night-time incubation in the sanctuary brought the dream or vision of healing. Asklepios was most often depicted with a snake. The snake entwined around the staff persists as the caduceus, the emblem of medicine today. The ascent of the snake from earth to light symbolizes the rise of psyche towards conscious understanding. A. has two children, but the dreamer has had none. So she is in the house of her friendly, maternal shadow – psychologically, an unknown side of her own personality which is not hostile to her. She wants no intruders in this house; she is afraid of outside influence. A woman with a negative mother complex is insecure in her own identity as a woman, unsure of the grounds she stands on and pessimistic. Only when she can look inside herself can she find this identity, so that she is not dependent on the influence of others and what they say either positively or negatively to, or about her. A room of one's own is usually a place of personal privacy, and this is what she needs: a place of her own in which she can reflect and find her own personal values. She sees two young boys, youthful animi, through a door. Her Logos principle is young – perhaps the collective femininity she has seen before and adopted as her own is too old. Jung says that, in a woman's dream, a young boy represents an honest endeavor. Doubling indicates a possibility of consciousness, and she has a need of youthful spontaneity and enthusiasm. However, she wants to push them out of the house, yet finds a huge snake lying across the entrance, preventing her from doing so. Snakes were long seen as guardians of the treasure in mythology. In Greece, in the garden of the Hesperides, a snake guarded the tree that bore the golden apples; in Rome, it was seen as the house fertility daimon. In India, serpents were supposed to carry a precious jewel in their heads and were the keepers of the life energy in earthly waters; they also guarded the vast treasures beneath the sea. "One of their important functions was that of door guardians ... they frequently appear at portals of Hindu and Buddhist shrines."[327] A giant cobra sheltered the Buddha from a rainstorm whilst he was meditating in a state of bliss. This woman has to keep her own

---

[327] Heinrich Zimmer, *Myths and Symbols in Indian Art and Civilization*, Bollingen Series VI, Princeton University Press, 1946, Chapter 3: "The Guardians of Life"

personality together, for it is her treasure. She must cut off outside influence, but retain what is part of her – the boys. This would be to introvert, to meditate on her dreams and on the meaning and nature of her new endeavor – in this case, her pregnancy.

In the main room, she sees many large, colorful snakes. She is afraid, but does not panic and gets up on a table, which would indicate an elevation to a more spiritual realm. Food is usually put on a table, which could also be taken to mean the food in and through which the inner world is made manifest. When one baby is conceived, a seemingly banal human event, the whole mystery of the Cosmos is repeated. The snakes, motionless, do not attack her; she is observing an irrational, impersonal event. The snakes are colored, implying life rather than death. Throughout Australia the Aborigines have a mythological figure, the Rainbow Snake, which is sometimes male and sometimes female. It is the embodiment of fertility and is always associated with the coming of rain. It is said to be the maker of the road along which preexistent spirit children enter the mother's womb. In a shamanic cult, the shaman has it as a spirit familiar and can use the rainbow to travel through the sky. Another snake associated with color is Quetzalcoatl, the Plumed Serpent in Mexico, the dying and resurrecting culture-bringer and hero. The snakes have drawings on their skin: geometric patterns and not random scribblings.

Figure 20. Labyrinth on the floor of the Cathedral of Chartres, France

Labyrinths of different types, sometimes in combination with spirals, are frequent in prehistoric rock engravings, often associated with female figurines. An abstract or geometric pattern is an attempt to express something in its essence rather than in its outer apparent form. Spirals signify a developing process with their rotation about a center which Jung has used as a simile for the individuation process. One is reminded also of the Kundalini snake (in Tantric Yoga) at which Sakti, the world-creating energy, lies quiescent in a spiral coil around the Shiva lingam on the lowest chakra, Muladhara. A labyrinth is designed to protect a center, which can be a religious temenos, or a consecrated ground with a link between the worlds of god and man. To enter such a labyrinth and follow its path is an initiation, and an endeavor to reach the center which is a place of psychological rebirth. Theseus, a hero of Greek mythology, met and slew the Minotaur in the Cretan labyrinth.

There are labyrinths on the floor of some European churches. In Chartres Cathedral, for example, penitents walked the labyrinth on their knees, and it was felt to be the equivalent of a pilgrimage to the Holy Places. In Malekula, a female devouring ghost figure sits outside a cave with labyrinthine designs on the ground before it. The newly dead have to traverse this to join the ancestors and renew life by joining them. The ghost erased half of the pattern, and the newly dead had to be able to complete it in order to pass to the beyond.

In the early centuries of the Christian church, certain Gnostic Christian sects honored Christ as a snake. The Perates held that the son, the Logos, was placed midway between the Father and Matter and as a Serpent moved eternally between them. The Serpent brought down the paternal models and ideas and imprinted them in Matter, and carried back up again those who had been awakened from sleep and resumed the features of the Father. The Ophites honored the snake in the Garden of Eden as the first appearance of Christ. They celebrated a Eucharist with bread in which their live snake had rolled, and kissed the snake. There is an Orphic cosmogonic myth reported by Damascius in which a serpent called Ageless Time (Chronos) or Unchanging Herakles was born from water and earth. It had wings and the heads of a bull and a lion on it with the face of a god in between. This serpent produced an egg from which was born the Orphic god, Phanes (the shining one), or in another version, Zeus, the orderer of all things. In yet another version, the egg split into two, producing Ge (Earth) and Ouranos (Heaven). Both Phanes and the *deus leontacephalus*, Zurvan (endless time) are depicted with a snake wrapped around them. The former is shown within an egg-shaped border of the zodiac signs, and the latter has them on the body between the coils of the snake. It is also said that the zodiac is borne on the back of the snake, which would express the time aspect of eternity in relation to the star constellations and thus to the projections humanity has made upon them.

The snakes of the dream could be seen as the carriers of a timeless mystery of creation, as mediators between the beyond and this world, and between divinity and matter. They are marked by lines expressing links between the worlds of God and man, and the spirals of creative energy as a developing process. Although they are motionless, they have the colors of life. In terms of the development of human consciousness, they are world-creating, and two of these snakes have eggs that correspond to them in color, again the threshold of the number two. Psychologically, an egg is an image of a creative germ of the preconscious totality. It contains everything within itself for development, but it must, in order to fulfill its potentiality, be incubated and given time and space in which to develop – that is, it must be sheltered, meditated upon, and kept warm and alive by concentrated attention. These are huge eggs, which could well hold a correspondingly huge potential, and they are on her right. An unknown small child takes the egg nearest to her and lets it fall. This could illustrate that either a childish shadow cannot destroy the potential, or that a divine, childlike part of her shows her that it is unbreakable. The Self is indestructible, but the attempt for its realization has to be made by ego consciousness; here, the potential is shown to the dreamer, and a task is laid before her.

The further course of this pregnancy was not given, but here it seems to me that the snake does not necessarily appear to warn of possible physical problems. They are immobile and show the dreamer, who was said to have a very negative mother complex, the creative possibilities of her pregnancy in terms of psychic development. She has to relate to her instincts and find their spiritual meaning, which is inherent in both the snakes and their eggs. The action in the dream is that of the dreamer and her psychic components, on the background provided by the snakes.

This is a very big dream with its connotations of the world-creating possibilities of an ego consciousness developed from and in harmony with the Self. The snake is the timeless link between the beyond and the dreamer, bearing the potentialities of the development of the microcosm in and from the macrocosm. In number terms, the pleroma, the non-one one, has given birth to the future, the threshold two, as there cannot be a one without another.

This dream occurred at approximately nineteen weeks in the third pregnancy of a thirty-two-year-old lady. The first pregnancy ended in a spontaneous abortion at three months, the second was uneventful, and a healthy baby girl was delivered vaginally at full term. In this pregnancy, she had to have a Cesarean section because of fetal distress: the cord was extremely long with two knots in it and was wound around the baby's neck and arm. The baby boy was healthy, and there were no further problems with mother or baby. She said that she had had no feelings of panic in labor or concerning the emergency Cesarean section. She stated that in the dream when the snake opened its mouth she felt that it wanted to tell her something. She felt good when she woke up from the dream.

Dream No. 52:

I am in the dining-room of my parents with my brother and sister. A fat grass-snake with a yellow stripe on its back is passing by. My brother wants to kill it, but not me, because I know they are useful. I go outside into the garden, the snake following. It seems to be nervous. I suggest it could go underneath the hen-house, but that is not a good place. There is a hole near a root, but the earth is too moist. Then, back in the garden, there is a small, deserted hut, about 1 meter high. One of its sides is protected from the rain, and the earth is quite dry. My brother is following now. I tell him that the snake would be all right there and that my father would not be able to harm it. I open something like a door, and then, with a pick, I am digging a hole into the ground. I tell my brother that we could

176

even find a treasure here. Then the snake looks at me, opening its mouth. It seems to be pressing. It is placing itself in the dip I have made, and I explain to my brother that it is about to lay some eggs. But it is giving birth to another snake, like itself but smaller. It was high time! I shut the door, and I feel confirmed. We are looking for a name, and I remember we found something that begins with "pump ..." Then I can see a coach with many people driving into the garden. One of the faces is laughing like mad.

The initial setting of this dream is in the house of the dreamer's parents. She is with her brother and sister in the room where the family food is eaten – where the precepts and values which they have to conform to are fed to the children. This lady said that her father was dominating, destructive to her and an alcoholic – a negative influence. The paternal Logos principle was negative. Her mother also was ruled by her husband. In this room, the parents are not there, and no food is mentioned; there is nothing she needs anymore. Her brother, who is extremely introverted, would be an animus figure in touch with her inner world, and her sister, a shadow figure. Three figures (the number three has been discussed in the dog chapter), and then the snake comes, the unknown fourth, to complete the quaternio. Four is the number of individuation. Her brother wants to kill the snake: the irrational is not acceptable in the parental house, but she says no and accepts it. She tells him she knows that they are useful. To be useful implies to be of a beneficial nature. She leaves the house, and the snake follows her. Snakes do not move in straight lines: they oscillate around the mid-position of a line. Jung said: "What Nature wants us to do is to move with a snake-like motion. ... The snake is the symbol of the great wisdom of Nature, for the too direct way is not the best way; the crooked way, the detour, is the shorter way."[328] The snake has a yellow stripe on its back, indicating that the way it travels is illuminated.

So, leaving her family complexes behind her, she goes out into Nature with the snake and tries to find a place for it apart from the family house. A sister shadow remains in the house, and she has to become aware that it represents a regressive pull to her old ways of being. The actual garden (as it was in the dream) was extremely large – a garden where domestic animals and chickens were kept. The hen house had a too wet or unconscious ground. As she is pregnant, she has to avoid the clucking maternal quality with its ready-made hole in the ground. She finds a small deserted hut with dry earth, and she opens the door. Children like to have little huts or tree houses to play in; this could be a necessary return to the area of her childlike innocence. Perhaps this could also be seen as a need to discard the overly rational conventions of the collective. One has to open the door, just as Jung did when he built little

[328] C.G. Jung, Visions Seminars, Book I, Spring, Zurich, 1976, pp. 84-5

villages and a church with stones at the shore of the lake. Her brother animus now follows her, and she tells him that she has found a new place, where the negative father complex cannot harm the wisdom of Nature. The first image of the masculine principle is the personal father. If he is negative, he can paralyze his daughter and cut her off from her feminine instincts so that she is left with only collective opinions and false spontaneity. This is well-illustrated in the fairy tale, "The Girl without Hands," which Marie-Louise von Franz has discussed in depth.[329]

One has to tell the animus how one feels oneself (one's own values), acknowledging his collective opinions but not necessarily adopting them as one's own. This she had already done, so now he follows her, and she tells him that she feels the treasure could be in her own earth. She has to work, to dig into it and make a nest where the snake will be safe. One can often have an intuition but then one does have to work to explore its potentialities. She felt the snake was trying to tell her something; earlier in the dream, it had seemed nervous, but now it settles itself in the dip she has made. She follows the snake's needs, and through this, she follows the guide of the absolute knowledge of the unconscious, and digs. She feels it is going to lay eggs, or produce potentials: it almost seemed to be in labor. Contrary to her expectations, it gives birth to another snake – smaller but like itself. The maternal wisdom of Nature, if sheltered and taken care of in one's own earth and by one's own efforts, can give birth to one's own instincts. It was important for her to have left her parent's house, for the snake was nervous there and judging by subsequent events wanted urgently to give birth. She felt it was high time; she had succeeded in separating from parental influences to find her own potential. She shuts the door to exclude outside influence and feels confirmed; that is, she now has the potential to become herself. The search for a name implies that something expressing the nature of the to-be-named has to be found. Jung says: "The act of naming is, like baptism, extremely important as regards the creation of personality, for magical power has been attributed to the name since time immemorial. ... Therefore to give a name means to give power, to invest with a definite personality or soul."[330] In the Biblical story, God created all the living creatures before He created Adam and brought them to Adam to see how he would name them. A name brings something to consciousness. A pump is something that raises liquid or a gas by increasing the pressure on it, so it would seem that the snake could give this woman increased access to two of the necessities of life: water and air.

This dream illustrates that one has to work on one's own realities and find out what one's instincts really are, rather than what one has been taught they

---

[329] Marie-Louise von Franz, *The Feminine in Fairy Tales*, Shambhala, Boston, 1993, pp. 80-103
[330] C.G. Jung, CW 5, § 274

were. One has to step out of the framework of collective precepts, go with the snake and become aware of its needs in order to find one's own wisdom, born of the eternal wisdom of Nature, which carries its own light. The snake is helpful in this dream. It points the way for the dreamer and shows her where she has to work. She has to introvert – to go into her own earth. She has to follow her dreams and fantasies and thereby allow the fertile wisdom of Nature to express itself.

The Tortoise

Among North American Indians and in Asia, there exists a widespread belief that the earth rested on the back of a tortoise or turtle. An Iroquois creation myth says that, before the earth was made, a woman fell down from heaven into the primordial sea. She fell onto the great turtle, which collected her on its back together with earth from the depths. Thus, the first land was made with the turtle as the supporting center. In inner Asia, a Buriat story tells that in the beginning there was nothing but water and a turtle. Then God turned the turtle on its back and built the world on its stomach. In India, the world rested on the back of four elephants who stood upon the great tortoise. As an avatar of Vishnu, the tortoise supported Mount Mandara when the gods churned the cosmic Milky Ocean to obtain Amrita, the elixir of immortal life. In China, where it is associated with the yin, the feminine principle, the turtle

Figure 21. Churning the Milky Ocean

179

symbolized the universe – its dome-shaped back shell representing the heavens and its flat belly shell being the earth. Between these two is the tortoise – the mediator between heaven and earth, the transcendent function. The Lo Shu mathematical order was said to be the gift of the turtle from the River Lo. The shell, when heated by fire, was used as an oracle to reveal the will of the gods. A life elixir could also be prepared from the shell. In Egypt, the tortoise, as well as the beetle and the frog were seen as heralds of the rise of the fertilizing Nile. The Dogons are a tribe in Mali near Timbuktu on the old trade route between Egypt and West Africa. According to their mythology, Amma, a creation god, divided and transformed a "placenta" into the sun and the tortoise. The placenta was presumably a generative prima materia. The tortoise formed in this way was a representation of the world and all its living things; its upper shell became the heavens and its lower one the earth. The tortoise was equal to the sun, which became one of the guardians of the world. Also, the sun and the earth are twins because they both come from the same "placenta." The tortoise, represented diagramatically, was associated with the passage of the sun through the sky; its liver reflected the apparently varying sizes of the sun as its altitude changed.

The head of Dogon families keeps a tortoise as the guardian of the world, and this tortoise is always given a taste of food and water before the family itself eats.[331] It is interesting that this myth from Africa has concepts of the tortoise as heaven and earth similar to those of the Chinese.

In Greek mythology, Hermes made the lyre from the shell of a tortoise and then gave it to Apollo in return for being allowed to keep the cows he had stolen. Plucking the strings of the lyre created music from the air, one of the gifts of Apollo. By taking the lyre, Apollo gained access to the world of Nature. The tortoise links the heavenly Apollo with the chthonic Hermes, the guide of souls. Thus the chthonic tortoise with the energy of earth and water can gain access to the celestial sphere of Apollo, one of whose maxims was: "Know thyself."

One of the most notable features of a turtle or a tortoise is its ability to withdraw its legs, head and tail into its own house. They move steadily and slowly and can be very long-lived. In a dream, it would indicate a change, possibly far in the future, and questionably for better or for worse. One should also exercise the tortoise's prudence and reticence and remain in one's own psychic house, and not become dissociated.

The following dream occurred at seventeen weeks in the first pregnancy of a thirty-one-year-old lady. The pregnancy was planned. It was a tiring pregnancy with nausea, back pain, severe uterine contractions and an inguinal

[331] For further details see M. Griaule et G. Dieterlin, *Le Renard Pâle*, Institut de l'Ethnologie, Paris, 1965, pp. 196-200

hernia. A healthy baby girl was delivered by Cesarean section because of a narrow pelvis.

Dream No. 53:

> *Suddenly I found my tortoise again. She was completely neglected. Her shell on the stomach side was softened because of a lack of chalk and food. I am feeding her, and she staggers around busily all over my kitchen.*

This lady had lost her tortoise, which was female; that is, she had lost sight of her personal feminine identity. She was no longer in touch with her instincts or their spiritual meaning, and the possibility of relating them to each other was also lost. Apparently, most of the neglect was seen on her earth or material reality side. The pregnancy was said to be tiring with many bodily symptoms. Very often, the expectation for women today is that they should be able to carry on as usual whatever happens, and this perhaps is what she has tried to do. Sometimes it seems that the idea of having a baby is uppermost, and the actuality of the physical and psychic demands of pregnancy are not adequately taken into consideration. There is a lack of harmony between spirit and instinct. Here, Apollo's "Know thyself" would be very relevant. Fortunately, she finds her tortoise, which indicates that what she has to do is to search for it. She has to prudently withdraw into her own psychic house. If she is extroverted, this could mean she should introvert and give more time and attention to her inner world. If she is introverted, she has to pay attention to her physical reality and give some attention to the outer world. In either case, she has to try to unite the two worlds. She feeds the tortoise, which would be to give careful consideration to what her dreams or active imagination say to her and to pay attention to what her body needs and what it says to her. Psyche and matter could be said to be two sides of the same unknown, and this unknown can "speak" through either, or through both at the same time. In material fact, pregnancy needs an adequate intake of calcium, the main constituent of chalk, for fetal bone formation – so this could be a message that she should be careful that she maintain adequate nutritional standards. The result of feeding the tortoise in the dream is that she starts moving busily around the kitchen. "Historically, the kitchen is the center of the house and is therefore the place of the house cults. The house gods were placed on the kitchen stove, and in prehistoric times, the dead were buried under the hearth. As the place where food is chemically transformed, the kitchen is analogous to the stomach. It is the center of emotion in its searching and consuming aspect, and in its illuminating and warming function, both of which show that the light of wisdom only comes out of the fire of passion."[332]

The tortoise then would be an entity whose activity reveals itself in the emotional sphere. The cold-blooded reptile and what it symbolically represents has to be brought into contact with the heat and light of emotion in order to be understood. It is perhaps difficult to feel enthusiastic about pregnancy when one is burdened by unpleasant physical symptoms, but negative as well as positive emotions carry their own light.

I feel that this woman, who possibly has a negative mother complex, would be helped by intensive depth analysis to help her find her own psychic and physical realities. It sounds as though the Cesarean section was known to be a possibility if not a certainty. Nowadays there is great emphasis placed on natural childbirth, and one might feel that one had failed if one had delivered in another way. According to the nature of the tortoise, it will take time but the dream says that she can find and feed her own heaven and earth if she looks for them. She must feed the tortoise by putting her emotion and energy into it. This is a first pregnancy so it would seem that, apart from the creation of a baby, it is an essential part of the dreamer's own individuation. For her, it is a new step into the world of the maternal feminine mystery and its part in the creation of life.

One cannot draw any firm conclusions from such a small number of dreams. However, I feel that the appearance of a reptile, especially of a snake, should make one more alert to the possibility of a physical complication of pregnancy. Three dreamers of snakes had complications and unplanned Cesarean sections – although the tortoise dreamer also had a Cesarean section. Fortunately, the babies were all born healthy and normal without further complications. Interestingly, the lady who killed the mechanical snake had no problems. One dreamer miscarried. The lady who dreamt of the snake that gave birth said that, from the onset of her labor, she felt "it wasn't quite right," but when the crisis arose, she did not panic: her instinct had warned and supported her.

It is important to remember, particularly in connection with the snake, that pregnancy is regulated by psychic and physical forces, of which the ego has little knowledge, and which it cannot control. Dreams bring in images, the objective messages from the Self – the God image in the psyche of man. Jung has defined the Self as the creative, inner guiding and regulating center, as well as the totality of the psyche, of which the ego is only a small part. A dream compensates the deficiencies of the conscious personality; it offers an enlargement of ego perspective. A symbol carries an essential message which, if understood, can enrich the personality of the dreamer. The symbolic image has to be understood not only by personal associations, but by consideration and amplification of the significance that has been attributed to it throughout the history of humankind. The snake has an enormous range of symbolic meanings, and both the snake and tortoise have world-creating mythological

---

[332] Marie-Louise von Franz, *The Interpretation of Fairy Tales*, Spring Publications, N.Y., 1978, p. 90 (revised edition published by Shambhala, Boston, 1996)

and religious associations. In these dreams, emphasis has been placed upon a need for better relationship to instinct, emphasizing that the development of ego consciousness has been too one-sided. Seen in personal terms, their presence in a dream would have the underlying implication that individual ego consciousness is world-creating. Some of the dreams above present the need to see pregnancy as part of the world-creating principle rather than just "having a baby." Pregnancy is also seen as a step in the development of psychic maturity.

We cannot step outside ourselves and see either psyche or matter in an absolute way. We can only view creation with the eyes that the mystery of creation has created. The creation of life is a mystery in both cosmic and personal terms, which we can only circumambulate and honor with both awe and respect.

5.2. Spiders

Irmgard Bosch

The first two dreams of this chapter stem from a study by Thomas Shroer, entitled "Archetypal Dreams during the First Pregnancy."[333] They were dreamt during the first trimester of first pregnancies. I shall deal with the spider-symbol per se a little later. Here is the first of these two dreams:

Dream No. 54:

> *I was in the shower and suddenly I noticed a clear plastic sack coming out of my body. I looked up and the school nurse was standing outside the tub as if to comfort me. The clear sack was near the drain now. It looked like it was filled with ants or little black objects. They were crawling all over each other inside the sack. They frightened me.*
> *I tried to get them down the drain. But they started to grow and change. They looked more like spiders now. I was frightened even now and tried again to get them down the drain.*
> *I looked up at my arms and there appeared to be leeches hanging on both of my arms. The nurse tried to help me free them from my arms. I kept pulling at my arms and succeeded in getting all but one down the drain. I was tired and relieved.*
> *But then the one leech began to grow. It was flesh in color and looked like a tiny seal. It was wet-looking. When it dried, it looked like a Maltese puppy.*
> *I was shocked at first but relieved that it was no longer an ant, spider, or seal but rather a puppy I was familiar with in childhood.*

The dreamer is in the shower, a place where we clean ourselves. What actually happens in the shower is a process of discovery about what is going on in her own body. She finds this process difficult to handle, and a school nurse, a female helper, is giving her a hand. In this sense, the shower is turning

---

[333] In: *Psychological Perspectives*, Vol. 15, No. 1, Los Angeles, 1984

185

into an initiation cabin, and the nurse is assuming the ancient role of the "female helper," i.e., helping the girl to become a woman.[334]

The dreamer has had a sack in her body and has just given birth to it, as it were. The dream actually represents a process of initiation and practice for the impending birth. The dreamer can see through the sack. This signifies that she has gained insight and that she is experiencing the fundamental realization of what it is that is growing inside her and wanting to be born. Her understanding grows from one stage to the next, parallel, as it were, to the development or transformation of the animals. To begin with, there is fear but also the comforting voice of the nurse. The impulse to get rid of the grisly animals persists. Something like the idea of an abortion can be heard ("down the drain"), however, it is not so much abortion that is at issue but the irrevocability of a transformation taking place, regardless of the individual's attempts to free herself.

According to C.G. Jung,[335] a large number of little animals such as insects, ants, etc. suggests that there is a physical irritation of the sympathicus, i.e., a disturbance or disharmony in the vegetative nervous system. This is an autonomously functioning sphere of the body-and-soul unity. It can cause psychological dissociation that, given a certain predisposition, can occasionally occur during pregnancy. But even among those pregnant women who are psychologically robust and stable, feelings tend to be highly contradictory. It is only natural for the feelings of joy and excitement about the child to struggle against those of fear and refusal.

Now the dreamer sees that as she tries to push the horrible bag down the drain, the ants begin to grow and change into spiders. She is still afraid and tries anew to get rid of them. Then she notices that she has several leeches hanging on her arms. She finally manages to free herself from all the leeches but one, and to put them down the drain.

The collective and disturbing multitude has now been overcome, and the confusing images of a growing life have now been reduced to one that is very typical of the situation: the child she is carrying can indeed be compared to a leech that is coupled to her circulation! She feels tired and relieved. A great job has been done.

Now the growing life is on a steadfast path – the little leech triples in size, takes on the color of flesh and then suddenly turns out to be a small wet seal! As it dries up, the dreamer recognizes with great relief that the creature looks like a Maltese puppy, bringing back childhood memories.

The graphic correspondence in this sequence of imagery with a growing embryo all the way to the child ripe to be born is striking! Having started at

---

[334] Alfred Winterstein, *Die Pubertätsriten der Mädchen*, p. 56 ff, in: *Märchenforschung und Tiefenpsychologie*, Wissenschaftliche Buchgesellschaft
[335] *Über die Archetypen des kollektiven Unbewussten*, Eranos, 1934, p. 227

the animal stage, the creature now approaches the human sphere, and the pregnant woman can enter into a genuine and loving relationship with it that reconnects her with her own childhood.

We notice in this dream that the dreamer's unconscious clearly formulates the developmental idea of a dual process in dreams. On the one hand, the dream comments on the natural process implicit in the growth of a child in the maternal womb. At the same time, the dream reflects the change the dreamer undergoes in her attitude to childbirth. Her subjective attitude has been differentiated, she has been able to "see through" the process and realize with relief that she is dealing with a higher stage in development.

It is not so much spiders alone but the massive appearance of tiny, disgusting animals that is typical. They represent an early stage of evolution.

Transformation in stages is the theme of another dream from Shroer's collection in which a comparable stage is represented by a flea. The following dream also describes evolution as a kind of a series of transformations. Instead of spiders we have a flea.

Dream No. 55:

> I was on the back porch. I had a little bird. – The little bird became a tiny little flea. I followed it and grabbed it. It became a big bug, like a daddy long legs, and I didn't like it, but I couldn't leave it. Finally, I blew on it. It came to me. I had mixed emotions. I still loved it, but I didn't like the bug. Then it turned into a plant in a glass dish, and frogs were all over it. I felt a longing for it to share with me what the frogs were saying to it. I knew it could understand the frogs ...

This dream, like the preceding one, takes us back to the very early stages of life – suggesting initiation on an even more elementary level and stage, namely, that of the plant. The plant in turn learns something from the frogs that are symbols of fertility of which our dreamer is not yet aware. Is it the secret of the growing life? The "glass dish" evokes the Alchemists' *vas* (retort) in which transformation should take place.

Almost everybody feels an aversion to spiders. Some otherwise brave people can get into a terrible panic, turn pale and run away. Sometimes they get into a rage and risk their life to kill the animal. The spider-phobia is a phenomenon similar to the snake-phobia. The reactions of the ego become unexpectedly unreasonable and irrational. This repulsion is common and almost insurmountable, and the fear is irrational, too, for in our regions, poisonous spiders are extremely rare, with the exception of the very South of Europe.

However, with the import of tropical plants, in isolated cases there have been insects that strayed into Europe, and the promising title, "The spider in the Yucca-tree," has indeed been given to a new collection of "modern legends."[336] But already long before this, the people who invented the horror-films had made successful use of the widespread fear of spiders.

Like snakes, spiders exercise a great fascination on people, which does not apply to other nauseating animals, such as lice, worms, rats or mice. The fascination probably springs from the wondrous work of the spider web, but also from the eight-legged, bizarre body and its remarkable behavior. The eight-leggedness may well be significant in that it is the doubling of four or "higher four" reminding us of a spiritual, higher wholeness as expressed in ancient Greece by Odin's horse or Pegasus, or in India by eight-limbed divinities, also a symbol of their totality.

The spider is often associated with the salutary effect of a spinning and weaving woman and in this sense can almost be seen as a symbol of female creativity.[337] An ancient Vedic saying says that the entire creation of the world and cosmos was brought forth – in the same manner as the spider's thread – from Brahma, the divine, all-embracing unity.[338] Another ancient conception of the world is the "veil of Maya." The image of the spinning spider suggests coming out of the Self and takes us to the subliminal meaning of the spider as a "central symbol." In literature, a general dread of the spider is prevalent. The encounter with one's Self is frightening. Its long, scrawny, threateningly skeleton-like legs make associations of death spring to our mind. The image of the female spider mercilessly sucking out and killing her husband immediately after the wedding makes of the spider a negative, vampire-like feminine symbol.

There are numerous horror stories involving spider-like vampires, particularly in science fiction. We also encounter them in modern fairy tales – for example, in the colorful tale of "The Hobbit" as the all-stifling stranglers in the dark woods. Jeremias Gotthelf has rendered their devilish aspect unforgettably in his story, "Die Schwarze Spinne" (The Black Spider): The woman who is the carrier of the spider has received it from the devil. The spider brings distrust, greed, the plague and death to the enchanting Emmental. Gotthelf uses for his story an ancient folktale from Emmental.[339]

In Zarathustra, what inspired Nietzsche's idea of "the eternal return of the same" was the image of the "slow spider crawling in the moonlight" that emanated a mysterious coldness and loneliness.[340]

The handbook of German superstitious belief has countless examples of customs and opinions concerning the great power and poisonousness of spiders. There is a harmless spider-oracle that we still know today although its

[336] Rolf W. Brednich, *Die Spinne in der Yukkapalme*, dtv, München, 1990

[337] M.-L. von Franz, "The Woman who became a Spider," in *The Feminine in Fairy Tales*, Spring Publications, 1972, p. 95 ff

[338] Melita Maschmann, *Eine ganz gewöhnliche Heilige*, Otto W. Barth Verlag / Scherz, Bern, München, Wien, 1990

[339] Bächtold-Stäubli, *Handwörterbuch d. dt. Aberglaubens*, Vol. 8, p. 265 ff

[340] Friedrich Nietzsche, *Thus Spake Zarathustra, III*, The Viking Press, New York, 1966

relevance is not entirely clear. It goes: "Spider in the morning – bad luck and sorrow. Spider at noon – the third day is a lucky day. Spider in the evening – invigorating and refreshing!" ("*Spinne am Morgen – Unglück und Sorgen. Spinne am Mittag – Glück am dritten Tag. Spinne am Abend – erquickend und labend!*"). Some people think it refers to the spinning of young ladies: those who did it in the morning were poor and had to earn a living with it. At noon, the brides spun their trousseau. Whereas in the evening, it served as convivial entertainment.

People were so convinced of the poisonousness of the cross spider in particular that they concocted poisonous drinks with them. A person wearing a seven-year dried spider around his neck fancied himself invulnerable. Recruits used to carry a cross spider with them for the call-up in the hope of avoiding conscription. Perhaps we are dealing with a secret bond with the Great Mother – mighty protectoress – or did they fancy themselves in league with the devil? In any event, it was certainly in league with a power that could oppose the state authority!

Spiders were dried, rubbed, pounded in a mortar and boiled, so that the evil disease would be confronted with an even more evil counterpart!

When the spider spins its web it turns into an artist or even a magician. In the South of Italy, the spider web is called "magaria," a work of a witch. Nowhere else in Nature except in the case of spiders do we witness the creation of such regular, concentric forms. Although flowers and crystals, too, may strike us as miracles of Mandala-like concentration, we can neither watch how they are being made nor who is behind these magnificent constructions. For this reason, the artistic construction of the spider web impresses us as being mystical or magical, especially when dewdrops twinkle on them. One is tempted to divine that the concentric symmetry conceals the

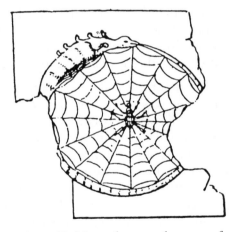

Figure 22. Maya, the eternal weaver of the deceptive world of the senses

"spirit" of Nature or the *lumen naturae* of Paracelsus and is startled at the idea that the little spider "knows" it.[341]

It is not only the magnificent web-technique that is fascinating about the spider web. Above all it has to do with the construction's concentration towards the center that the cross spider masters perfectly. Man is subliminally

---

[341] C.G. Jung, CW 13, *Paracelsus as a spiritual phenomenon*, § 148 f

reminded here of his very own psychic process from which he cannot escape or only by doing a great disservice to himself. Jung writes:[342] "We can hardly help feeling that the unconscious process moves spiral-wise round a center, gradually getting closer, while the characteristics of the center grow more and more distinct. Or perhaps we could put it the other way round and say that the center – itself virtually unknown – acts like a magnet on the disparate materials and processes of the unconscious and gradually captures them as in a crystal lattice. For this reason the center is – in other cases – often pictured as a spider in its web,[343] especially when the conscious attitude is still dominated by fear of unconscious processes."

We could continue: when we are little gnats that have got caught in the web, we are poor prisoners on a path that we cannot avoid in any way. Its goal, or the "central symbol" is the central cause of individuation, of our own wholeness. However, in his entire, very extensive work, Jung leaves no doubt that the process of approaching may be fatal.

From a negative point of view the spider in the web represents a clasping, sucking out and devouring unconscious, the caricature of the "great mother" and, subjectively speaking, the image of a negative mother complex. That is why spider dreams frequently occur at a time of vehement conflict with one's own mother. It is her keeping back and paralyzing, often through loving care, against which a young person has to fight. Oftentimes, the poisonous spinner already sits inside the daughter, covering her entire inner being with her suffocating threads of self-doubt and hatred.

The dreamer of the next dream had a miscarriage in her first pregnancy when she was three months pregnant. Around the same time, in her second pregnancy, which was likewise desired, she again had bleeding and subsequently had to lie still for three weeks. The rest of the pregnancy proceeded well and so did the birth of a boy, who was born on time and without any complications. The father lives with the family. Both children were wanted. – Other dreams by this woman reveal scenes of violent quarrels with her mother. We assume that she was suffering from anxiety at the time of the dream as the bleeding had started just then. However, the dream seems to point to another, hidden problem:

Dream No. 56:

> *I am dreaming of spiders in the apartment, a dead mouse, a dead cat and a dead dog.*

---

[342] C.G. Jung, CW 12, § 325

[343] Cf. *ibid.*, ill. 108, p. 217: Maya, eternal weaver of the illusory world of the senses, encircled by the Uroborous. – Damaged vignette from a collection of Brahminic sayings

When there are spiders in the apartment, the simplest explanation is that it has not been cleaned. The apartment consists of the rooms in which we live, our everyday, habitual environment. It seems as though in the dark, uncontrolled corners of our life and thoughts, some negative feelings and thoughts have settled. As we tend not to see them, they usually accumulate. Woman's negative thinking usually originates from a negative animus and can therefore be quite unconscious. Destructive thoughts, old feelings of reproach and envy (that have survived), have sneaked in or have simply been maintained over time. If they were conscious they would feel like vermin or dirt to which one would have to attend, particularly during pregnancy and in view of the new and still fragile unborn life.

The three dead animals – a dead mouse, a dead cat and a dead dog – form the other primary elements of the dream. They are domestic animals or pets, relatively close to man and are usually interpreted as helpfully functioning instincts.[344] Now, in our dream, these animals are dead.

It is interesting that there are four things – four kinds of animals. It is likely that this dream again addresses the process of wholeness but for now the only living thing in this quaternity are the wholly undesired spiders. The fact that the three "good" animals, which we interpret as instincts, are dead, shows the helplessness and dismay in the unconscious. The necessary instincts to help her in an unpleasant, perhaps dangerous situation, to unite opposites for instance, or to bridge something, in order to find a way out of a deadlock, are no longer alive.

We do not know whether the pregnancy has been the trigger in the unconscious to express these very violent and poisonous disputes with the mother that the analyst mentions in her commentary. Pregnancy can certainly bring them to the surface and shed light on them. In fact, all the maternal aspects are brought to the surface demanding a reaction, an opinion and clarification. This can be likened to cleaning up the apartment.

Our instincts are important in such situations. Instincts help us to act in accordance with the course of life. The dream illustrates this in the following way: having a good nose, sensing the trail or the way out (dog), knowing how to snuggle up and still retaining her freedom (cat), or swiftly disappearing into a hole when there is a danger ahead of getting trapped (mouse). The instincts can prevent us from getting into a panic in a hazardous, hopeless looking situation. Because they function practically automatically, they are far superior to the rational and moral consciousness that awkwardly weighs things up. Therefore, it is vital that the instincts be alive.

Seen in this light, the dream image is by no means harmless. The number 4 suggests that what is at issue is indeed "wholeness." Thus attending to her instincts at least as much as to the dark corners of her apartment could be

[344] Cf. Chapters 5 and 5.6

extremely important for the dreamer now. The problem with her mother seems to threaten her. Given the dead animals it is unlikely that the image is that of the positive "spinner" spinning the thread of life: it is far more likely that she has cut her daughter's thread!

The cruel conflict between mother and daughter that can turn into poisonous hatred (*spinnefeind*) is also described in an ancient legend told by Ovid after a Hellenistic piece of writing:[345] The girl Arachne challenges the goddess Athena to a contest in tapestry design. She weaves into her work scenes of the god's and goddesses' love affairs while Athena shows scenes of human arrogance. Athena is furious about Arachne's more beautiful work and rips it apart, whereupon Arachne wants to hang herself. Athena transforms her into a spider that from now on spins and weaves incessantly. In all the Roman languages, the spider is named after Arachne: *araignée* in French, *ragno* in Italian, *aranea* in Spanish.

We could see Arachne's ambition as an archetypal image of a negative mother complex. It would be similar to the problem of a woman "who is at daggers drawn with the goddess," and by challenging her to compete with her, she experiences the same destiny as Prometheus. The struggle for power between woman and goddess rarely ends in favor of the human woman or daughter. The violence or envy that, according to moral standards, seems unjust can, in a situation of rivalry, result in the daughter's self-destruction. It is one of these both ancient and ever new quarrels on earth, one of womanly ambition and jealousy of one another, of passion that can play a disastrous role, especially in conflicts between mother and daughter.[346]

Beyond that, the allegory of hanging on a thread suggests a danger for women of becoming too heady, that is, of not having both feet on the ground.[347] She then loses her ability to be a living intermediary between the air, heaven and the earth, and her negative thoughts can – when she is left alone – weave a tissue of secret envy and aggression turned against herself. In England, unmarried old women are called "spinsters." However, a negative mother complex can result in a negative animus possession, which could signify death of the positive instincts. This can also happen to young married women.

In the following dream, there are only spider webs and dead animals. It is worth noticing that the spider theme figures three times, and in two cases, it is coupled with dead animals! The dream occurred during a critical time – namely, when it looked as though the dreamer's husband had failed his doctoral exams. According to the dreamer's own words, she was in "shock" about it. When it turned out that the spouse had successfully passed after all, the two

---

[345] *Der Kleine Pauly*, "Arachne"
[346] Within the scope of this book it is not possible to discuss the "Oedipal" component.
[347] M.-L. von Franz, *The Feminine in Fairy Tales*, p. 103 ff

of them went to Indonesia as had been planned, not realizing, though, that she had become pregnant. The child was thus conceived during the time the dreamer had felt fear.

Dream No. 57:

> *I am in a dangerous spot and have to jump to the side. What happened is not clear.*
> *To rescue myself, I jump onto a lorry that, under the tarpaulin, has a kind of a cellar vault.*
> *The lorry is being driven by two men.*
> *There are a red deer and a dead dog lying in the cellar and there are several spider webs, such as one finds in a cellar vault.*

The dreamer is in danger and has to "jump to the side." Apparently something terrible is going to happen to her that she wants to avoid. But where does she jump in order to rescue herself?

She jumps onto a lorry driven by two men – i.e., a vehicle that is occupied by a "double male." This suggests an escape to find refuge in collective values and principles symbolized by the lorry transporting goods. This unconscious impulse is particularly weighty as it is personified by two men.

However, after this, she promptly falls into a cellar which is situated, astonishingly, under a lorry tarpaulin. The basement of this two-story lorry makes a good allegory for a deeper level of the unconscious, and it is likely that without the strong emotions and the feelings of hopelessness she had had before, she would not have gained access to this deep level. She too falls through (the German word *durchfallen* also means to fail, e.g., an exam), or rather fails, when in fact she wanted to drive off somewhere (in the lorry!).

In this basement, our dreamer discovers on the one hand something ugly and terrifying, and on the other hand, an opportunity to find out more about the strong manifestation of her animus: in the cellar, there are cadavers of animals "and there are several spider webs, such as one finds in cellar vaults."

We do not know why the deer and the dog had to die nor why they are in the cellar. To the dreamer, their death could signify the following: the free and light-footed deer and the reliable, scenting dog embody her own impulse of free movement and a healthy sense of where she stands in life; these instinctive powers could have come to her rescue at the time when she was in despair. Instead, though, the lorry – i.e., a strong collective impulse – provides a refuge or saves her from a dangerous situation. Perhaps, a desire to drive off somewhere also plays a role.

In the vault of the cellar, the dreamer notices spider webs. She immediately reasons that these are common in cellars, as if she wanted to immediately rationalize a fit of panic. However, the spider webs heighten the uncanniness considerably. In this dismal place, the spider webs seem like the traces of an uncanny work of spinning and slaughtering: they look too much like shrouds. Thus in the image of the spider web and the flight in the animus, we detect the constellation of a life-threatening aspect of the Great Mother. Something evil had been spun or woven here of which the conscious ego had no idea. This should be seen as a chance insofar as it showed the dreamer certain depths that confronted her with the consequences of an inadequate reaction.

The next dream stems from week twenty and again deals with fear. It is not the spider-like designs that actually inspire fear, and the spider dreams of our collection never suggest that the spiders themselves are dreadful or menacing. However, spiders and fear always occur together, which is why they seem to express one and the same thing.

C.G. Jung writes that where there is a prevailing fear of unconscious processes, even the central symbol sometimes presents itself in the form of a spider in a web.[348] In this sense, the radius of meaning of this image is rather extensive.

Dream No. 58:

> *I was on my way somewhere. I plucked out my toes, which had become decrepit, and with my hand, I stuffed them into my mouth. I found it extremely nauseating, and the chewing became more sickening. For some reason, I could not spit it all out and pulled the flesh out of my mouth, one by one. I felt even sicker.*
>
> *There were spider-like patterns crawling nimbly on the wall trailing their long legs that were the shape of a calyx, behind them. When looking closely at the patterns, you could see women's faces and bodies. Then there was nothing evil or frightening about them, only astounding.*
>
> *We returned to the classroom. I asked to open the window. I jokingly suggested that the ghost everybody was afraid of could also come through the window.*
>
> *The second B. from our class, the one I had asked, got stuck by the window. She was so afraid, she couldn't do anything anymore. Suddenly I realized that she was clinging to the window, hanging, her eyes rolled upward, paralyzed and quite insane from panic. I could see it was very serious and that she could fall out of the window and down into the schoolyard.*
>
> *I had to hold open a book and thought I couldn't move now and cried: Will you help one of the B's to shut the window! A man and a woman tried and as if contaminated, were seized and shaken by the same panic. A third woman, who was not free from fear either, eventually closed the window. Something rushed through the room, saying: I am your little*

---

[348] C.G. Jung, CW 12, p. 325

guardian. [The German *Bewacherin* is of feminine gender, thus the guardian is a female.]

The dreamer is very busy removing her own decrepit toes, i.e., her old standpoints that have become dated and frail. For this purpose, she stuffs them into her mouth to chew them up, which makes her feel extremely sick.

The rotten flesh is apparently very tough: she cannot process it with her teeth or spit it out but has to pull it out piece by piece – utterly revolting. It seems that she is finding it very difficult to distance herself from her old standpoints even though she is fundamentally opposed to them. Analyzing, dismantling them, in order to put a distance between them and herself and to get rid of them, does not seem to work. However, it is noticeable that the dream-ego is making a genuine effort to digest and finish with what has become old and hackneyed. Only, the processing tools, her teeth, which so far have worked, for some unknown reason do not seem to do the job anymore.

Despite the fact that the dream-ego has a most strange encounter, for the dreamer, there is "nothing frightening" about it: on the wall – she apparently has now approached the school building or is already in the hallway – are "crawling nimbly spider-like figures" that turn out to have beautiful women's faces and busts and trail along their legs, which happen to be flower cups. They are fantastic, mysterious creatures, but alive and nimble. The dreamer manages to examine them and finds them astounding but not frightening.

In his *Deutsche Mythologie*,[349] Jakob Grimm writes about spider oracles. Referring to a folktale by Arnim – "thus the kind-hearted fairy crawls along the ceiling as a spider and falls down as a woman" – he believes they are often a good prophecy. In the handbook of German folk belief,[350] under "spider" a legend from the Tirol is mentioned, according to which a spider comes to a kind-hearted farmer's wife in childbed, reveals herself as a beautiful woman and bestows charitable deeds on her. Marie-Louise von Franz similarly observed that a good contact to the tiny animals in fairy tales is practically always positive and important – there are those inevitable situations in which we rely on their help and would be lost without it.

Our dream also speaks of a mysterious connection between spider-like beings and women, with their beautiful feminine faces and breasts. The dreamer finds herself confronted with beings of mixed nature that are wholly alien and baffling to her consciousness; however, in the dream they do not cause feelings of repulsion or fear in her. Her taking a close look at them shows a similarly active, bold attitude in trying to process and eliminate the decrepit toes, i.e., parts of herself. This means that she subjects herself to a

---

[349] Jakob Grimm, *Deutsche Mythologie*, Akademische Druck- und Verlagsanstalt, Graz, 1968, p. 203
[350] *Ibid.*, Spider, p. 265 ff

process of renewal in the course of which she can face "strange things" without fear – however, only so long as she is not in the "classroom."

Having returned to it, she first asks to open the window. Perhaps it is too narrow in there for her or stuffy – after all she has seen things that school-knowledge would not even dream of – and she has tried to renew the foundation of the views she had held up to now. This has caused strong emotions in her. She seems to have experienced something outside that the people here apparently consider a "ghost," and she is tempted to let some of it in.

Because of the ambivalence of her experiences, the dream-ego is divided into several persons by the same name: "B." One of the "B's" got stuck by the window – that part in herself which is still the inexperienced student is seized with terror at seeing what is outside: this B clings to the window and is driven almost insane from fear. The dream-ego, on the other hand, now seems to want to stick to the studies, holding open a book and perhaps thinking it would prefer not to have anything to do with the "ghost" or the incomprehensible being that is trying to come in from outside. She holds onto the book and knowledge one finds in books just as the "other B" clings onto the windowsill and wants someone to help her shut the window. She herself does not move and watches how first a man and then a woman – this shows that reason has also been mobilized to counteract the fear – also fail and panic. Finally, a "third woman, not free from fear either, manages to shut the window." In vain, however, for "something" has already come in and "rushed through the room."

A breath? A spiritual being? A voice? What seems most likely is an idea that has been communicated to the panic-stricken scientists in an inexplicable way: something rushed through the room, saying: "I am the little guardian."

The sight of what goes on outside – perhaps in Nature? – is unbearable. Is it – what is understandably the case with many students – the fear of the ghost of a pregnancy? Regardless of the fear of an unwanted pregnancy, during intense intellectual training the collective attitude is virtually incongruent with the mysterious course Nature runs. Whenever we strive to bring things on a level governed by rationality and will and to deny the existence of anything non-researchable behind the researchable, we are given to panic in the face of the inexplicable and inevitable. Books do not teach us such things. Therefore the pursuit of serious studies during pregnancy easily results in feeling torn between two conflicting things.

On the one hand, as the dreamer knows, the studies must go on without interruption (she keeps her book open): she fends off the growing force that she is afraid will hem her in and will cause her to abandon the security of intellectual training. On the other hand, the dream-ego is fighting for a renewal. In this conflicting process, it is not clear to her whether what is coming should be shut out or let in. Being pregnant makes it particularly difficult for her to reconcile the two worlds.

Figure 23. Hoopoe (Egyptian relief)

5.3. Birds

Regina Abt

Man has been fascinated by birds since the very beginning of his existence. Their light-weightedness and independence of all gravitation, their sudden appearance from and disappearance to anywhere imaginable, surpass any concrete human experience. Therefore, more than any other animal, the bird represents a bridge between the human, terrestrial world and the hereafter, between earth and heaven.[351] In fairy tales, birds almost always know more and carry the heroine of the tale across the last stretch of the sea, to the end of the world. "Bird" in Greek means "prophesy, tidings" from the heavens. The Koran speaks of the language of the birds that Solomon understood, for it was the language of the gods. But not only in the Koran are birds angels – our angels have wings, too. The meaning of the word "bird" is often also identical to "fate" determined by the other world.

The Romans observed the birds' flight and singing for prophesy, that is, to predict the will and intentions of the gods.[352] In the Vedas, the bird is a symbol of friendship between the gods and mankind. It flies to an unreachable mountain and brings back Soma (Ambrosia) to the people. Furthermore, it helps man to fend off the demonic assaults of evil forces. For the Celts, the bird – in particular, the raven and goose – were divine messengers. Birds also belong to Odin (or Wotan). Rhiannon, the Gaelic goddess (also called "great goddess") is surrounded by birds, who with the sweetness of their singing, reawaken the dead or take the living to their death. The Taoists believe that the gods are incarnated in the bodies of birds. So everywhere, birds belong in some form or another to the divine, the world of the beyond.

In Kurdistan, birds are at the very beginning of all creation. God is depicted as a bird with golden wings even before heaven and earth existed. In our own history of creation (Genesis 1.1), God's spirit glides above the waters like a bird.

Related to fate, sent by the gods and standing at the beginning of all creation suggests that the bird has something to do with the spiritual world or

---

[351] Cf. also: J. Chevalier, A. Gheerbrant, *Dictionnaire des Symboles*, Vol. 3, p. 307 ff
[352] Ström, Ake v. Biezais H.: *Germanische und Baltische Religion*, p. 258

with spiritual notions, flights of thought and inspiration emerging from the unconscious. Any act of creation is initially preceded by ideas inspired by the unconscious. This is how we design our image of the world and of our destiny.

Paracelsus expressed this in his own fashion: for him birds' prophesy is based on the light of Nature, the *lumen naturae*, which is also the dream spirit. Here is a beautiful passage quoted by Jung:

> *It is, therefore, also to be known that the auguries of the birds are caused by these innate spirits, as when cocks foretell future weather and peacocks the death of their master and other such things with their crowing. All this comes from the innate spirit and is the Light of Nature. Just as it is present in animals and is natural, so also it dwells within man, and he brought it into the world with himself. He who is chaste is a good prophet, natural as the birds, and the prophecies of birds are not contrary to Nature but are of Nature. Each, then, according to his own state. These things which the birds announce can also be foretold in sleep, for it is the astral spirit which is the invisible body of Nature … .[353]*

Viewed from Christianity, inspiration is embodied in the dove, the symbol of the Holy Ghost. According to Jung, it corresponds to the female aspect of the Holy Ghost in early Christianity. In the Acts of Saint Thomas, the Holy Ghost is simply the feminine divinity, *Frau Gott*.[354] She corresponds to Paracelsus' *lumen naturae*.

Birds can also represent negative aspects, such as lunatic or devilish ideas. In China, a round yellow-red firebird with four wings and six legs symbolizes chaos. The Chinese believed that the bird destroyed its nest when chaos and uprisings broke out in the empire. In Buddhism, birds hovering around freely represent a destructive distraction. In English, we say, "he's gone absolutely cuckoo" and mean that he's gone mad, that his head is in disorder, or that he has foolish thoughts. To dream of black birds is often an expression of depression and anxiety. It is in the latter form that birds appear in one of the following dreams.

The bird has been the animal of the soul everywhere in the world and since the early epoch of humanity. On the prehistoric rock-carvings at Lascaux and Altamira, the soul is represented as a bird about to leave the body. Among various Berber tribes in India, in the Celtic world and among Altaic shamans, the souls descend into matter in the shape of birds. In Egypt, the immortal part of man, the so-called Ba-soul, that lives on after death, is depicted as a bird in the hieroglyphs. In Central-Asian, Siberian and Indonesian myths, birds, symbolizing the souls of men, sit in the branches of the cosmic tree.[355]

---

[353] C.G. Jung, CW 13, *Paracelsus as a Spiritual Phenomenon*, § 148, Routledge & Kegan Paul, 1967
[354] Jung, Seminars: *Kinderträume*, 72

The souls of the dead turn into birds and ascend to the cosmic tree from where the shaman, on his ecstatic flight to rebirth, can bring them to the earth, in the form of birds.[356]

Small birds usually represent the souls of children. In Central-Asian popular wisdom, a pregnant woman dreaming of a bird must try to detect its gender in order to know whether she will have a boy or a girl. The child's soul is disguised as a bird, as it were – in other words, she intuitively recognizes it in its future form.

Folklore in our culture says that the children are brought to us by a stork. This goes back to the Germanic belief, according to which the souls of the departed are renewed in the fountain of Hulda, and the stork brings them back to the earth. The bird in general and the stork in particular are typical for metempsychosis and hence are closely linked with death and rebirth as well as with psychic transformation.

Figure 24. Ani's Ba above the mummy in the tomb

Here follows a shortened version of a dream a woman had a few months prior to becoming pregnant.[357]

Dream No. 59:

> *I am in my kitchen, looking south at a wide open sky. In the brilliant blue air an enormous "craft" is approaching. Its shape resembles that of an aircraft, but it is gleaming white and silent like a bird, like a gigantic, stylized white dove. This image, the sight of it in the blue sky is very numinous. I stand entranced and open myself wide to whatever this beautiful unearthly, shining bird is or brings. I know it is coming for me, will come straight into me or through me, shatter the house – anything ... The next thing I see is the bird-craft gliding off in a beautifully swung curve to the East, still gleaming white and slowly losing size ... Suddenly two messengers stand next to me (insubstantial creatures, young and with golden curls – I take them to be angels). I presume that they had issued from the craft. They speak together: "We have come to bring you a*

---

[355] Cf. Dream No. 75, Chapter "Cat"

[356] *Dictionnaire des Symboles*, Vol. 3, p. 307 f

[357] By the same dreamer: No. 16, Chapter 3.2

message." I rescue one word only and write it on a scrap of paper. It is "Glocke" [bell] and the message had been that "the bell had been tolled" ... I took it to mean "your hour has struck," and attached great meaning to this message from another world.

This dream is not a pregnancy dream, and I shall discuss it only briefly. It demonstrates nicely how a new content, in the form of a dove or two angels, enters consciousness. The oak grove of Dodona, which was consecrated to Zeus, had doves; they were a part of the cult of Dione, the great Mother Earth, and were used for prophesy. In the Bible, the dove is the symbol of the Holy Ghost. The dove seems to announce creation, albeit in an abstract form. The dreamer still seems to have difficulties in accepting this new content with her feelings. Then they turn into angels, divine messengers who are almost humanlike and speak a language she can understand. They help to establish a connection, as it were, to Mother Earth or to the dreamer's own greater maternal side.

It is possible that this dream indeed points to the forthcoming conception and to the penetration of some other kind of unconscious content from the other world. In any case, it seems to communicate the "voice of God" or of the soul (bell).[358] Next comes something very important! Now, "your hour has struck." Something has been set in motion: a hint of something beyond the human manifests itself and imparts to the dreamer a feeling of great significance. A few months prior to the birth of her child, the same dreamer had the following dream:

Dream No. 60:

I look up towards the edge of the pine wood behind my hut. On the very tip of a pine-crown sits a white bird which now flies up. It glides beautifully, majestically and silently through the very blue sky. At first it looks like a duck, but then it turns into an elegant, white swan. It curves gently around towards me and the hut and even as I watch, it metamorphoses once more. It stretches and elongates and anthropomorphoses into an airy, white, lacey being like a ballet-dancer, like the human swan in swan lake, an exquisite amalgam of neat tan limbs and delicate lace tu-tu. This glorious creature lands – it seems quite voluntarily – in some kind of large aviary attached to my hut.

This dream has much in common with the dream we have just discussed. Again, a white bird comes down from heaven symbolizing an otherworldly, ghostlike or spiritual content. The duck is a prime example of an animal that is at home in different elements: water and land as well as air. The American

---

[358] Cf. R. Abt, *Die Heilige und das Schwein*, Chapter Glocke, Daimon, Zürich, 1983

Indians considered the duck a leader-animal because of its familiarity with the three elements. In a Siberian creation myth, a duck initiates creation from the water. For the Celts, it was the swan rather than the duck who had this role.[359] Owing to its radiant whiteness, the swan was associated with beaming perfection, purity and with both the sun and moonlight. This was so in Greece, Siberia, Asia Minor, in the Slavic and Germanic cultures. Sometimes the feminine and masculine aspects are united in an animal that has particular sacral significance. In a great many of our folktales, we can find motifs of otherworldly swan maidens who marry a mortal man. In several tales, these heavenly maidens become pregnant through the water or the earth, in order to give birth to the first man. This perception of the swan as a mythical maiden, as soft moonlight, prevails in all Slavic cultures, in Iran and Asia Minor. In Asia Minor, for a long time it was even believed that swans menstruated like women.

In her associations, the dreamer indicates that she understood the white bird to be a soul bird who deliberately alighted in a body to be in prison on this earth. Being able to move in all three elements, the duck would be particularly apt to represent the migration from the soul or the spiritual realm to body or material realm. As a swan and eventually swan maiden this new psychic content enters the human consciousness and ability of apperception. It becomes apparent that it is a feminine spiritual being of numinous quality.

The symbolism of the soul bird representing the soul of the future child is identical with the image of the supra-personal feminine being that we see as a personification of the dreamer's Self. It is possible that endowing the child with a living soul could also signify the concretization of an initially intangible and ghostlike fleeting content of the unconscious, or, a creative fantasy that eventually reveals the feminine Self. Those two aspects so intricately linked would appear to be a paradox! The Self is still in the state of a virgin bird, though no longer merely a notion or fantasy but not quite a human experience yet. The aviary attached to the house alone, or rather the thought of the unspeakable human restrictions can fill a woman with melancholy, and all the more so having to come to terms with the subsequent daily motherly responsibilities. And yet, what *élan* such a dream can bring to our narrow consciousness and to the experience of creating a child and becoming a mother!

The following three dreams deal with the difficult sides of imminent motherhood. The birds play a threatening and uncanny role. The first dream contains strong water symbolism and was therefore also discussed in the Chapter "Water." The twenty-five-year-old dreamer from South America, three months pregnant, was emotionally rather unstable during her pregnancy and did not eat properly, so it was unclear whether she was suffering from anorexia nervosa or not.

[359] *Dictionnaire des Symboles*, Vol. 2, p. 161 f

Dream No. 61:[360]

> *It was night. I was with my son on a deserted beach. After we walked to the other end, I realized I was so far away from Nature and from myself that I could barely see the sea. At this place where we were the sea was enraged, full of big waves. We were in a slightly elevated place. We were looking at the sea, and I was showing my son the waves coming and going. Suddenly, the sea surged up and almost made us wet. I thought of leaving, but there appeared many geese trying to bite us. Despite my pregnant belly, I took my son in my arms and ran away. The geese came after us, biting my son's legs.*

The geese in this dream, the messengers of Juno, the Roman Mother-goddess, have a clearly negative propensity for the dreamer and her son. It would appear that the dreamer is in a desolate, "darkened" state of mind (the deserted beach at night). She feels far away from Nature and from herself. The water, symbol of the unconscious, seems furious and menacing with its mighty waves.

In the same week, she had the following dream. The horses, which also symbolize the Mother-goddess – the "supporting instinct-foundation" – are desperate and in turmoil. In both dreams, the dreamer's son is in danger.

Dream No. 62:[361]

> *I was going to a country house with my husband and my son where other friends were already staying. Suddenly I saw my husband come running and my son in despair because there were three horses. Two of them were in despair, kicking. My husband escaped and left the boy behind. I went to the middle of the horses to rescue my son, who was alone and afraid. I rescued him and we both were okay. The sky was dark, and I saw the rain approaching. Three vultures [urubu – in Brazil, a sign of bad omen] came into the house, and I had to get rid of them all by myself. Then I saw that in reality the sky was only half-dark. I had eaten, because I was hungry.*

Not knowing the personal background of the dreamer, we can only say that something at the very bottom of her feminine-maternal instincts has apparently become dominated by negativity causing depression in her. We can infer this from the occurrence of water, geese, horses and vultures in the dream. While the deserted beach at night evokes feelings of desolation and abandonment, the waves have more to do with being inundated by emotions. The two kicking horses are an appropriate illustration of fits of despair and panic that

---

[360] Also discussed in Chapter 3.1
[361] Also discussed in Chapter 5.6

have become uncontrollable. The three vultures represent the kind of black ideas that feed on the sick, dying and dead. Depressive thoughts sometimes are like vultures sitting there, waiting before they swoop down on their rotting prey. They live on the adversity, as it were: the rubbish around and within us. For someone who is vexed, there are plenty of bad things in the world which can feed their vexation.

The dream of the geese shows clearly that it is the anger of the Mother-goddess herself turning against the dreamer. Geese, as the flying messengers of the Mother-goddess, symbolize an omen, from very far away, conveying that the dreamer's depression has to do with her maternal side, with her basic attitude to motherhood. Presumably, this is why her son is in danger.

In between these two dreams occurs a short dream about the dreamer's going to Mass and taking Holy Communion. Although it does not belong to the theme of birds, it is interesting in this context:

Dream No. 63:

> *I was attending Mass. I was the last to take Communion and went to the place where the Host is kept. There I saw a little chapel. Although it was the day before Passion, neither the Crucifix nor the image of Jesus were there.*

We know that the dreamer converted from Judaism to Christianity and that she is deeply interested in religious things. The dream shows that, at this point, she cannot find the Christian God. Instead of finding Him, she finds emptiness. The Mother-goddess' vexation could refer to the idea that, at the time of pregnancy and forthcoming birth, she should be rather more concerned with the mystery of the great goddess than the passion of Christ on the cross. We assume that behind the dreamer's depression lies hidden a profound religious or spiritual problem. It becomes acute during pregnancy possibly because pregnancy seems to require a spiritual or religious approach that is in harmony with feminine instinct.

Another twenty-five-year-old dreamer had a traumatic experience with a former partner and a previous abortion. Later, she was uncertain whether she might be Lesbian, but then she became pregnant again. After her initial bewilderment, she felt sure that she wanted the child. A few months later she was married.

Dream No. 64:

> *I was being attacked by "Quero-queros" [a kind of Brazilian southern region bird whose popular name, if it were translated into English, would be "Wish-wish"]. The Quero-quero-mother had a long beak, and I broke it to defend myself. Then came the Quer-quero sons to attack me. These*

205

*were like eggs with long beaks and two thin legs. After this, I felt guilty
because I had harmed their mother.*

The attack by the "wish-birds" could be interpreted as an invasion of wish-fantasies into the dreamer's ego. However, taking a closer look at the birds makes it a little more complicated. The son-birds look like eggs, with legs and long beaks. The egg and bird are motifs that, in various creation myths, are intimately related.[362] The egg contains the germ of the new but it also already contains the whole entity, like the seed of a flower or tree. It is an image of the not yet realized or preconscious totality. Sitting on an egg, brooding, in dreams suggests a possibility of reflection, of concentrating and reflecting about oneself.[363]

The eggs in this dream, however, are already young birds and have something dissociating about them. They are like unhatched "thought-eggs" that draw attention to themselves in the form of "wish-invasions." They could represent egotistical greediness or not yet hatched, unreflected needs of any kind. At the same time, they have an aspect of the germ of creation. As the dreamer is attacked by a mother-bird with her sons, it seems likely that the question of pregnancy and motherhood is being attacked. We do not know why the figure of the Great Goddess has come to represent something so negative for the dreamer. It could have something to do with the brutal manner in which the dreamer breaks off the mother-bird's beak. She may feel guilty about it; i.e., she can feel the inappropriateness of such an attitude vis-à-vis the "wish-bird" that is a part of her own maternal side. We assume that the initial desire for creation corresponds to a deep reproduction instinct that sets in motion Eros and the union of the genders. Underestimating or rejecting it offends and incenses Nature herself, which in negative thought-attacks, turns against the dreamer's Ego. We have widely observed that it is in the nature of creativity to turn destructively against the Ego if it ignores its impulses. This often manifests itself in a depression or sickness.

It is possible that through the earlier abortion and flirtation with homosexuality, our dreamer hurt her own femininity, suppressing a strong wish inside her, and that this resulted in guilt feelings. This could be the source of her continuing negative thoughts, be it in the form of self-destructive forces that make her insecure in her new role as a mother, be it inappropriate wishes and expectations regarding this very role.

---

[362] Cf. M.-L. von Franz, *Creation Myths*, Shambhala, Boston, 1995, p. 228 f. According to an ancient Greek myth, from the original chaos, Night, with her dark wings, gave birth to a wind egg. From it, sprang the god Eros, the one who arouses desire and has golden wings.
[363] *Ibid.*, p. 230

The next dreamer, whose pregnancy was overshadowed by a preceding miscarriage in month four and anxiety, had a difficult birth. At seven months she dreamt:

Dream No. 65:

> *I dreamt of two beautiful large birds resembling peacocks. One had a tail that was golden with dark red, the other one golden with dark green. They landed from high up on the left on the walls of what looked like a fortress, where I was with my husband and around it went a kind of moat in which grew lush trees. They flew into them, and it all looked like an Indian miniature painting. In the dream, I told my husband about the magnificent birds. Then, there was a child: a boy who brought a book and showed me the page where there were pictures and a description of these birds. They were called "Birds of Paradise." I awoke feeling utterly happy.*

This dream seems to bring something enormously helpful to the dreamer, and she wakes up filled with happiness. Birds are relatives of angels, and as the gods' messengers, they often render supernatural help during birth. This helper motif through the birds suggests corresponding impulses and insights on the part of the unconscious that originate in the helping Mother Nature.[364] This motif is well-known from the fairy tale, "Cinderella," where Cinderella's deceased mother appears as a bird.

The colors of the birds' tails are reminiscent of peacocks. The peacock, in its resplendent blaze of colors, has always captured man's imagination. It plays an important part in mythology and also in alchemy. It belongs to Juno (and to Hera), the mother-goddess. In China, it is also called a "mediator" and is able to make a woman conceive by casting a single glance at her. We can take this to be a spiritual conception, an intuition, or an insight. In the Greco-Roman as well as in the Christian traditions, because of its shining fan, the peacock is associated with the sun or rather the sun wheel. In India, it is the killer of snakes, the anti-pole of the sun to the earth. It transforms the snake's poison into the beauty of its feathers. Therefore, as in Christianity, the peacock is connected with resurrection and eternal life. For the ancient Christians, it is a symbol of the Savior and a relative of the phoenix, the Egyptian bird of resurrection, who incinerates itself and is born anew from its own ashes.[365] Thus, it possesses a significant aspect of psychic transformation that is only accessible to man, as it were, through a precious, intuitive, divine experience.[366]

---

[364] Cf. C.G. Jung, *Symbols of Transformation*, CW, Vol. 5, Bollingen Series Inc., 1956, § 546 and 538

[365] *Dictionnaire des Symboles*, Vol. 2, p. 352 f

[366] Cf. M.-L. von Franz, *Individuation in Fairy Tales*, Shambhala, Boston, 1990, p. 209

In alchemy, the *cauda pavonis*, the peacock fan with its abundance of colors appears directly before completion of the alchemical process, i.e., of individuation, which is what this dream is ultimately about.[367]

Gold, as an everlasting, indestructible value, combined with red, could be associated with blood, fire and heat. These are eternal, constant values in life penetrating consciousness, such as emotion, intensity of feeling, passion, anger. In addition, red has to do with the physical life. In contrast, green would stand for vegetative life, for biological growth but also for hope and resurrection (Osiris, the "green one," is the god of vegetation and of the dead). Green could also symbolize the unconscious spiritual life or a kind of "Nature-spirituality." Green and red then, are complementary colors and as such represent opposites. In the Orient, the peacock is considered a symbol of psychic opposites.[368] These complementary colors (from a physical point of view) contain all the basic colors – in other words, complete light, or totality. For this reason, we can regard the two peacock-like birds as a pair of opposites within the totality consisting of both the unconscious and consciousness.

The seemingly trivial detail of two birds in our dream clearly has a deeper meaning. It corresponds to an archetypal constellation that becomes recognizable where something new is being created. The creation myths of many different cultures therefore contain the motif of two gods of creation. Depending on the culture, as Marie-Louise von Franz writes, one god is more, the other less human, one more, the other less active, one darker, the other lighter; one is oriented towards life, the other towards death. This duality of the creation gods has to do with the polarity of the psyche that, according to Jung, governs all conscious and unconscious processes. Wherever there is light, wherever something enters consciousness, the rest lies in the dark or in the unconscious. This is why, in creation myths, most conscious processes of discrimination have an underlying duality: "... the discrimination of ego and the rest of the psyche, or of subject and object, outside and inside, and all other opposites ... no psychological process is imaginable for us without an underlying duality or polarity."[369] We have seen this duality with the two angels in the dreams discussed above.

Thus anyone who wants to be or is supposed to be creative will always be divided to a certain extent just like the creation gods, who tend to be more active or passive, or belong to the world of the living or the dead: something inside us wants it yet something else resists this task with a hundred pretexts. The task consists of allowing something new to well up from the unconscious over the threshold of consciousness. One current in the unconscious pushes towards consciousness, the other one against it. A woman often wants to have

---

[367] C.G. Jung, CW, Vol. 13, § 190 and 380
[368] *Dictionnaire des Symboles*, Vol. 2, p. 352
[369] M.-L. von Franz, *Creation Myths*, pp. 239-240

a child and then again she does not. Creative impulses also have this double aspect. Therefore, the conscious exertion required for each creative birth can sometimes result in complete depletion.

Before summarizing the various amplifications, let us look at the place of the dream action: the dreamer is in fortress-like walls surrounded by a moat lined by tall, growing trees. The picture is a perfect mandala or indeed a kind of a representation of paradise. In the center, there is the fortress that we can see as a work of man of times gone by – that is, as a medieval conscious perception or spiritual attitude. The fortress apparently is a ruin. Like the abandoned castles and fortresses of many fairy tales, it could be associated with the epoch of courtly love, where an appreciation of the feminine was on the increase. However, later, under the influence of the church, which steered all too strongly towards the Virgin Mary, it failed to take into account the whole feminine personality.

The story in the Bible of paradise and the notion of the original sin committed by woman resulted in people believing, in the early Middle Ages, – thanks to the interpretation of the church – that woman, being mainly driven by pleasure and sexual desire, should be placed under the control and guardianship of the spouse. She would otherwise, or so people thought, only be up to no good. It was also customary that a woman who could not produce heirs would be cast out without the slightest hesitation. Under the influence of the church, sexuality in marriage was altogether put in the service of procreation; otherwise, it was a sin.[370] This is what underlies the famous division in the image of the feminine: a childbearer, preferably a virgin, and a sinful temptress. This still presents a handicap to woman today because there does not seem to be a connection between her nature side in which sexuality, pregnancy and birth are united as one and the spiritual dimension of her personality. Our dream is almost a comforting answer to this pain that possibly underlies a depression. However, at the same time it points to a step towards a heightened consciousness of the opposites inherent in the feminine nature.

The two messengers of the great mother-goddess, the peacock-like birds of paradise, convey a spiritual premonition to the dreamer – a revelation from the unconscious, or an intuitive experience of the feminine wholeness and her own tension between the opposites of the physical, concrete side and natural spirituality. The whole thing looks like an Indian miniature. Indian representations of paradise mostly show the tree of paradise surrounded by birds.[371] They symbolize the inner center, the goal of Eastern thinking, the oneness before the split into the opposites. It is, as it were, the state of the preconscious

---

[370] Georges Duby, *The Knight, the Lady and the Priest*, Pantheon Books, New York, 1983. Cf. the legends of St. Godelive and St. Ida

[371] Cf. Dream 77, Chapter 5.4

totality, a state of *Nirdvandva*, preceding all creation and beyond all opposites.[372]

In her *Creation Myths*, Marie-Louise von Franz points out that this return to the beginning, a reversed creation myth, as it were (that in alchemy, e.g., begins with the animal and ends with the stone), is undoubtedly part of the symbolism of the individuation process. Images of the preconscious totality are often found in the symbols of the ultimate goal.[373] In this sense, then, the dream is a true individuation dream. It seems to provide our dreamer with a better idea of the meaning behind her suffering from the opposites of bodily discomforts and a psychic need having to do with her own feminine wholeness.

We may see the boy as a spiritual impulse bringing the dreamer a book or an "objective view." This could mean naming and classifying an intuition that has already been experienced and described by others. In this way, the dreamer is connected with the "knowledge of humanity," with a collective empirical knowledge that can lift her out of her loneliness and depression. Moreover, it could indeed be important now for this dreamer to study some appropriate books, which will enable her to order and formulate her experience and to anchor it in her consciousness.

The twenty-nine-year-old dreamer of the following dream had long wanted a child and had almost given up when she finally became pregnant. She was happy but concerned whether or not she would be able to bring a pregnancy to term. For medical reasons, the birth was planned for the seventh month, but then she ended up having her healthy baby boy, at around the due date, by a Cesarean section. She had the dream shortly before the birth.

Dream No. 66:[374]

> *I give birth to an eagle carrying a baby boy in his beak.*

The image of an eagle, majestically circling in the sky and soaring so seemingly close to the sun, has impressed people across time. The eagle has nearly always been related to the sun. Its feathers, in the American Indian headdress, represent the rays of the sun, and together with the bone pipe, are a part of the Red Indian Sun Dance. The eagle is regarded as the king of the birds and therefore symbolizes a higher spiritual state. It is likewise the bird of Zeus, the father of the gods. In our culture, the eagle is used in countless aristocratic coats-of-arms and is a symbol of power and superiority, victory and heroism. A need for domineering, tyranny and oppression, for pride and unbending,

---

[372] M.-L. von Franz, *Creation Myths*, p. 240
[373] Ibid., p. 240 and pp. 354-356
[374] By the same dreamer: No. 171 in Chapter 10 and No. 38 in Chapter 4.2

devouring power, but also an ability to be captivated through the spirit by a crazy or delirious idea, are the negative characteristics of the eagle.

As a bird of the sun, the eagle is also associated with higher insight and spiritual penetration.[375] During the ecstatic flight of the shaman, his soul is transported to the heavens by eagles. In the Psalms, like the phoenix (symbol of Christ), the eagle becomes a symbol of spiritual renewal. In alchemy, too, the eagle is synonymous with the phoenix. In *Psychology and Alchemy*, there is an image of an eagle rising from a retort symbolizing the spirit rising from *prima materia*.[376] Thus it is a symbol of transformation describing the process of psychic transformation or individuation. Another alchemical symbol shows the philosophical egg symbolized through the round, alchemical vessel from which the eagle or the phoenix arises. It stands for the soul that has become liberated and that, as Jung writes, is ultimately identical with the Anthropos (the archetype of the complete man), which according to the doctrine of the Gnostics "was imprisoned in the embrace of Physis" and had to be set free from there.[377]

The idea of an Anthropos-figure, spread out in matter and being liberated from it, is a primeval image that has never vanished. In alchemy, it was coupled through projection with the human soul that had to be freed.[378] The freeing of the soul from matter – the alchemical stage of sublimation (*sublimatio*), represented through the eagle, has to do with liberating the spiritual or psychic aspect in man.

The rise of the eagle from the alchemical cooking-vessel corresponds almost perfectly to the birth of the eagle from the maternal womb in our dream. In fact, the alchemical vessel or oven was often referred to as being a "uterus."

Therefore, our dream has primarily to do with a process of transformation and/or achievement of consciousness. The concrete child comes only after that, as a consequence, so to speak. It seems clear that what preoccupies our dreamer is a spiritual problem. Perhaps she has high-flying, ambitious ideas or even spiritual (winged) potential that is difficult to reconcile with the earthy weight of pregnancy and birth. However, in the dream, the birth of the sun-eagle and that of the concrete child coincide, as if they were identical. One is, in fact, brought forth by the other.

For some women, motherhood entails losing sight of certain spiritual objectives that can result in projecting onto the child high-flying unconscious fantasies of all kinds of things that the child should do in life.[379] Because we are dealing with women's dreams, we shall not say more about what happens

[375] Angelius Silesius wrote: *L'aigle regarde sans crainte le soleil bien en face.* [The eagle looks fearlessly and directly at the sun.]
[376] C.G. Jung, *Psychology and Alchemy*, Bollingen Foundation, Princeton University Press, 1968 CW, Vol. 12, Fig. 229, § 498
[377] *Ibid.*, § 306 and Fig. 98
[378] Cf. M.-L. von Franz, *Individuation in Fairy Tales*, p. 108

when fathers have such fantasies, but rather how these fantasies hinder the child's development. If, on the other hand, woman succeeds in bringing to consciousness her fantasies, to understand their function or to actually help them to be born, she will provide the best possible conditions for the real child's own development. In such a case, there is no contradiction in the opposites, as it were: one is rather the result of the other.

Giving birth to an eagle could be interpreted as giving birth to an inner, spiritual approach or a fantasy, of bringing a wish to the outer world and to reality; by rendering the wishful thought conscious or realizing it, it is bound to cause a transformation of consciousness. It is possible that this dreamer can only be granted access to her child once she has given a form to her own spiritual destination, her own spiritual demands and inner desires. The first need is to allow them to cross the threshold to consciousness, which in itself is a creative achievement! For other women, conceiving and delivering children is a natural process that simply happens and works out well – without its raising any questions or problems. This dreamer, however, seems to be walking on a different path. She only became pregnant when she had already given up. Mother Nature did not assume the task of bringing her fantasies to consciousness and realizing her own ideas for her. Other women have to go through this much later, when their children have already flown the nest. Thus, instead of projecting her wishes and fantasies onto the child, she has to realize them herself!

If this dream of a birth of an eagle and child reminds us of the symbolism of *sublimatio* or the liberation of the spirit from matter and of the birth of Anthropos, we can also infer that, from the point of view of the unconscious, having a child is the job of the "whole man." It involves a transformation of the personality: in other words, a birth of the Self, of which the Anthropos is a symbol. The birth of a child in the dreams of many pregnant women is scarcely different from the birth of a higher level of consciousness, or the Self. We feel that these dreams, of which we have found a large number in our selection, must therefore be taken as a clear indication that conception is in many ways fateful and beyond our control. These dreams can be particularly helpful when it comes to making the serious decision as to whether to have or abort a child. They can throw light on the problem from the point of view of the unconscious and thus provide an additional element to the rational position.

It appears that just like the other dreams that have birds "fall into them," something wants to be made human – that is, conscious: something wants to be incarnated in a concrete, human form. The incarnation can therefore refer to either the child or to the realization of a spiritual interest in the concrete, everyday life. The doves of Dione, the earth-goddess, could be a simile for woman's inner experiences – the essence of a woman's feminine intuition,

[379] Cf. Dream No. 88 in Ch. 5.6, where the father of the child is an eagle: it could be fantasies involving power, glory, honor or any other ambitions for the future son.

which could positively influence her environment, her children and her relationships. Irrespective of intellectual work, studies, profession or other outer activities, from the standpoint of the unconscious, this is of the utmost importance. These dreams show us that pregnancy and spiritual development are often only apparent opposites. In fact, they may be prerequisites for each other.

Figure 25. Bastet (Saqquara 600 B.C.)

5.4. The Cat

Regina Abt

The cat enjoys a special position among our domestic animals. It is the only pet that domesticated itself voluntarily, so to speak, and it has preserved its independence to this day. One side of its being is friendly, affectionate, human-oriented, playful and joyful, whereas the other side is shy, still wild, furtive, nocturnal, unfamiliar. These curious opposites of comfortable familiarity and mysterious distance have always intrigued man and have also been the basis of numerous positive, as well as negative, projections onto the cat.

Cats are distinctly maternal animals: cat mothers protect their offspring and bring them up in an exemplary manner. Delivery often takes place in hiding, as the cat father is not to be trusted. Cat mothers are also well known to bring up other animal offspring, such as hares, foxes, squirrels, etc.[380]

Various religions made of the cat a feminine-maternal goddess. With this, we are about to enter a world and iconology related to the cat which has interested man form time immemorial. Freya, the Teutonic mother-goddess, was represented sitting in a carriage drawn by two cats. In Egypt, whence all our cats originate, Bast or Bastet, the cat goddess, enjoyed the highest veneration for two thousand years. It was the vivacious and sensual aspect of the cat that was primarily venerated in her cult. Bastet celebrations were full of cheerful exuberance, sexual freedom and musical entertainment.[381] Particularly characteristic of the cat is its playfulness, which has to do with its highly creative side. We have seen earlier in the book that creativity often germinates during play or fantasy.

Sometimes Bastet is represented by Bes, a naked dwarf and god of music, dance and pleasure, but also marriage, fertility, pregnancy and birth. These mirthful, buoyant aspects of life relate to the creative content in the unconscious, for they bring forth things that get forgotten in the monotony of everyday life. It is for this reason that more or less orgiastic religious celebrations

---

[380] Cf. Barbara Hannah, *Seminar on Cat, Dog, Horse*

[381] M.-L. von Franz, "The Bremen Town Musicians from the Point of View of Depth Psychology" in: *Archetypal Dimensions of the Psyche*, Shambhala, Boston, 1997, p. 124

have a firm place in all cultures. Because of her connection with the sunny sides of life, Bastet was also the goddess of happiness, who granted wealth, power, honor, health and longevity.

Figure 26. Ra as the sun-cat killing Apophis, the snake of the underworld

Some cat statues carry on their forehead the Egyptian sun symbol of Scarabaeus. At certain times, Bastet was regarded as the daughter of the sun god, Ra, who is sometimes represented as a male cat. Every day anew Ra fights Apep or Apophis, the underworld snake, the chaos of the night, in order for the sun to rise again. Psychologically, Ra as a male cat stands for the ability to stave off darkness and "vermin," mice and snakes in the unconscious.[382]

Bastet was also called the solar eye of Horus, the heavenly god. Horus had one solar and one lunar eye. The solar aspects had to do with light or the light of consciousness, insight and foresight. This is how disaster could be prevented. The Egyptian name "Mau" signifies cat and seeing at the same time. The cat is considered a prophetess in various mythological contexts. Bastet was also called the goddess of truth. The solar eye, i.e., insight into the outer circumstances and relationships of life, is assisted by the lunar eye of Horus, another name by which she was known and which can see into the depths of the night. Bastet, as the moon goddess, corresponds nicely to the nocturnal aspect of our cat: the twinkle in her eyes, which mythologically have been associated with the moon, can see in the dark. The cat's secret life takes place in the night and until only recently remained an unsolved riddle to zoologists. Psychologically, the night side is the unconscious where things cannot be seen at all or only to the extent one can see them in the dimness of the moonlight.

The moon has to do with the cosmic movement of time – the tidal waves, the seasons and Nature's rhythms of death and rebirth, of dying and being born again. Bastet, the moon goddess, belongs to the feminine rhythm and fertility, and presiding over sexuality and *joie de vivre*, also to the feminine, instinctive nature.

The fertility of the moon goddess, symbolically speaking, is also the fertility of the night shining in the background of the soul, embodied by the moon and light of the unconscious. Bastet not only protects the physical pregnancy and birth but nourishing the "psychic" children, she is also in charge of the psychic

[382] B. Hannah, cf. *Lectures on Cat, Dog, Horse*

pregnancy and birth. The fact that Bastet, like Artemis and other ancient fertility goddesses, was worshipped as a virgin, may suggest that her children could also have been spiritual children.[383] Hence, when we dream of a cat in the context of a spiritual task, this independent creature who does whatever pleases it, can cause us quite a bit of trouble. For, the cat gives birth wherever and whenever it wants to. It won't be harnessed like a horse. Dealing with this strong-willed, unpredictable feminine creative principle, personified by the cat, is extremely difficult. This self-confident autonomy and independence is the most remarkable feature of the cat. The cat often emerges in dreams of women who would need to reflect more upon their independent feminine personalities because they are too dependent and insecure. The cat's independence is based on self-confidence and trust in itself. The negative side of this can be an egotistical lack of responsibility, quite analogous to the often hurtful behavior of our cats when they unexpectedly turn their backs on us.

The cat has this wonderful and enviable quality of imperturbability that stands out in our hectic everyday lives. The shadow side of it is laziness. There are many tales (e.g., Gubernatius) about cats who are too lazy to catch their own mice, so they trick others into catching the mice for them. This aspect, too, belongs to the shadow-side of the feminine. It is sometimes this very aspect that a modern young woman seems to be deprived of during pregnancy. On the other hand, laziness can lead to treacherous duplicity, especially when someone wants to fulfill a personal ambition with a minimum of responsibility.[384] Men still tend to project feminine deceitfulness onto cats. Therefore, with a man who actively hates cats, one would be well-advised to watch his anima!

In Egypt, Bastet was closely associated with Sechmet, the lion-goddess, who was also a war-goddess, and her breath was the hot wind of the desert. She was known as both a carrier and healer of diseases, including the plague. (Whenever the unconscious produces a neurosis, it can also heal it again!) When Hathor, the goddess of cows, appeared as a cat, it was said that she was Bastet when she was friendly and Sechmet when she was infuriated. The maternal element of infuriated Sechmet can easily put woman in a state of unpredictability, destructiveness and frustration. She can contaminate and render sick her entire environment! However, Hathor as Bastet – that is, the maternal in its positive form – can have a healing effect and can unite the opposites that are combating each other.

In Egypt as well as here in Western Europe, the value of the cat was mainly seen in terms of its being a hunter of mice and snakes. Bastet thus became the patroness against sickness, in particular against blindness, for mice and snakes were believed to be carriers of diseases. Eye-shaped cat amulets were

---

[383] P. Dale-Green, *The Archetypal Cat*, p. 155
[384] Cf. B. Hannah, *Lectures on Cat, Dog, Horse*

common. In our folklore, it was primarily the cat's tail that was considered to have healing powers. Its tail has an amazing power of expression and is an unerring indicator of its moods (*pars pro toto*). People therefore attributed magic and sometimes even bewitching powers to it. Thanks to its tail, a cat can keep its balance on the most narrow of garden fences. Psychologically speaking, it therefore has to do with the equilibrium of man's deeper, instinctive layers. One could say that the many contradictory states of mind, inclinations, moods and needs that can tear us apart if we cannot keep our balance like a cat, have to do with our own "tail." To experience healing through the tail of the cat could psychologically mean that a woman has learnt to accept and to deal with the part of her dark, instinctive cat nature – a part of that would consist of savage, untamed emotions.

The dreams that we are going to examine more closely now will initially show the negative, menacing or alienating aspect of the cat. In our cultures, we do not have a Bastet, which is why in folklore the cat has primarily negative characteristics – in fact, cat and witch are often considered to be one and the same. People believed that cats turned into witches at night or that witches rode on cats' backs up to the *Brocken* [a mountain in Germany], in order to make a pact with the devil. Black cats signified bad luck, illness or death and were closely associated with black magic. While in the pre-Christian era Nature's cycle of growth and decay belonged to the great mother-goddess, in certain Swiss mountain legends, Nature is dominated by a wicked weather-witch, who is responsible for lightning, thunderstorms, rock slides and flooding. The witches in these legends are frequently described as cats. The witch-like aspect has to do with elements pertaining to Sechmet – i.e., with destructive emotions, anger and moody frustrations that can inundate and possess us – as well as with mean intrigues, being unjustly critical and harboring negative fantasies about other people.

The beginnings of medieval witch-hunting also gave rise to cat-hunting. Cats were most cruelly tortured, hanged, drowned, burnt alive because it was thought that they belonged to or were themselves witches or demons. The individuality of woman and the ostensible darkness around the feminine represented by the cat's qualities of autonomy and unpredictability were suppressed and have largely vanished into the unconscious. This problem is the theme underlying many cat dreams of women today.

Marie-Louise von Franz writes: "In effect, the way a human being deals with animals is the same way he also deals with his own instincts, and thus also with the oldest gods, that is, the oldest psychic representation of our instincts, the animal gods."[385] The first dream that we are going to discuss will show how Bastet or Sechmet are alive in modern woman.

[385] M.-L. von Franz, *The Bremen Town Musicians*, p. 114

Five months pregnant and having had a series of complications, a thirty-one-year-old woman dreamt:

Dream No. 67:

> *I fished out a kitten from the lake and rescued it, placing it on the raft of the public bathing area. I hold it in a way that the water can come out of it. I apply mouth to mouth resuscitation. It comes alive again.*

The dreamer manages to lift the psychic content represented by the helpless kitten onto the land, i.e., into consciousness. Here, she can revive it, that is, let it be alive again in her own life. This kitten presents us with a new kind of independent femininity or maternal qualities that need to first establish some firm ground in the conscious ego. However, the problem has not been solved yet. One month later she dreams:

Dream No. 68:

> *A little kitten is being kept locked up (by an old man?), without food. I feed it. It is so hungry that it even eats salad.*

Here, the cat is under the control of an old man, an animus of which the dreamer is apparently quite unaware. The old man could represent an old conscious attitude, e.g., a religious attitude she has inherited from the ancients that put virtue, the law and uprightness before certain feminine values, such as enjoyment of the pleasures of life or even a certain amount of laziness and physical well-being. Cats are carnivores, and eating meat would point to something physical or sexual. However, the kitten is so famished that she eats salad, which seems incongruous. The animus can play the role of a kind of conscience and can cause woman constantly to do things she thinks she has to do. The instinct in pregnant woman, however, may in fact need to be more quiescent, may want to vegetate and let the body dictate the pace, or be sexually more active. The animus is telling her that that is improper in her condition.

A 24-year-old woman, in her first pregnancy, was undecided as to whether or not to have an abortion. She had been living with the father of the child to be for four years but did not know whether she should marry him. She dreamt:

Dream No. 69:

> *I am at the Federal University Summer Camp with B. Two old men look after the luggage we left in the TV-room. B. comes in but he doesn't want to help them. I am cooking. Dad and B. are at home. Some very small kitties enter through the kitchen. One is black. The two other ones are white or yellowish. I scream. We go outdoors. There is something mysterious about those cats. My father walks home with me. Suddenly he can't*

walk – there is a problem with one of his legs. Then he sits on the stairs. The corridors in the building get crowded with people who are puzzled about the kitties.

In this dream, the father and representative of traditional consciousness suddenly becomes lame as the kittens appear. The dreamer is cooking, performing a truly feminine activity, which we associate with warming-up, baking, or hatching-out. She is a metaphor, so to speak, for pregnancy. Something is not quite cooked yet – in German, "baked": *Jemand ist noch nicht ganz gebacken*, which means somebody is still green behind the ears or somebody is not quite of this world yet. At this point, the three mysterious kittens turn up, creating confusion for everybody and in a way making the male-fatherly standpoint shake. It seems as if here, despite the conscious ego of the woman, something managed to get an entry, a dynamic, light-dark feminine element that apparently causes some hefty unrest to the conscious daily course of life. This could be linked with the dreamer's still unsure attitude towards a firm commitment to a womanly life, be it the status of a married woman or assuming the responsibility for a child. It may well be in the interest of both that the father's one-sided, "one-legged" standpoint begins to shake! A healthy boy was finally born. After Dream No. 67, the same dreamer had the two following dreams, four and two weeks before delivery:

Dream No. 70:

The baby is born. At home I look at it and want to feed it. It is big, fat, red-haired, has sharp teeth, speaks and can already stand. I become suspicious: this cannot be our child! I show it to my husband. It must be a changeling. It is somebody else's child, who has something against Frau von Franz. I look for our cat, who has our real child. She runs away.

Dream No. 71:

I have to mind a large, heavy baby. Then it is a sweet, little kitten that I calmly carry in my arms through the noisy city.

Frau von Franz of the first dream has to do with a creative piece of work the dreamer was working on when she was pregnant, and Frau von Franz was a kind of a "spiritual midwife" to her and her work. Something seems not to be quite all right with this creative process. According to ancient folklore, a changeling is a child who has been maliciously exchanged by dwarfs.[386] It is not a normal human child. It is a real limb of the devil, for red hair and sharp teeth belong to the devil or to a vampire. The dreamer is feeding the wrong child – one who must have foisted maliciousness and envy onto her. It could

---

[386] J. Guntern, *Volkserzählungen aus dem Oberwallis*, No. 2012, and others

be ambition or envy foisting the wrong child onto her, in which case her creative work, that is also her "child," would not be her own. Perhaps her work indeed became infested with ambition and envy, and this had troubled her relationship with her spiritual teacher. The cat has the real child, but she runs away.

A cat participating in a creative process is rather like the feminine manner of absorbing an idea (*Einfall*), autonomously and self-confidently, without having an eye to success or approval. The cat follows its own course, which is why she is not always available when we need her. This idiosyncrasy of the feminine-creative has to become accepted. On a biological as well as spiritual level, the type of creativity pertaining to the cat or to Bastet, the moon-goddess, is rather different from the masculine active, efficient way of performing (intellectually, abstractly). It is more in the nature of having the ability to wait patiently, like a cat in front of a mousehole, concentrated and yet relaxed, until the right moment has come and the new content has revealed itself. We shall come back to this very different kind of creativity a little later.

In the last dream, two weeks before the birth of her child, the dreamer has to care for and then carry a huge baby. We assume that this is the burden both the spiritual and physical child represents to her. A little kitten, on the other hand, she can love and easily carry around with her. Thus in the unconscious we see how, parallel to the physical pregnancy, an additional creative process has unfolded: it is the creation of a new, instinctive feminine modus vivendi that despite all the noisy activity going on around her, will not run away. The dreamer finally gave birth, by Caesarian section, to a healthy, large baby-girl.

In the dream below, from a different woman, we return to the theme of "feeding the cat," which was already discussed in Dream No. 68:

Dream No. 72:

> I find myself in an old stone building. For me it has a romantic atmosphere. It is a sort of castle. I walk around this castle accompanied by a black male cat. It seems that I am responsible for it. Soon it is hungry. I give it something sucky to eat. It is very unsatisfied with this and goes by itself to fetch a better piece of meat, which annoys me somewhat. I find the cat is quite cheeky. – Later I am sitting with other people in a sitting room, my mother is there as well. We are all, I believe, working on a piece of handicraft. In the middle of the table is a huge block of chocolate. Suddenly the cat climbs on the table – as if paralyzed I watch it. It sits on top of the chocolate and produces a long excrement on it. My mother says to me about this: "You should not have allowed that". As if it were easy to deal with that cat.

221

This male cat is evidently not getting the right food. It is only given something to suck on. But it is bold and goes and fetches itself a good piece of meat. Perhaps our dreamer is trying to feed her unruly instinct by indulging it like a child. Some women behave like pampered babies during pregnancy, letting themselves be overindulged and looked after. However, the great mother's *Trabant*, the attendant of the witch, the black male cat, is not satisfied with this: it wants substantial nourishment – namely, meat – which, to a person with a Christian consciousness, smells of sin. This is why the dreamer gets annoyed. Then the male cat commits another atrocity. It produces a large excrement upon a huge piece of chocolate on the maternal "crochet-tea table," which is all too sweet for it. The maternal ladies' tea party with chocolates paints too traditional and Christian a picture of motherhood. Something in the dreamer strongly protests against this. The excrement illustrates her deep and very base sense of outrage. The male cat personifies a thoroughly ruthless mind and will that could not care less about conventions or about being amenable. And it is right!

The dreamer, of course, earns disapproval regarding the bad behavior of the cat over whom she has little control. She presumably lives in an atmosphere of a positive mother complex and is too much of a "good girl" – too childlike and passive, such that everything is done the way mother did it. An independent cat instinct, which wants different needs satisfied, naturally rebels against this.

Mythologically speaking, the castle amplifies a feminine symbol of the Self. The Virgin Mary is often depicted as a tower or palace, and in alchemy, the *"castrum"* is a symbol of the anima or mother.[387] This important symbol shows the dreamer that motherhood and the creation of a new life require her individual totality. For, along with the maternal, giving, life-bestowing aspect, Mother Nature has equally instinctive, self-willed, incomprehensible aspects, just like a black cat. The picture of the noble, kind, self-denying, self-sacrificing sweet little mother painted in romantic literature, is only a part of the feminine nature. The process of rendering conscious unknown or repressed aspects of the maternal-feminine in preparation for motherhood goes hand in hand with the growth of the child in the maternal womb.

The beginning of a process towards achieving consciousness frequently looks revolting and destructive. The following dream is an example of this:

Dream No. 73:

> *At a table with children. Horrible worms crawl out of the ceiling. The dreamer is immensely horrified. The worms turn into cats which start to*

---

[387] Cf. M.-L. von Franz, *The Cat. A Tale of Feminine Redemption*, Inner City Books, Toronto, 1998

chew the dreamer. Although she likes cats otherwise, she can't prevent her resistance to them. At last the children say: "Stroke them!" – which the dreamer immediately does. Immediately, the cat in her arms turns into a quiet little boy. "Now … be quiet, too. This battle is over, too."

In his *Dream Seminar*, Jung deals with the worm in great detail: it comes out of the earth, i.e., from below or from within, or psychologically, from the body as the body is our closest link with the earth. Worms do not have a brain but are entirely sympathetic and belong to a primitive stage of evolution. The worm has no center but consists of a series of separate ganglia. Jung says that when a worm comes to the surface it is an unconscious form of life that can be extremely destructive for us, for there is a danger of segmentation, disintegration and dissociation of consciousness into parts.

Human uterine development begins with the vegetative life of the less evolved animal species. Later, it develops into a sympathetic nervous system, then the brain. The nervous system signifies the prime origin of the disintegration of the perfect continuum of undifferentiated life. It is "the first beginning of the dissociation of the perfect continuum of undifferentiated life, and so the first beginning of differentiation is the beginning of destruction."[388] Therefore, the worm is the source of evil, already present in paradise. Yet, despite its destructive appearance, the worm symbolizes the beginning of a spiritual life – that is, a primeval germ of life or the beginning of higher consciousness and knowledge. Jung refers to certain early Gnostic philosophers, who believed that God had created the worm in order to create a spiritual world.

Furthermore, the worm is a symbol of the decomposition of the body after death. The body is eaten by the worms and becomes earth and a part of Nature's great life-cycle. According to Epiphanius' version, having been burnt, the proud phoenix reemerges from the ash as a worm.[389]

The worms in our dream signify the decay or demise of an old consciousness and the beginning of a newly reached level of consciousness or perhaps the interregnum between the death of an old attitude and the birth of a new one. This is signaled first on a very deep instinctive, physical layer. The dreamer is horrified by the worms, for they are so far removed from her conscious reason that she cannot relate to them in any way. But then the worms turn into cats – a higher type of animal that is much closer to human understanding. The children urge her to stroke the cats, i.e., to accept them. There seems to be a strong unconscious bond and affinity that children feel for animals, which is probably why they are so good at imitating them. Their manner of treating animals is completely spontaneous, unsentimental, at once empathetic and cruel, and unconscious, like Nature itself.

[388] C.G. Jung, *Dream Analysis, The Seminars*, edited by William McGuire, Bollingen Series XCIX, Princeton University Press, 1984, p. 237
[389] Jung, *Mysterium coniunctionis*, CW 14, § 472, Princeton University Press, 1970

The dreamer is supposed to spontaneously accept a new femininity, which is unpleasantly body-oriented and catlike, without even questioning it. This new awareness of the body's functions and needs, which are inevitable during pregnancy, can be a new and rather tedious experience for a woman. Part of this has to do with manifestations, such as physical discomfort, feeling moody, depressed or irritable, which are difficult to explain or to understand because they are a result of the deepest transformative processes in the body and psyche.

Yet to accept lovingly and to accommodate all this seems to cause a transformation on a higher plane. Suddenly, the dreamer has a little boy in her arms – not her own but a stranger's child, who has been created from a magical transformation process. The child is a new addition to her consciousness, and it was not "given" to her: it cost her quite some effort, courage and readiness to face the bothersome new contents from the deep instinctive layers of her personality. She feels as if she has just come from a battle of hostile parties intercolliding. The feeling of peace signifies the deliverance from the battle of the opposites without which we cannot reach a higher level of consciousness. The transformation of worms-cats-child in this dream again illustrates a process of struggling to achieve consciousness. The last stage is the child and it points to the Self.

The cat symbol occurs again in a dream by the same dreamer, about a month later, only a few days before delivery.

Dream No. 74:

> In a dream I am standing in front of a white wall. Suddenly a small cat jumps out of the wall and rolls on the ground. I watch this happening with mixed feelings – on one hand the cat is very sweet to look at, on the other it has a large growth on the front of its neck (throat?) which I found made me feel disgust. [Blister on husband's finger the evening before.] But I suddenly realize that this growth has something to do with the awaited birth of our child. Immediately the mixed feelings disappear and I feel curious and happy. At this moment two other kittens come out of the wall. They roll on the ground as well, now sitting beside them there is a large fat cat and I think: "That is surely the mother of the three kittens."

The original small cat has a repulsive growth or blister on its throat. The dreamer relates it to the expected child, perhaps because it, too, is lying in a watery sac. As she realizes this, she suddenly derives a feeling of happiness and curiosity about the little kitten, who is contentedly rolling on the floor.

The throat is the place where we feel the cat's purring sound. Cats love to be stroked on the throat. When a cat purrs, it expresses an extraordinary feeling of being at peace with itself. Cats purr much more frequently in the company of people than with members of their own species. They also purr in

224

the presence of their master or mistress when they are dying or suffering pain. Then, this strikes us as total submission to fate. It is a psychic attitude that is propitious in anticipation of the mystery inherent in the birth of a child.

To begin with, there are three kittens before a fourth, the mother cat, joins them. Let us take a look at the symbolism of the numbers: the three has to do with the flow of time, with the past, present and future and with the inevitable, irreversible and fateful aspect of time. As we have seen earlier in the book, the Nordic Norns and the Greek Moirai, the Greek goddesses of fate, had triple personalities. In addition, many moon goddesses, e.g., Hekate *triformis*, the mistress of birth and death, had three dog heads, or the Egyptian moon goddess depicted as three maidens and finally, the Celtic moon goddesses as three Bridgets.[390] We can therefore see the cats in a context of a feminine creation process under a lunar cycle or fateful temporal cycle.

The triple moon goddess always contains the light and dark moon or the fertility and ephemeral aspect of Nature. For our dream, this could mean that the conflict of "sweet little kitten" and repulsive blister on the throat – in other words, the dark and light aspects of becoming a mother – could be overcome by a third aspect: namely, conscious submission to life's fatefulness.

The third of the Arabian moon maidens, later the three daughters of Allah, is Manat, which means time in the sense of fate. The word Mana, derived from Manat is used by the Arabs for happiness.[391] Happiness is what the dreamer feels because she realizes the fatefulness of the impending birth and the expected child. Thus, it is not happiness in terms of fulfillment of personal needs – rather, it encompasses feeling secure and comfortable in the fateful current of life.

The number four has to do with orientation, with consciously dividing up our universe into all four directions, the year into seasons, the month into weeks, etc. This concept of four parts (quaternity)

Figure 27. Bastet

we can find in all cultures seeking optimal orientation or an expression of totality. The archetypal structure underlying our conscious functions is, as Jung has shown, fourfold.[392] Four has to do with an objective realization of something that had previously influenced or obsessed

[390] *Lexikon der germanischen und römischen Mythologie*, II, 1, p. 1341
[391] M. E. Harding, *Woman's Mysteries*, Harper & Row, New York, 1971, p. 218
[392] Cf. C.G. Jung, CW 6, *Psychological Types*

us in a fateful way – (the number three). We can now regard the four cats at the end of the dream as a potential, fundamentally new orientation of the dreamer's ego consciousness. Moreover, the cheerful cat quaternio, with all the warmth and serenity that is characteristic of Bastet, puts the young mother into an optimal frame of mind in preparation for the birth of her child.

Dream No. 75:[393]

I am at my mother's house, packing a lunch for work. I pack a sandwich, but see she has pickled eggs, too. I ask if I can have some, so I eat one, then I pack one. – Now I am in a parking garage. I am with some girlfriends. I think we are going to a conference or high school reunion. I pass by some young men who are familiar to me. I have met one before through my Dad. We all start downstairs. We hear that there are animals on the loose. As we go into a building we see behind us a large prehistoric cat (it is supposed to be a tiger, but it looks like a wet cat to me or a cat that is very scrawny and short-haired). We are sitting in the front room in front of a large picture window. We are trying not to move because it may pounce through the window if it sees movement. I am peering at it from behind the curtain, hoping it doesn't see me. It turns away, and we decide to try to make a break for it up the stairs. But as we start, it turns back and begins to get ready to pounce. My alarm went off so I don't know what happened.

The dream begins in the house of the dreamer's mother. She is getting a packed lunch of sandwiches and eggs to go to work. She is in her former daughter-situation, the way it used to be before she was married, pregnant and a mother herself. Her mother is still in possession of the eggs, i.e., the germs of creativity, albeit pickled, preserved. Then she is off to some conference or high school reunion with her girlfriends and young men, the way she used to perhaps when she was a student.

First, she goes down to some parking garage where it is usually dark, empty and possibly dangerous. If alone, one could get assaulted there, which is not a comfortable feeling. Apparently there are animals on the loose. This place is a perfect allegory for the unconscious, rather like the cellar every little child is afraid of. Being pregnant, the dreamer no longer really belongs to the world of her student years. This is why the unconscious unleashes animals, i.e., instinctive sides in her that may be tied up or locked up down there. When the large prehistoric cat suddenly emerges from behind a large window with a splendid view, it is not clear in which room the dreamer and her friends actually are. Glass windows are insulators: they protect us against all types of weather and variations in temperature, yet we can still see through them. Although the

---

[393] Dream by a Spanish dreamer. Many of the dreams throughout the book are hers.

dreamer can see this new menacing content of the unconscious clearly in front of her, she has not yet absorbed it emotionally. She is afraid and wants to run away upstairs, or back into the familiarity of consciousness. However, it is too late. She wakes up filled with fear just as the cat is getting ready to pounce on her. The outcome and lysis of the dream remain undisclosed to us.

The archetypal image of the prehistoric cat comes from the depths of the dreamer's unconscious. Erich Neumann held that at the beginning of the developmental history of human consciousness – belonging phylogenetically to the development of humanity and repeating itself ontogenetically in each human individual – there was a matriarchal stage. He is referring to the dawn of human history, a time in which the unconscious (and the feminine) still prevailed, and when consciousness (and the masculine) or the ego had not yet become autonomous and independent.[394] This epoch was ruled by the archetypal great mother with her close link to the rhythm of Nature and to the changes of the moon. Bastet, the catlike moon goddess, is born out of this context. Her creativity is of a feminine kind that is far removed from the academic knowledge the dreamer had to acquire at high school. It has rather to do with passive expectation, with letting grow and mature and with bringing to term something new.

Many women today, having developed their rational, masculine, active ego-consciousness, have removed themselves considerably from this kind of attitude. And yet, pregnancy is the time of the great mother. To go through it we still have to resort to her help, which is the help of the feminine instincts. The larger the schism between that deep matriarchal layer and today's consciousness in modern woman, the more dangerous are the newly emerging contents. In this dream, the opposites of the world of parking garages and the prehistoric cat are so immense that it looks as if the dreamer can only flee. Perhaps the shock of this dream has somehow affected the young woman. At best, it would have incited her to activate her imagination, i.e., to engage in an inner dialogue with this menacing cat. In such a way, consciousness can then turn to this new, uncanny, unconscious content – can introvert, as it were – in order to question its purpose. This kind of confrontation frequently results in the fact that the unconscious figure becomes less menacing and at the same time creates the potential for greater psychic maturity or a new attitude.

The following dream shows the possibility of a harmonious transition from the everyday conscious world to an experience of maternal archetypes and back. As these archetypes do not stand in contradiction to the dreamer's consciousness, they turn out to provide a wonderfully helpful experience.

[394] E. Neumann, *The Moon and Matriarchal Consciousness in Fathers and Mothers*, Spring Publications, 1973

Dream No. 76, twenty-six-year-old dreamer, five months pregnant with her second child:[395]

> *I sit with my husband and our two dogs in an open, uncovered carriage of some kind. We are leaving from a farm in Östergötland, the landscape where I was born. It is 12 o'clock, midnight, darkness. We have our cat Mio running around us, as we pass slowly along the small path or road, leading from the farm. In the darkness, I catch glimpses of many cats. They are large and like rounded and lie watchfully waiting. One of the cats is especially big. He is the ruler of all the other animals.*
>
> *The Nature has the form of several small hills. To the right a solitary tree grows. It is not a very high tree, maybe 3 meters, with symmetrically wide growing branches. It is an apple tree. The strange thing is that this tree shines from a light that radiates from the tree itself. In its mild moon-shine-like light, many bats, or maybe birds, swarm around. They are beautiful, look like birds in wonderful colors. In a way they look more like fishes because they do not move their wings but float or glide swiftly around, in the light under the tree. It is most beautiful and moving to look at. I know in the dream that this is a Holy Tree.*
>
> *On the next little hill to the left I see an elephant with her baby elephant. No, it is a Mammoth mother and her child. They have long-haired, grey, rough fur, ivory tusks and a trunk. The child follows its mother closely and they wander peacefully away. These two animals, like the shining tree, are numinous, and I watch them with deep love and respect. I think of Mio, our cat. I realize that if he is left alone here, he will not be able to find his way home tomorrow. I call for him. After some time, I notice that he is together with Frodo (our terrier) under my right arm. My husband drives the car away.*

Although the archetypal aspect of the Mother-goddess in this dream has nothing menacing about it, it evokes the supreme image of a numinous, entirely different world and dimension. It is midnight, a time when night turns to day, a transitory moment at which, according to the folklore of all cultures, otherworldly things happen. Spirits and demons, devils and witches, are on the loose and extra-human powers can be called upon for good as well as for evil purposes. The position of the moon is also taken into account here. It is Bastet's, the moon goddess' time and the time of the cats. Let us remember the Egyptian sun-cat, struggling against the underworld snake, who ensures that each night turn into day again. It is the moment of the birth of a new day or of a new light.

The dream setting is the dreamer's birthplace. Pregnancy and anticipated motherhood tend to take a woman back to the beginnings – to her mother's

---

[395] By the same dreamer: No. 28, Chapter "Fire"; No. 35, Ch. "Plants"; No. 42, Ch. "Tree"

land or to her roots, as it were. Whether she has accepted her own mother or not, an identification with her as the first maternal experience she has had is inevitable. However, what transpires unambiguously in this dream is that the land of the mother is in fact the land of the great mother-goddess. Thus behind Mio, the dreamer's personal cat, we see the *Trabants*, the divine cats belonging to the great mother. They are lying there, waiting, as the creation process in question is a time of waiting. Now, to the right, there is an apple tree which in the soft moonlight shines from within, and fishlike birds in all colors hover about the tree.

We have discussed the symbol of the tree in detail earlier. Let us only remember the tree of life often associated with the great goddess, water and the cosmic tree, whose branches reach into the heavens.[396] The cosmic tree is depicted here and there in the company of birds, horses or tigers. It is also the place where the ancestors' souls meet.

Without, for the moment, even taking into account the specifically feminine symbolism of the apple tree, it is clear that this dream's holy tree is the tree of the great mother-goddess. The bats or birds that are flying around it are presumably related to the souls of the ancestors or of yet unborn children. In most cultures, the soul of a deceased individual is represented with wings or in the shape of a bird, illustrating thereby that the body has disappeared but that the spirit has survived.[397]

The soft moonlight radiating from the tree is the "light of Nature" or the *lumen naturae* of the alchemists and Paracelsus, which Jung held to be the light of the wisdom pertaining to the feminine unconscious. For Paracelsus, the light of Nature is an intuitive conception of the circumstances, or a kind of illumination.[398]

The moonlike light also belongs to Bastet, the moon and cat goddess and her special role in the creative process, physical or spiritual. As Neumann explains in his essay on the moon and the matriarchal consciousness, the recognition of the moonlight is linked to periodicity and the changing quality of time[399]: the wisdom of the sun or intellectual, masculine wisdom is expeditious, calculating and abstract. The wisdom derived from the moon has to do with waiting, being patient, as in cooking or baking, bringing something to term, letting it mature in silence, transforming, allowing it grow. Understanding here means conceiving or receiving as opposed to intellectual registering, assimilating, classifying. When the time is ripe, recognition or the new

---

[396] Cf. M. Eliade, *Die Religionen und das Heilige*, p. 302 ff / *Patterns in Comparative Religion*

[397] M.-L. von Franz, *Individuation in Fairy Tales*, p. 147

[398] C.G. Jung, *Paracelsus the Physician*, CW 15, § 29 and 41, Routledge & Kegan Paul, 1966

[399] E. Neumann, *The Moon and the Matriarchal Consciousness*

emerges as an illumination. Hence the importance of the moment in time. Similar to any natural process of growth, we cannot force it: time alone determines it. Just as the cat sits in front of the mouse-hole, concentrating and yet totally relaxed, so it requires a kind of observant consciousness, a contemplative pondering upon, a circling around a content or a purpose, until the right moment has come for it to be apprehended with feeling. This kind of feminine wisdom is rather closer to life and Nature than it is to any abstract-intellectual mode.[400]

Today, there are many women in the world of science and among so-called intellectuals who are trying to prove themselves. They always run the risk, however, of placing too large a distance between their outer life and the side of their feminine being and thus easily fall prey to the animus. On the other hand, it is not uncommon for women to throw away their careers from one day to the next and to have a baby. It is very difficult to hold one's own with this kind of feminine creativity in a masculine-intellectual world. To recognize the light of the moon-wisdom as an independent feminine value and to defend it vis-à-vis the masculine style characterized by efficiency and purposefulness, seems equally difficult in the time of the biological process of pregnancy, birth and child-rearing.

Being the dwelling place of the spirits of the departed and at the same time a place of the creation of the life of a newborn, the tree is concomitantly the goal and source of the individuation process. In Jung's words, it represents the outer, visible appearance of individuation.[401] In the dream, the tree is on the right, the side of consciousness, i.e., of our right hand with which we conquer the world. The left side is where the heart is, the side of feeling and the unconscious. This is where the elephant or mammoth mother comes from. The right side is tied up with the light of wisdom, that is, Nature's wisdom and the manifestation of the spirit from the unconscious. On the one side, we have the specifically feminine-creative spirituality (the tree), on the other side, the mammoth mother, embodying the animal-instinctive foundation or the feminine-maternal creation process.

The mammoth being evidently a primitive form of our elephant, we must give it priority in our interpretation. From what we know about elephants today, they are exceptionally conscious of and oriented towards the members of the family and herd. For example, a herd has a veritable kindergarten, and all the mothers alternate in being in charge of it. The chief elephant cow, which in event of danger has everyone stand in a circle, reassures younger, more fearful cows by putting into their mouths carefully arranged little bundles of grass.[402]

---

[400] Cf. *ibid.*, p. 355 f
[401] Cf. C.G. Jung, *Alchemical Studies*, CW 13, Chapter IV, § 241
[402] Cf. Grzimek, *Lexikon der Tierwelt*, Chapter "Elephants"

In the Middle Ages, we knew very little about elephants. People believed that they lived to one thousand years and ascribed invincible bravery, a sense of dignity, generosity and intelligence to them. In Europe, the elephant became a symbol of Christ, and in Africa, it is considered to possess wisdom and arcane knowledge. Marie-Louise von Franz therefore held that the elephant represents a personality that has completed the individuation process.[403] There is a widely known medieval European fable that tells of an elephant couple in a kind of a paradisiacal garden where nobody can find them. There they feed on the legendary Mandragore fruit and other exquisite herbs. Then there is a mysterious wedding followed by a two-year pregnancy of the elephant cow. The latter is so frightened of the dragon that wants to devour the elephant baby that she disappears into the water, the sea or a river, and delivers it there.[404]

The Christian interpretation of this story was to see in the elephant mother the sinful man preoccupied with earthly things and the baptismal water having a regenerating and vivifying effect, like the water for the young elephant. I am more convinced by the elephant mother as a symbol of the feminine-maternal Self. In the dragon, we can see a correspondence to the snake in paradise. Let us not forget, however, that the snake also signifies the Christian beginning of the process of achieving consciousness of good and evil, feminine and masculine, in other words, of the opposites underlying our existence.

The elephant mother is part of the feminine archetypal nature aspect. The fable says that her baby will be born far away in the water or in the unconscious. That is where the mammoth mother is safe and strong. It is the great mother or the collective unconscious that contains every individual woman's unconscious and the mystery implicit in every birth. Our dreamer is made aware of this marvel through the touching image of the mammoth mother and her child. The destiny of individual woman fits into a larger context. The knowledge that things have always and everywhere been the way they are can bestow upon her confidence and security. It seems to me that women today can derive much support from these archetypal pictures given that the attitude propagated by the Christian church has very successfully estranged her from her deep-lying feminine instincts. Thus the emergence of the mammoth mother signifies the appearance of something extraordinarily primordial and primitive, a primeval vital content from the unconscious that cannot be influenced by volition.[405] A primitive conception of the mammoth would be a totem-animal incarnating the spirit of an ancestor. In the language of psychology, we call it ancestral instincts, or, as Jung puts it, the origin of physiological

---

[403] Cf. M.-L. von Franz, *Puer aeternus*, Sigo Press, Santa Monica California, 1981, p. 15

[404] Félice d'Ayzac, *L'une des acceptations mystiques de l'éléphant dans le symbolisme chrétien au moyen âge*, Revue Archéologique, 10e année, Paris, 1853

[405] Cf. C.G. Jung, *Dream Analysis*, p. 644

life.[406] A prehistoric animal represents a very primitive animal instinct. When it is helpful, it is like an immeasurable force from the depths which helps us to overcome difficulties that consciousness alone would never be able to master.[407]

The archetypal images of the cats, the light-emitting tree with the birds and the mammoth mother with the child impart maternal libido to the dreamer from the deepest layers of her personality. This experience is so powerful that the dreamer has to make sure that her own cat does not go astray and that it will find its way home again. This primordial imagery can hold so much fascination that returning to the domestic feeding bowl and the daily business of conscious life, like a good cat or dog, can go against the grain. One might want to escape into a dream world or an unconscious identification with the overpowering content. However, in the case of our dreamer, this fear is unjustified. She has both animals firmly under her right arm. In this sense, she returns to the familiar family situation of the departure point of the dream setting, the world of the conscious ego with its tasks and obligations.

The dream experience has helped the young woman in her innermost being to gain some access to the archetypal maternal course of events. This may be the crux of the matter. The cats, tree, birds and mammoth mother present her with various faces and aspects of the archetype of the great mother that can all display fate-determining powers, in one way or another. Whenever cats appear in a woman's life, what is at issue is always a kind of individual and autonomous femininity in which the dark and light aspects are equally active and harmoniously connected. Naturally, this femininity can also comprise a "masculine" dynamic as the "cat regent" and its attendants could suggest. Our dreamer happens to be in a phase in her pregnancy when she has to keep still and wait. The imagery of the moon-tree and mammoth mother seem to declare a time of perseverance, contemplation and intuitive exploration of a deep mystery, rather than the restless roaming about of a male cat in the springtime. This dream image could help our dreamer's agitated feminine creativity to find peace. She can now admit a state of mind that is expectant, peaceful, contemplative, a passive kind of allowing things to happen and grow.

The dreamer had an unusually easy delivery: a healthy boy was born within only fifty minutes.

---

[406] *Ibid.*, pp. 324-325
[407] See also Chapter "Water," Dream No. 7 about a dinosaur

Figure 28. Anubis, the 'Conductor of Souls,' on the tomb of Tutenkhamon

5.5. The Dog

Vivienne MacKrell

It is well established that dogs joined the family circle of man in the Upper Old Stone Age (50 – 12 thousand years ago) and that at the beginning of the Middle Stone Age, about 10,000 B.C., they had become thoroughly part of a significant relationship with man. How this started is uncertain but in a Stone Age hunter society, the advantage of having a domesticated animal with vastly superior senses of hearing and smell and greater speed in the chase, would be enormous. For the dog, man would be a source of more easily obtainable food and warmth, and identifying with the territory he now occupied, he would also give warning of intruders and defend it. Their innate friendliness and desire to be related to man make them the only animal to be domesticated by their will and not by captivity. They have sacrificed their ability to live in the wild in a desire to live in relationship with mankind. They have "allowed" their instincts to be partially subordinated by training for the use of man, upon whom they have become dependent. A dog in our society can no longer forage for himself as can a cat, for example. The faithfulness of a happy dog to his owner is proverbial, and they can only be reliably trained by friendliness rather than oppression. The enigmatical bond between the dog and his owner often just happens and is not inducible except, perhaps, that loving care for the puppy's needs allows favorable circumstances for it to develop. It has two sources: 1) the ardent love of a puppy for its mother, which in the wild dog disappears at maturity, is preserved as a permanent mental trait, the original mother love is transformed into master love, and 2) the submissive attachment to the pack leader and the loyalty to the pack of the dog is transferred to man – the owner becomes the pack leader. This last trait is more evident in Lupus (wolf) type dogs as the community life and loyalty to the pack of the wolf is extraordinarily well developed.

In partnership with man, dogs can be divided into four main categories: hunters, workers, entertainers and companions, and in all categories, the foundation for the dog's behavior is the Eros bond with the owner. It is this Eros quality of the dog which appeals to man's consciousness and to the unconscious psychic dog level in man. As the owner can, with proper care, utilize the dog's superior sensory abilities in the outer world, so can the inner dog become a bridge to man's own instincts, a psychopomp (one who shows the way, in psychology, the guide of the soul) to the inner world, and point the way to some understanding of the dynamics of spirit as it moves in matter. Dogs appear in folklore and myth all over the world in various roles; essentially, they are a threshold phenomenon, appearing when a step from one state of being to another is happening or should be happening. They relate man to something else, the other, something of which he may not be cognizant. "Because of its rich symbolic context the dog is an apt synonym for the transforming substance."[408] As transforming substance, the presence of a dog in a dream – even as a very minor participant – would indicate a potentiality for transformation of some kind. The way in which the dog behaves depicts the attitude of the dreamer and the relationship to the context of the dream.

Fully 80% of our body functioning is not under conscious ordering or control: it depends on the lower brain and autonomic system and not on the higher cognitive centers. The archetypal dreams of pregnancy will reflect what the collective unconscious "says" about this 80% unconscious oneness of mother and baby. The focus of attention would be on the new life to come and the instinctual and spiritual needs for the new state of being of them both. It is interesting in our survey that the preponderance of archetypal dreams occur in the first three months of pregnancy, when perhaps the most far-reaching changes occur, when the advent of the new is both physically and psychologically most immediate. It could be said that when an animal in a dream threatens the dreamer, whoever or whatever instinct that animal symbolizes is something that is repressed or is not understood in the dreamer's consciousness. An instinct not related to or understood in consciousness can enforce itself in an autonomous power manner and be acted out without meaning.

Jung's essay, "Woman in Europe,"[409] published in 1927 is not outdated: the basic premises are still valid today and even more important for our understanding. In it he states: "Woman's psychology is founded on the principle of Eros, the great binder and loosener. ... the concept of Eros could be expressed in modern terms as psychic relatedness."[410] "It is the function of Eros to unite what Logos has sundered."[411] In *Mysterium Coniunctionis*, he writes: "By Logos I meant discrimination judgment, insight and by Eros I meant the capacity to relate ...,"[412] and he describes them as "intellectually formulated equivalents of the archetypal images of Sol and Luna."[413] He further describes

---

[408] C.G. Jung, CW 14, § 174, footnote 280. Bollingen Series, Princeton University Press, 1970

[409] C.G. Jung, CW 10, Section II, Bollingen Series, Princeton University Press, 1970

[410] *Ibid.*, CW 10, § 255

[411] *Ibid.*, CW 10, § 275

[412] *Ibid.*, CW 14, § 224

[413] *Ibid.*, CW 14, § 226

Eros as "a Kosmogonos, a creator and father-mother of all higher consciousness."[414] Those two great archetypes underlie our ego consciousness and need to be realized together. The *participation mystique* and chaos of the unconscious Eros need the discrimination and insight of Logos to differentiate, and then with Eros to relate in a psychologically meaningful way.

The dog entered the Western world from Arabic alchemy. Sol and Luna were personified in theriomorphic form as a dog and bitch, and together, the dog and bitch "will beget a dog of celestial hue, and if ever he is thirsty give him sea water to drink: for he will guard your friend, and he will guard you from your enemy, and he will help you wherever you may be, always being with you in this world and the next."[415] The spiritual dog will be a protector and guide in this world and the next, and needs the salt water of wisdom of the collective unconscious to quench his thirst. The hierosgamos of Sol and Luna brings to birth something that is one and united – the lapis. The theriomorphic form indicates that the two are, in a way, like sensual appetites complementing the spiritual light (conscious) quality of Sol and the fluctuating, dark light quality of Luna: "The motif of the dog is a necessary counterbalance to the excessively praised 'light nature' of the stone."[416]

The dark side of the moon (Hecate) was considered to be its most dangerous aspect. The Greek Hecate is the ancient triform goddess of the underworld. She was considered to be the deity of black magic, childbirth and animal fertility, and of the crossroads, a goddess of marriage but also the devourer of children. She has a key, whip, dagger, and torch as her symbols and sometimes was depicted as a whelping bitch. The dog was one of her animals. "She represents a psychic power. ... exceedingly mysterious, underground, helpful but at the same time destructive, uncanny and working from the unconscious in a way man cannot understand. This is a witchcraft particularity that is especially in woman's unconscious."[417]

Dogs appear in so many dreams that only those in which they play a major role will be discussed in this work.[418]

Dream No. 77:

> *Now we have a German Shepherd pup (a dog) in a box, on the outer part*
> *of our terrace, on the little roof that covers the gas deposit. I am going to*

[414] C.G. Jung, *Memories Dreams and Reflections*, Vintage Books by Random House, 1963, p. 353

[415] CW 14, § 174

[416] CW 14, § 179

[417] C.G. Jung, *Seminar on Dream Analysis*, Bollingen Series, Princeton University Press, 1984, p 391

[418] A comprehensive survey of the dog in myth, folklore and religions rites can be found in *Dog*, by Patricia Dale-Green, Rupert Hart-Davis, London, 1966; and *God Had a Dog*, by Maria Leach, Rutgers University Press, 1960

take him the milk E. didn't want yesterday. Also a peacock appears. I say to myself: "This, with fortune, at the end of its life will succeed in exceeding itself if it is able to fly with his tail spread out in the just moment (at the moment of rut or something like this)." It came flying. Half-awake, I think if I will make a compost I will exploit food scraps and dog's dregs.

The dreamer is not primarily English speaking. She did the translation from her mother tongue into English by herself and gave some additional information. This was her second pregnancy, and a healthy baby boy was born without complications. E. is her young daughter with whom she was having problems, and she was angry with the child for not drinking her milk. The box was a neglected seedbed which had an anthill in it. She did not like it because she did not know how to get the ants to leave. "It was something I have to do, but I never find the moment." The little roof holding the box is further down so the box would be as if it were in the air.

The setting of this dream is outside the house of the dreamer: it is not yet part of her psychic make-up, and the anthill box is in mid-air, not yet grounded, although in an area attached to her. Ants are industrious, social colony insects. They symbolize parapsychological participation and the deeper instinctuality based in the body, which is not under conscious control. The puppy is specified as a German shepherd, which as well as being a related companion, is a dog whose natural instincts lead it to be an excellent protector and tracker detecting and warning of what is alien in the surroundings and following to secure it, if necessary. The puppy is on this anthill – a young, warmblooded new instinctual potential. In the first three months of pregnancy, the fetus is in the uterus but is not yet firmly embedded in the maternal womb; the switch-over to placental nourishment is usually at three months, and this pregnancy is only approximately eight weeks after conception. The new (the puppy) is still part of an unconscious participation, and for it to be brought into consciousness, it must be fed. Milk, a complete natural food, together with honey, is the heavenly food fed to the newly baptized in the Ophitic rites. It is a mild, appeasing, sober drink sacrificed to the gods of the underworld. It is apotropaic against evil but is also easily attacked by witches and devils. In this dream, the dark feminine is to be appeased and the positive potential nourished. The milk rejected by the very young feminine side that will not propitiate the gods will nourish the new. It is as though the unconscious participation has on it a potentiality for a relationship which can be fed by the dreamer but which her juvenile shadow aspect does not want. Today, many women have a baby with little realization of the deeper implications and psychic changes involved. The baby and the pregnancy are, so to speak, a peripheral issue: items which have to fit into the usual daily aims and activities, be they social or professional. They have to fit into the demands of the outer world and its collective norms.

When the dog is going to be fed, the peacock comes. The peacock, a symbol of renewal and resurrection, is an attribute of Juno, the Roman queen of the gods. The *cauda pavonis* in alchemy heralds the attainment of the goal. At the end of the nigredo, immediately before the albedo, all the colors appear just as if the peacock were displaying his beautifully colored fan of tail feathers. It is also called "the soul of the world, Nature, the quintessence, which causes all things to bring forth."[419] In the dream, this is associated with the rut: the peacock spreads his fan to attract the peahen to promote a joining to produce the fertilized egg – the germ of new being. The statement is that the peacock, with good fortune, can exceed itself (surpass itself) if it can fly in the courtship position. The furtherance of the *coniunctio* in nature occurs on the ground, so for the peacock to fly with spread-out tail feathers would be *contra naturam*. As the renewal here is to be an *opus contra naturam*, so indeed the development of human consciousness is an *opus contra naturam* to distinguish man from a state of *participation mystique* with his milieu and a purely materialistic existence. The peacock's tail, as it unfolds, presents a shimmering, iridescent glow of color, which would mean an unfolding of fantasy life – here to be centered on the child to come, with thoughts, feelings and wonderings about the mystery of being, rather than considering it all as only a biological event. "To this tremendous opus the woman does not only contribute consciously, but with her whole being and through her psychological substance. ... it is essential and positively important for the child that the fantasy should in the early stages be centered around the child ... this fantasy activity prepares a nourishing ground for the child to be born into."[420]

As is common in alchemy, the neglected unwanted holds the future potential – the gold is in the dung. The warmth of the contemplated compost production from the dog's excreta and vegetable waste would produce fertilizer and could be likened to an incubation – an introversion – to promote growth. In keeping with the dog as a threshold phenomenon, thoughts of the compost occurred when she was half-awake. It therefore seems that the development of a deeper understanding could be approaching the consciousness.

The next dream occurred approximately at the time of conception. The dreamer was Japanese, a twenty-nine-year-old woman, and this was her second pregnancy.

Dream No. 78:

The scene of the dream was in an information office for an employment examination. Two friends of mine were sitting at the information desk. Beside them, about three strangers were sitting side by side. The women,

[419] CW 14, § 391

[420] Marie-Louise von Franz, *The Feminine in Fairy Tales*, Shambhala, Boston, 1993, p. 46

*whom I recently felt to be nice, were to take the employment examination.
I did not apply for it at that time. I wanted to, but I did not think I could.
It seemed to me that I had a test different from the other people in the
place (which seemed to be for an employment examination). I was told
to make tea by an old woman, and so I did. Though I had confidence
about making tea it wouldn't foam at all. I asked her why this tea
wouldn't foam. The dog which was kept at the electric appliance store
where I worked appeared. I talked to the old woman about the dog, and
then I made friends with her. She seemed to like me. My friends sitting at
the information desk told me that I might be probably employed.*

The setting is in an office where one gets information about employment
and takes an examination to see if one is able to fulfill the work. The dreamer
has doubts about her abilities to do the test, and although she wanted to so,
did not apply. It seemed that her test was different from that of the other
people. Pregnancy is a new task, and the dream is concerned with the
dreamer's attitude to this. The emphasis is on her own test being different – as
if to tell her that every pregnancy is an individual, unique event, even though
the general course of physical change is much the same for every woman. Her
friends, shadow parts of her personality, want to do the usual test. This could
mean doing what everyone else does and not listening too much to one's own
feelings. Pregnancy is a most profound experience for a woman touching the
very depths of her being. The physical and psychic realities are like no other,
culminating, as they do, in the creation of a new being. Here, there are three
unknown women: "Three means time, and time is always identical with the
flow of energy. We can determine time only on the basis of movement. There
must be movement in order that time exists. Proclus says always where there
is creation there also is time. The neoplatonic god of Creation is Chronos, the
god of time."[421] One could think of these women as the three Fates or as an
unconscious dynamic triad. Colloquially, we say: "The time is ripe" – fate has
constellated it – and indeed, this seems to be so for the dreamer. "Three
signifies a unity which dynamically engenders self-expanding linear irreversible processes in matter and in our consciousness."[422]

Together with the dreamer, there are now six feminine elements. Six is a
perfect number – the number of the days of creation, the wedding number,
evolution, fertility and the macrocosm in the microcosm – the last being very
appropriate to the time of conception. The seventh, the old woman, as in fairy
tales, represents the deeper wisdom of the unrecognized feminine goddess.
Seven is regarded as the number of evolution in time – the development of

[421] C.G. Jung, *Seminare Kinderträume,* edited by Lorenz Jung and Maria Meyer Grass,
Walter Verlag, Olten und Freiburg, 1987, p. 220
[422] Marie-Louise von Franz, *Number and Time,* p. 106; see also Chapter 6 for the number 3 in depth, and in particular, its involvement in the R.N.A., and the *I Ching,*
Northwestern University Press, Evanston, 1974

psychological maturity. One thinks of the seven planets, the elements of which are represented in the horoscope, as the make-up of human personality. In Japan, the tea ceremony is one of communion in contact with eternity, the entry of the spiritual into the material, and this is what the dreamer is told to prepare. She is confident, but it does not go the way it should; she could not unite the spiritual and material. So often, the ego can be overconfident, trusting to its powers alone and neglecting the *Deo concedente*.

When she questions her ego assumption, the dog, the eighth (eight points to psychic completeness) comes to her from where she had worked before – her old habits and attitudes. The dog provides the link between the mature feminine and the ego. By means of an instinctual Eros and relationship principle, and through talking about it, the dreamer can communicate with and make friends with her unconscious, deeper, feminine nature. This could be done in an active imagination with the dog pointing the way and becoming a bridge to the new understanding. Then she is told she will probably be employed, for she now has the ability to enter into her new task. This dream points out to the dreamer that Fate is constellated, that she has to develop an individual religious approach and that her instincts will make a bridge for her to the feminine wisdom of Nature and to concentrate on this rather than on collective requirements. This, perhaps, compensates a rather too conventional, superficial approach that has to be discarded.

Dream No. 79:

> *I had a baby girl, and that was wrong: it was meant to be a boy, and eventually the baby turns into a dog.*

The dreamer said it was not a nightmare, and that often before an event, she dreamed about its going wrong. This was her fourth pregnancy, and there was a conscious desire for a boy as she already had three daughters. The baby, in fact, would be a girl, and she has dogs of her own and loves them. The time in her pregnancy when this dream occurred was not given.

In the Judeo-Christian heritage and patriarchal society, the masculine is esteemed more than the feminine, and the conscious desire for a son can, in collective society, stem partly from this. The carrying-on of the family name and inheritance have long been masculine prerogatives, although, in our time, there has been a gradually increasing awareness of the feminine principle. In this dream, the baby is a girl who changes into a dog. The needed progression, contrary to ego desire, is not a new masculine: the renewal, the new potentiality, lies within the feminine realm. That which is human changes into the dog as transformer and a friendly threshold instinct or guide to the dreamer's instincts. A change in the feminine was constellated as a compensation rather than a switch to the opposite. The dream says: "Be glad that it is a piece of Nature and of life and do not worry about masculine or feminine." It was not a nightmare which would indicate a receptive attitude on the part of the dreamer.

Dream No. 80:

> *I was in the church of my home place, and there stood a dog of middle size with the ugly unsympathetic face of a man with a mouth big like a duck's beak. I was afraid. The dog came whimpering to my side rubbing against my legs. I felt disgusted and judged the dog to be false. I tried to get away on another way. I saw the upper entrance of the church and jumped down carelessly from the clock-tower where I was and then saw that I was nearly falling over, so I turned to the ropes and tried to climb them. I was as though paralyzed from fear. I managed only a little bit and was in despair. Only when I changed my technique and didn't fight with my legs and pulled myself up with my arms did I achieve.*

This dream occurred at eight weeks in the first pregnancy of a twenty-eight-year-old lady. Five weeks before the expected date of delivery, there was a spontaneous rupture of the membranes and onset of labour. The baby was a healthy (2,650 grams) girl. In the church, that is, in the conventional religious setting of her home, something very unconventional appears, and the dreamer sees it as disgusting and false. Fearing it, she tries to escape and does so only by climbing ropes high from the ground. There is a message she wants to avoid. When a mixture of animals, which does not normally occur in Nature, appears in a dream, there is no appropriate vehicle in the consciousness of the dreamer to express the unconscious content. So here there is a mixture of dog and human with a little bit of a duck resemblance – something that wants to relate to the dreamer and is pleading for recognition. Usually when a dog whimpers, it is unhappy or in pain. This instinct has a human face with a mouth big like a duck's beak – so it could perhaps talk, for example, in active imagination. The more an unconscious content is repressed, the more it strives for recognition and the more aggressive it can become. So it could be said that, here, the Eros relationship as dog is combined with a masculine principle she describes as ugly and unsympathetic in appearance, and with a hint of bird as a more spiritual, intuitive nature. Ducks are at home on land, in the air and in the water. Unlike us, they can move in all realms of Nature: "… it represents the transcendent function, that strange capacity of the unconscious psyche to transform and guide the human being who has been blocked in a situation into a new one."[423] Something potentially human is repressed into animal form but still has a limited means of expression, or alternatively, something instinctual is acquiring human form in order to express itself. The dreamer cannot understand the language, the message of what seems to her to be ugly and false, and instead of trying to see what this is, to determine that

---

[423] M.-L. von Franz, *Shadow and Evil in Fairy Tales*, Shambhala, Boston, 1995, p. 265

it is not hostile, she judged it and ran away, denying her own receptive feminine principle. But she could not escape: she was as though paralyzed until she abandoned her standpoint – her feet would not help her (they hindered her) so she hauled herself up in the clock-tower, by using ropes, into temporal time measurement. Ropes in a church-tower (although not specifically stated as such in the dream) are attached to the church bells, which are rung to repel the demonic powers. There is a dog-headed saint, St. Christopher, in the Eastern Orthodox church. Nothing authentic is known about him but a vast amount of legendary material surrounds him. His particular power was to protect the faithful from sudden death.[424] Here, it could be the other way round; something human has been repressed into the animal creature, and instinctual Eros with a Logos face is longing to be accepted. The opposites are united in a form that the dreamer cannot appreciate. This dream, I feel, warns the dreamer that she is avoiding coming to terms with her grounded reality – that she has perhaps a too light and puella-type approach to life, and in this case, to pregnancy. She is refusing to leave the shelter of Christian morality and retreating even higher into the spiritual area of a church where feminine earth, instinct, chthonic masculinity and transforming potential are not sufficiently recognized. Climbing up a rope to avoid what she views with disgust as the devil on earth.

Dream No. 81:

> I am out with my two dogs. I walk along a meadow, and on my left hand is an enclosure with many horses.
> I meet a man who has an aggressive wolflike dog. I try to avoid them but they take the same way. First there is a violent fight between his dog and my Kastorp (a violent Great Dane). Then it tried to mate with poor little Frodo (a brindle Scottish terrier), who is not even a female. I ask the man to discipline his dog.
> Later I have a white poodle along. He looks like Plongen, the dog I had when I was a girl. Suddenly it falls on its right side in an epileptic attack like Plongen did before he died. I take him up in my arms.

The setting of this dream, which occurred at five weeks in a first pregnancy, is in Nature. On the dreamer's left, her unconscious side, her animal vitality and parapsychological perception are enclosed and separated from her.

Then, even though she tries to avoid it, her dog, a very big one, described as violent, is attacked by the aggressive, wolflike dog of an unknown animus figure, and a power battle ensues. The animus has an aggressive, indiscriminately promiscuous side, and apparently there is no Eros. The dreamer asks

---

[424] Zofia Ameisenowa, *Animal-Headed Gods. Evangelists, Saints and Righteous Men*, Journal of the Warburg-Courtauld Institutes, University of London, 1949, Vol. 12, p. 21

the man to discipline his dog, there is no attempt at an *Auseinandersetzung* [a coming to terms with or having it out with] to develop a relationship between the dreamer and the animus, she tells him, as his dog attempts to tell hers. One can be fairly certain in a dream that if one is attacked by a dog a relationship of some kind, either outer or inner, has been misvalued by the ego consciousness. Here, one could say that the Eros quality of the dog is repressed, so power enters, and the psychic dog becomes angry and aggressive. The wolf in our society carries the projection of a dangerously destructive evil force that desires to eat anything and everything. However, studies of wolves in their natural habitat have shown that they are exceedingly intelligent, usually mate for life and have a well-established family life. The pack is well-organized for hunting and of a size and with a range appropriate for the available game. The advent of man upset this ecological balance: the natural prey of the wolf was appropriated by man or driven out, the forests were cleared etc., so in the absence of prey, man's herds were attacked, and the wolf was hungry. The wolf is Apollo's animal, the dark shadow side, law and order to excess with disregard of it as a pure ethic, using it for gain, and then it turns into its opposite: indiscriminate, chaotic greed. In contradistinction to its related side, the dog is also promiscuous. Cerberus, in Greek mythology, who can be placated by an offering of honey cakes, ferociously guards the gates of Hades and lets no one in or out. Angry instinct blocks the way to the other world and needs honey, spiritual natural food, and recognition of its meaning made by man's efforts. Ego will has to be sacrificed in order to listen to what the angry instinct says: one must make a creative expression of some kind to allow it to talk.

Then the dreamer has with her a smaller white dog, like the dog of her youth. White is a transition color – either the union of all colors or the absence of all colors. White can be the albedo following of the *cauda pavonis* preceding the rubedo, or the cold, inhuman aspect of the unconscious objective psyche. Ghosts, which may be good or evil, are traditionally white. White can, so to speak, go two ways: either into life or into the beyond; it is the color of initiation, virginity and purity. This dog has an epileptic attack and falls onto its right (conscious) side. Her actual dog died after a similar attack. Epileptic attacks can result from a disturbance in cerebral function. The dreamer picks it up, takes up a childish relationship principle in a vain attempt to avoid the conflict apparent in the earlier part of the dream. It is as though this dream dog could serve to remind the ego that childish Eros has to die.

This dream is a message that the dreamer should discard a rather youthful puella-type approach to conflict. She is unconscious of the elemental powers, forces which are needed especially in pregnancy. She has to become aware of the need for animal vitality and the parapsychological participation between mother and baby, the darker, unknown, offended instincts and the animus, in order to mend a body-mind split rather than retreating into childishness.

Dream No. 82:

> *We were coming to a bigger hut, but underneath this hut it was uncanny. The dog crept under it and didn't come out for a long time, as if there was a long tunnel. I felt uncanny in the hut.*
>
> *It was in the Middle Ages. I had lost the favor of the duke and duchess when I defended witches, let one go and cried out: "The evil which you see in others is in you. Jesus said, 'Let the weed grow together with the wheat in order that you don't pull out the wheat by mistake.'\" I was to be burned as a witch. I fled, and I was betrayed. I had been hidden by a priest, then discovered and sentenced to be burned together with him. I saw a niche from which light was coming and a thin blue veil. I bent over and saw a pretty statue of Mary in the niche. I thought that even this pretty image would now be of no use for me any more. I imagined all the stages of my death by burning.*

These dreams occurred at nine weeks of pregnancy. Only the first will be considered here; the second has been interpreted in the "Fire" chapter (Dream No. 31). Two dreams in the same night or scene shifting in one dream can present different aspects which all focus on the same problem. Here, it seems that she is first shown how to proceed on her way, and then is shown what she will encounter if she does.

There is a widespread belief that a dog can lead one anywhere – especially into the beyond. In Zorostrianism, the dog was created by Ahura Mazda, the supreme god, and belonging to him was a sacred animal. As soon as a soul left the body, the evil demon, Druj Nasa, attacked; then the dog, by eating the flesh, would expel the demon.[425]

When a Parsi was dying, Parsis used to place a little dog on his chest with its muzzle applied to his mouth, so that it could receive the departing soul and deliver it to the waiting angel. The presence of the dog would also frighten the demon back to hell. The Cinvat Bridge to Paradise leads over the abyss to hell. For the righteous, it is wide, and for the sinner, as narrow as a sword's edge. The worthy man is met by Daéna, the rose of a hundred petals, the Anima Coelestis of man, who has two dogs. She and the dogs aid his passage, defending him from the demons that attack from below.[426]

The dream opens with the entry into a bigger hut – a larger container, a more embracing psychological situation, which has close contact with the other world, the unconscious. A numinous situation can indeed feel uncanny, and here, the opposites of conscious and unconscious are constellated, i.e., something other than the commonplace becomes apparent. Underlying the

[425] M.M. Dawson, *The Ethical Religion of Zoraster*, A.M.S. Press, 1969
[426] Henry Corbin, *Spiritual Body and Celestial Earth*, Bollingen Series, Princeton University Press, 1977, pp. 41-44

ground we stand on, our ego views of the world, is the unconscious – the beyond with its treasure house of symbolic images.

It is as if there was a long tunnel underneath the hut through which the dog entered into the realm of the Great Mother and the mysteries of life, death and rebirth. It crept into a deeper, older layer of the collective unconscious that is relevant for the dreamer (it is under the hut she is in). The dog is shown as a guiding instinct that can lead the way and can also, most importantly, come back and return to her. The dreamer can rely on her instinctual Eros. It will not desert her, and it will show the way to complete her task.

Dream No. 83:

> *A man with an aquiline nose is standing up in front of the lost temple of the ancient Egyptian god, Anubis. Nobody gets to enter into it: but suddenly, when he is there, it [the temple] comes to life again like long ago, and the man finally enters. I am afraid something will happen to him because Anubis – that is, a black bronze dog – is the dead: its profile is very similar to the man's. Inside the temple, there is a sort of trial perhaps judging this man, but nothing frightening is happening.*

The dream occurred one month before the baby was born. The dreamer said the place of the temple was on the "outskirts, dunghill, abandoned place," and the temple itself was "closed, mysterious." The trial "seemed to be a religious ceremony."

In this dream (the first dream in the "dog" section was also hers), which occurred one month before delivery, the dreamer is observing and not participating. Something is shown to her as being no longer alive – though it does become alive again when the unknown animus figure is there. Here, the animus figure is in the right place, leading into the lost temple, doing what she will later have to do for herself, showing the way into a religious mystery.

Anubis, depicted as a jackal-headed man, dominated the embalming process in the funerary rituals of the ancient Egyptians, so perhaps one could say that the mortuary chambers, which were closely associated with the tombs, were his temples. In the myth, Anubis accompanied Isis in her search for the parts of Osiris which, after Seth had killed him, were scattered far and wide. Anubis helped Isis and was with her when she reassembled the dismembered god and made him immortal and incorruptible. The funerary rituals, imbued with magico-religious meaning, were designed to facilitate the entry into immortal life for the dead to become like unto Osiris, he who resurrected, and to produce the eternal, immortal nucleus of the individuality of the person. The agent of the resurrection with the mortal body, as the starting point, is represented by Routi, depicted as either a double lion or two lions facing in opposite directions with the solar disc on their backs. "This double lion was called 'Yesterday and Tomorrow' and was somehow the mysterious agent of the resurrection. He represented the god who personified that incomprehen-

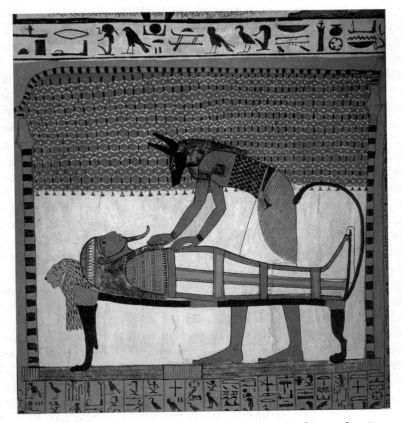

Figure 29. Anubis bending over a mummy (tomb of Sennedjem)

sible process on the earth by which the dead return to life and is at the same time also an image of the human soul."[427] He represents the process by which eternity becomes apparent in linear time, in matter and psyche, a creative energy by which divinity becomes manifest in the human realm. Sometimes two of the jackals of Anubis replace the lion and are stated to be "the openers of the way, the agents of resurrection" in the inscription below them. The dog as Anubis is thus a psychopomp into the other world for rebirth into immortality. The "dog" in man, the psychic relatedness, can be the factor necessary for entry into the psychic mystery of being for renewal of the sun of consciousness.

In the Hall of Judgment, Anubis presides over the Balance, the scales in which the heart of the deceased is weighed against the feather of Truth (Maat). Thoth, the Logos, scribe and messenger of the gods, records the results. The hearts of those who fail are eaten by the tri-formed beast Am-mit, the "Eater

---

[427] M.-L. von Franz, *On Dreams and Death*, Shambhala, Boston, 1984, p. 15

of the Dead," who lies waiting. This would be the factor that strictly observes where one has deviated from one's inner truth, and it appears in the voice of conscience. If one deviates from one's own truth, one does indeed get eaten up.

The unknown animus of the dreamer is being judged – how far does he depart from the inner truth? Apparently, it is all right – nothing frightening is happening. Anubis is not only the dead that she is afraid of but guardian of the threshold and a guide to renewal. To give up one's collective morality to find one's inner truth is not a death but a rebirth. In outer life this would be to test one's collective opinions and morality against the voice of the Self: to attend to the dream message, the guide of conscience and conscious action. As she describes Anubis, he seems rather to be Hermanubis, a union of opposites, on one side of his face the golden – the guide to heaven and leader of souls to Osiris – on the other, the black, for he was also the incarnation of death and decay. In the Graeco-Roman period in Alexandria, the Greek Hermes and Anubis merged into this one figure: Hermanubis, who played a great part in the mysteries of Isis and was her constant companion. His primary duty was to guide the souls of the dead through the underworld; he was also a protector of pregnant women, and the caduceus, the opener of all ways, was one of his emblems. The dreamer does not know this masculine component of her psyche; she says that his profile is similar to that of Anubis. The dream points out the personal and how it fares in contact with the eternal. In times past, maternal mortality was very high, the hazards of childbirth were great, and women feared death – so this dream could compensate a deep, age-old, buried fear. For the unconscious to be incarnated into this world is a sort of death – a confining unto mortal limits. New creation implies a death of the previous stage. This lady has to let her old ideas and conventional attitudes die and relate to her new tasks: physically, to give birth to a baby, and psychically, to a new concept of life as eternally related rather than wholly personal. Jung says: "The decisive question for man is: 'Is he related to something infinite or not?' That is the telling question of his life. Only if we know that the thing which truly matters is the infinite can we avoid fixing our interests upon futilities."[428] As the Egyptian ritual was one of preparation for entry into eternity, this dream, in the context of pregnancy, is the reverse: the entry of eternity into the now – or the mystery of divinity becoming manifest in the human realm – the heritage of which this new baby is the tangible result.

As a whole, these dreams insist on the need for an enlargement of ego consciousness and the development of a deeper relationship to the unconscious. Generally, they point out to the dreamers that they are not sufficiently in contact with their instinctual natures and rely too much upon conventional collective rules and ideas. They do not seem to be specifically related to pregnancy except for the dreams of new employment at the time of conception and the baby girl's changing into a dog.

---

[428] C.G. Jung, *Memories Dreams and Reflections*, p. 325

The dog appears as a new instinctual potential growing on top of an unconscious *participation mystique* that can, with introverted fantasy, transform the dreamer's attitudes. Acting as a bridge for her new task, the dog relates the dreamer in friendship to an older, as yet unknown, feminine principle. The disregarded dog-part of the dreamer's nature is in union with an also disregarded masculine factor, but it wants to get into contact with her. It is appealing for recognition: the voice of the transcendent function cannot be disregarded; and conventional Christian morality is no real defense against the demands of the Self. Where there is no Eros there is power – and outraged, the dog protests against the lack of relationship. It appears as a compensation for an ego desire for a boy as a transformed baby girl – a newborn feminine instinctual side. The role of psychopomp to another world is shown clearly in the last two dreams: the dream of the hut and the Anubis dream. The latter, with its mythological connotations, is a dream that shows most clearly the conscious-unconscious opposites and the need of linking them together in a more comprehensive and religious appreciation of the divine in the individual and the part the individual has to offer to the divine.

At the end of the *Mahabharata*, the great Indian epic, there is a wonderful story about a dog. Prepared for death, the five heroic Pandava brothers, their shared wife and a dog climb the Himalayas towards the holy world mountain, Meru. Along the way, the wife and four brothers fall and die, one by one. Yudhishthira, the eldest brother, is the only one considered to be pure enough to have the honor of entering Heaven in the flesh, so he and the dog go on alone. Then, with a clap of thunder and in a blaze of light, Indra, the King of Heaven, appears in his chariot to take Yudhishthira to Heaven. Yudhishthira stands aside to let the dog enter the chariot first, but Indra is aghast – dogs cannot enter heaven as they are unholy and would defile it. Indra begs Yudhishthira to send the dog away, and they argue, but Yudhishthira refuses. He declares that the dog has always been devoted and loyal and to abandon him would be the greatest sin. He could not live happily in heaven with this on his conscience, so he refuses Heaven for the sake of the dog. At this, the dog transforms into the shining god, Dharma, who is the god of the sacred order of Life and absolute justice. This story illustrates that the lowliest, despised, unclean part of Nature holds within it the highest seeds of both the mortal and divine orders of being, which find a parallel in the alchemical opus.

Individuation is a psychological process of inner growth and centralization to become oneself – to approach the Self for guidance rather than to rely on worldly maxims. In pregnancy, the mother can, as well as giving birth to a baby, give birth to new and deeper aspects of her own personality. It can be an essential part of her individuation process. The physical and psychical demands of pregnancy are but a prelude to the opus of greater development for mother and baby. It is an irreversible big step into Fate. *Vocatus atque non vocatus Deus aderit* [Summoned or not, the god will be there] – the inscription which Jung chose to be carved above the door of his house.

Figure 30. Horse with the pillar of the universe rotating around the center, with the sun wheel (Spain, 1 year B.C.)

5.6. The Horse

Regina Abt

The horse-to-man relationship has a long history. And indeed, none of our domestic animals has influenced history as markedly as the horse. The first evidence of companionship between man and horse, and of the first domestication attempts, can be found in the Spanish cave drawings that are 20,000 years old. However, first indications of the beginnings of cultivated riding can be found only in the last millennium B.C. This tells us that, for many generations, horse-riding (the cart on wheels was invented earlier) represented an unsolvable problem. The achievement of horse-riding, therefore, represented a genuine cultural feat. In Western Europe, saddle-riding had developed to an exceedingly high level over the past centuries – the harmony between horse and rider being of paramount importance, altogether dissociated from the original functions of the horse as pastoral horse, means of transportation, martial horse or plough and carriage horse.

The advent of cavalry or performance-oriented military riding marked the beginning of the fall of this riding culture and sees its continuation in competitive, high-performance sports today. Military compliance, precision and later high-performance sports gradually replaced the jovial interplay between the rider and horse that had been individually worked with and trained. The art of riding – as opposed to riding as a means of performance – as well as the animal generally were sacrificed for our rational, utilitarian thinking. The genuine companionship underlying the harmonious interplay between man and horse was, and still is, man's dream. Time and again, the horse appears in the dreams of modern man, pointing to something that apparently contains very deep emotional meaning. The actual experience of this harmony or being carried in perfect accord with the horse can have a numinous quality. It is an archetypal experience, for it symbolizes the harmonious interplay of man's consciousness with the unconscious, vital instinctive libido. The best illustration for this is the mythical figure of Chiron, the centaur. He was a healer and teacher of Aesculapius, the god of healers, whose serpent we continue to find on all pharmacies to this day.

Figure 31. Peleus taking Achilles to Chiron

Symbolically, this proverbial harmony between man and horse signifies that the consciousness which has developed from the unconscious animal nature has been reconnected with the instinctive libido that is both its nourishing ground and supporting force. The painful barrier that through the development of our consciousness has separated us from the instinctive ground is thus lifted to a certain extent. In this manner, man attains wholeness again. The horse thus signifies man's vital life force without which he is only half a man.

In mythology, the horse virtually plays a cosmic role.[429] The carriage of the sun god in Hellas traversing the heavens is drawn by white horses, and the carriage belonging to the god of the night and moon is drawn by black horses. This suggests the perpetual life cycle going from light to dark and through the darkness to the light. Therefore, symbolically, the horse represents the instinct responsible for setting in motion and maintaining the advancement of consciousness.[430]

Poseidon, the Greek god of the sea and master of the depths of the waters, originally represented as a horse, is said to have given man the horse and to have also taught him how to ride and use the bridle. The horse is, in simple terms, a part of the unconscious, an instinctive force that one can learn to handle, in order to be carried and drawn by it. At a certain developmental stage of consciousness, this presented a problem. In an ancient German legend, a horse emerges from the sea and ploughs the land for man; but then it sometimes hurls both plough and plowman into the abyss, or, if a person wants to ride it, it vanishes back into the sea with the horseman still on its

[429] Cf. Julius von Negelein, *Das Pferd im Arischen Altertum*, Königsberg, 1903
[430] v. Franz, *Shadow and Evil in Fairy Tales*, Shambhala, Boston, 1995, pp. 307-8

back.[431] In legend, therefore, the people had not yet managed to control it or to give it a direction.

In shamanism, the horse plays an important role. The shaman goes on a trip on horseback to the land of the beyond during which he leaves his body. The poles the shaman takes on his voyage are fitted with horse-heads. Here, the horse is an escort into the other world. Perhaps we could call it an instinctive, intuitive energy that can carry a creative man along to higher insights.

It is this context that in our culture led to associating the horse with an aspect of ghosts and spookiness, in other words, with supernatural perception. Many folktales tell how a horse announced future events, e.g., births, weddings, death but also places where a future church or cross was to be erected or a coffin lowered into the earth. Oftentimes, horses would find hidden springs. Thus the horse recognizes future potentialities, good as well as bad ones. In this sense, the horse represents an instinctive, semi-conscious, creative and most importantly, spontaneous side that can signal dangers, tendencies or new impulses from the unconscious. The conscious ego has to trust it and let itself be carried along, so that the horse's spontaneity can come forth.[432]

Pegasus, the winged horse and son of Poseidon, on which Bellerophon, a mortal, wanted to ride too high into the heavens (the domain of Zeus), also represents creative intuition or creative libido. The angered gods sent down a horsefly that stung Pegasus so that he threw off his rider, who from then on had to wander about the earth blind and lame.

We can see that the creative libido from the unconscious is far from harmless, particularly if it is used to avoid the painstaking, detailed work of the mortal or to try to be on a par with the gods. This is inflation and has to be paid for with deflation. This is a specific problem of the Puer-Aeternus type and woman's puer-animus that cannot content itself with its own creative possibilities within the limited reality of human life, always involving work.[433]

Folklore explained the horse's proneness to panic by its connection with the supernatural. Some kind of imperceptible influence was apparently responsible for the fact that the horse would suddenly be given to destructive panic attacks. It is also a part of our own psyche – an emotional, invisible background of the unconscious that can suddenly cause a terrible panic. Jung said that although the unconscious itself was not dangerous, panic emanating from the unconscious could be very dangerous. A horse panics mainly if its freedom

---

[431] Julius von Negelein, *Das Pferd im Arischen Altertum*, p. 73 f

[432] M.-L. von Franz, *Shadow and Evil in Fairy Tales*, 302-3

[433] Cf. M.-L. von Franz, *Puer Aeternus*, Sigo Press, Santa Monica, 1981. *Puer Aeternus* is the name of a god of antiquity and means "eternal youth." In depth psychology, it indicates a certain type of man who remains in adolescent psychology for too long: he has trouble committing himself to anything whatsoever and has great difficulty in adapting to the social, including professional, situation.

of movement is obstructed or if it is exposed to an ostensible or real threat that it cannot avoid in a natural way. Psychologically, this would mean that consciousness prevents a natural instinctive reaction to an unconscious impulse. Panic is the instinctive reaction to this obstruction.

In mythology, the winged horse as well as the ordinary horse are closely associated with the air, the wind, storm, fog, clouds and lightning. The name of Wotan, who like Poseidon, was represented as a horse in ancient times, is etymologically related to violent, stormy movement. He rides Sleipnir, the eight-hoofed stallion, personifying the speed of the stormy wind. Odin, the Nordic god of wind, has his horses pasture in the branches of Yggdrasil, the world ash tree.

Figure 32. Epona, the Celtic goddess, tutelary goddess of the horses, of horse-breeding and rider, sometimes also represented as a fertility goddess

As we have seen, in mythology, the horse belongs just as much to water as it does to the air. It represents strong, dynamic potential in both domains. A horse coming out of the water rather suggests that it penetrates the conscious ego in the form of an emotional manifestation from the unconscious. On the other hand, the domain of the air indicates an equally dynamic force characterized by direction, structure and meaning. Lightning-horses and riding gods of lightning – which also exist in Greek, Indian and Slavic legend – have to do with the attributes of natural lightning, i.e., lightning intuition, insight or synopsis. Most of us have experienced seeing the entire nightly scenery surrounding us in one flash of lightning.

A "supernatural perception" in the form of archetypal spiritual imagery and ideas thus comes from those two domains, i.e., the collective unconscious.

This perception is not only essential for survival but it also aims at expanding and maturing the consciousness. It is the positive aspect of the Great Mother in which the horse plays an important role in mythology. So the Great Mother, both mistress of the animals and ruler over the sea, earth and air, often winged, is a chthonic as well as a celestial goddess.[434] We have earlier already encountered Demeter, the great chthonic goddess of corn and fertility, who has also been represented with a mare's head and horse mane. In the Celtic cultures, she is called Epona.

Carrying and drawing man, the horse works for man. In this function, it corresponds to the physical, instinctive energy, to sexuality, hence to the entire domain of Mother Nature's body and instinct. This is the *prima materia* of alchemy, the basic instinctive drives and source of all further development. It is also the sphere with which pregnant woman has to be in touch if something new is to grow from her.

Although, thanks to modern medicine women generally no longer die in childbirth, life and death in woman's unconscious are never nearer each other than during pregnancy. At no other time can she be more aware of fate's being either benevolent or pernicious. The unconscious, i.e., dreams can bring forth this aspect of "being in the hands of fate" and consequently challenge an attitude which may otherwise be overly optimistic – too easily taken in by the "feasibility-mentality" of the modern conscious ego.

The perilous side of the mother-goddess and her instinctive sphere, symbolized by the horse, is widely represented in mythological tales. One of them is the story of Lamia who, seduced by Zeus, became pregnant, but Hera, out of revenge, ensured that she could only give birth to dead babies. From then on, she tried to have all newborn babies slain. This is where the "Lamias," the female spirits called "nightmare," originate: they are night-spirits that threaten expectant women and steal newborn babies. They ride their victims or are themselves spectral horses, who carry their riders away at a mad gallop. In fairy tales, the witch-like mothers devouring men and children correspond to the child-murdering Lamias. Contrary to the nurturing, giving Mother Nature, they illustrate the cruel, ruthless re-devouring aspect of Nature. Hel, the goddess of death, rides a three-hooved horse.

In folklore and in legend, these spectral horses are frequently associated with sexuality. The sexual drive can, as is known, manifest itself in the form of a "ghostlike" obsession and rob man of a night's sleep. In Christian cultures, these horses are usually associated with the devil and especially with witches. The "ghost horses" carry man off at night or sit on his chest in the form of a nightmare. The unconscious sexual drive has turned destructive, be this because it has been "demonized" or otherwise repressed by a denigrating

---

[434] E. Neumann, *The Great Mother*

conscious ego, or be it because the natural instinctive dynamics threaten the conscious ego as a result of an otherwise inadequate attitude to it.

It is generally true that, in our dealings with a horse, much depends on how skilled or talented we are. The conscious ego is perfectly able and in fact should make it its responsibility to provide the instinct embodied by the horse with direction and limits, without, however, oppressing it.

The following dreams do not contain all the aspects of the horse symbol we have mentioned above. In some instances, they are nevertheless present in the background. It is therefore useful for us to know as much as possible about this symbol even though our dream material represents only a limited selection.

The first dream stems from a twenty-eight-year-old woman, who is one month pregnant with her first child. She and her husband are both taking their doctoral degrees at this time.

Dream No. 84:

> *There should be a competition. We rush into the water where, at a partic-ular spot, we are supposed to take hold of the horses. From this spot, I saw how many dove under like dolphins. I did not do so and grabbed my horse by the neck, in the water, without having seen it, and the competi-tion began. My horse was special – I knew that. It carried me safely across the pathless beginning of the racing track. Then it became dangerous, and precipitous, and the narrow path was lined with bushes, and I frantically tried to hold onto them. Then the horse said to me that it was no good to hold on frantically and to be frightened and that this way we would not get anywhere: I should relax and not be frightened. I tried it and realized that the dangerous part of the track was quite short and already lay behind us. Then the horse took a paste into its navel, so that it would have hallucinations. It tore off galloping. I rode it. It really was a special horse, a kind of a leader, and I was sure to win the race.*

Together with others (women?), the dreamer is by the water. They are each supposed to get hold of a horse for a competition. The others dive under like dolphins; however, our dreamer does not join them, grabs a horse by the neck and rides off with it.

Let us recall the most important aspect of water. In its quality of *the* life-giving primary substance, it is at the beginning of every creation. It contains, as it were, the sum of all possibilities. Many cosmogonies, e.g., in India and Babylon, tell of the creation of the universe from the primeval waters – because in the water, the creative powers are so concentrated that contact with it or immersion in it has a regenerating or fecundating effect. In the folklore of most cultures, water cults pertaining to the renewal of fertility of the earth, animals or women play an important role. Immersion in water signifies a ritual of regeneration for the purpose of rebirth and renewal. Folk belief holds the idea of a "water mother" bringing the children into the world. In Switzerland, there are many places where one can find so-called "children's ponds" – fountains and springs where people thought children were begotten. Another widespread mythical fantasy is that a woman could conceive a child from or in the water. In the fairy tale of "The Sleeping Beauty," for example, the queen's wish to have a child is fulfilled while she is sitting in the bath.[435]

The Moon and goddesses like Ishtar and Isis are closely related to water. Ishtar was born of the waters of the River Euphrates just as Aphrodite was born of the sea. Isis is represented through a water bowl carried along in a procession. Water, i.e., the tides, the moon, the cyclical element of Nature's growth and fertility and woman's cycle are seen as part of one and the same context by archaic man.

Viewed with an archetypal background of symbolism, the dreamer's plunging in the water together with *others* (the impersonal form could indicate that she is in a collective situation), is an immersion in the fertile domain of the primordial mother from which a child will eventually be born. Immersion in water always signifies regeneration and renewal, an example of this being baptism, symbolizing the renewal and rebirth of man. For woman, pregnancy can also be likened to being reborn into a new condition – namely, the condition of motherhood, which is uniquely different from another woman's.

The others dive under the water like dolphins. Our dreamer does not do that. Dolphins, like fish, belong to the symbolism of water fertility. The moon-goddess herself was sometimes represented as being half-fish – perhaps a forerunner of our mermaids.[436] To become like or turn into a fish probably has to do with being wholly dedicated to the maternal-feminine or to the instinctive side of motherhood. When women live their feminine-instinctive drive, disconnected from feeling, they are sometimes said to be "cold as a fish." The image that comes to mind is that of a mermaid or a siren, seducing a man and pulling him down into the depths of the waters. The dolphin has less of that disconnected coldness of a fish. It is an intelligent mammal, as we know today, thus a personification of an aspect of the Great Mother Water that is closer to humankind. "The others" could suggest their identification with her, or with a state when woman gives herself up completely to motherhood and the physical condition of pregnancy, albeit unconsciously – like an animal, as it were. Some women would like to be pregnant all the time because they feel so very well in that state. They are at one with the physical, and identical, as it were, with the amniotic fluid and the creative function of the unconscious maternal body.

[435] Cf. Chapter 3.1
[436] E. Harding, *Woman's Mysteries*, p. 54, Figure p. 161

Figure 33. Fishes and horses, on a Greek vase between bands of rue, symbols of fertility

Our dreamer, however, is either unable or does not want to do that. Without dipping her head into the water, she manages (like the others) to take hold of a horse, who will carry her to an unknown destination.

Now, the horse embodies that instinctive force from the maternal domain and the emotional background associated with motherhood, carrying her along the troublesome path that lies ahead of her. There is a very strong physicality in the horse that reflects well the particularly strong relationship with woman's own body during pregnancy. Women frequently find it very difficult to come to terms with "their horse," i.e., they have to endure all kinds of physical discomforts, and their instinctive nature often behaves in an unruly manner – there is either too much of it or too little.

Let us now examine the theme of the race in the dream. A part in us might want to reject the idea of associating pregnancy with a race or competitive performance. Perhaps this links up with the dreamer's personal situation, i.e., the fact that she and her husband are about to obtain their PhD.'s. Indeed, for some intellectual women, having a child is part of their ambitions in life – something they have to prove: "Can I do it without giving up my profession or studies?" (I have had students tell me proudly: "In the meantime we've 'made' another child!"). Nevertheless, our dream takes us to a much deeper level and shows us what kind of a competition is at stake.

The dreamer here is carried by some goal-oriented dynamics of which she is as yet unaware. This frightens her at first, and she is tense. Along with the aspects of anticipation and endurance involved in maternal brooding, pregnancy comprises also the dynamics of a development that is unstoppable, striding forward until it reaches the goal that is the birth and culmination of a dynamic process of Nature. It is better to go through this process serenely and without fear. This is beautifully expressed by the image of horse-riding as a harmonious interplay of consciousness and the instinctive energy carrying woman along, which is of particular importance to a pregnant woman.

Now, we have the strange motif of the horse using some paste on its navel, in order to have hallucinations. Then *"It tore off galloping. I rode it. It really was a special horse, a kind of a leader, and I was sure to win the race."*

The navel is that central point where mother and child are attached by the umbilical cord before it is cut at birth. In folklore, the navel is highly significant. It was apparently thought that the point from which the child's autonomous life begins is also where its fate is determined. For this reason, much oracular practice revolved around the navel and umbilical cord. The so-called "umbilicomancy," for example, dealt with interpreting the lines of the skin around the navel, or the knots and coils of the umbilical cord, with regard to the future life of the child. The most ancient reference to this custom dates back to Abu Masar (886 A.D.), an Arabic scholar, but the custom has been preserved in our cultures up to the 19th century.[437]

The paste serving to engender hallucinations is reminiscent of Soma, a drink of the Indian gods, granting ecstasy and inspiration, but also renewal of life, illumination, wisdom of Nature and immortality. According to one tradition, the soma was created by stirring the cosmic ocean, the primeval waters. According to another tradition, it was brewed from the fruit of the moon tree. Ambrosia, the Celtic counterpart to Soma, is brewed in Hymris, the magical bowl that lies at the bottom of the ocean or a lake. This drink, too, imparts immortality and eternal youth.

The horse reaches beyond the personal-physical and in fact opens doors to the wisdom of the other world. We can assume that this is the reason why this horse is "the leader" on which the dreamer will be the first to reach the goal. Moreover, the dreamer's horse can probably convey to her an idea of what really lies behind pregnancy, namely, the Great Goddess, who will determine the destiny of her child, too. Seen in this light, the horse in her dream is an escort to the beyond, just like the shamans' horses.

To place oneself in the hands of the horse would also mean to trust one's instincts – for they have the magic spell, the potential to disclose the world of the unconscious through visions, dreams and fantasies. This again makes it possible to see the dynamic processes involved in the creation of a new child in a larger context. Dreaming and fantasizing about the baby to be is thus essential, and many mothers do it quite unconsciously while sitting and knitting baby-clothes.

Unlike the undefined number of "the others," the dreamer now has access to a deeper insight into or a higher awareness of what is happening to her. It is, besides the physical changes, a spiritual creative process she is engaging in. For, as we have seen, horses possess a quality of creative intuition and a close connection to the spiritual and sensual spheres. The horse can see otherworldly things; that is, it can build bridges so that things from the beyond can reach the world of the here and now.

Three months later, the same dreamer had the following dream:

---

[437] *Handwörterbuch d. dt. Aberglaubens*, Bd. 4, p. 1307 f

Dream No. 85:

> *We were sitting in a garden. Two wild horses flew at each other, but two giants restrained them with a strong hand, even when one of the horses attacked them. Afterwards, these giants were admired as heroes.*

In this dream, the horse plays an entirely different role. There seems to be a conflict on the creative-instinctive level. Two horses clash, and as Marie-Louise von Franz has shown in *Creation Myths,* this division in the unconscious is part of the creative process. Many creation myths have at the beginning two creation gods that are often only slightly different from one another: one is a little more active, the other a little more passive, one a little fairer, the other a little darker, one a little more masculine, the other a little more feminine, etc. From the initial uroborian primary oneness or the conscious-unconscious wholeness of the psyche, an active aspect strives towards creation while what has been left behind lies passive and inactive. When we want to or are supposed to be creative, there is always an inner pro and contra struggling against each other. Therefore, every creative process or every conscious realization is preceded by this schism. A conscious ego that is more active and focused may have as its counterpart one that is passive, dreaming and self-indulgent, lacking the necessary will for real work, prone to inertia and feelings of inferiority and as a result unfit for the creation of something new.

The two fighting horses suggest a creation conflict on the instinctive level. The positive maternal instinctive libido supporting pregnancy and child and wanting to bring it into the world, on the other hand faces a negative aspect of the instinctive libido. It is the death aspect of the Great Mother and of pregnancy that is fundamentally destructive. This conflict underlies many superficially perceptible pregnancy conflicts.

One of these conflicts of opposites is between the maternal passive "hatching" and sitting at home and the active life the woman led before she became pregnant. These opposites can tempt woman again and again to run away from the tedious bodily discomforts and the enforced passivity. Or it could be the conflict of sexuality during pregnancy. Something in woman wants it, perhaps even to a greater extent, another part in her rejects it and wishes to be left alone.

The yes-no-libido, the feeling divided and the chaotic confusion resulting from the opposing instincts must somehow be resolved and given a direction. In the dream, the two giants take on this task. In comparison with the horses, they represent a form of emotional instinctive force that is closer to man, an already as it were, more human form of consciousness. It still contains the pure emotional quality and instinctive force of the animal unconscious. Giants are often helpers in the creative process. In certain medieval legends, it is said that saints tricked them into building cathedrals. Thus, if we succeed in keeping control over them, they can indeed be very useful helpers.[438]

Figure 34. Solar carriage, Trundholm, Denmark

Marie-Louise von Franz mentions a dream Jung had at a time when he had to write *Psychological Types*. He had collected an enormous amount of material. He dreamt that he saw a huge ship heavily laden with goods that should now be towed into the port. An elegant white horse was attached to the ship by a rope, clearly incapable of pulling the boat in. Then a red-haired giant appeared, cut the rope, killed the horse with an axe and tugged the ship onto the land. After this, Jung wrote the book down in a tremendously enthusiastic mood, with great creative élan, "hammering together" all of the complex material.[439]

To bring order into the chaos of material for a book is a creative achievement, in a way similar to the creation of the world from the chaotic primeval waters, or managing to go through pregnancy with its often hostile instinctive counter-positions, or the creation of a child. The dream makes use of the same mythological motifs.

Our dreamer's giants are being celebrated as heroes after their deed, for not only did they withstand the attack of one of the horses but they also managed to control them with a strong hand. According to Marie-Louise von Franz, in a pre-creative stage giants usually have to do with ego-inflation caused by a tremendous surge of affect or emotion.[440] Creative work can often only be carried out with the help of a giant, or a gigantic emotional surge. We are

---

[438] M.-L. von Franz, *Creation Myths,* 268 f
[439] *Ibid.*, p. 267
[440] *Ibid.*, p. 275

carried by a state of inflation, and once we have completed our work, deflation or depression sets in – just as after the birth of a child, when a woman suddenly can fall into the well-known "post-natal depression."

Prior to this, however, the giants perform heroic deeds – for apparently, our dreamer harbors such aggressive, destructive impulses in her unconscious that it takes an heroic deed and a forceful affect to tame a mind that had already been made up. The dreamer must summon all of her feeling and stand up for her decision to have a child. She must bridle her dissociating "yes-no-thoughts," moods and impulses. For her, this is an heroic deed. The hero is the symbol of the ego-complex or consciousness that withstands the chaos of the dissociating instinctive patterns and the futile quarrel of the archetypes. The dreamer's conscious ego seems to be in need of the help of a primitive-emotional force, in order to cease being driven by mood swings and to see the creative process through. The dream points to this possibility. We do not know whether she succeeded. A healthy child was born, albeit five weeks prematurely.

A twenty-five-year-old woman, two months into pregnancy, had the following dream. In her first pregnancy, four years earlier, she had had a great deal of anxiety concerning the future and the welfare of her baby. This time, she was preoccupied by problems with her parents and husband. In addition, her health was unstable as she was not eating enough.

Dream No. 86:

> *I was going to a country house with my husband and my son, where other friends already were staying. Suddenly I saw my husband come running and my son in despair because there were three horses. Two of them were in despair, kicking. My husband escaped and left the boy behind. I went to the middle of the horses to rescue my son, who was alone and afraid. I rescued him, and we both were okay. Then the sky was dark, and I saw the rain approaching. Three black vultures [=urubu: in Brazil a sign of bad omen] came into the house, and I had to get rid of them all by myself. Then I saw that in reality the sky was only half- dark. I had eaten, because I was hungry.*

We are again dealing with the motif of horses "in despair," or in panic, which is typical of the horse. For some reason, panic and aggression seem to be developing in the dreamer's unconscious. Later, three vultures penetrate the dreamer's house – heralds of death and bad omen.

Interestingly, we have the number three in both three horses and three vultures. The odd number, three, tends to have masculine connotations. It corresponds to our Christian Trinity, the upper masculine Trinity of the Father, Son and Holy Ghost. In contrast, the horses have to do with instinctive sexual libido, the dynamic aspect in the lower, physical and at the same time emotional sphere of the feminine.[441]

Two horses are lashing out in a panic (literally "in despair"). Among horses, panic often occurs when their natural freedom of movement is being impeded. The "lower Trinity" of the horses in the dream, i.e., the emotional dynamic-instinctive domain of the lower feminine, the very domain of the dark maternal, seems not to be given adequate consideration. This state of affairs tries to come near the dreamer's conscious ego in the form of reactions of "panic." This can express itself in the dreamer's personal life in aggressive outbursts against husband and child. Her husband, however, as well as her own masculine-sensible side cannot help out here, for these reactions are wholly irrational. They are rather like the nature of panic in that the triggering issue is usually totally disproportional to the reaction. When we are in a panic we are momentarily nearly insane, just like horses that in their panic put their environment into danger.

Our dreamer had converted from the Jewish to the Catholic faith and took her religion very seriously. In the official Christian creed there is a representation of a feminine figure in contrast to the purely fatherly religion of Yahweh of the Old Testament. However, for a human woman, she is rather remote or at least situated below the masculine Trinity. In addition, she lacks the dark, earthy-maternal features that folkloric traditions had justly reattributed to her. We can find them in the black madonnas, in fairy tales and other stories of black maidens, witches and the devil's grandmother. There is a strong connection between this domain and the physical, instinctive part of the feminine nature that is particularly important during pregnancy. If it is entirely repressed or even rejected, woman usually experiences pregnancy as a burden and suffers from various kinds of ailments.

Panic has broken loose in the domain of the lower Trinity, of the unconscious counterpart to the Christian conscious perception of a higher Trinity. Given the state of the maternal instinctive libido that is supposed to carry through the dynamic creation process, we can understand the dreamer's insecurity and fear.

The three vultures represent another aspect of the lower Trinity. They are related to the fate-determining spirit of the unconscious that becomes particularly evident in the archetypal situations of pregnancy and birth. It manifests itself in the dreamer only in a very negative manner, overwhelming her consciousness and producing mainly dark thoughts regarding the future of the world and life of the child. The darkening sky and rain correspond to the

---

[441] C.G. Jung, Seminar 1938/39, p. 143. Jung speaks of a lower trinity or a lower chthonic triad that stand in contrast to the upper trinity as a "correspondence in reverse." Cf. also C.G. Jung, *The Phenomenology of the Spirit in Fairy Tales*, CW 9 I, § 425 f. For a discussion of "threeness," cf. also Chapter 5.4

gloomy mood of the dreamer. On the other hand, rain also signifies alleviation like the flow of water after a period of drought. Things can begin to "flow" again – something new can be born from the depression.

Having dealt with the vultures, she realizes that the sky is only half-dark. It would appear that she has been able to free herself from her gloomy outlook and black thoughts. She can now recognize that light and dark actually balance each other, or rather, hold each other in equilibrium. The terribly light image of the feminine, inspired by the church figure of the Virgin Mary, leaves the instinctive bodily domain of the feminine nature unnourished. Only now the dreamer feels hungry and is able to eat.

The dreamer manages to rescue herself and her son from being attacked twice by dark contents: first by the horses, then by the vultures. Although at the end of the dream she feels better, she never has a conscious confrontation with the contents attacking her from the unconscious. We shall see that the following dream, which I shall only briefly discuss, seems to take up this problem again.

Dream No. 87:

> *My daughter and I got to the beach, by car or bus. We see through the bus windows a little beach, between rocks. It is very nice. I think it will fill up with people at once. A white horse is running across the sand. The trip goes on, and now having got off the bus, we are both walking on a large beach, looking for my husband. There are a lot of people. Suddenly, just passing some dunes, we see a little estuary between dunes, formed by little brooks and the sea, a loop out of sight from the rest of the beach. And so there is my husband, with other men. They look like homosexuals, like everybody there. I feel very bad. Then I'm looking for my daughter: she has disappeared. I have a feeling she has been asphyxiated or has drowned. She appears exhausted or lifeless on the shore. I pick her up, and she finally revives. What a scare! My husband comes with me. All seems to straighten up. I have felt very bad, but in the end, this feeling disappears.*

This dream shows similar motifs to the preceding dream. The horse galloping along the beach, like Poseidon who originally appeared as a horse, belongs to the sea and therefore to the territory of the Great Mother.[442] Being white, it is a special horse, has something "unnatural" about it because it breaks all the camouflage rules of Nature (except in the snow). This is why Albinos are particularly exposed. Many tales and legends center around white animals (e.g., Melville's *Moby Dick*) having some connection with otherworldly, super-

---

[442] E. Neumann, *The Origins and History of Consciousness*, Bollingen Series, 42, Princeton University Press, 1970

natural things. White is the color of the beyond, of spirits, and so the white horse easily becomes a ghost horse.

We do not know the dreamer's associations with homosexuals. All we know is that in the dream she feels dejected seeing her husband with homosexuals.

As Marie-Louise von Franz explains in *Puer Aeternus*, homosexuality can be a disorder of a man with a very pronounced mother-complex.[443] This type of homosexual has got stuck in the adolescent phase, when the separation from the mother should have taken place. In mythology, he corresponds to Attis, Tamuz, Adonis, the youth-gods and son-lovers of the Great Mother Goddess, the Phrygian Cybele, the Syrian Astarte and the Ephesian Artemis.[444] Being castrated and sacrificing their masculinity is part of the destiny of these youths. A man who corresponds to this type seems to be deprived of his own masculinity. He projects his masculine side towards the outside and thus remains under the control of the maternal unconscious, putting projections and illusions onto other men and determining his relationship in this way. He lacks a strong masculine ego that would allow him to take on the heroic fight with the dragon, the fight against the unconscious Great Mother that controls him.

The dreamer feels miserable because she sees her husband in the company of homosexuals. It is only natural that, in her pregnant condition, she longs for masculine protection and sharing of the responsibility. In the dream with the horses in a panic threatening her son, the man played the role of a weakling who took to his heels instead of rescuing the child from the horses that lashed out. In this dream, too, the dreamer's first child is in danger. The child is a part of herself. On the subjective level, it is a part that can be childlike, spontaneous and full of potential growth. It is also the "divine child" that, according to Jung, is a symbol of the Self.[445] Like the children in our two dreams, this child too is often in danger.

The dream seems to suggest that pregnancy not only requires devotion to the maternal but equally a certain masculine strength of the ego. In other words, an animus is needed that can give a sense of goal and direction, so as not to lose our very own growing, new personality to the all too powerful maternal. The dreamer could be in danger of "drowning" in her condition of motherliness and thereby of losing sight of the potential of her individual personality. The white horse is like a vision of this other, otherworldly or spiritual aspect of the unconscious. It can give personal meaning that reaches beyond the maternal reduced to the purely biological-brooding aspect – the homosexuals on the beach seem to be under that spell, too – striving towards

---

[443] M.-L. von Franz, *Puer Aeternus*, p. 9

[444] E. Neumann, *The Origins and History of Consciousness*, Bollingen Series, 42, Princeton University Press, 1970

[445] C.G. Jung, *The Psychology of the Child Archetype*, CW 9 I, § 259 f

a deeper understanding and broadening of consciousness. However, as the horse also belongs to the maternal domain, the dream reflects both sides of pregnancy and motherhood. It is interesting that the risky side is depicted with the child in danger of suffocating or drowning which symbolically can be viewed as being cut off from oxygen, from the breath of life, i.e., from spirituality. At the same time, there is a danger of being flooded by unconscious-rendering emotions.

The dénouement of the dream shows that, despite everything, the dreamer succeeds in saving the child – that part in her which is her very own – and protecting it against the superpower of the mother-archetype that drives her to join the collective and unconscious. She succeeds once she "takes things into her own hands." Her husband reappears as if he had realized where his place was – namely, by the side of his wife and child. Hence, a psychic equilibrium has been reestablished in the dreamer: an equilibrium between the purely instinctive maternal, which is in the hands of Nature and its biological goals on the one hand, and on the other, the possibility of an individualized, more conscious existence, in which the animus can fulfill a valuable function.

I believe that while woman is put in the hands of the blind principle of Nature, what in fact underlies her urge for emancipation is precisely the desire and need to develop her own personal spirituality. This seems to be the red thread going through most of the dreams we have discussed so far. The horse motif is suggestive of its being closely linked to the spiritual or meaning aspect. It is, however, a kind of nature-spirituality that should not contradict maternity and pregnancy but, on the contrary, should become especially meaningful because of it.

The following dream comes from a thirty-four-year-old woman, who is pregnant with her first child having earlier had a miscarriage. A healthy boy was born and later another two. The same dreamer provided the dream in which she had become a tree.[446]

Dream No. 88:

> *The dreamer is in the living-room. Her oldest brother and his wife are also there. [The latter is in reality a super active "power-woman," very independent]. The dreamer does not like that. So dependent, so helpless. Her brother and herself are dressed in black. It is night. They are getting ready to go out. They are partisans, who have to blow up a strategically important bridge. Her brother's wife stays behind. The dreamer thinks that that was typical of women: of course they wouldn't participate, didn't have any sense of responsibility for the world, for politics, etc. They leave. The other partisans they are meeting now are also all dressed in black. The*

---

[446] By the same dreamer, No. 39, Chapter "Tree"

dreamer is the only woman present. It is night, cold, unpleasant. She has a baby under her black jacket. They are mounting the blasting composition. She realizes: "Now my child is going to catch her death of cold." She also realizes that she has to distance herself from the partisans because of the child. This is a painful conflict. She struggles and finally runs off with the child. She has a warm maternal feeling for the child, yet at the same time, she regrets the separation from the partisans.

Now she climbs up a mountain path through thorny brushwood. Suddenly, the sun comes out, and it gets warm. All of a sudden, she realizes that she is, in a way, split in two halves: on the one side (the left side), where the sun is shining, she is wearing a soft, fluttering, feminine fabric. On the other (right) side she is still wearing the hard, black fabric. On the left side, she can see a vine. She thinks: "Now I'm losing sight of the city, the valley, the partisans and of all they have been doing." In order to have a better view, she has to turn her left side to the valley and walk a short distance ahead. She sees that the entire city has been destroyed, burnt down, bombed. The partisans did not manage to prevent destruction, to help the people. One has to go on fighting. She turns her left side away again with a feeling of having to say good-bye to the armed conflict. At this moment, she sees a large plateau and walks up to it. Now her entire body is covered with the soft, feminine fabric. The plateau is like a steppe (Tibet, or something like that). An eagle is circling above her head. She looks up, has a momentary feeling of being in love, thinking: "I see – this is the father of my child." She walks on. She places her child in a cave. The years now go by as if in quick-motion-effect. She is standing in front of the cave, her legs bandaged up in fabric, earthy, at one with the earth. She protects the child while it grows up. Her hair grows very long, all the way down to the ground. At this point, the child has grown up, to age seventeen or so. She frees the entrance to the cave so that the child can come out: it is a boy. Now the eagle is again circling above them. She can feel a pang in her heart knowing that the father is going to come down to claim the son, so that he will rebuild the dead city. He shows him the way. The son follows his father until they reach the edge of the plateau, turns around briefly and goes off. She feels "shitty," worn out; she has served him, protected him, and now they're simply disappearing. She turns away. Now she spies a white horse, far away at the other end of the plateau. She thinks: "Aha! This is what they've left me – that is my life." She can hear music. She can see herself leap towards the horse in great bounds. With every leap and every time her feet touch the ground, there is some green grass growing. In the end, the entire plateau has become completely green.

The dreamer had this striking dream at around the time of conception. The woman, who is extremely active, got married at the same time. Her brother's "power-wife" is presumably a shadow-figure. The dreamer feels contempt for this side in herself, which associates marriage and motherhood with a false kind of "middle-class security." She would like to remain open and politically active. Partisans fight against the governing power structures. When the dreamer realizes that she has a child, she has to leave this masculine world in which her child would perish. This means a very heavy sacrifice on her part. In the dream, the unconscious seems to point out to her what her pregnancy is really about. It very likely compensates the dreamer's conscious attitude, which underestimates the meaning of pregnancy and bringing up children in comparison to a masculine activity, which is trying to improve the world.

The dreamer and her child have to negotiate their way through thorns to go up a mountain. At the top of the mountain and in the sunlight, she realizes that she is dressed half as a woman, yet half still in those masculine black clothes. We could say that she is on a thorny road as long as she does not recognize her state of being split in two. On the right and conscious side, she continues to be bound up with the masculine, hard world. On the left, the side of the unconscious or her natural personality, she suddenly feels soft, feminine clothes, warmth and femininity. For a woman, clothes are an expression of her inner state of being, and thus the dreamer finally becomes aware of her own femininity.

The vine is a fertility symbol and belongs to the mother-goddess. At the same time, it has to do with wine, the blood of Christ and with sacrifice. In the Baroque period, the Lamb of God was often depicted as standing between thorns and grapes.[447] The vine presents her with the idea of sacrifice that symbolically, however, results in resurrection and eternal life. After this, our dreamer is definitively and painfully made aware of the fact that she will never again participate in the partisans' efforts of saving the city. She has to distance herself from the combat. Because of its cohesive and mandala-shaped structure, a city in dreams symbolizes a personality that is outwardly solid. Behind the fascination by the outer, masculine, active form of life there is the projection of the Self. The people who must be helped represent the "lower" aspect of the dreamer herself that wants to be liberated from the clutches of a tyrannical power. During pregnancy, however, a woman must become conscious of her femininity and must renounce her masculine type of activity. It is as if the dream wanted her to walk on a different path though ultimately leading to the same destination – namely, the growing into a new personality.

Now, let us look at the eagle. It is the father of her child. It reminds us of the idea of the totem-animal that, according to an ancient belief, discloses itself to the individual during an ecstatic experience. Neumann holds it to be

---

[447] Cf. J.E. Dirlot, *Dictionary of Symbols,* London, 1978

an "ancestor with a claim to originality of spiritually procreative ideas."[448] This animal is put under a taboo and surrounded by strong rites, for it represents a personal experience of God from which stem not only the initiation rites of the primitives but also the mysteries of antiquity and all the foundations of the great religions.[449]

In alchemy, the eagle symbolizes the winged Mercurius, the spirit of the unconscious. In *Psychology and Alchemy*, we can find an illustration of the eagle as "a symbol of the spirit ascending from the *prima materia.*"[450] Like most birds, the eagle is associated with flights of thought and with fantasies and intuitive ideas. In antiquity, the bird's flight was interpreted as the will of the gods. Birds were the gods' messengers and established a connection with the beyond. The eagle is mainly associated with height, proximity to the sun, and in Egypt, with light, warmth, origin and day. In our dream, too, the warmth of the sun exists as an important element.[451]

Interpreting the eagle positively, we could say that the dreamer encounters her personal totem-animal, the divine, creative spirit of the unconscious. It is the father of the child and the one the child ultimately belongs to. Not realizing that the child is not her own work and not her property, she will feel "shitty," if later she has to give it up. What she must understand is that the seventeen years she has spent being feminine, passive, at one with the earth and "lasting out" to bring up the child, has been a sacrifice she made to God and her feminine contribution to the rebuilding of the bombed city. Neither woman, mother nor even father can solve the collective problems of the world. They are entirely in the hands of God, whom he and she can merely serve in a modest kind of way. As we have already seen in the chapter on birds, the eagle could have to do with power, with a fantasy about the future child and its great future mission in the world. Many mothers silently nurse such fantasies. If, in this sense, the child had had an eagle for a "godfather," that is, a power-fantasy of his mother's, the second part of the dream would be even more meaningful.

As the years go by, so the dream says, the dreamer's hair grows down to the ground. Hair growing out of her head signifies thoughts and fantasies growing out of the unconscious. However, in those long years during which she apparently does little else apart from watching and protecting her son's growing up, something else has grown as well. In the eyes of primitive man, hair is a carrier of mana. It carries, as it were, the spiritual substance of life. Above all, very long hair is an attribute of femininity. The long time of passivity provides

---

[448] E. Neumann, *Ursprungsgeschichte des Bewusstseins*, 160 f (excerpt transl. by V.N.)/ *The Origins and History of Consciousness*, Bollingen Series, 42, Princeton University Press, 1970

[449] *Ibid.*, p. 451 f

[450] C.G. Jung, *Psychology and Alchemy*, CW 12, Bollingen, 1953, Fig. 229, p. 417

[451] Cf. Chapter "Birds"

fertile ground for the development of her feminine fantasies and thoughts as well as her own spirituality imparting *mana* to her, that is, a certain distinctive aura of feminine value.

On a higher plane (the plateau), she now comes to recognize the white horse, symbol of the Great Mother closely linked with the spiritual and the hereafter. The dream seems to say: "Life is not over when woman is left by her children." For, when she has sacrificed her masculine, dynamic outer activities, Mother Nature endows her with her own powers as expressed by the beautiful allegory: every time her feet touch the ground, new green grass grows. This goes to show the fruitful effect she has on her environment. Her touching the earth, which is reality, life, the environment and other people, results in new growth. Thus, her real goal becomes perceptible. It is not what she thought at the beginning of the dream – a partisan comrade-in-arms (who was, moreover, denying her own femininity). It has to do with letting herself be carried by a feminine-instinctive natural spirituality that is directed towards the Self.

The following two dreams address a different problem. We know that this thirty-seven-year-old, one month pregnant woman was told by her doctor that her child would probably be born dead and that she should think about having an abortion. At first she rejected this possibility. But when the diagnosis became a certainty, she agreed to it. The child was indeed found to be dead. The night after her visit at the doctor's, she had the following dream:[452]

Dream No. 89:

> *I was with a woman from the Third World. She had a number of children and was squatting on the ground in the midst of her poverty. She wore a veil over her face. The woman looked very poor and neglected, and her children were in a similar state. Both the mother and children were hungry.*

This dream suggests, in quite a brutal manner, why the child could not live. When we think of the Third World, images of poverty, misery, hunger and death come to mind. This simple, natural world is suffering from hunger and malnutrition. The simple woman within the dreamer – the one who is having a child – is hungry. Psychologically, this means that she lacks the necessary nourishment; in other words, her conscious ego either refuses or fails to give her a certain amount of caring attention that she needs. The nourishment represents the purely biological aspect of the maternal, the primitive maternal element that is indispensable for the creation and life of a child. It is this maternal element that seems to elude the dreamer's consciousness. She had,

[452] I am using these notes, which were enclosed with the dream, with the kind permission of the patient and her analyst.

in fact, led an extraverted life – one that was influenced by collective opinion. She was also greedy for power and unpredictable in her actions. Finally, she had to bear the cruel consequences of the unconscious, i.e., the death of her child.

The night after this dream, she dreamt:

Dream No. 90:

> I gave birth to a baby-horse.

Now, the dream of the birth of the baby-horse offers great consolation. It would appear that, despite everything, new growth can now occur – moreover, that this, in fact, is the purpose of all the suffering. The little horse is, as it were, a present from the Great Mother that will one day carry her along in life. Precisely because she had wanted to stand behind her child but had to lose it all the same, her maternal instincts, containing all potential growth, could be awakened inside her.

A thirty-seven-year-old woman, seven months into her first pregnancy and suffering from depression, had a similarly comforting dream:

Dream No. 91:

> I sat alone, silent and preoccupied. My brain felt dull and exhausted. I tried to open the window and go out, but I couldn't. I was a goner. A large horse came. It had large and beautiful eyes. I asked a favor of it. It nodded. Then I woke up. I could not restrain my tears. I felt as if I had been saved by the horse, with tears pouring down my cheeks.

In this dream, the dreamer asks a horse for help as she is sad and exhausted by the demeaning thoughts of her confused brain. As in many fairy tales, a horse comes to the rescue of an individual once his or her situation is desperate. Barbara Hannah wrote, referring to a passage from Jung's *Visions Seminars* describing a picture of an animal painted by a patient.[453] I find this passage so moving that I will reproduce it in its entirety:

> She made a picture of a face with the melancholy eyes of a beast. What really happened was that they [the animals] not only traveled back to ancient Greece, but went even further: the animals led her back even into the animal age. You remember that the purpose of the Dionysian mysteries was to bring people back to the animal; not to what we commonly understand by that word, but to the animal within. She looks directly into THE EYES OF AN ANIMAL, AND THEY ARE FULL OF WOE AND BEAUTY BECAUSE

---

[453] C.G. Jung, *Visions Seminars*, I, pp. 153-4; B. Hannah, *Lecture on Dog, Cat, Horse*, p. 118 (my emphasis)

271

THEY CONTAIN THE TRUTH OF LIFE, AN EQUAL SUM OF PAIN AND PLEASURE, THE CAPACITY FOR JOY AND THE CAPACITY FOR SUFFERING. The eyes of very primitive and unconscious men have the same strange expression of a mental state before consciousness, which is neither pain nor pleasure: one doesn't exactly know what it is – it is most bewildering – but undoubtedly she sees here into the very soul of the animal, and that is the experience she should have. Otherwise she is disconnected from Nature.

The dream seems to show the dreamer that she can trust Nature and her own instinctive foundation. She will be dealt what she deserves in her difficult pregnancy. What is essential, however, is that she asks. We can find the motif of the missed question in many myths and folktales, e.g., in the Legend of the Holy Grail. Gawain, the knight, sleeps through the moment when the Grail King would have been prepared to reveal to him the mystery of the Holy Grail if he had only put the question to him. The unconscious often only answers our questions when we beg it to. Many individuals have powerful dreams, but as long as they do not take any active interest in them, they will not receive any explanation regarding their meanings. More often than not, there has to be a strong sense of urgency and of suffering before we are willing to ask. Only then will the animal soul help us.

Dream No. 92:[454]

I received a gift of two lively, cheerful brown horses, whom I immediately found frisking about on a green meadow. After that, I was in a church. Standing there were many old men – my father-in-law and my husband's godfather and others – and they were all trying to move forward in order to say the "Credo," which each one of them had written down on a scrap of paper. It was a personal "confirmation." I felt this to be terribly important and meaningful in view of the birth of a new being.

This dream came shortly before a happy and easy delivery of a boy, who was the dreamer's third child. The horses on the green meadow evoke a feeling of a rich instinctive life suggesting a birth without complications in contrast to the previous one, which had ended in a miscarriage. In addition, a "personal confirmation" now takes place. This can be interpreted as a religious initiation process, a confirmation or reinforcement of a new state having to do with a consolidation of the personality.

It is interesting that there are only older men in the church, together with the dreamer's husband, his father and godfather. The three "fathers" belong together. They are the human representatives of the Christian religion headed by a masculine Trinity. The latter is handed down through dogma and ritual,

[454] By the same dreamer: No. 24: Chapter 3.2, No. 65: Chapter 5.3, No. 36: Chapter 4.1, No. 112: Chapter 6, No. 98: Chapter 5.8

from father to son, written down and read again by each generation and confirmed with the Credo. Now, the three horses on the green meadow make up the missing feminine-maternal element, which represents the fourth element. The masculine community and the act of confirmation in the church point to an acceptance of the Christian-patriarchal tradition, including its clearly defined value system. The dreamer's unconscious does not perceive it as something negative, but on the contrary, as something meaningful in view of the birth of the new baby-boy. I think that the three fathers and the continuity of the religious tradition symbolize for the dreamer an assurance, as it were, and firmness or strength (*confirmare* – "to confirm, render firm") of the masculine, conscious values committed to Christianity. Set against this are the horses, expressing her feminine temperament. This is the gift pregnancy bestows on her – becoming conscious of that aspect of her femininity. This results in another consolidation, namely, the personal confirmation of her own religiousness, in harmony, as it were, with the tradition of the fathers.

Jung reiterated again and again that it was not a question of throwing overboard our Christian myth but that it was essential to develop our own understanding of it. Many of us, in our present day and age, find little satisfaction in "reading the Credo." People are looking for a lively, personal relationship with religion. Jung tries to show a way of opening the doors by shedding some light on the symbolism, thereby translating the Christian mythology into the language of today. Maybe our dreamer had a tendency to reject indiscriminately all the longstanding values, which seemed to her like empty religious shells. However, as Jung held emphatically, religious systems have a therapeutic function of regulating man's confrontation with the archetypal powers, and without them, our dreamer would have been lost in the face of the onrush coming from the unconscious. She depends on this form of support represented in her dream by the religious system (confirmation). At the same time, however, becoming aware of her instinctive femininity, the ground on which she can realize her own personal relationship with God within the framework of traditions has now been prepared for her. This is what is most likely to be essential for the new child.

Over the centuries, alchemy, numerous fairy tales and other teachings running parallel to the Christian doctrine have demonstrated the values of the earthy, feminine temperament. This dream adds these elements in a natural, unproblematical way to a religious *Weltbild* in which the Trinitarian, masculine conception prevails.

273

Figure 35. Boar-headed mother-goddess (India, 7ᵗʰ cent. A.D.)

5.7. The Pig

Regina Abt

In our Christian cultural consciousness, the pig has almost exclusively negative connotations. We associate it with dirt and gluttony, sexuality and sin. We say in English, "he's made a pig of himself" when we mean someone ate or drank too much, or we call someone a "swine" – meaning he is mean or immoral. The German word, *Schweinerei*, is likewise used to express a sense of outrage about something indecent. Regardless of what the ancients already knew and what modern zoologists and ethnologists have rediscovered – namely, that pigs are clean, sociable and intelligent animals provided they are kept in an animal-friendly way – "swine" or "pig" are still among the most widely used swearwords: "he eats like a pig," "she behaves like a pig," "her room is a pigsty," etc. Pigs used to be, and sometimes still are, kept in the most shady places of the farm in stables that are dismal holes.

Where do these unfavorable opinions regarding the pig come from? This has not always been so. Even in our culture, there are remnants of a very different sense of reverence for the pig: for instance, for the New-Year's-piglet or the good-luck-piglet. The origins of this custom go back to an age when the pig was positively associated with arable land and the plowing culture. It played an important role in harvesting rites, for its exceptional fertility, which signified wealth, food and growth to the peasants, greatly impressed the ancients.[455] The pig thus became a symbol of growth and fertility and of the blessing of Mother Nature. Having a large family was a part of it. For this reason, numerous customs connected with pregnancy and birth, but also prophesy regarding a future spouse, number or gender of children, etc., revolve around the pig. Folklore has it that a pregnant woman kicking a pig with her feet will experience a difficult birth. Pigs are also useful in magic, especially in issues of love, marriage, fortune, fertility but also to fend off evil. The pig, even more so than the cat or horse, symbolizes the abundantly wholesome, fertile side of Mother Nature, comprising a warm, animalistic instinctive aspect of the feminine and maternal, as well as Eros, feeling and sharing.

---

[455] James G. Frazer, *The Golden Bough*, and *Handwörterbuch d. dt. Aberglaubens*

Figure 36. Demeter sitting on a pig (Hellenic, Southern Italy)

The ancient Greeks associated the pig with Demeter, the great goddess of fertility and corn. She is portrayed with either a pig in her arm or by her side or riding on it. In Egypt, the pig also ranked among the gods. Nut, the Egyptian sky goddess, was depicted as a mother pig with suckling piglets.

According to European folklore, the pig can scent treasures, guard springs and treasures and track down sunken bells. In fairy tales and legends, the treasure signifying the highest hidden value is a symbol of the most precious inner value – the Self – whereas the sound of a bell was perceived as the voice of God or of a saint, *vox dei*. In psychological terms, it is the voice of the Self. That it could be found by a "dirty pig" of all things may well be possible in folkloristic thinking but hardly in Christian-ecclesiastical conception. As the Christian rejection of all things associated with the animalistic, instinctive, natural world and its hostility to the physical spread more widely, the pig was turned into an animal of the devil, a riding animal for witches and demons and a symbol of carnal temptation. The hermit, Anthony, is supposed to have fallen prey to it in the desert. Thus, the only remaining associations with the pig were the projections of greed, sexuality and sin while its positive aspects of feminine fertility and sexuality, maternal-animal warmth and nourishment were discarded from man's consciousness. Thus, an essential facet of the feminine-maternal nature, indeed vital for woman's wholeness, was lost to the unconscious. It was no longer "known" and venerated. It seems to me that many women today acutely suffer from this Christian heritage and have to bear the consequences. They suffer from the devaluation of what the pig represents. What is more, they themselves devalue it frequently, finding it impossible to admit this vital part of their nature. Naturally, however, the entire feminine-maternal domain of the psyche rebels against the suppression of the "pig side" in her, particularly at a time of pregnancy and birth. For, to reject the image of the animal-instinctive, warm, motherly qualities of the pig mother with all her feeding piglets, apparently cannot be done without causing some damage. In the following two dreams, the "pig-like aspect" or "piggishness" seems to want to come into the dreamer's life. Around the time of conception, expecting her third child, a woman dreamt:

Dream No. 93:

> *I was looking through a window in a parlor. A pig entered. He bit my hand. Someone aided me.*

Prior to a Cesarean section delivery of her fourth child, another woman dreamt:[456]

Dream No. 94:

> *A wild boar appeared suddenly. Although I tried to run away from him, it was impossible to free myself. He attacked me, but I felt no pain or fear.*

What may seem peculiar at first sight is the fact that they are male pigs menacing the dreamer. Mother Nature goddesses frequently have male, sometimes destructive, attendants, e.g., a boar or he-goat.[457] They are seen as a masculine attribute of the feminine that can have a negative influence.[458] This masculine-aggressive side, which will be discussed in this context in detail in Chapter 6, belongs to the maternal-feminine. Other cultures approach it with great caution. The menacing side of the Great Mother is best represented in the figure of the Indian Goddess Kali or the Greek Gorgo. Both are depicted with boar tusks. They are also goddesses of death, for death is the other side of fertility, and Nature's fertility is intricately bound up with the fading-away of old things.

Despite the threat by the boars, neither of the dreamers feels real fear or pain. "Someone helped me" – presumably the positive side of the Great Mother or the pig symbol itself. The intruding boar restricts her freedom ("it was impossible to free myself") and her freedom of action ("he bit my hand"). Inexplicable, terrifying and paralyzing impulses attack the dreamer, yet at the same time, they can be overcome without her having much to do with it. A helpful instinct carries her over the difficulties. Something inside her does the adapting to the situation for her, as it were, almost without her own contribution.

Consciousness tends to underestimate or suppress the pig aspect of the maternal, whether it be an all too childlike attitude towards pregnancy and future motherhood, or a momentary decline in interest substituted by a strong spiritual pursuit. In either case, the limiting, dark, perilous element, the death-aspect of the new feminine task can unexpectedly surface from the unconscious. It is the threatening, constricting, frightening side of the world of sexual and instinctive drives. This can manifest itself in an unaccountable

---

[456] By the same dreamer: No. 27, Chapter 3.3

[457] Cf. figure in: Buffie Johnson, *Lady of the Beasts*, Harper & Row Publishers, San Francisco, 1988: The boar-headed mother-goddess sitting on a lotus throne representing the changing phases of the moon, continually dying to be reborn again.

[458] E. Neumann, *The Great Mother*

sense of dissatisfaction, aggressiveness and irritability. Some mothers do not want to breastfeed because they either find it restricts their freedom or they believe they are unable to. They also frequently feel that excessive demands are being made upon them for other reasons, perhaps through a lack of contact with other mothers-to-be or other experienced women, who could give them support, or because of a husband, who may be away a great deal. The little babies with their constant demands make them nervous, irritable, unloving and very often, out of the resulting bad conscience, the mothers become overly concerned. This again reinforces the sense of overburden and irritability. It brings up the negative animus-side. The attacking boars could be an image for this.

Sexuality goes alongside with "piggishness," of course in a positive sense. Therefore, the attacking boars could also be interpreted as aggressive sexuality, which is incongruent with the condition of a pregnant woman. Her dream in this respect could be a warning signal. As we do not know the dreamer's personal circumstances and associations, we cannot tell which possibility applies to her.

Pregnant with her third child, a woman dreamt:[459]

Dream No. 95:

> *A large number of pigs were crowded together. Their heads looked like black dots which symbolized the heads of the crowded people in the cartoons. They all bowed their heads to me. A captain pig among them came to me and bowed again. He asked me to ride on him. I refused to do so, but all the pigs were saying all at once: "Please ride on him, Ma'am, he is safe." I finally rode on him.*

"A large number of pigs were crowded together" speaks of a distinctly collective situation that in many ways corresponds to the expectant mother. Seemingly, she must be or become like the masses of women, living out their maternal instinct and having children. It is similar to the aforementioned feeling of constriction, imprisonment, and of feeling "crowded in."

However, in this dream, the individual conscious ego is given a leading role. All the pigs, including the "captain pig," bow to the dreamer as if wanting to reassure her about the uncanny and collective side of the maternal world of sexuality and instinct, and grant her the leadership. Riding the captain pig, she becomes captain or leader herself. Symbolically, they thus confer upon her the role of "mistress of the animals," that is, Mother Nature herself. As the goddess, the feminine Self, she is the one who rules over and controls the various animals, that is, the variety of their instinctual drives. She is in charge of the body and the abundance of its functions and so creates a kind of unconscious

[459] By the same dreamer: No. 27, Chapter 3.3

"spiritual" order of the totality. In many mythologies, the human figure of the mistress of the animals is described as a spiritual force in man that is superior to the instincts.[460] The bullfight, for instance, belongs to the rituals of the Great Mother Nature. Moreover, the animal offering, in other words, the sacrifice of the instincts, their restriction and control equally belong to the mistress of the animals.[461] The order of the mistress of the animals is an unconscious natural order embracing at once death, cruelty and arbitrariness as well as planning, creation, sensuality, etc.[462] The fact that the dreamer's small ego is offered the leading role could suggest that the instinctive world is in want of meaning and reason. In other words, a guiding principle that makes all the individual instinctive elements fall into place, so to speak, wants to become human, thus conscious. This will result in consciousness being connected with and carried by the instinct. The dreamer becomes both being led and a leader. A woman, putting herself in the hands of the collective symbol of the pig, is guided and carried by maternal instinct and a femininity that includes and represents Eros, human relations and a nurturing feeling in the family social fabric. (Pigs have a highly sophisticated family and social life that becomes evident provided they are kept in groups and with plenty of room to run.)

It would seem that, in our day and age, it is not considered sufficient for woman to unconsciously submit to the feminine maternal nature. What is demanded is a very conscious devotion to those elements that distinguish her as woman or mother.[463] This permits reconciliation between the apparently absurd perpetual repetition of an unconscious instinctive determination with its variety of faces, on the one hand, and the spiritual goal of a consciously recognized meaning, on the other. Many women among us, particularly those brought up in a Christian culture, are frequently no longer able to fulfill their feminine-maternal functions in an unconscious-natural way. Pregnancy is sometimes marked with depression, anxiety and physical discomfort. For these women, only a higher consciousness of the manifold aspects of their natural condition can help them to see the meaning of it all and to accept consciously the sacrifice they have to make: the sacrifice of their liberty, self-will, individual life-plan, and finally even of the maternal devotion the Great Mother demanded of them.

An eight-months pregnant twenty-three-year-old woman had the following terrifying dream:

---

[460] Cf. Neumann, *The Great Mother*

[461] *Ibid.*, p. 265

[462] *Ibid.*, p. 263

[463] Cf. Esther Harding, *The Way of All Women, A Psychological Interpretation*, Longmans, London, 1933; see also Chapter 9

Dream No. 96:

> *An unknown insane woman comes to a garden party. She brings an uncooked pig. She eats it by tearing it apart with her teeth. When we look at this macabre scene, she spits the piece at us and then chases us to devour us, too.*

Figure 37. Kali on Shiva, dancing (India, 19th cent.)

The uncanny figure of the insane woman is an image of the destructive, devouring side of the Great Mother. An example of these cruel features can be found in the Indian earth-goddess, Kali. Kali drinks warm blood from a skull; chopped-off heads are dangling around her neck, and she is attended by beasts of prey. She also holds a ladle or food bowl as well as a snare, an iron hook or scissors, with which she can sever the thread of life. She has a beautiful body but has tusks for teeth shooting out of her mouth and a long tongue.[464] The devouring Greek Gorgo also has boar tusks, a tongue sticking out and in addition, a beard. Among these goddesses, the dark destructive will, the aspect of death prevails over the life-giving side that is also present. While the life-bestowing aspect is connected with life per se and with the gift of Nature, the daily exposure to the natural elements, hunger and death were perceived as coming from the merciless, dark Mother Nature. For woman, facing her own primeval feminine principle can be like facing the Great Mother, of which the mother of death is also a part.[465]

Viewed psychologically, the latter represents the most threatening aspect of the unconscious, namely, one that can reclaim at any time what the unconscious has once given. Hence, not only a new child but also the birth of new consciousness, which apparently lies in the will of Nature herself, are always potentially at risk. Nature often destroys the very things it has brought forth –

---

[464] H. Zimmer, *Myths and Symbols in Indian Art and Civilization*, Pantheon Books, Washington, 1946

[465] S. Birkhäuser, *Die Mutter im Märchen* [*The Mother: Archetypal Image in Fairy Tales*], p. 47

particularly if human consciousness fails to firmly counter her unpredictable attitude.

On the other hand, the aspect of death belongs to the Great Mother's fertility just as blood sacrifices of human beings and animals, e.g., pigs belong to her fertility rites. Killing and dismemberment are a precondition for fertility and renewal of life. Given that the word "Kali" is structurally linked to time (Kala), the time may be propitious to accommodate the fruitful aspect of Mother Nature and to live consciously the instinctive and sexual femininity pertaining to the maternal nature. At a later moment in time, however, it is sometimes necessary to sacrifice again this very aspect, in order to prevent it from being turned into something destructive by the unconscious, negative, devouring side of the maternal nature.

Particularly caring mothers, having fulfilled their maternal duty with utter devotion over many years, often find it impossible to comprehend, why, from a certain age their children show only negative results of their upbringing. Their relations with their children appear to be seriously troubled or influenced by some destructive force. Perhaps a form of the instinctive motherliness (the pig) had not been sacrificed or the detachment from the children did not take place at the right moment – or with the necessary conscious and painful renunciation. It is as if in the unconscious, the destructive side of the Great Mother has unnoticeably taken hold of the pig and now produces its effects. We could therefore say, that if the sacrifice is not made voluntarily, the goddess herself will claim it. The time has evidently changed and so has the face of the archetype.

Like Gorgo with a long tongue, beard and boar tusks, she has suddenly distinctly masculine features. On the collective level, this means that the archetype of the Great Mother can – perhaps unexpectedly – show its destructive, dynamic side. An example of this could be the great collective obsession phenomena. For example, the destructive side of the dark Mother Nature or the unconscious can form the basis of terrific outbreaks of emotions resulting in war. On a personal level, the positive maternal aspect can transform itself into a destructive animus effect of which the woman is mostly completely unaware. Towards the outside, though, she is still the caring, loving mother.

Let us now return to the personal level of our dreamer. She is young and expecting her first child. Although the problems we have just discussed do not concern her, they could have been her mother's problems. This type of psychic constellation frequently results in destructive manifestations in the daughter, especially at a time when she herself is about to become a mother. Then it becomes a problem. Unconscious patterns of attitudes taken over from her mother make her own motherhood difficult. An example of unconscious thoughts stemming from such attitudes could be: "I feel sorry for the children who are born into this world that is doomed!"

In psychological terms, the insane woman could represent a form of a mother complex that has a destructive effect on the maternal instinct. What could have been a pregnancy guided by natural instinct is now dominated by unconscious contents of aggressiveness and a deadly kind of unconnectedness affecting the dreamer's conscious ego with insecurity and fear. It is not our dreamer's personal mother but an unknown female figure. This indicates the dangerous aspect of the archetype of the dark feminine that manifests itself in the dreamer's unconscious. The emergence of this archetype means that the dreamer is in danger of being gripped by something immensely powerful that could destroy her animal motherly instinct. Sometimes terribly "good" mothers are tormented by sudden exaggerated attacks of rage and inexplicable aggression. It is the "insane" side that can cause a mother to be beside herself and to lose the warm instinctive feelings she has for the growing child. Our dreamer seems to be in great trouble, although a month later, she delivers a healthy baby-girl.

In the Christian tradition, the pig belongs to the devil. In folklore, however, Saint Anthony, being supposedly deeply in touch with his instinctive sides, is associated with a pig. In this way, he is brought closer to man. Women are frequently too "saintly" and therefore tend to infuriate the Great Mother or the unconscious. A little more dirt, e.g., a pig-like mess or piggish laziness could sometimes allow a bit more stable warmth. Children can relate to spontaneous, warm instinctive reactions. It provides a counterbalance to the cold scientific approach gaining ground nowadays in education and in fact in most other spheres of life.

Suppressing these spontaneous emotional reactions causes a damming up of dangerous potential in the collective unconscious. Today's youth has good reason to yearn after spontaneity and feeling. The general lack of these can turn into a collective outburst of destructive emotions with which we are no longer equipped to deal. For this reason, it is important for our children that mothers be on good terms with their own "pig instinct."

Some fathers might ask themselves where all this leaves them, what do their problems contribute? Knowing how important it is that the anima, i.e., the feminine side in a man, his soul and feeling, play an active role in his life, it becomes clear that all the facets of the feminine brought up by the dream imagery, are naturally part of the feminine side in man. It would be interesting to look at the dreams of the pregnant women's spouses; however, that would reach far beyond the scope of our present study. It is, however, worth noting that pregnancy – a condition during which a woman is intimately connected with instinctive and physical processes – brings up imagery and produces archetypal aid that is primarily specific to the maternal-feminine life.

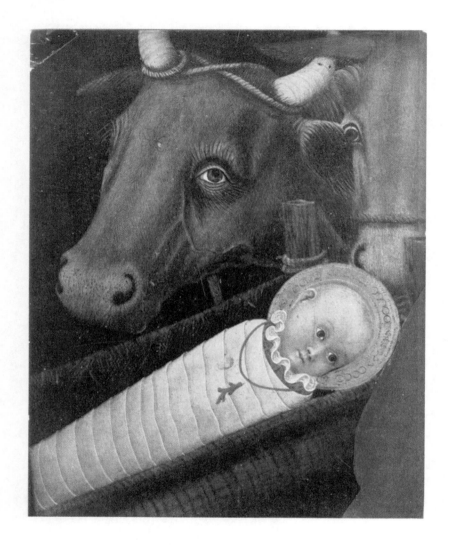

*Figure 38. Detail from: "The Adoration of the Shepherds"
by P.d.G. d'Ambrogio (15th cent., Siena)*

5.8. The Cow

Irmgard Bosch

It may surprise some readers to find that, in our extensive collection of pregnancy dreams, there are so few containing the motif of the cow despite the cow's manifold associations with pregnancy: the production of milk, the growing belly with its burdensome weight, an increase in appetite, the need to rest and to be more attentive to the body. These are all things belonging to the realm of consciousness, however, whereas the unconscious tends to address the more profound and enigmatic issues. In this chapter, we are going to discuss dreams involving the cow motif that turned out to be very revealing.

Since the Neolithic Period, most people lived with and on cattle: their milk, their meat and blood and parts of the body, such as the hair, skin, bones, horns, hoofs, etc. They used the cow dung to make fire and fertilize the soil, and they also harnessed them. For thousands of years, to all intents and purposes, the cow embodied a foundation and source of life, and from time immemorial, the highest goddesses were worshipped through the cow. The bull cult is one of the most ancient cults we know of. On the feminine side, we have the following examples: Hathor, the ancient Egyptians' great goddess, was depicted as an enormous cow, and squatting under her belly was Pharaoh, as the representative of humankind, drinking from her udder. Isis, the Egyptian goddess, equally wore horns. Hera, Zeus' sister and wife, originally had cow's eyes. In India, a myth of the origin of the world describes it as having come from milk: together with the demons, the gods swirled the milky ocean from which the earth was brought forth.[466] In India, sacred cows continue to be venerated to this day.

The cow, mythologically seen as something great and maternal, stands mostly for a "beginning." Krishna, the Indian god, played as a child with the milk-girls and cows on the pasture. The birth of Christ is unthinkable without the donkey and ox. Even among the ancient, weatherbeaten Nordic peoples, the creation myth of Snorri Sturluson's Prose *Edda* (ca. 1200 A.D.) tells of a cow licking the first man out of the glassy infinity of ice.

---

[466] Cf. Figure 21, p. 179

285

Figure 39. The Heavenly Cow (Egyptian)

As a dispenser of nourishment and milk, the cow evokes an aspect of the feminine that has almost been forgotten. It is the symbolical maternal foundation of all life. The character of the cow (whose domestication occurred millennia ago) is mostly gentle and giving willingly: it thus corresponds to an ancient mother-ideal. Entering an older cow shed, you can still feel the cows' warm breath. This reassuring, as it were, vegetative atmosphere we can feel particularly in the presence of ruminating cows – so peacefully at one with their bodies and concentrating so naturally and steadily on their digestive processes. We often wish just a little bit of "cow-being" for our pregnant friends today when either because they want to or have to, they so bravely try to "get pregnancy over with" – sideline it, so to speak.

The focus of the following dream is upon a conflict between the dreamer's animus aspects and her maternal-animal psychic components. The report of the dream being very long, I am reproducing it here in a shortened form:

Dream No. 97:

> *The first part of the dream takes place at a girlfriend's wedding-party, and after this in an antique shop, where a funny, impish artist bursts into overwhelming enthusiasm over the ancient objects in the shop. These antique items are deeply meaningful to him and also have deeply religious references. He picks everything up, dancing around with them in ecstasy.*

286

The dreamer is enraptured by his archaic behavior. When he ritually turns her into a cow by putting cow horns on her, she is entranced and dances with him. She can scarcely keep her balance with the horns that are hung with veils of all different colors.

After this fantastic scene, the dreamer returns to her friend's house, or more precisely, to the terrace at the back of the house. It is very much the back side of partying and celebration, for there is nothing to remind one of "dancing and veils" but instead, of sobriety and work. On this terrace, there is a lot of washed clothing and ordinary bed linen hanging up to dry – pointing to the practical side of everyday life. On the other hand, washed clothing also has a firm place in the archetypal scenery of encounter (e.g., Odysseus and the Phaeacians).

On the back terrace, by the washing, the dreamer meets a young man. He looks like the Pueblo-Indian, Koshare, *who plays an important role in the Indian corn-dance: a fertility rite. Again, the encounter with the dancing male figure bears upon something archaic-religious. However, the dancing man cannot unfold freely. First, he is obstructed by the washing, then by several "healthy-looking cows," who evidently frighten him. His thought of a shortcut – right across the house – or "head first through the wall" – turns out to be illusory.*

The "healthy-looking cows" are an impenetrable wall for this animus-spirit, for they heavily contradict his favorite life-style of a free imagination and freely floating ideas. This means that the dancing aspect of the unconscious has little bearing on the material, maternal reality that he shies away from even though he explicitly invokes fertility and is fascinated by it. Just as in religion, idolization is not sufficient in real life.

Now the dream-ego wants to move. The dancer is to perform a difficult deed: namely, pushing the cows aside and slapping them lightly, thereby doing something with his hands. Although the dancer looks worried, he eventually dares to touch one of the cows.

Unfortunately, another obstacle comes up that the dream-ego itself seems to have put in the way. The dreamer is amazed to notice that the cow is just starting to dance in a hesitating manner, like a horse on its hind legs, without actually moving. Suddenly, she realizes that she had been holding the cow's ear firmly on the windowsill! As soon as she lets go of it, the animal calms down and lets the corn-dancer pass by unharmed.

For the interpretation of these peculiar scenes, let us refer to Emma Jung's apt animus descriptions in *Animus and Anima*, where she says: "Unquestionably, the animus is a spirit which does not allow itself to be hitched to a wagon like a tame horse. Its character is far too much that of the elemental being; ... [it may] confuse us with unruly, flickering inspirations, or even soar entirely away with us into thin air." [467] Woman's imagination and fantasies are to a large extent determined by the animus. Her artistic and spiritual work, for example, based on the production of inner images and ideas are carried largely by the animus function. In contrast, pregnancy, birth and bringing up children involve large steps towards the concrete and physical "matter" which for the animus can be an obstacle that is difficult to overcome. These steps are made at the cost of great strength. Marie-Louise von Franz once said that the fear so many young women had of the stark contrast between having children and raising them and their spiritual-creative work was not completely unjustified. The animus, having exerted much influence before, could put up quite a strong resistance.

Our dream shows something about this animus conflict with the feminine reality. Nevertheless, the male dancer in the dream is enchanted by the archaic-feminine antiques, the colorful veils and the cow horns, and he is intoxicated with the divine-archaic aspect, causing an almost religious frenzy in him. However, faced with the wet linen and the fat cows, he becomes blocked and afraid, for here, he would be asked to participate in sober work and the "rude health," which strongly gravitates towards the earth.

There is an additional inhibition coming from the dream-ego itself. Although the dancer finds the courage to touch and push aside the fat cow, the cow still does not move as the dreamer unwittingly had been holding onto her ear! What does this final scene tell us?

The animus has now to bridle his urge to go into an uncontrolled frenzy over the mystical-religious enigma of sacred womanhood. He must also learn to actually touch the feminine "matter," the fat healthy cows, and if need be, to push them aside a little as well as to respect the walls of the house and the washing that is hanging out to dry. The dream-ego, too, i.e., the dreamer's consciousness, must learn to trust Nature fully from now on. Clinging to the cow's ear could mean that her ego is still too concerned with exercising control over the natural process of pregnancy. She wants the cow to listen to her and obey her so that everything will go the way it is "supposed" to. For this reason, she holds onto her ear. It is possible that she read too many good books about pregnancy and birth. ...

This dream focuses on the ambivalence inherent in becoming a mother. The confrontation with a lively, spiritually oriented animus has been described extremely clearly. Impending motherhood in the form of a fat, healthy cow represents an obstacle for him – an issue the dreamer now has to address actively. The dream-ego's advice, simply to touch a cow and literally to get a grip on the matter, served well. Having stopped wanting to desperately

---

[467] Emma Jung, *Animus and Anima,* The Analytical Psychology Club of New York, 1957, p. 40 (also Spring Publications, 1974)
Cf. also Chapter 6

cling to the cow or her maternal instincts, it looks as though pregnancy and motherhood could, after all, coexist in harmony with the needs of the animus!

Cows are frequently perceived as obedient, boring creatures. The following dream will provide us with a different view.

Dream No. 98:

> *I was in the old house where I had grown up. The house had a small garden behind the kitchen. A lion was strolling there. I was scared. I shut the door tightly.*
> *An old woman visited me at that time. She said: "It is not a lion, but a cow that has been given to you by your ancestors." I couldn't agree as I saw the mane of the animal.*
> *I couldn't help opening the door, though.*

The dream setting is the dreamer's house in which she grew up. Pregnant women frequently see childhood imagery in their dreams, especially their childhood homes and their mothers. These images suggest a new beginning, a new phase of a woman's orientation towards the Self after the storm of puberty. They point both to her own maternal future and to the past. A pregnant woman will often encounter another, older mother, be it the grandmother or any unknown elderly woman: these are all figures belonging to the archetypal Great Mother, who is constellated during pregnancy. We have already seen an example of their surprising wisdom in Dream No. 12.

An old woman appears in the dream of the "lion-cow" just as the dreamer, looking out of the window and glimpsing a lion roaming about in her beloved vegetable garden, gets a terrible fright!

She knows this place extremely well, having so often stood there as a child with her mother in the kitchen and looked out into the small garden. The latter is a protected area where a woman grows herbs to season the food, as well as growing flowers, lettuce and other vegetables. The garden was a place where she could be undisturbed. It corresponded to the role woman had in those times and represented a reasonably-sized, intimate and rather important feminine domain. In the garden, where she was still more in harmony with Nature than in the kitchen, she grew things that were essential for the well-being and contentment of the whole family. It is common knowledge that taste, spices and smells that are often associated specifically with "mother," turn out to be the most intimate, earliest and strongest memories. "Mother's cooking was always so tasty," is often a way of commenting on her unnoticeable but life-promoting effect on the atmosphere in the house and on the general mood. (The most important precondition for this is, of course, that she herself be contented!)[468]

As our dreamer casts a glance into this familiar feminine area of activity, there is a real lion roaming about. Psychologically, the lion expresses a mighty, highly dangerous instinct that suddenly and completely unexpectedly manifests itself. The dreamer was never aware it even existed, let alone in this very feminine domain. The lion is the King of the animals. He has always stood for a natural, inexorable power, though also for savagery and aggression. Everyone can and must hear its roar!

The presence of the lion extinguishes the idyll of the little vegetable garden from one moment to the next. As it is clear from the start that the lion is out of place in the garden, we have to consider this on the subjective level. Could it be that, in a hidden part of the dreamer, a lion emerged, presenting a threat to her femininity? The little vegetable garden would undoubtedly be too constricting for a super strong, powerful masculine instinct. It would become a prison. Now, a woman who kept a lion here would certainly want to rule, that is, to tyrannize or completely devour (out of love) her husband and child, but she would herself be so frustrated in this narrowness that all hell would break loose, and she would have to get away as quickly as possible.

The dreamer is afraid and carefully locks the door. This reaction could indicate that she thinks power is evil; therefore, she does not want to risk becoming devoured by it, or in psychological terms, becoming unconsciously possessed by it. In fact, she does not want to have anything to do with it!

In the "Cat" chapter, there is more about the symbolism of the lion. In many cultures, he personifies the power and grandeur of the sovereign. The lion is also considered a symbol of rebirth and of conquering death. Egyptologists explain this by the fact that he alone is able to withstand the scorching heat of the sun in the desert. We assume, however, that the connection lies much deeper and possibly beyond rational explanation. Doors and passages to tomb chambers (e.g., Sennedjem in Luxor) were flanked by two lions, and between them, there was a sign for "horizon": one had its eyes turned backwards, towards the night, the other forwards, into the new day. They embodied "the mystical moment of transition between death and resurrection"[469] symbolizing a mysterious and dangerous transition. The marble table on which the ruler was embalmed and prepared for eternal life had lion's paws and two lion heads facing in opposite directions at either end (e.g., Memphis). The monumental lion-shaped Sphinx representing the Pharaoh in his eternal form is an unambiguous illustration of the lion as a symbol of time and eternity.

The power of the king or ruler symbolized by the lion represented not only power on earth but also divine supremacy. Therefore, in Christianity, too, it

---

[468] The recently developed Aroma-Therapy testifies to the importance of smells and tastes and illustrates how deeply they can affect people. This method has shown some success after serious physical or psychological breakdowns.

[469] M.-L. von Franz, *Individuation in Fairy Tales,* Spring Publications, 1977, p. 35 ff

signified spiritual power, the overcoming of death and resurrection. Countless portals and stairs to Romanesque and Gothic cathedrals are adorned with magnificent lion figures that, as the guardians of the Lord, compel man to show Him proper respect. The pillar on the back of the lion not only represents the triumph of the church over the "evil" worldly paganism, as we seem to read in art guides time and again, but the lions are also the supporting pillars, even for the church. Another example of their role as an embodiment of protection of the king and his palace are the enormous lions on the famous Lion Gate of the Palace at Mycenae. Artemis, the great goddess of the animals, has been depicted with two lions since a very early period, and the Great Mother, too, is represented sitting on a lion throne.[470]

The lion appears in our dream as a dynamic content of the unconscious that is far stronger than the human ego. The latter could easily be devoured in an unprotected encounter; in other words, it could be destroyed in an inflation (megalomania).

But our dreamer is not alone nor is she unprotected. An old woman comes to visit her. On the subjective level, it is as if recognizing great potential danger, a helping force, an archaic feminine force or being, has emerged from within her in the form of the old woman. She imparts to her the following, surprising wisdom:

"It is not a lion but a cow that has been given to you by your ancestors."

Although the dreamer – seeing clearly the mane of the lion – cannot quite believe this – she involuntarily opens the door ("I couldn't help it")!

This action is at the same time surprising and convincing. Despite the seeming contradiction and her fear, our dreamer spontaneously opens up to the uncanny appearance, ready to receive the strange message containing an almost irreconcilable contradiction.

Before we try to tackle the riddle, let us consider for a moment the figure of the old woman-visitor. She most likely belongs to those "unknown visitors in fairy tales and dreams" that Marie-Louise von Franz calls one of the archetypal phenomena known to many cultures.[471] According to M.-L. von Franz, such unknown visitors, sometimes dressed in rags and looking uncanny or odd, revealed themselves, usually at the end or when it was too late, as divine beings or God himself. Furthermore, she emphasized that in fairy tales and legends, they tended to behave in a highly curious manner, did or said incredible things but often had a gift for those who took them seriously and did not turn them away. In conclusion, she writes: "It seems to me to be one of the

---

[470] Buffie Johnson, *Lady and the Beast*, Part II, "The Lion"
[471] M.-L. von Franz, "The Unknown Visitor in Fairy Tales and Dreams," in: *Archetypal Dimensions of the Psyche*, Shambhala, Boston, 1997, p. 73

greatest contributions of Jung and his work that it taught us to keep our door open for the 'unknown visitor.' "

Figure 40. Hathor with solar disk and uraeus

The main point in our dream seems indeed to revolve around the trust in the old visitor. Her words seem to command supernatural authority for the dreamer to have the courage to open the door. Perhaps some of the inexplicable lion strength has already been imparted to her.

Subjectively, the lion represents her own power or a rather dominant instinct in her that she can now confront in the dream without feeling too threatened by it. The old woman explains to her its true nature, for she knows that "power" can have feminine, fructifying, nourishing qualities, which have been given to her like a precious inheritance from her ancestors or women-ancestors, to be more precise. Therein lies an obligation.

Getting to know the lion within her – that is, a positive power instinct that can be feminine and giving – the lion has a well-developed sense of responsibility, is strong and patient, – is very valuable and important for the dreamer. Like the cow, he belongs to the Great Mother, mistress of the animals.

I believe that the seemingly virtually irreconcilable discrepancy between the lion and the cow can serve the dreamer as a call for a profound development towards a reconciliation of opposites, which must still appear to her as a task that is next to impossible. How she will go about solving this problem is beyond the boundaries of this dream. However, in this context, I recall something important that C.G. Jung pointed out: "The unconscious conversion of instinctual impulses into religious activity is ethically worthless …," unless "one is conscious of the conflict in all its aspects."[472]

[472] C.G. Jung, *Symbols of Transformation*, CW 5 § 106

The act of "opening the door" is equal to facing the incredible and surprising or disturbing nature of the mysterious animal duality and thus to admitting it to the threshold of consciousness. I believe the dream here is trying to show the dreamer a way of reconciling the opposite instinctive forces that seem to exclude each other in the dream.

The dream suggests the necessity of a redirection of the libidinal energy in a pregnant woman: the symbol of the lion changes into the cow, a transformation from the stage of a perfectly free, gloriously powerful life to the maternal powers of responsibility and an attitude that is compatible with motherhood. In short, the dream's message is the old woman's saying to the dreamer: the lion "is" the cow. This ancient feminine wisdom enables the dreamer to actually live with the mystery of these contradictory principles. Marie-Louise von Franz commented: "A renewed healthy relationship with the dualities of the unconscious allows vital life processes to flow again."[473]

In general terms, the dream aims at the very core of the feminine-masculine-issue of our times. It can be seen as a guideline on how to further develop feminine thought and imagination in a lively and creative manner, so that feminine consciousness can integrate the polarity or opposite nature of reality. To this, Jung said: "The ego keeps its integrity only if it does not identify with one of the opposites, and if it understands how to hold the balance between them. This is possible only if it remains conscious of both at once."[474] The archetypal insight displayed in this dream could help not only pregnant women but also a great many individuals.

At the end of this short series of cow-dreams, I would like to present a simple dream that does not actually require any interpretation. Two days after an uneventful and short delivery of a baby-son, who was a third child, a woman dreamt the following:

Dream No. 99:

> First, I was going up a hill in a public bus. I got off at a bend, crossed a clear stream and on the other side, climbed up an open field. That's where I found standing on the slope the large blue old-fashioned pram. I knew U. lay in there. My husband was lying on the grass, waiting for me.
> Then we were in a village at the top of the hill. At nightfall, the large bells were ringing of the biggest and most handsome bull and the biggest and most beautiful cow, who were going to mate. Then all the animals of the village followed suit: there was one great "wedding," and the bells of all different sizes were ringing. They awoke me, and I felt very happy.

473 M.-L. von Franz, *Shadow and Evil in Fairy Tales,* Spring Publications, New York, 1974, p. 46
474 C.G. Jung, CW 8, § 425

This dream is about love. First, on the grass on the meadow where the newborn child is already lying in the blue pram next to the couple, then in the mountain village where – with all the large and small bells ringing and resounding – the animals celebrate the union of the happy pair.

On the subjective level, the image is one of man seized with all his strength, instincts and sexual drive (the animals) by the bliss of the union of love. There is no trace of a split, no doubt about the value of physical love. There is a clearly sacred feeling to this picture of an animal-wedding celebrating the natural and instinctive with the bells ringing the ceremony in just as for a church service. It also evokes something like the "love in paradise" when man and animal, soul and body, still represented a peaceful union. The union of love is the only moment in which that mystical union can be imagined.

However, some doubts could arise. According to the myth, paradise is no longer on earth, for the love between the sexes severed the union and caused human consciousness: Adam "realized" that Eve and he were naked, their eyes were opened, and they knew the difference between good and evil (Ge. 3). How are we to understand this?

Our dream also somehow emphasizes the place of the union. It is at the top of the mountain, and the woman must first cross a clear stream, in order to reach it. It is outside the world of ordinary life that such a love occurs. It is also significant that they are not wild beasts celebrating the union but domesticated animals, who are a part of human culture.

But let us stop here. The rupture of the union and the expulsion from paradise that in the myth started with the arrival of the snake, is an immense mystery, which is not the theme of this dream. What seems to be at issue here is rather the gift our dreamer has – at least at the time of the dream – of being in complete harmony with her strong but tamed nature side.[475]

---

[475] Cf. Dream No. 24 by the same dreamer

Figure 41. The Lady with the Unicorn (Tapestry, Musée de Cluny, Paris)

5.9. The Unicorn

Irmgard Bosch

Among the uncommon and strange animals appearing in the dreams of pregnant women (and of other people) the unicorn plays a role that is not always easy to grasp.

Apart from the rhinoceros and the narwhal, no other animal with only one horn exists. Throughout history, the great variety of descriptions of "single-horned animals" (for instance, one-horned horses, asses, fish, dragons, scarabs, etc.) shows that the "unicorn is not a single, clearly defined entity" but a fabulous being, and that we are therefore "more concerned with the theme of the single horn (the alicorn)."[476] The fact that the unicorn is a "purely fabulous" being still comes as a surprise to many of us.

The picture of an animal with a single, long horn on its forehead dates back to ancient times. Literary evidence has existed since antiquity: Aristotle, Plinyus, Horace and Strabo reported strange things about it, and stories regarding the unicorn have been spun in the West since the early Middle Ages. The tradition goes back even further: illustrations of unicorns can be found on seals of the Neolithic Valley of the Indus Culture (before Mohenjo Daro) as well as on Assyrian Friezes, where it makes obeisance to the solar disk.

Naturally, we do not know exactly what the image represented in these early cultures. Later, in Indian-Buddhist legend, the unicorn symbolizes seclusion from the world, and the absolute, intent, unswerving spiritual strength of the Sadhu, the Indian pious hermit. Thanks to *Physiologus*, the late classical, highly esteemed work on Nature based on Aristotle, the unicorn became known in the West early on.

In the Old Testament, too, its enormous strength is taken as a known fact ("the strength of a unicorn").[477] In the Jewish culture, the horn was a symbol of the procreative, primeval power of God and is always referred to as "singular." It seems likely that certain translated Bible passages of "the exalted horn" contributed to the widespread ideas of the unicorn.[478]

---

[476] C.G. Jung, CW 12, § 518
[477] Numbers, 23, 22

It is interesting that, in the Jewish tradition, the horn is represented as pointing in the opposite direction, as compared to Indian legend: The God of the people of Israel always points towards man. [479]

C.G. Jung has devoted quite a detailed study to the "paradigm of the unicorn."[480] He follows its history in the Christian and alchemical allegory and finds that there is a close connection between alchemical symbolism and the language of the Church. In early Christian writings (church doctrines of the 2nd and 3rd centuries A.D.), God is called "one-horned." As Jung said, Priscillian's *"Unicornus est Deus,"* is a parallel to the term *"Unigenitus,"* the uniqueness of Christ the Son.

The image of the concentrated energy of God contained in one long, pointed horn, is of course striking and closely related to the Hindu *"lingam"* (Greek = *phallos)*. The peculiar feature of "strength protruding from the head" makes of the unicorn a symbol of God's spirit as a creative spiritual power. The sexual component cannot be ignored and is testified to in the continuation of unicorn tales. Apart from its healing powers, medieval descriptions ascribe to the unicorn an unsurpassed physical strength and speed, a mysterious treacherousness and wild sexuality, the characteristics of a terribly shy and hermit-like creature, whom no hunter can ever catch.

Already in the above-mentioned Buddhist legend, which reached the Occident in Hellenic times, there was a feminine counter-image to this masculine primeval force: a tender, gentle princess, who was supposed to catch and tame the dangerous animal. Legend has it that subsequently it made the dying king well again. All the later unicorn tales presuppose that its horn contains mysterious and highly effective healing powers – which only work, however, provided the animal has been caught and tamed by a virgin.

Thus it appears that, historically speaking, a "motif-migration" from East to West took place. The deeper reason for this phenomenon of migration lies in the fact that the symbol has an underlying archetypal context that underwent several new adaptations or differentiations. The steep pointedness of the single horn suggests a kind of goal-oriented power of the Divine. Its objective however, from a Christian and psychological point of view, is the archetype of the human soul in the figure of the immaculate Virgin. The purity of the soul alone is able to receive the savage nature of the unicorn, i.e., the spiritual elemental power of God, and thus to transform its radical and destructive side into medicine or healing power.

---

[478] Psalms 92, 10; 89, 17 and 24; 132, 17; 148, 14

[479] A much more ancient, theriomorphic (animal-shaped) image of a deity may gleam through from beneath this symbol of which were preserved only unintelligible fragments at a time when the Jewish people had already consciously separated from the belief of other Eastern peoples of the old Covenant (2nd cent. B.C.)

[480] C.G. Jung, CW 12, § 518 ff

Hence, the unicorn is a symbol of the Holy Ghost, as is the dove. It eventually became a symbol of Christ, who lay down in the lap of the Virgin – according to Tertullian.[481] Jung writes: "The symbol of the unicorn as an allegory of Christ and of the Holy Ghost was current all through the Middle Ages. ..." He goes on to quote St. Ambrose's saying that "the origin of the unicorn is a mystery, like Christ's procreation." Nicolas Caussin (16th cent.) observes that "the unicorn is a fitting symbol for the God of the Old Testament, because in his wrath he reduced the world to confusion like an angry rhinoceros (unicorn) until, made captive by love, he was soothed in the lap of a virgin."[482]

In this significant comment, we can see an indication of a change in the image of God from the Old to the New Testament. Furthermore, it expresses the conception that the healing and completion of the Creation occurred through the conception of Christ in the lap of the Holy Virgin. Generally speaking then, the motif of the "Virgin with the unicorn" is a symbol for a psychic and spiritual event or a fundamentally religious matter of the

Figure 42. The Virgin Mary taming the unicorn (Martin Schongauer, Colmar, 15th cent.)

very first rank. In the time when this idea was most widely propagated (13th-16th cent.), one could guess in the encounter of this unequal pair the potential union of two opposites and thus paint a picture of a profoundly religious mystery.

The motif of the Virgin and the unicorn was frequently embroidered on carpets and tapestries in convents. The most remarkable example of an ensemble of six magnificent tapestries is to be found in the Musée de Cluny in Paris.

---

[481] *Ibid.*, § 521
[482] *Ibid.*, § 519 and 522

The feminine figure is represented as a handsome, chivalrous lady – not yet as the Virgin Mary.

Although it may seem to the reader of today that they are being taken for a ride, as late as the 16th century, the "hunt for the unicorn" was described in the following way:

> This is the Unicorn you see /
> He is not found in our country.
> Arlunnus says these animals
> Lust greatly after pretty girls.
> This way to catch him is the best /
> A youth in women's clothes is dressed
> And then with mincing steps he flaunts
> About the Unicorn's bright haunts.
> For when this creature spies a maid
> Straight in her lap he lays his head.
> The huntsman / doffing his disguise /
> Saws off the horn and wins the prize.[483]

In folklore, those drinks and powders supposedly concocted from the unicorn's horn – in reality, from the stag's horn or the horn of the narwhal – were correspondingly highly valued and rare to come by. *Unicornus*-preparations were considered the strongest *alexipharmakon* [antidote]. One cup of unicorn would render any poison ineffectual. *Unicornus* was also used for gynecological complications and in obstetrics.

Sometimes the unicorn appears as a buck or a donkey (for instance, in the painting of the Romantic artist, Arnold Böcklin); at other times, as a stag (as in Dream No. 100) or as a bull (as in Dream No. 101). Within the scope of the present work, we cannot take into account the complete symbolism of the stag, bull, buck and donkey. I would, however, like to mention that the stag's antlers were also credited with healing and beneficial powers, and medications were prepared from them. In folktales, a stag frequently finds the saving source of water. *Springerle*, the traditional German Christmas cookies, originally bore pictures of stags – symbolizing the renewal of life and light at wintertime.

What is the meaning of the unicorn motif in pregnancy dreams? In order to shed some light on the psychological context, the ancient symbolism of the unicorn could help us.

---

[483] *Ibid.*, § 518, quoted by C.G. Jung from: Amman, *Ein neuw Thierbuch*, Verses by G. Schaller, Frankfurt am Main, 1569

Dream No. 100:

> *Dr. X and I are on our bikes. We are on an island, where we encounter a strange animal that looks like a stag. Its antlers consist of a single strong branch of a tree that, being bent from right to left, covers the upper half of the large animal's head.*
>
> *Dr. X. assures me that it is quite harmless, but I cannot help thinking that it will attack me because it is a male animal. And indeed, it follows me around a tree, sniffing me. (We are in a forest).*
>
> *Amidst the trees I can see the female grazing peacefully. Then, as we walk on, we come upon her fawn.*
>
> *Before I enter a house, located by the edge of the forest, I notice on the other side, to the right of the entrance door, a high fence behind which there is a monkey jumping about agitatedly. In its paw, it has some dung, which it tries to throw after me, grimacing. It is jumping so high now that it could almost jump over the fence.*
>
> *I go into the house, for I feel scared. As I close the door behind me, I notice that half of the door belongs to a stable. Behind it, set free, I can see the monkey now trying to push down the inner door latch from the outside, in order to come into the house. I can still see a remnant of dung in its paw. It runs after me: I get frightened and try to escape.*

The first part of the dream has that "strange animal that looks like a stag" whereas the second part (the monkey) sheds some light on a different aspect of the problem.

The setting of the dream is an island where the analyst and the dreamer are riding their bikes in a forest. With the analyst she dares to enter the murky Nature-domain of the unconscious. When the dreamer meets the stag, she knows – despite the reassuring words of the therapist – that this male animal is dangerous. It is woman's primitive fear of the male sexuality. The single, bent branch is clearly evocative of an erect "penis on the forehead." Most traditions about the unicorn speak of their fierce sexuality.

And "indeed, it follows me around a tree, sniffing me." Like a male animal following a female scent, it chases the young woman around a tree. She is peremptorily forced into a circular movement, a real *circumambulatio* around a tree – a symbol of life – and at this precise moment, she glimpses "the peacefully grazing female and then the fawn." It is as if from her current, somewhat burdensome perspective of a pregnant woman, she catches a glimpse of a future, where calm has been restored and where there is, in addition, a child.

"Circumambulating" the tree,[484] even if it happens involuntarily, signals that this dreamer's quest is to come nearer to something central: to her Self. The strange animal pushes her towards this.

Regarding the individuation process and its central point, Jung reflected the following, which I believe can be helpful for the understanding of our dream: "Often one has the impression that the personal psyche is running round this central point like a shy animal, at once fascinated and frightened, always in flight, and yet steadily drawing nearer."[485]

In this part of the dream, our dreamer is on a profound level of her psychic life and therefore rather far removed from consciousness. The emergence of the strange animal gives rise to a true opportunity to realize herself, or rather her Self, both as a woman and mother. One could say she is now walking along the "central path of her life." The unicorn and its fawn's peaceful grazing suggest the healing power and hidden, deeper side of the savage-male character. The final forest-scene of the dream leaves us with a feeling of hope and of peace in Nature. The grass the grazing unicorns eat to fortify themselves is a free gift from Nature signifying hopeful, thriving growth. The preternatural animal has given our dreamer this insight.

But she is apprehensive and flees from Nature into the protection of a house, i.e., into the sphere of culture and civilization. Here – and how could it be otherwise? – everything pertaining to animal elements is locked away, in a cage. It is nevertheless present, in the shape of a black monkey agitatedly jumping up at the railings and trying to throw dung after her; soon, the monkey breaks out of the cage and opens the half-stable-door from the outside, its paws still soiled with dung. The protection of the house has failed; the frightened dreamer tries to run away.

This scene describes the distress the woman feels illustrated through another animal. A black monkey is a shadow, a dark animal caricature of man. It is half-human or almost human. We often perceive the monkey as being indecent like no other animal.[486] The monkey is upset because it is prevented from giving free rein to its devastating instincts. This ferocity the woman perceives as "dirtying" because it embodies sexuality (including her own) which, from her standpoint of being in a respectable house, disgusts her.

Dung carries abundant symbolism. It is an organic substance in a state of fermentation, and it stinks while it changes. It is also the pride of the farmer and invaluably precious for the fertility of the fields. For the alchemist, it is that abject place where the treasure or the "stone" can be found.[487] Despite its

[484] C.G. Jung, CW 12, Bollingen, 1953, Fig. 264: *Mandala of the Unicorn and the Tree of Life*, Verteuil tapestry (15th cent.), "The Hunt of the Unicorn"
[485] *Ibid.*, § 326
[486] Cf. Hansueli F. Etter, *"Mensch, du Affe!," Zur symbolischen Bedeutung unserer nächsten tierischen Verwandten*, in: Jungiana Reihe A, Band 5, p. 47 ff

malodorous sordidness, it is at the same time productive. The black monkey's impulse of throwing dung after her can be seen as a desperate attempt of a dark, dissociated part of herself to unite the seemingly incompatible opposites (respectable house, forest, animals, dung). This attempt at achieving consciousness at this point comes as a shock to her.

Thus the question is raised of whether her conscious ego is able to admit the first scene of the dream: the strange unicorn, circumambulating the tree and that mysterious peacefulness of the Nature in the forest. The dream indicates that while her exploration of the unconscious is under the guidance of analysis, she could perhaps gain access to a deeper meaning of sexuality. On the other hand, while she is in the house of a respectable life, it only disgusts and distresses her.

Subjectively, the unicorn and monkey are aspects of her own chthonic powers, which are apparently very strong and in need of integration. They could ultimately endow her with unsuspected powers. In the first dream scene she was "simultaneously fascinated and frightened" – already on the spiral path of life that Jung called the process of individuation.

The dreamer of the next dream was thirty-three years old and married. The pregnancy had been planned: a healthy baby-daughter was born, and there were no complications. There had been a previous pregnancy, however, which had been terminated at two months. (Dream No. 97 is from the same dreamer.)

Dream No. 101:

> *I dreamed that I was one among a procession of robed figures, perhaps my graduate school classmates, and we entered the grounds of a Gothic cathedral through an archway. Two men were standing on either side of the gate holding upraised right fists as a blessing upon our passage. My best friend was the man on the right, and when I passed and asked whether he would give me his blessing, too, he lowered his fist and sneered.*
>
> *Once inside the cathedral, we were seated in groups according to class. We were instructed to give "the sign" – raising the right fist gracefully. I never raised mine but a pale girl on my right raised hers. The "sign" seemed too limp and feminine for my comfort, yet I felt sad to be unable to participate. Next, I am in a Romanesque crypt. On a low platform under bright illumination is a young woman sitting in lotus posture. She wears only the white cotton gown of a hospital patient.*

---

[487] Cf. Eva Wertenschlag-Birkhäuser, *Das Gespräch zwischen Khalik und Morienus über den Stein*, in: Jungiana Reihe A, Band 1, p. 44

Doctors in white lab coats stand around her, reciting her failings for our instruction. One of them says: "She goes back and forth."

Finally, I stand in an underground tunnel before a wizard, who explains to me the nature of the girl's psyche. He holds up his hands, palms facing one another, about a foot apart. Between them appears an image of the ocean with waves capping towards the center. He said that, like these waves, she was a freak of Nature.

Intuitively, I grasped his meaning and said to him in great excitement: "Yes, just like the bull who runs backward!"

At that moment, a young bull with curly black hair and a single black horn protruding from the center of his forehead ran from the darkness on my left. As he passed between us, I grasped his horn and led him into an enclosure. A young black woman held the gate open for us. Within was a docile female mate for the bull. The black woman, who tended the animals, closed the gate after I stepped back into the passageway.

Allow me to summarize:

In the course of an exploration of herself in the form of a descent into the depths of the soul – culturally speaking, from the Gothic down to the Romanesque period and further down into subterranean caves – the dreamer has undergone a critical self-examination. The stations resemble a difficult initiation ritual. She has just been rated as a failure, a mistake or "freak of Nature," someone who goes "back and forth," i.e., who does not advance. This very negative evaluation is made by scientists, examining "doctors" and in addition she is exposed to pitiless glaring light – "bright illumination" (reminding one of the lighting in an operating theatre). The image of a "young woman" being analyzed and pulled apart by hostile men indicates a state of severe self-doubt.[488]

The verdict – she is "not right" – hits her like an illumination, and the young woman submits to it with humility (lotus posture) thus attaining an even deeper level, an underground tunnel. This cave is almost devoid of any human influence; it is almost Nature in its pure form and a magic world where word, image and action directly fuse into one another. A magician or spirit, a clairvoyant using imagery instead of words is able to impart to her those aspects of her personality she must improve. Huge waves come surging from between his hands; however, they cannot spread but collide in the middle being thereby blocked by elemental power.

Suddenly, the dreamer can clearly see her problem; she is deeply moved and exclaims: "Yes, just like the bull who runs backward!" At this very moment, a "bull with curly black hair" comes running towards her from the

---

[488] Cf. C.G. Jung, CW 7, 1953, § 332: "This collection of condemnatory judges, a sort of College of Preceptors, corresponds to a personification of the animus."

left (the side of the unconscious), out of the dark. It has a single black horn protruding from its forehead. Now something wonderful happens: the dreamer takes hold of the horn with her hands and calmly leads the wild bull to an "enclosure" where a gentle, feminine mate is waiting for him. A young, black woman closes the gate again.

Now an animal wedding will undoubtedly take place, a *coniunctio* in the instinctive sphere. What is being united in the depths of the unconscious and rendered fertile are her own chthonic powers. The futile struggle of the natural elements, such as the colliding ocean waves, has now been appeased. The bull no longer runs backwards.

We could almost say that down there, in the depths of her dream, the dreamer grabbed the "horn of salvation" by "taking the bull by the horns," whereupon she found peace. On that perilous path to a greater knowledge of her Self she was able to admit, no matter what it would turn out to be, that she had grown, as it were, an almost supernatural courage. This greater knowledge was the goal of her initiation.

The animals are tended by a dark feminine figure. The dreamer watches her guide the animals to their special pen. Psychologically, this indicates that deep down in the unconscious of our pregnant dreamer, there is a calm and composed feminine strength enabling her to take appropriate action, if necessary. Furthermore, this indicates that there is a good chance her conscious ego will change its attitude and eventually defeat the tormenting self-condemnation as well as the deep doubt about the "correctness" of her own nature.

The black woman symbolizes her positive shadow and at the same time her unconscious image of her Self that could show her how to live with her chaotic and wild sides (the waves or bull) without their mutually destroying each other but on the contrary letting them become fruitful and productive.

It is as if, in this dream, the dreamer assumed something of the role of the "Virgin": she took hold of the horn and thus managed to soothe the ferocious animal. I believe that this could be a moment of grace for her. Pregnancy could be an opportunity to impart to the conscious ego an idea of this great potential of maturation and healing. I doubt that otherwise she would have had this important dream of initiation.

Figure 43. Babylonian god Tesup with trident, axe and sword

6. Man – Father – Wise Old Man

Regina Abt

In pregnancy dreams, as in all dreams, we come across masculine figures of all shades. When they appear as clearly positive figures, and particularly if they derive from personal experience, it is easy to read them as positive masculine aspects from within ourselves: courage, assertiveness, target-oriented determination, initiative, objectivity and clear thinking come to mind. To interpret certain masculine dream figures as inner figures from the unconscious when they appear in a dubious, foreign, even evil form, on the other hand, becomes more difficult. Where within me is there a tramp, a drug-addict, a fighter pilot, a poacher, a convict or, for that matter, simply an unpopular pal from school? Or which part within me might possibly be the president of the United States, a dictator of the Middle East, the devil or a saint? The possibilities are endless. For, contrary to what woman represents in her conscious life, these masculine figures or figures of the animus, illustrate or personify, so to speak, elements of the opposite sex from the unconscious.[489] And as such, they "cause" life, as it were, from behind. This is why woman can only acknowledge them provided they have already existed in her own thoughts. Hence, many of her convictions pertain to this kind of unconscious masculine figure but not to the conscious personality of woman. While subliminally fascinated by the animus, woman is not entirely herself, as we never are when we are in the hands of unconscious powers. However, once she succeeds in consciously thinking about "who" stands behind her and "what" he is trying to impart to her, she is able to accommodate him. He can then occupy a place in her life and personality so far as he belongs to her personal unconscious. She can benefit from his strength. He is "that masculine or spiritual element that corresponds to woman's own nature and that develops into a conscious attitude and can be integrated into the whole of her personality."[490] However, where the animus is unconscious, very often his function

---

[489] M.-L. von Franz in: C.G. Jung, *Man and his Symbols*, Aldus Books, London, 1979, p. 189

is being possessed by thoughts, ideas and opinions or by convictions laid down by certain authorities. For woman, it is naturally in the first place the father, who was the first to form her masculine spirit. Therefore, her judgment and opinions are interspersed with what her father was and thought, even if this may often be far removed from her own reality.

Now, the animus also offers woman creative insights, spiritual knowledge and truths which transcend the personal: they are of an impersonal, objective, archetypal nature. This animus appears in dreams as a higher masculine spiritual principle of divine quality on the order of a soul leader. At times, he may be a kind of a teacher or savant, at other times, a kind of animal-spirit personifying an exceptional kind of natural wisdom. In this way, he can bring about spiritual profoundness and spiritual introversion.[491] First, however, woman must perform the enormously toilsome Cinderella tasks, in order to become conscious of both the negative and positive effects of the animus, to sunder them and to free herself from the unconscious captivity of both. Only then can her *Weltanschauung* and *Lebensanschauung* develop into something mature, which has its roots as much in her feminine, natural life as in her spiritual background.

The animus occasions woman time and again to say or do things in her daily life which do not correspond with her true feelings at all. She can say things unwittingly, which later cause her immeasurable grief because she realizes that she made a blunder, and yet did not mean it at all. This results in a conflict and at the same time the possibility to find out "who" had (in fact) smuggled in this utterance. However, more often than not woman is convinced that the view she holds is her very own.

Examples of this are collective prejudices, which frequently occur during pregnancy, along the lines of: "children rob you of your freedom," or "you command less respect because you are no longer working." In our selection of dreams of pregnant women, a large number of animus dreams are of a negative, ominous kind. Nowadays woman is no longer necessarily prepared to perform the role of wife and mother as she was in the past. Man no longer carries out all of the (traditionally) masculine and spiritual activities in her place, while woman is dedicated to feminine obligations, household and family. Today, she, too, assumes masculine roles and intellectual work. She has a job, a degree and holds her own in the professional world. It would appear that the projection of woman's own inner masculine part onto man has dissipated, and it now stimulates woman's unconscious. The problem of the spiritual has become acute but not necessarily resolved. For, much of woman's outward masculine activity is now dominated and defined by her inner man, while her

[490] *Ibid.*, p. 195

[491] Emma Jung, *Animus and Anima*, The Analytical Psychology Club of New York, Inc., 1957, p. 39

feminine personality may not be aware of it nor in keeping with it. Woman is often possessed by her masculine occupation, which can entail losing or putting her femininity at risk. It is not surprising, then, that persecuting, negative masculine figures often appear in the dreams of both pregnant and other women.

The problem with the animus that wants to become conscious in modern woman remains unresolved – even during pregnancy, that momentary, uniquely feminine state of nature. In fact, he seems at this point to become particularly pressing and also particularly destructive.

The male component or animus in the woman has been named by Jung but was not his invention, as people (particularly women's animus) will sometimes impute to him. In myths, fairy tales, poetry, etc., this psychic reality has continually and vividly been represented in a multitude of facets. But also in film, television, theatre and in all other productions of contemporary culture we can find these ancient figures in new clothes. Moreover, at every turn of her life woman encounters men seeming to mirror her own inner masculinity, and in this regard, they hold a curious fascination for her. Therefore, the animus not only organizes her relationships to the highest degree, but it also often falsifies the true image of the male and causes her feeling for him to turn into something unreal, or else forbids it completely.

When his workings are negative, he can surround her in something like a magic circle of judgments and misjudgment, ranging from disparaging to destructive, in a prison where there is no exit. The same situations tend to repeatedly poison her human relationships where the negative animus guarding the prison tries to convince her that she will never leave it again: "My life will never change – I shall never be able to have a true relationship; I shall always be alone." These are the kind of recurrent, agonizing thoughts woman is prey to.

One of the prevailing themes in fairy tales is, for instance, to free the princess from the captivity by a wicked troll, demon, magician, robber or father, so as, ultimately, to reunite her with the prince belonging to her. Or it may be a theme about redeeming a prince who has been transformed into a beast or a monster, as in "The Beauty and the Beast," a tale that has traveled in many variations through many countries and centuries. It belongs to the Amor-and-Psyche type of fairy tale, which essentially revolves around a young girl being married to a man whose appearance is that of a beast or a demon. She then loses him, either through disobedience or heedlessness, and must then undertake a long and arduous search in order to find and redeem him.[492] It is essentially a matter of becoming aware of the animus, the inner companion, who in altered form, cuts woman off from her relationships. In "The Beauty and the Beast," the young woman must live with the beastly monster in his

---

[492] Cf. M.-L. von Franz, *The Golden Ass of Apuleius*, Shambhala, Boston, 1992, p. 77 ff

castle, cut off from all contact with the outside world, until she manages to redeem him – to recognize his true, regal nature and to enter into union with him forever. As stated by M.-L. von Franz, the monster shows all the archaic-emotional, instinctive characteristics of woman's spirit, which have not yet been differentiated.[493]

In certain fairy tales, the heroine of the tale is under the spell of a kind of moon-spirit or spectral stranger, a personification of another aspect of the animus. He stands for the fascination of a speculative-nebulous fantasy-world in which a woman can lose herself. This kind of animus can pull a woman away from life, and it is as though she were not quite there. She can quietly nurse a fantasy, which can sometimes quite suddenly invade her life in a manner that is surprising and unrealistic to everyone else.

We shall discuss only a few aspects of the animus here. Although there is a great variety of male figures bustling about in our dreams, we can at least examine certain groupings of characters which we shall encounter in the dreams that follow. Investigating the problem of the animus today, in the era of woman's emancipation, seems to be more timely than ever before. More-over, pregnancy – a time when the feminine nature assumes leadership – could constellate the counter-pole, the spiritual-male side, particularly strongly. As Emma Jung points out, the problem of the animus consists of uniting the opposites of spirit and nature, a creative task comparable to that of bearing a child.

Dream No. 102, in the first month of pregnancy:

> *In Valencia's or Madrid's market, a fellow aims at me with a pistol. We struggle, I catch his pistol and turn it to himself. He still gets it in his hands. Then somebody pulls us apart, and he pursues me. I am very nervous, because I can not get rid of him. Now I see a policeman looking at a bookshop window. I tell him what has happened to me. Then the man (the pursuer) and me are going to be put in jail. The policeman and the man and me were in a large building with a lot of windows. But finally, only the man will be convicted. I feel that this is happening again and again, and that the man is still pursuing me.*

Vicious men, with or without pistols, knives, automatic rifles, arrows or other pointed or cutting tools against which woman is desperately fighting – and mostly in vain – aptly illustrate the essential being of the animus. They keep surfacing at any time of life, and in their own way, menace or overwhelm the feminine Self. Knives, pistols and other sharp objects symbolize injurious, destructive impulses from the unconscious. In mythology, gods often send wounding or sick-making arrows, as shown by Marie-Louise von Franz in her

---

[493] M.-L. von Franz, *The Interpretation of Fairy Tales*, Shambhala, Boston, 1996, p. 176

book, *Reflections of the Soul*. For example, Apollo sends the plague, and Artemis or Mars (in Rome) bring disease and death, etc. These gods, seen as fate-determining powers, are constant factors pertaining to the nature of the unconscious psyche, behavior patterns of the emotional and imaginative personality, which Jung denoted as Archetypes.[494] Being struck by the missile of a God, therefore, signifies at the same time being struck by an archetype, by a mood that overwhelms conscious life.

Being "shot at" by the animus does not so much affect the mood (as in the case of anima) but rather manifests itself as a sudden idea, a thought, an opinion, or a judgment. Seen from the outside, these animus thoughts seem be prompted out of the blue: they can transform woman from one minute to the next, without her even being aware of it. Only with great difficulty can she herself differentiate between these animus thoughts, which suddenly surge up from her unconscious, and her conscious personality. Often she cannot even recognize them as being negative and dangerous and consequently is at their mercy.

In the dream above, the woman gets involved in a gunfight with the assailant in which she tries to defeat him with his own weapon. But this does not work. He manages to hold onto it. Shooting at the animus turns out to be futile and shows that the animus cannot be brought down with the same weapons: that is, the assailant cannot be reasoned with. He always has the last word.

It is useless to try to eliminate aggressive thoughts, directed against pregnancy, child, husband or oneself, with masculine-oriented counter-arguments: they linger about, be it only during sleepless nights. Not even the policeman seems to be of any help, proceeding to lock up both the victim as well as the aggressor. The policeman is the guardian of law and order, of the collective norm, symbolized by the large "official" building. Although the pursuer is convicted, meaning that reason and judiciousness seem to triumph over the unacceptable behavior of the animus, the chase continues: "It is happening again and again." Reason and the claim to "adapted collective" behavior first even evoke visions of being locked up. The pressure of general norms of behavior ("that's disgusting – as a future mother and wife, you simply don't entertain such thoughts") does not help but periodically feels more like a prison in which a woman is locked up together with the animus. Marriage, too, can at times represent a prison, not only for man but for woman, even though it concomitantly means protection and a kind of structure for her own life as well as for that of their children.

Many dreams describe total helplessness on the part of the woman when the animus suddenly appears "in her own house" and in his most despicable

494 M.-L. von Franz, *Projection and Re-collection in Jungian Psychology*, Open Court, La Salle, IL, 1980, p. 21

form. A woman had the following dream, when she was three months pregnant with her third child:

Dream No. 103:

> *It is night. I'm alone with my children. When I realize that there is a man in my house whom I know, I'm overcome with a paralyzing fear. My daughter comes into my bedroom. She complains of diarrhea and has a temperature. I'm glad that she needs me, which distracts me from my own fear. Together, we go downstairs to the changing table while my husband is still asleep. The man comes after us. He tells me, before he kills us all, that I have to write the house over to him and sign the document with my own blood. I'm thinking of writing a good-bye-letter to my husband. When I hear my neighbors' telephone ring, I cry for help. Thereupon, the man runs up the stairs in order to fetch his pistol. It occurs to me that I could quickly pull up the blinds and escape with the children. Finally, I wake up, drenched in sweat.*

A dangerous burglar penetrates the dreamer's house at night – in the darkness and quiet of the night, when the evil spirits are awake, the brutal animus attacks the feminine ego. The animus is what, in folklore, is called spirit or demon.[495] In many fairy tales, this type of dangerous animus appears as a male figure of the Bluebeard type, keeping a young woman prisoner in his house.[496] She is strictly forbidden to enter a certain room of the house, which is always kept locked. Of course, she enters the room anyway and discovers all the women he killed before her, but is caught in the act. At the very last moment, she receives help from the outside to fight against the murderer, who wants to kill her. It is this type of negative spirit that is here threatening our dreamer and her children. He demands the entire house and wants it written over to him with her own blood. He takes over the ownership of her house, or in psychological terms, she becomes "possessed" by him. Something possesses her that could be described as abstract, cold, masculine thinking. It frequently starts with a negative view of something, which is followed by an impulse of wanting to change things brutally, pick a fight, force a sudden decision on someone and so forth. On the other hand, it can simply be a depressive state of mind with regard to herself or the circumstances she finds herself in. She becomes helplessly stuck and cannot see a way out. The Bluebeard-animus has a highly destructive effect on a woman's life. Such women frequently become bitter and lonely. They feel unloved and have difficulty in finding a partner.

Signing a pact with the devil with one's own blood in legends and fairy tales signifies becoming his slave, irrevocably, as if one could never escape and be

---

[495] Cf. v. Beit / v. Franz, *Symbolik des Märchens*, Francke Verlag, Bern, 1957, p. 610 f
[496] Cf. *ibid.*, p. 615 f

free again. It is this power of persuasion the negative animus possesses that is one of its most conspicuous characteristics: "Things will never change, anyway." Thus, strangely resigned to her fate, the dreamer accepts the gangster's proposition. Luckily, the ringing sound of the neighbor's telephone reminds her that she is still connected to the human world, and she cries for help, which shows that she can still react. This is a first attempt to free herself from the obsession. To pull up the blinds and jump out of the window would mean to jump out of the oppressive power of the animus through her own will and strength. In other words, she has to become active, a little bit more like a man, for she lacks precisely what the positive aspect of the animus could impart to her: a kind of active resistance against being flooded with aggressive impulses. Woman is often helpless because she is so angry at being prey to unfavorable circumstances, e.g., a difficult marriage driving her directly into the hands of the animus. Passivity and feeling completely powerless are closely linked with destructive behavior from the masculine side of the personality turned either outward or inward. If woman succeeds in breaking free from the negative masculine impulses, then they can be transformed into a positive force, a kind of determined and controlled resistance and clarity that is also in good accord with the feminine part of the personality.

What does "breaking free from an obsession" actually mean? How can the conscious ego help? Can it do anything at all if it has fallen prey to supreme inner figures? How can it deliver itself from the brutality, wild affect and paralyzing emotional frigidity of the negative animus if the solution is not a superficial police model (another animus thinking pattern), but individual, profound and in harmony with the feminine nature?

In the fairy tale of "Bluebeard," the woman has to wait for last minute help from outside, afforded to her by her brothers. It is as if the only thing that can possibly save her in the face of this demonic and absolutely supernatural figure is a moment of benevolent fate. Amplifications of the Bluebeard-figure almost all take us to Wotan, or in the south, to the ancient death gods.[497] During pregnancy, a time of *abaissement du niveau mental*, of closer proximity to the maternal unconscious, this dangerous proximity to the archetypal contents of the collective unconscious can far exceed the limits of the personal level. Being overwhelmed by such contents can, in some cases, lead to a pregnancy-psychosis. For this reason, our dreamer's fear is understandable, for behind the negative experience with the animus is lurking the danger of Bluebeard. However, perhaps the animus in this dream is rather close to the ego-personality, and pulling up the blinds and breaking free, thanks to a broadening of consciousness, is, in fact, possible.

---

[497] v. Beit / v. Franz, *Symbolik des Märchens*, p. 616

In *Aion*,[498] Jung says that animus and anima are factors transcending consciousness and also beyond the reach of perception or volition. They are autonomous, i.e., despite the integration of their contents, and for this reason, Jung says, they should be borne constantly in mind – for the more unconscious they are, the mightier they are. Dealing with all this frequently requires help from outside, as in our dream. Talking to other people about feeling tormented and threatened could also help. Human warmth and relations, including responding to and respecting the feminine nature (as opposed to the often arrogant judging of the kind: "Oh well, there she is again in that negative animus mode" as we often hear men, using psychological jargon, say), can counteract the loneliness the animus manages to cause in woman. In fairy tales and dreams, loneliness or feeling isolated or imprisoned through a negative animus figure is one of the most common themes. Likewise, in our material on dreams of pregnant women, the negative-animus-problem takes up considerable space.

The following dream stems from a twenty-six-year-old dreamer, who was two months into her first, unplanned pregnancy.

Dream No. 104:

> *I am about 16 years old. I am walking up the street to go home. I see a black man walking behind me. I start running for home, but when I get there, it is dark, all the lights are off, and the doors are locked. I keep yelling for my mother to let me in. I see the black man coming around the bend. I run out into the street. I notice that my arms and legs are bleeding. A bus is coming up the street. I fall in front of it. The bus driver gets out and helps me onto the bus. I turn around, and the black man is sitting in the back seat. I keep begging the driver to let me off but he won't. The black man comes up and puts his arms around me, telling me not to worry, that everything is okay. I start screaming.*

The dreamer sees herself as 16 years old, pubescent, that is, in a time of transition into a new form of feminine life. Animus figures of various kinds now become important: actors, sport champions, relationships with fellows, etc. Looks take on paramount importance, and it is the exception for a girl to accept the way she is or looks. It is a time of major insecurity. The young chick has left behind the eggshells and the fuzz but she cannot yet entirely rely upon the new feathers. At this time she is particularly dependent upon the approval and recognition of her father – the first man in her life. Times of transition are, as a rule, times of insecurity, fear of the new and of irrevocable change. According to folklore, this is when the spirits are on the loose – for example, during the night of New Year's Eve or at midnight or at the time when night

[498] C.G. Jung, *Aion*, CW 9, II, § 40

turns to day. It seems as if her constellation as a pregnant woman has a common denominator with herself at age 16.

The bleeding arms and legs could point to an injury she incurred at that time and that now manifests its effects or is recurring now. While it might have been her father then, today it is the father-animus within her that continues to attack her. Perhaps he had said how ugly and useless she was and that she had better stay at home (stay with him of course) as she would never find a husband anyway, etc. Today, the negative animus-figure is the black man who brings back her old fear of not being "up to scratch," not being able to master the new life-task or to keep her husband, etc. An affiliation with the animus-world can indeed badly undermine the ability of being a mother.[499]

The dreamer is unable to find protection from the pursuer with her mother. Instead she lands on a bus, i.e., she "falls" right in front of it. The bus, as a collective vehicle not allowing for any individual routes, could signify various things: the path everyone has to walk, or perhaps general ideas of how to be a mother, woman, wife, etc. or what girlfriends, aunts and the psychology column of a woman's magazine have to say. Our dreamer "falls" into these hands. However there seems to be no escape, for neither the pursuer nor the driver or leader of collective opinions let her get off. Apparently she can only help herself by finding her own individual solution. For, the flight into the collective, into "what is done," lands her directly in the clutches of the negative animus.

Symbolically, arms have to do with actively coping with reality whereas legs represent the standpoint or ability to stand (in) reality. This is presumably the point where our dreamer was hurt and condemned to passivity. We can only speculate about our dreamer's life at 16 and how the heavy criticism of a destructive father could have stripped her of all courage and positive élan to tackle life and its challenges. Passivity is a common result of a negative animus. Not always does a negative animus render a woman aggressive and too masculine. He often forces a woman to remain inactive as any activity immediately gives wings to the pursuer wanting to make it quite clear that she does not stand a chance. It is therefore likely that in her current situation she finds herself unable to confront confidently the negative animus or the black pursuer within her.

The comforting manner in which the black man puts his arms around her does not reassure her in any way, for she screams with alarm. We could almost say: thank heavens, for, similar to the anima in men signifying sirens and mermaids, the animus in a woman's psychology can bring about a kind of strange alienation from reality.[500] This can result not only in the marriage suffering but also in domestic and maternal life generally becoming a constant

---

[499] Cf. v. Beit / v. Franz, *Symbolik des Märchens*, "Das Märchen von der Frau, die keine Kinder haben wollte," pp. 627 and 629

strain. Symbolically, then, the arms and legs cannot fulfill their function effectively enough. The animus can seduce a woman into entertaining idle fantasies nurtured by film, television and women's magazines that reinforce and feed on them. In her outward life, too, she can become involved in unrealistic relationships with men, which then jeopardize her marriage.

The animus in our dream has a strange double function: on the one hand disparaging, and on the other hand, enticing her to have unrealistic fantasies. Both functions are equally paralyzing and dangerous. This problem reaches back into the dreamer's childhood, and I suspect that this moment of a fateful transition period must serve as a ground on which to explore and eventually understand it. Escaping and trying to find salvation in collective behavior mechanisms could be most dangerous now.

Here is another dream by the same dreamer, which highlights the problem in a most interesting way.

Dream No. 105:

> *I am walking through a large pavilion. As I walk, I notice that a black man has started to follow me. It is not certain that he is after me, but I feel menaced. I start to run and so does he. I tear down a flight of stairs and out onto the street. I go quickly so that I think I might escape. I can't. He catches me. The next sight I see is a tall black woman, in a fetal position, lying in a corner. She has long bruises on her skin. I know this is what the man did. She is alive but hurt.*

The pursuing animus has hurt a black woman who is lying in a corner in a fetal position. The black woman is a shadow-figure with the qualities of a kind of dark, nature-bound femininity. Her feminine and maternal nature is intrinsically primitive and instinctive. The fetal position of the hurt woman could suggest an inner adult figure that inhabits the woman as well as a kind of innate feminine instinctive behavior. By the same token, the hurt woman concerns something that evidently has to be born yet (fetal position) – in other words, that has to become conscious. Whenever the father-animus has considerably reinforced the destructive influence of the animus in woman's life, she tends to be deprived of a natural, unconscious access to her feminine instincts. It seems as if, by way of compensation, she has to live her femininity all the more consciously; moreover, she must protect it against the intrusion by the animus much more consciously than other women. Our dream thus reflects the fact that this kind of confident femininity must first be born in her and that the negative animus is not going to give her a hand but will try to stop this birth time and again.

[500] Cf. v. Beit / v. Franz, *Symbolik des Märchens*, "Das Märchen von des Nebelbergs König," p. 625 f

The following dream describes how a woman sometimes has to intervene consciously and actively in unacceptable animus situations. A twenty-eight-year-old woman dreamt this when she was one month pregnant, having had a miscarriage prior to that when she was three months pregnant. Before she had her second child, she again miscarried after three months:[501]

Dream No. 106:

> *It is a pitch-dark night, and I am walking within 2 to 3 meters distance to the side of a man who is completely black and wearing a large felt hat. The atmosphere is dramatic. The man is a stranger. I feel terribly tense and afraid of him. Suddenly, he begins to run and runs off to the right. Then there is another man running up from behind: he passes me and also runs off to the right. Somehow, there must be three parties present: enemies, friends and the police. I quickly go up to a man who is walking in front of me and whom I believe to be a friend. This is indeed so, and I try to rescue myself through him. It turns out that we must have met before at the Teachers' Training College. We walk on together. A physician's white coat suddenly appears from around the corner. We feel that something must have happened that makes this night seem so dramatic. As we approach the corner, the place transforms into a room with a glass door behind which there is the doctor with a woman lying on a stretcher about to give birth. But her spouse has locked her up behind this glass door. I simply know that I have to do everything possible to help this woman have her baby even if it means smashing the glass door.*

The first part of the dream paints a picture of darkness; a sense of drama is in the air; hostile, as well friendly men and policemen are present. The dreamer is distressed, unsure of who is a friend or who is a fiend. The scene reflects an image of her own night-side: her own unconscious. As becomes transparent in the second part of the dream, the reason for all this is evidently an impending birth that is being prevented because the woman in labor has been locked up behind a glass door by her husband. From the fact that it is not the dreamer herself but another woman, we can assume that there is something in the dreamer that should be given birth to – a second birth, as it were, in the dreamer's unconscious.

If, in a woman's unconscious, something is supposed to be born, it means the birth of a new content that consciousness should admit. In fairy tales, mythological or heroic children are frequently in danger of being eliminated by the ruling king. It is similar to the story of Christ's birth and the murder of the children by King Herod, or the story of the baby Moses being abandoned in a reed basket. The prevailing consciousness, symbolized by the king, dreads

[501] By the same dreamer: No. 56, Chapter 5.2

renewal and will do anything to undermine it. In a woman's unconscious, it is the negative animus (often projected onto the spouse) that wants to thwart the birth of a new step towards consciousness, or a spiritual child.

In fairy tales, children who are not supposed to live are often locked up somewhere: in a tower, cave, glass mountain, grave. These images aptly reveal the possessiveness of the negative animus, the feeling of being held captive from which a woman is often unable to break away without help. However, the dream seems to suggest that the reason for the dreamer's acute animus problem, which is disorienting her, confusing her and making her anxious, lies much deeper: it is as though something in her unconscious is possessed by a destructive content, so that the birth of a new step towards consciousness is impossible. Being locked up behind glass reveals this remarkably clearly. This motif we can find in many fairy tales: anima figures or female figures representing a woman's actual personality, have been cut off from life and kept imprisoned in a glasshouse, glass coffin ("Snow White"), glass mountain ("The Raven"), etc.[502]

To be behind a glass wall signifies in colloquial language to be cut off from other people and emotionally inaccessible. This kind of inadequacy is rather difficult to grasp. Although the barrier is transparent, it still interrupts the contact.

The "higher personality" of the dreamer that, with the birth of a child, is supposed to bring a new element and a new attitude to the world is apparently behind a glass wall. The animus sees to it that that higher personality is cut off from the dreamer's real feelings. Although women often do have access to their "higher personality" or their Self and benefit from this valuable experience, sometimes from one moment to the next, it can change radically: then all the problems become insurmountable again because the rationality of the animus is there to prove it. Next, a feeling of loneliness and of being cut off from life and relationships, or simply of being "behind a glass wall" again takes possession of her. Creative impulses become quickly stifled by the animus so that it is literally impossible for a woman to give birth. Therefore, the birth has to take place in the feminine part of our dreamer's personality. This amounts to the birth of a change in her feminine attitude. It runs parallel to the concrete forthcoming birth of her child.

The dream ends with the realization that something has to be done. The glass wall has to be smashed so that the woman can deliver the baby. The emotional barrier the animus has set up between the dreamer and her higher, inner personality must be smashed in a deliberate *coup de main*, an intentional affect. The part in the dreamer allowing creative rebirth is apparently in the clutches of the animus, ensuring that she is emotionally detached. Not being able to relate emotionally to her creative impulses, she falls into a depression,

---

[502] v. Beit / v. Franz, *Symbolik des Märchens*, p. 712

a feeling of pointlessness and fear and disorientation (as is described in the beginning of the dream).

What is required here is not so much suffering and tolerance, but an active resolve: this cannot go on – we have to put an end to it. The feminine life of the dreamer, including her pregnancy, can thus make sense again – her inner personality being allowed to mature and to be creative anew. It is this kind of determined resolve that sometimes causes a breakthrough and puts an end to the animus' destructive reasoning – for, unless she is vigilant, she will continue to fall victim to the animus. If, on the other hand, she succeeds, the path to creative work becomes free, and life can flow again.

The dream is most probably a reaction to the pregnant woman's attitude of depression and disorientation. It reflects the source of the problem and shows insight into how she can deal with it and fight it.

The following dream comes from the dreamer of Dream No. 103 (concerning the blood pact with the black man).

Dream No. 107:

> *I'm with a stranger who wants to have sexual intercourse with me. When I refuse, he becomes so infuriated that, by means of magic powers, he tries to surgically remove, at a distance, my unborn child from my belly. Only because I'm holding a round stone in my hands and pray to God incessantly do I manage to prevent him from doing this. The man comes nearer to me, threatening me and gesticulating. We are surrounded by people who are smiling at me condescendingly. As long as I don't waver and continue praying, the man cannot do anything to me.*

This dream shows when and how a woman can defy the destructive animus. Again, a still unborn child is at risk. The dreamer is protected as long as she concentrates upon holding the stone tightly and praying. No activity is indicated here, or even possible. She has to wrap her capacity to act around the stone, so to speak, or around the innermost, indestructible core of her personality. In other words, turning her undivided attention to the center, praying, amounts to absolute introversion.[503] Neither confrontation nor fighting against the over-powerful animus are indicated here. However, there seems to be some change taking place, for three weeks later she dreams that she is able to free herself from the prison of the negative thinking pattern dominated by the animus and that, in fact, she is able to escape from the reign of the father-animus.[504] It is likely that the dream is telling her that she can and must do something against the more personal aspects of the animus whereas the over-

---

[503] Cf. same dream, No. 19, Chapter 3.2
[504] ditto

powering archetype of the black magician can only be counteracted by white magic or the strength of the Self.

The dream is reminiscent of one of Grimm's fairy tales entitled, "The Girl without Hands." This is the story of an impoverished miller who sells his daughter to the devil. In order for the latter to accept her, however, the miller has to chop off her hands, for they are too pure for the devil. Nevertheless, the daughter's tears which are shed over the stumps of her hands are so purifying that the devil refuses to take her. She leaves her father and is found by a king. They are married and have a son. But the devil reappears, whereupon she is forced to abandon the castle and to go and live in a forest for seven years, accompanied by an angel. She names her son *Schmerzensreich* – "Sorrowful." At the end of the seven years of exile, the king finds her again.

The miller represents a father who tries to get himself out of trouble by cheating and to do so has to sell his anima or his own soul to the devil. He may well be a successful businessman but neglects his emotional side, which results in his daughter's emotional undernourishment. Therefore, "… a destructive, devilish intellectualism, a devilish animus of some sort, will take possession of her. She will either be very ambitious or very cold, or she may do the same thing as her father, continuing his life pattern in the calculating, cold way of her animus."[505] However, in this fairy tale, the girl is aware of the danger. With her type of a father complex, a daughter is often reduced to staying away from everything touching the spiritual side. Having her hands chopped off renders the heroine of the fairy tale incapable of performing any kind of activity in life. Although she is safe from the devil, she is condemned to passivity and isolation. The long years in the forest mean deep introversion, retreat from any kind of animus opinions and from any impulse to the activities which are required in life. In addition, she has to suffer the resulting loneliness.[506] Like the stone, the forest suggests the side in us that is closest to Nature and absolutely unconventional, which is also why the people smile at our dreamer mockingly. In the fairy tale, a helpful angel appears. In other versions, this might be a bird, a messenger of the gods or God the Father Himself. Psychologically, this would be interpreted as a numinous or a religious experience. This brings us back to the symbol of the stone: an experience of the incorruptible, everlasting core of the personality.

To sum up, holding onto the stone and praying means to introvert, to turn to what the absolutely unique Self (the alchemists called it "the speaking stone") in the most extreme or abject circumstances is able to bring forth: namely, a miracle. It seems miraculous, for instance, that our dreamer can break away from her prison – from the dominance of her father or the negative animus. This has to be preceded, however, by consciously suffering through

---

[505] M.-L. von Franz, *The Feminine in Fairy Tales*, Shambhala, Boston, 1993, p. 89
[506] Cf. *ibid.*, "The Fairy Tale of the Girl without Hands," p. 80

the conflict. *Schmerzensreich*, "Sorrowful," is born from the long period of suffering and isolation which belongs to the fate of a woman with a negative father complex. Without this suffering, there can be no redemption – though this is often difficult for a woman to accept. Her animus says to her: "Why should I always be the one to suffer? Why must I be alone when I feel isolated from life, anyway? Why can't I live a normal life and be happy like everyone else? Why is my marriage not like everybody else's?" It is not easy to argue with this kind of animus reasoning, for indeed, who knows why things work out felicitously for some and not at all for others? Our dream says that, as long as the woman is not distracted from the stone and the prayer, she will be protected and draw nearer to the meaning of her life. Expressed differently, we might say that she will then give birth to Sorrowful. Marie-Louise von Franz writes: "He is the fruit of the woman's life that has passed through the whole experience of suffering and thus acquired serenity and wisdom."[507]

A thirty-one-year-old woman, periodically suffering from depression, dreamt at five months pregnancy:[508]

Dream No. 108:

> *I'm coming out of a multistory building where our apartment is. A man with an unkempt poker face stops me physically in the street, asking me when my husband would be released from prison. He threatens me and forces me to answer: "Tomorrow morning." I should call him right away at this number. I end up letting him write down the number for me. ...*
> *Then I run away, trying to shake off potential pursuers and accidentally pass the prison. I can see that on the other side of the door, my husband is sitting on a bench, presumably because he will secretly be released that night.*
> *I pick him up. We go out together and make our way to the apartment, reaching it only towards the morning. I've told my husband everything, and our plan is to take a few things with us and then escape from the gang. ... When we finally do escape, it is the time the man mentioned. We are wondering whether we should leave the building by taking the stairs. We do that, but promptly run into the arms of the gangsters.*
> *We try to think how to get out of town. My husband tells me he has a few stolen cars, which nobody knew to be his, standing in a row a few blocks away from here. The cars are partly camouflaged as rose bushes.*

The dreamer's husband is in prison in this dream. In reality, though, he is not; moreover, whether or not, in some respect, he may be in any kind of prison in his life is unknown to us. A "prison" primarily signifies limited

---

[507] *Ibid.*, p. 101
[508] By the same dreamer: Nos. 1 and 4, Chapter 3.1

freedom – being locked up in rigid rules of behavior prescribed by the collective. People can easily feel that they are, figuratively speaking, in a prison if, for instance, they have to carry out inflexible, spiritually or intellectually deadening work or if they are prevented from living their own lifestyles. On the inner plane, the dreamer's husband is an animus that is either too limited, somehow locked up within himself, or feeling this to be the case. Many women feel in their marriage or pregnancy as if a part of them were locked up in prison. They tend to be dissatisfied or frustrated because their masculine activity and independence seem insufficient to them. However, in this dream, the spouse is to be released – which apparently brings a dangerous gambler type – indeed, a whole gang – into the picture.

Bearing in mind the emancipation efforts of the women's liberation movement – which after all and among other things, is intent upon liberating woman's spiritual side from being forced into child-rearing and conventionally imposed housewifery – it is remarkable how difficult this, in fact, is to realize. The transition to freedom is always problematical. In former East Germany, where the "prison walls" of the Communist ideology with its inhuman restrictions and disrespect for the individual finally collapsed, gangs of skinheads and other brutal, aggressive extremists suddenly began to wage a new terror: a primitive, Wotan-like spirit breaks free, throwing out of the window any progress human culture has attained.

When woman's spiritual side, having been confined for too long in a narrow, conventional form of life, is liberated, there is a danger that at first it will be dominated by a primitive-aggressive animus, i.e., a negative form of the new spirituality. Jung said in a seminar on children's dreams that the animus does not usually appear as an angel but manifests itself in a highly unpleasant manner. Instead of going home with her newly released husband, the dreamer directly falls into the hands of the pursuers. Thus, instead of liberation, what ensues is being possessed. Many marriages are broken because the wife destroys everything the couple has in common with one sweeping blow. Freedom, in such cases, results in destruction.

However, in the dream, it is still possible to escape. What is the meaning of the cars hidden a few blocks away and camouflaged as rose bushes?

I suspect that the husband's time in prison has to do with the stolen cars. The car symbolizes a vehicle carrying us through life, allowing us to move freely including our individual freedom of movement. Hence, stolen cars would refer to a means of transport that had been unlawfully appropriated. In other words, the dreamer's animus would have secretly laid hold of means of advancing herself to which she had no right. As the animus stands for woman's spiritual attitude and *Weltanschauung*, they would be stolen attitudes. Such foreign "animus-mobiles" can be observed when a woman's thinking is invaded by psychological or other theories that she has read or adopted from the media and that interfere with her family life and personal relation-

322

ships. If a rose is seen as a symbol of love between man and woman, then the rose bush camouflage of the "animus-mobiles" would point to a false Eros relatedness. Women often use psychological theories, wanting to help or caring about human relations as a cloak for stolen animus vehicles promising further advancement and ultimately more power. Many women manipulate their environment with acted, ungenuine, superficial feelings. It is a way of securing power, and it is very difficult to see through this artifice or mechanism.

We do not know whether they successfully escape from the nasty animus-pursuers. The suggestion for this way out comes from the husband-animus of our dreamer. If he sat in prison because he stole cars, it could mean that the uncanny source of our dreamer's oppressive feelings regarding a lack of spiritual freedom, are the general opinions or *Weltanschauung* her animus has stolen. Therefore, we must assume that the escape with one of the stolen cars can only be a short-lived solution, sufficient for the moment to avoid getting into more trouble. There is a danger of projecting the sense of oppression felt through spiritual restriction onto the marriage, family and pregnancy. This would mean giving the destructive animus a real chance.

Dream No. 109 (by the same dreamer as Dream No. 101, at two months):

> *A crazy young scientist with a big-headed and little assistant, who provides him with human rests, made an instrument or weapon, like a shot or a missile, that regenerates the rests (remains of the body) and produces sickening and dangerous life. The weapon disappears in my parents' bedroom.*
>
> *It is dangerous, it could go off just by itself. Suddenly it turns into a film (this story), and the scientist and his assistant tell me that at the end the regenerated human rests will be destroyed. But the film is not finished. I'm afraid of them (the demonic figures) stalking. I wake up.*

In this gruesome dream, the work of the animus has quite a different kind of frightening face. The dreamer sees the crazy scientist as a man "possessed" by something. About the big-headed assistant, she remarked: "He is like one of Frankenstein's helpmates, or something like that."

Looking at the world outside, it is hardly difficult to see the crazy scientist obsessed with an idea. In our dream, he stands for an arrogant intellectual spirit whose dangerous scientific discoveries and new inventions for life on earth have become a threat to humanity. Because he has forgotten that there is something more vital than reason, he is obsessed by it. Obsession is one-sided. The feeling function, evaluating things correctly, has failed as a regulating factor. In folktales and myths, there are often demonic figures consisting of a head only, or those who are one-legged or one-eyed and so forth; in other words, these figures are incomplete. They represent a one-sided, disfigured

323

human image and illustrate the one-sided and distorted influence of an autonomous complex overwhelming or taking possession of the ego.[509]

Scientific, intellectual thought detached from feeling rationally works on individual facts separated from the living context. Although it may reach scientific knowledge, it can lead to logically correct but – as far as the feelings are concerned – completely wrong decisions. Thus relating to scientific discovery with reason alone, excluding feeling and emotions can lead to monstrosities – a conspicuous, present-day example of which is the manipulation of genes. The reanimation of bodily remains into demonic, life-threatening beings is an apt simile for this. In all the domains of animal husbandry and the raising of livestock, the exclusively rational pursuit of certain goals has lead to partly unnatural, life-threatening symptoms, such as cows becoming overweight and sluggish for the benefit of increased meat or milk production. Respiratory problems and sterility are common symptoms among cats and dogs as a consequence of pursuing certain aesthetic ideals, etc. The assistant with the large head is a Frankensteinian horror vision, for nothing will stop the purely intellectual "head-dominated thinker." Everything is possible for this type of mind, for it lacks the feeling for differentiating and seeing things in a larger context, with a sense of moral responsibility or conscience that would act as a break. Black can be turned into white and vice versa as long as the ultimate goal requires it. In this way, everything becomes feasible or justifiable. Human arrogance knows no boundaries. Everything can somehow be rationally argued and justified, even wars, the extermination of dissidents, etc.

Just as the reanimated bodily remains in the dream are life-threatening, so are the intellectual structures, concepts or discoveries emanating from the rational one-sidedness of the negative animus. When the animus becomes one-sided, woman's spiritual understanding and insight lose their balance. The animus makes use of seemingly logical, rational arguments. This enables it, according to the dream, to animate any random facts. We sometimes come across this kind of reasoning when everything a woman brings up regarding her life, her childhood and adolescence is logical but consistently negative. The conclusions she draws mostly aim at devaluating all the positive things that she developed so far in her life and at undermining her relationships. This really makes one feel as if negative, one-sided demons were on the loose. One is often quite at a loss as to how to help the woman, for the individual parts seem to prove a certain logic, but then looking at it as a whole, one gets the distinct feeling that it is not right.

Issues from childhood that have not been dealt with or overcome, infantile fears, demands and expectations, negative experiences, repressed or disconnected elements as well as other facts that have been separated from the

---

[509] Cf. M.-L. von Franz, *Projection and Re-Collection in Jungian Psychology,* Open Court Publishing Company, La Salle, IL, 1980, p. 103

emotional context – these are all "bodily remains." The revival of such contents occurs in the dream by means of a "shot," that is, by means of a projection. To project means literally to throw out, most often onto other people, a content from a person's own inner personality. This results in negative, critical judgment and preconceived ideas. They debilitate family life or bring down a partnership.

The negative animus can creep into all the crevices where injuries, unresolved misunderstandings and other differences have been repressed or left in the dark for reasons of insecurity, cowardice or some kind of false altruism. What can happen then is that quite unexpectedly and in a different context a person gets ambushed with an acerbic remark and is surprised and hurt. If we then go back to try to clarify the misunderstanding, reestablish the emotional connection, we can see more clearly how the animus animates these bodily remains. Instead of distancing themselves from a certain person or from their own animi, women are too easily intimidated. Moreover, in order to catch her own animus animating bodily remains, a woman sometimes has to undertake toilsome detective-like investigations.

The animus that uses intellectual knowledge split off from feeling usually relies on some theory. Many women rely on scientific literature for a "correct way" of bringing up their children. Or they join some school or other of psychology because they do not trust their own feeling-judgment or their own common sense. It goes without saying that the confidence with which we assume the parental role very much depends upon how we experienced our own parents. It seems fashionable today to explain everything in terms of the behavior of one's own parents, and the rational attempts to explain things in terms of the early days of one's psychological existence are still in force today. For a one-sided rational animus, this is the very grist to his mill. Consequently, we often do not have a good word to say for our parents. The problem for a future mother, in this case, is that she lacks a parental image that can serve as an identification model which could help her to grow into the new role in a natural, spontaneous manner. In our dream, it is the dreamer's own parental image as well as the parental bedroom that are at issue: it is the place of matrimonial relations or the place where parenthood begins. This type of negative animus represents a danger to it.

The crazy scientist's weapon disappears in the dreamer's parents' bedroom. This signifies that the dangerous projection of the possessed animus onto the parental image has become unconscious. The dreamer is unaware of the extent to which a wrong intellectual attitude can put her parenthood at risk. However, the situation can explode at any time: there can be a fierce affective attack from the young mother which no one, including herself, would have expected. This can undermine the bonding feeling in the young family. The fierceness of the ensuing conflict and the exaggerated nature of it all point to an inner, unconscious image, which is attached to the projection of the entire parental situation.

Marie-Louise von Franz wrote: "When an archetype is immediately and intensively constellated, the experience is like being hit by a projectile sent by an overpowering being that transfixes us and brings us into its power. At the same time, we are assailed by fantasies and imaginary images experienced either as proceeding directly from the inner world (for example, as an obsessive idea) or, more often, as caused by an outer object. An attack of aggressive hatred, for example, is felt by us as coming not from Mars but rather from an 'evil adversary' who 'deserves' to be hated (shadow projection), erotic passion not from Cupid but from a woman who arouses this passion in a man (anima projection). *Ultimately, however, it appears that projections always originate in the archetypes and in unconscious complexes.*"[510]

Apart from the weapon in the parents' bedroom, at the end of the dream there are still animated bodily remains. They are the spirits and demons that have been created by the animus obsession and have obtained life-threatening autonomous dynamics. There is something inhuman, robot-like about them that has gotten out of control. These spirits represent unhealthy thoughts that are hostile to life and convince our dreamer of the absurdity of parenthood or the hopelessness regarding any life on our earth. "They [spirits] are either pathological fantasies or new, but as yet unknown, ideas."[511]

In this particular case, the spirits are harmful because they tend to focus only on a partial aspect of life – naturally a negative one – which amounts to a distortion of the whole. It is rare that, for instance, a marriage and family situation are only bad, but the "remains-animus" can make something grave out of a more or less harmless marital conflict and conclude cold-bloodedly that the husband does not love his wife anyway and that divorce will have to be considered.

The dream ends with the crazy scientist and his assistant trying to reassure the dreamer that all this was merely a film, and that in the end everything would be all right. The dreamer is still afraid, however, knowing that this was not the end of the film. She wakes up. I am not certain that the reassuring words should be seen in a positive light. I rather feel that it is very much in the nature of the intellectual animus to find such clever excuses so as to make us feel no longer directly and personally concerned. The intelligent woman is particularly predisposed to integrate the effects of her negative animus in her conscious system, so that everything looks absolutely reasonable. Our dreamer, however, awakens with fear enabling her possibly to realize fully what her animus is capable of doing. Therefore, a potential exists for her to

---

[510] *Ibid.*, p. 24
[511] Cf. C.G. Jung, *The Psychological Foundations of Belief in Spirits*, CW 8, § 597

distance herself from this false spirit and to consciously exclude it from her Self.

Six months later, the same dreamer had the following dream:

Dream No. 110:

> *A couple with a boy stays for a day and a night at home. They hardly worry about the boy's meals. My elder daughter (she is very dear, I can't treat her as she deserves) goes to say good-bye to the man. He is half-Gypsy (he reminds me of a bricklayer who did a botched job for us). He starts to play with my daughter. They move to a distance from me, along the street. I call her. ... After a while, I go running after them, but they don't stop. ... At last some unspecified person appears, with a folder from some kind of clinic, with drawings of regenerated hearts. (This man reminds me of some foremen trying to convince us of their ideas, convenient for them principally for their self-interests, I suspect). Everything seems to suggest that they are carrying my daughter to this place. I am half-awake. I am afraid for her, I think that he, heartless, has taken her there to use her as material for the transplantation. My fear and grief are great. I reproach myself for not having controlled her more close up. I don't see clearly the possibility of retrieving her safely. I awake, and I plot and plan to give them money to bring her back. Finally, I decide to get up and see if she is in her room, but even so, the impression lasts strongly.*

The crazy scientist of the preceding dream comes back again. He wants to take away the dreamer's daughter and then remove her heart. He tries to obtain the heart of a living person in order to implant it in a person with a heart disease. Here, scientific spirit has run amok: human life has to be destroyed in order to maintain another human life. Much of this has long been going on in the context of medical experiments performed on animals. Extending this to man, as in the dream, would merely be an extension of the same fundamentally immoral approach. The role medicine has played in certain modern totalitarian states is equally known to us.

As a medical student, Jung already warned of the loss of the feeling value in science. In a lecture to his fellow-students, he said:

"In the first place, we must institute a 'revolution from above' by *forcing* morality on science and its exponents through certain transcendental truths ... In institutions that offer training in physiology, the moral judgment of students is deliberately impaired by their involvement in disgraceful, barbarous experiments, by a cruel torture of animals which is a mockery of all human decency. Above all, in such institutions as these, I say, we must teach that no truth obtained by unethical means has the moral right to exist."[512] In the same context, Jung goes on to quote Kant and his idea that a belief in a reality lying beyond the crudely material world alone could guarantee an ethical approach to life.

Our dream reflects this terrible collective problem, which at the same time, seems to be a personal problem of the dreamer. She is a part of the collective problem through which she is connected to the collective unconscious, just as we all are. Her daughter equally represents an aspect of feeling that is threatened in our culture as well as her own childlike, spontaneous feeling.

With the first abductor, she associates an incompetent bricklayer who has "botched" a job; with the "heart specialist," an untrustworthy foreman who is only interested in his own profit. These two dubious figures intend, as it were, to procure a heart transplantation for themselves by illicit means. Something is evidently wrong with their hearts. They are sick. The bricklayer type deals with material in a sloppy way. He wants money without showing any real work for it. The "heartless" heart specialist also represents a materialistic attitude marked by greed and exploitation.

Now, what is the meaning of this kind of animus laying violent hands on the dreamer's child?

We have always associated the heart with feeling. The dreamer's child symbolizes an inner image of her Self that is still childlike-spontaneous and capable of development. Therefore, the heart of the child presumably has to do with genuine feeling – the central part of the feminine developmental process – in other words, with the seat of the soul that alone can be creative.

Next, the negative animus apparently runs a clinic where he uses the hearts of strangers for transplants. The unknown other people we assume here to be personality parts that ostensibly acquire more vital energy than Nature has afforded them. The drawings of the hearts suggest the theoretical concept of the animus wanting to invest energy where it is promised returns. However, until now, men or women with a foreign heart have not lived substantially longer. The success is relatively short-lived and still, in the wake of it, there is death.

If the heart of a child is being transplanted by a materialistic animus-figure, there is a danger that essential feminine feeling and creative energy are being wasted on a trivial project. It is not uncommon for women constantly to get involved with new people, new situations or to spend their energy forever looking for new commitments but without ever finding real satisfaction. The real children, on the other hand, tend to be deprived of adequate affection, and the inner child, the essential creative core of the psyche, seems also to perish. The reason why a woman does this is usually quite "sensible" – even scientific, so to speak; however, it completely ignores feeling. One can't really say any-

---

[512] C.G. Jung, *The Zofingia Lectures*, translated by Jan van Heurck, p. 45. Supplementary Volume A of the *Collected Works*, Bollingen Series XX, Princeton University Press, 1983

thing against it. But one can still sense that something is not right: that is, one can often feel an "upset mood" (*Verstimmung* = "out of tune with one's feeling"), rather like the exaggeration in euphoria, irritability, unpredictability or depression. Since the animus can never maintain the life of the wrong "heart patients" for long, in the aftermath, a "deathlike" emptiness or deep fatigue is bound to set in again. For, the whole thing has been done at the expense of woman's essence: namely, the feeling for meaning. Such women often feel a need to have yet another child, as if (without consciously realizing it), in this way, they could rescue the inner child who is threatened time and again.

We are now coming to the last one of these "negative" animus dreams! It was dreamt by a twenty-five-year-old woman, a week before the birth of her first child:[513]

Dream No. 111:

> *I heard some noise outside. Somebody was wildly knocking at the door. So tired, I couldn't open my eyes. I muttered at my husband, trying to wake him up. He didn't answer anything. He must have fallen into a deep sleep. I knew from the sound of footsteps that my mother came down from upstairs. Suddenly the noise stopped. My mother shouted at me, "Don't come out!" It was absolutely silent, then. A devil must have been knocking and caught my mother. She was taken to some place? It was a horrible and shaky experience. I tried to wake up my husband, but he was still sleeping. I couldn't get my body up either.*

It would help if we knew more about the dreamer's relationship with her mother. If she had a bad one, we could perhaps say it is right that she go to hell or be carried off by the devil, so that the dreamer could find her own more positive maternal qualities. (It is possible that the real mother is being taken away by one of her own devils.) However, if the mother-daughter relationship is good (which is what we assume, because the mother warns her daughter of the devil), we must consider the devil as the dreamer's animus causing her maternal feelings to go astray. Should we really simply accuse the dreamer of having such a devilish animus in her?

During pregnancy, a woman is particularly strongly connected with the collective unconscious, and this tends to bring up super-personal, i.e., archetypal, figures such as demons, gods and devils. They exceed by far the limits of the dreamer's personality and must be recognized as such: namely, as not belonging to her. Demons, evil spirits and devils have always been perceived as a particular threat to pregnant women.

---

[513] By the same dreamer: Nos. 115 and 116 of this chapter, No. 26 of Chapter 3.3

The devil is the shadow of our Christian culture: the enormously evil entity, the unruly opponent of the virtuous God. As Jung has demonstrated in *Aion*, the Christian era is marked by the disintegration of the divine opposites of good and evil into a good God and his evil counterpart, the devil or Antichrist. In folklore, the devil is frequently associated with the grandmother, i.e., with the Great Mother; and in our culture, it corresponds to what, in other religions and mythologies, is personified by more or less dark, menacing demons and divine figures.

Figure 44. The Demon Pazuzu
(Assyrian bronze statue)

In the Kabbalistic tradition of Satan or Samael,[514] the "prince" of demons or leader of the fallen angels is the counterpart to Lilith, the strangler, a devouring feminine goddess. This connection is important, for Lilith becomes particularly dangerous for newborn babies, stealing them from their mothers and slaying them as soon as they see the light of day. Lilith is also mentioned as the wife of Asmodei, the demon-prince. According to ancient Babylonian mythology, Azazel, the demon of the desert, is in their service, and Lilith, as a child-robber, is represented as a winged creature with a bird's feet and talons.

In this form, she resembles other demonic winged creatures/beings, such as Pazuzu, a masculine divinity, who is half-man, half-animal, or Lamashtu, a feminine nocturnal goddess with a bird's feet, who is attended by owls. There were also feminine and masculine "Lilins." Pitted against all these demonic figures, who could harm the newborn or the mother, there were numerous apotropaic practices, amulets, magic circles, prayers, etc. In Aramaic magic texts, the "Lilins and Liliths invoked … are conjured up or invoked to leave the bewitched person and his home and possessions alone. Thus, all demons,

[514] Anne Lewandowski, *The God Image, Source of Evil*, p. 71 f – *"The Kabbalistic Equivalent of Satan, also known as the 'Other God,'"* Diploma thesis, Jung Institute, 1977.

devils, Saans and Liliths who live under the lintel of the door or who lurk on its threshold are forced to remove themselves. Because wherever there is some kind of entrance, demons lie in wait. Above all, Lilith is warned not to appear at night in dreams nor during the slumber of daytime."[515]

The intrinsically transitory element of pregnancy and the moment of birth were as hazardous then as they are today. In dreams and during day-time naps, the demons still appear. It is apparently a reality we have to live with. In our culture, it was customary to keep secret the midwife's path to the woman in childbed because of the evil spirits, and one had to ensure that there was plenty of light to protect the woman during childbirth. The midwife would cut off a lock of hair from the boy and throw it to the devil, and that would make him turn on his heels.[516] Legend has it that the Holy Birth was a bitter disappointment for the devil. For this reason, he tries to deceive Mary or to steal her milk.[517]

Therefore, the vulnerability of mother and child by the devil, as described in our dream, is a motif that can be traced back to the most ancient times. As we have said before, pregnancy facilitates access to the collective unconscious; hence, there is a higher risk considering the archetypal psychic powers. The appearance of the devil in the dream of a modern, pregnant woman suggests an impersonal, archetypal event that pregnant women have always been particularly exposed to.

Countless myths, fairy tales and legends share the motif of the hero or heroine having to know or write down the name of a god or demon, in order to protect themselves against their destructive powers. In a magic text of ca. 4 A.D., Lilith, the child-strangler, too, declares to Salomon, the god of spirits and demons, that the women merely had to write her name on a scrap of paper, and she would vanish. In Ancient Greece, it was the knowledge of *Logoi Hekatikoi* (name for Hecate) that should protect one from her intrigues. Knowing the name of a god in modern language signifies being conscious of his powers. In contrast, the unconsciousness of the work of the devil in our Christian culture has become one of the most serious individual and collective hazards. This unconsciousness originates from the attitude of the Christian Early Fathers, who failed to concede to the evil an autonomous divine reality with independent powers and influence – the reason being that evil had to be denied. The name of the dark side of God that was dissociated from Him was lost, and simultaneously, the protection that consciousness and relatedness to it could grant. Like the great demons, the devil is a divinity. He has forcefully taken the place of the good God, who seems to have lost his place in today's religious life. Being conscious of that and knowing his name is therefore not

---

[515] S. Hurwitz, *Lilith, The First Eve*, Daimon Verlag, 1992, p. 95
[516] *Handwörterbuch des deutschen Aberglauben*, 3, p. 1589
[517] *Ibid.*, XIII, p. 741 f; S. Hurwitz, *Lilith, The First Eve*, pp. 118-119

only a necessity in the delicate transition period of pregnancy – a time when the gates to the underworld are open – but in our precarious era generally. At the end of the dream, our dreamer, too, finds it difficult to wake up, that is, to become conscious.

The devil in the dream being so overpowering is an allegory for a state of obsession or identification with cold, ruthless, destructive judgments and opinions causing the maternal feelings to fall apart. How should a woman deal with this? It hardly helps her to try to emulate the Christian ideal of altruism, which is often disguised in a more or less artificial attempt to "think positively." This is too sentimental and will never suffice to cope with evil, the shadow of human nature or the dark, unjust side of God. For, we all know that contrary to committing evil deeds, virtuousness often does not guarantee success. As far as raising children is concerned, for instance, wanting to be "good" frequently not only has little or no effect at all, but even a contrary one. The more the desperate parents try to "preach" to their children, the more unruly they sometimes become.

The desire to be kind and the ideal of altruism tend to get a woman even more deeply enmeshed in the seemingly irreconcilable opposites of good and evil. It seems to prompt not only the shadow but also the negative animus to rise to the surface. If, on the other hand, she succeeds in seeing that the animus does not belong to her personal feminine essential being, perhaps she can then establish her own differentiated "feeling-relatedness" with her environment and herself. This would then allow her to see the opposites in a softer light. Jung described this moonlike quality of feminine consciousness in *Mysterium coniunctionis:*[518] "Her consciousness has a lunar rather than a solar character. Its light is the 'mild' light of the moon, which merges things together rather than separating them." Jung characterizes the moonlike, binding, feminine consciousness with *Eros*, which connects – whereas *Logos*, ascribed to the masculine consciousness, has more of a differentiating, judgmental and perceptual quality. This Eros of human relationships has no need of being involved in elaborate negotiations of "who is right" or "who is wrong," and therefore differs from the idea of being "absolutely good all the time." Children can often be distracted from a quarrel by inconspicuously drawing their attention to something more interesting. This way of dealing with a problem is also indicated, in order to stop the unpleasant negative, argumentative animus. Simply to redirect it can be most helpful. This can easily be done if one gives it a new creative challenge. For behind this type of animus is often an unrealized creative potential. An unconscious content appearing at the threshold of consciousness with a tremendous demonic negative force can take possession of a woman's personality. "The demonic, therefore, would be the creative *in statu nascendi*, not yet realized, or 'made real,' by the ego."[519]

[518] C.G. Jung, *Mysterium coniunctionis,* CW 14, § 223

And indeed, unrealized, creative impulses belong to the most destructive forces in existence. The animus, the feminine spirituality or Logos in woman is a content of the unconscious that wants to be realized and obtain its rights in woman's life.[520] This realization is in itself a creative achievement no matter where or how it eventually finds expression. An additional immense complication and danger for woman is the fact that the animus will show archaic primitive features in its initial undifferentiated form. However, admitting to consciousness the obsessive states and the suffering they cause can also lead to transformation: for, both demon and liberator belong to the same inner figure or the same inner force that will sometimes reveal one, sometimes the other face.

Dream No. 112 (the dreamer is seven months pregnant with her third child):[521]

> *First my husband and I were in the process of writing a book, or rather translating a book from an ancient language (possibly Latin). It was a scientific text about flowers: large yellow male alpine flowers. ... I climbed up high mountain slopes surrounded by a multitude of such blooming flowers. It was in Graubünden, my favorite Swiss canton. We had some controversy that we brought before an elderly woman, who seemed to be an authority. The problem was about the location in the book, that only "Disentis" should be mentioned. I suggested that we should put "Graubünden," at least in brackets, for the book would be read in Germany as well as other countries, and not everyone would know that Disentis was in Graubünden. This was done in the end. The yellow flowers and blowing clouds of pollen on the mountain slopes gave me – in the midst of it all – a feeling of happiness.*
>
> *Then, together with other young people, I went to a rustic peasant church, which was also in Graubünden. ... As we were looking around inside, an effusive young minister suddenly began to give a sermon with great vivacity, performing one ceremony after another. The entire ritual captivated everyone. I was sitting on a kind of altar or in the dock or more likely alternating between the two. When it was all over, the show was over, and we stepped outside, I felt as if I had been put through the wringer. Here is what I felt: "Now you have gone through the whole ceremony one more time – just as you were supposed to – but it doesn't mean anything to you. It doesn't concern you; it doesn't touch you in the least; it isn't even your religion." I left thinking that it was time I grasped that I had to find my*

[519] Cf. M.-L. von Franz, *Projection and Re-Collection in Jungian Psychology*, p. 105

[520] Cf. v. Beit / v. Franz, *Symbolik des Märchens*, p. 604

[521] By the same dreamer: No. 24 in Chapter 3.2, No. 36 in Chapter 4, No. 92 in Chapter 5, No. 65 in Chapter 5.3

own religion and that I had nothing to do with any of what was going on there.

Next, I was a young girl going to a family with four children. Before this, I went to buy a pair of shoes. It was the place where I grew up. I couldn't decide between a pair of light-elegant-kitschy "Gigi" shoes and a pair of lovely boots which I ended up buying. I then made my way to the house in those boots. Before everything started, I wanted to go to the toilet. To my dismay, however, I realized that my period had started and that this was going to make me late. Then the hostess came in, and noticing my problem, very kindly helped me. She told me not to worry about unpacking as we were all – including my grandmother – going on a long journey.

The first part of the dream speaks of a scientific piece of work about yellow flowers that the dreamer and her husband were engaged in translating. Our dreamer had to translate from an ancient language, and at the same time, to write about it. Although this may seem paradoxical, we do exactly that when we study ancient myths – for instance, fairy tales and legends or the writings of the great religions – and we try to translate their symbolic language into our own. Examining our dreams in analysis we equally realize that these symbolic images and traditions from the past are components of them. Therefore, analysis of the unconscious always entails scientific work – that is, a creative, new formulation of old contents. Trying to understand what the ancients were thinking enables us to bring alive deep religious statements and insights and discoveries about the nature of the soul, even though they may come to us from seemingly outdated, dried-up paper. In this way, we can shed light on our own dreams.

A yellow or golden flower is an ancient symbol of the Self, a simile for the Eternal in man. In the Orient, the golden flower corresponds to enlightenment. The Chinese Taoist text (published by Richard Wilhelm with a commentary by C.G. Jung) entitled *The Secret of the Golden Flower* describes this flower as a "new being," which unfolds from the dark inner depths of silence through meditation. Jung called this the experience of the Self an experience of immortality beginning already in this life.[522]

The variety of yellow flowers on the mountain slope swept over by the wind-driven pollen are a beautiful picture for a genuine religious experience. Jung explained that the original meaning of spirit (*pneuma*) was in fact "air in motion," and that animus and anima are connected with *Anemos* [= wind].[523] In the dream, the flower, an expression for the feminine Self, is connected with the wind, the primordial manifestation of the spirit or animus. The wind and pollen signify fecundation, exemplifying the procreative aspect of the spirit.

---

[522] Quotes by M.-L. von Franz, *Dream and Death*, p. 58, and M. Mijuki, *Kreisen des Lichts*, Barth Verlag, 1972

[523] C.G. Jung, *The Phenomenology of the Spirit in Fairy Tales*, CW 9 II, § 387

Marie-Louise von Franz said that the animus "either contains the Self of the woman or, if it does not make her possessed, helps her to find the roots and the essence of the feminine personality."[524] Hence, the elderly lady, the feminine higher authority, is also of the dreamer's opinion that the yellow flowers have to be regarded in a higher context. This contradicts the husband's view – the dreamer's personal animus – who is apparently too narrow-minded about it all and not paying much attention to it. Perhaps he stands for an attitude that is too scientific and rational and that fails to include feeling. Oftentimes, we only understand things correctly once we have decided upon their relative importance; but for this, we need our feeling function in order to make a judgment. Thus the scientific work is followed by a strong emotional experience and a deep feeling of happiness on the mountain slope. After this experience of an original union of Spirit and Nature in the flowers and the wind, the dream leads us to the root of the problem of today's world: namely, the separation of the Spirit and Nature, as our ecclesiastic Christianity has implemented it.

The separation of the original union of above and below, of heaven and earth, which was also how it was at the beginning of the Christian creation myth, corresponds to the natural human process towards achieving consciousness. In Christianity, however, making this necessary distinction between Spirit and Nature led to an over-emphasis on the masculine-spiritual side, which was perceived as superior to the "lower" aspect of all things intrinsically Nature-bound. "Good" was associated with "above" and "bad" with "below," which is how it came to be that – because of the rigid adherence to the principles of "good and evil" in ecclesiastical Christianity – Nature and femininity were placed "below," and thus together with "evil."

The minister of the second part of the dream embodies this kind of attitude. But for the pregnant woman who had already experienced in her unconscious the mystery of the union of the Spirit and Nature or of masculine and feminine, this attitude is no longer valid. Her personal grasp of the spirit is not housed in an outer masculine authority despite the fact that the animus still oppresses her with its values of good and evil. The animus could detract from her very own religious experience by causing her to belittle it as "only dreams" or "only psychology," etc. or even to condemn it to the categories of good and evil.

Many women lack the confidence to stand up for their femininity, their womanly roles or their feminine bodies because they are somehow imprisoned in the clutches of a too Christian animus, which is critical of any and every irrational or instinctive emotional reaction, or of the genuine need simply "to be" in congruence with their very natures. If, on the other hand, women are active professionally or politically, the animus will tend to force them into

---

[524] v. Beit / v. Franz, *Symbolik des Märchens*, p. 601 (trans. V.N.)

the roles of masculine heroes, which then leaves them in a state of possession by the animus, and above all, cut off from their feminine feelings.

The third section of the dream contains the lysis in this conflict. On the one hand, there is a genuine, individual religious experience in which the feminine and the animus, in its original form as a manifestation of the spirit, are at one. In stark contrast to this there is the collective Christian religion, which underestimates the feminine nature, along with the resulting schism between Nature and Spirit. The animus-minister's sermon has put the dreamer in a situation where she feels "split": that is, her feminine ego and the animus face each other as opposites. Now, what counsel does her instinct, i.e., the dream, give her?

First of all, it would seem that the dreamer has to turn her attention to her physical femininity. To her help comes the hostess or the mistress of the house, signifying her domestic side and "life-at-home," which are so often regarded as "inferior." Then she is to go on a journey with her grandmother, which, apparently, is both the goal and the solution. To accomplish this, she first needs a new pair of shoes, i.e., a fundamental change in her basic attitude. Fortunately, she chooses the robust boots, i.e., a firm, consistent attitude with which she can step onto the stage of the outside world. The "light-elegant-kitschy" pair would correspond to a frivolous, short-lived attitude along the lines of "try something new" (as is fashionable not only in the field of psychology). The sturdy boots symbolize being firmly in touch with reality – the reality of her life as a housewife and mother. Furthermore, they symbolize "standing her ground," and most importantly for the moment, pursuing her interest in the journey with the grandmother or the Great Mother. The journey is the search for her feminine Self that is concomitantly the search for her own religion. Thus, fulfilling the role of femininity, I believe is also a spiritual goal for our dreamer. What often seems to be the case is that, in order for a woman to gain access to her individual creative spirit, she first has to resolve a problem with her mother and/or her own maternal side. Using her feminine instincts and her feminine nature, the daughter initially has to overcome the mother's animus, as it were, for which the Christian minister-spirit is a befitting image. If she does not manage to do this, however, there is a danger that the animus will interfere with the new child's development as well as with the young mother's own spirituality.

Dream No. 113:

> *I am in the countryside with my husband. Going along a country lane, I feel as if I am being pursued and threatened by a ghost, and I fly into a panic. We run away and arrive at an old, well-kept timber house. An old farmer's wife lives in it. She tells us that the ghost was a young man who needed to be near people, in order to collect strength from them. She said*

that he was very sad and lonely, but that people felt cold in his presence and became frightened. He would follow people just as long as they were running away. Within a certain radius around the house, he had power over her and would recharge himself with her energy. He was living with her.

Inside, he is harmless. I can now watch him calmly. I feel very sorry for him because he looks so abysmally sad. Once I have gotten used to his presence, I take him in my arms and hold him tightly. I caress him. This way he can come alive and become stronger. He has taken on some material substance and already looks more like a human being. Later, I sleep with my husband. We learn from the old woman that it is better if the young man does not know about this, however, as it could harm his healing process. The old woman has found some interesting jobs for us in town, so we have to leave this place (temporarily?). I'm a little sad because the boy is not quite well yet. I hope he'll soon be healthy again.

It is as if this dream came out of one of the sagas people told in times past. These folktales speak of ghosts and specters coming from the beyond to disturb and menace people's lives. There were specific behavioral rules one had to observe in their presence. Naturally, no one could prove their existence, no matter how vividly and credibly the tale was told. What is remarkable is the strong resemblance of motifs with dreams. Gotthilf Isler says in his book on the psychological interpretation of sagas: "We cannot be sure about the thing in itself; however, we cannot differentiate it phenomenologically from psychic manifestations. Therefore we can conceive of them as archetypal projections of the unconscious psyche. Thus, although physically they are not necessarily true, psychologically they are."[525]

In folklore, ghosts are usually unredeemed souls of the dead whom the living have to attend to, in some form or other, in order to deliver them. Psychologically, this would mean that an unconscious content welling up in a negative possessive form can be made to disappear or become transformed through care and love. What does this mean, though?

Here, the animus is the unredeemed spirit which is sapping energy from the consciousness. The animus, a youth, has certainly to do with new ideas, inspiration, intuition, images from the unconscious and creativity – though on the other hand, perhaps with unrealistic fantasies, which ensure that he can remain free and uncommitted. In this form of fantasy and day-dreaming, he could indeed be a harmful figment of the mind or a sick, dangerous phantom. To gain strength, he seeks proximity with people. In the unconscious, he is

---

[525] G. Isler, *Die Sennenpuppe*, p. 12. "In other cases, too, where projection has to be ruled out, where factually the psychic behaves identically to the psychological (and vice versa), namely, in the case of synchronistic events, the 'underlying' archetypes are perceptible."

only a son of the Great Mother (in the dream, he lives with her), without any substance of his own. With her, he is harmless but nevertheless sick. Many women function rather well in their feminine domains, in their families and social lives, and yet their animi are not well: their spiritual-creative sides have not found adequate forms of expression or realization in their conscious lives. I believe that there is a general tendency of the animus to demand more energy and substance, i.e., increasingly concrete manifestation in a woman's life. We are often taken aback when the animus reveals itself in the form of obsession, cold argumentation and inflexibility, forbidding any real exchange of ideas. Men sometimes complain that some women in politics are poor at achieving consensus, instead easily becoming involved in confrontation or resentful arguments. This is the negative animus at work with its separating or divisive rather than uniting "logic."

The farmer's wife's house is where the ghost-animus can be healed through the loving care of our dreamer. It is also the maternal place where the primordial feminine tasks of caring and loving, nourishing and protecting new life take place. The young man is the animus who could seduce her into being uncommitted and perhaps excessively mobile and extraverted. She must recognize that the source of his nastiness and destructiveness is his mourning his loss of strength and power. Embracing him might be a way of admitting that a part in her mourns his powerlessness in her life. Perhaps something in her still wants the freedom she had before she had a family, wants to let her fantasies and ideas roam about freely, and make plans. If she does not waste this inner strength through extraversion but contains it as an inner problem (embrace!), she can transform him into a creative spirit helping her to find meaning in her life, her activities and fantasies.[526] In her book, *Puer Aeternus* Marie-Louise von Franz has described the youth-animus in all its facets of problems and potentialities. As long as our dreamer's animus continues to haunt her in the outside world, she will always feel somewhat dissatisfied and drained in her maternal role – as if somewhere or someone were sapping her energy.

Living in a three-bedroom city apartment or in an urban housing estate makes it particularly difficult for many women to allow their *puer-aeternus*-spirits to live without wearing themselves out in superficial extraversion. The modern homes we live in, where some kind of Nature-relatedness or creative potential is reduced to a minimum, may be a reason for the high number of erring "animus-ghosts."

However, it looks as though in the dream we have just discussed, the dreamer succeeds in recognizing in the youth-animus a personal psychic component, accepting it and thus transforming it into a human, i.e., conscious form to which she can relate. It is always better to recognize a problem, to

[526] E. Jung, *Animus and Anima*, p. 26

confront it and not to let it wander about in the unconscious, thereby allowing it to create various kinds of damage.

Dream No. 114:[527]

> *I am on a long, long journey from East to West – like a life's pilgrimage. China is mentioned at one point, and I travel on foot by a path going often through wild and desolate country, beset by all kinds of dangers from dreadful precipices to wild animals. I wander on plateaus, through deep valleys and narrow mountain ridges, reminding me of descriptions by Gurdjieff of traversing the wilder regions of the Caucasus and Hindukush ranges. But: I am not alone. With me is a black man (or very dark brown skin, not necessarily Negroid, just very dark). I love him from the depths of my heart. I trust him utterly and completely. While he is there, I am safe even on such an exhausting and treacherous journey. And he, in turn, is devoted to me. We must have been companions for a long, long time to achieve such mutual esteem. But he is the Master, I am the child. … At this point, I awaken.*

This dream was dreamt one week before the mother's fourth child was to be born. She is on a trip from East to West, from sunrise to sunset, journeying through unknown, dangerous, remote land. The sunrise is the symbol of the birth of light and therefore also of the birth of human consciousness. By contrast, the setting of the sun symbolizes the extinction of the light of consciousness in the obscurity of death. The unknown land with its animals and treacherous Nature is the land of the Great Mother, which a woman enters with pregnancy. It is no less the land of rebirth than the land of death. Nearing confinement, woman is also near death, for Nature signifies both life and death. The way to the West can therefore mean death just as much as rebirth, for in Nature, every death simultaneously signifies a transformation into new life. In an unperturbed natural cycle, each time a plant, animal or man dies there seems to be a corresponding renewal of life. In spite of all the modern medical science and technology, when expecting a child, women have in the past and will always enter the unknown and dangerous land of the Great Mother.

A dark-skinned companion, guide and lover accompanies the dreamer. It feels as if they had always known each other, always been together.

Lovers of all times have described this feeling when in their lover they suddenly find their inner companion. The animus here is a leader figure through the treacherous land. His dark skin indicates his archaic-instinctive and emotional characteristics. For the white man, the black man still carries the projection of something primeval, connected with the instincts, something

---

[527] By the same dreamer: No. 60 in Chapter 5.3, No. 43 in Chapter 4.2

from a remote land and also something uncanny. This type of animus personifies primary strength and courage but also a kind of instinctive, intuitive
knowledge from the unconscious. It is an extremely positive and yet obscure
psychic leader-figure, a psychopomp with a double aspect of light and dark.
All natural psychopomp figures have this more or less pronounced double
aspect (masculine-feminine or good-evil).[528] When we try to live in accordance
with our instincts and are not at war with our unconscious, then we are
permanently grappling with our conscious needs as well as those of the unconscious. The dark soul leader in our dream is probably a guide in this process
of coming to terms with the unconscious or with individuation.

With the East the dreamer associates "strong spiritual and religious connotations," and the journey for her is a "life-pilgrimage." The journey through the
treacherous land indeed resembles the hero's or heroine's quest in myths and
fairy tales, but also the shaman's journey of initiation as well as the inner
journey of the mystics. The goal of the initiation journey, according to Jung, is
the encounter with the Self or the inner experience that grants man the experience of anchoring and the goal of his individual life in a higher meaning that
is enduring and will guide him throughout life. The "great journey" is a typical
representation of the psychic maturation process – particularly in the second
part of life.

Figure 45. Sibirian Shaman

One of the dangers of this inner
journey can be the negative animus: it can be not only a leader
towards the Self but can also
entice us into an unreal dream-
land. This type of animus figure
can be found in fairy tales about
the *Elfenkönig*, *Wassermann* or
other seducers into the Land of the
Hereafter or also in the tale of the
rat catcher *von Hameln*. In real
life, it sometimes happens that the
libido becomes irresistibly
attracted to something, thereby
drifting away from consciousness
and everyday life into another
world. "... the world into which we
go is a more or less conscious
phantasy or fairy land, where

---

[528] v. Beit / v. Franz, *Symbolik des Märchens*, 781

everything is either as we wish it to be or else designed in some other way to compensate for the outer world."[529]

This is a possibility in our dream, too; however, I believe it rather likely that the forthcoming birth of our dreamer's fourth child will invite her, so to speak, to the beginning of a spiritual journey whose path will take her to the West, the beyond or the sunset of life. This task, belonging to the second part of life, is ultimately a religious one, which seemingly will only be completed with the close of life.

Young women, whose daily lives have been "filled out" with children over the course of several years, tend to lose sight of this task. Once the children have grown up and flown the nest, they often face a precipice before them as if their lives would end just there. The unconscious uses for pregnancy the same image as it does for what the future has in store for us when our children have left us. The birth of the Self corresponds to the birth of a child.

The dream gives a striking demonstration of how the animus can turn into the leading authority of the unconscious provided a woman manages to transform its destructive side. Not only can the animus convey courage and a power of endurance in view of pregnancy and birth, but it can also convey a more conscious, deeper way of coming to terms with the unconscious. The animus becomes a mediator of creative and religious experiences, whereby life acquires an individual meaning.[530]

The prince of the following dream has much in common with the animus-figure of the dream we have just discussed:

Dream No. 115:

> *Many people were crowded in the square. They were waiting for some ceremony. I stood behind them. A tall and handsome guy appeared high in front of the square. An old lady came to me and proposed to me that I marry him. I said: "No, I am already married." She explained that the tall guy was the prince of this country and wanted me to be his bride. She asked me to divorce my husband. I was finally forced to go to the handsome prince by her. I felt guilty, but excited too. The prince and I stood face to face. He knelt down before me and kissed my hands. The people blessed us with some shouting words.*

The same dreamer had the following dream shortly after the one above:

---

[529] E. Jung, *Animus and Anima*, p. 36
[530] M.-L. von Franz in: C.G. Jung, *Man and His Symbols*, "The Animus: The Man Within," pp. 194-195, Aldus Books, Ltd., London, 1979

Dream No. 116:

> *The prince visited me again. He wanted to go out with me. As he was so attractive, I couldn't say no, even though I felt guilty. I worried about my husband. "He must be so frustrated if he knew I met another handsome guy." The prince and I went to the countryside where a pretty pond was glistening.*

The dreamer had these dreams in the first few weeks of her pregnancy.[531] She is irresistibly drawn to this handsome, tall prince, who has chosen her as his bride. Perhaps the union with him is also in the interest of the mother-figure. This would imply a positive, close connection with the unconscious as the animus not only represents the inner component that is not realized in the outer life but is also the symbol and the driving power for woman's introverted spiritual life.[532] As we have seen, if a woman does not pay enough attention to the animus, it can become autonomous and destructive and negatively over-grow the feminine. This so-called "animus-possession" always involves a loss of the feminine, of the feminine gift for human relationships and of her motherly instincts. This explains the fact why fairy tales – where the tasks that are set have to be *fulfilled* – produce such important feminine symbols, which can be understood as symbols of the Self.[533]

Our dream, too, ends with the wonderful image of a glistening pond in the countryside, evoking a symbol of the feminine and maternal or of woman's Self.

Now the dreamer is not sure whether she should be with the prince or with her husband. She feels as if she were being unfaithful to her husband. When a woman begins to turn to her unconscious, e.g., in analysis, and she begins to develop her spiritual side, her husband may have good reason to be concerned: this development can feel as if he were up against an unknown rival who is suspicious, for his wife is in the process of changing because of him. If he does not blame psychology for putting strange ideas into his wife's head, it is still likely that, to a certain extent, he will perceive his wife or her image as being unfaithful.

As an inner figure, the husband corresponds to an animus that is closer to consciousness and more integrated in the personal sphere, whereas the prince is rather an archetypal, super-personal power. The personality-animus has to do with those masculine qualities that are familiar to her from her husband and that can occasion a realistic adaptation in the dreamer's life. To give an example: if a woman is rather shy and introverted, an extraverted animus with a masculine kind of initiative can be very useful for her.

---

[531] By the same dreamer: No. 111 of this chapter
[532] v. Beit / v. Franz, *Symbolik des Märchens*, p. 586
[533] *Ibid.*, p. 605

The prince, as the future king – the archetype of a woman's logos – is, by comparison, a guiding spiritual principle in her behind which ultimately lies the Self. Her conscious ego is inexorably drawn to the archetypal content of the unconscious that he symbolizes. As we have already seen in the previous dream, when a pregnant woman opens herself to the world of collective imagery, it can happen that she is so fascinated that she enters a fantasy world far removed from her everyday life. It is therefore wise of the dreamer to feel that she does not want to leave her husband. In any event, coming to terms with a tormenting personal animus and one's own husband cannot be avoided. These dreams demonstrate the strong fascination archetypal images exert and the conflict they engender in the conscious ego. And yet, there is nothing destructive in the lysis of the dream. Finally, whether the archetypal images can serve an individual as life-supporting, divine forces or merely as destructive ones, entirely depends on the attitude and the strength of the conscious ego. Pregnancy takes us to the boundaries of consciousness. On the threshold to the unconscious dreams, fantasies and thoughts emerge also containing an aspect of the spiritual-creative, i.e., insights and truth of a purely objective, impersonal nature. "The mediation of such knowledge and such contents is essentially the function of the higher animus."[534]

In our next dream, this will become visible, too. The dreamer was 31 years of age when she was expecting her first child. The pregnancy was very difficult. A healthy baby-girl was born by Cesarean section.

Dream No. 117: [535]

> *We are supposed to go on an expedition into a mountain to see the tombs of Tutankhamon. It is dangerous, still unknown. We are only a small group, and we are the first ones. Before this, we are in a room where one after another is being put into a bathtub. A doctor and nurse, both dumb and uncanny, are spraying something into our eyes and faces. I'm the only one who is naked. I don't want it. I'm afraid of those two and of the drops that are stinging my eyes. Everybody is doing it including the only man among us who is keeping a sharp eye on everything that's happening. I ask him why they are doing this to us. He says that as a man experiences the outer world he also experiences it within – that the world affects us outside as well as inside. The mountain was something so enormously, overpoweringly dark that one could not bear it within oneself. The sea, too, was unearthly when one dove down into it. (I find it so on a high mountain, too.) This was the reason, he said, that they were*

---

[534] E. Jung, *Animus and Anima*, p. 21
[535] By the same dreamer, Dream Nos. 67, 68, 69, 72 in Chapter "Cat"

> *"fogging-up" our view with the drops. I also end up undergoing the pro-cedure. Next Tuesday we should start.*

We again find ourselves on a journey, or rather an expedition, to the bowels of a mountain and the tomb of Tutankhamon, the Egyptian Pharaoh.

When Tutankhamon's tomb was discovered and opened by Carter in 1922 (the only tomb of pharaohs that had not been plundered), they found not only the coffin containing the pharaoh's mummy, but also a precious treasure of gold, utensils, replicas of servants, animals: in short, everything a pharaoh might need in the Other World. The wall paintings in this tomb show how Tutankhamon is being received by Nut, the Egyptian sky-goddess, and how he and Osiris, the god of life-after-death, become one – or more precisely, how he himself becomes Osiris. Osiris is the dying and resurrecting god, and the ruler of the kingdom of the dead. At the same time, he guarantees fertility of life, and after each drought, he causes everything to sprout up again. He is also depicted as the nocturnal sun in the form of which he, starting in the West, traverses the underworld in a solar bark, in order to be reborn in the East the following morning, rejuvenated. In the tomb of the dead king, the new king performs the death and resurrection rituals on the mummy.[536] Thus the tomb of Tutankhamon is an illustration both of death and the continued existence after death. The dreamer seems to be drawn towards this mystery, for which the doctor and nurse have to prepare her. It would appear that this procedure has to do with healing. She is put in a bathtub, and she is without any clothes. Bathing and undressing could mean that she is being cleansed or purified and freed from unnecessary things. Approaching the Other World requires an attitude concentrating on the essence, on the "naked," as it were, or original man, without all the superficialities of the profane world. Cleansing, undressing and acquiring new clothes is an important element of initiation rituals transforming man into a new form of life and thereby into a new attitude.[537] This is precisely the issue addressed in this dream: for birth signifies an initiation into "motherhood," an entirely different form of life replacing the old form, which, effectively, has to "die." Although modern young mothers some-times tend to pass over this important transition and separation from the teens, the unconscious usually marks these transitions quite notably.

Moreover, Tutankhamon's tomb also relates to a real death, which is why we understand the double fear of the dreamer involving unknown, new terri-tory as well as a realistic possibility of death that is present at every childbirth. In former times, this dreamer, together with her child, would have had to die: given the size of the child and the too narrow birth canal, natural birth would not have been possible. This reality, it seems, would have been too overpower-

---

[536] Cf. Erik Hornung, *Geist der Pharaonenzeit*, Artemis, 1989

[537] Cf. M.-L. von Franz, *Redemption Motifs in Fairy Tales,* Inner City Books, Toronto, 1980, pp. 21-31

ing; therefore, the dreamer has something trickled into her eyes, "fogging up" her eyesight.

The animus plays a helpful role here: it observes everything closely and explains to the dreamer what it means. Being a part of the dreamer, the animus naturally undergoes the same procedure, although it has a somewhat more objective view of it. Through the animus, the dreamer can understand why this expedition is dangerous and why the eye drops are necessary – for it reveals to her the overpowering reality of outer and inner nature, the collective unconscious containing the mystery of death and rebirth, towards which she is drawing nearer. We have earlier already mentioned that pregnancy and birth are moments in life when the unconscious gains prevalence and can engender a psychosis. The ego, being covered by the dark mountain cloak or drowned in the sea, is an apt image for such a potentiality.

The "fogging-up-drops" protect her from seeing all this too clearly. Although she is exposed to the danger and must face the superior power of Nature, with the help of her animus' sensible objectivity, she can avoid succumbing to panic. This is particularly problematical for women with a negative mother-complex for whom motherliness is not the nurturing soil one could entrust oneself to. Thus, the animus mediates a kind of psychological insight, showing the dreamer an appropriate approach or behavior in the face of this frightening situation Nature has brought on. The experience of pregnancy and birth is depicted in a way that could have a healing effect on the dreamer and fundamentally change her approach to death and life. In fact, pregnancy and birth – despite the negative mother-complex causing her again and again to lose her courage to face life – can create new firm ground for her to stand on. The animus in this dream is clearly on the side of life.

The following dream was dreamt by a twenty-nine-year-old woman around the time of conception of her second child.[538]

Dream No. 118:

> ... A man was sitting next to me. On the top of his head which was not covered with hair but covered with something like foam, grass was growing and flowers were blooming.

This peculiar dream image once again takes us to Ancient Egypt, along with one of the most important gods there: Hapi, the god of the Nile River. He is depicted with papyrus and lotus flowers growing from his head. He is a positively life-bestowing water god, the annual inundation of the River Nile guaranteeing the land perpetually recurring fertility and renewal.[539] His Greek

---

[538] By the same dreamer: No. 78, Chapter 5.5
[539] Wallis Budge, *From Fetish to God in Ancient Egypt*, Oxford University Press, London, 1934, p. 11

counterpart is Priapus, a son of Dionysos and Aphrodite, and also a god of fertility. Priapus has fruits on his lap, like a female goddess, and a rosebush on his head.[540] People sang hymns to Hapi, the Egyptian god, and one of them goes:[541]

Hail to you, Hapi,
Sprung from earth, …
Of secret ways,
A darkness by day,
To whom his followers sing!
Who floods the fields that Re has made,
To nourish all who thirst;
Let's drink the waterless desert, …
Lord of the fishes,
Maker of barley, creator of emmer,
He lets the temples celebrate. …
When he floods, earth rejoices,
Every belly jubilates, …
Gives bounty to the poor. …
As he spouts, makes drink the fields,
Everyone grows vigorous.

Hapi is not only the god of darkness, "of secret ways" and the one bringing prosperous life, but also a god who dispenses happiness, love, festivities, i.e., Eros, in the broadest sense of the word. Although he is a male god, he has all the attributes of a female goddess of fertility and in fact is depicted like a woman, with swelling, pendulous breasts.[542]

With regard to our dream, a man with flowers and grass on his head could represent a fertile, masculine spirit from the unconscious, having a reviving effect and an aura of Eros and connectedness. A woman connected to this kind of spirit is not at war with her femininity or with her animus. Because it is the spirit of Nature, serving life and renewal, she can be both feminine and spiritually creative. Hapi is a water god promoting life-furthering impulses from the unconscious. This extends to religious life (thou makest the temples to keep their festivals) as well as to human relationships. Contrary to the "clergyman-animus" of Dream No. 112, Hapi symbolizes a harmony between Spirit and Nature. This kind of animus can inspire any kind of creative work – a book, for instance, that will bestow a nourishing feeling upon the reader. A

---

[540] Jocelyne Bonnet, *La Terre des Femmes et ses Magies*, p. 129
[541] Miriam Lichtheim, *Ancient Egyptian Literature: A Book of Readings*, Vol. I: "The Old and Middle Kingdom," Berkeley / Los Angeles / London, 1973, pp. 204-207
[542] Wallis Budge, *From Fetish to God in Ancient Egypt*, p. 11

Figure 46. Hapi, the god of the Southern Nile and Hapi, the god of the Northern Nile, with flowers on the head and female breasts

woman with this kind of animus will have a vitalizing and harmonizing effect on all her activities and on the way she leads her life, and her environment will benefit from it. She will not have to "extravert" to a point where she has to enter into competition with men but will have the freedom to live her own creative life.

If the dreamer suffers from a sense of dissatisfaction – because she feels she can now only live her womanly side and is thereby cut off from spiritual inspiration or from life itself – the dream can compensate these feelings and indicate to her that there is potential for the contrary, too.

Summarizing the animus dreams we have discussed, I believe that frequently they serve as an explicit warning: the animus in its negative form during pregnancy represents a specific danger for a woman as it seeks to undermine her confidence in herself and to strip her of her sense of security in her womanly role. Furthermore, the animus can interfere with her social life or general need to feel connected, which are indispensable for her well-being. Finally, the animus can seduce her into a wishful-thinking mode, thus making it more difficult to cope with everyday life. Although none of this is unique to pregnancy, the greater proximity to the unconscious at this particular time can provoke the demonic, super-personal aspect of the animus more than at other times in a woman's life.

The various positive animus aspects, such as courage, strength, being focused, active and having initiative, seem to have played a minor role in the dreams. This can be explained by the fact that pregnancy and birth are a wholly feminine business and have more to do with passive "hatching out." However, we have also seen that in the face of the dark, menacing sides of nature, where strength and courage are needed, the animus can have a helpful function. If, on the other hand, the animus appears as a creative-spiritual principle, it seems to have some secret link with the Great Mother or even the feminine Self.

The animus and the mother imago seem to be in a reciprocal relationship. Many fairy tales demonstrate to us that, on the one hand, being attached to the animus-world can complicate maternal life; on the other hand, a negative mother image can be an obstacle in relating to the animus.[543] In its hostile attitude towards corporeality, the negative animus impairs the instinctual sphere and the vitality of woman so that becoming a mother can seem an enormous burden. In dreams where a woman is cut off from her own femininity, it is often the animus of the mother or the grandmother that render her insecure and cause depression. In fairy tales and myths, the Great Mother frequently has masculine features, is accompanied by male attendants or is in fact portrayed as a male (for instance, a wolf, beggar, dead man or old man). Finally, the masculine – aggressive to malicious – unconscious component of the mother can put a spell on the daughter's animus, so that the daughter herself becomes possessed by an evil animus.[544]

Tackling the mother-problem – which becomes an issue, at the latest, when a woman has her own child – generally brings with it, as it were, the animus-problem. The dreams we have discussed have shown us how dangerous this can be for the new inner and outer child as well as for the feminine destiny or realization of the feminine Self. If, on the other hand, we manage to successfully address the problem and come to terms with it, our individual animus can turn out to be a guiding and benevolent power of the unconscious.

The Father – The Wise Old Man

One of the masculine figures personifying woman's animus is, of course, the personal father. The father is the first example of a man for every young girl and therefore also the first animus image. In this function, Jung said that the father conditions her spiritual temperament, her relations with spiritual things per se and also her overall approach to spiritual or religious questions.[545] Although our present collection contains a large number of animus dreams, only in a very few of them does the personal father appear. This may be accidental; however, I think we can assume that at the time of pregnancy,

---

[543] v. Beit / v. Franz, *Symbolik des Märchens*, p. 625.
[544] Cf. v. Beit / v. Franz, *Symbolik des Märchens*, Francke Verlag Bern, 1952
[545] M.-L. von Franz, *Passio Perpetuae*, Spring Publications, 1980, p. 85

compared to the maternal-feminine themes, the personal father rather remains somewhere "backstage." At this time of life, a woman primarily turns to the Great Mother, who can help her to master her biological task. The personal father has little say here (apart from interfering when he should not). This problem is largely manifested in the negative animus-dreams, which we have studied above.

In some dreams, though, the father appears in an impersonal or super-personal form. His image transcends the ordinary and becomes the wise old man, the grandfather, or occasionally, the magician or an uncanny nature-spirit.

Let us take a closer look now at the image of the "old man" or the "wise old man." Most of us are familiar with this figure in fairy tales: he always appears when the hero or the heroine is in a desperate situation from which only profound reflection or a fortunate idea – in other words, a spiritual function or an endopsychic automatism of some kind – can extricate him or her. But since, for internal and external reasons, the hero cannot accomplish this himself, the knowledge needed to compensate for the deficiency comes in the form of a personified thought, i.e., in the shape of this sagacious and helpful old man.[546] "Indeed, the old man is himself this purposeful reflection and concentration of moral and physical forces that comes about spontaneously in the psychic space outside consciousness when conscious thought is not yet – or no longer – possible."[547] "…not only in fairy tales but in life generally, the objective intervention of the archetype is needed which checks the purely affective reactions with a chain of inner confrontations and realizations. These cause the who? where? how? why? to emerge clearly and in this way bring knowledge of the immediate situation as well as of the goal."[548]

The old man in fairy tales, who already knows the goal and the way to attain it, therefore personifies knowledge, wisdom and intuition. As a positive character, he is helpful and well-meaning. The helpful elves of our folktales belong to his world. The old man, as an archetype of the spirit, and like all archetypes, has an ambivalent character. Occasionally, he may be an evil spirit, feeding on human flesh, or a magician. Then the feat of the hero or heroine consists of succeeding in escaping. For flight is always indicated when a negative spirit or the dark side of an archetype promises to impart power to the personality. This signifies a moral decision that eventually leads to the goal, that is, to the princess.

The wise old man can be encountered in many cultures, be it in the person of an old peasant living in the mountains, impressing us with his placid personality, which has been toughened by the storms of life, be it in spiritual or

---

[546] Cf. C.G. Jung, CW 9, I, *The Phenomenology of the Spirit in Fairy Tales*, § 401
[547] *Ibid.*, § 402
[548] *Ibid.*, § 404

religious leaders, shamans, medical men or saints like Saint Francis of Assisi or Niklaus von Flüe. These figures become part of a culture's active store of imagination. In dreams, it is often the grandfather personifying this superior spirit from the unconscious and helping the conscious ego to attain a broader view. The following dream serves as an illustration of this. It comes from an unmarried twenty-four-year-old woman who had had an abortion but wanted to keep the second child against the will both of her family and of the father of the child. In fact, the father never wanted to see the child. After a very difficult pregnancy, a healthy baby-girl was born by Cesarean section.

Dream No. 119:

> *I was about to bring forth. There came a boy, but I was sure he was not my son. My grandfather showed up and said: "This is not your child, for he is a man, and he is going to continue the lineage of the blue eyes."*

The appearance of the grandfather in this dream of a young woman expecting a "fatherless" child is particularly touching. Moreover, the grandfather seems to possess superior knowledge, something an ordinary grandfather would not normally have. He unveils himself as a spirit announcing the birth of the "divine" child that she has conceived. The child will "continue the lineage of the blue eyes" – eyes which are the color of the sky or a symbol of the spiritual view, which over many generations was considered to be in the father's line, despite the fact that the mother seems to have been abandoned to the feminine-maternal domain.

Two days before the delivery of her daughter, she dreamt:

Dream No. 120: [549]

> *I dreamed Saint Francis of Assisi was blessing me and her.*

Saint Francis of Assisi is known for his love for the poor and for the animals and thereby represents a spirit taking care of the abandoned mother and child together with her whole "animal," instinctive natural predisposition. Many saints are said to have had a wondrous contact with animals.

This feature is conferred upon them by the wise old man, who, as a spirit of the unconscious, is connected not only with the superhuman but also with the animalistic-subhuman in its dark, threatening form. Saint Francis of Assisi is dedicated to lightness and virtue. In his Song to the Sun, he implores the animals not to eat each other up in the saintly-naïve ignorance of the fact that in this case, a major part of the animal kingdom would be condemned to death. However, above all, he is a spirit of love and a patron of the weak trying to defy Nature's law of the "survival of the fittest." He can give the young abandoned mother the strength to assume her destiny and to survive, even on

---

[549] This dream is also mentioned in Chapter 7.

Figure 47. Saint Francis with the Birds, Giotto (1266-1337)

a stony road. Being associated with light, he can compensate for the negative experience of the "father" who refused to be one.

Dream No. 121:

> *I find myself sitting at a scoured white wooden table in a subterranean chamber of a cave-citadel by the sea. It is quiet and peaceful in this cool room. Next to me is sitting a man of my age who is said to have accompanied me in my life and to be married to me. From the depths of the mountain, there is a corridor leading out to the vault where we are sitting at a table in silence. Then I notice that an old man with a white beard is approaching us from the dark corridor, issuing from the deep interior of the mountain. ... He has a venerable, old face that, at the same time, has a look of freshness. The young man next to me silently arises to yield his place to the old man, then moves towards the opposite wall of the chamber. Now I understand that my life-companion wants to leave me. I wish to call after him, but the entreating cry becomes stuck in my throat – for, at this very moment, I see something dreadful: as soon as the young man reaches the wall, he goes through it, becoming invisible like a spirit. ... It was Mephistopheles himself! This realization makes me shudder. Meanwhile, the old man has sat down next to me. I feel I am in his hands.[550]*

The dreamer is a thirty-two-year-old woman and by profession, a lawyer, who could not have a child for a long time and was very sad because of this.

Finally, her husband and she decided to adopt a child. However, she began to have such terrible headaches and nausea that they had to give up this idea. A little later, she went to see an analyst having had several very interesting dreams. The dream above came shortly after she became pregnant, i.e., after she had missed her first period.

It is not difficult to recognize an animus figure in the young man, the ghostlike companion who had apparently been accompanying the dreamer throughout her life. His Mephistophelean nature – that is, his seductive ambivalence – is revealed to her only at the end of the dream. He may well have promoted her intellectual rise and success in the legal profession, but perhaps at the cost of her femininity. One of the prerogatives of a lawyer is to be "right" – furnishing the animus with an ideal playground. Now that she has conceived a child and is turning a page in her life, the animus must disappear and make room for a new spirit of wisdom. This transition is terrifying, and without the powerful figure of the wise old man, who has "a venerable, old ... look of freshness" in his face, in whose "hands" she is – that is, whom she has to follow from now on – it would have been a nightmare instead of a dream. Her shudder signifies a genuine fear of God: she is struck with reverential awe, for the transition into the new form of life is fateful and irrevocable and will require a complete change in her spiritual attitude. The dreamer, at that time, had several other very powerful dreams that dealt with her instinctive femininity and the initiation into her new state of femininity. Thus, the unconscious assumed the task that, in primitive cultures, was performed by initiation rites: namely, the promotion of a change of attitude and the maturation process of a woman about to take on a new responsibility.

---

[550] This dream is quoted in; Carol Baumann, *Seelische Erlebnisse im Zusammenhang mit der Geburt, Eine Voruntersuchung.* Sonderausdruck: *Schweizerische Zeitschrift für Psychologie*, Bd. 16, Heft 2

7. The Child

Irmgard Bosch

The motif of the child in pregnancy dreams is, of course, a pivotal theme. "Motif" (Lat. *movere* = "to move") signifies motivation or drive. The child is both the goal and the content of pregnancy as well as the literal content in the pregnant belly.

Although we are primarily going to consider the child in the light of pregnancy, it is one of the most common symbols worldwide and like every true symbol, its meaning is of great complexity, working on different layers and pointing at once forward to the future and backward into the past. Although we mostly associate with it its promising aspect of renewal, the motif of the child as an image of immaturity or childishness can equally be negative.

Countless fairy tales begin with the urgent desire of a couple to have a child and revolve around the child motif. The fairy tale often develops from a strong need for rejuvenation or renewal.

From a psychological standpoint, the link between the child motif and pregnancy is not as evident as it may seem, for it can relate to developmental aspects that may touch the dreamer's entire life. Men, too, can dream of birth and children. In German, we say, "that was a difficult birth or delivery" – meaning a difficult job or decision. Indeed, it is often hard to know whether a child-dream relates to a future child – i.e., a specific psychic development resulting from pregnancy – or a fundamental problem in the woman's life. As such, life and pregnancy are inextricably linked: the latter is now a part of life.

The problem of the "origin" of children is as great a mystery today as it has ever been. It continues to stimulate the human mind and imagination. First of all, it emerges in early childhood: "Where do babies come from?" The answer: "from mother's tummy" makes sense to children presumably without concretely understanding it. Behind that, the uncontested idea of heaven or paradise, as being the place where children originally come from, still remains true. Perhaps, too, the idea of "paradise" or heaven bears an unconscious resemblance with the security of the maternal womb.

Figure 48. Jesus as a child, blessing (Siena, ca. 14th cent.)

Allegorically speaking, the birth of humankind could be seen in terms of the dramatic expulsion scene from the Garden of Eden in the Jewish creation myth.[551]

Upon examining the myths of other cultures, we find that in the background of many traditions concerning the places of the origin and birth of man, lies predominantly the earth as *Terra Mater*. In Ancient Greece, for instance, Gaia was the primordial mother of all creatures. The birthplaces of the gods and of men were caves, the earth was matter (Adam) and Mother Earth fed her children with its springs. Already the earliest known rock carvings at cave entrances engraved by hunters in the Ice Age unmistakably represent female vulvae. We can find examples of this in the Dordogne, in France.[552] Traditions of entrances to the lap of Mother Earth have survived in numerous cultures and across the millennia – for example, the Zeus-cave on the island of Crete. Eastern European churches preserved this image in the birth of Christ. The ancient myth of Mother Earth can offer us consolation when we bury our beloved ones.

Another widespread belief is that children originate from the water. The knowledge of water as a source of all life is a primal experience of all creatures and is much older than humankind itself. We have already talked about the *Kindlibrunnen*, etc. in Chapter 3.1 and about the myth of the stork bringing the children from ponds, which has very ancient roots and is popular in various cultures (cf. Chapter 5.3).[553]

Let us now look at the following peculiar dream, which I believe addresses the question of "the origin of children" in a most significant way.

The dreamer is thirty-one years old, married and so far without children. Although the pregnancy has come unexpectedly, she gladly accepts it. A healthy child was born. The dreamer lives in South America – in the "New World," so to speak – which seems here to be of some relevance. The dream is reproduced below in a slightly abbreviated form.

Dream No. 122:

> From on high, I can see an old ship – a caravel – which approaches an ancient European city through a very narrow river whose waters are very deep and murky. The river is so narrow that I think the ship has just one direction: to keep going on further and further, with no chance to turn back.
>
> It's silent, gloomy and mysterious. Reaching a harbor, the ship comes alongside. There are ancient houses along the river banks, narrow and high like in Holland or Denmark.

---

[551] Ge. 3, 23
[552] Cf. Chapter 3.2.
[553] Some local names, such as *Kindlibach*, may derive from a place of a child murder kept secret.

The mystery continues. Now I'm on the anchored ship. Someone gives me a white-covered book and tells me I should write a title on it. I wish to open it, but I am deeply afraid. I look again at the white cover. Now it shows a title in golden letters: "The World of Children's Subconscious' Waters" or "The World of Children's Waters' Subconscious."

This dream reflects the ancient maternal symbol of "water" in the form of a narrow stream. The narrow passage evokes the image of the birth canal. There is no going back. The water is deep, dark and murky.

The quietly approaching ship, which is confined to one passage and direction, is again a maternal symbol, given the ship's belly and its feature of carrying. The same symbolism applies to *Kirchenschiff*, the German word for "nave," and to the English Christmas carol, "I Saw Three Ships Come Sailing In." On Christmas Day in the morning, a ship brings the Holy Family with the child to the shore. We can call the ship in our dream a "life-ship" in contrast to the "death-ship," which, according to Germanic legend, carried the deceased off to the sea.[554] The solar bark of the Egyptians is a life-ship which journeys through the nocturnal sea of death; and finally, there is Noah's Ark. In the above examples, the ship symbolizes being carried through a difficult or perilous passage in life. The caravel of our dream is steadily sailing nearer to the land of the living, which is here the "Old World" ("Holland or Denmark"). The scene, on the whole, seems to imply an occurrence of a deep feminine-maternal nature, such as the mysteriousness of pregnancy.

The dreamer, who is now on board the anchored vessel, in a mystical atmosphere, clearly states: "The mystery continues." Someone hands her a book with a white cover, asking her to write a title on it. She wants to open it, but does not dare. A sudden fear overcomes her: the content of the book could entail something terrifying.

It would appear that her dream-ego has an intuition of the unfathomable depths of the event and that the mystery is so great that any premature or ignorant thought could invoke tremendous danger, even death. The human language is inept to formulate the ungraspable. It is rather in the archetypal sphere that the dreamer has to look for an answer, in the "unentered, not to be entered" (Goethe, *Faust II*). The white book-cover is a blank sheet in the truest sense of the word. Perhaps one day its title will say something about the fate of her child – which she cannot anticipate under any circumstances. Its square shape could point to the proximity with the Self. Because she feels such an acute sense of alarm, as if she were standing on the edge of a precipice, she does not open the book.

Perhaps the golden letters appear on the book precisely because she has realized that it is a crucial moment. She reads on it: "The World of Children's

---

[554] Martin Ninck, *Wodan und germanischer Schicksalsglaube*, Jena, 1935, p. 137, p. 210

Subconscious' Waters" or "The World of Children's Waters' Subconscious" – a sequence of words not logically linked – in other words, a content that could not be expressed logically by any means. On the other hand, the golden letters reveal how immensely valuable it is. The dream characterizes the ancient image of the "waters of the unconscious," i.e., the mystery of the origin and the essence of children as something highly precious but mysterious – without, however, going as far as to unveil it.

I wonder whether each birth of a new child might not represent the novel and fresh element, the divine water that has to flow into the "Old World" or even, the superannuated world of Europe? The atmosphere and particularly the somewhat unintelligible end of the dream express for me or allude to the mystery of the origin of children but do not disclose it, for it will always remain a mystery, even at the age of genetics and biology. We cannot really claim to have surpassed St. John's knowledge (1 A.D.): "... but canst not tell whence it cometh, and whither it goeth: so is every one that is born of the Spirit." [555]

Just like having a real child, so dreaming of a child primarily addresses the issue of the perception of the new, unknown and also of an adequate attitude to it. At the same time, as the birth of the child draws nearer, we often recognize that we are dealing with something ancient and familiar, something we feel "has always existed."

As to the origin of children, the occurrence of the element of air in dreams is much less frequent – neither is the image common in the old traditions. The wind, on the other hand, that "bloweth where it listeth," was thought to be both fertilizer and a procreator. Ideas of the origin of children's souls lying in the heavens could also be derived from the wind as a carrier of seeds. [556]

As far as the elements go, there are even fewer dreams or fantasies about fire as a place of birth. In mythology, birth from fire is ascribed exclusively to the gods: for example, to Agni, the Hindu god of fire. The goddess Demeter, in charge of the upbringing of Demophon and wishing to make him immortal, held him over fire at night, burning away his mortal elements, so to speak. A spiritual quality was attributed to fire. [557]

The symbol of fire often means spirit (see the Chapter on Fire). This helps us to understand better Jesus' words concerning the (re)birth of man of "water and of the spirit" (St. John, 3, 5): in order to create a "new human being,"

---

[555] St. John, 3, 8

[556] Cf. also Dream No. 66, Chapter 5.3, of an eagle carrying a child in its beak

[557] The alchemical fiery processes, whose end product was designated "son," can be seen as purification processes. Their goal would be man's maturing to a new quality of "child-being" that does not imply being infantile. This would coincide with Jesus' words: "... Except ye be converted, and become as little children ..." (St. Matthew, 18, 3). Jung commented with regard to this that Jesus did not say "be children" but "become as children."

opposite worlds have to come together. This idea is familiar from Catholicism where the burning candle, dipped into the holy water font, symbolizes fire and water becoming one. Therefore, in Christian symbolism, the fiery element plays a major role in the creation of man.

The most eminent symbol of fire is the sun as symbolizing the origin of all life. In mythology, many tribes retrace their origin to the sun. The chief, including all of his tribal members, were "children of the sun." Let us, for a moment, try to imagine how one's feeling for life might be affected by this image.

During her third, unplanned pregnancy which had presented some health problems at the beginning and caused her to worry about an abortion, a woman dreamt:

Dream 123:

> *In one of the most impressive dreams of my life, I dreamt of a single image of a baby boy sitting in sunlight on a dirt road, playing in the sand. He was big, healthy and blue-eyed. A voice whispered in the dream: "This is the child." K. [the dreamer's husband] and I were overwhelmed with joy. – (I felt the decision to have the baby was made on the ground of my being – and, yes, it was a big, healthy, blue-eyed boy).*

Here, two opposite elements come together: sun rays on the child and the dirty road, a symbol of the earth's dust. A terse definition of the existence of a child (and of man in general for that matter): bathing in the warmth and light of the sun with the attention turned to the earth, heedless of dirt or dust. It is a positively encouraging image, and the dreamer perceived it as such. She interpreted it as a decision in favor of carrying the child to term, which had been made in the depths of her soul.

The following dream stems from a thirty-five-year-old teacher, who is eight months pregnant (and who had wished for this pregnancy).

Dream No. 123b:

> *My husband and I were in the bedroom, in the dark. The door opened, and a boy ran in the room. He was tall, lean. He crossed the room: he was the expression of life! He was lit by a sunbeam. We were bewildered!*

According to the dreamer, the slim boy looked like "the quintessence of life." The striking element in this image is the sunbeam, which is illuminating the child in the darkness of the night.

Another Nature image in myths – the tree – was also traditionally seen as a birthplace for children. There are numerous tales of a maternal tree or also of the devouring, entwining tree.[558]

As in myths and fairy tales, in dreams, too, children are frequently born from certain parts of the body. Athena, for example, was said to have been born from Zeus' head, which he had bid Hephaestus, the god of metals and metallurgy, to split open with an axe. This kind of midwifery was appropriate for the future warrior goddess, incarnating the belligerent soul of her father. She was armed with a spear and aegis (a kind of goat-skin breast plate) as she leapt from his head. Dionysus was born from the thigh of Zeus, inside of which he had been sewn and carried to term after his mother, Semele, at the sight of her divine lover, was consumed by the flames of her love for him (Zeus, the father of the child).

The dreamer of the following dream is twenty-four years old. She was seven months pregnant when she had this dream (at which point she was having health problems). A healthy child was finally born:

Dream No. 124:

> My child is born out of my left ear. It is painless for me, and the baby is healthy and normal.

Besides signifying a comforting aspect (don't be afraid, everything will be all right), the easy and painless delivery "from the ear," might also indicate that for this woman the hearing sense is particularly fruitful. The ear is the entrance gate to something that has developed in her and that now sees the light – the "fruit of the hearing." Consequently, the child is healthy. To hear means also to listen, or eventually, to obey: the dream image is reminiscent of old paintings representing the Annunciation to Mary where the word of God or the Holy Ghost – depicted as a golden thread – of God the Father in majesty is conveyed by a dove to the ear of the kneeling Mary. Mary replied: "Let what you have said be done," whereupon she gave birth to the Christ child.

Whether the dream relates to a real child or to a spiritual fruit, we cannot discern. However, since the dream appeared during pregnancy, I believe it is legitimate to see both aspects.

Some pregnancy dreams in our collection contain the motif of an ugly or unsuitable place where a child is born or found. The following dreams speak of the often awkward arrival of a child on the earth.

Dream No. 125:

> The baby is born, in an odd place, perhaps here, on the ground floor of home. He is in the cradle, dressed. He nearly speaks to his Dad. He is healthy. We (husband, E., first child, baby and me) go by car on a trip to "England" (there is a big store, where I tend to forget time and everything, sometimes I buy useless things). The car is full. I have to feed the baby. My breast is full, and I have hardly place to do it. ... [abbreviated][559]

---

[558] C.G. Jung, CW 5, § 367; see also Chapter 4.2

Figure 49. "The Birth," Pierro della Francesca (1439-1492)

This dream describes a typical situation of an unsuitable place for delivery and multiple problems for the mother and child (lack of space in the car, a huge, crowded department store, full breasts, no place to feed the baby).

Distress at the time of birth or after birth is an archetypal image with which we are familiar from the birth of Christ. It bears upon the deepest layers of human experience. "There was no room for them in the inn." It is as if two opposite worlds collide at the time of the birth of a human child: a spiritual-psychic one and a hard, perplexing, earthly one (call it what you may) – which almost inevitably creates distress and is very often a serious hazard.

Although giving birth on the floor has again become one of the preferred methods today, our dreamer was not prepared for this – hence, it was perceived as "odd," or perhaps silly and inconvenient. Nevertheless, the child is healthy and surprisingly precocious.[560] But then, all kinds of problems set in for the mother, as if she hardly had enough room in her life for the delivery and the child!

[559] Cf. dream interpretation No. 44, Chapter 4.2

360

The dream we are discussing turns out to be an overture to a long and detailed initiation dream in the course of which the woman is being introduced to her immense potential for development. It would appear that a trying beginning must simply be a part of it! The child itself, as well as the novel seed in her, as it were, must begin their growth from below, so as to prepare the ground first.

This idea is reflected in the image of the floor as a birthplace. It reminds me of the countless artistic representations of the birth of Christ in which the infant Jesus, contrary to the evangelical text of the Story of Christmas, lies naked and uncovered on the ground in the stable with sometimes only a minimal amount of straw.[561] I believe these paintings communicate the archetypal idea that Jesus' arrival on the earth ("odd place") presupposed landing in the pitilessness of the real world. The presence of the animals, the scanty barn or the somber cave are further explicit images of the arrival of the human (and divine) child.

When the circumstances of the arrival of a child are very disadvantageous, it is surprising how many compensatory impulses the unconscious may bring forth. From the remarks about of the following case, we know that the attitude towards the forthcoming birth was extremely negative. The child was unwelcome for both its father and the dreamer's mother and all the rest of the family. The dreamer was alone with her wish for a child – a very difficult situation! Her first pregnancy had ended, for health reasons, in an abortion. Her second pregnancy was also marred by serious complications, and she had to deliver by Cesarean section. She dreamt:

Dream No. 126:

> I dreamed of a little girl who told me she loved me. She told me I should do her no harm. (That child resembled greatly my expected daughter G.)

Dream No. 127:

> I was going to live alone near Gaia's father's house. From afar he watched me, ever afraid to come closer. I was doing Gaia's room. Her bed looked like Jesus' straw cradle.

It would appear that the dreamer's unconscious stands very much behind her pregnancy despite the above-mentioned problems. The unconscious gives her strength from the very depths of her soul. Let us regard the little girl as a

---

[560] An unusually fast child development and outstanding abilities of the infant are archetypal images and occur in countless legends of heroic and divine children, e.g., Hermes, Heracles.

[561] Painting by Hugo van der Goes, "The Adoration of the Shepherds," Triptychon Portinari, Florence, Uffizi

symbol of the Self. She already feels close to her mother. This love, emanating from her own psychic center, equips the dreamer with a means of coping with the pressures issuing from outside. The child, whose mother she is about to become, shows her the potential she has for self-realization at this period of her life.

In the second dream, the dream-ego prepares for the child to live in an adequate environment. The unconscious sees a religious sense in this birth alluded to in the similarity of the infant's bed with the baby Jesus' manger. It should be noted that it is the dreamer's unconscious drawing the parallel with Jesus, and were this a conscious thought, she would have to be careful not to nurture too high expectations of her "heavenly child." ... Now, since the image was produced in her unconscious under very adverse circumstances, the dream can be interpreted on a compensatory level, effecting comfort and encouragement.

The same woman had another dream some time later that seems like a continuation along the same line:

Dream No. 128:

> *Two days before G. was born I dreamed that Francis of Assisi was bless-ing me and her.*[562]

Here, the way her unconscious perceives and expresses her attitude towards the child and her destiny is even clearer: "The world will be against you. You shall be poor and lonely, but St. Francis, who loves the poor, gives you and your child his blessing." In other words, the dire straits you are in are under his blessing; therefore you will go unharmed.

A child growing in a woman's body generally causes her (particularly if the pregnancy is wanted) to introvert and to enter a new and satisfying phase of introspection. Fundamentally, intuitions and genuine visions are no different from dreams. However, nowadays it is much more difficult to summon the strength and flexibility to allow even a temporary retreat from a busy life and to permit a woman's thoughts and feelings to revolve around the child. For, the attitude required of women today is dominated by studies or a profession and is oriented accordingly towards the outer world. But positive fantasies can still prepare something like a warming cloak for the child. Expectations set too high or negative fantasies, on the other hand, can have a destructive or restric-tive effect on the child's development.

Sometimes a certain kind of fatigue during pregnancy causes an *abaisse-ment du niveau mental*, which facilitates introversion. In former times, intro-version used to come more naturally with the kind of daily tasks young women carried out involving much more routine work, handiwork or cooking. It

---

[562] This dream is also mentioned in Chapter 6, No. 121.

allowed room for a certain amount of day-dreaming and relaxation, which are forsaken in a professional life accompanied by hectic activity and traffic. Women would benefit from a return "to the old ways," that is, a general and natural acceptance of taking more time and rest during the enormous hormonal and spiritual-psychic changes pregnancy entails. By the same token, it should be considered a "time of normalcy," not involving exaggerated indulgence either.

Despite the tension of our times, women continue to have intuitions and dreams during pregnancy regarding the child's gender, for instance. (Perhaps this will become increasingly rare with modern technology, e.g., ultrasound, etc.) Although such psychic experiences do not always turn out to be true, astonishingly enough, they often do. The dreamer who saw St. Francis of Assisi blessing herself and her child (Nos. 194, 195) mentions in her commentary that everyone had predicted a boy: she alone was certain it would be a girl – "for I could feel what was inside me" – which turned out to be correct. From a symbolical point of view, we could say that, in addition, the girl of her dream was also her own feminine being, which she could feel growing inside her.

The following dreamer hears a voice, pronouncing in a determined tone:

Dream No. 129:

> *"You are going to have a girl ..."*

– after which (and already in the dream), she stopped seeking a name for a boy. The dream turned out to be right.

Dream No. 130 (at four months' pregnancy):

> *I look down at my bare stomach. At first, I think I see the baby's foot pushing against the inner wall and pushing outward. As I look closer, I realize that I can see the outlines of the baby's face on my skin – the eyes, nose and mouth. The baby is about three inches long and so new and young. Its eyes are closed. I'm amazed and deeply moved.*

This dream suggests a loving introversion on the part of the woman resulting in an (in)sight into the child's being that deeply moves the dreamer.

The phenomenon of pregnant women discovering a name for their child in a dream or semi-conscious state by suddenly hearing or simply knowing it, is actually quite common.

On the theme of an inexplicable knowledge of the unconscious, we received the following report from a psychotherapist.

Dream No. 131:

> *A woman told me that, when she was two months pregnant, she suddenly began dreaming in black-and-white, i.e., did not see any colors any more in her dreams. Shortly afterwards, her doctor diagnosed the death of the fetus. The same thing happened to her in her fourth pregnancy, which also ended in a miscarriage.*

The expectant woman had realized, before she knew of the death of the fetus, that she was suddenly dreaming in black-and-white. Colors are life signs. It is possible that subliminal changes – e.g., of the metabolism in the womb – influence dreams. It is certainly impressive how clearly the unconscious expressed itself: it mourned the life that had been extinguished.

It is very common that pregnant women see themselves or the child they are carrying exposed to terrible threats and injuries. This has been a continuous theme throughout the dreams we have dealt with in this book. Most of us have had dreams describing a terrible failure (which, in reality, then turned out differently – e.g., failing the exam of the next day, missing a train before an important appointment, etc.), and we immediately tend to feel that these must be bad omens. Pregnant women can become extremely anxious when they have had bad dreams. The present study aims at providing some guidelines to try to understand these dreams better and to experience them with less fear.

I do not believe that certain widespread collective apprehensions regarding the future constitute the underlying reason for the terrifying imagery appearing in pregnancy dreams. Although a general negative or apprehensive attitude towards the future of humankind may have some influence on the dream life, what in fact happens is that dreams tend to describe the "other side" – that is, they tend to compensate for the conscious ego. In the context of birth and childhood, images of perils and death have always existed in good times as well as in bad times – universally. Indeed, it is as if imperilment and destruction are as much a part of the "image" of the infant as is the bliss of a new beginning.

Death and birth have always been close neighbors. In legends, fairy tales and the mythical imagination – that is, in the collective unconscious and dreams of all cultures – extreme forsakenness and exposure to life's dangers are extremely common among tales about children and birth. It seems both fundamental and natural. Heroic and divine children are especially prone to this fate. Moses as an infant, Krishna as a child and Zeus, Dionysos and Hermes as children are all said to have been exposed to extreme danger. In the Bible, we can read St. Matthew's report of the baby Jesus.[563] The imperilment of the child is archetypal.[564]

---

[563] Matthew, 2, 16 f

What, or mythologically speaking, who puts the obstacles in the way of the growth of a child? In myths, it is predominantly the reigning king's hostility towards a potential successor (Freud described this manifest dynamic as the "Oedipus complex"), even though rejuvenation is equally necessary and desirable.

It is surprising how often an oracle and prophesy, or fixed, negative preconceived ideas and opinions, play a crucial role. Examples of this are the birth oracles of the myths of Perseus and Oedipus, and not least, the Evangelist St. Matthew's book.[565] Was it not the fateful question of the three Wise Men from the East asking: "Where is he that is born King of the Jews?" instilling in King Herod the fear for his throne and making of him a child murderer?!

The Greek legends about the very first gods are continuously interspersed with the embittered enmity between a forefather and his own children, who only survive thanks to the tireless arrangements and tricks of the respective foremothers (Rhea, Gaia), in order to eventually found a new lineage: it is precisely the dominant masculine power that is out to prevent a "new" lineage. This kind of fatherly self-protection is destructive and often ends in tragedy.

In ordinary life, too, a daughter may be unlucky and have an "old king" for a father, who is overpowering and hostile to novelty and interferes with her own, new impulses. This is how a woman develops a negative animus threatening her from within and impairing and rejecting her femininity as well as her creative ideas. Therefore, the "war of the sexes" is primarily an inner problem – a fight within woman herself.[566]

However, the child's mythological fiend is not only the "old king," or psychologically, the ruling consciousness resisting renewal. Feminine figures after the child's life or out to prevent a birth occur at least as frequently in the countless tales about a raging Great Mother, who is threatening, killing or devouring (e.g., the Indian goddess Kali or the Greek Hera).[567] In folklore, this phenomenon of the imperilment of the child is often symbolized by the image of the stepmother or the witch. This power usually works secretly or subliminally. It does not so much represent the ruling consciousness as the dark maternal side, an unconscious struggle for power, untamed passions, but above all, jealousy.[568] The effect of unbridled, overpowering maternal love is psychologically dangerous, too, as may be illustrated by expressions such as –

---

[564] Cf. C.G. Jung's detailed commentary in: *Einführung in das Wesen der Mythologie*, Karl Kerényi, Amsterdam, 1941, p. 103 ff

[565] Mt., 2, 2

[566] On the question of the succession of the old king, see M.-L. von Franz, *Interpretation of Fairy Tales*, Shambhala, Boston, 1996, pp. 52-4

[567] Cf. Chapter 9

[568] Gotthilf Isler, *Die Überwindung der Hexe*, Vortrag auf der Brunnenburg/Südtirol, unpublished manuscript, 1988. Cf. also Chapter "Mother"

"I love you so much that I could eat you up ..." – an unmistakable manifestation of the "devouring mother."

In the Middle Ages, "to see something inadvertently" [*Versehen*] was considered to be a serious potential hazard. It was believed to have a detrimental "imprint" on the pregnant woman through a sudden shock at the sight of a wild animal, a fire or an accident, or simply through the effect of an "evil eye." People had thus invented various means to prevent any subsequent bad influence on the child, such as antidotes, sayings or amulets. Even present-day medical research, prenatal experiences and impressions of the embryo are taken into account again. Many pregnant women have again become aware of the fact that their unborn child can already hear and feel.

In times past, reason for fear of any kind of damage to pregnant women or to their children was immense compared to today: the mortality rate among infants and young children, as well as of women in childbirth, was shockingly high. Looking at the genealogical table of W. A. Mozart, for example, illustrates this: of seven brothers and sisters, only Mozart and Nannerl survived the first year; of Mozart's own six children, also only two survived. How much sorrow and suffering must have been inflicted upon these families and especially upon the women!

Although it would be difficult to say anything universally valid about the most frequent hazard to the life of a child – namely, the intentional termination of a pregnancy – the dreams in our study clearly testify to a compensatory response of the unconscious. In the public consciousness, abortion is without doubt a highly controversial issue.[569] I would like to compare three dreams that stem from a time of an intentional pregnancy termination. Perhaps they can show that the unconscious reacts subjectively to the problem of a conscious decision to abort in a variety of different ways, although an objective aspect seems to be present nevertheless.

The following dream was dreamt just before or in the first days of pregnancy. The woman decided not to have the child. That is all the information we received.

Dream No. 132:

> *She stood by the washbasin and was washing a little sack filled with soft stones, pebbles or rock fragments, in order to keep them moist. Among them was a bone splinter. She knew these were parts of the baby. She was unable to fit the parts together.*

It would seem that the dreamer's unconscious apprehends the situation as extremely conflicting – possibly even before the occurrence of the supposedly

---

[569] This difficult problem is discussed more at length in: Eva Pattis, *Gorgo 22*, Milano, 1992, pp. 39-53

unwanted pregnancy. If, in the dream, the woman soaks the sack of stones and the bone splinter in water, it means that her dream-ego tries to keep the "parts of the child" moist, thereby perhaps making it capable of staying alive (or at least, not letting them dry out and die). The dream-ego might have hoped for life, but "she was unable to fit the parts together": the experiment is unsuccessful. Water has to do with feelings; according to the view of the Ancients, it is the very element of man's soul. Tears are made of water, and "keeping moist" also corresponds to the feminine YIN-principle of the Chinese *I Ching*. I perceive the action as an expression of an integration of feelings; i.e., the dream-ego is trying to unite something and create a potential for growth. The final sentence – "she was unable to fit the parts together" – suggests that her activity at the washbasin is not merely of a cleansing nature.

While a conscious decision against having the child had been taken, the dream also illustrates that something, to which the feminine principle would naturally aspire, has gone wrong. Thus, it shows the intense psychic effort of bringing something together that is in pieces and confused. The unconscious impulse is temporarily lost. The conscious ego could, however, accommodate and further develop it in terms of a potential transformation, which would certainly amount to a positive development or growth of the personality.

The following dream describes a very different situation. It is a recurring nightmare that was dreamt here for the seventh time, prior to a pregnancy termination:

Dream No. 133:

> I am walking in the woods late at night. There is a full moon, and I can see my way easily; nevertheless, it is frightening because of the play of the shadows from the trees caused by the moon. I have the feeling that I am being followed, and am concerned for my baby. After a time I see a wolf behind me, a long way off, and notice that he is followed by other wolves. The wolf pack keeps its distance, but continues to follow me. I am afraid for my baby and begin to walk faster. The wolves walk faster, too. I begin to run. The wolves begin to run, too. They get closer and closer and, at last encircle me, howling horribly, their red eyes shining in the dark. I hold my baby in the air, high above my head, screaming as I do so.
> Then the wolves attack and knock me down, the baby falls and is devoured by the wolves, while I lie there watching …
> Then I awaken, screaming "My baby, my baby! What have you done with my baby!"

Described above is the ghostly hour of the soul and a heart-wrenching tragedy, unfolding in a particularly distinct and complete way. There is nothing cozy or romantic about the nocturnal woods nor in the pale moonlight; all things here present in Nature are black and cast black shadows onto the dreamer's path. The woods and darkness symbolize a deep layer of the unconscious. The full moon shines eerily; it is the light of the night rendering the unconscious processes perceptible.

The moon and the moon-goddess, Luna, have been feminine symbols since beyond memory: the phases of the moon rule Nature's fertility. The sprouting and growth of plants (the sowing- and harvest-calendar) as well as the processes in a woman's body (menstruation) are influenced by the changes of the moon. The variability of the moon is a primordial image of Nature's cycle of growth and decay and beyond that, of changing feelings and states and of secrecy and concealment. The moon is equally strongly associated with illness and death (new moon) as well as with the world of the spirits. A clock working "according to the moon" is something irrational. In rational terms, this simply does not work or at least would be totally imprecise.

When, as is the case in our dream, the moon is full, the lunar force is particularly strong (spring tides). The moon, as a perfectly round disk, can be perceived as a symbol of the feminine Self. Therefore, the dream scene is of great portent for our dreamer. We could say that her situation is being illuminated entirely from a feminine standpoint.

She is carrying her baby and is worried for its safety. On a subjective level, she is not only carrying the expected child but rather also a newly created and apparently unconsciously valued, precious seed of her psychic development, which seems to coincide with the possibility of becoming a mother.

But the uncanny content of the woods at nighttime – which are the psychic ground available to her – is not kindly disposed towards this developmental step. It takes the concrete form of a pack of wolves following the dreamer from behind and from a distance – at first, always from the same distance, but as soon as she begins to run, they follow suit, as if they were a part of her. Subjectively, they are indeed unconscious parts of her psychic inventory. "From behind" not only means "from the shade of the unconscious," but also from the past. Something horrible pursues her that she has left behind and that her dream-ego also wishes to leave far behind.

Who are the wolves? Women and children have always dreaded them. The wolf was always a symbol of evil. Adults used to frighten children by saying: "Be a good little girl or boy – otherwise the wolf will come to fetch you!" Our imagination has stored several images of this, e.g., the dreadful image of Hecate persecuting women in labor and their infants at night, howling, or the idea of the werewolves or witches that were after little children. One of the most conspicuous devourers is the well-known wolf disguised as grandma in "Little Red Riding Hood." The wolf is an image of voracity, and in particular, the voracity for life and young blood, which is closely related to the dark mother.

The most powerful negative image of the wolf in Europe is Fenris, the wolf of Northern mythology: Fenris is a son of Loki, the fiend both of the gods and of humankind; he menaces the entire world. According to the Edda, during the final battle, Fenris will devour the sun, and the "wolf age" will commence when the world comes to an end in the glacial cold. Once the voraciousness of beasts of prey becomes rampant, what else is left in the world, apart from a ghastly, glacial cold?

The pack of wolves in the present dream approaches steadily from behind. The "red eyes shining in the dark" are reminiscent of Cerberus, the insatiable dog, who guards the entrance to Hades. The dreamer holds her baby high up above her head – a gesture indicating that she holds the highest regard, respect and love for it. She tries to rescue it from the hounds. But the wolves attack, pull her to the ground and tear the child to pieces while she is lying there, watching it happen.

Our dreamer appears to be completely paralyzed in the face of the attacking wolves, or subjectively speaking, vis-à-vis the murderous aspect within herself and her own unconscious voraciousness. Her lying there passively while the wolves are tearing her child to bits and her cry – "What have you done to my baby!" – powerfully illustrate this. Although she is clearly horrified and desperate about the child, she remains completely impotent in the face of the predatory instincts and can only passively watch them.

The dream can be taken for a warning, saying something along the lines of: "It is as if you were haunted by a wolfish voracity and have passively to watch the destruction of the very thing you deem highest. If you will not definitively change your attitude, the devouring aspect hidden in the depths of your soul will literally overwhelm you. The dreamer's conscious ego could listen to the dream-ego's horrified reaction and recognize the alarming situation not only of the child but of her whole personality. It seems to me as though the unconscious made a desperate attempt by producing this dream. It has not given up yet.

The next dream came with a detailed commentary from the dreamer. She was nineteen years old at the time and had just been deceived by her boyfriend, who had deliberately made a hole in the condom because he wanted to force her to marry him. When the dreamer learned of this trickery, and in addition found out that he was having an affair with another girl, she immediately decided she would have an abortion. She was fully aware of the fact that her religious parents would throw her out of her home and permanently ostracize her, which is what happened. Her father never recovered from this blow, and her mother continued to reproach her for her crime for many years. In spite of all this, the dreamer wrote: "This dream affected me so powerfully during that desperate and chaotic time of hardship and loneliness that it actually kept me alive." Later she married another man and had two children with him and in addition, even adopted several children.

Dream No. 134: [570]

I dreamed that I saw four tulips. Two of them were yellow and two were red. They were completely closed and in their bud-state. They were arranged in a square with their stems meeting below in a bunch. A voice said: "Look!" I looked carefully at the buds, and while doing so, they slowly began to unfold: the green encasing petals pulled back and allowed the golden and red flowers to emerge fully. As the buds opened in this way, the light changed, too. An increasingly stronger, golden light from above appeared until the four tulips were fully open and stood in all their splendor in the full, golden light that flooded them. I was astonished and amazed at this beautiful sight and asked: "What does this mean?" The voice replied: "This means light and life." It was said in a tone of calm reassurance and caused a sense of peaceful certainty with which I awoke from the anaesthetic.

Some additional information from the dreamer is: Having told this dream to my gynecologist, he said to me: "Keep this in you memory. Whatever it may mean, it is a good dream. When you confront your family, think of this dream, for once they find out what happened, things may get rough for you."

A morally discordant decision creates a kind of chaos. However, the dream manifests an unconscious psychic process going on in the dreamer. The words "light and life" suggest that the dreamer is in full possession of the powers she had thought were swamped forever. The four flowers, arranged in a mandala unfolding in the golden light, are undoubtedly an image belonging to the personality's regulating center, i.e., the Self. As Jung frequently emphasized, images of the Self tend to appear at moments of grave or seemingly hopeless crises in life.

The dream image is an anticipation of a usually slow development towards the central goal of one's existence taking place internally. In the case of this particular dreamer, it tells us that even though she has decided not to carry the child to term, her individuation process is underway. Furthermore, we can infer that the dreamer's later life has been shaped by the traumatic experience of the abortion and that (interestingly) other children were to benefit from all this. Confronted with the extremely painful and distressing nature of the problem – whether to unnaturally interrupt a pregnancy or let it proceed normally, the circumstances fatefully woven into each individual's fabric of life that determine the outcome are always unique.

The following horrifying dream comes from a twenty-three-year-old woman, who is twenty-eight weeks pregnant. There were no health problems, and her first child, a healthy girl, was born on time.

---

[570] This dream has been discussed in Chapter 4.1, No. 33

Dream No. 135:

> *I am together with some tourist-guides in a foreign country where canni-*
> *bals live. I am their victim. Before they decapitate me, I am told that they*
> *will later eat my unborn child.*

The dream is set in a "foreign country where cannibals live." It is not clear whether the tour guides are also in the hands of the cannibals or was it they who took the dreamer there? "Tourist-guides" represent, on the subjective level, an interest and volition impulse aiming at getting acquainted with the unknown.

I assume that being a "tourist" signifies a semiconscious interest (initiated by the animus) in exploring a hitherto unconscious domain, rather like Safaris or expeditions. However, "the child is unborn," i.e., psychologically the conditions – that is, maturity and a capacity to deal with the elementary, primitive world – have not been prepared yet. A journey into the innermost realm is certainly timely during pregnancy, as we have already seen several times. However, unless the ego-organization is sufficiently strong, being over-whelmed from the depths can involve hazards, such as a pregnancy-psychosis. The journey of the dream is too perilous; the unborn child's place is in human-ity and not in the jungle.

The primitive powers of the unconscious are described as perfectly inhu-man – wanting to decapitate the dream-ego – to make it "headless," as it were – and eat the unborn child. In other words, these primitive powers want to annihilate the new life that has yet to differentiate and realize itself. This dream describes a serious personal risk. It would appear that the dreamer has immersed herself too deeply in the archetypal sphere – was she seduced by the tour guides? – and reached the periphery of the human in an archaic-inhuman world, where she and her unborn baby are exposed to immense danger.

Like the Great Mother Nature, the unconscious itself perpetually brings forth life and devours it again in the natural way of renewal. The individual, however, the human differentiation into consciousness perceives this as fun-damentally precarious. The new, still fragile life is being swallowed back. Dreams are a psychic reality. Therefore, the force of the "nightmare" will not be broken because it is a dream, but rather because life goes on offering new chances every day.

However, judging by the dream, deep inside of her it is shaky and upset, so that there is a concrete danger of her becoming psychologically devoured. The powers of the "dark continent," i.e., of the collective unconscious, can be inhuman, and dangerous, so long as the ego is not consolidated or prepared for this type of journey. The shaman venturing on the soul-journey must be equal to the dark powers; so must the medical doctor and every human ego. As we have seen, a curious but naïve Safari-attitude is insufficient. The unborn child – that is, the future potential for growth – is put at risk.

Nevertheless, our dreamer seems to possess an indomitable urge for transformation and rebirth.

The following dream reflects her psychic condition very lucidly, which is why I feel it should be added here, though it does not contain a child motif. She had the dream at 33 weeks, 4 weeks after the one above.

Dream No. 136:

> *I am visiting Sicily. Together with my old schoolmates, my husband and I go for an excursion to an ancient, sacred mudpool (Taormina). We bathe, and we enjoy it. Somehow it is difficult for me to get into the pool. I think my husband is careless when he jumps into the water. Later, all of us are chased away. We hide behind a fence, and we are not caught.*

Here, the desire to be in touch with the deepest layers of the soul has gained a less daredevil form: The dreamer enjoys a bath in a sacred mudpool – a stark contrast to a trip to the land of cannibals. Her husband and she plunge into a chthonic renewal-bath, as did the Romans in honor of Demeter, the fertility goddess. The company of old schoolmates indicates that it is appropriate in terms of their status. Those of us who have been in a mudbath or bog lake can sympathize with the exquisite pleasure one can derive, as if experiencing a primal state. Animals love mudbaths, too: they cause a feeling of being reborn, and I believe the central issue of this dream series is rebirth.

What was missing in the preceding dream – an important boundary line – is finally manifest in this dream. The husband, an animus figure, jumps into the murky mudpool, unprotected, which the dream-ego now finds irresponsible: the dream-ego is right, too! The ending scene clearly reinforces this feeling: Enough is enough, so to speak; everyone is being chased away but manages to hide behind a fence without being "caught." The fence protects them. It is a boundary.

I believe that "bathing in a mudpool" is a most apt image of pregnancy, suggesting a kind of initiation into a Nature-bound, chthonic stage as well as into a kind of self-protection: respectfully putting a boundary line between ourselves and the non-human, archetypal aspects of the Great Mother Nature. Jung perceived the entire unconscious – including the collective unconscious – as an unfathomable realm of Nature. Seen in this light, such dreams teach us that to "become a part of Nature" is far from being merely harmless or romantic.

Dreams of pregnant women produce a great variety of other fatal menaces to the child. Those cases where the origins clearly lie with the mother, e.g., the motif of letting a child starve to death or die of cold, will be discussed in the chapter entitled "Mother."

Dream No. 137:

> ... *The child was waxen and stiff, but each time I picked it up and held it in my hands, it became quite lively.*

Little explanation is needed here. All of the "manual work" caring for an infant involves a great potential for well-being and contentment. Bodily contact with the child will generally help to overcome an initial fear and alienation towards the newborn baby. Feeling the skin and the limbs of the infant can engender a deep feeling of happiness resembling a kind of homecoming. It is possible that it invokes memories of the mother's own childhood.

When we pick the baby up and hold it in our hands, we automatically and with a natural sense of responsibility direct our attention and affection to the new being. These are life-promoting gestures.

Dream No. 138:

> *A newborn child is being taken away from its mother and tied to the leg of a strange old lady. When the mother can eventually see her baby after three days, its skin is pale and on the point of turning blue. The dreamer knows that the reason for this is the separation from her. Therefore, she urgently wants to have the child back and to be in close physical contact with it.*

Again there is the problem of separation or distance between the mother and child that apparently makes the baby feel cold, as it were. Being tied to the old lady's leg deprives it of a sufficient amount of maternal warmth. On the subjective level, it means that something within the mother is like an old lady whose legs feel like lead with the weight of the child; that is, the child is a handicap. However, the dream-ego rightly claims more contact with the child!

Dream No. 139:

> *A baby lies on the floor. One looks for help.*

There seems to be a discrepancy (contrary to Dream No. 125) between the helpless child on the floor and an unwillingness or inability to do the appropriate thing, namely, to pick the child up. If the dreamer herself does not pick up the child, but "one looks for help," she or the pregnant woman has not yet established a relationship with the child. On a subjective level, the dream image could symbolize a deep fear of being abandoned and a desperate cry for help in her own, still relatively undeveloped and weak unconscious personality: the baby on the floor in need of help is she herself. It is therefore possible that the dream unveils a time in her early childhood when she "lay flat" in her own development which, according to more recent theoretical knowledge, could have resulted in a "narcissistically injured personality" that is incapable of normal emotional reactions.

Pregnancy commonly constellates early childhood fears of abandonment, and psychotherapeutic help is sometimes indicated, particularly in order to ensure that the child will not be used as a substitute for all those things we were deprived of in our own young life. It is reassuring that the dream clearly announces that help will be sought.

The dreamer of the following dream is forty years old and two months pregnant. She has been married for six years, is a judge by profession, and has a first son aged five. The pregnancy had been planned.

Dream No. 140:

> *She turned over herself, on the floor the open-mouthed head of a baby ran after her.*

We can interpret this dream on either the subjective or objective level. Objectively, it may refer to the expected, physical child who, for the moment, consists of a mere "head" in the woman's imagination, which seems to run after her, wanting something from her. In her mind, the child is only a "head," i.e., a pitiful phantom, or a kind of intellectual child theory that persecutes her.

The subjective level, on the other hand, "... conceives all the figures in the dream as personified features of the dreamer's own personality."[571] Something coming "from behind" psychologically means that it belongs to the shadow or is the shadow itself. In analytical psychology, the shadow represents those constituents in the personal unconscious that could reach consciousness provided we could see them. However, these contents usually remain in the dark and would create pain and shame, as well as a loss of self-esteem, were they illuminated by consciousness. It is for this very reason that we instinctively tend to keep these items hidden from ourselves. A major part of the work in analysis is dedicated to coming to terms with the shadow. If the effort is successful, the personality can heal.

The difficulty in recognizing the shadow is also expressed by the Greek word *metanoia* indicating a radical turn-around, as John the Baptist had demanded it.[572] The burden of life is lifted after the turn-around, i.e., once the shadow aspects have been acknowledged.

"She turned over," it says in this dream. Perhaps pregnancy enabled her to fulfill this psychic "turn-around or turning over to the other side" when she was "on the floor," too, so to speak. But what a horrifying sight must she endure: the head of an infant running after her, open-mouthed!

Subjectively, as we have already said, these are all aspects of her own personality: i.e., the turning over or around, the wretched baby head on the floor and its desperate running after her from behind her back. It looks as if

---

[571] C.G. Jung, CW 8, § 509, Bollingen Foundation, N.Y., 1960
[572] Mt. 3, 8; Lu. 3, 8

she is being persecuted by an infantile, bodiless spirit. The baby head has its mouth wide open, as if to scream or to say that it is starving. The bodiless head is full of deficits. All this has little to do with the real child: it is a part of the dreamer herself!

"Head-spirits" appear in many folktales, legends and fairy tales. They are usually frightening and menacing. Owing to their grave deficit, i.e., deprived of a body (like all spirits and specters), they often look for a baby they can inhabit, to be close to a human and to upset him or her out of revenge. Because of their incorporality, they are not tangible, and our dreamer, the judge, was therefore unaware of their existence.

Marie-Louise von Franz interpreted a fairy tale from the circum-polar tribes (Eskimos) in which a timid, man-despising girl loves a handsome head of a young man that she takes into bed with her and has wonderful conversations with. She does not know that he is the moon spirit. The girl's father does not see any "use for a son without a body who could not hunt for us when we are old!"[573] The father wounds him with a meat skewer, then throws the head out onto a rubbish heap. The girl loves her head so dearly and is so devoted to him, though, that she leaves home and follows him to the moon. Never again does she return to the earth, and she turns into a spider. She begins to "spin" and turns into a spinster.

Among Eskimos, and also among African tribes, people believed in the existence of such heads rolling about as skulls and causing damage. Sometimes they are departed ones that cannot find peace because they died unjustly and have not yet been avenged. Skull cults were widely practiced, and they are supposed to exist still today in remote regions of Borneo and in parts of India. The skull, according to these beliefs, contains the essence of man, that is, his spirit. For this reason, too, skulls were used for prophesy.

Considering the baby's head's rolling along in isolation, it leaves an impression of a split-off personality component (complex) craving for acceptance, or integration into the woman's life. If she continues to run away, it can overcome her from the back. Alternatively, it can die by falling ever deeper into the unconscious and producing inexplicable symptoms from there.

This type of incorporeal, to the highest degree one-sided and unconscious head-dominance in a woman, we refer to as animus possession. An animus-possessed woman is unconsciously driven by rigid, mostly negative opinions and judgments (cf. the Chapter "Animus"). At the same time, however, she can be haunted by a secret and childish, even an excessive longing for love and security.

In our dream, the mouth of the baby-head is open, or hungry. It wants to live and be fed and noticed by its cries. It took a turn of 180 degrees – that is,

[573] Marie-Louise von Franz, *The Feminine in Fairy Tales*, Spring Publications, Zurich, 1972, pp. 95-96

an actual metanoia (which was only possible thanks to her pregnancy) – for our dreamer to look behind her back and notice the helpless being (= a part of her Self) running after her.

In terms of compensation, we can assume that the conscious life of this woman is marked by success and esteem, which is in stark contrast to the grisly picture of the baby-head. Hence, it will be that much more difficult for her to admit the ghastly baby spirit. Turning over in the dream has enabled her to see her shadow. Therefore, there is a real chance that she can outgrow the persistent infantility through the relationship with her child.

Dream No. 141 (around the time of conception):

> *People got together for a seminar. There was a large building nearby, and we went there. It turned out to be a tall, spacious hall and at the far end of it, there was something like a tabernacle. I remembered that in earlier dreams, I had been here and had always been sneaking around a very fascinating but dangerous center in the shape of a woman or man. Now the hall was being prepared for some social event.*
> *I remembered that formerly the mystery of the room was at the entrance of the other end, but when I went there, the mystery was gone. A few people in the group wanted me to give them a kiss. The last one of them brought a child with him, to whom I gave a very affectionate cuddle. It came into my bed and asked for a tear in its skin to be sown up. It looked like a tear in a flower. I didn't dare to touch it.*

The tall and spacious hall is reminiscent of a church, particularly because there is something like a tabernacle in front. The tabernacle [Lat.: "tent, hut"] on the altar is the Holy Shrine for The Most Holy Sacrament.

Now the dreamer remembers that in her dreams she has been here many times before and that she was "always sneaking around a very fascinating but dangerous center" that concealed a mystery "in the shape of a woman or man." In the dream we are discussing, when she gets to the spot where she remembers the mystery to be, it has gone. It is possible that this open question of gender and sexuality is indeed a central question that she circumvents in shyness. Perhaps she has obscure ideas of a primal and concealed masculine/feminine wholeness of God, symbolizing precisely that: an essential mystery. The mystery is likely to be the content of the tabernacle.

In her dream, the mystery was "fascinating but dangerous," presumably a kind of a taboo impelling her to "sneak around" it. Imagining her movement as a drawing on the floor, what emerges is the ancient hallowed sign of a spiral. C.G. Jung describes this figure as a symbol of the timid attempt of the individual soul to come nearer to the mystery of the Self: "Often one has the impression that the personal psyche is running round this central point like a shy animal, at once fascinated and frightened, always in flight, and yet steadily drawing nearer."[574] This movement is also called *circumambulatio* and is practiced by the Tibetans at the holy Stupas or by Hindus at holy mountains and temples. At issue is always a central content that the ego can only circumambulate but not possess.

In the present dream, the hall is no longer sacred, and "the mystery has gone"; instead, they are preparing "some a social event." It has to do with kissing – some "wanted me to give them a kiss." The forthcoming event seems therefore to be a love celebration or a kind of a wedding (the dreamer being the bride?). There is something erotic going on whereby, interestingly, the dreamer is supposed to kiss others. She is asked to make a gift of love until "the last one of them" brings her a little child for which she feels great affection.

Given that the dream took place around the time of conception, it seems fair to assume that the unconscious had an intuition of the conception. For, it is the child who clearly awakens her unconscious affection, whereas kissing is something others want from her. However, the dangerous and fascinating mystery "at the entrance of the other end" around which she used to sneak, has gone. Instead, she suddenly has a child in her bed. What is the meaning of this?

At first, one is tempted to interpret the dream details in terms of sexuality: The mystery that has disappeared is the mystery of conception or the sexual taboo that now, after the act, is no longer one. We are hardly assuming that this was the dreamer's first sexual contact, although the full unfolding of the personal sexuality happens in stages, even in marriage. Kissing, bed, cuddles, "tear in a flower," including the ending phrase: "I didn't dare to touch it," all suggest sexuality.

Upon closer examination, however, another dimension to the dream is found. Jung has repeatedly shown how both the openly and the masked sexual dream image should be considered as a symbol of a psychic-spiritual context. As the action here takes place in a kind of a church, which formerly had a tabernacle, the dream must be conveying something about the symbolism of sexuality.

Let us inquire further into the action of the dream: After kissing, the dreamer receives a child in her bed, quite plainly suggesting conception. On a subjective level, however – i.e., looking at the child as the component of the dreamer that has remained a child – it would be appropriate for this childlike aspect to be offended by sexuality and its presentation of "profane" collectivity. Thus, as long as the child is the component that has remained a child in the woman herself, she cannot accept the "tear" and wants it to be mended or wants the old, intact child-state to be reestablished.

---

[574] C.G. Jung, CW 12, § 326

The dreamer, or rather the child in her saw the "seminar" [Lat. *seminare* = "to sow"], that had once been a sacred place, as now being only profane. It is as if the dreamer is disappointed that the holy mystery of man and woman has suddenly disappeared and has been replaced by Eros or sexuality, which she has to share with a whole group of people. This, precisely, can be an highly painful experience for an ideal-minded young girl or young man.

Nevertheless, part of the painful process of growing up consists of this realization! For, all of a sudden the dreamer has a tiny, tenderly loved child in her own bed turning to her, as an adult, and looking for security. It has an injury – "a tear in its skin" and the dreamer comments: "It looked like a tear in a flower." This evokes the folkloristic expression "flower" for the female genitalia as well as "defloration" for the rupture of the hymen through the first sexual intercourse.

An archetypal situation is unfolding here approximately at the time of conception. The theme of being "injured" is an ancient motif playing a major part in many stories and fairy tales. For example: the drops of blood in the snow in the opening scene of "Snow-White," those in Wolfram's "Parsifal"[575] and the still very popular image of Amor's arrow shot into the lovers' hearts! "Being wounded" signifies a state of being struck by a power which is trying to enforce a fundamental change.

In our dream, it could be mourning the rupture of an original totality: namely, the destruction of the unscathed child as something original, intact as it makes the transition to a new form of being, where it will develop and change. Like the child, the flower is an image of the Self.

According to Jung's concept of the Self, a "rupture in the flower" would not involve any impairment to the Self. The latter is indestructible, imperceptible and acts upon the center of man. This was contained in the "fundamental mystery," the tabernacle of the beginning of the dream.

We usually encounter in dreams such centered, abstract as well as concrete mandala forms, such as a flower, crystal, star, circle, house, but also tree, man, woman, child, etc., as images of the Self or of God. In the course of every man's life and probably in that of every culture, a wound is created by "the incest taboo, which cuts a man off from the security of childhood and early youth, from all those unconscious happenings that allow the child to live without responsibility as an appendage of his parents."[576] There is no contradiction between this deeper explanation of the wound and that which mirrors the unconscious side of the above-mentioned disappointment. The "rupture" only refers to the image of the Self, not the Self itself, as it were. Thus, the time has come for the image to transform itself. The loss of childhood is painful. The young, albeit long married woman, is in the process of a separation from a

---

[575] Wolfram v. Eschenbach, *Parzival*, Vers 281, 10 - 283, 23
[576] C.G. Jung, CW 5, § 351

certain stage of life, and the dream offers a glimpse into how the psyche is dealing with the changes in her life. They are part of those "difficult acts of adaptation," a period of temporary regression but also of revitalization.

Let us now return to the dream. On the subjective level, the dreamer is not only the child but also the adult accepting the child in her bed and loving it. This indicates that she is inwardly ready to turn towards her own vulnerability and towards the child within her, in a loving and already maternal way. It is a positive response of the dream-ego to the Self. The "tear in the flower" cannot be sewn up: it can only grow over, and the dreamer intuitively knows that she cannot do anything: she does not "dare to touch the flower." If, factually, she were hurt – that is, if a component in the dreamer (that has remained infantile) is currently "hurt" – then, in order to attain a new attitude, it is first necessary to realize this fact sincerely. Her lovingly and comfortingly taking the baby into her bed psychologically signifies an integration of an infantile shadow aspect into her psychic wholeness. So, there is hope for healing and restoring wholeness – not merely for "patching-up."

Overgrowth or continuation of growth would imply a transformation. Considering the flower as a blossom, the next step in Nature would be the ripening of the fruit. Only a little child, unable to understand this developmental step, will want to alter or hold back this process of growth. I would therefore consider the flower image in this dream to be an indication of the Self and an image of totality and perfection. At the same time, I see it as a preliminary stage or form of the Self, just as the image of the "child" represents a preliminary form that is dynamic as opposed to static. Its youth marks the continuation of growth.

Our dreamer will be able to accomplish healing and a maturing of the infantile component within herself primarily through the growth of her own real child, for it will irrevocably set in motion her transition to motherhood, which can give woman a new opportunity to achieve wholeness.

It is most appropriate for the dreamer, or rather for the adult dream-ego, not to concede to the child's demanding to be mended. The lysis points out: healing and becoming whole are always brought about by the Self. The reverse does not work; i.e., the ego cannot restore the Self.

Figure 50. Tellus-relief of Ara Pacis. Detail (10 B.C.)

8. The Duplication Motif

Irmgard Bosch

Although no twins were born among the pregnant women participating in our study, several of them had dreams containing the duplication motif. The element of duality or duplication brings up dramatic and wide ranges of relationships. Perhaps it is an intrinsic and fundamental structure of our existence and thus emerges already in the earliest creation myths, as we shall see in more detail in the chapter on creation dreams.

The duplication motif is present in the legends of all cultures. In Western cultures, Cain and Abel[577] spring to mind, or Horus and Seth, the hostile brothers from ancient Egyptian mythology. Further, there is the unequal pair in the Mesopotamian epic of Gilgamesh and Enkidu. Countless fairy tales revolve around variations on this theme, such as the Iroquois tale of the twin brothers, which C.G. Jung interpreted.[578]

Although the examples cited above describe the opposite natures and conflicts of siblings emanating from the same maternal womb, there are just as many stories of remarkably loving and sharing brothers and sisters. Let us only mention the most well-known pairs: Castor and Pollux and Romulus and Remus from the Greek or Roman cycles of legend. There are also many fairy tales about a pair of brothers or sisters. Twin-gods or twin-heroes frequently are humane and compassionate gods and goddesses, who support each other and can be called upon for help.

The fact that the duplication motif appears so frequently in the imagination of all peoples, throughout history, indicates that a psychological basis underlies it. This clearly transpired in our collection, although none of the dreamers expected twins. (Let us not disregard the fact, though, that the thought of having twins or a progeny of a multiple birth has undoubtedly crossed every pregnant woman's mind.)

---

[577] Ge 4, 1 ff
[578] Cf. C.G. Jung, CW 13, § 132

The duplication motif in stories of twin brothers has always been perceived as something extraordinary, whether the twins are "identical" or not. However, in Nature, no phenomena can be said to be "identical," and as soon as they are "almost identical," it raises questions of difference or confusion.

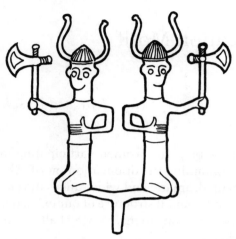

Figure 51. Divinity-figures of the Danish Bronze Age (Grevens Vaenge) from a drawing of the 18th cent.

Even a duplication that is only optical, such as a reflection, always has something irritating about it – we ask ourselves, "Where is the reality? Here or in the reflection? Do I also exist in the outer world?" The "outer" and "inner" can, in fact, perhaps only be apperceived thanks to the duplication or mirror image, which is a crucial experience for consciousness.

Reflection can be dangerous. An illusionary image of the Self fascinates the ego and can inflate it. In the Greek legends, Narcissus was so in love with his own reflection that he became totally isolated (he could only love himself), and this led to his ruin. The mirror was supposed to have magical powers: it was used to fend off evil – as described, e.g., by the hero Perseus' battle against the petrifying eyes of Medusa: Perseus broke her mesmerizing spell by putting a mirror (his shining shield) in front of her, thereby avoiding any direct eye contact with her.

The shadow belongs to the duplication phenomenon, too. There comes that moment in every child's life when it discovers its own shadow and learns to play with it. The shadow is alive, after all, but then, is it "something," or is it "nothing"? Does it belong to me? In former times, the shadow was regarded as something real. In some cultures, it is even forbidden to step on it, while in others, it is used to perform magic.[579] The shadow is a duplication of our own figure; it is, therefore, of the same sex. It is in this sense that the notion of the shadow is used in analytical psychology.

As concerns the phenomenon of duplication, Jung said: "… when unconscious contents are about to become conscious and differentiated … they split, as often happens in dreams, into two identical or slightly different halves corresponding to the conscious and still unconscious aspects of the nascent content."[580]

[579] Baechtold-Stäubli, "Schatten"
[580] C.G. Jung, CW 9/I, § 608

This psychological insight will make an understanding of the peculiar dreams of twins and duplication easier and should explain, at least to a certain extent, why it is so common for pregnant women to dream of twin births: it is as if, for them, psychologically the child lies on the threshold of the unconscious and consciousness, and in this sense, it "duplicates." Looking at the phenomenal world around us, we will never find two natural creatures who are exactly identical. Identical twins do not have identical personality structures even though, genetically, they are identical. We know and must always assume that they have individual souls and are, despite their similarities, individual beings.[581, 582]

In ancient times, people believed that every man or woman had a kind of "double" or twin in the invisible world.[583] There is still a widespread belief that every child has a double or an "alter ego," which has a different psychic structure, but is always with him/her, like a shadow. It is likely that the idea of a guardian angel (or fairies who magically "adopt" a child) is closely linked to this.[584]

In many places, the afterbirth – i.e., umbilical cord, fetal membrane and placenta – was considered to be this "other part," and after close examination (birth oracle), it would carefully be buried – though it should also live, in the other world or in Nature, and from there it should protect and guide the newborn. Sometimes people would plant a tree or a flower on that burial spot, which was supposed to symbolize vitality and indicate the development of the child. Trees and other plants, e.g., rose bushes, figure in many a fairy tale about sisters and brothers. On them the heroes or heroines would be able to read their fate (cf., *Snowhite and Rosered*).

In ancient Rome, the men's invisible companion was called "Genius," and the women's was called "Juno." People would give them special offerings on their birthdays. Socrates wrote that, according to Plato, the Greeks' named this being *daimonion* and

Figure 52. Female statue with twins (West Africa)

[581] For this reason, we tend to dislike the idea of genetically cloned animals. We tend to feel repulsion and fear for uniqueness and for our own individuality which is already at risk in our technologically ever more perfected world.

[582] According to the latest results in twin research, surprising parallels can be found in the most trivial details of twins' biographies. Scientifically, this has yet to be proven.

[583] Marie-Louise von Franz, *Projection and Recollection*, Chapter 7: "The Inner Companion," Open Court Publishing, La Salle, IL, 1980

that he could even hear its voice.[585] The Greeks depicted the genii with wings symbolizing their free and mobile, "volatile" spiritual quality, similar to the angels of the Western cultures. Among some Hellenistic Gnostics,[586] it was held that man is only partially born: his most noble part remained above, in heaven, and the two parts only became reunited in death. This basic idea – namely, a separation from one's original divine unity – is also shared by the post-Biblical Jewish theory on the Shekhina, a daughter of the creation god, who was dispersed in this world. It is similar to the idea of the heavenly sparks of light inhabiting individual human souls and waiting to return home, that is, to be reunited with God. The dreams in which only one of the twins is born alive are reminiscent of this belief.

We would not wish to speak here in detail of the various forms of duplication were it not for the fact that motifs of astonishing similarity appeared in the dreams of pregnant women. Sometimes, they almost literally correspond to certain features of folktales, strongly indicating the existence of an underlying archetypal psychic disposition prevalent all over the world.

The following dream appeared three times:

Dream No. 142:

> *I have had my baby – and it was twins!! Beautiful, perfect, healthy twins. I got hold of a second basket and wrapped them both up and put them down to sleep. I myself was in a curiously elated, almost exalted state, partly pride and joy, but also caused by being slim and mobile again. I could not help running and skipping.*

The duplication of the children is a duplication of joy! Both babies are fully developed and healthy, and the mother reacts in the most natural way, taking care of both of them. Then she gives free expression to her joy, dancing around. Her joy is twofold, too: the delivery went well, and she is mobile and slim again! – the thing all pregnant women dream about ...

In this duplication motif, I do not see any hidden clash of opposites. It rather suggests that, along with the birth of the child, a second thing was born to which the dream-ego responds with exuberant joy: it fathoms spontaneously that a birth of twins signifies beautiful completion and perfection. More-

---

[584] If, however, the conscious ego becomes split, it can indicate a serious psychic illness (schizophrenia). One of the most remarkable accounts of the appearance and persecution by the "double" is Dostoyevsky's Ivan in *The Brothers Karamasov*

[585] Marie-Louise von Franz, *Projection and Recollection*, p. 147

[586] Philosophical-religious school of thought, widespread in several schools of the Greater Greek-Mediterranean World, fought against and suppressed by the Early Fathers. Some basic Gnostic ideas (e.g., the dualism of "this world") and a "spiritual" hereafter partially infiltrated into Christianity. In esoteric teachings they play a major role.

Figure 53. Chnum, the God of the Ram, forming the Pharaoh and his Ka. Hathor granting life to them.

over, that this event is not merely an individual child but also something of the order of an "epiphany," a visible manifestation of the true twofold figure of man constituting at once individual as well as super-individual aspects that reach far beyond the individual case. We encounter the motif of the two mothers in several traditions. Krishna, the Indian God, had two mothers: a divine one, who gave birth to him, and a human one, who cared for and raised him.

Let us for a moment turn our attention to a semi-destroyed ancient Egyptian relief of the Greco-Roman Empire: under the orders of the highest god Amun, Chnum, the pottery god, forms the body of the new pharaoh. The sculpture represents a birth. Hathor, the goddess with the cow horns, blesses him with Ankh, the sign of life.[587] However, what we see on the pottery god's

[587] Helmut Brunner, *Die Geburt des Gottkönigs*, Tafel 6, S. 67, Wiesbaden, 1986, Otto Harassowitz-Verlag. While making pottery, Chnum says: "I give you a full life, all the welfare you want, longevity and a place in my huge heart. I give you all the health...."

385

table are two boys! For, according to the ancient Egyptian conception, the king's body is at once divine and human, a religious fact the Egyptians represent in an archaic "literal" manner in the same way as our dreams, and as most children, do.

Dream No. 143 (the dreamer is thirty-eight weeks pregnant with her third child; the baby girl is born with no complications):

> *During the delivery at the hospital, everybody gets into a flurry (of excitement). As the baby is sliding out, we suddenly notice a second, smaller, weaker baby behind it. Twins! But we've only prepared for "one"!*

Here, duplication does not cause pure joy. A second, less fit baby is born and there is immediate reason for concern: "What are we going to do now? We only expected one baby!"

How should we interpret such a dream? I believe it implies a broadening and deepening of the dreamer's idea of a child. It may be saying something like: this is, as it were, "more than a child" that wants to come out. The knowledge of this other being is still very faint. The unconscious realizes that the preparations, that is, the conscious attitude, is weak and one-sided. For the real child everything has been done. But what to do with the "other child," or with the other side of the child? It seems to me that this dream challenges the dreamer with this question in a gentle way.

Psychologically, it is interesting to see, how, in this dream, the event of the birth is represented as something "emerging" in the same way as Jung described a new content of consciousness. At the moment of birth, or of becoming conscious, there is a constituent that is already fully illuminated, i.e., conscious, followed by a second one less illuminated: in our dream, it is the "weaker" one.

Sometimes the "other" constituent remains in the unconscious and cannot be recovered by consciousness. Dreams often indicate this through the death or disappearance of a figure. Marie-Louise von Franz quoted the following, millennia-old Indian stanza relevant to our theme:[588]

> Two birds, inseparable friends,
> cling to the same tree.
> One of them eats the sweet fruit;
> the other looks on without eating.

She explains: "In many primitive civilizations, every person born is believed to have a twin brother: his placenta. Rather than enter the world, this twin is dried and wound around the neck and thus remains as a spirit in the Beyond.

---

[588] *Mundaka Upanishad*, quoted from M.-L. von Franz, *Shadow and Evil in Fairy Tales*, Shambhala, Boston, 1995, p. 131

At the moment of death, the two halves meet again."[589] In other words, to return to our dream, psychologically speaking, the twin does not enter the world although he continues to form a basic union with his brother, like the two birds in the above-cited poem, sitting on the same tree – the tree of life.

As we have mentioned before, pregnancy is a time that in concentrated form demonstrates the intricate link between the opposites of life and death as well as many others. Immense joy and tremendous pain can go hand in hand.

Dream No. 144 (the dreamer is thirty-eight weeks pregnant):

> *I am in the waiting room of an obstetrician. I am lying on a bed with my husband. Close to the door of the consulting room stands a girl, who is about fifteen years old, with her mother. She is very sad, and I feel sorry for this girl. At the same time, we are happy about our baby. Two doctors come from the consulting room. One of them has tears in his eyes because of the girl's abortion, but the other one is happy. We look at each other, knowing that it is time for me to go in and give birth to my baby.*

The sad young girl, whose unhappiness touches our dreamer, personifies an aspect of the dreamer herself. For this reason, the dream has a duplication aspect. Furthermore, polarity is patent throughout the dream: the two doctors show opposite feelings.

A dream-figure suffering or dying means that a psychic content, a life stage or a relationship, is ending and/or disappearing in the unconscious. It is as if different levels of the same development are going on at the same time, belonging to the same subject: The sad young girl with her mother is certainly part of the pregnant woman. The "lost child" could be the childlike side in the dreamer herself, from which she knows at this fateful moment, she must part forever. Her empathy with the sad girl suggests something like a secret identification – it is not really herself, although she, too, has lost a "child": her own childhood. On the other hand, she is a grown woman who long ago made the step to adulthood and who, together with her husband, looks forward to the forthcoming birth of her child.

There is much depth in the ancient Indian poem that we looked at above. It shows the mysterious gap, but also the belonging together, of the opposites. (This does not mean, however, that the opposites have been explained or that the suffering has been alleviated.)

---

[589] *Ibid.*, p. 131

Dream No. 145 (the dreamer is thirty-nine weeks pregnant):

> *I go to have a shower. Liquid flows from inside. I ask my husband to come and see if this is amniotic liquid. We have to go to the hospital. But first, as my husband tells me, we have to go to the cemetery to bury the little baby girl of my sister-in-law.*
>
> *(Dreamer's commentary: My sister-in-law does not have a little girl and was not pregnant lately.)*

The woman seems to undergo a process of transformation. The water helps her and her husband to realize that she is now ready for the birth, the waters (amniotic fluid) having broken. However, there is something entirely different that has to be done first. Her husband informs her that they have to go to the cemetery to bury her sister-in-law's little girl. The husband-figure personifies her unconscious masculine, spiritual side, pointing out to her an unexpected aspect of the event of which her conscious ego, as well as her dream-ego, were perfectly unaware.

The sister-in-law can be considered as one of the dreamer's shadow figures. An unconscious feminine part of herself has lost a little girl. Before she herself can assume her maternal role, this little girl has to be "buried." This is to say, something had to pass away in her – namely, the "little girl in her" – for the new child to be able to live.

Therefore, her dream-husband or animus, bringing to her consciousness something from the very depths of her unconscious, suggests an intense maturation process of the kind that is typical for pregnancy.

Dream No. 146 (the dreamer is twenty-five weeks pregnant with her first child; the birth takes place without complications):

> *I am having an ultrasound examination of the uterus. I can look at an X-ray film of my child. I see that there are two! I can also see that they are both boys. When the doctor comes back, he says that I am perfectly healthy and everything is normal: "You have twins: one is dead, but that is normal."*

At first, the doctor's statement seems shocking. However, let us remember that the death or disappearance of a twin corresponds to an archetypal phenomenon to which each of us is subject to a certain extent. It is indeed "normal" that a part of our inner potential "dies off," that is, it disappears in the unconscious. We only manage to realize a fraction of our total potential and thereby often lose our better part, or our "twin," who could embody still "undreamed-of," hidden psychic powers.

It is important, however, to remain in touch with them, without endlessly mourning them, but rather consistently attempting to resuscitate that "dead brother or sister" and eventually to bring it to a realization. This would imply believing in our hidden psychic potential without its being subject to the will of the ego. It is perhaps rather like what, in the past, people called "having faith in God."

The following dream may render this a little clearer:

Dream No. 147 (the dreamer is a thirty-three-year-old woman who is twenty-three weeks pregnant with her third child; there are no complications at birth):

> *I give birth to twins. They are both very small. I can hold them in my hand if I form it like a bowl. Then I lose one of them. I search and search for it. I wake up crying.*

The mother's efforts to hold the wee tots in her hand suggest a good maternal attitude of her unconscious. She wants to bestow upon the tiny beings her maternal protection, just as she did when they were still in her womb. But she cannot yet quite "grasp" them: her ability for grasping is not yet quite sufficiently developed. The fact that they are so very tiny might suggest that the new element in the dreamer is still growing.

In the background of the dream, there is again the image of man's otherworldly double or twin, i.e., the unconscious part of himself. The dream also illustrates a sense of nostalgia for the lost soul that was once there and that usually follows the inner man or woman like a distant intuition.

"I search and search for it" expresses the mourning over the distance to our own wholeness represented by the twins.

The following dream also belongs to the duplication motif. The dreamer commented that she had not at all been shocked in the dream that the child had two heads.

Figure 54. The Heavenly Twins (West Africa)

Dream No. 148 (the dreamer is twenty-nine weeks pregnant with second child; there are no problems with the birth):

> *I am together with my family. I meet a woman with a pram in a market-place. The child in the pram has two heads. It sounds strange, but in the dream, it was natural. The child was very pretty. The mother said, and I agreed, that it was not strange to have a child with two heads. At a certain age, one of the heads is to be amputated.*

This dream is an interesting, if rather gruesome, variation on duplication dreams. There is no indication of a possible miscarriage or anything abnormal; on the contrary, the child is supposedly "very pretty." What, then, is the meaning of the two heads?

The woman in the marketplace could be seen as the dreamer's shadow figure. It is equally likely that the dream is emphasizing on the dreamer's own too strong but not conscious, "headedness," meaning that her thinking is excessively dominated by her intellect. For example, her head may have certain expectations about the child. At the end, the dream soberly states that the "spare head" would be removed later – amputated: with time, she would lose the "excess head."

This kind of development, especially among intellectual young women, is very common. In most cases, though, the children themselves ensure that their mother manages eventually to let go of her theories!

In conclusion, I would like to present the reader with the following dream about two artificially conceived children:

Dream No. 149 (the dreamer is twenty-eight weeks into a wanted pregnancy; the dreamer and spouse are taking their doctoral degrees; a healthy girl is born five weeks prematurely):

> *We discovered a forgotten room under the roof and made an important find: amidst ornate stones, we discovered an ancient grave of a magician. When he was lifted out, I saw his green mummified head. It was slightly scary. Even more amazing was the fact that, in his arms, he held two retorts with tapering middle parts in which were two small but complete children. They were his children.*

The ground, cellars and caves are not the only places where surprising and unusual things can be discovered – so are places high up, such as lofts. In the attic, among old, weird lumber or "forefathers' household," draped and spooky, it can be as uncanny as in the darkness of the cellar. Children usually do not want to go to the cellar or to the attic alone. Perhaps the old lumber is not quite dead, after all.

How do cellar and attic differ? The "house," the inhabited realm, is man's conscious room and conscious identity. Cellars in dreams are usually interpreted as the unconscious foundations or prerequisites for consciousness. For example, "supporting" vaults are seen as the realm of the unconscious in whose deeper layers we imagine vital resources and potentialities to be stored (provisions in the cellar). Much of what is stacked away in this domain must not be exposed to light.

By contrast, in an attic, people put away things that need to be kept "dry," e.g., old furniture, writings, letters, old clothes – items that are vessels of memories and stories. In the olden days, for the more mature children, the attic was a place where the most intense and exciting play went on and to which the parents had no access. In the forbidden attic at the top of C.G. Jung's house (forbidden because the floorboards were worm-eaten and rotten), for example, the young boy kept in a pencil-case a tiny puppet which he had carved himself and to which he had given a little oblong stone that he had painted with watercolors. He hid it on a beam under the roof. He perceived this statue, together with its stone, as his personal good fairy. Jung writes in his memories: "I contented myself with the feeling of a newly won security, and was satisfied to possess something that no one knew about and that no one could get at. It was an inviolable secret which must never be betrayed, for the safety of my life depended on it."[590] This "little double" became a refuge during the boy's psychologically fragile childhood. Later, he forgot about the statue – until he was about thirty-five and engaged in the preliminary studies for his book, *Symbols of Transformation* [CW 5]. In his reading, he came upon the Australian *churingas* [a cache of family soul-stones] and discovered that he had, somewhere in his memory, quite a definite image of such a stone, though he had never seen any reproduction of it.[591] Thus the little statue in the attic provides another example of a double or twin.

The dreamer tells of an "important find" made "in a forgotten room under the roof," thus in a room that had once been used as a part of the house, but had then become forgotten. It had slipped into the unconscious, moreover, out of the intellect or the memory function. The dream has reawakened her memory. The find of a grave in an attic is also unusual. The dream suggests thereby that this discovery is not an everyday occurrence, but concerns a "higher" issue, something spiritual or metaphysical.

A magician had been buried up there, but the room had been totally forgotten: how are we to understand this? I assume that we are dealing with an exigent but virtually obsolete, forgotten spiritual domain. Furthermore, the magician is presumably a spirit of high esteem, his deathbed lying beneath ornate stones. He had once been honored, but subsequently forgotten – just like the room and the entire spiritual domain that he represented. His skills were lost, too, not in the depths but high up, i.e., in spiritual spheres or theories.

As would be expected after lying in an attic for a prolonged period of time, the magician's skull, or spirituality, has dried up and become mummified (in contrast to the moist quality of emotions and vitality). And yet, surprisingly, it is "green" – the color of life and vegetation. All this is "slightly scary" remarks the dreamer quite understandably. Jung said: "For a woman, the typical danger emanating from the unconscious comes *from above*, from the 'spiritual' sphere personified by the animus...."[592]

---

[590] C.G. Jung, *Memories, Dreams, Reflections,* Vintage Books, New York, 1965, p. 21 f
[591] *Ibid.*, p. 22 ff; cf. also Chapter 3.2

Up to this point, what has been uncovered in the attic is quite contradictory. On the one hand, the forgotten room is evocative of an important spiritual domain, on the other hand, the dead magician lies buried under "ornate stones," pointing in fact to the earth or a chthonic domain. Moreover, what are we to make of the two babies – "his children" – in the retorts that he is holding in his arms, with respect to the woman who is twenty-eight weeks pregnant?

Viewing the house in terms of the habitual world of consciousness, the attic by contrast, could signify the collective memory (the attic is available to everyone as a storage place), general historical knowledge, or to be more precise, oblivion. Here, a testimony to a spiritual life that has died out is suddenly being recovered. This is what happens with countless conceptions: once they no longer fit into the *Weltbild* or present-day philosophy, they sink into oblivion. If the spiritual foundation of the age changes again – for instance, in the case of major convulsions setting free forgotten contents – they can then be "rediscovered." This took place to some extent in the case of medieval alchemy, whose complicated procedures were rediscovered by C.G. Jung and decoded as valuable evidence of psychic processes occurring place in those participating in the *opus*.[593]

The discovery of the "dead magician" can be regarded as an issue of collective, historical interest. Nevertheless, I believe that our dream is also deeply personal, for it appears during pregnancy and closes with the two children in the retorts.

Let us go back to the beginning: We are dealing with the grave of a "magician." A magician is a person capable of causing matter to transform, of making visible things disappear and causing invisible things to appear. He is wrapped in mysterious gowns and works with obscure means, through magic alone. Performing magic is a highly developed art of trickery; therefore, "the devil must be in it" – i.e., it is irrational or supernatural. However, magic also likes to present itself as a divine, creative power and is related to shamanism and alchemy, where – through using mysterious tricks – hidden life or spirit is supposed to be restituted from dead matter. This is redolent of the ancient (Promethean and demiurgic) human dream that is to assume the place of the creation god – to "make" man, thus to become the supreme creator of him.[594]

Beyond this, the mummified magician's head is reminiscent of the mummy of Osiris, the Egyptian God of the Dead and of Transformation, who could bring the dead back to life. He was also venerated as the god of vegetation. His

---

[592] C.G. Jung, CW 9/I, § 559

[593] This regards transformational phenomena taking place in the individuation process that the alchemists projected into the chemistry of matter. – Cf. Jung's research and discoveries in Volumes 12-14 of the *Collected Works*

[594] Cf. Mircea Eliade, *The Forge and the Crucible*, University of Chicago Press, Phoenix Edition, 1978

color was green, and in Ancient Egypt, his deathbed was furnished in his honor with fast-sprouting germs in slivers of clay or seeds – a symbol of resurrection – were strewn into the bandages (cf. Dream No. 118). The appearance of a mummified green magician therefore strongly suggests the idea of transformation and resurrection. The dreamer need not know anything about Osiris or Adonis: it is the dream itself that communicates the theme of transformation.

Benedicta viriditas or "the praised greening" constituted an important stage in the process of alchemical transformation. Jung discovered, in the otherwise incomprehensible representations of the alchemists, projections of psychic processes that moved him deeply.[595]

The magician in our dream holds two retorts with "two small but complete children" in his arms. It would seem that he has been occupied with the art of "man-making." The emphasis of the last sentence of the dream is clearly on: "They were his children." They were made purely by a male or magic trick, excluding any female element. To call them "head births" would therefore be correct. Although they may be complete or perfect, they have not been able to live but had to remain in their retorts, sterile and isolated from the world.

Nobody knows these child spirits: they rested in the grave with their father and interpreting them as spiritual germs or impulses of the dreamer would mean that they have no part in the present work (doctor's degree) and obviously play hardly any role her present life. However, let us not ignore their duplication. As Jung has shown, the duality motif always appears "when unconscious contents are about to become conscious and differentiated. They then split, as often happens in dreams, into two identical or slightly different halves corresponding to the conscious and still unconscious aspects of the nascent content."[596] The motif of twins seems to correspond quite well to the present situation of the pregnant woman – the child being partly conscious, partly unconscious.

At the same time, however, we are dealing with death. With regard to the dreamer as the subject, we must therefore ask: "What meaning does the dead magician have in the totality of her psyche, and what does the duality of 'his' children signify?" I believe the magician is a deceased animus figure or a kind of intellectual activity that has atrophied in our subject. Perhaps during some time in the past, she left a creative piece of work, or the ideas for it, unfinished. It is also possible that, in her pregnant condition, she has rediscovered an earlier spiritual creativity.

---

[595] The unintelligibility of the symbols in alchemy is partly traditional, partly deliberate coding because of the opposition from the church. The language used is incomprehensible because alchemical contents are understandable only through symbolism.
[596] C.G. Jung, CW 9/I, § 608

A strong animus in the form of a "green mummified head" of a dead magician does not strike me as bizarre.[597] Thinking and the way thoughts create their objects is magic in many ways. Moreover, the fact that a dehydrated head has a green color suggests a possibility of his resurrection and rebirth of his (i.e., the dreamer's) creative core.

Today, here and there, there are signs of the understanding that the ancient efforts of the Alchemists failed in the sense of producing any tangible results. I see an allusion to this in this dream or in our dreamer's unconscious. The Alchemists could not produce "gold" or the "philosophical stone." Their goal was further-reaching: they aspired to reach those mysteries in matter that touched upon "life." The crucial ideas of their prescriptions consisted of transformations and crises, and finally, in "the wedding of the king and queen" – that is, in a unification of the feminine and the masculine. The old magician of our dream, a masculine spirit in the head of a woman, had evidently constructed his children by some strange means – but in theory, without a woman, therefore in isolation. The connection to the feminine ego of the dreamer and her spirituality had been lost in a similar fashion as has happened, for the most part, in science. In the Christian Western cultures, notwithstanding a few exceptions, the feminine spirit has not succeeded in developing to the same degree of intensity as the masculine one. The green color belonging to the magician's head could suggest that this masculine spirit is about to transform itself. It is being "discovered" by the woman. Moreover, the duplication of the children is a clear sign: the dreamer's (feminine) consciousness is about to be connected – which, in view of her pregnancy, most likely has to do with real children!

[597] For "animus," cf. Chapter 6

Figure 55. Demeter of Cnidos (ca. 330 B.C.)

9. Mother

Irmgard Bosch

Like the image of the child, the image of the mother in pregnancy dreams can refer either to the future or the past, e.g., the woman's own childhood. In many dreams of pregnant women, the relationship with the personal mother plays a role as these women tend to undergo an intense process of transformation at this particular time. Behind and beyond that, the powerful general human dynamic of the mother-archetype manifests itself in the most multifarious actions and imagery. We have already discussed the more or less superpersonal maternal aspects from various standpoints. Whenever the mother appears as a human figure, she is considerably closer to the conscious ego than in her symbolic manifestations, e.g., as the earth or an animal, such as a cat or cow.

The word "mother" primarily designates a domestic function or role. In former times, women used to find fulfillment in this structure of reciprocal relationships, sometimes even to the point of exhaustion. She was carried by a maternal image, which on the one hand, was irresistibly nourished by instinct, while on the other hand, she was largely confined to her role (albeit with cultural differences). Her individuality took a step back. Bearing and bringing up children and devoting her ego to the maternal responsibilities filled her life with meaning.

Because of the far-reaching changes in women's lives in modern societies – including, among other things, the emancipation from the family role, her professional qualifications and perhaps even a common feeling of an imperiled planet Earth (overpopulation, environmental damage, etc.) – serious questions have now been raised making the concept of the "mother" seem very problematical, or sometimes even unsolvable.

The fact that we consciously plan and integrate motherhood into our lives has brought about enormous changes. The fact that there is now a choice about whether to have children or not has undoubtedly meant a tremendous progress for women. For men, too, it is a progress, as well as a chance even to assume maternal functions from time to time! Motherhood – being now reduced to a limited passage in her life, "the family phase" – has lost much of the weight it used to have in a woman's biography. A more conscious perception of the necessity for motherhood is required again, in order to comprehend that the maternal relationship is an indispensable part of our inner development. The mother, being a child's "first object" in the world, conditions its first orientation. She is a part of the child's own psyche. Involuntarily, she will become her son's first anima and the first self- or shadow-image of her daughter. Thus, she plays a major role in their inner maturation process.

What do the dreams of today's pregnant women – each one of whom experiences the process of becoming a mother in her own unique and individual manner – express regarding the theme of the "mother"? Do their dreams reflect problems of a general order and/or do they provide answers to personal questions and difficulties?

It seems to me that the transition from girlhood to motherhood is greater today than ever before. To become pregnant is no longer the uniquely "natural" path for a woman to take. It is at least assumed that she and her partner have consciously decided upon this step, even if the decision was made only after the fact, partly unconsciously or not at all. This effect of free will (to the extent it actually was free) can be a great help for the adjustment the new mother subsequently has to make. Pregnancy itself will show her how important, but also how minimal, this act of free will is compared to the inevitable natural process that is about to run its course. In favorable circumstances, this experience can lead to a calm, imperturbable composure and to an inner security of a kind she has never before experienced.

In the course of this book, we have spoken of the manifold rituals and social forms of initiation that existed to help us to cope with the crucial transitions in life. Marie-Louise von Franz often made a point of remarking that some of these orientations now had to be taken from dreams. The following dream, dealing with initiation, will illustrate this thought in a rather conspicuous manner. The majority of the dreams on the theme of the mother also contain elements of initiation:

Dream No. 150 (the dreamer here is twenty-one weeks pregnant; this was her second, planned pregnancy with complications, necessitating a Cesarean section):

> *Dr. von Franz and I are in a kind of a tower or some other old building. She climbs up a set of stairs, which remind me of the stone stairs in Jung's old tower.*
> *I remain downstairs in a kind of a closet that looks like a stalactite cavern. Dr. von Franz is talking upstairs. It sounds like a sermon; it is about having little babies and the mother-goddess.*

From the ceiling of the stalactite cavern, water drips down onto me in the
form of (or like) transparent precious stones.
I am deeply moved. It is a sacred event.

The tower is an ancient feminine symbol. It is a plain image of a closed and protected spiritual room.[598] The dream can also symbolize a prison, as it often does in folktales. However, in our dream it signifies the innermost room of the soul, where our dreamer can introvert and concentrate on the part of her Self that is buried in the center of her soul. Furthermore, the tower is a symbol suggesting femininity as a safe interior as well as masculinity in its erectness. In uniting the feminine and masculine, the tower is above all a symbol of the Self. What goes on in its interior is a mystery.

In 1923, C.G. Jung began to build his "dwelling tower" in Bollingen by the lakeside of Zurich. He wrote: "The feeling of repose and renewal that I had in this tower was intense from the start. It represented for me the maternal hearth. ... a place of spiritual concentration. ... In Bollingen, silence surrounds me almost audibly.... Here, the torment of creation is lessened; creativity and play are close together."[599]

As an opening, Dr. von Franz climbs up the stone stairs. Going up stairs or steps symbolizes a transition to a higher level. Like the tower, stairs are an ancient symbol for connecting the heavens and the earth, as we have already seen with Jacob's ladder.[600] Stairs or a ladder ensure a potential connection between above and below. By climbing up the stairs, Dr. von Franz transcends into a higher being. From there, she speaks from a higher plane, like a priestess.[601] Psychologically, she represents a figure of the dreamer's Self. The woman remains below in a kind of a closet looking like a stalactite cavern.

It is interesting that what follows takes place in a cave – in a stalactite cavern, moreover – which appears to stand in contradiction to the image of the "tower." The design of many Christian churches comprises both of these spiritual tendencies: the towers express aspects of man's upward-striving towards the light, elevation and power; the crypts symbolize submersion into withdrawn, devout meditation and the mysteries of religious life.

From time immemorial, caves have been home to the sanctuaries of numerous feminine divinities. They belonged to the earth, the chthonic element, as well as to the humid and obscure (as characterized by the Chinese Yin). Every

---

[598] Mother-goddesses of the ancient Orient and Egypt were represented as a tower or wall, e.g., protecting city-goddesses with crowns made of a wall, or tall city gates with images of a protecting goddess. There is a litany praising the Virgin Mary as a tower (Lauretanical Litany).

[599] C.G. Jung, *Memories, Dreams, Reflections*, pp. 224-226

[600] Cf. footnote No. 340

[601] Priests and priestesses at the altar are not supposed to embody human beings but should serve the religious cult.

cave signifies a lap of the earth (cf. the Chapter "Earth, Stones, Precious Stones"). Eilithya's, a pre-Greek goddess of birth's place of worship, was a stalactite cavern near Knossos on Crete. Demeter, the Goddess of Fertility, was also venerated in a cave near Enna, Sicily (belonging to Greece at the time) and another one near Agrigent.

Figure 56. The birth of Christ in the cave (Rumanian-Byzantine)

It is not surprising, therefore, that certain cave cults have survived to this day in various places on the earth. They correspond to an ancient psychic need and to a feminine archetype.

In 1850, Bernadette's visions of Mary marked the beginning of the great pilgrimages to the holy springs of Lourdes, France, where to this day, people hoping to be healed still dip into the springs and sprinkle themselves with the springs' water. Since then, many Catholic churches have larger or smaller Mary grottos, usually trimmed with stalactites, which are popular places for prayer. The icon of the Orthodox Church (cf. Fig. 57), depicting the birth of Christ in a cave, testifies to the same source.[602]

What is being said in the upstairs room strikes our dreamer, who remained down in the cave in devout meditation, like an initiation. Deep inside her she can feel what is being imparted to her without being able to hear it all. She grasps those words that are crucial in this phase of her life: mother-goddess, birth and having little babies. The entire spectacle is an inauguration for the forthcoming phase of life, which she realizes in a state of deep introversion.

The transparent crystal drops of water dripping down are an obvious sign of a blessing: she is being baptized, as it were, in her new role as a mother-to-

---

[602] Ernst Benz, *Die heilige Höhle in der Ostkirche*, in: Eranos Jahrbuch 1953, Band 22, S. 365 ff

be or elevated to a higher status, as a new person. The dreamer is deeply moved. The drops, reminding her of precious stones, show the perpetual and imperturbable spiritual value of the event.

The fact that the dream-ego has recognized and accepted the sacred happening, but that she has psychically remained on the ground and with herself, is suggested by the concluding sentence of the lysis: "It is a sacred event." We could not find a more apt way of describing what has happened, it is like an inner baptism that her ego experiences through her feminine Self, in order to be fundamentally invigorated and prepared for her new life as a mother.

I feel that this initiation dream is one of the most precious examples of how the Self sometimes unveils its proximity to God.

The word "mother" is also used for collective concepts: Mother Church, little Mother Russia. Underlying this is the archetypal image of the Great Mother. She is all-encompassing, watches her children, gives birth, protects and keeps them – but she also swallows everything back. She is as much a mother of life as a mother of death.[603] Numerous languages, as is known to everyone, share the word Ma or Mama. Sometimes it is used as an honorary title – even for childless women.

Psychologically, what is important is that the mother is essential for the child's survival for a certain time. There were early cultures that took this principle into account in the social order. But already in the Greek myths of the classical period, the story – along with other creation myths – according to which the beginning of all creation was owed to Gaia, the Mother Earth, had faded into distant memory.[604] Since the pioneering work of Bachofen, the research of matriarchal forms of societies has covered hitherto unknown territory but has not yet been concluded.[605] It seems that, already in prehistoric times, both the predominance of man as well as of woman had existed.[606] However, social order is not our topic here, although this, too – like dreams – has archetypal roots.

In certain regions of the earth we can still feel influences of matriarchal cultures, e.g., Dravidian South India, the hinterland of Mediterranean regions and regions in Africa.[607] Jung observed matriarchal remnants also in North America and speculated about a secret survival of a lost Indian psychic condition in the collective unconscious of the US Americans.[608] Even in our lati-

---

[603] Cf. Chapter 3.2

[604] Cf. Chapter 3.2 and Dream No. 13

[605] Johan Jakob Bachofen, *Versuch über die Gräbersymbolik der Alten*, 1859; *Das Mutterrecht*, 1961; *Das lykische Volk*, 1862 (cf. *Mutterrecht und Urreligion*, Leipzig, 1926)

[606] Lucidly presented from an angle of depth-psychology: Ingeborg Clarus, *Wer war zuerst?*, *Mythologischer Exkurs über die Wechselwirkung sich ablösender weiblicher und männlicher Vorherrschaft*, Anal. Psychologie 1989, 20, pp. 241-256

[607] Cf. C.G. Jung, *Memories, Dreams, Reflections*, p. 254 ff

[608] C.G. Jung, CW 10, § 790

tudes, people spontaneously cry out: *Mama!* or *Mother!* in a state of shock or extreme danger – even though, consciously, creativity is predominantly associated with the masculine.

Primordial imagery in many cultures comprises the coming together of opposite primal beings, primal elements or primal gods, whose masculine-feminine union caused creation. I believe that these basic principles testify to a more mature attitude: more mature or wiser than the psychologically well-founded attitude of an absolute primacy of the mother (rooted in an infantile sensibility) and wiser than the power-oriented and one-sided idea of a single, male God of creation.

There are two developments in pregnancy that mutually overlap or in fact presuppose one another: one is the intrauterine child developing into an individual living being; the other is the pregnant woman developing into a mother. We can even observe them in an adoptive mother having had to wait for a long time for the arrival of her first adoptive child. In her commentary, she writes that, at the time, she felt exactly like a pregnant woman.

The mother of the dreamer is, in reality, rather tall, and she is the chief of an influential clan whose "black sheep" is our dreamer. In the dream, she is not waiting for her child but for her mother.

Dream No. 151:

> *I am at the Denver Airport meeting my mother. As I approach her, I realize that she is tiny – like a midget. I have to sit down to hug her. She feels round and solid and small.*

We first notice the change in height: The stately mother is now small, like a midget; the dreamer has to sit down to hug her. On a personal level, this could mean that the powerful woman, against whose reign the dreamer had rebelled, has now become much smaller. Because the dreamer herself is about to assume maternal responsibilities, she has grown taller.

But the relative heights have, in fact, not normalized. The tall mother appears as being the size of a small child. The dreamer hence embraces at once the child and the mother.

The change of reality points to the subjective main aspect of the dream. The mother is a symbol here, she is the maternal being or motherhood per se, i.e., the feminine-responsible principle. The latter approaches the waiting woman in the form of a small child, and she has to bend down to hug it. The dream thereby expresses that the expected child brings with it maternal elements or aspects of motherhood that the dreamer lovingly accepts. All in all, we could say that the dreamer's psyche is so flexible in its development – she can easily "bend down" – that she manages to reach the child.

This dream very plainly implies again this fundamental fact: the mother is contained in the child and vice versa.

Many pregnant women fill out the waiting period with practical preparations (to the extent that they are in a position to do so). They knit, crochet or sew for the baby. In some cases, the father puts together a crib or they line a bassinet with fresh fabric, and the siblings paint pictures for the baby. Through these preparatory actions and constructive fantasies of the mother as well as the entire family, the child is being swaddled in loving thoughts and given the warmth and attention it needs for the arrival in the harsh reality. The stitches that have been patiently and meticulously made can be likened to the threads and material of its life, including the physical constitution that has to be built up from countless vital building blocks.

From the point of view of the unconscious, the waiting period is a fruitful time. A pregnant woman "invented" in her dream a particularly lovely image of a protective mantle she wishes to prepare for the child:

Dream No. 152:

> *Aunt Emmi, who in reality has no children, has had a baby boy. Together with other relatives, I was allowed to wait in the room nextdoor, in order to then look at the boy, as soon as he would be dried. Aunt Emmi had just fed him. A doctor took him and held him on his lap because the mother had a runny nose and did not want to infect the infant.*
>
> *The sister had promised to leave the placenta for me, so that I could make something from it. I made an Easter nest from it.*

The dreamer has to wait in the room nextdoor. Being pregnant, she is already in a state of waiting, that is, gradually approaching the birth of the child. "Aunt Emmi," too, seems to keep a cautious distance from the child. The dream reflects how the dream-ego is not yet ready for the birth as such, but only for the preparation or the nest-building. Even though the egg has already been laid, so to speak, priority must be given to the preparation of the nest. The dream has selected the placenta for creating a nest, which, biologically, makes a great deal of sense! It is a manifestation of how the dreamer's unconscious, affected by a purposive, happy anticipation, desires that the child be born into a nurturing environment. The "Easter nest" provides a rich symbolism for this.

Dream No. 153 (the dreamer is twenty-eight weeks pregnant):

> *I have a little baby girl. She is very small – almost like a little doll. I am having trouble taking care of her. My mother is helping me.*
>
> *She takes her in her arms so that I can give my breast to the baby.*

The dreamer is concerned about the tiny size of the baby and does not quite know how to take care of the fragile little doll. But her mother, symbolically her own maternal forces and qualities that she had seemingly been quite unaware of, come to help her. When the dream says, "she takes the baby in her arms so that I can give my breast to the baby," it is the maternal side within her that is enabling her to breastfeed the baby.

Figure 57. Mary, St. Anne, her mother and baby Jesus with a lamb (Leonardo da Vinci, 1501-1507)

This dream image presents more than prompt help with feeding: it is a mother's most natural passing-on of what the new being needs in order to survive. It is reminiscent of the infinite line of maternal ancestors passing down their experience and wisdom. The painting depicting St. Anne with Mary and the baby Jesus is an illustration of this archetypal fact of the line of maternal ancestors ensuring close ties within the human race.

A similar situation occurs in the following dream from the very first days of a pregnancy that was strongly desired.

Dream No. 154: [609]

She was giving birth to a baby boy: her mother and her paternal grandmother (who has the same name as she) were helping.

Already in the first days of pregnancy, all the mothers – including the "Great Mother" – have come to help her. Remarkably strong maternal feelings have been awakened in the dreamer, emphasized by the fact that the grandmother has the same name as the dreamer, suggesting that she, too, is a part of herself. This dream is also a "St. Anne with Mary and baby Jesus" dream.

Dream No. 155 (the dreamer is thirty-four weeks pregnant):

In the dream, I could clearly feel the toe of the child stick out of the abdominal wall. I could touch and feel each individual toe by stroking over them with my fingers. ... Gradually, more and more of the child

[609] By the same dreamer: Dream Nos. 168 and 172

moved up to the surface of the belly. You could see the whole child like a relief; it was only kept inside my belly by a very thin layer of skin. When I wanted to show it to my mother, the skin burst, and the baby was born. I immediately held it in my arms ... and put it to my breast. It drank immediately. It was handsome baby, and I was incredibly happy.

By stroking over the belly, the pregnant woman begins to love the baby's body. The child becomes more concrete, grows bigger, and once her own mother joins her, the "maternal instincts" have become so acute that the abdominal wall bursts; i.e., the tension becomes too intense, and the child is born in the dream. It is as if a newly achieved mother-consciousness has already been born.

The following dream is from a woman who is eight weeks pregnant. She had several dreams before she became pregnant, which showed her unconscious concern with fertility. However, this professionally very active woman had not aspired for pregnancy.[610] When she actually did become pregnant, the news struck her like lightning. She was dismayed, perplexed and unhappy. Her conscious ego could not accept such an abrupt interruption of all her plans and aspirations, but the unconscious continued to send her conscious ego images of a different inner development.[611]

Dream No. 156:

My mother is inscribing symbols in a stone like a monolith. Some are astronomical signs. Then I see many little eggs. Someone wants to see what is inside. I say that only roaches can come out of such eggs. But the person keeps insisting about opening the little eggs.
Then he finally opens two eggs, and two small white rabbits come out of the eggs. – They belong to me.

The persons in this dream are: the mother, the dreamer and "someone." We consider the persons in terms of representing inner figures of the dreamer herself – her own mother being an already vital part in her – and we assume the "someone" to be a positive animus.

Prehistoric monoliths are known to be associated with stars, the sun and moon and their orbits, and were used for calendars. They were usually perceived as feminine. They had to do with fate and fertility. Fertility rites were performed near such stones.[612, 613]

---

[610] Cf. interpretation of Dream No. 13 by the same dreamer
[611] Cf. Dream No. 40
[612] Frank Teichmann, *Der Mensch und sein Tempel* and *Megalithkultur in Irland, England und der Bretagne*, u.a., p. 43 ff
[613] Cf. Dream No. 63

Imprinting or inscribing astronomical signs into a large stone symbolically represents pregnancy, or more precisely, the moment of conception itself: i.e., the stone receiving or being "impregnated" with cosmic symbols from the Great Mother. The dream-mother inscribes the signs: she is behind the curtain, as it were. It is the greater mother or the mother principle that is inside the image of the personal mother.

Conceiving a child in the body of a woman is not an isolated, accidental or purely material happening. It seems to correspond to higher events governed by cosmic laws. The dream points to a context of meaning that compensates for the rejecting attitude of the conscious ego. For the unconscious, this pregnancy does not imply a temporary disturbance, a breakdown or an accident. What the mother inscribes exists in the dreamer's own unconscious: a more knowledgeable, maternal part of her being that establishes a connection with a larger horizon and with the true meaning of the event.

Now, the dreamer sees numerous little eggs. Eggs are a more familiar and widely known symbol of fertility and new life: Easter eggs spring to mind along with creation myths from other cultures. According to an Ancient Egyptian legend as well as a Greek myth, the entire universe was brought forth from an egg.[614]

A masculine "someone" appears in the dream, wanting to know what is inside the eggs. In the context of growth, curiosity can sometimes be harmful – but it is not so here. It is rather an urge for knowledge serving the goal of the dream, which is to try to understand the meaning of the mother's inscriptions in the stone. Here, the animus function is of the kind Jung has described as ideal: closing the gap between the unconscious and the conscious.

The dreamer's conscious ego does not want a child and the dream-ego is equally dismissive, thinking that "only roaches [freshwater fish] can come out of such eggs" – and what has that to do with her?!

Although the dream-ego is intent upon pushing these eggs out of its mind, so to speak, it has touched upon a secret image that was discovered by Jung and discussed in *Aion*.[615] The fish played an important symbolic role, not only in early Christianity. Christ, the Redeemer, was referred to as "ichtys," the fish. Bearing in mind that the fish is a creature of the sea – psychologically speaking, a content of the collective unconscious – this cryptic image no longer seems so farfetched.[616]

However, even without the religious background of the fish symbol, it is interesting to see how rapidly the dream imagery now advances. The intrigued participant will not give in and opens two of the eggs – "and two small white

---

[614] Karl Kerényi, *Die Mythologie der Griechen*, p. 22 f / *The Gods of the Greeks*
[615] C.G. Jung, *Aion*, CW 9/II, § 162 ff
[616] Barbara Hannah, *The Religious Function of the Animus in the Book of Tobit*, in: The Guild of Pastoral Psychology, Guild Lecture 114, London, 1961

rabbits come out. ..." Then the dream-ego promptly realizes: "They belong to me!" It spontaneously claims ownership, thereby indicating an altered tendency of the unconscious, i.e., showing what "it" wants. Rabbits and eggs are also common folkloristic symbols of Easter: the bunnies bring the eggs, not vice versa! But for the tale in the dream, this is of no concern: Easter, the holiday of resurrection and new life, has brought about the irrevocable turn in the dream.

Furthermore, the duplication of the rabbits could suggest that this symbolism is already on the threshold of consciousness.[617]

The dreamer's words, "they belong to me!" could be referring to precisely that: "Fertility and the new young life belong to me because I say so!" For the moment, it is the dream-ego speaking; however, I believe that the dreamer's unconscious attitude in this dream will help her with the difficulties she will experience in her new situation.

To conclude this section of the "positive" mother-dreams, here is another dream conveying the super-personal aspect of pregnancy.

A woman, who is thirty-nine weeks pregnant with her third child, having no complications at birth, dreamt:

Figure 58. Birth-goddess with fetuses and children (Mesopotamia)

Dream No. 157:

> *My cousin is also pregnant but it doesn't show because she is a little plump. The baby is due on December 24, but it will be like Spring then.*

The cousin (who is forty-five years old, with two children) personifies an aspect of the dreamer that is in tune with Nature. Pregnancy, there, is nothing extraordinary, or virtually normal for a woman who is naturally maternal,

---

[617] On motifs appearing in pairs, cf. Marie-Louise von Franz, *On Divination and Synchronicity*, Inner City Books, Toronto, 1980, p. 107

thanks to her figure. The 24th of December, the date the baby is due, suggests the intrinsically religious and cosmic significance of every human birth, and by the same token, of motherhood. Although at Christmas time it is still cold in our latitudes, the turning point-towards the emerging increase of light happens exactly when the position of the sun is lowest.

The hour of birth is also associated with Nature, – "it will be like Spring" – which, psychologically, can be regarded as a redeeming turn of events, like the birth of the Savior. In this kind of attitude, birth is not an isolated event but a vital element of the greater Nature and consequently of the will of God.

We must now turn our attention to the darker side of the mother-theme that is just as present in the dreams of pregnant women: dreams of not merely an ambivalent or "somewhat uncanny" but also plainly malicious mother-figure. These types of dreams belong to the most intense experience of terror that pregnant women (as well as other men and women) can have in dreams.

The Negative Mother and her attendants: Monster, witch, seductress, the mother who cages you up, and devouring mother-figures

To begin with, we are going to look at a dream we have discussed in Chapter 3.2. In Dream No. 20 "The Ring Robber," a savage man appears whose mother intervenes in a fight, trying to restore order and pacify the situation. We called the aggressor the dreamer's negative animus. But who is his "mother"?

The dream read: "I found many rings on the ground and put them on all my fingers. A strange man tried to rob me of all the rings. Then, an old woman appeared. She was the mother of the strange, wild man. She told him to give me only one ring that I could have: the ruby ring."

The woman appears confident, powerful and intelligent – like a queen or a goddess. She could personify the dreamer's Self. The odd thing, though, is that she has an evil "son." How can he be hers? We come upon similarly mysterious family relationships in the tale of "The Devil's Grandmother." She is sitting in a dark hole together with the devil but nevertheless helping those out of their fix who have landed there.[618] This motif exists in many tales. Such multi-layered mother figures are usually bound up with evil.

The German fairy tale, *Hansel and Gretel*, illustrates the most common problems resulting from a negative mother in a condensed manner. How is it possible that Hansel and Gretel, a pair of innocent children, banished from their own unfeeling mother, fall into the clutches of a child-devouring witch? Does this exist, psychologically? The cold mother, who turns out her own children, and the false fire-witch in her sugar-candy hut, are only different

---

[618] E.g., Grimm, *The Complete Grimm's Fairy Tales*, Pantheon Books, 1944, Nos. 29, 125 and 172

Figure 59. Gorgon (Syracus)

facets of the same archetype: namely, of the negative mother-archetype. The story of *Hansel and Gretel* stands for many fairy tales from various cultures. It addresses the danger and the overcoming of a negative, or more precisely, paralyzing or constricting maternal power. The term "negative mother" is a more modern name for what formerly used to be called, more graphically, a witch, evil sorceress, female demon or even dark mother-goddess, who were consistently held to be extremely powerful.[619]

In some cultures, savage, fire-spitting feminine divinities, or terrifying goddesses of fury and raging destructiveness, had their own recognized cults and sacrifices. People remembered how real they could be and endeavored to pacify them gently. Examples of this are Sechmet, the feared lion-headed goddess of Ancient Egypt,[620] and to this day, the black Kali of the Hindu religion. She is venerated as the Great Mother with her tongue sticking out and skulls dangling around her neck, wading in blood. Despite this, or rather as the Indians say, because of this, Kali is the great, highly venerated, protecting mother.

However, the inexplicable rage against one's own offspring, which will be the theme of the following dream, has long existed in myth, among the maenads, for instance. Pentheus was torn to pieces by his mother, and Medea killed her children in a rage of jealousy. In the classical myth, the once beautiful Lamia, whose children had been killed by Hera out of jealousy, was feared as a child-devourer because she would threaten expectant mothers at night and steal the newborn.[621] Lilith, the Near Eastern feminine demon – also a rejected woman – had a similar reputation, which extended all the way into Middle Europe,[622] and pregnant women wore amulets, in order to protect themselves against her. Remnants of this fear (e.g., of the evil eye) continue to exist in Southern Europe.

Hecate, the Goddess of the Moon and of Crossroads, was invoked for good deliveries in the entire Mediterranean region as she supposedly helped women in childbirth. At the same time, Hecate was known to be the one who oppressed them dreadfully.

One might be somewhat surprised by the descriptions of evil mothers in fairy tales, mythology and in the dreams of modern women. Are mothers not generally and by nature the most loving creatures in existence – full of good will and devotion to their children? Where, then, do their evil doings – which,

---

[619] The following two books contain a rich selection of interpretations of fairy tales regarding the theme of the mother: Marie-Louise von Franz, *The Feminine in Fairy Tales*, and Sybille Birkhäuser-Oeri, *The Mother: Archetypal Image in Fairy Tales*, Inner City Books, Toronto, 1988

[620] Cf. Chapter 5.4.

[621] Karl Kerényi, *The Gods of the Greeks*, Pelican Books, London, 1958

[622] Siegmund Hurwitz, *Lilith, The First Eve*, Daimon Verlag, Einsiedeln, Switzerland, 1992, p. 149 f

in some cases, actually have lifelong damaging effects – come from? Of course, the negative aspects of the maternal archetype can be equally destructive for men. We must admit that examining the ambivalence contained in the mother image from the standpoint of depth-psychology, does not explain or solve it. Although we may often ask why this is so, we do not always have the answer. What does seem to help sometimes, though, is to recognize the problem.

In myth, a helping hand and a menace are often represented by the same feminine figure. This type of mother-figure is, first and foremost, powerful and only secondarily either evil or good, or both. In contrast, the Christian Mary personifies exclusively the good, luminous and helping sides of the feminine. In accordance with the Catholic dogma, her femininity is fruitful but immaculate. It is a sad fact that this purification of the Christian mother image has been disastrous for the real woman. For a long time, any inexplicably bad or perilous things were attributed to those women who were believed to know things that could have only come from an evil spirit or from the devil himself: for example, secret knowledge about a woman's body, about illnesses, popular medical practices, and in particular, those involving birth, which had been considered to be impure. An unconscious feeling of dread and a strong tradition kept the men away from all this. Exactly what the women assistants did during a delivery was kept secret among the them and was considered heathen. For centuries, therefore, women were suspected of performing witchcraft and were persecuted.[623]

In the following dream, the mother-figure is patently dangerous. The dream appeared in the third or fourth week of the dreamer's first, planned pregnancy. We are in possession of a series of dreams by the same dreamer, which is helpful for the interpretation. Jung said of such series of related dreams: "They form a coherent series in the course of which the meaning gradually unfolds more or less of its own accord."[624] The first dream of the series (preceding the one below) contained the image of a giant, "prehistoric cat" that terrified the dreamer, for the giant cat was about to come through a glass wall at any moment.[625] Perhaps at the time she had a faint intuition about conception. In the following dream, though, she knew for sure that she was pregnant:

Dream No. 158:

> *I'm with friends and my husband out in a farm land. I see a woman who has many children start the woods and fields on fire with gasoline.*
> *I say that we need to go back and help to put it out. We go down to the woods and put it out. The woman invites us into her house to eat dinner. When we go inside, she tells us that we're never allowed to leave again.*

[623] Baechtold-Stäubli, *Schwangerschaft*, Bd. VII, p. 1407 ff
[624] C.G. Jung, CW 12, § 50
[625] Cf. Chapter 5.4, No. 75

*I find a knife that one of the children had left out. I'll use it to escape, but
one of the children tells the mother, and she takes it away.*
*Finally, we get out and run into a village. But here they won't let you
escape either. There are police out looking for us while we hide and try to
make our get-away.*

Our dream is set in the woods and fields, not far from a village. For every
pregnant woman, Nature takes on a special importance. The prehistoric, giant
cat is also an image of primal nature – interestingly, behind a glass wall. The
dream reflects perfectly what seems to be the dreamer's acute problem.

The action is clearly structured: first the "fire-setting" mother, then, the
putting out of the forest fire, being held captive by the mother, the unsuccessful attempt to escape, hiding from the police, and finally no lysis.

We must not consider the terror-inspiring mother as an ordinary human
being, but rather as a powerful figure of the Great Mother in the surroundings
of the forest and fields as a kind of Mother Nature or fire-witch.[626]

The dreamer, her husband and friends are in the open countryside. What
do we look for in the countryside? Fresh air, being close to Nature, taking deep
breaths, relaxing. But she finds everything that is not relaxation: something
desperately alarming is going on.

The dreamer tells everyone to help to put out the fire. This shows that the
dreamer is courageous; however, it is strange that she does not question the
dreadful arsonist or her children in any way. The problem is not solved,
although much cannot be wrong in trying to extinguish a forest fire! The
arsonist's next sly move is to invite everybody to dinner – a trap into which the
dreamer falls directly. This could be due to an unconscious fear causing a
strong urge to appease.

The two women are worlds apart – and yet, the false witch is just what the
dreamer soon wishes to become: a mother! We have come upon an unfortu-
nate entanglement, which is becoming ever tighter. Realizing that the dreamer
is "the entire dream herself," we begin to imagine how impossible it is to
straighten things out.

Seduction for the purpose of taking away someone's liberty turns the house
of a nurturing mother into a veritable prison. The imprisonment of Hansel and
Gretel springs to mind where the fairy tale witch, just like the mother in the
dream, triumphantly declares that no guests will ever leave this place again!

The dreamer attempts to escape; she finds a child's knife and wants to use
this to escape. A child's knife is, of course, inadequate – suggesting that the
dreamer is not equipped to defend herself against a negative maternal power.
As long as the "child in the dreamer" does not grow up and reach a certain
degree of wisdom, she will never be able to free herself.

The next scene takes place in the village: the police are after them, and the

[626] Sibylle Birkhäuser-Oeri, *The Mother: Archetypal Image in Fairy Tales*

terror continues. The fiendish mother has already mobilized another team of hers: nothing less than the authorities responsible for public order. She has everything in her hands: morality and the law, which makes her immune. The dreamer and her friends can but hide and continue to hope to escape. The dreamer is paralyzed, for the morality is within herself. The police represent her unconscious and compulsive control as well as her perseverance and the discord with her Self. The police also stand for a principal animus or norms: in this respect, too, she is caught.

By contrast, Gretel of *Hansel and Gretel* was much more able to cope with the sorceress who tried to lock her up.[627] The knife could have been an instrument for liberation as it can separate things neatly. Psychologically, it has the function of an objective analysis leading to deeper insights. However, in this dream, it is merely a child's knife: too small and probably not sharp enough. Hence, the dreamer, despite a rational decision to get away, is too infantile or still "too good" to make a success of it: she is not equipped to stand up for herself in a conflict with the confining mother.

Let us return now to the initial fire. Given that the fire was kindled artificially and with the help of children, we suspect the presence of a certain shrouded psychological message or at least of something contradictory.

Taking the subjective approach, it is likely that an unconscious impulse within the dreamer deliberately kindled the fire due to a lack of other available means. It is as if the gasoline signified a means of deliberately, albeit artificially, providing some heat for the dreamer's affective function. I can see unconscious tactics on the part of the dreamer whereby using the children – i.e., a means of sexuality, pregnancy and birth – she tries to kindle the fire of love and human affective warmth. However, this turns out to be a self-destructive act with the correspondingly detrimental consequences.[628]

Thus the rational attempt to extinguish the fire turned out to be a vain operation, for no attempt had been made to come to terms with the initiator of the fire – in other words, with the dreamer's own negative-feminine unconscious.

Now, looking at all this objectively, a personal negative experience seems to be at play: the mother-image appears to be severely perturbed. In the dreamer's inner life, there seem to be irreconcilable opposites violently confronting each other. The domain of "fire" – that is, being passionate, warm, or instinctive – seems to be so drastically split off that it can only manifest from out of the shade, in a manner hostile to life.[629] For a pregnancy, this can entail an oppressive inner burden.

---

[627] *Ibid.*
[628] Barbara Hannah, "The Problem of Women's Plots" in *The Evil Vineyards*, The Guild of Pastoral Psychology, Guild Lecture 51, London, 1948
[629] Cf. the ominous giant cat behind glass wall in Dream No. 75, Chapter 5.4

The following dream describes another basic problem, namely maternal coldness. We know from the commentary that the pregnancy was not planned and not wanted by either of the partners. However, the thirty-nine-year-old dreamer is still aware that this may be her last chance to become pregnant. She is therefore unsure as to what she should do.

Dream No. 159:

> *Her refrigerator was closed, and she couldn't open it. She was angry because she was hungry. At last she opens it, with difficulty. Inside, she found a very small, frozen baby. She was desperate.*

Hunger in a dream represents an instinctive, forward-pushing condition that is driven by the survival instinct. It is, in actual fact, the vital instinct that can manifest physically as a stomachache, and emotionally, as anger.

Feeling hungry drives her to find something that will satisfy her. This suggests that there is somewhere a deep psychic dissatisfaction: this could have to do with her job or partnership or the attitude to life she has hitherto had.

The feeling of hunger apparently impels her to open the fridge, or herself, as she is both the fridge and the baby, as it were. The dream allows this, then challenges her to feel that she needs to feed herself or her soul more adequately than she has so far done. A vital instinct has awoken in her.

Her innermost being, "her child" – i.e., something of essence – had been drastically undercooled and, figuratively speaking, she had allowed her own fertility to wither away. In the dream, she immediately recognizes this and is overcome with desperation. In reality, the fetus within her is alive, albeit unwanted. It has, however, crossed her mind that this could be her last chance to have a child.

In the deepest layers of her soul a much more far-reaching conflict goes on, for which the dream produces this dramatic imagery. Although the fetus is still alive, the glacial aura surrounding her feelings and the anticipation of a possible abortion have already killed it – that is, killed the psychic potential it represents in the eyes of the unconscious. The dream suggests this quite unambiguously. The refrigerator symbolizes inner coldness, or a lack of the warmth of Eros. This leads us to associate the words refrigerator or fridge with "frigid." Whether or not, medically speaking, our dreamer is indeed frigid, we do not know, though psychologically, this certainly seems to be the case, given that she has a hard, tightly shut shell (the fridge) in which it is horribly cold.

A further aspect: it is possible that the child, whom we interpret as being a vital impulse from her Self, was "put on ice" at a certain time in her life and that she had intended to make use of it when it would suit her. This attitude would be too egocentric, however, for no child or new impulse can grow without warmth or devotion.

Therefore, the dream image shows not only a danger of freezing the child, but also a danger of devouring it: although the dreamer has opened the refrigerator, which could lead her to a painful insight into herself, it seems evident that there is also a possibility of her using her real child to feed herself – that is, that, psychologically, she would devour it. There is only one way out of this dilemma: namely, to let the hunger enter the consciousness and to try to come to terms with it.

As we have already mentioned, the baby as representing a part of herself, is a young but immature, stunted aspect in her that is in urgent need of warmth and needs to develop its own warmth in order to survive. For this reason, it is good that the lysis of the dream reveals her feeling of desperation. This is where her soul is coming alive.

Whether or not she can carry a child to term we cannot tell; however, we received several other dreams that seemed to indicate that an inner development had commenced. One of them is about a little box that she finds under her bed, and having become curious, she puts it on her bed and covers it with a sheet, in order to protect it. This image is suggestive of a tendency towards a new attitude vis-à-vis life. It points to a definite improvement from the image of a fridge containing a frozen baby.

In the course of our research, we have frequently come upon the theme of death for the sake of potential rebirth. Dreams are images of a psychic reality. When they manifest death, a dismembered body, blood and putrefaction, we can, as a rule, view them in terms of symbols. This does not render them harmless by any means, but they must be interpreted on a plane other than a concrete one. This is important since pregnant women can be exposed to the most terrifying ideas or intuitions through dreams about death, blood or dismemberment. However, these images usually signify transformation, that is, the end of something that has been outlived and therefore has to die, in order to make room for a new approach. This aspect is also present in the dream about the baby in the fridge: the sense of despair and despondency is the inevitably painful beginning of a new attitude.

Dream No. 160 (this is the dreamer's first wanted pregnancy; the birth of the child is five weeks premature; both parents are taking their doctoral degrees):[630]

> *I kept returning to a spot that was walled-up; I took away the stones and found something. I also complained about it somewhere. I went there again and again.*
> *It was already covered with tar.*
> *I accidentally pulled a large stone out and found a small child in the arms*

---

[630] following dreams by the same dreamer have already been discussed: No. 141 in Chapter 7, No. 84 in Chapter 5.6, No. 58 in Chapter 5.2

of a knocked-over Madonna statue, which had been discarded by the church. I pulled the child out of there and held it in my arms, tenderly. It was a little boy.

I expressed my indignation to those who were present. An elegantly dressed woman denied that she knew anything about it. But she betrayed herself by showing me the "ham corner" where boys could deposit food for the little child. All I could say and repeat, as I followed the woman holding the child, was: "Murderess! Murderess!"

It would appear that the dreamer, who in reality is preoccupied with her doctorate, "discarded" an important psychic content that she had deemed to be useless. According to her comments, she had already had several dreams in which something was buried but still somehow alive.

In the present dream, the dream-ego is worried about something that has not been finished and tries to investigate, although the spot behind the wall was by now "covered with tar," as she says. This clearly implies that somebody (or she herself) had once wanted to get rid of something, had decidedly covered up a problem or "swept it under the carpet," so to speak. But now that she is pregnant, the problem has come back to her, bothering her. Again and again, she goes to the same spot and finally pulls out a large stone, which had been blocking her "in-sight."

Her discovery is devastating: a Madonna statue that has been cast aside holding a living child in her arms! She pulls the child out and affectionately takes it in her arms. She also complains to whomever is there, which suggests that we are dealing with a personal, but also with a collective problem.

The dream-incident with the "elegantly dressed lady" could mean that, although she denies having anything to do with it, she also tries to justify herself, thereby indicating the secret chance of survival the buried child has.

On a subjective level, therefore, there were still secret, relatively infantile impulses (the boys) in her that endeavored to rescue "baby Jesus," i.e., to feed it and secretly to keep it alive. It is as if the dreamer had preserved a kind of childlike belief in the "Madonna with Child," but that this had become incompatible with the more scientific-rational *Weltbild* she had constructed. Moreover, they (she) had energetically supported her loss of the belief, for now the spot was "covered with tar."

It is through such pregnancy dreams that one can discover that something may be wrong in the depths of the soul. Previously, the dreamer had been unaware that "burying and forgetting" might imply a deeply moral problem, too. In the dream, she perceives this as murder, calling after the elegant lady: "Murderess! Murderess!" – to make it clear that she is the culprit. But who is this woman?

She is a facet existing within the dreamer herself – a shadow-figure representing a part in her that wanted to have nothing to do with the mother-child-problem but instead sought elegance, success and prestige. Because the elegant woman is among the group of bystanders – i.e., the public, as it were – we can call this psychic figure her *persona*, which Jung called "a segment of the collective psyche."[631] Here, it could define our dreamer's attitude of not wanting to bother about inner growth or maturation, maternal devotion or the responsibility of having children, but rather seeking esteem in the outside world.

I suppose that the dreamer is not wholly unconscious of this ambitious side in her but she evidently did not think she could be punished for it. The elegant lady could furthermore stand for the way the dreamer thought she could elegantly get her doctorate and pregnancy under one umbrella. However, the unconscious is giving out signals by producing compensatory imagery proposing a very different view of things. In the buried Madonna, the dream invents a drastic image so as to broaden and correct her conscious attitude. Should she succeed in becoming conscious of the one-sidedness of her present attitude: this, in turn, could result in a deeper understanding of pregnancy as well as of her religious feelings.

Another negative mother-dream by the same dreamer had appeared just before she became pregnant:

Dream No. 161:

> *Two women were running, following me. I was also running, very frightened, get into a room and leave for another one. Finally, I get into a room without exit. I sat down in the corner, on the floor, holding my knees. Then, I noticed that there was just one woman, and she was my mother (who died sixteen years ago). At first, I was surprised, but then I said: "Don't kill me, mother. I do not want to die yet." She answered that she did not want me but the one I was carrying in my womb. I screamed: "But I am not pregnant!" –"Yes, you are," she told me, "and I am going to put some little drops on you, so you will miscarry."*
> *I was desperate, and crying, I screamed: "I do not want to be pregnant, but if it is true, no one will take away my son!"*

To begin with, there is the motif of being persecuted by an evil mother, similar to Dream No. 158; however, here the menace is directed towards the child of whose conception the dreamer is still unaware at this point. The mother, having been dead for sixteen years, reappears like an evil spirit, shortly before the conception. We do not have any information about her (and will not speculate about whether or not the dream mother objectively represents her real mother). On the inner, subjective plane, our dreamer is still haunted by the fears she has always had with regard to her mother. Although

---

[631] For the concept of the *persona*, cf. Dream No. 20, Chapter 3

at first she is chased by two women, she then realizes that it is her mother alone who has "cornered" her.

What does this mean? First, it is a partially conscious, partially unconscious, rather generalized duplication of a feminine image persecuting her – until she notices that it is only her own mother, who had died sixteen years earlier. It is likely, therefore, that her mother had always threatened her and inhibited her growing.

The dream shows the malicious and threatening fantasies about the mother that are still at work in her unconscious. Thus, even if, in the past, she tried to come to terms with her mother, this could only have worked on a distant, rational level. What is alarming, however, is that the aggressive mother is out to kill the daughter's unborn child and plots to do this with little poisonous drops – or quiet critical remarks: she can kill off the "germs" that are growing in her daughter.

The unconscious has thus created a mother image capable of poisoning her daughter by quietly denigrating, drop by drop, the part in her that was young and growing (the child in her womb) – presumably attempting to destroy everything that mattered most to her.

We have no way of knowing whether a negative aspect of the mother-archetype is acting autonomously, appearing in the figure of the personal mother, or whether they are unconscious reminiscences of her that have produced the evil image: the ultimate effect, though, is the same. However, the daughter has learned to stand up for herself. Moreover, she is able to state the facts: "I do not want to be pregnant, but if it is true, no one will take away my son!" Her unconscious proves to be superior to the evil mother. In reality, despite a difficult pregnancy and already being the mother of two, the dreamer struggled through, fully accepting the third child. At the end of her pregnancy, she had Dream No. 47, which expresses her being in a fundamental harmony with the natural process going on in her body.[632]

---

[632] Cf. Dream No. 47, Chapter 5.1

Figure 60. Mother with child (Italy 5ᵗʰ-6ᵗʰ cent.)

9.1. Breast, Breast-feeding and Breast Milk

Irmgard Bosch

Breast-feeding is important for the well-being of both the mother and child.

After existing in the timeless, perfect security of the maternal womb, followed by the brutal expulsion through the birth canal into the unaccustomed cold of the outside world, the period of drinking from the maternal breast provides a partial continuation of the former warmth. This preconscious experience or the nostalgia that surrounds it is likely to be one of the fundamental experiences conditioning human relationships. Being nursed, as a temporary relief of the separation from the mother, signifies the first reconciliation with the world: a world that, initially, consists uniquely of this one entity called mother, wet nurse or nurse – the very person nurturing us after the expulsion from paradise.

Examining the earliest known representations of man, we cannot fail to notice the conspicuous breasts of feminine statuettes from as early as the Paleolithic Age.[633] We often find breasts held or touched by hands, as if they were precious vessels.

The early Egyptians depicted the rain streaming from the breast of Nut, the Goddess of the Sky. They painted the Spring of Life into the branches of the Tree of Isis, who is feeding the pharaoh.[634] Artemis, as a deity of Nature, was depicted with a hundred breasts. In all cultures, we encounter the image of the mother with a child at her breast: Mary with the infant Jesus, Isis with Horus as a boy, or Demeter with Kore.

In India, the waters of the rivers that are considered feminine – primarily, the great rivers Ganges and Jamuna – are venerated

Figure 61. Isis as a Tree-goddess, feeding the pharaoh

[633] Cf. Erich Neumann, *The Great Mother*
[634] Cf. Figure 62: Thutmosis III suckled by Isis in the guise of a Sycamore-tree, 16th-14th cent. B.C., from: *The Tree of Life*, New York, 1974. Cf. also Chapter 4.2, Figure 14

for rendering holy, cleansing and nourishing all the Hindu as well as Moslem peoples. There are incalculable connections to milk, to the cow and to ghee [clarified butter], the quintessence of milk that is used as an offering to the gods. According to the ancient Hindu Scriptures, the *Puranas*, the entire universe was brought forth by the churning of Ksiroda, the primal Milky Ocean in which Vishnu lay in a deep, contemplative sleep.[635] Hence, for a religious Hindu, milk bears a spiritual content.

The Hebrews seem to have had a similar idea. They called their promised land "the land flowing with milk and honey"[636] expressing at once the infinite mercy of God that their land promises.

In Antiquity, milk generally stands for the light and comforting side of God. Let us not forget that to the people of those times, milk tasted far sweeter than it does to contemporary man, who has become so used to sugar! Marie-Louise von Franz comments: "In the ancient mysteries, milk plays an important role as being the nourishment of the spiritually reborn (*in novam infantium*). In the Phrygian mysteries, for instance, the mystic abstained from eating meat "and moreover, he fed on milk as one newly born."[637, 638]

In Christian antiquity, milk was considered a medium for spiritual instruction – for example, in the first Epistle of Peter: "As newborn babes, desire the sincere milk of the word, that ye may grow thereby: If so be, ye have tasted that the Lord is gracious."[639]

"That the Lord is gracious" and that He can be loved in innocent love, is "the milk of piousness," that is the special purity of a heart that trusts the Lord – which is, without doubt, what has become the goal of Christian life and thought – with all the consequences this one-sidedness has shown: "Blessed are the pure in heart: for they shall see God."[640]

However, like everything that looks pure, milk easily spoils. The witches were particularly keen on fresh milk because of its purity. There were countless rituals, in order to protect the precious milk from their evil eye and other bad spells (for example, immediate straining, covering, crucifying or bespeaking[641]). Breast-feeding mothers had to be carefully protected against magic effects perpetrated by envious spirits and female demons, such as Lilith, Hecate and the Lamia. According to folklore, they could transform the mother's milk into blood or poison or let the milk of mothers and cattle completely run dry.

---

[635] Volker Möller, *Die Mythologie der vedischen Religion und des Hinduismus*, in: H.W. Haussig, *Wörterbuch der Mythologie*, I, S. 135

[636] Ex. 3, 8

[637] Marie-Louise von Franz, *The Passion of Perpetua*, Spring Publications, University of Dallas, Texas, 1980, p. 33

[638] Karl Wyss, *Die Milch im Kultus der Griechen und Römer*, Giessen, 1914

[639] 1 Peter, 2, 2/3

[640] Mt. 5. 8

[641] Bächtold-Stäubli, *Handwörterbuch des deutschen Aberglaubens*, Vol. 6, p. 243 ff

Breast-milk played an important role in the love play, e.g., as a remedy against impotence. Beneficial animals living in and around the house, such as snakes and toads, were given their daily bowl of milk with the idea of preserving their own, and thereby everyone's, life in the house.[642] Offerings of milk were also made to the dead – perhaps to appease them, too.

We have seen in Dream No. 153 that experienced women – usually the mother, a mid-wife, friend or formerly, a neighbor – would help the young mother with breast-feeding. However, as a first dream on the theme of the breast and breast-feeding, I would like to present the rare dream-image of a helping old man because of the highly archaic image it represents.

The dreamer's unconscious appears to be preoccupied with fertility. It was not certain that she was pregnant, although the pregnancy was planned. The dream is from Brazil.

Dream No. 162:

> I am naked. I am sitting on a beautiful meadow. It is late afternoon, it will be dark soon.
> An older man with gray hair and a beard is near me. He holds a long needle in his hand. He pricks my breasts all around the nipples, not the red part, but the white skin.
> Milk flows out of the little holes he made.
> I wake up. I am happy.

We notice that the pricking is not painful. At first, an old doctor comes to mind giving an injection or drawing blood. Taking a closer look at the scene, we realize that we are dealing with an archaic situation.

The dreamer is naked, sitting on a beautiful meadow. She is in a primordial state, like Eve in Eden. The sun is setting in the dream: we descend to an even lower layer of the unconscious, creating room for a unique paradisiacal experience.

Who is the old man with a gray beard? Is this an image of the Lord, the Father and Creator? As if for the first time, God creates the openings of the breasts and has milk flow from them. The dreamer's happiness at the end leads us to believe that she has a good spiritual attitude corresponding to a positive animus. This could be, for example, a natural and deeply rooted religious feeling that will enable the dreamer to have trust in the events. She awakens feeling happy: her breasts turn into spring fountains; she can become a mother.

Thus the old man turns her into a true Eve – in Hebrew, a "mother of life." The meadow, gay with flowers, adds the healthy vegetative soil, the basis of growth and thriving.

---

[642] Grimm, *The Complete Grimm's Fairy Tales*, No. 105

At the same time, the procedure is evocative of the painful initiation practices of primitive cultures, such as puberty or fertility rites, that were often done through incisions. (Circumcision and tattooing still exist among many cultures today.) The old man could thus be reminiscent of a medicine man or a shaman.

Our dreamer's unconscious seems to say here: yes, it is a turning point, or an incision. One that God makes and that makes me happy.

Although Eve may be "the mother of life," let us nevertheless not disregard the other aspects of the feminine. Adam did not have one, but two wives!

According to Zohar and other mystic Jewish texts, Lilith was created together with Adam, as his equal and female fellow human being. According to these traditions, only after she had rebelled against her "inferior" position and was driven away did God take a rib from Adam and make of it Eve, who then became the mother of humankind.

Lilith, the ancient goddess of the moon, the changeable-feminine, the outcast, turned into a seductive, savage demon. Until a few decades ago, women with bare breasts were associated with magic or witches – even in our latitudes. The dream images do not seem to take any notice of topless beaches and the fashion that has rendered breasts less sensitive. The dreams seem to indicate archaic conditions and a raging war of the sexes.

The upsets and provocations produced by the mixed signals of bare breasts tend to get blown away and defeated. Instead we are seized by tender and loving feelings in the presence of a nursing mother. The image seems to create an aura of perfect peace, of renewed innocence and fantasies of a blissful primal state that has temporarily been attained.

Breast-feeding for the infant is not only a comforting continuation of the physical contact with the mother, but it also offers the new mother an indispensable time of peace and quiet with the child in which she can reconcile herself to her maternal role and the beginning of a new life. It is in these moments that the love-threads are spun, which under favorable circumstances, can last throughout their lives. The eye contact between mother and child that is established within a few days, if not immediately, is the natural channel for an exchange of feeling during the time of a very close physical and psychic union between them. The eye contact at feeding time gradually helps to dissolve any last remnants of fears or doubts the mother may have. This also applies when children have to be given a bottle instead of the breast.

Figure 62. Hathor with child Horus

Sometimes, breast-feeding can be a source of worry and frustrate both the mother and child. Nevertheless, the theme of breast-feeding in our dream collection shows relatively little drama or ambivalence. Once the child is known to be healthy and the afterpains are over, the pains, dangers and anxiety are easily forgotten.

The extraordinary powers of breast milk are also illuminated in an ancient Indian fairy tale: A Yakkhini, a child-devouring demon, seduced a newborn prince. When they search for her, she hides in a water-pipe. In the narrow space of the pipe, the newborn accidentally grabs her nipple. "She felt maternal love awaken in her and raised the boy...." An Arabian fairy tale tells of a monster, who is incapable of harming the hero because he had previously secretly sucked her nipples.[643]

The picture of the mother with the child at her breast has become a symbol of heavenly peace. In Mediterranean regions, the image has existed long before Christianity, and it is thought to originate in matriarchal socio-cultural forms of the time.

The following dream comes from a woman, who was three months pregnant:

Dream No. 163:

> *I have had my second baby, a girl. I am sad, I would have liked a boy. I cry at night.*
> *One day, as I am breast-feeding it, it has turned into a little tiger-cat, the kind I would have always loved to have. Perhaps I shall want a third child....*

After the disappointment of the newborn's not being a boy, breast-feeding soon helps to establish an inner bond with the child: As the mother gives it the breast, the child is transformed into a tiger-cat, something the dreamer has always wished for. This signifies that the instincts have been awakened and now that she is a "tiger mother," as it were, it no longer matters whether the child is a boy or a girl, as long as the child is healthy and feeds well. The dreamer has suddenly become aware of an ongoing fertility, causing her to play with the idea of having yet another child.

Pregnancy dreams about breast-feeding often address the relationship to one's own mother or to motherhood in general. It can be an indication that pregnancy is an opportunity to try to solve the problems in the mother-daughter relationship that occurred during puberty. We generally find that tensions between mothers and daughters decrease with the daughter's having her own children and that the help offered by the mother is then more easily requested or accepted (see dreams Nos. 155, 156).

---

[643] *Buddhistische Märchen aus dem alten Indien*, Leipzig, 1961, No. 4, and *Arabische Märchen*, Fischer Taschenbuch No. 480, Frankfurt, 1977, p. 66

If the way to a reconciliation with one's own mother is nevertheless not smooth and painless, it is partly due to the fact that, today, a woman's attitude to her own feminine position is characterized by a deep ambivalence. In some cases, tensions prevail throughout their lives. Given the far-reaching changes models and ideals of womanhood have undergone, daughters are no longer able to take guidance from their mothers. It is useful to reflect on this very consciously.

The following dream appeared on the 2nd or 3rd day after the birth of this woman's child. The dreamer is impatient to see whether or not she will be able to breastfeed her child. After having nursed her baby for the first time, she dozed off and dreamt:

Dream No. 164:

> *I am alone with my mother – am I visiting her or do I live with her? In any case, the atmosphere is bad. I feel like a spoilt daughter. I am torn between feelings of anger with myself or for my mother, and feeling sorry. At some point, I lose control over my anger and I deliberately do something – I can't remember what – to upset her. Now I'm feeling worse than before and oppressed by a bad conscience.*
> *Later, I lie down on a bed. I want this inner tension to ease off. Just before 11 o'clock, my mother comes and sets the table.*
> *My anger comes back, and I feel nervous. Why does she bring food now? I'm not hungry, but she always wants to make things better with food; that's what she used to do when I was depressed, but she just hasn't found the right tone. The tension inside me becomes unbearable.*
> *Now she comes in with a huge pot of rice. I want to insist, but all of a sudden the whole tension has gone: I feel that my mother really wants to do something to please me. She agonized over what she could cook for me: she does what she can.*
> *Life is strange, I say, we always have to start over again.*

This dream refers to a very common mother-daughter-problem: the mother seems to continue to play the somewhat helpless role of the food-provider – the one trying to communicate or act through nourishment, as it were. It is a typical image of a mother who never quite let go of her own nursing instinct! Her feeding efforts, to say the least, were not at all appreciated by her daughter, who, at the time, was growing up and had to cope with all her insecurities about her own feminine body. It is a common conflict: the mother resorts to food, not knowing how else to help the depressed adolescent or how to fight the threat of a breakdown of communications. Behind this can be a mother's own fear of loss: "Come, have something to eat (perhaps you'll want to talk to me…)."

The road to independence is indeed difficult for a young person, particularly because there are strong regressive tendencies that want to pull the girl back to a protected childhood. A girl has to learn to accept the inevitable manifestations of her feminine body while at the same time she is hungry for freedom, independence – and above all, for spiritual nourishment rather than for soup. Her animus becomes active in her struggle with the mother, frequently resulting in much mutual injury.

In such times of crises, sometimes life-threatening ones (anorexia, bulimia, running away), a mother is tempted to concentrate on ensuring that there is plenty to eat. A hair's breadth of more care than the daughter can tolerate provokes in her a feeling of being patronized and not being given enough independence, which leads to anger and rejection (particularly if she represses the fact that the mother has only the best of intentions). Better to go hungry than to remain a small child!

We find that the daughter, who is in this situation in her dream, has just given the breast to her baby for the first time. She relives in the dream what happened in her adolescence – her anger becomes unbearable. The mother was unable or did not want to respond to her daughter's confusing needs and instead had remained on the biological food-supply-level. In turn, the daughter was not prepared to recognize her mother's signals of love, which reached her in the wrong form.

Now, reality has added something new to the dreamer's life: she herself has become a mother and has assumed the ancient task of feeding an infant. In a flash, it strikes her (feeling, not just rationally knowing it) that her mother "really wanted to please her"; that is, she can suddenly empathize with her mother: "She does what she can." All the tension disappears instantaneously. Her unconscious has grasped the situation – a reconciliation takes place. The lysis of the dream comes with a big sigh: "We always have to start over again."

The following dream appeared immediately after a delivery:

Dream No. 165:

> It's summer in a public swimming pool, a big muddle. I've lost my bearings. There are many people and I know only my mother and Gregor. In order to collect myself I, go to the WC. I squeeze my nipples; at first a little premilk comes, but then little worms wriggle out of my breasts. Then I know that the right milk will flow. I feel very happy about this.

The dream reflects how the dreamer's unconscious perceived the birth that is only just over – namely, as a large public swimming pool with crowds of unknown people among whom she can recognize only her husband and her mother.

The overwhelming event of the delivery is perceived like plunging into the water. In pregnancy dreams, this is a common image as the movement of the waves are like the "flowing and ebbing" of the contractions. She has lost her bearings and perhaps, to orient herself, she looks for a WC, where she can be alone and collect her thoughts. The WC also frequently figures in dreams as symbolizing a protected place for creativity. Children's usual spontaneous attitude towards what they are "producing" there quietly is a product of creativity. The close proximity of the anus and the genitalia as well as the pushing reminiscent of the bearing down at delivery, as well as the elementary necessity of allowing it to happen, have provided for a number of analogies.

The dream produces a strange image to show how she furthers her own creative process: she squeezes her nipples and is excited to see how after a bit of "premilk," little worms wriggle out of the breasts – another analogy for a delivery. Now she knows that the right milk will flow soon.

Worms are an archaic image representing the life coming from the bowels of the earth: something amorphous turns into something living. The production of nourishment from the breast is another one of those "magic" deeds of Nature, and our dreamer performs her own act of initiation in a highly independent way.

During a desired pregnancy that proceeded without any complications, an American medical doctor dreamt several times the following dream that frightened her greatly:

Dream No. 166:

> *I'm playing with my baby. Suddenly, I realize with terror that he is silently dying in a corner, absolutely motionless! I had forgotten to nourish him!*

The dreamer's unconscious produces a drastic image to manifest its state of distress. It would appear that something as elementary as nourishment is missing, suggesting a psychic deficiency, e.g., warmth or a failure to understand instinctive needs. The "child" is psychically starving to death because it is being played with before its basic physical needs have been fulfilled. The dream could be saying that the young mother should now concentrate on the more elementary and simple things pertaining to her new situation. Having children and raising them is not "mere child's play."

Viewing this on the subjective level, the starving child could represent a neglected young creative side in the dreamer that she does not take sufficiently seriously (playing with the child) and that, moreover, she forgets, perhaps because of the rather strict rationality required in her profession.

In dreams of pregnant women, breast-feeding and mother's milk frequently stand for the totality of the feelings the mother can or wishes to give the child. A woman dreamt she added ovaltine – a nutritious concentrate – to the breast milk!

Sometimes, children are surprisingly demanding in dreams. Here follows the end of a detailed dream about the birth:

Dream No. 167:

> ... *Much family around. My baby was hungry, but he didn't want to drink milk: he wants spirits.*

Let us first interpret this excerpt objectively: surrounded by all the family, the child needs spirits, or symbolically speaking, spiritual nourishment. Furthermore, motherhood extends beyond breast-feeding and cooking porridge. Looking at it on a subjective level, "my baby" could refer to a new impulse in the dreamer's psychic household telling her that it needs urgent attention and spiritual nourishment!

The dreamer of the following dream had polio when she was three years old and therefore limps with her left leg. Both she and her husband wanted a child. Earlier dreams show a positive attitude towards pregnancy:

Dream No. 168:

> *She gives birth to a baby ... a small but well-built child. She gives him her right breast, since the left one produces a mixture of milk and blood.*

The milk and blood mixture may be directly connected with the fate of the dreamer. The left side is the side of suffering and sorrow: it is lame. The unconscious seems to correct this by pointing to her right side, where normal milk flows. It is as if the unconscious made a pun on the word "right," and that for the dreamer, the right side is the correct side. It is right to feed the infant the "normal," white milk and not (yet) to let it taste the mother's sorrowful, "mixed" left side.

The pair of opposites of milk and blood is an ancient symbol. They occur together in several languages, e.g., in German and Russian, where to describe a face that is the very picture of health, one says, "a face of milk and blood," meaning its freshness and innocence on a background of ephemerality and death. Milk and blood are both different in color but also relatives: both are vital bodily fluids, or "saps of life." However, when red and white occur together they symbolize vulnerability, love and pain or sorrow. An example of this is the fairy tale, *Snow-White*, in which the queen sees the drops of blood in the snow and wishes for a child in these colors. She dies in childbirth, and her fantasies could be said to be a "pregnancy dream." In Wolfram's *Parsifal*, a few drops of blood in the snow of a dead wild goose that had been killed by a falcon spellbind the hero, for he sees in them the love and suffering he has inflicted upon his wife by leaving her.

Coming back to our dream, we could say that it is inappropriate to burden the infant with such ambivalent emotions and that it should have pure white milk without adding blood to it. Thus, the dreamer's attention is drawn to her healthy and normal side with which she can feed her child.

10. Creation Motifs

Regina Abt

In the preceding chapters, we have seen an extraordinary wealth of themes in pregnancy dreams. These dreams do not only outline the child's specific, personal origins, but they also present a *recapitulation of the creation of life on earth as a whole.* Just as the physical fetus in the womb repeats the biological evolution in man in a shortened form, so pregnancy dreams offer a mythological description of the psychic evolution of humankind.

Viewed in this light, each child who has been conceived is not only a statistical billionth continuation of its species, but also a *cosmic primal event* each time. This has to do with the cosmogonic meaning of human consciousness, which C.G. Jung spoke about in his memories.[644] In each new human being the unconscious spirit of the world (*Weltgeist*) opens its eyes and sees itself for the first time.[645] The following dream of a twenty-year-old woman illustrates this in a powerful way:

Dream No. 169:

> I am sitting on the globe together with a dragon. Out of one of his heads the dragon conjures up a silken blanket with the sun, moon and stars. The blanket is very soft and moves like light waves. My skin turns into fire, and yet it is cool like water. The dragon spits out one sun after another into all directions. Steam rises from his nose, and his eyes become red-hot. His skin is hard and rough. He seems not to feel anything through it. Our globe carries us into a storm. The earth turns to the other side, and flashes of lightning go through the air. Whenever another planet comes too close to ours, the dragon swallows it up. I fear for the world because the (dragon)-monster near me is in such a rage. But taking a closer look, I realize that it is sending birds out from one of its four eyes. The birds keep a look out for what is lacking on the other planets. The

---

[644] C.G. Jung, *Memories, Dreams, Reflections,* p. 255 f
[645] Verbal formulation from Dr. M.-L. von Franz

431

dragon is going to have these things sent to them. Depending on the needs, he will rain, spit fire or will drop rocks down like scales from his horny skin. Everything is in motion and changing all the time away and towards each other, unpredictably, fermenting. While he follows the goings-on around us with his eyes, he now turns to me and says he wants to make love to me. When he touches me, his skin is not of horn but like the little hairs of a thousand fruits, and his breath is like the breath of a thousand animals. Unlike a colossus, he moves easily on the waves of our blanket and glides through the fluid air everywhere at the same time. His eyes are made of lava, shifting from one side to the other because of the heat – thus creating new pictures. He permeates all my pores, and his touch is like light sailing over me. His long, silky hair covers me all the way down to the earth. It feels as though he is sleeping within me whereas, in fact, he never sleeps. He sleeps from eternity to eternity. In his sleep, he moves inside my belly and dreams. He is growing and keeps on turning round. He grows to be tall and round and rolls out of my belly to join the other worlds. Once he is among them, he unravels himself and skips away. He can walk! The dragon is still next to me and telling his stories in my ears. He asks me whether I like him and rains softly over my skin. He becomes a bird, a bull, a cat and a louse, and I know that nobody ever let me be so beautiful. He points to the former belly that is jumping about among the other worlds and says: "Look here, my son!"

We presume that this was not a pure dream but at least partially imagination and fantasy – which are, however, also expressions of the unconscious. We shall restrict ourselves to expounding upon the symbol of the dragon.

In the *I Ching*, the Chinese *Book of Changes*, the dragon represents the cosmic energy that stands behind all creative processes on earth.[646] He has been presented as a kind of agile-electric arousing force manifesting itself in storms, thunder and lightning. In the winter, this force is reabsorbed into the earth and reemerges in early summer. The dragon is "the arousing," bursting forth from the earth and soaring up to the thundery sky. It needs the dragon, the creative act of God, in order to originate creation in the beyond from all things in their germinal form. In the beyond, everything pertaining to the future still rests in the form of primal images or ideas that are waiting to be shaped into life by the divine creative power. The dragon marks the beginning and conception of all creatures. It is the creative power of Nature signifying perpetual development. The outer image of the creative is the heavens. The dragon is the force propelling him on tirelessly. He embodies the intrinsic force of creation.

---

[646] Wilhelm and Baynes, *I Ching, The Book of Changes*, Bollingen, 1987

According Ibn Arabi, the great Arabic Sufistic mystic who lived in Andalusia in the twelfth century, God created the universe having imagined it. In doing so, God manifests and reflects His own divinity in His creatures. Each creature has one of the infinite names of the otherwise hidden, invisible God. Thus, the human soul is the form through which the divine existence is declared. The numerous divine names are pure potentialities without any concrete existence. Only through the soul can they "be," that is, become recognized. Thus, the divine essence of man declares itself in an individual as one of the divine names. For this reason, Ibn Arabi said that every creature has its divine dimension, its own angel. Without this relationship, man is lost in the religious or social collectivity – which is also why, according to him, there was not one God for All but every man had his own particular God. Furthermore, man's active imagination is a moment of divine imagination representing God in every mortal creature. This is why it is creative. It shows that creation is a cosmic event.[647]

The above fantasy is suggestive of such cosmic perspectives. It compensates, as it were, the banal modern perception of the birth of a new human being.

Contrary to the fantasy, the following is a genuine dream by a thirty-six-year-old woman, who is two months pregnant.

Dream No. 170:

> My menstrual period is starting. Is it a miscarriage? I give birth to a small parcel, in the form of an embryo, wrapped in three blankets. I remove two of them, the third one only when my friend Urs is with me. He embraces me. It is lovely. We are sitting at a table. There are students with us. Now I unwrap the third blanket and open up everything very carefully. I can see little figures. Each of them is a type of a human being. They all wear the mark of Cain on their forehead. In the end, Mother Mary appears. She is round, maternal (like an Italian), at one with herself and content. Now I can see the inner side of the blanket (which is now very large). It has on it a beautiful mosaic illustrating the Garden of Eden, the paradise with two rivers, people and animals. Urs is deeply engrossed in it and explains to us the imagery and symbols. We are all very impressed. On the reverse side of the blanket more symbols have been woven in – among others, a cross that has been rounded-off.

Biologically, menstruation is a kind of premature birth or even a miscarriage. The mucous membrane of the uterus that could accommodate a fertilized egg is discharged because no egg has nested. The mucous membrane of the uterus is the maternal foundation for the new germ, being there before the

---

[647] Henry Corbin, *Creative Imagination in the Sufism of Ibn Arabi*

egg. We are therefore dealing with a kind of a psychic premature birth or something that psychically appears before man has become conscious – a psychic secret that is gradually unveiled. Urs, in real life a musician and theologian, represents a positive animus, that is, the dreamer's spiritual side that is able to establish a connection with the unconscious and to explain the symbols. The little figures are reminiscent of the Greek Cabiri, those arcane Chthonic gods, the sons of Hephaestus, who were ascribed with magic powers. They are creative, dwarf-like divinities toiling away in secret like our Tom Thumb or brownies.[648] They are of small stature but of immense force. They are archetypes or great gods of human fate.

Just as the genes determine the individual type of a person, the archetypes constitute his or her specific psychic disposition. Here, too, lies the meaning of a horoscope: the constellation of the archetypes at the moment of birth. In astrology, the assumption is that, at the very moment of birth, when an individual fate is being discharged into its own outer world and order, there still exists a correspondence of meaning between the macrocosm, the world of the planets, and the inner microcosm of a human being. Further, it is assumed that a horoscope contains symbolically, in the constellation of the stars, the meaning or purpose determined by the moment in which a man is born. The outer image reflects the corresponding inner one.[649] The planets remain the same but their constellation changes. The specific qualities of the appearance of the planets, as well as their movement through the sky (which man has observed for more than 4000 years) were associated with gods – with Mars, Jupiter, Pluto, Uranus, etc., from very early on. In mythology, they correspond to the archetypes, and their behavior can be said to describe what is happening in the human psyche.

The archetypes or determining factors of human fate, as it were, keep on changing and shifting similar to the constellation of the planets. They set the *Zeitgeist* that influences and to an extent shapes every man and woman in much the same way as the year with its specific weather conditions influences the taste of the wine.

Before we go on with the interpretation of our dream, I would like to mention the following four little dreams. They illustrate how the unconscious views the coming-into-being of a new child as an astrological event that is at the same time the archetypal background of the psyche.

A thirty-six-year-old woman, who has been married for seven years, dreamt the following, ten days prior to the birth of her sixth child:[650]

---

[648] C.G. Jung, *Symbols of Transformation*, CW 5, § 180
[649] E.v. Xylander, *Lehrgang der Astrologie*, Origo Verlag, Zurich, 1971, p. 32 f
[650] By the same dreamer: No. 130 in Chapter 7

Dream No. 171:

> *I am standing outside with my sister-in-law, looking up at the sky. The night is dark, so I can see hundreds of stars. Suddenly, I see a shooting star. Then another and another and another. ... They move across the sky and are magnificent to see! I wake up, remembering the Bushman belief that a shooting star announces the birth of a child.*

A twenty-nine-year-old woman, who will have her first child, dreams this, shortly before conception:[651]

Dream No. 172:

> *In the countryside with her husband: It is night, and she carefully observes the starry sky. The myriad stars forming the Milky Way have now produced a zodiacal constellation. She urges her husband to come and see the exceptional show: first the sign of Scorpio appears. It is followed by the image of the god Horus.*

A twenty-nine-year-old student of law, living separately from her partner and having already had a miscarriage, was unsure about whether or not to have the child because of her studies and professional career. She dreamt at one month into pregnancy:

Dream No. 173:

> *I was a star in the sky. Suddenly, I fell from the sky down to the earth.*

She did not keep the child.

The following dream stems from a twenty-nine-year-old mother of two small boys. She was three months pregnant and had given up a career as an artist in favor of the children. She was now considering taking her artistic career up again:

Dream 174:

> *A star in the sky falls down to the earth. It's exploding and very beautiful. A UFO is landing in X-town.*

In his investigations into synchronicity, Jung discovered that when in one of his patient's life an archetype was activated and as a result of this a state of strong emotional tension was generated, the symbolic imagery and dreams they produced curiously coincided with external-world events. Most of us have experienced such coincidences of inner images suddenly being reflected in an

---

[651] By the same dreamer: No. 39 in Chapter 4.2, No. 66 in Chapter 5.3, No. 168 in Chapter 9

external occurrence or vice versa, and it usually leaves a strong impression on us. "In such moments, psyche and matter seem no longer separate entities but arrange themselves into an identical, meaningful symbolic situation. ... This unitary reality Jung called the *unus mundus* (the one world)."[652] The constellation of the stars and the psychic constellation of a child at the moment of birth are connected through their equally meaningful coincidence, which has been an object of study for millennia and which man always assumed to represent a legible or understandable picture.[653] The star-dreams above can perhaps impart to the dreamers a premonition of this *unus mundus*, a notion of a much larger context from which their child was born.

Let us return to Dream No. 170.

All the little figures have the mark of Cain. Cain, the son of Adam and Eve, who killed his brother out of envy was punished and banned by God and marked on his forehead, so that someone else would not kill him. The mark of Cain signified being in Gods hands, that is, in the hands of his cursed fate. The same mark on the little figures suggests that the gods of fate, although well disposed towards humankind, could also kill or put them under a curse. For this reason, man, from Antiquity, sought liberation from Heimarmene. It is a self-centered and arrogant attitude of the men and women of the present age, who have ceased to believe in anything, to deem that they are in control of their own fate. However, the ancient dependencies sneak in through the back-door in the form of, for instance, magazine horoscopes, fortune telling and all varieties of clairvoyance. Liberation is illusory. In the dream, liberation comes through the merciful Mother Mary representing an image of the Self. Therefore, she is "round and maternal," earthy – like the Catholic Madonnas of the Middle Ages. For any mother, not knowing what fate will have in store for her child, the image can provide comfort and calm. Only the Self can help us to overcome the inexorable destiny that, through our personality traits and unconscious background, seems to determine our lives. It is ultimately the Self, and not the ego, that can avert the fate determined by the constellation of the stars. To convey this knowledge with its symbolism is the goal of this dream.

Now, the inner side of the blanket is spread out: in other words, the inner spiritual aspect of conception and birth is revealed.

In creation myths, the world is frequently woven on a loom, in particular if a feminine Nature-goddess is involved in the creation. In India it is Maya, the goddess whose immensely large colorful veil represents the entire world of appearances. In a pre-Socratic creation myth, "the Sky God married the Earth Goddess, and he wove the whole world as a big mantle and spread it over an

---

[652] M.-L. von Franz, *Psyche and Matter: The Psychological Experience of Time*, Shambhala, Boston, 1992, p. 113 ff
[653] *Ibid.*, p. 99

oak." [654] For many Nomadic tribes, the carpet signifies their world, their own mother soil and a piece of their homeland. This is why the carpet travels with them everywhere. The patterns of Oriental carpets tend to depict, in more or less abstract forms, the paradise, the tree of life, the animal world and various other images whose symbolism suggests the origin of creation or the beginning of fate with all its complicated life patterns.[655] The individual pattern of life or of fate is inextricably linked to the divine creation. Cosmic mother-goddesses frequently have a spindle with which they spin people's threads of fate. In India, men, women and children are all regarded as part of the great web of the Godhead. They are re-born souls, who come and go – just as the threads woven in a fabric appear and disappear. The pattern that is being woven would be analogous to a certain pattern of psychological and biological inherited factors with which the child is born.[656] From an arcane woven cloth of all the "ancestral threads," a new life pattern is created – the eternal repetition of a unique creation process.

In our dream, the Garden of Eden with two rivers is depicted on the "creation cloth." Simon Magus, the Gnostic, amplified this in a helpful way. We know from early Christian literature that Simon Magus was a contemporary of Jesus belonging to a movement of the so-called heretical Gnosis (Gnosis = knowledge/insight). The orthodox church persecuted the movement for being heretical because it was outside the official Christian dogma. Through intense introspective observation (i.e., concentrating on inner images during meditation) the Gnostics reached a "psychological knowledge whose contents derive from the unconscious" in the form of symbolic imagery.[657]

According to Simon Magus, man is created from *pneuma*, which – unless it is transformed into an "image" – only remains a potentiality and goes down with the cosmos, that is, does not enter the life cycle.[658] God, on the other hand, shapes man in Paradise, which is the maternal womb. From the land of Eden, the navel is created that divides first into two canals – one for blood, the other for pneuma, then into the four origins, i.e., the four rivers of Paradise that feed the embryo. The four senses or the child who is made in Paradise are thereby created: the face, sense of smell, taste and feeling. The four rivers have to do with man's four functions of consciousness with which he apprehends

---

654 Cf. M.-L. von Franz, *Creation Myths*, Shambhala, Boston, 1995, p. 135 f

655 Cf. M.-L. von Franz, *The Interpretation of Fairy Tales*, pp. 75-77. Also: H.U. Etter, *Der Schöpfungsteppich von Girona*, Jungiana, Reihe B, Bd. 1, p. 26 ff

656 M.-L. von Franz, *The Feminine in Fairy Tales*, Shambhala, Boston, 1993, pp. 45-48

657 C.G. Jung, CW 9/I, § 350

658 According to the perception of the Gnostics, the world is a perpetual cycle of growth and decay, a kind of power struggle that is contained within itself. Everything is brought forth from "one" and everything disintegrates again into the same "one." Eternity becomes temporality, temporality again eternity. God creates the cosmos and the cosmos becomes God again. H. Leisegang, *Die Gnosis*, p. 75 and p. 98.

the world: thinking, intuition, sensation and feeling. For, whenever a psychic content is divided into four aspects, it means that it has undergone a differentiation through the orientation functions of consciousness. In our dream, there are two rivers, suggesting the two attitude types of extraversion and introversion. According to the Gnostic symbolism of the blood and pneuma canals, they, too, need first to be established and then built up. In simplified and figurative terms, blood would correspond to the inner aspect, and pneuma, or the spirit, to the outer one.

According to Simon Magus, the "great man" or the Anthropos springs from this creation act.[659] Thus each human birth reflects a divine birth. The great man or Anthropos symbolizes the soul of a giant man spread over the entire cosmos. This cosmic man personifies the wholeness of the unconscious soul, or the Self that emerges at each birth.[660]

The outer side of the blanket bears the cross as a primary symbol, for every human life is a crucifixion. The cross symbolizes the divine suffering for the deliverance of mankind, God's suffering because of the world and His collision with it, or rather with the world's prince, the devil. At the same time, the cross is one of the most primordial symbols of order.[661] In the face of chaos, the cross signifies a structure providing order, similar to the cross-hairs on a telescope and the fixing of a middle-point through their two intersecting lines. Man's devotion to the cross was, to the Gnostics, a "coming together of the unstable," an order in chaos, the uniting of disharmonies and a centering in the middle-point. The latter was to them not only the center of mankind but, by the same token, the center of the universe.

If, in accordance with this conception, crucifixion creates "order in chaos," then we come upon such opposites as good and evil, above and below, a spiritual and material world, consciousness and the unconscious, etc. As we have already seen, psychologically, this division into four causes a differentiation of consciousness. In Jung's words, "...the progressive development and differentiation of consciousness leads to an ever more menacing awareness of the conflict and involves nothing less than a crucifixion of the ego, its agonizing suspension between irreconcilable opposites."[662] At the same time, the cross has the psychological function of an order-creating center in which the opposites are united. Through devotion to the cross, a bridge can be established between consciousness and the unconscious. For this reason, the cross symbolized the goal – the salvation and the exaltation of man.[663] In addition, the cross, like the circle and quaternios in general, have been a symbol of God

---

[659] H. Leisegang, *Die Gnosis*, 75
[660] M.-L. von Franz, *Individuation in Fairy Tales*, Shambhala, Boston, 1990, p. 108
[661] Cf. C.G. Jung, CW 11, § 250
[662] C.G. Jung, CW 9/II Aion, § 79
[663] *Ibid.*, CW 11, § 445

or of wholeness expressing *Weltgrund* (world foundation) and divinity since time immemorial.[664]

In our dream, the cross is "rounded off" presumably meaning that it is closer to a circle. With the exception of the point, the circle is the simplest symbol of wholeness and of the divine image.[665] "God is a circle whose center is everywhere and the circumference nowhere."[666] God is the beginning and the completion in a perfect cycle. According to the conception of the Alchemists, in the circle the opposites are united.

The extensive symbolism in our dream takes us to the wheel, one of the most ancient symbols. The wheel rotating around a middle point is an extension of the circular movement of the circle. Our astrological system, too, consists of a wheel or a circular procession of gods and archetypes, the wheel of birth. Originally, the underlying idea was that of the heavenly pole and the starry vault of heaven rotating round it.[667] The observation of the regular circular motions of the stars and planets probably underlies the fact that almost all the ancient cultures perceived time as cyclical or as an eternal circular movement.[668] Hence, there exists the idea of the wheel of time determining the fate of all living creatures.

As a symbol of life and decay, the wheel of time belongs to Fortuna, the goddess of fortune, but also to Cairos, the Greek God who personified the moment of time, with the most propitious constellation of circumstances, in which to act. In India, it is the swastika, i.e., the wheel of fortune. The signs of the circle and the wheel visible in the cross are also reminiscent of the samsara, the Indian wheel of rebirth man enters. The horoscope, too, is a wheel of time. The first two of

Figure 64. Celtic stone cross (Scotland)

the four little dreams we have mentioned, belong to this context, for astrology (the knowledge of the stars and planets) deals with man's entrance into time. We will come back to the aspect of time a little later.

[664] *Ibid.*, § 285
[665] *Ibid.*, CW 13, § 457
[666] *Ibid.*, CW 9/II, Aion, § 237
[667] C.G. Jung, CW 9/II, § 352
[668] M.-L. von Franz, *Psyche and Matter*, p. 73 ff

Figure 65. The Lateran Cross in Rome (early Christian mosaic with the cross in the center of the world and the four rivers of paradise)

The cross that is rounded off and tending, so to speak, towards a wheel that has been divided into quarters, brings up the problem of the quadrature of the circle. It was of great interest to the medieval mind, and it appears in the visions of our dreams and fantasies, too. It belongs to the very central archetypal motifs. The four rivers of paradise, according to the teachings of the Naassenes, are also based on the quadrature of the circle. So is the magnificent, 800-year-old carpet representing the creation in Girona, Spain, which pilgrims from all over the world still come to see today.[669] The squaring of the circle also plays a role in the work of the Alchemists by dividing the originally chaotic unity into the four elements and then combining them into a higher unity.

In comparison with the torn-up opposites in the crucifixion, the complete circle emphasizes unity and represents the quaternion as a unity. Eastern mandalas are usually based upon the squaring of the circle. Meditating on these pictures is supposed to help one concentrate on the center of one's personality. "The energy of the central point is manifested in the almost irresistible compulsion and urge to become what one is, just as every organism is driven to assume the form that is characteristic of its nature...." Fate is thus determined by this center or the Self, as opposed to the "blind compulsion of the planets" or the constraints that our unconscious and contradictory complexes put on our lives. Everything the circle holds – in particular, the paired

---

[669] Cf. H.U. Etter, *Der Schöpfungsteppich von Girona*

opposites that make up the total personality – belongs to this innermost point, which is the center which is the Self.[670]

Summarizing the extensive symbolism of the cross with the rounded off corners, we can say that, in our dream, it seems to allude to the birth of the potential wholeness of the new child. This entails, as we have seen, a life of crucifixion and of the perpetually necessary uniting of the opposites. The Self relates the opposite components of fate to the center and unites them. The dream clearly suggests that, in this phase of pregnancy, the constellation of the fate of the future human being already crystallizes.

The birth of this marvelous creation blanket in the dream serves to bring its rich symbolic content to the light of consciousness so as to pass on to the dreamer some insight into the mystery of human life. Given that she has a positive animus, which can understand the symbols, she can gain access to this super-personal dimension of her pregnancy. It also seems likely that something in her wants to become conscious of these connections. This is the right moment for it.

The following dream was dreamt under anesthesia during a Cesarean section. Dreams under the influence of medication or drugs tend to lack a certain order or clarity. The dreamer, whose personal background we know fairly well, did not think this was the case. On the contrary, the dream turned out to be crucial for her life. We shall soon see why:

Dream No. 175:

> *I am in a large dark hall. There are display cases, round balls in which you can see figurations that look like molecular chains or atomic models. I go from ball to ball looking into them. I can hear a murmur in each ball. E.g.: legs to walk, legs to walk. Or: arms to grasp something ... or ....*
> *Fascinated, I stroll about among the balls until I realize that all these balls seem to drift in a certain direction, floating. Amazed, I drift along with them. There are always more balls: the stream becomes bigger and more compact, and the speed increases. Finally, above a torrential stream of balls, I float out into the horizon. The murmuring of the balls is now an excited giggling and chattering. The stream pulls me in ecstasy into a large ball / cave / hole. A tremendous force seizes me, expands me, brutally turns me inside out and lets me contract again on the other side. This moment is somehow terrifying: I come very close to my own destruction, but I end up composed again.*
> *Now I'm standing at a huge gate, and from high up, I look out onto an alpine landscape with a mountain range in the background. It is morning. Beneath me, I notice the same stream of balls pouring into the world.*

---

[670] Cf. C.G. Jung, CW 9/I, § 634

Suddenly, I have to laugh: if they knew that it is all the same here, only mirror-inverted! I let myself drift out. (I awoke from the anesthesia and was convinced that I was dead. It was truly hard for me to try to think about it in detail and to convince myself that this could not be the case. For a long time afterwards, I was sometimes unsure as to whether or not I was in fact living in the mirror-image of the world).

The beginning of the dream seems to describe the coming together of the child from various initially chaotic individual parts. The torrential stream of the balls flowing ever faster reminds one of the movement of the time, which is what the dreamer called it in her associations. The course of time has intuitively been perceived as streaming or flowing throughout the ages.[671] This intuition is behind all time-measuring devices based on the flow of a substance or liquid, i.e., sandglasses, water clocks, mercury clocks, etc.[672] Time was personified as a living river of growth and decay in the god, Oceanos. This river was also known by the name of *Chronos* (Greek = time). The movement of time was originally perceived by man as the divine secret of the stream of life.[673] The stream of balls or "life-building-blocks," pouring into the world in the dream, presumably has to do with entering the time principle, an event taking place each time a human being is conceived.

The ancient Egyptians believed in the otherworldly primal waters of the Nile, or the first primeval mass of water called Nun, from which all life is brought forth and in it renewed again. According to a myth, the Nile rises from a cave near Aswan, which is where all life originates. This is, as it were, the geographical point of transition from one world into the other, for at the time, the First Cataract in the Nile formed, in reality, a natural boundary with the foreign Nubian South. This foreign, other world on the other side of the boundary line, mythologically represented the world of the mirror-image that strongly influenced the ancient Egyptians' belief in the beyond.[674]

In this world of the mirror-images, everything exists in an inverted form. Thus, the Nile of the beyond flowed backwards to its source. In the evening, when Ra, the old and weary sun-god "goes down," his solar bark takes him "backwards," to the source of the Nile. By floating on the river of life, which is at the same time the river of renewal of life, he rejuvenates, in order to be born again at the end. This is how the mysterious renewal of the sun, during its

---

[671] M. Eliade, *Images and Symbols: Studies in Religious Symbols,* Princeton University Press, 1991. In Buddhism, time is represented as a flowing river (*Samfang*). The flow of time has to do with the ultimate non-reality of the present moment, which continuously transforms itself into the past and not-being.

[672] M.-L. von Franz, *Psyche and Matter*, p. 69

[673] *Ibid.*, p. 65

[674] These observations stem from an unpublished manuscript by Theodor Abt, *Grundzüge der Alchemie*, 1995

nocturnal sea-voyage, was explained. Thus, from the otherworldly river of life, in the form of a little child through the sacred scarab, the sun-god is released across the horizon into the day.[675]

This dream caused the dreamer to make an essential step, not only in terms of connecting with her child, but also in terms of her own life. Before she was put to sleep for the emergency Cesarean section, she had been in labor for many hours and was at the end of her tether when she had the following experience:

Dream No. 176:

> *I'm falling into darkness. Time, space, everything ceases to exist. I do not know for how long this goes on. It seems only for a short while (in fact, as I discovered over a year later, it went on for hours). Gradually, a light appears towards which I'm sailing. It becomes brighter and brighter and fills everything out. I'm flooded with a sense of bliss and warmed by it. Now I can see unfolding before me a meadow in flower with fruit trees. Everything is bathing in a golden glow, in light and blissfulness. The meadow lies before me, and overcome with joy, I want to throw myself into it. At that moment, I hear a male voice say: "Stop, you have to deliver your child first!" I am pulled back. I am enveloped by blackness. I am thrust back into consciousness and know, to my unspeakable horror, that I almost killed my child. I feel like a murderess. (I am going in for the emergency Cesarean.) My only wish now is to have my child saved. I myself wish to die.*

This powerful death-dream shows how close the dreamer came to her own destruction, and to her child's. Not for anything did she want to murder her child while she had nothing against murdering herself – that is, her own future and individuation. Death was too tempting. Then comes the dream under general anesthesia, and she immediately realizes that death is no "solution," for the here and now and the hereafter are mirror images. Furthermore, she realizes that it is useless to try to escape from one side to the other, for the psychic reality is the same on both sides, and one cannot not escape one's destiny. The anesthesia-dream, therefore, turns into a genuine birth-dream – not only for her child, but she, too, is re-born into life, as it were. We know from the dreamer's biography that her own birth came after the tragic miscarriage of her baby-brother and that, as a result of this, she had felt all her life that she had no right to exist, since the little brother was supposed to have been born in her place. This precarious anchorage in life found an end in the dream under anesthesia, and the twofold experience of the birth of her child. She now realized that there was a core in her personality that was identical

---

[675] *Ibid.*

here as well as in the beyond – moreover, she realized that this core of consciousness came from a pre-conscious existence and would also eventually
outlive death. For, only this kind of core of consciousness that she later found
again in the symbolism of the Self could impart to her in the dream this view
of the two worlds. She also found it extremely valuable to realize that her
present life was not accidental, but that it was reflected in the beyond and that
it was her duty to assume responsibility for her own life.

The dream liberated the young woman from her previous approach to life,
which had been too restrictive and had made her feel ill at ease. It gave her an
insight into an existence beyond time and space, where a birth into time is
only a stop along the way of a long journey transcending time. She had been
on a "journey in the other world," at the end of which was not only the birth
of a new child but in fact the birth of a new sun, a new light – a new life and a
new vital life-consciousness. This can be seen as the conclusion of the dream
that is missing, as it were, at the end of the anesthesia, and because the
dreamer does not quite know where she actually is, she awakens – whether in
the world of ordinary time or in the timeless world. It is one of those "big
dreams" that speak of the myth of the creation of humankind.

After this experience, our dreamer began to assume responsibility for her
own life. She studied her dreams, and it became clear to her that they were
about the potential birth of the Self. Thus the birth of her child became a
fundamental turning-point in her own life.

The following dream comes from a thirty-year-old woman, who was four
months pregnant:

Dream 177:

> *I am sucked through space, as if in a time tunnel, to a place where there
> are many eggs. There are various stages of formation. Some have small
> chickens inside.*

In this transparent and vivid dream, it is as if the dreamer herself is going
through a birth. The birth canal is a "time tunnel," propelling her through
space to the "egg place." Regarding this dream, Marie-Louise von Franz said
that each birth means entering time from Eternity. For, the subjective realization of the course of time is contingent upon the functioning of individual
consciousness. If we are woken up abruptly, we realize that we have fallen out
of time and need to reorient ourselves in time. In many fairy tales and legends,
the hero or heroine has somehow landed in the "other world," apparently only
for a day, but when they return home, their family and friends have long been
dead, whereupon they realize that they have been away for a hundred years.
These narratives tell us that, in the preconscious world, time is relative or even
nonexistent.[676]

Entering the time principle at the moment of birth signifies the simultaneous birth of the seed of our consciousness. In our dream, this is illustrated with the eggs. In many creation myths, eggs are the germs from which a creation god forms the cosmos through brooding upon them and dividing them in half.[677] In Egyptian mythology, the first creation act begins by making an enormous egg that was held in the hands of He and Hehet, representing the eternal and creative aspects of the time principle: they also embody the eternal and creative aspects of the order of time. From an egg springs Ra, the Sun God who then becomes the immediate cause of all life on earth.[678] Therefore, the sun is born anew, every day, by the hen. The birth of the sun from the egg – that is, the birth of consciousness – is a common motif in mythology. The egg contains the preformed totality of a future being as a seed or a germ. Some of the eggs in our dream already contain little chickens, while others are still purely in a germinating stage. These are the seeds of the soul in a preconscious form, or archetypes, from which the instincts are the first to develop.

The fact that the dreamer experiences this creation process in her dream seems to me to suggest that she herself is partaking in a process of birth through her child. Its goal is the development of a new consciousness. Viewed from the unconscious, both births are identical. Nowhere else in our collection do the dreams say more about the origin of a child or the emergence of consciousness from the beyond than in this little dream of the time tunnel. I believe it is the last thing we will ever know, for what lies beyond the time tunnel in the timelessness of space continues to remain a mystery. It is the pure not-time that, in China, was represented as an empty hub of the wheel – the symbol for the indescribable center of the Self.[679]

I thank Dr. Marie-Louise von Franz
for her valuable help in this chapter.

[676] Cf. M.-L. von Franz, *Psyche and Matter*, Shambhala, Boston & London, 1992, p. 296
[677] M.-L. von Franz, *Creation Myths*, p. 226
[678] *Ibid.*, p. 227, and M. Eliade, *Images and Symbols*
[679] Cf. M.-L. von Franz, *Psyche and Matter*, Shambhala, Boston, 1992, p. 122

Conclusion

Regina Abt

Using C.G. Jung's method of depth psychology, the treatment of the present dream material has shed light upon several important questions. Although at first view, the dreams of pregnant women hardly differ in imagery and structure from the dreams of other people, the connection to pregnancy becomes very apparent upon more careful examination. The common ground is due to the fact that the symbolism pertaining to pregnancy and birth is often identical with that of the individuation process. In other words, pregnancy gives rise to a process not only involving the growth of a new life in the womb, but gives rise equally to a *process of psychic growth* ultimately aiming at *a new consciousness*. Symbolically, the latter is a new child in the mother's soul as well as the real child growing within her body. The dreams of pregnant women therefore contain numerous symbols of the Self – of which one is, of course, the child. In many myths and religions, not least in Christianity, we encounter it as the "divine child" or a symbol of a potential wholeness.[680] Other symbols of the Self in our dreams manifest as stones, flowers, animals, the Great Mother and many other images.

Our dream material has contained an enormous *variety of motifs and themes*, extending from the stone, the potato in the earth, the spider and snake to the cosmic tree, the planets and the great mother-goddess. It is as if the dreams simultaneously reflected two processes running on parallel tracks: on the one hand, each concrete fetus represents the biological evolution of man in condensed form. On the other hand, the dreams mirror the psychic development of an individual as well as the psychic evolution of humanity as a whole. Marie-Louise von Franz said this had to do with what Jung described as the cosmogonic meaning of human consciousness[681], an insight he had while contemplating the vast herds of wild animals in Africa. He wrote: "... that man is indispensable for the completion of creation: that, in fact, he

[680] Cf. C.G. Jung, *The Psychology of the Child Archetype*, CW 9/I and *Aion*, CW 9/II
[681] Cf. Chapter 10

446

himself is the second creator of the world, who alone has given to the world its objective existence – without which, unheard, unseen, silently eating, giving birth, dying, heads nodding through hundreds of millions of years, it would have gone on in the profoundest night of non-being down to its unknown end. Human consciousness created objective existence and meaning, and man found his indispensable place in the great process of being."[682] It is, as he said, our own myth that bestows meaning upon human existence. For, without the birth of consciousness, we would be trapped in what he called a "cheerless clockwork fantasy" in which life is viewed as "a machine calculated down to the last detail, which, along with the human psyche, runs on senselessly, obeying foreknown and predetermined rules."[683] According to this kind of world view (*Weltbild*), woman would be little more than a birth machine contributing to the misery in the world caused by the growth in population. However, our dreams seem to confirm this "myth of our own," according to which each new human being is a cosmic primal event[684] – namely, the birth of human consciousness.

In this cosmic framework, woman is neither a disinterested observer nor is she a mere performer. Just as the invisible process of transformation takes place in the uterus, so it happens in the soul of the mother, as we could see in a multitude of dreams. In the life of a young woman who is expectant for the first time, pregnancy signifies a maturation process involving *bidding childhood farewell* and entering a new phase and form of life that is fundamentally different from the previous one. Folklore and ethnological studies from all over the world show that this transition was always considered momentous and was marked and supported with corresponding rites. Today the boundary lines between the different life stages have become blurred. We lack the so-called initiation rites that could assist and stand by women in this grave transition to motherhood. The more youthful woman's maternal image is, the more she is accepted in a society where looking young and being dynamic till old age seem to rank highest in people's order of values.

However, regardless of the modern trends on the surface of our collective consciousness, a dream continues, as ever, to produce symbolic imagery containing instinctive knowledge. It derives from the collective human fund of experience that is stored in the great depths of our souls. If we try to "translate" its symbolism into a contemporary language, then the dreams and their symbols in fact assume the function of initiation rites whose roots lie in the same foundation.

Drawing upon this fund of knowledge contained in the unconscious layers of the instincts, our material shows that we can *find guidance as well as detect*

---

[682] C.G. Jung, *Memories, Dreams, Reflections,* p. 256
[683] *Ibid.*, p. 256
[684] Quote from M.-L. von Franz, cf. also Chapter 10

danger in the same manner as women have throughout history. They have altered no more than has the biological process of pregnancy and birth since the creation of humankind. This is also why we can interpret pregnancy dreams without resorting to women's personal associations, as we have done for the present study. A more personal interpretation must then follow in each case based upon individual circumstances. The universal human symbolism, however, puts a woman in touch with her instinctive layers, and it is through this alone that a fundamental emotional transformation can be achieved.

Many young mothers today are *extremely detached from their instincts,* or from the laws of Nature; hence, there is a frequent appearance of animals in the dreams – helpful ones as well as threatening ones. They both mirror and compensate a woman's relationship with the animal instincts and serve to help her to go through her pregnancy in a more instinctively appropriate way. Moreover, a woman who is experiencing pregnancy and birth is not only subject to the immense forces of creation but equally subject to the dangers of death and undoing – including the gods with their light and dark sides. She can only respond either instinctively correctly or incorrectly to their presence. If it is correct, she feels in harmony with life and with herself. If on the other hand, she cannot adapt to these powerful forces, she will lack a certain inner support and tend to be neurotic, easily exhausted and unable to cope with the discomforts of pregnancy. These same difficulties may persist once the child is born because the transition to the new form of life was not made consciously or adequately.

Some of our dreams have conveyed a feeling of a *mysterious fatefulness determined by the Self,* as if fate had already been decided in the maternal womb. St. Nicolas von Flüe is said to have had a vision of a star, a stone and the holy oil already in the womb and also to have seen his baptism. Marie-Louise von Franz believed that Brother Klaus' visions of prenatal events and his baptism happened in a dream. According to the Bible, John the Baptist also "recognized" Christ while in the womb. In many myths, the future savior and religious leader knows of his predestined electedness at the time of being in the maternal womb.[685] About Buddha, it is said that his mother Maya dreamt of a white elephant, when she carried him beneath her heart. The elephant is a symbol of wisdom and fortitude as well as of an individuated personality, and in Maya's dream, this would therefore point to the elected destiny of the future spiritual guide. Parallels in religious history and mythology with prenatal fatefulness seem to suggest that the latter underlie a basic archetypal structure. A saint or religious founder would thus be an archetypal example of the "wholeness" in man lying dormant as a potential within each individual.

---

[685] M.-L. von Franz, *The Dreams and Visions of St. Nikolas von Flüe,* Lecture 1, Jung Institute, 1957, p. 9

CONCLUSION

Viewing pregnancy and birth in the light of the dreams of our study would result in a tremendous enhancement, strongly contrasting with the present-day, rational conception of the manipulability of the elementary processes of life. The dreams do not provide us with general recipes (e.g., for or against abortion). However, what seems generally to transpire is that dreams, i.e., the unconscious, contain a reliable source of insights that could be most useful if only the conscious ego were able to pay more serious attention to them.

This also applies to the external circumstances a woman has to learn to master. The dreams in this book can be seen as mirroring the external events affecting our lives, and in this sense, they can provide "answers." The answers are firmly rooted in the archetypes and are thus of universal validity. What precisely these answers mean with regard to the dreamer's personal life, her relationships and her problems lies beyond the boundaries of this study. The fathers, family structure, social environment, professional life and many other important spheres of the conscious life of a pregnant woman have only been taken into account insofar as they might be affected by an "archetypal" answer. To analyze dreams in terms of the position of the unconscious with regard to the aforementioned spheres could be the object of further research.

Considering pregnancy as a holistic event, embracing *the tiniest aspects of life as well as the great cosmic processes* – that is, not merely as a means of human reproduction but as a cosmic event – means to value it in terms of a much more far-reaching event. One might think that women would, in that case, want to have more children, and what would that lead to? I do not believe this would be so. Many women today still have children because it is the only way they feel accepted as a woman. They feel compelled to have a child in addition to realizing themselves in their professions or studies and all the other things men also do. Or, they hope a child will consolidate their marriage or solve other problems they may have. These are egocentric and egotistical motivations that, with a profounder attitude, would become redundant, in which case, one might say that the instinct would regulate the number of births. So much for the individual sphere.

Now, faced with problems of a higher order – such as the pressing overpopulation of our planet – we shall have to wait and see whether man will find a way of including the regulating impulses and guidelines, which the instincts can provide, before it is too late, or whether Nature herself will intervene. However, it seems to me that an inner high authority producing the dream-meaning (Jung called it the archaic man or woman in us), or the dream spirit, is not yet weary of promoting the development of human consciousness. I believe that, from our study of these dreams, we can conclude with certainty that it is important to what extent we can emotionally grasp and respect the mysteries involved in the perpetual renewal of life.

Bibliography

Aarne, A. & St. Thompson, *The Types of the Folklore*, Helsinki, 1981

Abt, Regina, *Die Heilige und das Schwein*, Daimon, Zürich, 1983

Abt, Theodor, *Grundzüge der Alchemie*, unpublished manuscript, 1995

Ameisenowa, Zofia, *Animal-Headed Gods. Evangelists, Saints and Righteous Men*, Journal of the Warburg-Courtauld Institutes, University of London, 1949, Vol. 12

Amman, *Ein neuw Thierbuch*, Verses by G. Schaller, Frankfurt am Main, 1569

Arabische Märchen, Fischer Taschenbuch No. 480, Frankfurt, 1977

Ayzac, Félice d', *L'une des acceptations mystiques de l'éléphant dans le symbolisme chrétien au moyen âge*, Revue Archéologique, 10e année, Paris, 1853

Bachofen, Johan Jakob, *Versuch über die Gräbersymbolik der Alten*, 1859; *Das Mutterrecht*, 1961; *Das lykische Volk*, 1862 (cf. *Mutterrecht und Urreligion*, Leipzig, 1926)

Bächtold-Stäubli, *Handwörterbuch des deutschen Aberglaubens*, Berlin & Leipzig, 1927

Baumann, Carol, *Seelische Erlebnisse im Zusammenhang mit der Geburt, Eine Voruntersuchung*. Sonderausdruck: *Schweizerische Zeitschrift für Psychologie*, Bd. 16, Heft 2

Beit, Hedwig v. / Marie-Louise von Franz, *Symbolik des Märchens*, Francke Verlag, Bern, 1952

Beit, Hedwig v., *Gegensatz und Erneuerung im Märchen*, Francke Verlag, Bern 1957

Benz, Ernst, *Die heilige Höhle in der Ostkirche*, in: Eranos Jahrbuch 1953, Band 22

Bingen, Hildegard von, *Heilkraft der Edelsteine*, Aschaffenburg 1990

Birkhäuser-Oeri, Sybille, *The Mother: Archetypal Image in Fairy Tales*, Inner City Books, Toronto, 1988

Bolte, Joh. / Georg Polivka, *Anmerkungen zu den Kinder- und Hausmärchen der Brüder Grimm*, Olms, 1963

Bonnet, H., *Reallexikon der ägyptischen Religionsgeschichte*, Verlag Walter de Gruyter, Berlin, 1971,

Bonnet, Jocelyne, *La Terre des Femmes et ses Magies*, Éd. Robert Laffont, Paris, 1988

Bosch, Robert, *Das Automobil als Selbst-Symbol*, unpublished lecture, 1990

Bousset, Wilhelm, *Hauptprobleme der Gnosis*, Göttingen und Zürich, 1973

Brednich, Rolf W., *Die Spinne in der Yukkapalme*, dtv, München, 1990

Brosse, J., *Mythologie der Bäume*, Walter Verlag, Olten, 1990

BIBLIOGRAPHY

Brunner, Helmut, *Die Geburt des Gottkönigs*, Otto Harassowitz-Verlag, Wiesbaden, 1986

Buddhistische Märchen aus dem alten Indien, Leipzig, 1961

Budge, Wallis, *From Fetish to God in Ancient Egypt*, Oxford University Press, London, 1934

Chevalier, J.+ & A. Gheerbrant, *Dictionnaire des Symboles*, Seghers, Paris, 1969

Clarus, Ingeborg, *Keltische Mythen*, Walter Verlag, Olten, 1991

Clarus, Ingeborg, *Wer war zuerst?, Mythologischer Exkurs über die Wechselwirkung sich ablösender weiblicher und männlicher Vorherrschaft*, Anal. Psychologie 1989, 20

Corbin, Henry, *Creative Imagination in the Sufism of Ibn Arabi*, Princeton University Press, 1981

— *Spiritual Body and Celestial Earth*, Bollingen Series, Princeton University Press, 1977

Dale-Green, Patricia, *Dog*, Rupert Hart-Davis, London, 1966

— *The Archetypal Cat*, Rupert Hart-Davis, London, 1966

Dawson, M.M., *The Ethical Religion of Zoraster*, A.M.S. Press, 1969

Der Kleine Pauly, Lexikon der Antike in fünf Bänden, Alfred Druckenmüllerverlag, Artemis, München, 1975

Dirlot, J.E., *Dictionary of Symbols*, London, 1978

Duby, Georges, *The Knight, the Lady and the Priest*, Pantheon Books, New York, 1983

Edinger, Edward, *Anatomy of the Psyche*, Open Court, La Salle, IL, 1985

Eliade, Mircea, *Die Religionen und das Heilige*, Wiss. Buchgesellschaft, Darmstadt, 1976, quoted in *The Forge and the Crucible*

— *Images and Symbols: Studies in Religious Symbols*, Princeton University Press, 1991

— *Pattern in Comparative Religion*, Sheed and Ward, London and New York, 1958

— *Shamanism, Archaic Techniques of Ecstasy*, Bollingen Series, Princeton University Press, 1974

— *The Forge and the Crucible*, University of Chicago Press, 1978

Enzyklopädie des Märchens, Handwörterbuch zur historischen und vergleichenden Erzählforschung, Walter de Gruyter, Berlin, 1993

Eschenbach, Wolfram v., *Parzival*

Etter, H.U., *Der Schöpfungsteppich von Girona*, Jungiana, Reihe B, Bd. 1

— *Mensch, du Affe! Zur symbolischen Bedeutung unserer nächsten Tierischen Verwandten*. In: Jungiana, Reihe A, Bd. 5

Franz, Marie-Louise von & Emma Jung, *The Grail Legend*, G.P. Putnam's Sons, New York, 1970

Franz, Marie-Louise von, *C.G. Jung, Man and His Symbols*, "The Animus: The Man Within," Aldus Books, Ltd., London, 1979

— "The Bremen Town Musicians from the Point of View of Depth Psychology" in: *Archetypal Dimensions of the Psyche*, Shambhala, Boston, 1997

— "The Unknown Visitor in Fairy Tales and Dreams," in: *Archetypal Dimensions of the Psyche*, Shambhala, Boston, 1997

— "The Woman who became a Spider," in *The Feminine in Fairy Tales*, Spring Publications, Zurich, 1972

— *Alchemy: An Introduction to the Symbolism and the Psychology*, Inner City Books, Toronto, 1980

— *C.G. Jung and the Problems of Our Time.* Analytical Psychology Club, Perth
— *C.G. Jung's Rehabilitation der Gefühlsfunktion in unserer Zivilisation.* In: Jungiana, Reihe A, Bd. 3, Verlag Stiftung für Jung'sche Psychologie, Küsnacht 1991
— *C.G. Jung, His Myth in Our Time,* C.G. Jung Foundation for Analytical Psychology, New York, 1975
— *C.G. Jung,* Inner City Books, New York, 1975
— *Creation Myths,* Shambhala, Boston, 1995
— *Die Erlösung des Weiblichen im Manne,* Insel Verlag, Frankfurt, 1980
— Essay "Bei der Schwarzen Frau" in: Märchenforschung und Tiefenpsychologie, ed. by W. Saiblin, Wiss. Buchgesellschaft, Darmstadt, 1965
— *Individuation in Fairy Tales,* Shambhala, Boston, 1997
— Lectures: *The Dreams and Visions of St. Niklaus von Flüe,* Jung Institute, Küsnacht, 1957
— *Number and Time,* Northwestern University Press, Evanston, Illinois, 1974
— *On Divination and Synchronicity,* Inner City Books, Toronto, 1980
— *On Dreams and Death,* Shambhala, Boston & London, 1986
— *Projection and Re-Collection in Jungian Psychology,* Open Court Publishing Company, La Salle, IL, 1980
— *Psyche and Matter: The Psychological Experience of Time,* Shambhala, Boston & London, 1992
— *Psychological Interpretation of Fairy Tales*
— *Puer Aeternus,* Sigo Press, Santa Monica, 1981
— *Shadow and Evil in Fairy Tales,* Shambhala, Boston, 1995
— *The Bremen Town Musicians,* in: Zeitschrift für analytische Psychologie und ihre Grenzgebiete, Berlin
— *The Cat. A Tale of Feminine Redemption,* Inner City Books, Toronto, 1998
— *The Dreams and Visions of St. Nikolas von Flüe,* Lecture 1, Jung Institute, 1957
— *The Feminine in Fairy Tales,* Shambhala, Boston, 1993
— *The Golden Ass of Apuleius,* Shambhala, Boston, 1992
— *The Interpretation of Fairy Tales,* Shambhala, Boston, 1996
— *The Passion of Perpetua,* Spring Publications, University of Dallas, Texas, 1980
— *The Psychological Meaning of Redemption Motifs in Fairy Tales,* Inner City Books, 1980
Frazer, J.G., *The Golden Bough: A Study in Magic and Religion,* Macmillan, London, 1980 [or New York: St. Martin's Press, 1990]
Gélis, Jacques, *History of Childbirth: Fertility, Pregnancy and Birth in Early Modern Europe,* Northeastern University Press, Boston, 1991
Gennep, Arnold van, *The Rites of Passage,* The University of Chicago Press, 1980
Goethe, J.W. von, *Faust,* The Penguin Classics, Penguin Books Ltd., 1959
Griaule, M. et G. Dieterlin, *Le Renard Pâle,* Institut de l'Ethnologie, Paris, 1965
Grimm, Jakob, *Deutsche Mythologie,* Akademische Druck- und Verlagsanstalt, Graz, 1968
— *The Complete Grimm's Fairy Tales,* Random House, 1972
Grzimek, B., *Lexikon der Tierwelt*
Guntern, J., *Volkserzählungen aus dem Oberwallis,* Basel, 1978
Hannah, Barbara, "The Problem of Women's Plots" in *The Evil Vineyards,* The Guild of Pastoral Psychology, Guild Lecture 51, London, 1948

BIBLIOGRAPHY

— *The Cat, Dog and Horse Lectures,* ed. by Dean L. Franz, Chiron Publications, Wilmette, Illinois, 1992

— *The Religious Function of the Animus in the Book of Tobit,* in: The Guild of Pastoral Psychology, Guild Lecture 114, London, 1961

Harding, Esther, *The Way of All Women, A Psychological Interpretation,* Longmans, London, 1933

— *Woman's Mysteries,* Harper & Row, New York, 1971

Harnik, Avo, *Seele und Kristall,* Diploma thesis at the C.G. Jung Institute in Zürich, 1982

Holmberg, U., *Weltenbaum,* in: Annales Academiae scientiarum fennicae. B XVI, Helsinki, 1922

Hornung, Erik, *Das Totenbuch der Ägypter,* Artemis, 1979

— *Die Nachtmeerfahrt der Sonne*

— *Idea Into Image: Essays on Ancient Egyptian Thought,* Timken, New York, 1992

Huizinga, J., *Homo ludens: A Study of the Play Element in Culture,* J. & J. Harper Editions, New York, 1970

Hurwitz, Siegmund, *Lilith, The First Eve,* Daimon Verlag, Einsiedeln, Switzerland, 1992

Isler, Gotthilf, *Das rätoromanische Margaretenlied – eine seelische Tragödie,* in: Terra Plana, Vierteljahreszeitschrift für Kultur, Geschichte, Tourismus und Wirtschaft. Mels 1988, Heft 4

— *Die Sennenpuppe,* Krebs Verlag, Basel, 1971

— *Die Überwindung der Hexe,* Vortrag auf der Brunnenburg/Südtirol, unpublished manuscript, 1988

Janov, Artur, *The Primal Scream*

Johnson, Buffie, *Lady of the Beasts,* Harper & Row Publishers, San Francisco, 1988

Jung, C.G. / Wilhelm, *The Secret of the Golden Flower,* Kegan Paul, London, 1931

Jung, C.G., *Dream Analysis,* The Seminars, Routledge & Kegan Paul, 1984

— *A Modern Myth,* CW 10

— *Aion,* CW 9, II

— *Alchemical Studies,* CW 13

— *Instinct and the Unconscious,* CW 8

— Introduction to Frances G. Wicke's *Analyse der Kindesseele,* in CW 1, § 90 f

— *Memories Dreams and Reflections,* Vintage Books by Random House, 1963

— *Mysterium Coniunctionis,* CW 13+14

— *Paracelsus as a Spiritual Phenomenon,* CW 13

— *Paracelsus the Physician,* CW 15

— *Psychological Aspects of the Mother Archetype,* CW 9, I

— *Psychological Types,* CW 6

— *Psychology and Alchemy,* CW 12

— *Seminar on Dream Analysis,* Bollingen Series, Princeton University Press, 1984

— Seminars: *Kinderträume*

— *Symbols of Transformation,* CW 5

— *Synchronicity,* CW 8

— *The Phenomenology of the Spirit in Fairy Tales,* CW 9

— *The Philosophical Tree,* CW 13

— *The Psychological Foundations of Belief in Spirits,* CW 8

453

— *The Psychology of the Child Archetype*, CW 9 I
— *The Spirit Mercurius*, CW 13
— *The Visions of Zosimos*, CW 13
— *The Zofingia Lectures*, translated by Jan van Heurck. Supplementary Volume A of the *Collected Works*, Bollingen Series XX, Princeton University Press, 1983
— *Visions Seminars*, Spring Publications, Zurich, 1976
— *Word and Image*, edited by A. Jaffé, translated by Krishna Winston, Bollingen Series, Princeton University Press, 1979

Jung, Emma / Marie-Louise von Franz, *The Grail Legend*, Princeton University Press, 1970

Jung, Emma, *Animus and Anima*, The Analytical Psychology Club of New York, 1957 (also Spring Publications, 1974)

Kerényi, Karl, *Einführung in das Wesen der Mythologie*, Amsterdam, 1941
— *Humanistische Seelenforschung*, Langen & Müller, München/Wien, 1966
— *The Gods of the Greeks*, Pelican Books, London, 1958

König, Marie, *Unsere Vergangenheit ist älter, Höhlenkult Alteuropas*, Krüger-Verlag, Frankfurt, 1980

Leach, Maria, *God Had a Dog*, Rutgers University Press, 1960

Leisegang, Hans, *Die Gnosis*, Kröner Verlag, Leipzig, 1924
— *The Mystery of the Serpent in The Mysteries*, Bollingen Series XXX2, Pantheon Books, New York, 1955

Lewandowski, Anne, *The God Image, Source of Evil*, – "*The Kabbalistic Equivalent of Satan, also known as the 'Other God,'* " Diploma thesis, Jung Institute, 1977

Lichtheim, Miriam, *Ancient Egyptian Literature: A Book of Readings*, Berkeley / Los Angeles / London, 1973

Lurker, Manfred, *Dictionary of Gods and Goddesses, Devils and Demons*, Routledge and K. Paul, London, New York, 1987
— *The Gods and Symbols of Ancient Egypt: An Illustrated Dictionary*, Thames and Hudson, New York, 1980

Mann, U., *Der Ernst d. hl Spiels*, Eranos Jahrbuch 1982, Insel Verlag, 1983

Maschmann, Melita, *Eine ganz gewöhnliche Heilige*, Otto W. Barth Verlag / Scherz, Bern, München, Wien, 1990

Mijuki, M., *Kreisen des Lichts*, Barth Verlag, 1972

Möller, Volker, *Die Mythologie der vedischen Religion und des Hinduismus*, in: H.W. Haussig, *Wörterbuch der Mythologie*, Stuttgart 1969

Negelein, Julius von, *Das Pferd im Arischen Altertum*, Königsberg, 1903

Neumann, Erich, *The Great Mother. An Analysis of the Archetype*, Bollingen Series 47, New York, 1955
— *The Moon and Matriarchal Consciousness in Fathers and Mothers*, Spring Publications, 1973
— *The Origins and History of Consciousness*, Bollingen Series, 42, Princeton University Press, 1970

Nietzsche, Friedrich, *Thus Spake Zarathustra*, The Viking Press, New York, 1966

Ninck, Martin, *Die Bedeutung des Wassers im Kult und Leben der Alten*, Wiss. Buchgesellschaft, Darmstadt, 1967
— *Wodan und germanischer Schicksalsglaube*, Jena, 1935

Onians, R.B., *The Origins of European Thought*, Amo Press, 1973

Portmann, A., "Die Erde als Heimat des Lebens," in: Eranos-Jahrbuch Vol. XXII

BIBLIOGRAPHY

Roscher, W.H., *Lexikon der griechischen und römischen Mythologie*, Olms Verlag, Hildesheim, 1977

Rosenberg, Alfons, *Das Herzensgebet, Mystik und Yoga der Ostkirche*, Barth Verlag, München, 1955

Schiller, Friedrich von, *The Lay of the Bell*, in: The Poems and Ballads of Schiller, translated by Sir Edward Bulwer Lytton, Bart. Leipzig, B. Tauchnitz Jun., 1844

Schroer, Th., "Archtypal Dreams during the First Pregnancy," in *Psychological Perspectives*, Vol. 15, No. 1, 1984

Ström, Ake von / H. Biézais, *Germanische und baltische Religion*, Kohlhammer, Stuttgard/Berlin, 1975

Teichmann, Frank, *Der Mensch und sein Tempel* and *Megalithkultur in Irland, England und der Bretagne*, Urachhaus, Stuttgart 1983

Wertenschlag-Birkhäuser, Eva, *Das Gespräch zwischen Khalik und Morienus über den Stein*, in: Jungiana Reihe A, Band 1

Widengren, Geo, *Manichäismus*, Darmstadt, 1977

Wilhelm & Baynes, *I Ching, The Book of Changes*, Bollingen, 1987

Wilke, H.-W., "On Depressive Delusions," in *Analytische Psychologie*, Vol. 9, No. 2, Basel, 1978

Winterstein, Alfred, Die Pubertätsriten der Mädchen, in: *Märchenforschung und Tiefenpsychologie*, Wissenschaftliche Buchgesellschaft

Wyss, Karl, *Die Milch im Kultus der Griechen und Römer*, Giessen, 1914

Xylander, E.v., Lehrgang der Astrologie, Origo Verlag, Zurich, 1971

Zimmer, Heinrich, *Der Weg zum Selbst, Lehre und Leben des Ramana Maharshi*, München, 1989

— *Myths and Symbols in Indian Art and Civilization*, Bollingen Series VI, Princeton University Press, 1946

List of Dreams

List of Figures

461

Index

Index

ENGLISH PUBLICATIONS BY **DAIMON**

C.A. Meier
Healing Dream and Ritual
Ancient Incubation and Modern Psychotherapy
168 pages, 10 illustrations, indexes, ISBN 3-85630-510-6
C.A. Meier calls for modern psychotherapy to honor the role that the dream has played in the healing process, from ancient times to the present.

Healing Dream and Ritual is one of the most significant and lasting witnesses of how far beyond immediate psychology the implications of Jung's work stretches. This book is, in my feeling, as important for today's healers as was the early work of Paracelsus to the redirection of medicine in the Renaissance.

– Sir Laurens van der Post

Harry Wilmer
How Dreams Help
190 pages, ISBN 3-85630-582-3
'Growing numbers of people are fascinated by the dream world. From psychological scholars and analysts to spontaneous groups and cults, the dream has a compelling voice. ... I make the point in this book that our dreams are our most creative inner source of wisdom and hope. ... The criterion for selection is simply that each one illustrates a common human life experience that all readers have had or are likely to have.'

– from the Introduction by the Author

Available from your bookstore or from our distributors:

In the United States:

Continuum	Chiron Publications
P.O. Box 7017	400 Linden Avenue
La Vergne, TN 37086	Wilmette, IL 60091
Phone: 800-937 5557	Phone: 800-397 8109
Fax: 615-793 3915	Fax: 847-256 2202

In Great Britain:

Airlift Book Company
8 The Arena
Enfield, Middlesex EN3 7NJ
Phone: (0181) 804 0400
Fax: (0181) 804 0044

Worldwide:
Daimon Verlag   Hauptstrasse 85   CH-8840 Einsiedeln   Switzerland
Phone: (41)(55) 412 2266   Fax: (41)(55) 412 2231
info@daimon.ch
www.daimon.ch

Write for our complete catalog!

ENGLISH PUBLICATIONS BY **DAIMON**

Abt / Bosch / MacKrell
- *Dream Child – Creation and New Life in Dreams of Pregnant Women*

Susan R. Bach
- *Life Paints its Own Span*
- *Images, Meanings and Connections* (ed. by Ralph Goldstein)

E.A. Bennet
- *Meetings with Jung*

George Czuczka
- *Imprints of the Future*

Heinrich Karl Fierz
- *Jungian Psychiatry*

von Franz / Frey-Rohn / Jaffé
- *What is Death?*

Liliane Frey-Rohn
- *Friedrich Nietzsche*

Yael Haft
- *Hands: Archetypal Chirology*

Siegmund Hurwitz
- *Lilith, the First Eve*

Aniela Jaffé
- *From the Life und Work of C.G. Jung*
- *The Myth of Meaning*
- *Was C.G. Jung a Mystic?*
- *Death Dreams and Ghosts*

Verena Kast
- *A Time to Mourn*
- *Sisyphus*

Hayao Kawai
- *Dreams, Myths and Fairy Tales in Japan*

James Kirsch
- *The Reluctant Prophet*

Yehezkel Kluger & Nomi Kluger-Nash
- *A Psychological Interpretation of Ruth*

Mary Lynn Kittelson
- *Sounding the Soul*

Rivkah Schärf Kluger
- *The Gilgamesh Epic*

Paul Kugler
- *Jungian Perspectives on Clinical Supervision*

Eva Langley-Dános
- *Prison on Wheels: From Ravensbrück to Burgau*

Rafael López-Pedraza
- *Hermes and His Children*
- *Cultural Anxiety*

Gitta Mallasz (Transcription)
- *Talking with Angels*

Alan McGlashan
- *The Savage and Beautiful Country*
- *Gravity and Levity*

C.A. Meier
- *Healing Dream and Ritual*
- *A Testament to the Wilderness*
- *Personality*

Laurens van der Post
- *The Rock Rabbit and the Rainbow*

Rainer-Maria Rilke
- *Duino Elegies*

Miguel Serrano
- *C.G. Jung and Hermann Hesse: A Record of Two Friendships*

Helene Shulman
- *Living at the Edge of Chaos*

Susan Tiberghien
- *Looking for Gold*

Ann Ulanov
- *The Wizards' Gate*
- *The Female Ancestors of Christ*

Ann & Barry Ulanov
- *Cinderella and Her Sisters*
- *The Healing Imagination*

Erlo van Waveren
- *Pilgrimage to the Rebirth*

Harry Wilmer
- *Quest for Silence*
- *How Dreams Help*

Luigi Zoja
- *Drugs, Addiction and Initiation*

Jungian Congress Papers:

Jerusalem 1983
- *Symbolic and Clinical Approaches*

Berlin 1986
- *Archetype of Shadow in a Split World*

Paris 1989
- *Dynamics in Relationship*

Chicago 1992
- *The Transcendent Function*

Zürich 1995
- *Open Questions in Analytical Psychology*

Florence 1998
- *Destruction and Creation*